# BUSINESS RESEARCH METHODOLOGY

**J.K. SACHDEVA**

Editor:
Journal of Global Economy,
Mumbai.

Himalaya Publishing House
ISO 9001:2015 CERTIFIED

| | | |
|---|---|---|
| First Edition | : | 2008 |
| Reprint | : | 2009 |
| Second Revised Edition | : | 2011 |
| Edition | : | 2013, 2014, 2015, 2016 |
| Third Revised Edition | : | 2017 |
| Reprint | : | 2018, 2019, 2021 |
| **Reprint** | **:** | **2023** |

---

**Published by** : Mrs. Meena Pandey
for **HIMALAYA PUBLISHING HOUSE PVT. LTD.,**
"Ramdoot", Dr. Bhalerao Marg, Girgaon, Mumbai - 400 004.
**Phone:** 022-23860170, 23863863; **Fax:** 022-23877178
**E-mail:** himpub@bharatmail.co.in; **Website:** www.himpub.com

**Branch Offices** :

**New Delhi** : "Pooja Apartments", 4-B, Murari Lal Street, Ansari Road, Darya Ganj, New Delhi - 110 002. Phone: 011-23270392, 23278631; Fax: 011-23256286

**Nagpur** : Kundanlal Chandak Industrial Estate, Ghat Road, Nagpur - 440 018. Phone: 0712-2721215, 2721216

**Bengaluru** : Plot No. 91-33, 2nd Main Road, Seshadripuram, Behind Nataraja Theatre, Bengaluru - 560 020. Phone: 080-41138821; Mobile: 09379847017, 09379847005

**Hyderabad** : No. 3-4-184, Lingampally, Besides Raghavendra Swamy Matham, Kachiguda, Hyderabad - 500 027. Phone: 040-27560041, 27550139

**Chennai** : No. 34/44, Motilal Street, T. Nagar, Chennai - 600 017. Mobile: 09380460419

**Pune** : "Laksha" Apartment, First Floor, No. 527, Mehunpura, Shaniwarpeth (Near Prabhat Theatre), Pune - 411 030. Phone: 020-24496323, 24496333; Mobile: 09370579333

**Cuttack** : Plot No. 5F-755/4, Sector-9, CDA Market Nagar, Cuttack - 753 014, Odisha. Mobile: 09338746007

**Kolkata** : 3, S.M. Bose Road, Near Gate No. 5, Agarpara Railway Station, North 24 Parganas, West Bengal - 700109. Mobile: 09674536325

**DTP by** : **Sunanda**

**Printed at** : Geetanjali Press Pvt. Ltd., Nagpur. On behalf of HPH.

**TO**
**ABHISHEK**
**&**
**MANREET**

# Preface

## (To Second Edition)
## Business Research Methodology

I am humbly presenting the revised editions. The shortcoming in earlier edition has been removed. New sample project reports have been added. Chapter on development of research has been improved. New definitions have been added. Chapter on generalization has been improved. More solved examples have been added to sub-chapters on quantitative techniques.

I hope improved version will be helpful both to teachers and students.

Comments are welcome to improve the contents.

**J.K. SACHDEVA**
**sachdevajk@hotmail.com**
**09892728281**

---

# Preface

## (To Third Edition)
## Business Research Methodology

I humbly present third revised edition. The shortcomings in earlier edition have been removed. New sample project reports have been added. Chapter on development of research has been improved. New definitions have been added. Chapter on generalization has been improved. More qualitative research techniques for business have been added. More solved examples have been added to sub-chapters on quantitative techniques.

I hope improved version will be helpful both to teachers and students.

Comments are welcome to improve the contents.

**J.K. SACHDEVA**
**sachdevajk@hotmail.com**
**09892728281**

# Preface

## (To First Edition)
## Business Research Methodology

The book '**Business Research Methodology**' has been written as per Indian University Syllabus. The book covers both theoretical explanations and quantitative techniques of research required in business. The contents include defining research problem, development of research methods, research designs, problems of measurement, issues and problems of validity, sampling techniques, qualitative and quantitative analysis, report writing, etc. Chapters like case study method, survey, focus group discussion and multivariate analysis are add-ons explaining the techniques in detail but in a simple way. Chapter on report writing explains methods of writing research article, a project report and a dissertation.

Quantitative techniques of data analysis include chapters as ANOVA, Regression with all tests, multivariate regression analysis, testing of hypothesis of means, proportions and comparison of means, Chi-square. Induction of Factors Analysis, Cluster Analysis, and Discriminant Analysis has been given. Quantitative techniques have been explained by taking solved examples. Each chapter of quantitative techniques has enough solved examples and unsolved problems for practice so that students may grasp the techniques with ease.

A special chapter has been added to explain the use of computer in research. Use of spreadsheet in Excel has been explained to get ANOVA, solve problems of regression and other data analysis. How to use SPSS and other software in research is another special feature of this book.

A unique feature of the book is sub-chapters "**How to do**", after every chapter. It is learning by discussion. Two research scholars **'Jolly and Dolly'** discuss the issues in research in a simple language. Fifteen research projects contributed by expert researchers from various colleges and universities are discussed and analysed by these research scholars. It is learning by role play method. Language in conversation is colloquial and simple. Serious researchers should take it easy. While discussing the research projects, objectives and methodology of the study have been criticized from various perspectives. Contributors, researchers and readers should take it positively as academic debate.

I hope the book will be helpful both to teachers and students.

Comments are welcome to improve the contents.

**J.K. SACHDEVA**

**sachdevajk@hotmail.com**

**09892728281**

# Acknowledgements

Research Methodology is not a new branch of learning and I am not the first person to write on the subject. Since Aristotle, there have been many developments to the area and technique. While concluding a research project, Sugata *et al.* (1997) wrote "Theoretical examples are based on the broad range of writings on the subject." Some of the conclusions will not be novel, as they have been dealt with elsewhere in the literature. Though a unique way has been adopted while presenting the topics, I shall not deny that researchers, whom I have referred, have already contributed a lot to the subject. I am humbly representing the already established knowledge.

I shall always remain thankful to Dr. S. Mahendera Dev, Prof. C.S. Murty and Dr. G.K. Mitra from CESS (Centre for Economic and Social Studies), Hyderabad. It is the divine grace that I am affiliated to them.

I am thankful to the following researchers who have contributed research projects for the sake of discussion in research methodology:

1. Dr. R.M. Chennaveer, Chairman, Social Works Department, Davangere University, Karnataka.
2. Mr. Gangadhar B. Sonar, Assistant Professor, Social Works Department, Karnataka University P.G. Centre, Bijapur, Karnataka.
3. Dr. Ram Krishna Mandal, S.G. Lecturer in Economics, Dera Natung Govt. College, Itanagar-791113, Arunachal Pradesh.
4. Dr. Mrs. Gunmala Suri, Faculty, University Business School, Punjab University, Chandigarh.
5. Dr. Pratibha Desai, Lecturer in Sociology, SIVAJI University, Kolhapur.
6. Prof. S.N. Salwade, Lecturer in Political Science, Walchand College of Arts and Science, Solapur.
7. Dr. A.M. Suresh, Mr. Raja K.G. and Mrs. S. Vijayalakshmi, Faculty Members Post Graduate Department of Management Studies, Dayanand Sagar College of Management and Information Technology, Bengaluru.
8. Dr. M. Dhanabhakyam, and K.R. Vijaysanthi, Faculty Members, Department of Commerce, Bharathiar University, Coimbatore.
9. Dr. P. Chellasamy and J. Udhaya Kumar, Faculty Members, Department of Commerce, Bharathiar University, Coimbatore.
10. Dr. Suramaya Joshi, Department of Home Management, Faculty of Home Science, M.S. University of Baroda, Vadodara, Gujarat.

I have not done any justice personally to them. Instead of appreciating their work, I have put them to harsh criticism of methodology. I have no words to feel sorry for the treatment they get during discussion in the book.

There are hundreds of other researchers who have contributed to this cause but due to space constraints, I am unable to write their names.

I am thankful to my wife Mrs. Meenu Sachdeva, Executive Editor of Journal of Global Economy, who stood by me through thick and thin giving me all technical assistance. The project has seen the light due to her.

It has always been blessings from Mr. D.S. Bawa, Chairperson Research Centre for Social Sciences, who has always been a moral support to all my causes.

I am indebted Dr. C.S.· Adhikari for his continuous moral support.

Last but not the least, it was continuous motivation from Shri S.K. Srivastva, that the book is born.

Thanks to Pandey Brothers of Himalaya Publishing House Pvt. Ltd. for their support.

Thanks are due to faculty and staff members of various institutes to which I have been attached with as an adjunct and full-time faculty.

The book is presented to my children, Abhishek and Manreet.

**J.K. SACHDEVA**

# Contents in Details

CHAPTER

# Business Research Methods

## Structure

## 1.1 Introduction

Organizations often want to know everything about their products, services, programmes, policies, etc. Business research is a systematic way to collect information and get knowledge out of it with a methodology so that the derived knowledge can be used to make decisions. Usually, managers face major issues like ongoing complaints from customers, need to convince financers/ bankers for advances, unmet needs among customers, the need to polish an internal process, issues while managing men, machines, materials and money, issues of forecasting and future plans. Research helps us decide rationally. Business research is the process and the tool needed to reduce risk in managerial decision-making. Business research is a systematic inquiry that provides systematic knowledge to guide managerial decisions. More specifically, it is a process of planning, acquiring, analysing, and disseminating relevant data, information, and insights to decision-makers in ways that mobilize the organization to take appropriate actions that, in turn, maximize business performance.

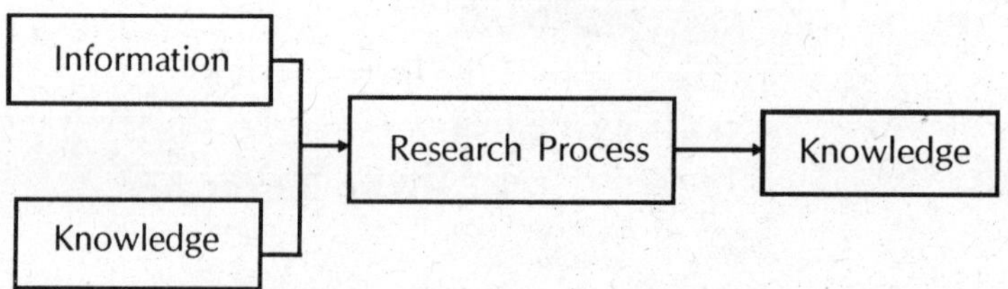


Assume for a moment that you are the manager of a service unit. You are experiencing significant turnover in one of your front desk worker, and a loyal customer has commented that the friendly atmosphere, which has historically drawn him to your unit, is changing. How will you solve the problem? Similarly at macro level, if you are the Cabinet Secretary of department of transportation, charged with determining which roads and bridges will be resurfaced or replaced in the next fiscal year. Usually, you would look at the roads and bridges with the heavy traffic in combination with those representing the biggest economic disaster if closed. Your assistant suggests that business research should be carried out to make your decision, as the decision is one with numerous operational, financial, and public relations ramifications. Will you carry out the recommended research?

Decision-makers can be found in every type of organization: businesses, non-profit organizations, and public agencies. Regardless of where these decision-makers are found or whether their resources are abundant or limited, they all rely on information and derived knowledge to make more efficient and effective use of their budgets.

## 1.2 Why Research?

There are several interesting factors which motivate you to study Business Research Methods:

1. **Business Competition:** Competition in business is increasing day by day. You need to know about customers, products and industry competition.

    a. **Customers:** You need to know about your customers, their needs, their perceptions and future requirements. Research helps you to find out the variables and factors which are significant for increasing customer loyalty and adding new customers.

    b. **Products:** Research helps you to know consumer need and this in turn is used to develop new product. To decide about pricing, positioning, packaging, branding, sales promotion and other promotional techniques, we need to carry out business research.

c. **Industry competition:** You need to know what other companies are doing to increase their market share, factors responsible for increase and decrease of market share, and trends in industry growth.

2. **Business Environment:** Business environment is the totality of all those factors which affect the business but are not under the control of managers. Economic and non-economic elements of environment include economic system (ownership rights like in capitalism and socialism), economic anatomy (structure of households whether manufacturing, trading or agriculture society), Government legislations, Government policies, movement of policies, velocity of policies, fiscal and monetary policies, ideology of ruling party, social ideology, social values and systems, social structures, etc. Changing environment affect the business. You need to know the trend in environment and factors responsible for change in environment.

3. **Maturing of management as a group of disciplines:** The quality of theories and models to explain tactical and strategic results in human resources, marketing, operations, and finance is improving, providing managers with more knowledge. In turn managers are expected to use these models to specific field they are attached to; business research can help managers to understand these models and their use in specific situation.

4. **Explosive growth and influence of the Internet:** The explosive growth of company websites, e-commerce, and electronic publications brings extensive amounts of new information, but this information does not help us to make decisions. (We shall read in the coming chapters that information is not knowledge). Information need to be processed to arrive at knowledge. This knowledge can be helpful to have competitive advantage.

5. **Stakeholders demanding greater influence:** Customers, workers, shareholders, and the general public demand to be included in company decision-making; armed with extensive information, they are more sensitive to their own self-interests than ever before and more resistant to an organization's stimuli.

6. **More global competition:** Competition, both global and domestic, is growing and often coming from unexpected sources; many organizations re-focus on primary competencies, while they seek to improve operations by reducing costs and converting customers to advocates.

7. **More government intervention:** Governments continue to show concern with all aspects of society, becoming increasingly aggressive in protecting various segments of society with various policies. This throws challenges to managers to be alert to various factors which are not under their control. The decisions under such circumstances can be made after the use of managerial and business research tools.

8. **More complex decisions:** Managers have more variables to consider in every decision, increasing their need for more and better knowledge and greater insights from that information.

9. **Lower-cost data collection:** Computers and telecommunications lowered the costs of data collection. Everybody has access to data. Research helps to convert information into knowledge, hence knowledge is easily available, This drastically changes knowledge about consumers at both store and household levels; employees at the position, team, and department levels; suppliers and distributors at the transaction division, and company levels; and machines at the part process, and production-run levels resulting into increased competition. Due to heavy competition among companies and also due to easy availability of data, continuous research process is required.

10. **Better visualization tools:** With the use of technology, it is possible to download at high speed. High-speed downloads of images allow researchers to visualize complex concepts, which enrich measurement capabilities and in turn help consumers to arrive at better decisions of purchasing the products. Researchers can develop new techniques to create images which can be more competitive.

11. **Powerful computations:** Sophisticated techniques of quantitative analysis are emerging to take advantage of increasingly powerful computing capabilities. Computer advances permit businesses to create and manage a data warehouse, an electronic storehouse where vast arrays of collected, integrated data are ready for mining. The power and ease of use of computers offer us the capability to analyse more data more quickly to deal with complex managerial problems. Yet, the quantity of collected raw data overwhelms users, necessitating a means to manage it. Early efforts to provide a flow of information to managers used a Management Information System (MIS). Now the challenge of database management from an MIS perspective has increased which include removing obstacles like resistance to use, keenness of managers to disclose fully their information needs and decision criteria, decreasing costs of single-user report generation, system design time, increasing adaptation to changing organization structures, and decision relevance (standard versus tailored reports). While routine MIS reports are useful for well-structured problems and those amenable to a standardized set of procedures, data must be more than timely and standardized; reporting must be customized to be truly meaningful to the user.

12. **Advanced analytical tools for enhanced insights:** Organizations increasingly practise data mining, applying mathematical models to extract meaningful knowledge from volumes of data contained within internal databases. Enormous quantities of research data are reduced to relatively straightforward equations with statistical models. Expert systems, and outgrowth of artificial intelligence, and data mining entered the 21st century as important tools for research. Advanced analytical tools are available to answer a variety of research questions. Traditional topics open to modelling—market share, price elasticity, the cannibalization of one product's sales by the introduction of another product, the effects on productivity of changing an employee compensation system, to name a few—create decision support models that reflect the behaviour of individuals, households, and industries. Programmes that combine modelling and decision support systems evolved in the latter part of the 20th century to provide the most utility to users.

13. **New perspectives on established research methodologies:** Older tools and methodologies once limited to exploratory research are gaining wider acceptance in dealing with a broader range of managerial problems.

## 1.3 Business Strategy

Let us understand some terms in decision-making. The decision-maker should have a broad knowledge of the firm's environment. A business intelligence system (BIS) is designed to provide the manager with ongoing information about events and trends in the technological, economic, political and legal, demographic, cultural, social, and, most critically, competitive arenas. Such information is compiled from a variety of sources. It is often data from a DSS or BIS that stimulate the question, Should we do business research?

### Strategy

**Strategy** is defined as the course of action with general approach an organization will follow to achieve its goals. Strategy is the course of action which is decided by all levels of management–top level, middle level and lower level. Knowing that it costs less to retain a customer than to capture a new one, most managers place a high value on keeping their customers buying repeatedly. This explains why customer satisfaction, customer loyalty, and customer assessment studies represent a significant portion of business research studies. Now, we have a goal to achieve continuous customer loyalty and satisfaction.

A firm usually implements more than one strategy at a time. With regard to training, one organization may train its data warehouse employees with mostly classroom activities, while another will use on-the-job training. Another strategy might describe how an organization handles maintenance on its machines, rigorous periodic maintenance versus repairs only when a machine breaks down. A strategy may describe how an organisation can best position its particular goods and services to fulfill customer needs. The discovery of opportunities and problems and the resulting strategies is often the task of the BIS.

## Tactics

Business research also contributes significantly to the design and selection of tactics, those specific, timed activities that execute a strategy. In the earlier example of worker in service unit, service floor manager may have changed a product tactic so that entries can be prepared faster (production tactic) and delivered to clients more quickly. The manager may have instituted a new sales programme (a promotion tactic), one that discouraged the front desk staff from making small talk with patrons and rewarded efficiency. Business research is often used to help a manager decide which of several tactics is likely to be successful in executing the desired strategy.

So the purposes of business research can be listed as:

- To identify and define opportunities and problems.
- To define, monitor, and refine strategies.
- To define, monitor, and refine tactics.
- To improve our understanding of the various fields of management

## Internal Research

Not all decision-makers rely on research to make decisions. Such firms usually have an internal research department or an individual who co-ordinates research initiatives. The structure and scope of these operations are as diverse as the management dilemmas that they research. They range from one-person operations, where the individual primarily co-ordinates the hiring of external research suppliers, to small-staffed operations that do some survey or qualitative studies, to large-staffed divisions that more closely approximate the structures of research companies.

## External Research Suppliers

Research Firms help in research. There are many firms who do research as a service industry. There are many types of research firms like custom researcher, proprietary methodology researchers, speciality research firms, syndicate data provider, omnibus researchers, trade associations and consultants.

**A proprietary methodology** is a research programme or technique that is owned by a single firm. It may be a slight twist on an established methodology or may be a method developed by that firm. Firms often brand these methodologies to establish distinction in the minds of prospective clients. Proprietary methodologies grow from significant expertise in a given methodology or a given industry and develop over many years' working on thousands of client projects.

**Speciality researchers** represent the largest number of research firms and tend to dominate the small research firms operated by a single researcher or a very small staff. These firms may establish a speciality in one or several different arenas:

- Methodology. The firms (methodology specialists) may conduct only one type of research (for example, survey research, customer satisfaction research, ad copy testing, packaging evaluation, focus groups, retail mystery shopping, or retail design research).
- Process. The firms usually contribute to only a portion of the research process (for example, sample recruiting, and telephone interviewing, or fielding a Web survey).
- Industry. The firms become experts in one or a few industries (for example, pharmaceutical research or entertainment research or telecommunications research).
- Participant group. The firms become experts in a particular participant group (for example, Latin-Americans, or children, or doctors, or country club golfers).
- Geographic region. The firms may operate in only one region of a country — as is true for many mystery shopping firms — or a single country or group of countries.

One large group in this speciality research category includes firms that conduct focus groups.

Research companies in India

1. Delphi Research Services Pvt. Ltd., Bangalore
2. Diksha Research, Coimbatore.
3. Market Pulse, New Delhi.
4. Samsika Marketing Consultants (P) Ltd., Mumbai.
5. Multiple Action Research Group, New Delhi

**Syndicated Data Providers:** When managers want comparative performance and opinion data, pitting themselves against their competitors in sales, market share, share of voice, image as a corporate citizen or employer, or salary and benefit levels, they turn to researchers that are syndicated data providers. For a substantial fee, often millions of dollars per year, managers subscribe to receive the periodic data as well as the interpretation of these data. A syndicated data provider tracks the change of one or more measures over time, usually in a given industry. For example, a syndicated data provider might track product movements through various retail outlets and wholesale environments. The tracking of sales performance measures during promotional events like coupon drops, distribution of product samples, special events (like the appearance of a celebrity at a charity event), and advertising is often the key to successful strategic planning. These research firms are also responsible for providing decision-makers with measures of price elasticity. Each syndicated data provider determines the frequency of data collection and reporting based on the heeds of the members in the syndicate. While some studies provide data monthly or weekly, not all such studies are done as frequently as sales tracking studies. Some syndicated data are collected only once per year or once every few years. Other syndicated data are collected several times per year during designated collection periods. In India, CMIE and Indiastat.com are data providers.

**Omnibus Researchers:** Sometimes the decision-maker needs the answer to one or a few questions to make a quick tactical decision, such as when it faces a crisis caused by a product recall or the indictment of a company staff for fraud, there are research providers who help instantly.

## 1.4 What Research is Not?

Let us understand what research is not.

- **Research isn't information gathering:** Gathering information from resources such as books or magazines isn't research as there in no contribution to new knowledge.
- **Research isn't the transportation of facts:** Merely transporting facts from one resource to another doesn't constitute research because there is no contribution to new knowledge although this may make existing knowledge more accessible.

**Research** is the systematic process of collecting and analysing information (data) in order to increase our understanding of the phenomenon about which we are concerned or interested.

The following kinds of projects usually don't make for good research:

- Self-enlightenment.
- Comparing data sets.
- Correlating data sets.
- Problems with yes/no answers.

## 1.5 Methods and Methodology

**Difference between 'Methods' and 'Methodology'**

| Method | Methodology |
|---|---|
| • Techniques for gathering evidence. | • The underlying theory and analysis of how research does or should proceed, is often influenced by discipline. |
| • The various ways of proceeding in gathering information. | • "an *epistemology*" is a theory of knowledge. It is the theory that decides what can be observed. |

Research originates with a question or problem, requires clear articulation of a goal. It follows a specific plan or procedure and often divides main problem into sub-problems. It is guided by specific problem, question, or hypothesis. It accepts certain critical assumptions. Procedure requires collection and interpretation of data and is Cyclical (helical) in nature.

**Good research requires:**

- The scope and limitations of the work to be clearly defined.
- The process to be clearly explained so that it can be reproduced and verified by other researchers.
- A thoroughly planned design that is as objective as possible.
- Highly ethical standards are applied.
- All limitations are documented.
- Data should be adequately analysed and explained.

- All findings are presented unambiguously and all conclusions should be justified by sufficient evidence.

The research involves an eclectic blending of an enormous range of skills and activities. To be a good researcher, you have to be able to work well with a wide variety of people, understand the specific methods used to conduct research, understand the subject that you are studying, be able to convince someone to give you the funds to study it, stay on track and on schedule, speak and write persuasively, and on and on. So more focused you are about what you want to gain by your research. The more effective and efficient you can be in your research, the shorter the time it will take. Otherwise it will cost you in your own time, the time of your employees and the time of a consultant.

## 1.6 Features of a Good Research

Good research generates dependable data that are derived by professionally conducted practices and that can be used reliably for decision-making. In contrast, poor research is carelessly planned and conducted, resulting in data that a manager can't use to reduce his or her decision-making risks. Good research follows the standards of the **scientific method:** systematic, empirically based procedures for generating replicable research. Following are the features of a good research for managerial decisions:

1. **Purpose clearly defined.** The purpose of the business research, the problem involved or the decision to be made should be clearly defined and sharply delineated in terms as unambiguous as possible. Getting this in writing is valuable even in instances where the same person serves as researcher and decision-maker. The statement of the decision problem should include its scope, its limitations, and the precise meanings of all words and terms significant to the research. Failure of the researcher to do this adequately may raise legitimate doubts in the minds of research report readers as to whether the researcher has sufficient understanding of the problem to make a sound proposal attacking it. This characteristic is comparable to developing a strategic plan for achieving an objective before developing a tactical plan or an action map.

2. **Research process detailed.** The research procedures used should be described in sufficient detail to permit another researcher to repeat the research. Except when secrecy is imposed, research reports should reveal with candour the sources of data and the means by which they were obtained. Omission of significant procedural details makes it difficult or impossible to estimate the validity and reliability of the data and justifiably weakens the confidence of the reader in the research itself as well as any recommendations based on the research. This characteristic is comparable to developing a tactical plan.

3. **Research design thoroughly planned.** The procedural design of the research should be carefully planned to yield results that are as objective as possible. When a sampling of the population is involved, the report should include evidence concerning the degree of representativeness of the sample. A survey of opinions or recollections ought not to be used when more reliable evidence is available from documentary sources or by direct observation. Bibliographic searches should be as thorough and complete as possible. Experiments should have satisfactory controls. Direct observations should be recorded in writing as soon as possible after the event. Efforts should be made to minimize the influence of personal bias in selecting and recording data. This characteristic is comparable to developing detailed action plans for each tactic.

4. **High ethical standards applied.** Researchers often work independently and have significant latitude in designing and executing research projects. A research design that includes

safeguards against causing mental or physical harm to participants and makes data integrity a first priority should be highly valued. Ethical issues in research reflect important moral concerns about the practice of responsible behaviour in society. Researchers frequently find themselves precariously balancing the rights of their subjects against the scientific dictates of their chosen method. When this occurs, they have a responsibility to guard the welfare of the participants in the studies and also the organizations to which they belong, their clients, their colleagues, and themselves. Careful consideration must be given to those research situations in which there is a possibility of physical or psychological harm, exploitation, invasion of privacy, and/or loss of dignity. The research need must be weighed against the potential for adverse effects. Typically, you can redesign a study, but sometimes you cannot. The researcher should be prepared for this dilemma.

5. **Limitations frankly revealed.** The researcher should report, with complete frankness, flaws in procedural design and estimate their effect on the findings. There are very few perfect research designs. Some of the imperfections may have little effect on the validity and reliability of the data; others may invalidate them entirely. A competent researcher should be sensitive to the effects of imperfect design. The researcher's experience in analysing data should provide a basis for estimating the influence of design flaws. As a decision-maker, you should question the value of research where no limitations are reported.

6. **Analysis adequate for decision maker's needs.** Analysis of the data should be extensive enough to reveal its significance, what managers call "insights." The methods of analysis used should be appropriate. The extent to which this criterion is met is frequently a good measure of the competence of the researcher. Adequate analysis of the data is the most difficult phase of research for the novice. The validity and reliability of data should be checked carefully. The data should be classified in ways that assist the researcher in reaching pertinent conclusions and clearly reveal the findings that have led to those conclusions. When statistical methods are used, the probability of error should be estimated and the criteria of statistical significance applied.

7. **Findings presented unambiguously.** Some evidence of the competence and integrity of the researcher may be found in the report itself. For example, language that is restrained, clear, and precise; assertions that are carefully drawn and hedged with appropriate reservations; and an apparent effort to achieve maximum objectivity tend to leave a favourable impression of the researcher with the decision-maker. Generalizations that outrun the evidence on which they are based, exaggerations, and unnecessary verbiage tend to leave an unfavourable impression. Such reports are not valuable to managers wading through the minefields of organisational decision-making. Presentation of data should be comprehensive, easily understood by the decision-maker, and organized so that the decision-maker can readily locate critical findings.

8. **Conclusions justified.** Conclusions should be limited to those for which the data provide an adequate basis. Researchers are often tempted to broaden the basis of induction by including personal experiences and their interpretations — data not subject to the controls under which the research data were gathered. Equally undesirable is the all-too-frequent practice of drawing conclusions from a study of a limited population and applying them universally. Researchers also may be tempted to rely too heavily on data collected in a prior study and use it in the interpretation of a new study. Such practice sometimes occurs among research specialists who confine their work to clients in a small industry. These actions tend to decrease the objectivity of the research and weaken readers' confidence in the findings. Good researchers always specify the conditions under which their conclusions seem to be valid.

9. **Researcher's experience reflected.** Greater confidence in the research is warranted if the researcher is experienced, has a good reputation in research, and is a person of integrity. Were it possible for the reader of a research report to obtain sufficient information about the researcher, this criterion perhaps would be one of the best bases for judging the degree of confidence a piece of research warrants and the value of any decision based upon it. For this reason the research report should contain information about the qualifications of the researcher.

Good business research has an inherent value only to the extent that it helps management make better decisions that help achieve organizational goals. Interesting information about consumers, employees, competitors, or the environment may be pleasant to have, but its value is limited if the information cannot be applied to a critical decision. If a study does not help management select more effective, more efficient, less risky, or more profitable alternatives than otherwise would be the case, its use should be questioned. Alternatively, management may have insufficient resources (time, money, or skill) to conduct an appropriate study or may face a low level of risk associated with the decision at hand. In these situations, it is valid to avoid business research and its associated costs in time and money. Business research finds its justification in the contribution it makes to the decision-maker's task and to the bottom line.

## 1.7 Fallacy in Research

A *fallacy* is an error in reasoning, usually based on mistaken assumptions. Researchers are very familiar with all the ways they could go wrong, with the fallacies they are susceptible to. Two important types of fallacies are discussed below.

The **ecological fallacy** occurs when you make conclusions about individuals based only on analysis of group data. For instance, assume that you measured the math scores of a particular classroom and found that they had the highest average score in the district. Later (probably outside school in a garden) you run into one of the kids from that class and you think to yourself that she must be a math whiz. It is a fallacy because she comes from the class with the highest *average* doesn't mean that she is automatically a high-scorer in math. She can be the lowest math scorer in a class that otherwise consists of math geniuses.

An ***exception fallacy*** is sort of the reverse of the ecological fallacy. It occurs when you reach a group conclusion on the basis of exceptional cases. For instance you meet a school student on a way and after interaction you may find her to be math whiz and may conclude that her class may be of math geniuses. This is the kind of fallacious reasoning that is at the core of a lot of sexism and racism. The stereotype is of the guy who sees a woman make a driving error and concludes that "women are terrible drivers." It may wrong or it is fallacy.

Both of these fallacies point to some of the traps that exist in both research and everyday reasoning. They also point out how important it is that we do research. We need to determine empirically how individuals perform (not just rely on group averages). Similarly, we need to look at whether there are correlations between certain behaviours and certain groups

## 1.8 Important Terms in Research

Some concepts and terminologies used in research:

**Theoretical And Empirical Research:** These **terms** are often contrasted with each other. Research is theoretical, meaning that much of it is concerned with developing, exploring or testing the theories or ideas that a researcher has about how the world operates. But it is also empirical, meaning that it is based on observations and measurements of reality and what we perceive of the world around us. We can even think of most research as a blending of these two terms- a comparison of our theories about how the world operates with our observations of its operation.

**Nomothetic:** Nomothetic refers to laws or rules that pertain to the general case (nomos in Greek) and is contrasted with the term "idiographic" which refers to laws or rules that relate to individuals. It means that most research is concerned with the nomothetic, the general case, rather than the individual. We often study individuals, but usually we are interested in generalizing to more than just the individual.

The nomothetic deductive method is the one that is used by researchers who want to learn something about social regularities — things that apply to people in general. The nom in "nomothetic" appears in words like "autonomy," "economy," and "astronomy" — all words that describe systems of laws or principles that govern different aspects of reality. Nomothetic research attempts to discover what those systems of laws or principles are, while idiographic research is interested in describing only a single event, person, or situation. Since it is interested in discovering the laws or principles that govern aspects of reality, nomothetic research cannot depend on information that describes a single individual. It needs information that describes enough cases so that general patterns or relationships can be seen.

An idiographic study is one that explores a single person or event or situation in detail.

Although the researcher doing idiographic work would learn a great deal about the idiosyncratic thoughts or behaviours of the person or situation that was investigated, this information would apply only to that specific person or situation. Although it might give the researcher some idea of what to look for in the wider context, it can't be used to describe the population from which the case studied was drawn. It tells little, if anything, about social regularities — things that apply to people in general.

On the other hand, nomothetic research cannot depend on information that describes a single individual. It needs information that describes many cases — perhaps hundreds or thousands — enough so that general patterns or relationships can be seen. Ideally, it would use information that describes all people, events, or situations. Because this is clearly impossible, a different approach is taken. Inferential statistics, a set of logical tools based on the relation between an entire population and a subset of that population, assuming the subset is chosen in the right way, makes it possible to learn about the population by studying the much smaller sub-set.

**Probabilistic:** Research is ***probabilistic***, or based on probabilities. The inferences that we make in research have probabilities associated with them. Part of the reason we have seen statistics become so dominant in research is that it allows us to estimate probabilities for the situations we study.

**Causal:** Please note that it is spelled as *causal* not *casual*, hence means to relate with effect. In research we attempt to study cause effect relationship. This doesn't mean that most studies actually study cause-effect relationships. There are some studies that simply observe, for instance, surveys that seek to describe the per cent of people holding a particular opinion. And, there are many studies that explore relationships, for example, studies that attempt to see whether there is a relationship between gender and salary. Probably the vast majority of applied social research consists of these descriptive and correlational studies.

**Cross-sectional and longitudinal studies:** Time is an important element of any research design. A *cross-sectional* study is one that takes place at a single point in time. In effect, we are taking a 'slice' or cross-section of whatever it is we're observing or measuring, for instance, a study of young students pursuing MBA. A *longitudinal* study is one that takes place over time. It is the historical data and time series, e.g., study of exports during a particular period. A further distinction is made between two types of longitudinal designs: ***repeated measures*** and ***time series***. There is no universally agreed upon rule for distinguishing these two terms, but in general, if we have two or a few waves of measurement; you are using a *repeated measures* design. If you have many waves of measurement over time, you have a *time series.*

**Variables:** A ***variable*** is *any entity that can take on different values.* Anything that can vary can be considered a variable. For instance, age can be considered a variable because age can take different values for different people or for the same person at different times. Similarly, *country* can be considered a variable because a person's country can be assigned a value. Variables aren't always 'quantitative' or numerical. The variable 'gender' consists of two text values: 'male' and 'female'. We can, if it is useful, assign quantitative values instead of (or in place of) the text values. An ***attribute*** is a specific value on a variable. For instance, the variable *sex* or *gender* has two attributes: *male* and *female.* Another important distinction having to do with the term 'variable' is the distinction between an ***independent*** and ***dependent*** variable. This distinction is particularly relevant when you are investigating cause-effect relationships. The ***independent variable is what we (or nature) manipulates*** — a treatment or programme or cause. The ***dependent variable is what is affected by the independent variable*** — our effects or outcomes. For example, if we are studying the effects of a new educational programme on student achievement, the programme is the independent variable and our measures of achievement are the dependent ones. Another example, consumption (C) depends upon income (Y), which means C is the function of Y, i.e., C = f(Y). Here C is the dependent variable while Y is the independent variable.

**Hypotheses:** A hypothesis is a specific statement of prediction. It describes in concrete terms what we expect will happen in our study. Not all studies have hypotheses. Sometimes a study is designed to be exploratory. There is no formal hypothesis, and perhaps the purpose of the study is to explore some area more thoroughly in order to develop some specific hypothesis or prediction that can be tested in future research. A single study may have one or many hypotheses. Some examples of hypotheses are: 'All trains are running on time', 'it rains heavily in the month of July', 'Girls like colourful clothes', 'Boys like white collar jobs', and 'Inflations is rising'.

We define a proposition as a statement about observable phenomena (concepts) that may be judged as true or false. When a proposition is formulated for empirical testing, we call it a hypothesis. As a declarative statement about the relationship between two or more variables, a hypothesis is of a tentative and conjectural nature. Hypotheses have also been described as statements in which we assign variables to cases. A case is defined in this sense as the entity or thing the hypothesis talks about. The variable is the characteristic, trait, or attribute, in the hypothesis, is imputed to the case. For example, we may create the following hypothesis:

Brand Manager Abhishek (case) has a higher-than-average achievement motivation (variable).

If our hypothesis was based on more than one case, it would be a generalization.

**For example:** Brand managers in Company Z (cases) have a higher-than-average achievement motivation (variable).

**There are two types of hypotheses:** 1. descriptive Hypotheses and 2. Relational Hypotheses. Relational Hypotheses can be Correlational or Causal.

**Descriptive hypotheses** state the existence, size, form or distribution of some variable. Descriptive hypotheses format has many benefits:

- It encourages researchers to crystallise their thinking about the likely to be found.
- It encourages them to think about the implications of a supported or rejected finding.
- It is useful for testing statistical significance.

In descriptive research, the goal is to obtain a complete and accurate description of events, conditions, circumstances, processes, and relationships surrounding the situation under study. What were the conditions? What were relevant interpersonal, familial, social, economic, political, religious, or educational features of the situation? How many people were involved? What type of people were involved? What kind of relationships did they have with one another? How typical were their experiences? While this kind of research might tell me what was happening, it won't explain the causes of what I saw.

To get at explanations of causal relationships between events and circumstances, a different kind of research would be more useful. When we are interested in causal relationships, we do explanatory research. For example, how do the educational backgrounds of your parents influence the way they relate to you? Is the way parents interact with their children influenced by the number and kind of relationships the parents had with their parents? ...with their siblings? ...with their friends? Is the extent to which parents are socially integrated related to the ability of their children to form strong intimate ties when they become adults? Explanatory research is the most demanding kind of research, and it requires the use of special methods to identify causes and effects.

There are different kinds of generative forces in theories. Each leads to a particular form of explanation. The simplest kind of generative forces are ordinarily called "causes." A cause is an antecedent condition (something that happens first) that produces a consequent effect (something that happens later as a result of what happened earlier) over which the people involved have no control. The effect happens whether or not the person or people involved want it to; it is an unavoidable consequence of the cause. A theory that explains patterns by reference to uncontrollable antecedents employs causal explanation and is called a law. (ex: Because they are naturally more aggressive and solitary, men make more assertions and give more orders than women; because they are naturally more co-operative and social, women ask more questions and make more requests than men. Men and women behave like this because they are men and women, not because they want to or they think they should.)

A second, more complex, type of generative force is the rule. A theory that explains behavioural patterns by reference to norms or social customs employs rule-based explanation and is called a rule of behaviour. Rules can take many different forms. At Simon Fraser University, for example, people almost always cover certain parts of their bodies when they are in classrooms, regardless of how warm or cold it is. They do this because it is a social norm — a rule. On roads where the traffic goes in both directions, people almost always drive on the right side of the road. They do this for two reasons: first, because there is a law (a particular type of rule) that says you should do this; second, because they do not want to crash head-first into a car coming from the other direction. Note that it is quite possible to break these rules, although there is usually a price to be paid if you are caught.

A third type of generative force is the reason. A reason refers to the pre-existing goals, needs, and desires of a person that explain patterns of behaviour and social activity. A theory that explains patterns by reference to goals or subjective reasons for acting is called a teleological explanation. A great deal of research energy is directed toward understanding the dynamics of human behaviour by focusing on how people's goals and their efforts to achieve them affect how they interact with one another.

Generative forces are what make things happen. They are the connections between causes and effects; they are the social forces, customs, pressures, and motivating forces that govern the behaviour of people in social groups; they are the rewards and goals which people try to attain and the costs and pain they try to avoid. Each type of generative forces requires its own particular form of explanation. It is important that you choose the right type of explanation for the generative force acting in the situation you are trying to explain. For example, causal explanations are good for explaining why people fall on icy sidewalks; rule-based explanations are appropriate for descriptions of what people say in particular ceremonial social situations; teleological approaches are probably the best ones to use when you are interested in how people behave when they are trying to achive a desired goal. If people's behaviour is determined by social norms, a causal explanation will be a waste of time. If personal goals are the motivating force, a rule-based explanation will not shed much light.

## Relational Hypotheses

The research question format is less frequently used with a situation calling for relational hypotheses. These are statements that describe a relationship between two variables with respect to some case. For example, "Foreign (variable) cars are perceived by American consumers (case) to be of better quality (variable) than domestic cars." In this instance, the nature of the relationship between the two variables ("country of origin" and "perceived quality") is not specified. Here we have two interpretations. The first interpretation (unspecified relationship) indicates a correlational relationship; the second (predictable relationship) indicates an explanatory, or causal, relationship.

Correlational hypotheses state that the variables occur together in some specified manner without implying that one causes the other. Such weak claims are often made when we believe there are more basic causal forces that affect both variables or when we have not developed enough evidence to claim a stronger linkage. For example: 'Young women (under 35 years of age) purchase fewer units of our product than women who are 35 years of age or older.' 'The number of suits sold varies directly with the level of the business cycle.' 'People in Atlanta give the president a more favourable rating than do people in St. Louis.' By labelling these as correlational hypotheses, we make no claim that one variable causes the other to change or take on different values.

With explanatory (causal) hypotheses, there is an implication that the existence of or a change in one variable causes or leads to a change in the other variable. As we noted previously, the causal variable is typically called the independent variable and the other the dependent variable. Cause means roughly to "help make happen." For example of explanatory hypotheses: An increase in family income (Independent Variable) leads to an increase in the percentage of income saved (Dependent Variable). Exposure to the company's messages concerning industry problems (Independent Variable) leads to more favourable attitudes (Dependent Variable) by employees toward the company.

In research, a hypothesis serves several important functions:

- It guides the direction of the study.
- It identifies facts that are relevant and those that are not.
- It suggests which form of research design is likely to be most appropriate.
- It provides a framework for organizing the conclusions that result.

## Theory

Hypotheses play an important role in the development of theory. How theory differs from hypothesis may cause confusion. We make the general distinction that the difference between theory and hypothesis is one of degree of complexity and abstraction. In general, theories tend to be complex, be abstract, and involve multiple variables. Hypotheses, on the other hand, tend to be more simple, limited variable statements involving concrete instances. A person not familiar with research uses the term theory to express the opposite of fact. In this sense, theory is viewed as being speculative or "ivory tower." One hears that managers need to be less theoretical or that some idea will not work because it is too theoretical. This is an incorrect picture of the relationship between fact and theory to the researcher. In truth, fact and theory are each necessary for the other to be of value. Our ability to make rational decisions, as well as to develop scientific knowledge, is measured by the degree to which we combine fact and theory. We all operate on the basis of theories we hold. In one sense, theories are the generalizations we make about variables and the relationships among them. We use these generalizations to make decisions and predict outcomes. For example, it is midday and you note that the outside natural light is dimming, dark clouds are moving rapidly in from the west, the breeze is freshening, and the air temperature is cooling. We may predict that something decidedly wet will probably occur in a short time!

A theory is a set of systematically inter-related concepts, definitions, and propositions that are advanced to explain and predict phenomena (facts). In this sense, we have many theories and use them continually to explain or predict what goes on around us. To the degree that our theories are sound and fit the situation, we are successful in our explanations and predictions.

Let us take another example. In marketing, the product life cycle describes the stages that a product category goes through in the marketplace. The generalized product life cycle has four stages (although the length and shape of product life cycles differ): introduction, growth, maturity, and decline. In each stage, many concepts, constructs, and hypotheses describe the influences that change revenue and profit. Definitions are also needed for communicating about the claims of the theory and its consistency in testing to reality. For example, in the growth stage, companies spend heavily on advertising and promotion to create product awareness. In the early period of this stage these expenditures may be made to fuel primary demand (construct), improving product class awareness rather than brand awareness. Also, high pricing may reflect skimming (concept) to help the company recover developmental costs. The product manager may alternatively use low pricing, or penetration pricing (concept), to build unit volume. In the growth stage, sales increase rapidly because many consumers are trying or actually using the product; and those who tried, were satisfied, and bought again—repeat purchasers (concept)—are swelling the ranks. If the company is unable to attract repeat purchasers, this usually means death for the product (proposition). The maturity stage is a good time for the company in terms of generating cash (proposition). The costs of developing the product and establishing its position in the marketplace are paid and it tends to be profitable. Firms will often try to use extension strategies (constructs). These are attempts to delay the decline stage of the product life cycle by introducing new versions of the product. In the decline stage, "products will consume a disproportionate share of management time and financial resources relative to their potential future worth" (hypothesis). To make this hypothesis fully testable, we would need operational definitions for disproportionate share, time, resources, and future worth.

"Grounded theory" is a name for the results of the data-to-theory method of theory construction. When the scientist begins by making observations and then constructing a theoretical explanation that would account for the observed patterns, the logic is called data-to-theory and the logical method being used is inductive. The logical pattern is to move from the specific to the general. This approach is useful for the creation of theories in areas where there hasn't been much previous research. However, one weakness of this approach is that theories created in this fashion always match the data upon which they are based. Looking to see how well the theory "fits" the data only tells how good a job the theorist did while describing the data; the data cannot be used to test the theory. For this reason the data-to-theory approach is combined with the theory-to-data approach.

When the scientist begins with a theory and then tests it against observed data, the logic is called theory-to-data and the logical process being used is deductive. The pattern here is to move from the general to the specific — exactly the opposite of the inductive method. In the theory-to-data method, data are used to test the theory. A failure of the data to fit the theory is usually taken as an indication that there is something wrong with the theory, with the measurement methods (and thus with the data), with the methods being used to compare the data to the theory, or with the logic leading the researcher to expect the theory to fit the data.

In practice, the two logical modes are complimentary: the inductive approach is used in the development of theory and the deductive approach is used in the verification of theory. Used together, the two methods are much stronger than either one used separately.

Perspicuity is clearness. A perspicuous theory is clear, lucid, readily understandable, and unambiguous. Because it is precisely stated, it leads to clear, unequivocal predictions.

Parsimony is defined by my dictionary as "extreme care in spending money; reluctance to spend money unnecessarily." In the context of theory, it means "extreme care in the use of concepts; reluctance to use more concepts than are absolutely necessary." Is the theory parsimonious in its use of concepts and relations, or is it a complex network of relations tying numerous concepts together in several different ways? A parsimonious theory is one which uses few concepts and relationships among them. In this sense, it is more straightforward, more likely to be internally consistent. Because it is not a complicated mess of many concepts tied together in many ways, it is easier to connect with reality and more likely to lead to unambiguous and unequivocal predictions.

Utility in this context means three things: First, does the theory go "where no one has gone before"? Does it explain previously inexplicable phenomena? Does it explain things previously thought to be unrelated? Second, does it have heuristic value — does it set the stage for further conceptual developments and empirical research? Does it suggest new areas for research? Third, should anyone care about the theory? Does it matter in the sense that the knowledge based on the theory will have an effect on peoples lives?

Laboratory research is conducted in an artificial environment, all aspects of which are controlled by the researcher. Field studies take place in a natural environment where people normally are found in the course of day-to-day life. Laboratory studies are useful because the high degree of control allows the researcher to rule out possible disturbances or "contaminations" that would probably cause the results to be less reliable or valid than they otherwise would be. Field research, on the other hand, leaves the research open to the complexities and messiness of ordinary life. The researcher who wants to learn about how people in small communities behave when their houses are destroyed by a tropical storm can't answer the question with a controlled laboratory study; he has to wait for a hurricane or typhoon to develop. With field research you can address issues in the context in which they ordinarily occur. With a laboratory study, you must isolate the focus of inquiry from its normal context in order to prevent biasing the results. This clearly poses a dilemma: are the complexities of the field a greater threat than the certain distortions caused by the decontextualization demanded by laboratory research?

To say empirical research is "positive" means that it deals with questions about what is and why it is, rather than what ought to be. The book mentions a master's thesis about assisted suicides. The researcher asked who participated in the suicides, how they felt about what they did, and what arguments they made about the correctness or appropriateness of their actions. These were all valid topics for scientific enquiry. Science could not, however, determine whether it is wrong to assist someone to commit suicide. This is a question of societal norms, personal values and individual beliefs. While an empirical researcher can ask what people believe and what their personal values are, the researcher who argues that one set of beliefs or values are better than another has left the research arena and stepped onto the realm of the politician, the preacher, or the ideologue.

### Models

The term model is used in business research and other fields of business to represent phenomena through the use of analogy. A model is defined here as a representation of a system that is constructed to study some aspect of that system or the system as a whole. Models differ from theories in that a theory's role is explanation whereas a model's role is representation.

Early models (and even those created as recently as the 1990s for mainframe computers) were enormous expensive and often incomprehensible to all but their developers. Modelling software, such as Excel, has made modelling more inexpensive and accessible.

Models allow researchers and managers to characterize present or future conditions: the effect of advertising on consumer awareness or intention to purchase, a product distribution channel, brand switching behaviour, an employee training programme, and many other aspects of business. A model's purpose is to increase our understanding, prediction, and control of the complexities of the environment. Descriptive, predictive, and normative models are found in business research.

***Descriptive*** models are used frequently for more complex systems. They allow visualization of numerous variables and relationships.

***Predictive*** models forecast future events (for example, the Fourt and Woodlock model could be used to calculate revenue from a market segment).

***Normative*** models are chiefly for control, informing us about what actions should be taken. Models may also be static, representing a system at one point in time, or dynamic, representing the evolution of a system over time.

Models are developed through the use of inductive and deductive reasoning, a model may originate from empirical observations about behavior based on researched facts and relationships among variables. Inductive reasoning allows the modeller to draw conclusions from the facts or evidence in planning the dynamics of the model. The modeller may also use existing theory, managerial experience, judgment, or facts deduced from known laws of nature. In this case, deductive reasoning serves to create particular conclusions derived from general premises.

Models are an important means of advancing theories and aiding decision makers. Because the inputs are **often** unknown, imprecise, or temporal estimates of complex variables, creating and using models in the decision-making process can be a time-consuming endeavour.

## 1.9 Steps in Research Process

Issues in scientific research process will be discussed in second chapter. Research steps can broadly be written as follows. But it needs hard work for every step.

(a) **Define Problem:** How to define a problem is a big problem. We have hundreds of social and personal problems. There are thousands of problems at our workplace. Since you get up in the morning till you go to sleep, you observe hundreds of problems. Despite visible and observed problems, researchers are unable to find the problem for research. If they are able to narrow it down, they are unable to define it. We shall learn in coming chapters how to resolve these issues.

(b) **Review Literature:** After defining the problem, review literature. Details about literature reviews will be explained in coming chapters. However, you should understand this stage that lakhs of researchers are working on problems every day. You are not the first person to pick the problems. If you search good journals, you will find your problem has already been worked out by many researchers. The problem definition may not be same but scope and area may be same. Review their findings. Can you conclude from their findings? Can you find gap what has not been done by other researchers? Many researchers feel that literature review can give you good induction.

(c) **Set Objectives of Study:** The problem should be converted into objectives or sub-problems. Objectives should be achievable. A good guide will advise you whether these objectives are achievable or not. You should foresee whether you will be able to get data or not. Will you be able to analyze the data or not? Do you know tools of analysis or not? Will you be able to relate to your findings with your objectives or not.

(d) **Frame Hypotheses:** Sub-problems are converted into hypotheses. Hypothesis is a tentative statement which needs to be validated. The validated statement becomes your finding. You can relate your findings with your objectives.

(e) **Research Design:** We should properly plan our research. If it is experimental research, research design should be well defined and planned. Researcher should be clear in his mind whether it is going to be formal design or informal design. More has been written in the coming chapters.

(f) **Gather Data:** Gather data as you have decided in your plan or research design. Take care of sample size and sample frame. Methodology to gather data should be well planned.

(g) **Analyze:** You should be expert in analyzing the data. Qualitative analysis is very difficult to analyse. Observing the data by qualitative methods and then generalizing it, is very difficult. Many researchers take the help of psychologists. Many researchers are comfortable with quantitative methods. Quantitative methods help us in deductions. Hypothesis can be validated easily by quantitative techniques.

(h) **Write Report:** Research is not done for self-enlightenment or self-satisfaction. People must read your finding. Report should be written after everything has been done. Features of a good research report have been written in coming chapters.

## 1.10 Types of Research

There are three types of research in business

- Exploratory Research
- Descriptive research
- Causal research

**Exploratory Research:** The objective of exploratory research is to gather preliminary information that will help define problems and suggest hypotheses. Exploratory research is a type of research conducted because a problem has not been clearly defined. Exploratory research helps determine the best research design, data collection method and selection of subjects. Given its fundamental nature, exploratory research often concludes that a perceived problem does not actually exist.

Exploratory research relies on secondary research such as reviewing available literature and/or data, or qualitative approaches such as informal discussions with consumers, employees, management or competitors, and more formal approaches through indepth interviews, focus groups, projective methods, case studies or pilot studies. The results of exploratory research are not usually useful for decision-making by themselves, but they can provide significant insight into a given situation. Although the results of qualitative research can give some indication as to the "why", "how" and "when" something occurs, it cannot tell us "how often" or "how many."

Exploration is particularly useful when researchers lack a clear idea of the problems they will meet during the study. Through exploration researchers develop concepts more clearly, establish priorities, develop operational definitions, and improve the final research design. Exploration may also save time and money. If the problem is not as important as first thought, more formal studies can be cancelled. Exploration serves other purposes as well. The area of investigation may be so new or so vague that a researcher needs to do an exploration just to learn something about the dilemma facing the manager. Important variables may not be known or thoroughly defined. Hypotheses for the research may be needed. Also, the researcher may explore to be sure it is practical to do a formal study in the area. Despite its obvious value, researchers and managers alike give exploration less attention than it deserves. There are strong pressures for quick answers. Moreover, exploration is sometimes linked to old biases about qualitative research: subjectiveness, non-representativeness, and non-systematic design.

**Descriptive Research:** The objective of descriptive research is to describe things, such as the market potential for a product or the demographics and attitudes of consumers who buy the product. Descriptive research, also known as statistical research, describes data and characteristics about the population or phenomenon being studied. Descriptive research answers the questions who, what, where, when and how. Although the data description is factual, accurate and systematic, the research cannot describe what caused a situation. Thus, descriptive research cannot be used to create a causal relationship, where one variable affects another. In other words, descriptive research can be said to have a low requirement for internal validity **(we shall learn about validity in coming chapters)**. The description is used for frequencies, averages and other statistical calculations. Often the best approach, prior to writing descriptive research, is to conduct a survey investigation. Qualitative research often has the aim of description and researchers may follow-up with examinations of why the observations exist and what the implications of the findings are.

The basic difference between exploratory and descriptive research is the research design. Exploratory research follows a format that is less structured and more flexible than descriptive research. This approach works well when the marketer doesn't have an understanding of the topic or the topic is new and it is hard to pinpoint the research direction. The downside, however, is that results may not be as useful in aiding a marketing decision. We use this method because in addition to offering the marketer basic information on a topic, exploratory research may also provide direction for a more formal research effort. For instance, exploratory research may indicate who the key decision makers are in a particular market thus enabling a more structured descriptive study targeted to this group.

**Causal Research:** The objective of causal research is to test hypotheses about cause-and-effect relationships. In this form of research the marketer tries to determine if the manipulation of one variable, called the independent variable, affects another variable, called the dependent variable. In essence, the marketer is conducting an experiment. To be effective the design of causal research is highly structured and controlled so that other factors do not affect those being studied. Marketers use this approach primarily for purposes of prediction and to test hypotheses, though it can also be used to a lesser extent for discovery and explanatory purposes. In marketing, causal research is used for many types of research including testing marketing scenarios, such as what might happen to product sales if changes are made to a product's design or if advertising is changed. If causal research is performed well marketers may be able to use results for forecasting what might happen if the changes are made.

If the research study happens to be an exploratory or a formulative one, wherein the major emphasis is on discovery of ideas and insights, the research design most appropriate must be flexible enough to permit the consideration of many different aspects of a phenomenon. But when the purpose of a study is accurate description of a situation or of an association between variables (or in what are called the descriptive studies), accuracy becomes a major consideration and a research design which minimises bias and maximises the reliability of the evidence collected is considered a good design. Studies involving the testing of a hypothesis of a causal relationship between variables require a design which will permit inferences about causality in addition to the minimisation of bias and maximisation of reliability. But in practice it is the most difficult task to put a particular study in a particular group, for a given research may have in it elements of two or more of the functions of different studies. It is only on the basis of its primary function that a study can be categorised either as an exploratory or descriptive or hypothesis testing study and accordingly the choice of a research design may be made in case of a particular study. Besides, the availability of time, money, skills of the research staff and the means of obtaining the information must be given due weightage while working out the relevant details of the research design such as experimental design, survey design, sample design and the like.

### Literature Review

The literature review section examines recent (or historically significant) research studies, company data, or industry reports that act as a basis for the proposed study. Begin your discussion of the related literature and relevant secondary data from a comprehensive perspective, moving to more specific studies that are associated with your problem. If the problem has a historical background, begin with the earliest references.

Avoid the extraneous details of the literature; do a brief review of the information, not a comprehensive report. Always refer to the original source. If you find something of interest in a quotation, find the original publication and ensure you understand it. In this way, you will avoid any errors of interpretation or transcription. Emphasize the important results and conclusions of other studies, the relevant data and trends from previous research, and particular methods or designs that could be duplicated or should be avoided. Discuss how the literature applies to the study you are proposing; show the weaknesses or faults in the design, discussing how you would avoid similar problems. If your proposal deals solely with secondary data, discuss the relevance of the data and the bias or lack of bias inherent in it.

The literature review may also explain the need for the proposed work to appraise the shortcomings and/or informational gaps in secondary data sources. This analysis may go beyond scrutinizing the availability or conclusions of past studies and their data, to examining the accuracy of secondary sources, the credibility of these sources, and the appropriateness of earlier studies. Close the literature review section by summarizing the important aspects of the literature and interpreting them in terms of your problem. Refine the problem as necessary in light of your findings.

We shall study more about these techniques in the chapter research plan.

## 1.11 How to Do?

Jolly and Dolly are siblings. They discuss their studies at home. Their Dada also participates in discussion sometimes. Jolly has just completed his MBA and registered himself for Ph.D. with a reputed university. Dolly is the first semester student of MBA with a business school. When Dolly attended her first introductory lecture, she was told about the course curriculum she was going to take in her first semester, she got confused. She came home and in the afternoon while taking tea she said to her brother:

Dolly: "Brother, MBA is full of confusion. First, they say it is multidisciplinary study. It does not concentrate on one area or discipline. I wish to learn only marketing, then why to study accounts, finance, statistics, operation research, economics, etc. Second, there is a subject like Research Methodology. Why should I study research? I am not going to become a scientist."

Jolly: "Dear Dolly, your reply is in your question. When you say you wish to learn marketing, you will have to learn everything about marketing. For instance market is a place where buyers and sellers meet. You should know all about buyers and sellers, their buying and selling behaviour, selling powers of manufacturers, costs, prices, profits, segmentation, environment, competitors, etc. These attributes also interact and affect each other. For instance if a manufacturer can manufacture at lesser cost and wishes to earn less profit, he can sell more quantity. So we have to learn accounts, maths, statistics, economics, psychology, etc. Therefore management is multidisciplinary study....."

Dolly: "By why I should study research?

Jolly: "See, all the branches of management like finance, HR and Finance especially marketing are full of opportunities and threats. Research is required to identify and define opportunities and problems, to define, monitor, and refine strategies, to define, monitor, and refine tactics and to improve our understanding of the various fields of management. Business is not carried out in exclusion. To study the factors which are controllable as well as uncontrollable is the need of the day and is a continuous process. A manager should analyse all the factors and forecast the future by proper study of past".

Dolly: "How is it done?"

Jolly: "You have just started the course. You need to know a lot of interesting things about research. You appear to be anxious to learn all the techniques in a day"

Dolly: "Yes, yes, tell me in short and I wish to learn today only".

Jolly: "No, dear, research is a process which needs thorough understanding of the concepts and techniques, but just to give you some idea; researcher should know what the problem is. Yes, defining the problem is a major problem. Let us take the problem of the use of mobile phones in colleges. Students use their sets and disturb others."

Dolly: "Yes, this is a serious problem".

Jolly: "Students from Walchand College, Solapur, were so disturbed that they wanted to study the benefits and abuses of mobiles in college and surveyed their fellow students, I suggest that just getting some idea about research, read this report and we shall discuss the other issues tomorrow".

Dolly: "Do you want me read the report - Impact of Mobile Phone Usage on Academic Environment: A Study from Management Prospective By Prof Gangadhar Sonar and Mr. Santosh Jainapur."

Jolly: "Yes, it is a good descriptive report, it will give you an idea how research is carried out"

Dolly: "See you tomorrow".

✦ ✦ ✦

Research Project I

## 1.12 Impact of Mobile Phone Usage on Academic Environment: A Study from Management Perspective

*Gangadhar B.Sonar*[1] *and Santosh M. Jainapur*[2]

### Introduction:

Cell phones are the need of everyone. All over the world, tens of millions of people press them against their heads for hours every day. In the U.S. alone it was estimated that there were at least 100 million cell phone users, as of early 2002. However, this number has continued to rise. Many studies have shown that mobile phones at academic environment have a positive as well as negative impact on students' achievement, learning motivation, classroom atmosphere, and on the teachers. It seems that many of the positive expectations that are associated with the use of mobile phones in academic environment could be confirmed in some of the recent studies. However, the studies referred above are tainted with various problems: First, the results are mainly based on questionnaire and interview data exclusively, which is known to be biased in several ways. Behavioural and observational data to confirm the self reported data is missing in most studies. Also, many studies did not investigate control groups so as to clarify the effect of the mobile phone usage. Finally, results are sometimes based on rather short observation periods and small student samples.

Beside limitations in academic environment, cell phones are also harmful to health. They emit microwaves to send and receive signals. Microwaves, as it is known, are used to cook food. As the radiation penetrates tissue it causes heat. Due to source of the emission against brain, there are claims that people have had brain tumours in the exact size, shape and position as the antenna on their cell phone. Therefore, use of mobile phone in academic environment has multi-dimensional impacts. It may have an affect on students, teachers, management and the society. However, if students get affected, the overall academic environment gets affected. They may lose concentration, motivation and commitment. It may give scope for student unrest. As a result of it failures, malpractices and such unhealthy practices may take place at a large.

In view of this, following objectives have been formulated.

- To look into the general background of the students using mobile phones;
- To know about utility of mobile phones;
- To understand consequences of mobile phone usage; and
- To make suggestion for management of mobile phones in academic environment.

### Methodology:

To satisfy the objectives of the study, qualitative methodologies along with quantitative techniques were employed. The study is descriptive in nature. Total 90 students were administered questionnaire with different faculties in Solapur city. Students of MSW, MBA and BE were covered

---

* The report has already been published in Vol 2 No. 3 (Oct, 2006 issue) of Journal of Global Economy, Mumbai. Published with permission from authors and editors.

[1] Lecturer, Walchand College of Arts and Science, Department of Social Work, Walchand Heerachand Marg, Ashok Chowk, Solapur, Maharashtra state.

[2] MSW student, Walchand College of Arts and Science, Department of Social Work, Walchand Heerachand Marg, Ashok Chowk, Solapur, Maharashtra State.

in the study. Each group consisted of 30. The primary data were collected from the students and teachers with the help of semi structured interview schedule. Besides, participant and non-participant observation and focused group discussions were made to triangulate information and to get holistic understanding of the subject.

The secondary data were collected from, magazines, newspapers and Internet websites published on different aspects of mobile phone. The data collected from the students of selected faculties were subjected to verification, quantification and coding by referring a coding key. The coded data was keyed into computer for data processing and analysis. The statistical package for social sciences (SPSS) has been used to calculate percentile and frequency distribution.

## Analysis and Interpretation

Most of the mobile users, students, are males and belonging to age group of 22 to 23 years. They hail from urban areas. With reference to caste and religion most of them belong to open castes and Hindu religion. Many of the students are living in nuclear family. Their fathers are working as government servants and mothers are housewives. The students purchased mobile phones during the last one year. It was offered by the parents and regular expenditure is also met by them. Students spend average amount of ₹ 200 on mobile phone per month.

Many students use mobile phone to receive incoming calls. They receive incoming calls mostly from their friends. The frequency of receiving incoming calls in a day is minimum of 5 and maximum of 10 calls. A few students use mobile phone for outgoing purpose mostly to call friends. The duration of incoming calls varies from 1 to 30 minutes. Beside incoming and outgoing calls, students get 4 to 8 missed calls in a day. Short messages are also sent to friends, 4 to 8 messages in a day and receive 4 to 5 messages in a day. Though they have mobile phone, students also use public phones 4 to 5 times in a day.

### General background of the surveyed mobile phone users (students)

| **Gender** | **Frequency** | **Percentage** |
|---|---|---|
| Male | 70 | 77.8 |
| Female | 20 | 22.2 |
| Total | 90 | 100.0 |
| **Age categories** | **Frequency** | **Percentage** |
| Below 19 years | 6 | 6.7 |
| 20 to 21 years | 19 | 21.1 |
| 22 to 23 years | 37 | 41.1 |
| 24 to 25 years | 24 | 26.7 |
| 26 years and above | 4 | 4.4 |
| Total | 90 | 100.0 |
| **Domicile** | **Frequency** | **Percentage** |
| Rural | 13 | 14.4 |
| Semi-urban | 17 | 18.9 |
| Urban | 60 | 66.7 |
| Total | 90 | 100.0 |
| **Type of family** | **Frequency** | **Percentage** |
| Joint | 32 | 35.6 |
| Nucleolus | 56 | 62.2 |

| | | |
|---|---|---|
| Extended | 2 | 2.2 |
| Total | 90 | 100.0 |
| **Father's occupation** | **Frequency** | **Percentage** |
| Government servant | 42 | 46.7 |
| Private work | 7 | 7.8 |
| Business | 25 | 27.8 |
| Agriculture | 8 | 8.9 |
| Factory worker | 2 | 2.2 |
| Labour | 2 | 2.2 |
| Not applicable | 4 | 4.4 |
| Total | 90 | 100.0 |
| **Mother's occupation** | **Frequency** | **Percentage** |
| House wife | 73 | 81.1 |
| Government servant | 15 | 16.7 |
| Private work | 1 | 1.1 |
| Business | 1 | 1.1 |
| Total | 90 | 100.0 |

## About Mobile Phone Utility

| **Use of mobile phone for incoming** | **Frequency** | **Percentage** |
|---|---|---|
| Yes | 85 | 94.4 |
| No | 5 | 5.6 |
| Total | 90 | 100.0 |
| **Whose calls they receive more** | **Frequency** | **Percentage** |
| Parents | 26 | 28.9 |
| Friend | 48 | 53.3 |
| Business | 4 | 4.4 |
| Any other specify | 4 | 4.4 |
| Not applicable | 8 | 8.9 |
| Total | 90 | 100.0 |
| **Use of mobile phone for outgoing** | **Frequency** | **Percentage** |
| Yes | 78 | 86.7 |
| No | 12 | 13.3 |
| Total | 90 | 100.0 |
| Minimum duration of talk time | **Frequency** | **Percentage** |
| Up to 1 minute | 56 | 62.2 |
| 1 minute to 5 minutes | 21 | 23.3 |
| 6 minutes to 10 minutes | 6 | 6.7 |
| 11 minutes to 15 minutes | 2 | 2.2 |
| Above 16 minutes | 5 | 5.5 |
| Total | 90 | 100.0 |
| **Use mobile phone for messaging** | **Frequency** | **Percentage** |
| Yes | 81 | 90.0 |
| No | 9 | 9.0 |

| Total | 90 | 100.0 |
|---|---|---|
| **Minimum messages received in a day** | **Frequency** | **Percentage** |
| 0 to 4 messages | 63 | 70.0 |
| 5 to 8 messages | 10 | 11.1 |
| 9 to 12 messages | 9 | 10.0 |
| 13 to 16 messages | 3 | 3.3 |
| 17 to 20 messages | 5 | 5.6 |
| Total | 90 | 100.0 |
| **Switch off mobile phone in the night** | **Frequency** | **Percentage** |
| Yes | 12 | 13.3 |
| No | 78 | 85.6 |
| Total | 90 | 100.0 |
| **Keep mobile phone in silent mode in classroom** | **Frequency** | **Percentage** |
| Yes | 83 | 92.2 |
| No | 7 | 7.8 |
| Total | 90 | 100.0 |

It is interesting to know that students never switch off their mobile phone during night. Further, they keep mobile phones in silent mode while attending classes. When students were asked about allowing mobile phone in the classrooms, it was strongly expressed that mobile phones should not be allowed in the classrooms as it disturbs classroom environment.

### Consequences of Using Mobile Phone

| Sr. No. | Consequences | Frequency/(Per cent) | |
|---|---|---|---|
| | | Yes | No |
| 1 | Got vulgar call/message | 22 (24.4) | 68 (75.6) |
| 2 | Disturbed from vulgar call/message | 12 (13.3) | 12 (13.3) |
| 3 | Health problem due to mobile phone | 09 (10.0) | 81 (90.0) |
| 4 | Lack of concentration due to mobile phone | 29 (32.2) | 61 (67.8) |
| 5 | Disturbed classroom environment | 58 (64.4) | 32 (35.6) |
| 6 | Met accident due to mobile | 26 (28.9) | 64 (71.1) |
| 7 | Disturbed because of mobile phone usage | 35 (38.9) | 55 (61.1) |
| 8 | Got threatening call | 19 (21.1) | 71 (78.9) |
| 9 | Malpractice in examination through mobile | 20 (22.2) | 70 (77.8) |
| 10 | Misuse through camera | 30 (33.3) | 60 (66.7) |
| 11 | Misuse through recorder | 22 (24.4) | 68 (75.6) |

With reference to consequences of mobile phone usage, a few received vulgar calls and many received vulgar messages. A small number of students feel headaches, impatient, and are disturbed after using mobile phones for a longer duration. Some students lose concentration quite often in classroom due to mobile. They get disturbed sleep during nights. Some received threatening calls from stranger or known. Some of the students saw others misusing mobile phone for malpractice in the examinations, taking photos and recording voice without concern, viewing vulgar films, etc.

**Conclusions:**

Open ended questions also revealed important information. Students use mobile phones in academic environment just for fun and to show their status. They spend maximum of time with mobile phones due to one or the other reasons. Some use mobile phones as FM radio, others as MP Player. Some play games on mobile phones. They lack understanding of proper use of mobile phones. Therefore, students get disturbed and lose concentration in academic environment. Most of the classes are disturbed due to mobile phones. It has got more demerits than the merits if not used in a proper way. Now, many university and colleges have banned cell phones in campus. Using mobile phones in classrooms need to be strictly banned as it spoils the main purpose of academics. It has got many negative consequences. Therefore, progressive utility of mobile phones need to be focused among student, teacher and parent community for better academic achievements. The students should be punished seriously if mobile is used for malpractices in academic environment. The college authorities may arrange alternate communication for students in case of emergency purposes.

Though study is restricted to a particular college and samples were known to interviewers closely, bias cannot be denied. It may be an attempt to generalise that mobiles are necessary evils. Students use then more for fun than necessity. Another serious study is required with larger sample size so that important factors may be found out, which influence the students to use mobiles so frequently.

CHAPTER

# DEVELOPMENT OF RESEARCH METHODOLOGY

## *Structure*

Aristotle's works contain the earliest formal study of logic. Together they comprise a highly developed logical theory, one that was able to command immense respect for many centuries. Aristotle's logic revolves around one notion: the **deduction** (*sullogismos*). Aristotle says: A deduction is speech (*logos*) in which, certain things having been supposed, something different from those supposed results of necessity because of their being so. Each of the "things supposed" is a **premise** (*protasis*) of the argument and what "results of necessity" is the **conclusion** (*sumperasma*). The core of this definition is the notion of "resulting of necessity" (*ex anankês sumbainein*). This corresponds to a modern notion of logical consequence: X results of necessity from Y and Z if it would be impossible for X to be false when Y and Z are true. We can therefore take this to be a general definition of "valid argument".

## 2.1 Induction and Deduction

Deductions are one of two species of argument recognized by Aristotle. The other species is **induction** (*epagôgê*). He has said far less about induction than deduction, doing little more than characterize it as "argument from the particular to the universal". However, induction (or something very much like it) plays a crucial role in the theory of scientific knowledge in the *Posterior Analytics*: it is induction, or at any rate a cognitive process that moves from particulars to their generalizations, that is the basis of knowledge of the indemonstrable first principles of sciences.

Inductive reasoning moves from specific observations to broader generalizations and theories. Informally, we sometimes call this a "bottom up" approach. In inductive reasoning, we begin with specific observations and measures, begin to detect patterns and regularities, formulate some tentative hypotheses that we can explore, and finally end up developing some general conclusions or theories. For instance we have observations:

$O_{1:}$ Ram is mortal, $O_2$: Shyam is mortal, $O_3$: Hari is mortal, like this $O_{4,}$ $O_{5......}$ We can generalise every body is mortal.

Deductive reasoning works from the more general to the more specific. Sometimes this is informally called a "top-down" approach. We might begin with thinking up a *theory* about our topic of interest. We then narrow that down into more specific *hypotheses* that we can test. We narrow down even further when we collect *observations* to address the hypotheses. This ultimately leads us to be able to test the hypotheses with specific data, a *confirmation* (or not) of our original theories. For instance, we know demand falls with the rise in prices, all other things remaining same. This is theory. One may collect observations (data), to test it. If it is not valid, theory is falsified and a new theory can be developed by continuous process of testing by collecting data with time and space difference, etc.

Despite its wide generality, Aristotle's definition of deduction is not a precise match for a modern definition of validity. Some of the differences may have important consequences:

1. Aristotle explicitly says that what results of necessity must be different from what is supposed. This would rule out arguments in which the conclusion is identical to one of the premises. Modern notions of validity regard such arguments as valid, though trivially so.
2. The plural "certain things having been supposed" was taken by some ancient commentators to rule out arguments with only one premise.
3. The force of the qualification "because of their being so" has sometimes been seen as ruling out arguments in which the conclusion is not 'relevant' to the premises, e.g., arguments in which the premises are inconsistent, arguments with conclusions that would follow from any premises whatsoever, or arguments with superfluous premises.

Of these three possible restrictions, the most interesting would be the third. This has been interpreted as committing Aristotle to something like relevance logic.

These two methods of reasoning have a very different "feel" when you're conducting research. **Inductive reasoning, by its very nature, is more open-ended and exploratory, especially at the beginning. Deductive reasoning is narrower in nature and is concerned with testing or confirming hypotheses.** Even though a particular study may look like it's purely deductive (e.g., an experiment designed to test the hypothesized effects of some treatment on some outcome), most social or business research involves both inductive and deductive reasoning processes at some time in the project.

## 2.2 Scientific Methods

### Positivism

Positivism is a rejection of metaphysics. It is a position that holds that the goal of knowledge is simply to describe the phenomena that we experience. The purpose of science is simply to stick to what we can observe and measure. Knowledge of anything beyond that, a positivist would hold, is impossible. He believed that psychology could only study what could be directly observed and measured. Since we can't directly observe emotions, thoughts, etc., these were not legitimate topics for a scientific psychology.

In a positivist view of the world, science is seen as the way to get at truth, to understand the world well enough so that we may predict and control it. The world and the universe are deterministic; they operate by laws of cause and effect that we can discern if we apply the unique approach of the **scientific method.** Science is largely a mechanistic or mechanical affair. We use deductive reasoning to postulate theories that we can test. Based on the results of our studies, we may learn that our theory doesn't fit the facts well and so we need to revise our theory to better predict reality. The positivist believes in *empiricism*, - the idea that observation and measurement, is the core of the scientific endeavour. The key approach of the scientific method is the experiment, the attempt to discern natural laws through direct manipulation and observation.

### Post-positivism

In our views of science, things have changed since the middle part of the 20th century. Probably the most important has been our shift away from positivism into what we term *post-positivism*. Post-positivism is a wholesale rejection of the central tenets of positivism. A post-positivist might begin by recognizing that the way scientists think and work and the way we think in our everyday life are not distinctly different. **Scientific reasoning** and common sense reasoning are essentially the same process. There is no difference in kind between the two, only a difference in degree. Scientists, for example, follow specific procedures to assure that observations are verifiable, accurate and consistent. In everyday reasoning, we don't always proceed so carefully.

One of the most common forms of post-positivism is a philosophy called ***critical realism***. A critical realist believes that there is a reality independent of our thinking about it that science can study. This is in contrast with a ***subjectivist*** who would hold that there is no external reality. Positivists were also realists. The difference is that the post-positivist critical realist recognizes that all observation is fallible and has error and that all theory is revisable. In other words, the critical realist is *critical* of our ability to know reality with certainty. Where the positivist believed that the goal of science was to uncover the truth, the post-positivist critical realist believes that *the goal of science is to hold steadfastly to the goal of getting it right about reality.* Because all measurement is fallible, the post-positivist emphasizes the importance of multiple measures and observations, each of which may possess different types of error, and the need to use ***triangulation*** across these multiple sources (full of errors) to try to get a better bead on what's happening in reality.

The post-positivist also believes that all observations are theory-laden and that scientists are inherently biased by their cultural experiences, world views, and so on. This is not cause to give up in despair, however. Just because I have my world view based on my experiences and you have yours doesn't mean that we can't hope to translate from each other's experiences or understand each other. That is, post-positivism rejects the ***relativist*** idea of the ***incommensurability*** of different perspectives, the idea that we can never understand each other because we come from different experiences and cultures.

Most post-positivists are ***constructivists*** who believe that each of us construct our view of the world based on our perceptions of it. Because perception and observation is fallible, our constructions must be imperfect.

Positivists believed that **objectivity** was a characteristic that resided in the individual scientist. Scientists are responsible for putting aside their biases and beliefs and seeing the world as it 'really' is. Post-positivists reject the idea that any individual can see the world perfectly as it really is. We are all biased and all of our observations are affected (theory-laden). Our best hope for achieving objectivity is to triangulate across multiple fallible perspectives. Thus, objectivity is not the characteristic of an individual; it is inherently a social phenomenon. We never achieve objectivity perfectly, but we can approach it. The best way for us to improve the objectivity of what we do is to do it within the context of a broader contentious community of truth-seekers (including other scientists) who criticize each other's work. The theories that survive such intense scrutiny are a bit like the species that survive in the evolutionary struggle.

Clearly, philosophers have been debating these issues for thousands of years and there is every reason to believe that they will continue to debate them for thousands of years more. Those of us who are practicing scientists should check in on this debate from time to time. We should think about the assumptions we make about the world when we conduct research. But in the meantime, we can't wait for the philosophers to settle the matter.

## Scientific Methods and Popperism

According to Karl Popper, philosophy is a necessary activity because we, all of us, take a great number of things for granted, and many of these assumptions are of a philosophical character; we act on them in private life, in politics, in our work, and in every other sphere of our lives – but while some of these assumptions are no doubt true, it is likely, that more are false and some are harmful. So the critical examination of our presuppositions - which is a philosophical activity – is morally as well as intellectually important.

Popper, in his philosophy, offers a solution to the problem of induction. The problem, in basic terms, can be understood by example: given that the sun has risen every day for as long as anyone can remember, what is the rational proof that it will rise tomorrow? How can one rationally prove that past events will continue to repeat in the future, just because they have repeated in the past? Popper's reply is characteristic, and ties in with his criterion of **falsifiability**. He states that while there is no way to prove that the sun will rise, we can formulate a theory that every day the sun will rise—if it does not rise on some particular day, our theory will be disproved, but at present it is confirmed. Since it is a very well-tested theory, we have every right to believe that it accurately represents reality, so far as we know.

Popper concluded that all we know is but "a woven web of guesses," that while empirical generalizations may not be verifiable; they are, at least, falsifiable. It was through this process that Einstein turned Newtonian physics on its ear.

When we enter a new situation in life and are confronted by a new person, we bring with us the prejudices of the past and our previous experiences of people. These prejudices we project upon the new person. Indeed, getting to know a person is largely a matter of withdrawing projections; of dispelling the smoke screen of what we imagine he is like and replacing it with the reality of what he is actually like. Before we as individuals are even conscious of our existence we have been profoundly influenced for a considerable time (since before birth) by our relationship to other individuals who have complicated histories, and are members of a society which has an infinitely more complicated and longer history than they do (and are members of it at a particular time and place in that history); and by the time we are able to make conscious choices we are already making use of categories in a language which has reached a particular degree of development through the lives of countless generations of human beings before us. We are social creatures to the innermost centre of our being. The notion that one can begin anything at all from scratch, free from the past or unindebted to others, could not conceivably be more wrong.

Most criticisms of Popper's philosophy are of the falsification, or error elimination element in his account of problem solving. In interpreting these, it is important to bear in mind the aims of his idea. It is intended as an ideal, practical method of effective human problem solving; as such, the current conclusions of science are stronger than pseudo-sciences or non-sciences, insofar as they have survived this particularly vigorous selection method. He does not argue that any such conclusions are therefore true, or that this describes the actual methods of any particular scientist. Rather, it is a recommended ideal method that, if enacted by a system or community, will over time lead to slow but steady progress of a sort. It has been suggested that Popper's ideas are often mistaken for a hard logical account of truth because of the historical coincidence of their appearing at the same time as logical positivism, the followers of which mistook his aims for their own.

Popper's falsificationism can further be questioned logically, by asking about statements such as "There are black holes", which cannot be falsified by any possible observation, yet which seems to be a legitimately scientific claim. Similarly, it's not clear how Popper would deal with a statement like "for every metal, there is a temperature at which it will melt", which can neither be confirmed nor falsified by any possible observation, yet which seems to be a valid scientific hypothesis.

## 2.3 Paradigm Shift

**(Thomas Kuhn)**

If Popper sees the essence of science in divergent thinking and fundamental disagreements, Kuhn sees the essence of science in convergent thinking and consensus. In other words, if the hall-mark of science, according to Popper is critical thinking, the hallmark of science according to Kuhn is tradition bound thinking. In fact, according to Kuhn what distinguishes science from other areas of creative thinking is that whereas in science, one finds institutional mechanism of enforcing consensus, the other areas suffer from perpetual disagreements even on fundamentals.

If Popper considers the individual to be the locus of scientific activity, Kuhn bestows that status upon the scientific community. Both positivists and Popper looked upon science as the sum total of the works of individual scientists working in accordance with a method, though the positivists and Popper differ on the characterisation of that method. As opposed to this individualistic account of scientific enterprise, Kuhn propounds collectivistic view of scientific activity.

Thomas Kuhn (in his book *The Structure of Scientific Revolutions*, 1962), analyses the history of science. According to him there are three phases of scientific development. The first phase, which exists only once, is the **pre-paradigm phase**, in which there is no consensus on any particular theory, though the research being carried out can be considered scientific in nature. This phase is characterized by several incompatible and incomplete theories. The actors in the pre-paradigm community eventually gravitate to one of these conceptual frameworks and ultimately to a widespread consensus on the appropriate choice of methods, terminology or experiments may not contribute to increased insights. In the second phase, normal science begins. As long as there is general consensus within the discipline, normal science continues. The third phase is that of revolutionary science, which usually follows a period of crisis. A period of crisis is a time when an anomaly or anomalies in research reveal weakness or incompatibility of a paradigm. The period of research that yields a new paradigm is called the period of revolutionary science. A science may go through these cycles repeatedly, though Kuhn notes that it is a good thing for science that such shifts do not occur often or easily. According to Kuhn, the scientific paradigms preceding and succeeding a paradigm shift are so different that their theories are not comparable (incommensurable). The **paradigm shift** does not merely involve the revision or transformation of an individual theory, it changes the way terminology is defined, how the scientists in that field view their subject, and, perhaps most significantly, what questions are regarded as valid, and what rules are used to determine the truth of a particular theory. Kuhn observes that they are incommensurable — literally, lacking comparability, untranslatable.

## 2.4 Feyerabend's Radical Thoughts

Feyerabend was critical of any guideline that aimed to judge the quality of scientific theories by comparing them to known facts. He thought that previous theory might influence natural interpretations of observed phenomena. Scientists necessarily make implicit assumptions when comparing scientific theories to facts that they observe. Such assumptions need to be changed in order to make the new theory compatible with observations. The main example of the influence of natural interpretations that Feyerabend provided was the tower argument. The tower argument was one of the main objections against the theory of a moving earth. Aristotelians assumed that the fact that a stone which is dropped from a tower lands directly beneath it shows that the earth is stationary. They thought that, if the earth moved while the stone was falling, the stone would have been 'left behind'. Objects would fall diagonally instead of vertically. Since this does not happen, Aristotelians thought that it was evident that the earth did not move. If one uses ancient theories of impulse and relative motion, the Copernican theory indeed appears to be falsified by the fact that objects fall vertically on earth. This observation required a new interpretation to make it compatible with Copernican theory. Galileo was able to make such a change about the nature of impulse and relative motion. Before such theories were articulated, Galileo had to make use of 'ad hoc' methods and proceed counter-inductively. So, 'ad hoc' hypotheses actually have a positive function: they temporarily make a new theory compatible with facts until the theory to be defended can be supported by other theories.

Feyerabend's position is generally seen as radical in the philosophy of science, because it implies that philosophy can neither succeed in providing a general description of science, nor in devising a method for differentiating products of science from non-scientific entities like myths. It also implies that philosophical guidelines should be ignored by scientists, if they are to aim for progress.

## 2.5 Objectivity in Research

According to *empiricism* and *positivism*, the observer must be *separate* from those observed, and is required to be neutral about the nature of the phenomena. Yet, this separation fails, because the process of observing, selecting and naming phenomena is itself a normative act reflecting the social and ethical norms of the individual and society, as well as the actual concepts and descriptions. Weber argued for a *value free sociology*. While he conceded that in social science debates will exist about ends and normative standards of values, he maintained a fact-value distinction, arguing that from knowing the facts of something, we cannot determine its value, and knowing the value of something does not lead us to a factual description. Social science should only deal in questions of facts, and remain ethically neutral on the question of values. Weber's general strategy is to *understand* the meaning of actors' practices and values, but not to take sides on those values. Social science can make a reference to values without making value judgements. Weber maintains that researchers can provide a factual and objective assessment of actors and their practices. They assess whether actors are rational in undertaking their means to achieve their ends. *Rationality* and cost-benefit analysis, thus, provide the tools by which to investigate social situations.

Yet, the act of understanding requires the researcher to decide between values. For instance, to understand actors' acts of racism and sexism means also to *judge* and *evaluate* their understanding of the social situation; i.e., do racists or sexists have a flawed and wrong understanding of their situation, because they misrecognise events and misidentify causal mechanisms and structures behind the phenomena?

Here lies a paradox: Weber espouses value neutrality, yet values are unavoidable in the practice of social science (e.g., undertaking research on domestic violence *presupposes* that it is wrong and undesirable, and should be tackled, otherwise why do the study!). The objects of social science are constituted by values, and this presupposes an appreciation of those values. Without this appreciation, researchers cannot evaluate the phenomena under investigation, and their research is without relevance. Inevitably, the researchers will bring their own presuppositions into the research field; e.g., in the study of economy and society, is it analysed from a Marxist perspective and its values (such as equality and freedom from exploitation and domination), or from a liberal perspective and its values (such as liberty, choice and autonomy)? Researchers' own biography will shape their evaluative framework by which they assess social actors' understanding. They cannot remain neutral, as there is no 'view from nowhere'.

However, Marxists argue that the views of those who are powerful in society come to be regarded as the truth. Truth is shaped by *ideological* considerations of the ruling classes, so to achieve objectivity requires transcending social conditions (e.g., capitalist, or state authoritarian, property rights of the means of production of knowledge and communication) that serve to mask and distort its attainment. In this way, *false conscious* is removed.

For Marxism, knowledge is not merely an outcome of contemplation, but a dialectic process between ideas and material circumstances. Importantly, there is a link between power and knowledge, whereby the ownership and control of the means of production of knowledge (such as media) dictate what is regarded as valid and legitimate knowledge. The claim of value free social science is a bourgeois concept, masking the real relations of domination and causal explanations. 'True' objectivity, thus, can only be established under non-capitalist and non-bourgeois relations of production. Yet, Marxists fail to provide an account of what objectivity looks like, and whether under a non-capitalist organisation of production different forms of distortions and false conscious would not emerge as it did in the Soviet era.

Following Marx's concern with ideology and alienation, critical theorists emphasise that theory and research must serve *emancipatory* interests, to create a world that satisfies the needs and powers of social actors. Research is never undertaken merely to accumulate knowledge for its own sake, but rather to bring about the progressive social forces. The value of theory is not simply to satisfy the formal criteria of truth, but rather to inform actors on how to *intervene* and transform the world.

Critical theorists came to see the social sciences (e.g., economics and psychology) as uncritical and characterised by instrumental rationality, in particular rationality had become a servant of capitalist interests. In contrast, critical theory offers to provide ethical and social criticism, moving away from the orthodox interest of technical control and prediction towards emancipatory interest of liberation and real freedom of the oppressed classes.

Yet, critical theorists fail to outline clearly the nature of the emancipatory project, and also remain uncritical of their own value position that informs their social criticism. Both Marxism and critical theory do not explain on what basis we can come to know how whether to know things is the right one without some theories about knowledge in the first instance. Also, if ideology is so successful and all pervasive, how can we know whether we have transcended it?

Similar to Marxism and critical theory, feminism argues that social position largely determines what a person may know; i.e., it is not the consciousness that determines the being, but the being the consciousness. Feminist standpoint theories argue that women as an oppressed class can come to occupy a privileged epistemic position.

Feminist standpoint epistemologies make several claims: knowledge (especially scientific knowledge) is a social product; i.e., an outcome of social processes; society is patriarchal; i.e., scientific practices are androcentric; material life structures and sets limits on understanding; i.e., what we do shapes what we know; women have fuller and richer experiences (e.g., child-birth, family chores and community networking) than men.

Combining the above points, feminists claim that men lack everyday experiences, and do not nor can possess complete and undistorted knowledge. In contrast, women's knowledge comes from a position of being the subject of domination, and their experiences have the potential to produce more complete and less distorted knowledge claims. Unlike the empiricist and positivist views, where objectivity lies in method, or critical theory where this depends on coming to understand society in its contradictory totality, feminist standpoint epistemologies confer objectivity and *epistemic privilege* on women.

In addition, feminists argue that the production of feminist knowledge is grounded in *feeling*. Scientific objectivity and rational values derive from masculine ways of feelings for technical control, prediction, planning and domination over nature and people, as evident in physics and economics. In contrast, feminine ways of feelings for understanding, care, support and co-operation question rationality and objective values, technical control taken to be constitutive of science, regarding the latter as distorted knowledge based on unacknowledged and unexamined myths of masculinity. Here, scientific objectivity and rationality are not simply values, but masculine values, prioritising male values and cultures over those of female ones.

Yet, there are some weaknesses in the feminist standpoint epistemologies. First, if men-centred knowledge represents a partial view of the world, women-centred knowledge will also remain androcentric if it pursues objectivity, whatever its form. Second, it is unclear whether female experiences are common to all women. If women have different experiences based on class, ethnicity, age, sexuality, etc., then there is no single female knowledge, but knowledges. This suggests that there is no single privileged epistemic position, but rather *many*, so that objectivity is reduced to *relativism*. Third, some of the women's experiences can be part of men's experiences as result of class, ethnicity, etc. Consequently, it is unclear in what ways female experiences are closed off to males other than by women's biology. This suggests that women need not occupy a privileged position at all.

## 2.6 Ethics in Research

Some times research is used for political, financial and other motives. Manipulation of research at strategic level has proved dangerous for many. Freedom for research means that outside bodies should have little institutional authority over research. This places even greater demands on the will and ability of researchers and the research community to meet ethical demands and to take ethical considerations into account. Research must be regulated by ethical norms and values, even where there is disagreement over which ethical norms are applicable. Some norms express general ethical values which are absolutely fundamental. In other areas ethical views are less clear and considered, or may even be mutually contradictory. Because research gives us new insights and opportunities on which we are unable to take immediate ethical stands, such unclearness and disagreement often arise in research. In such cases, researchers bear a special responsibility for helping to resolve ethical problems. The ethical obligations of research relate partly to norms in the research process and partly to responsibility for the consequences of research.

There are a number of key phrases that describe the system of ethical protections. The principle of ***voluntary participation*** requires that people are not to be coerced into participating in research. This is especially relevant where researchers had previously relied on 'captive audiences' for their subjects — prisons, universities, and places like that. Closely related to the notion of voluntary participation is the requirement of ***informed consent***. Essentially, this means that prospective research participants must be fully informed about the procedures and risks involved in research and must give their consent to participate. Ethical standards also require that researchers not put participants in a situation where they might be at ***risk of harm*** as a result of their participation. Harm can be defined as both physical and psychological. There are two standards that are applied in order to help protect the privacy of research participants. Almost all research guarantees the participants' ***confidentiality*** — they are assured that identifying information will not be made available to anyone who is not directly involved in the study. The stricter standard is the principle of ***anonymity*** which essentially means that the participant will remain anonymous throughout the study — even to the researchers themselves. Clearly, the anonymity standard is a stronger guarantee of privacy, but it is sometimes difficult to accomplish, especially in situations where participants have to be measured at multiple time points (e.g., a pre-post study). Increasingly, researchers have had to deal with the ethical issue of a person's ***right to service***. Good research practice often requires the use of a no-treatment control group — a group of participants who do *not* get the treatment or programme that is being studied. But when that treatment or programme may have beneficial effects, persons assigned to the no-treatment control may feel their rights to equal access to services are being curtailed.

Even when clear ethical standards and principles exist, there will be times when the need to do accurate research runs up against the rights of potential participants. No set of standards can possibly anticipate every ethical circumstance. Furthermore, there needs to be a procedure that assures that researchers will consider all relevant ethical issues in formulating research plans.

## 2.7 How to Do?

Dolly was again in problem and as soon Jolly came home, she bombarded him with questions.

Dolly: "Now, what is this induction or deduction? Why should I study the development in research methods?

Jolly: "Relax, dear. Have you read the report on Mobile phone usage?"

Dolly: "What is in that? They have a problem and went though some related studies, surveyed 90 students and described their behaviour"

Jolly: "Can we generally say that mobile phones are good?"

Dolly: "No, it is an observation and we cannot conclude anything in general"

Jolly: "Good, it means it is only a descriptive study and does not want to test anything. Now research is of three types as we discussed in the previous chapter. The research types are exploratory, descriptive, and causal"

Dolly: "Yes"

Jolly: "Exploratory research is a type of research conducted because a problem has not been clearly defined. Exploratory research relies on secondary research such as reviewing with available literature and/or data, or qualitative approaches. The objective of descriptive research is to describe things, such as the market potential for a product or the demographics and attitudes of consumers who buy the product. Descriptive research, also known as statistical research, describes data and characteristics about the population or phenomenon being studied. The objective of Causal research is to test hypotheses about cause-and-effect relationships."

Dolly: "I understand that".

Jolly: "Good, these methodologies have not been framed or learnt in a day".

Dolly: "Yeah!"

Jolly: "So you need to understand the development of research methodology so that if there is any new technique or you want to develop a new technique, you should have the idea how methodology is developed."

Dolly: "So you want to say exploratory or descriptive studies are inductions and causal studies are deductions."

Jolly: "So you are on the line, but not exactly how developments have taken place, it is a debatable issue".

Dolly: "I also think so".

Jolly: "When you gather any information or data, there are two important issues, you should know why you wish to gather data, there is some underlying assumption or theory, second while collecting data you are somewhat biased where this data is going to be used. Theory and biased behaviour are behind the scenes which affect your data collection as well as testing the data".

Dolly: There is an issue, in my childhood I wished to be a writer. Can you explain me the difference between artistic writing like novel, stories, poetry and research work?

Jolly: Very good question. I can't write with any authentication but generally following is the difference between artistic work and research work.

| Literary/Artistic Work | Research Work |
|---|---|
| • Highly Subjective in nature<br>• Creativity lies in experience and synthesis<br>• Needs expertise in skill<br><br>**Example:** Story writing, Novel writing, Music composing, Painting | • Highly Objective in nature<br>• Creativity lies in observation and analysis<br>• Needs expertise in alertness, theory and observations<br><br>**Example:** Research Report, Scientific Experiments |

Dolly: "So objectivity and ethics are very important for a researcher".

Jolly: "Now you have started grasping the meaning, Good. Now I suggest you to read another exploratory study **"Khadi and Village Industries in North East India with Special Reference to Arunachal Pradesh: Retrospect and Prospect"**. This is a very good study conducted by Dr. Ram Krishna Mandal, Faculty D.N. Government College, Itanagar, Arunachal Pradesh. You may say it is another induction method which explores Khadi trade in Arunachal Pradesh".

Dolly: "I wish to read now; I want to know about Arunachal Pradesh".

Jolly: "You should 'know', not just get information. Knowledge is derived after processing information. Bye, see you tomorrow"

RESEARCH PROJECT 2

## 2.8 Khadi and Village Industries in North East India with Special Reference to Arunachal Pradesh: Retrospect and Prospect*

RAM KRISHNA MANDAL[1]

### Historical Review

Originally, Gandhi conceived khadi as the best instrument for giving concrete expression to the 'Swadeshi' spirit and for making effective the boycott of foreign goods in general and foreign cloth in particular. Khadi was also expected to provide an opportunity to India for cultivating self-discipline and self-sacrifice as a part of non-co-operation movement. For co-ordinated development of Khadi throughout the country, Gandhiji set up, the All India Khadi Board (AIKB) with branches in all provinces in December, 1923. This organization was an integral part of the Indian National Congress and worked under its control. Initially the first phase of khadi movement in India started in 1918 and ended in 1924.

The second phase started in 1925 with the formation of an autonomous body called All India Spinners Association (AISA) of Akhil Bharat Charkha Sangh. It was organizationally an independent of Indian National Congress. However, Gandhiji continued to distinguish and play an important role in the affairs of the Sangh. In 1930 Gandhiji's intention was to form other village industries; as a result the All India Village Industries Association (AIVIA) was established on the basis of a resolution passed by the Indian National Congress in 1934. The association under the Chairmanship of Gandhiji did distinguish service for the development of village industries. He wrote; "Khadi is the central sun around which the other village industries revolve like so many planets. They have no independent existence nor Khadi can exist without other village industries, they are absolutely interdependent". Among those that conceded a role for KVI, some stressed the need for adopting better technology and a flexible attitude to the use of machine. It was an answer to these doubts and hesitancies, Gandhiji wrote in the *Harijan* dated June 20, 1946 as follows: "Khadi (including Village Industries) is the only true economic proposition in terms of the millions of villagers until such time, if ever, when a better system of supplying work and adequate wages for every able bodied person above the age of sixteen, male or female, is found for his field, cottage or even factory in every one of the villages or displace the villages so as to give the villages the necessary comports and amenities that a well regulated life demands and is entitled to". "What I object to is the craze for machinery, not machinery as such. The craze is for what they call labour saving machinery. Men go on 'saving labour' till thousands are without work and thrown on the open street to die of starvation. I want to save time and labour, not for a fraction of mankind, but for all".

Perhaps, the first move to make Khadi, a Governmental programme was made in 1946 by the Government of Madras, which deputed a senior officer to obtain advice from Gandhiji and set up a department of khadi soon thereafter. This was followed by the Central Government's recognition of the importance of rural cottage industries in the Industrial Policy Resolutions of 1948. The Constituent Assembly also included development of cottage industries in rural areas among the Directive Principles of the Constitution in Article 43. These ideas were elaborated in the First Five Year Plan, which began in 1951-52. According to the First Five Year Plan, Village

---

* The article has already been published in Journal of Global Economy Vol 3 no. 2, April, 2007 issue. Reprinted with permission from author and editors of Journal.

1 Dr. Ram Krishna Mandal, S.G Lecturer in Economics, Dera Natung Govt. College, Itanagar-791113, Arunachal Pradesh.

industries have a central place in the rural development programme and their development should be matter of State's concern. The Government of India setup the All India Khadi and Village Industries Board (AIKVIB) in January 1953. The main function of the Board was to prepare and organize programmes for the development of KVI, including training of personnel, manufacture and supply of equipment, supply of raw materials, marketing and research and study of the economic problems of different village industries. Again Khadi and Village Industries Commission (KVIC), a statutory body was created by an Act of Parliament (No.61 of 1956). Accordingly KVIC was established in April 1957 to look after the work of the former AIKVIB.

This paper is based on a study which encompasses the following objectives.

1. To ascertain the present scenario of KVI in North East States.
2. To chart out the growth and development of KVI in Arunachal Pradesh.
3. To find out the problems faced by the KVI for its growth and development in Arunachal Pradesh.
4. To search the solutions of these problems and conclusion follows.

## Present Scenario of KVI in North East States

In order to have better implementation and monitoring of KVI programme in the North East States, KVIC took an initiative to put a foothold of its presence and established its field officials in the entire region. KVI occupy a unique position in the rural economy of this region and a collaborative approach has been initiated. Spices Board of India and Khadi and village Industries Commission have jointly extended financial and technical support for setting up of spices making units in Assam and Arunachal Pradesh. The Central Leather Research Institute (CLRI) under its Leather Technology Mission has extended support for setting up leather products manufacturing projects in Manipur and Nagaland.

**Table 1**

**Summary of Performance of KVI in NE States and India (2002-03)**

**(₹ In lakhs, employment in lakh person)**

| lIndia/NE State | Production | Sales | Employment | Earning |
|---|---|---|---|---|
| India | 856936.82 | 1019333.80 | 66.45 | 330507.44 |
| North East | 26079.27 | 28619.14 | 2.91 | 12300.77 |
| Arunachal Pradesh | 317.88 | 446.85 | 0.01 | 150.86 |
| Assam | 6074.74 | 5721.56 | 1.2224 | 16.18 |
| Manipur | 5997.52 | 5656.74 | 0.62 | 2632.11 |
| Meghalaya | 3100.46 | 3842.30 | 0.251 | 949.88 |
| Mizoram | 3769.44 | 5063.82 | 0.23 | 1492.67 |
| Nagaland | 4583.94 | 5508.02 | 0.30 | 3011.71 |
| Tripura | 2235.29 | 2379.85 | 0.28 | 647.3 |

**Sources:** Annual Report of KVIC (Ministry of Agro and Rural Industries, Govt of India 2003)

The North East has a great diversity in respect of culture, tradition and ethnicity. They have a tradition of artistic craftsmanship wide variety of crafts such as weaving, painting, pottery, smithy work, basketry, wood curving, etc. Therefore, development of KVI activities in NE region is considered as priority area under KVI programme. In addition to this, attention is focused on to provide better infrastructure facilities and liberalized assistance to motive rural population of the region to take up KVI programme in a large way. Accordingly, various policy decisions were taken from time to time for the benefits in this region. A major policy decision was taken for allocating 10 per cent of KVIC's budget in the NE region. During the year 2002-03 the Government of India also earmarked separate budget allocating under KVI programme exclusively for the region. Under Rural Employment Generation Programme (REGP), concession facilities are extended to the weaker section. Accordingly, 30 per cent Margin Money is provided to the entrepreneurs of north east region, whereas margin money for other than north east is 25 per cent. In spite of many concessional facilities extended to the region, Table-1 shows that contribution of KVI sector is not satisfactory, though KVI has a bright future in this region.

## Growth and Development of KVI in Arunachal Pradesh

Prior to independence, the present state Arunachal Pradesh had nothing in respect of industrial sector with exception of home-crafts. In view of the craft practices in the territory, the Department of Cottage Industries came into function in the year 1952-53. The Arunachal Pradesh Khadi and village Industries Board (APKVIB), a statutory body of the government of Arunachal Pradesh was lately created by an Act of Legislative Assembly viz. the APKVIB Act 1989.The board started its function in 1991-92 under the administrative control of the Department of Textile and Handicrafts, Government of Arunachal Pradesh. The Act was further amended during the year 1998 as per Government of India's direction which has ensured that State Government exclusive control over administrative affairs of the board. The APKVIB has a Chairman, who is non-official head of the board. The Secretary, Industry to the Government of Arunachal Pradesh is the ex-officio, Member Secretary of the board. The Director, Textile and Handicrafts, is the ex- officio, Chief Executive Officer of the board. The board has a full time Executive Officer.

**Table 2**

**Growth of KVI in Arunachal Pradesh (1991-2003)**

**(₹ In lakhs, employment in lakh person)**

| Year | Unit (in No.) | Employment (in No.) | Investment (₹ in lakh) |
|---|---|---|---|
| 1991-92 | 14 | 52 | 26.33 |
| 1992-93 | 52 | 71 | 25.86 |
| 1993-94 | NA | NA | NA |
| 1994-95 | 73 | 94 | 37.36 |
| 1995-96 | 40 | 175 | 84.25 |
| 1996-97 | 34 | 81 | 36.69 |
| 1997-99 | NA | NA | NA |
| 1999-2000 | 9 | 101 | 43.71 |
| 2000-01 | 80 | 590 | 290.79 |
| 2001-02 | 13 | 178 | 87.60 |
| 2002-03 | 11 | 133 | 66.19 |
| Total | 326 | 1478 | 698.78 |

**Source:** Director of Textile and Handicraft, Itanagar.

In spite of having abundant natural resources and tradition of artistic craftsman KVI programme is not visible in ground level. In cursory observation, KVI programme is suitable for the State like Arunachal Pradesh and should keep priority for growth of KVI to solve the unemployment problem. APKVIB being catalyst agent of KVI sector in the State, a number of KVI units have come up. Table-2 shows that as on 31.03.2003 there were 326 units with investment of ₹ 698.78 lakhs and 1478 persons engaged in this sector.

Table 3

**Districtwise Distribution of KVI unit in AP as 31.03.2003**

**(₹ In lakhs, unit and employment in No.)**

| District | Unit | Investment | Employment |
|---|---|---|---|
| Papum Pare | 138 | 282.21 | 582 |
| Lower Subansiri | 67 | 140.72 | 309 |
| Upper Subansiri | 7 | 9.91 | 22 |
| East Siang | 46 | 121.39 | 256 |
| West Siang | 28 | 78.11 | 163 |
| Changlang | 23 | 14.09 | 39 |
| Dibang Valley | 1 | 9.77 | 20 |
| Tawang | 1 | 0.54 | 1 |
| West Kameng | 3 | 10.82 | 20 |
| East Kameng | 4 | 28.65 | 58 |
| Tirap | 4 | 0.80 | 4 |
| Lohit | 4 | 1.20 | 4 |

**Source:** Director of Textile and Handicraft, Itanagar.

Revival and revitalization of the traditional handlooms, handicrafts and best utilization of local raw materials available in the State should be the basic aims of the KVI programme because fundamentals of the KVI establishment is to relieve poverty by finding employment for the villagers and make equitable distribution of goods produced. Further, Mahatma Gandhi opined that KVI was symbolized economic freedom and equality. Therefore, Arunachal Pradesh, a land of beautiful handicrafts, traditional craftsman and natural khadi and village industries' potentiality in every district should use KVI as tools for rural development. For this, APKVIB should identify and uplift the economic condition of those who fall below the poverty line and encourage them to enter into KVI activity. Table-3 reveals that there is a wide difference in the growth and development of KVI programme in different districts. Some districts of the State have yet to open account of the KVI activity. There is also dispersion in terms of establishment in all districts of the State. Therefore, APKVIB should sincerely implement the programme in view of equal distribution.

Industrial Policy Resolution of 1948, while appreciating the role of heavy and basic industries, emphasized the role of cottage and village industries as having a very special role in the national economy, because it is most conducive for employment generation, decentralization of economic and industrial concentrate, and for a more equitable distribution of national wealth. Less populated, industrially backward but growing States like Arunachal Pradesh should take advantage of KVI programme, because KVI sector is useful for mobilizing resources of small and middle class for investment in industrial ventures and it facilitates a more even distribution of incomes originating from village industries sector through a large number of retails outlets. Further, it is suitable for better utilization of local resources and for the achievement of local self-sufficiency in respect of certain types of essential consumer goods like food, cloth and agriculture equipment, etc.

Table 4

Bank Term Loans to KVI Sector in AP as 31.03.2003

| Bank | KVI unit (in number) | Amount (₹ in lakh) |
|---|---|---|
| 1. Centralized Bank | | |
| (a+b+c) | 46 | 151.41 |
| (a) SBI Bank | 24 | 48.90 |
| (b) UCO Bank | 19 | 87.25 |
| (c) Vijaya Bank | 3 | 15.26 |
| II. Arunachal Pradesh Bank (d+e) | 68 | 166.90 |
| (d) A.P Rural Bank | 67 | 160.54 |
| (e) A.P Co-op. Apex Bank | 1 | 6.36 |
| Total (I+II) | 114 | 318.31 |

**Source:** Director of Textile and Handicraft, Itanagar.

Finance is rightly regarded as the lifeblood of any commercial enterprises irrespective of its size and nature. Inadequacy of finance prevents the process of raising industrial growth. As such banks and financing institutions are a vital importance in the process of industrialization. Many times the committee is constituted to look into various aspects relating to the flow of institutional credit to KVI sector. They have submitted their report after study and observations regarding institutional credit flows and recommended different pattern and sources of finance to KVI sector. However, recommendations could not support both positive and pro-active to the KVI Programme in one way or other.

Presently KVIC introduced a Margin Money Scheme with the adoption of project approach. In respect of KVI in rural areas, credit can be made available by nationalized banks to the enterprises directly, up to ₹ 10 lakh for individual units and up to ₹ 25 lakh for institution, for which 25 per cent of project outlay would be the margin money granted by the KVIC/State KVIB. Margin money eligibility in respect of weaker sections including women and special area like NE States, 30 per cent of the project cost up to ₹ 10 lakh. Hence, bank finances 95 per cent of the project cost in the form of term loan to the Arunachal Pradesh Scheduled Tribe beneficiary/ institution and 5 per cent in the form of beneficiary contribution, in the process KVIC/APKVIB grant 30 per cent of the project cost as a subsidy.

Table 4 shows the term loans granted by bank to KVI sector in the State and disbursed ₹ 318.31 lakh of which centralized banks disbursed ₹ 151.41 lakh and Arunachal Pradesh banks ₹ 166.90 lakh. Thus nationalized bank have got prospect of credit for the KVI sector in the State. In spite of having many inhabiting factors in the development of agriculture sector; the State is exclusively reliant on it. Understanding the increasing population and limited employment absorption capacity in agriculture and Govt. job, it is desirable to go for alternative source of income generation, employment expansion. One desirable alternate may be the rural industrialization through KVI programme, because this sector has distinct advantages over large and medium scale industries. KVI provides immediate large employment, ensuring more equal distribution of wealth. This sector is labour intensive, less capital, less skill and has short gestation period and advantage of decentralization. KVI programme is good for accelerating the tempo of rural industrialization in the State. But the success of KVI programme is largely dependent on the dedication of KVIC and APKVIB officials, degree of co-operation from various concerned agencies and the involvement of people, their honest and fair participation which can make KVI programme a success and living reality. Thus the industry receives considerable help from the state government in the form of finance, improved looms, accessories and raw materials at reasonable rates. To promote production of handloom and handicraft products and generation of self-employment, the Directorate of Textiles and Handicraft is running eighty-eight of weaving and craft centres and six Handloom Development and Quality Dyeing units in the State.

With a view to popularize handloom and handicraft products being manufactured by the industrial units in the State, the department has been participating in various fairs, festivals and exhibitions. Besides running eighteen Emporia and five Show Rooms cum Sales Counters in the State, there are two Emporia functioning in Delhi and Kolkata. The department has also acquired a plot of land in New Mumbai for establishment of a Guest House and an Emporia to exhibit the State's traditional craft with a view to develop rich heritage of handloom and handicraft products of Arunachal Pradesh. The Department has taken up number of schemes viz. participation and organizing of Exhibition to create awareness amongst the local entrepreneurs and artisans of the State. The achievement of Craft/Weaving Centres during 2003-04 is shown in Table-5.

## Problems

The KVI are not commercially viable due to (i) lack of interest of weavers, (ii) lack of raw materials, (iii) lack of working capital, (iv) lack of marketing facilities, (v) lack of capacity-utilization, (vi) lack of technical know-how, (vii) shortage of organizational strength, (viii) competition from power loom and other modern products, (ix) lack of entrepreneurial knowledge, (x) lack of power, (xi) lack of transportation, etc. Some of these problems are discussed below in brief.

**Table 5**

**Physical Achievement of Craft/Weaving Centres in Arunachal Pradesh during 2003-04**

| Sr.No. | Particulars | Unit | 2001-2002 | 2002-2003 | 2003-2004 |
|---|---|---|---|---|---|
| 1 | 2 | 3 | 4 | 5 | 6 |
| 1 | Craft/Weaving Centres | No. | 88 | 88 | 88 |
| 2 | Trainees in Craft/Weaving Centres | No. | 247 | 302 | 303 |
| 3 | Handloom Development Centre and Quality Dying Units | No. | 6 | 6 | 6 |
| 4 | Value of Production of Cloth/Craft | ₹ in lakh | NA | NA | 28.59 |
| 5 | Emporium | No. | 15 | 15 | 18 |
| 6 | Show Room-Cum Sales Counter | No. | 3 | 3 | 5 |
| 7 | Annual sales proceed of Emporium and Show Room cum Sales Counter | ₹ in lakh | 39.80 | 40.09 | |
| | Cash<br>Credit | | | | 6.72<br>38.26 |

**Source:** Director of Textile and Handicraft, Itanagar.

## Market

Market is not necessarily confined to any particular geographical location in which buyer and seller are brought into contact with one another. The buyer may be in Delhi and seller in Mumbai or even in London. What is essential for a market is that the buyers and the sellers are able to get in touch with one another so that the exchange of goods and services for money takes place between them. The contact for the exchange of goods can be performed with the help of E-mail, internet, telephone, telegraph, ordinary post, etc. It is undisputedly accepted that the success of an industry depends on the market of its products. It has no well organized market outside this State and even inside the State. It has no worldwide website and no regular advertisement through T.V. and Radio and not even in daily newspapers inside or outside the State. Again there is no organized agent to whom its products are sold. Only the local entrepreneurs are encouraged to participate in different Faires and Expos inside and outside the State like N.E. Trade Expo, Indian International Trade Faire, New Delhi and Regional Level Exhibitions where the products of KVI are exhibited and sold.

## Inner Line System

After independence, the Government of India decided to continue to follow the restriction of the Inner Line System. But the purpose for which the Inner Line had been designed in 1873 was changed. The main purpose of the Inner Line is to restrict the free movement of Non-Arunachalees in NEFA now Arunachal Pradesh, i.e., the free flow of entrance of Non-Arunachalee is prohibited in the State. A Non-Arunachalee who wants to cross beyond such Line has to get first an Inner Line Pass (ILP) issued by Arunachal Pradesh Government authorized Gazetted Officer for a limited period of time after fulfilling some formalities.

Again, it is thought that the territory is located at strategic point from the stand point of defence. Besides, the Government of India feels it necessary to protect the land and forest of the innocent tribal people of the State from the Non-Arunachalees' hunger of grabbing. It is well thought that the protected Arunachalees can make economically a smooth progress. They will not be disturbed from their socio-cultural and economic dimension.

Globalization refers to a process of increasing economic integration and growing economic interdependence between countries in the world economy. It is associated not only with an increasing cross-border movement of goods, services, capital, technology information and people, but also with an organization of economic activities which crosses national boundaries. Broadly speaking, the term 'globalization' means integration of economies and societies through cross country flows of information, ideas, technologies, goods, services, capital, finance and people. Globalization says cross country flows among countries. To get the good effect of globalization in the State it needs first cross state flows among the states in India.

Industrialization is recognized as a real tool of economic development as it indicates a higher standard of living of the majority of population. Once, Nehru said that real progress might ultimately depend on industrialization. During the last fifty-eight years after independence, our country has been bringing a noticeable growth in industrial production. But the North Eastern Region of our country has, till now, been lying neglected. Therefore, Inner Line System stands as a main hindrance for the growth and development of KVI as well as globalization.

## Licence Issuing System

The people from outside of this State come for the activities for which they are to obtain licences in the name of some tribal people who get the rent from the businessmen for their licences. These trading people earn money and mostly siphon off in their respective home because they do not get the right to buy the property for independent business and trade. This situation hugely restricts the private investors in coming and opening up manufacturing units within this territory. Banking credit for establishing business and industries are available to the local people but they lack entrepreneurial skills and show little interest in industrial production activities. Therefore, Inner-Line Permits system and government policy in issuing licences only to local people most likely has worked against the opening up of KVI in this part of the country.

## Entrepreneurial Lack

Economic development of any region is an outcome of purposeful human activity. Both the developed and the underdeveloped countries look at the industrialization process as an important key to economic development. Most of the social scientists agree that man stands at the centre of economic activity and he assumes various roles in the development process, namely, as an organizer of human and material resources, worker, consumer and exchange agent. Out of these multiple roles, his role as the organizer of human and material resources is the most important and basic one.

It is widely accepted that the availability of entrepreneurship is the most important determinant in the process of industrialization. The government in its efforts to create entrepreneurship in the underdeveloped regions provides for various monetary and non-monetary incentives like the development of an infrastructure, assistance in marketing and procuring raw materials, providing finance or granting subsidies on investment. With this thrust in view, the state governments have created various institutions to cater to the different needs of entrepreneurs.

It can be argued that lack of entrepreneurial skill of the local people and their deficient interest to invest and innovate has contributed in preventing the evolution of modern economic system in the State. One example of their lacking interest in manufacturing activities is that those tribal boys and girls who go for crafts training do not want to have their own business but like to join as craft teachers in government organizations (Krishna, 2000). The mindset of the tribal is not to establish their own enterprise or business but to venture either in politics, contract business, or government services to earn "easy money". This mindset can be termed as a psychological barrier which has emerged very strongly in the context of present socio-political context of the State. Some tribal people within a very short period of time have experienced income and wealth inequalities to a high degree. Very few of them have been found to become very rich over night and enjoy luxurious life and prefer conspicuous consumption which has been adversely affecting the rest of the society. The income inequalities in the tribal society are very much strong. Some are very rich and some are very poor. Some peoples in rural areas are living on self growing food and common property resource forest products without functioning of money. The presence of high degree of corruption at all levels and existence of underground economy has also gone against in development of market economy.

## Power

The modern economic development involves large-scale use of power. Regarding the set up of an industry the State needs infrastructural facilities of which power is one. Due to its geographical location and its hilly terrain, Arunachal Pradesh has an immense hydel potential to use the power of water to produce electricity in comparison to the other states of the country. The state is of turbulent perennial rivers and major streams, which possess enormous hydro-electric generation potential. In addition to water resource, the state has oil, natural gas and coal resources that can be used in the production of electricity. Presently, there is a vast gap between the availability and the requirement of power. As per 2001 Census, out of 2,12,615 households, only 1,16,275 households (54.7%) are having electricity facility and out of 3649 numbers of villages (as per 1991 Census), only 2339 numbers have been electrified accounting 64% of total villages till the end of March 2003. Arunachal Pradesh, having untapped estimated hydro-power potential of 49,000 MW, may emerge as powerhouse of India when this potential is fully harnessed (Source: Deptt. of Power, Govt. of Arunachal Pradesh).

## Transportation

The service of Transportation is a precondition of economic development. Revolution in transport and communication would take place first before the advent of industrial revolution. It is a well known fact that the prosperity of a country depends on the development of agriculture, mining, industry, services, banking, etc. But without prior development of transport, any type of development is not possible of a region.

As such in the development plans, the government has been attaching high priority to the construction of roads and as a result, the total length of roads constructed in the State stood at about 15021.80 kms. including 399.80 Kms. under National Highway giving the road density of 17.9 kms. per 100 Sq.Kms. of area at the end of March, 2004 as against the all India average of 74.9 Kms. per 100 Sq.kms. during 1997. Thus in comparison to the all India road density, the State has a very low road density in the country, which is the basic barrier to the development of industry. Again, a peculiarity of surface transport of the state is that most of the district head-quarters are not interconnected, i.e., one cannot move from one district headquarter to other specially the old district headquarters in Arunachal Pradesh without going down to Assam. The state does not have lateral roads connecting district headquarters and sub-divisional headquarters of the districts. In other places, roads run vertically connecting places of Assam with the places of district headquarters in the state. As a result, the transport cost is not only high but also the state is affected by disturbances and insurgency activities in Assam.

Arunachal Pradesh being predominantly a hilly terrain, there are a lot of constraints in the development of railways. In fact, the state was brought under the railway map of India for the first time with the opening of Balipara (near Tezpur, Assam) to Bhalukpong in West Kameng District of Arunachal Pradesh in 1989 with only 1.26 Kms. (metre gauge).

## Solutions

The following suggestions may be considered with a view to strengthen the KVI in Arunachal Pradesh.

1. This industry needs well organized advertisement for its product through T.V., Radio, even through daily newspapers outside and inside the state. It must have own website.
2. The State government should give priority to develop border trade with Bhutan, China and Myanmar. If border trade comes into effect with undivided sincerity, I hope, it will give fillip not only generating a new avenue of employment but also it will make a self-generating and self-sustaining economy of Arunachal Pradesh. In this way the market for Arunachal products including KVI will be automatically developed.
3. A comprehensive techno-economic survey of entire region of Arunachal Pradesh by a competent agency should be performed to find out the potentiality of such type of small scale industries.
4. Establishment of various technical and managerial institutions should be set up for imparting training to the existing and potential entrepreneurs.
5. Complete financial support and its use in a proper way in any probable selected unit should be shouldered by the government agent.
6. The flow of relevant information relating to these small scale industries should be circulated in a regular way so that the entrepreneurs can get up-to-date information about technology, man power planning, etc.
7. The bank has to play a more vital role in addition to lending credit assistance to such type of small scale industries. Bank may offer a special scheme to the entrepreneurs so that they can take short-term interest free loan. The bank can detect the sickness of industrial units and draw up a nursing plan for their rehabilitation. It can set up a special cell for close monitoring during the rehabilitation period until the unit becomes self-sufficient again.

8. Tourism industry must be developed on the priority basis as this State has a great potentiality regarding this so as to attract large number of tourists to come in Arunachal Pradesh. The development of tourism industry will bring the development of KVI in the State.

9. To bring small scale industrial development, the State should be self-sufficient in raw materials, technical knowledge, machine and tools, skilled labourers, technicians and over all marketing facilities.

10. In the context of to-day's global liberalization, the existence of inner line between Arunachal and the rest of the economy of India may be deemed irrelevant as because, the observance of inner line is obstructing the inflow of capital, other inputs and technology. In such a situation, how can Arunachal Pradesh expect to avail of the benefit of liberalization so as to boost up the state market economy? Here, precisely, I may be within reasonable limit while recommending that the inner line should go.

## CONCLUSIONS

In the process of industrial development the importance of cottage industries should not be ignored. To set up heavy industry is not so much possible in different places of this State as its major portions are not easily accessible. But to set up small scale industries in the State is not so much difficult. That is why top priority must be given to those small scale industries like Khadi and Village industries which need light machine tools and other equipment in order to produce qualitative products because today a State's progress is measured by the quality of goods it produces.

To strengthen the economy of the State, the Government should provide larger scope to the private sector. At the same time, a number of changes in policy should be introduced with regard to industrial licensing to the non-tribal, removal of Inner Line, technology upgradation, fiscal policy, removal of controls and restrictions, rationalizing and simplifying the system of fiscal and administrative regulation and improving law and order problems so as to encourage for free flow of goods, capital, technology and labour from other States to this State. All these changes will be directed towards creating an uninhabited climate for private sector so that private sector investment can get a big boost to modernize the economy approaching towards global economy.

## References


1. Bhattacharjee, R.P (2000), "Economic Development of Arunachal Pradesh", Himalayan Publishers, Delhi, Itanagar, P. 147 & 236.

2. Borgohain, H., "Development of Industries and Handicrafts in Siang Region" in . Pandey, B.B. (ed), "Patterns of Change and Potential for Development in Arunachal Pradesh," Himalayan Publishers, Itanagar, New Delhi, P. 133 – 139.

3. Das G.D (1995), "Tribes of Arunachal Pradesh in Transition", Vikas publishing House Pvt. Ltd., Jangpura, New Delhi, P 30 – 33.

4. Das N.C (1998), "Handloom Development Programme under Five Year Plans in Assam" in Bhorali, D.(ed), "Economic Development of the North-Eastern Region", Spectrum Publication, Guwahati, Delhi, P. 177 – 185.

5. Govt. of Arunachal Pradesh (2000, 2001, 2002, 2003 & 2004), "Economic Review of Arunachal Pradesh", Directorate of Economics and Statistics, Itanagar.

6. Jha, S.D. (1985), "The wealth of Arunachal Pradesh" Mittal Publication, Delhi, P. 375.

7. Joram,A.(2006),"Khadi and Village Industries Movement in Arunachal Pradesh", Arunachal Review,Vol.VII.No.19,Sept.-Nov. PP.1 – 4.

8. Krishna, Sumi (2000), "Arunachal Pradesh", in M.S. Swaminathan (ed.) Gender Dimensions in Bio-Diversity Management

9. Mandal, R.K. (2005), "Arunachal Economy: Socio-Economic Transformation" Champion Publisher and Distributor, Itanagar P. 90 – 91.

10. Mandal, R.K. (2006), "Constraints of Eonomic Development in Arunachal Pradesh With Special Reference to Globalisation and Inner Line System",The Indian Economic Journal, Vol.54.No.3.

11. Mandal, R.K. (2006), "Arunachal Pradesh as Emerging Power House", Journal of Global Economy, Vol.1, No.4, Oct.-Dec.P. 223.

13. Mandal, R.K.(2005), "Emergence of Marketing of Handloom and Handicraft Products of Arunachal Pradesh" a paper presented in the 7th Annual Conference of North Eastern Economic Association (NEEA) held at Rajiv Gandhi University, w.e.f. 21st to 22nd October.

...✎...✎...✎

CHAPTER

# Defining Research Problem

## *Structure*

The most difficult part of any research is its beginning. 'What is the problem?' is a problem. What should we do and begin with? Defining the problem is a complex issue. Where do research topics come from? Problems can relate to performance variance, demand, revenue, finance, cost, consumer behaviour or any. Probably one of the most common sources of research ideas is the experience of **practical problems in the field**. Many researchers are directly engaged in at macro level like social, health or human service programme implementation and come up with their ideas based on what they see happening around them. Others aren't directly involved in service contexts, but work with people who are in order to learn what needs to be better understood. Many of the ideas would strike the outsider as silly or worse. For instance, in IT sector, there is great interest in the problem of backache among programmers. It's not necessarily the thing that comes first to mind when we think about sector. But if you reflect on it for a minute longer, it should be obvious that programmers do an awful lot in performing their jobs by sitting together for hours. If five or ten out of every hundred programmers were to strain their backs on average over the period of one year, the costs would be enormous. Even a minor problem can result in increased absenteeism. Major ones can result in lost jobs and expensive medical bills. So, even though it might seem silly at first, many of these practical problems that arise in practice can lead to extensive research efforts.

Another method is to look into your organisation. Study the case properly and define the problem. Another source for research ideas is the **literature in your specific field.** Certainly, many researchers get ideas for research by reading the literature and thinking of ways to extend or refine previous research. And let's not forget the fact that many researchers simply **think up their research** topic on their own. Of course, no one lives in a vacuum, so we would expect that the ideas you come up with on your own are influenced by your background, culture, education and experiences.

As soon as you get an idea for a study, you begin to think about whether the study is feasible at all. There are several major considerations that come into play. Many of these involve making **tradeoffs between rigor and practicality.** To do a study well from a scientific point of view may force us to do things we wouldn't do normally. We may have to control the implementation of our programme more carefully than we otherwise might. Or, we may have to ask programme participants lots of questions that we usually wouldn't if we weren't doing research. If we had unlimited resources and unbridled control over the circumstances, we would always be able to do the best quality research. But those ideal circumstances seldom exist, and researchers are almost always forced to look for the best tradeoffs they can find in order to get the rigor they desire.

There are several practical considerations that almost always need to be considered when deciding on the feasibility of a research project.

- First, you have to think about **how long the research will take** to accomplish.
- Second, you have to question whether there are important **ethical constraints** that need consideration.
- Third, can you achieve the **needed co-operation** to take the project to its successful conclusion, and
- Fourth, how significant are the **costs** of conducting the research.

Failure to consider any of these factors can mean disaster later.

## 3.1 Problem Definition

The most difficult part of any research is its beginning. 'What is the problem?' is a problem. What should we do and begin with? Defining the problem is a complex issue. Where do research topics come from? Problems can relate to performance variance, demand, revenue, finance, cost, consumer behaviour or any. Probably one of the most common sources of research ideas is the experience of **practical problems in the field**. Many researchers are directly engaged in at macro level like social, health or human service program implementation and come up with their ideas based on what they see happening around them. Others aren't directly involved in service contexts, but work with people who are in order to learn what needs to be better understood. Many of the ideas would strike the outsider as silly or worse. For instance, in IT sector, there is great interest in the problem of backache among programmers. It's not necessarily the thing that comes first to mind when we think about sector. But if you reflect on it for a minute longer, it should be obvious that programmers do an awful in performing their jobs by sitting together for hours. If 5 or 10 out of every hundred programmers were to strain their backs on average over the period of one year, the costs would be enormous. Even minor problem can result in increased absenteeism. Major ones can result in lost jobs and expensive medical bills. So, even though it might seem silly at first, many of these practical problems that arise in practice can lead to extensive research efforts.

Another method is to look into your organisation. Study the case properly and define the problem. Another source for research ideas is the literature in your specific field. Certainly, many researchers get ideas for research by reading the literature and thinking of ways to extend or refine previous research. And let's not forget the fact that many researchers simply think up their research topic on their own. Of course, no one lives in a vacuum, so we would expect that the ideas you come up with on your own are influenced by your background, culture, education and experiences.

As soon as you get an idea for a study, you begin to think about whether the study is feasible at all. There are several major considerations that come into play. Many of these involve making trade-offs between rigor and practicality. To do a study well from a scientific point of view may force us to do things we wouldn't do normally. We may have to control the implementation of our program more carefully than we otherwise might. Or, we may have to ask program participants lots of questions that we usually wouldn't if we weren't doing research. If we had unlimited resources and unbridled control over the circumstances, we would always be able to do the best quality research. But those ideal circumstances seldom exist, and researchers are almost always forced to look for the best trade-offs they can find in order to get the rigor they desire.

There are several practical considerations that almost always need to be considered when deciding on the feasibility of a research project.

- First, you have to think about how long the research will take to accomplish.
- Second, you have to question whether there are important ethical constraints that need consideration.
- Third, can you achieve the needed cooperation to take the project to its successful conclusion, and
- Fourth, how significant are the costs of conducting the research.

Failure to consider any of these factors can mean disaster later.

In fundamental research, sources of research problems are

- **Observation:** We face thousands of problems every day, yet unable to decide which topic should be selected for research. There may be many reasons for instance topic is not of your interest or area, or you may feel that you may not get relevant data, or you may not be well versed with tools to analyze the data or you may think the process may take a long time, or the process is very costly. The beginners have many worries and are not sure of possible outcome.
- **Literature reviews:** The research problem can be formulated by reviewing the literature. The literature here means the research work conducted by other researchers. This research work must have been judged by experts to be published in good journals. Such research articles can be good source of getting good problems. More has been written below about literature review.
- **Professional conferences:** Researchers should attend professional conferences. These conferences should be organized by professional without any interest to show numbers to Government agencies, Universities, etc. Conferences should be conducted for advancement of knowledge. Researchers can get idea what problem they can work on. They can also find gaps in the work of researchers, and work on the gaps. Many new tools can be learnt to analyse the data.
- **Experts:** If observations, literature review, and professional conferences do not help or problems needs further development and clarity, experts can help. Usually experts are of three types – guides, resource persons and subject experts. Guides help you at micro level in your work. But donot expect spoon feeding from guides. Guides help you at every level. They may be officially appointed by University or it may your personal choice. Resource persons are helpful to give you general guidelines on methodology, books, general topics and literature review. Resource persons are guides in general. Experts help you in specific helps. They may be specific subject experts like marketing tools, marketing finance, marketing visuals, advertisement or data analysis experts like econometrics, non-parametric tests, business mathematics, and verbal or non-verbal behavioural observation experts. You may need such persons during your work.

## 3.2 The Literature Review

One of the most important early steps in a research project is reviewing literature. Literature does not mean subjects related to their topic. A literature review is designed to identify related research, to set the current research project within a conceptual and theoretical context. When looked at that way, there is almost no topic that is so new or unique that we can't locate relevant and informative related research.

**(We should first concentrate on the *scientific* literature)**. Try to determine what the most credible research journals are in your topical area and start with those. Put the greatest emphasis on research journals that use a blind review system. Following procedure is adopted by the editors of Journal of Global Economy (published from Mumbai). In a blind review, authors submit potential articles to the journal editor who solicits several reviewers who agree to give a critical review of the paper. The paper is sent to these reviewers with no identification of the author so that there will be no personal bias either for or against the author. Based on the reviewers' recommendations, the editor can accept the article, reject it, or recommend that the author revise and re-submit it. Articles in journals with blind review processes can be expected to have a fairly high level of credibility. Second, **do the review early** in the research process. You are likely to learn a lot in the literature review that will help you in making the tradeoffs you'll need to face. After all, previous researchers also had to face trade-off decisions.

The literature review is useful; in many ways.

First, you might be able to find a study that is quite similar to the one you are thinking of doing. Since all credible research studies have to review the literature themselves, you can check their literature review to get a quick-start on your own.

Second, prior research will help assure that you include all of the major relevant **constructs** in your study. You may find that other similar studies routinely look at an outcome that you might not have included. If you did your study without that construct, it would not be judged credible if it ignored a major construct.

Third, the literature review will help you to find and select appropriate measurement instruments. You will readily see what measurement instruments researchers use themselves in contexts similar to yours.

Finally, the literature review will help you to anticipate common problems in your research context. You can use the prior experiences of others to avoid common traps and pitfalls.

Many management researchers feel why they should review the literature when the problem is firm or industry specific and may not find anything related to the subject. They are wrong in their approach. By reading the research on subjects, researchers can get the idea how other researchers have dealt with such problems. What methodology they have adopted. Models used by earlier researchers can help us to frame new models to resolve our issues.

## 3.3 Concept Mapping

Social scientists have developed a number of methods and processes that may be useful in helping you to formulate a research project. Brainstorming, brain-writing, nominal group techniques, focus groups, affinity mapping, Delphi techniques, facet theory, and qualitative text analysis are other important methods to define the problems. Concept mapping developed by Trochin, is very important. Concept mapping is a general method that can be used to help any individual or group to describe their ideas about some topic in a pictorial form. There are several different types of methods that all currently go by names like "concept mapping", "mental mapping" or "concept webbing." All of them are similar in that they result in a picture of someone's ideas. It is primarily a group process and so it is especially well-suited for situations where teams or groups of stakeholders have to work together. The other methods work primarily with individuals. Second, it uses a very structured facilitated approach. There are specific steps that are followed by a trained facilitator in helping a group to articulate its ideas and understand them more clearly. Third, the core of concept mapping consists of several state-of-the-art multivariate statistical methods that analyse the input from all of the individuals and yields an aggregate group product. And fourth, the method requires the use of specialized computer programmes that can handle the data from this type of process and accomplish the correct analysis and mapping procedures.

Although concept mapping is a general method, it is particularly useful for helping social researchers and research teams develop and detail ideas for research. And, it is especially valuable when researchers want to involve relevant stakeholder groups in the act of creating the research project. Although concept mapping is used for many purposes — strategic planning, product development, market analysis, decision-making, measurement development — we concentrate here on it's potential for helping researchers formulate their projects.

***Concept mapping is a structured process, focused on a topic or construct of interest, involving input from one or more participants, that produces an interpretable pictorial view (concept map) of their ideas and concepts and how these are inter-related***. Concept mapping helps people to think more effectively as a group without losing their individuality. It helps groups to manage the complexity of their ideas without trivializing them or losing detail.

## 3.4 How to Do?

Jolly: "Have you gone through 'Khadi and Village Industry in North East...'?"

Dolly: "Oh, yes. It is quite exhaustive. What I understand it is an exploratory study with only literature review and also descriptive."

Jolly: "Do you understand what the problem is?"

Dolly: "To study Khadi and Village industry in Arunachal Pradesh".

Jolly: "It has following sub-problems like

1. To ascertain the present scenario of KVI in North East States.
2. To chart out the growth and development of KVI in Arunachal Pradesh.
3. To find out the problems faced by the KVI for its growth and development in Arunachal Pradesh.
4. To search the solutions of these problems and conclusion follows. And they are main objectives of the study. Do you think the author has achieved it?"

Dolly: "Oh yes, they have been explored very nicely. First, present scenario of KVI has been discussed followed by growth and development of KVI and later problems have been explored. But in the earlier paper there was no reference section and in this article a reference section has been given".

Jolly: "We shall discuss the issues relating to writing a report later".

Dolly: "Let me revise what we learnt so far".

Jolly: "Yes".

Dolly: "Decision-makers rely on information and derived knowledge to make more efficient and effective use of their budgets. Business research is carried out to identify and define opportunities and problems; to define, monitor, and refine strategies and tactics, to improve our understanding of the various fields of management. Research isn't information gathering. It is also not transportation of facts. Research is the systematic process of collecting and analysing information (data) in order to increase our understanding of the phenomenon about which we are concerned or interested.

There are three types of research in business Exploratory Research, Descriptive research and Causal research.

A hypothesis is a specific statement of prediction. It describes in concrete terms what we expect and will happen in our study. Not all studies have hypotheses. Sometimes a study is designed to be exploratory. There are two types of hypotheses: 1. Descriptive Hypotheses and 2. Relational Hypotheses. Rational Hypotheses can be Correlational or Causal.

Inductive reasoning moves from specific observations to broader generalizations and theories. We may call this a "bottom up" approach. Deductive reasoning works from the more general to the more specific. It may be called a "top-down" approach.

In a positivist view of the world, science is seen as the way to get at truth, to understand the world well enough so that we may predict and control it. Science is largely a mechanistic or mechanical affair.

Post-positivism is a wholesale rejection of the central tenets of positivism. A post-positivist might begin by recognizing that the way scientists think and work and the way we think in our everyday life are not distinctly different. Most post-positivists are ***constructivists*** who believe that each of us construct our view of the world based on our perceptions of it. Because perception and observation is fallible, our constructions must be imperfect.

Popper has different view and he concluded that all we know is but "a woven web of guesses," that while empirical generalizations may not be verifiable; they are, at least, falsifiable.

According to Kuhn, the period of research that yields a new paradigm is called the period of revolutionary science. A science may go through these cycles repeatedly, Kuhn notes that it is a good thing for science that such shifts do not occur often or easily. According to Kuhn, the scientific paradigms preceding and succeeding a paradigm shift are so different that their theories are not comparable (incommensurable).

Research starts with a problem. Problem can be defined after consulting experts, reviewing the related literature or concept mapping.

Jolly: "It is not so simple, practically you may use a mix up all these concepts and techniques".

Dolly: "Thanks, today you have not told me to read any other article".

Jolly: "Ha! Ha! But today I wish you to write your own article of research."

Dolly: "Me! No baba, I cannot. It is difficult."

Jolly: "It is not difficult, just think about some common problem, collect articles and books relating to your topic, read, write their abstracts, logically adjust them and try to find two things –(a) what do you conclude from these studies (b) what is the gap which no body has discussed".

Dolly: "What if cut and paste?"

Jolly: "Cut and paste is not all that bad. But people blunder while cutting and pasting (a) articles chosen should not be from internet sites, news papers or magazines. The articles should be research articles by some known researchers. The articles so chosen should be peer reviewed. The views expressed in these articles should not be personal. Remember the term – objectivity in research. The conclusions from other researchers are going to be your assumptions, a logical truth, (b) while cutting, note the name of the article, its author, where it has been published and year of publication, people forget it (c) people blindly cut and paste, they may not be findings of the researchers, they may just be interventions and or points of further study, (d) people even don't read what they cut or paste."

Dolly: "How many articles or books do you want me read to write an exploratory study"?

Jolly: "Wrong question! You may have to read 100 articles or 20 books or more. For instance you wish to write an exploratory article on 'Inflation'. Read a good article from a renowned journal like 'Journal of Global Economy', 'Economic and Political Weekly' or 'ICFAI journals'. Read a good article. See its references — the author has taken the concepts from. Search those books or articles from library or on net. You may not be able to find all the articles or books from your library or on net.

Some articles of the net may be paid. Whatever is available, read and at the same read the references given by authors. Continue this process, till you get the same material and logic and it appears to be a replication of what have you have read from other articles."

Dolly: "Exploratory study is not so easy, I shall be old but still exploration shall never end."

Jolly: "Dear, people claim to write 200 or 300 research articles. They are good researchers, but in your life if you can carry out research only on one problem properly, you attain self-actualisation."

Dolly: "Godliness, you talk something great."

Jolly: "Researchers forget their subjectivity and achieve objectivity in life. We are going away from business."

Dolly: "Let us see what can be the problems in our organisation."

Jolly: "Both micro and macro."

Dolly: "Let us name a few:

1. "Customers complain that after-sales service is poor."
2. "There is always a cash crunch in treasury."
3. "Customers' acceptance of a new product."
4. "Attributes of the product."
5. "Demand of the product."
6. "Substitute of the product"
7. "Students' perception of the management college."
8. "Middle management is lethargic."
9. "Relationship of demand and price of our product."
10. "Export of Gem Stones."
11. "Style of Corporate Management and Goals."
12. "Increasing productivity through labour management co-operation."
13. "Foreign Reserves and Management Risk."
14. "Supply Chain Management."
15. "Theory and practice in value management."

Jolly: "The problems are okay, objectives should be specific and clearly defined. For instance when you want to analyse 'export of gem stones', you should specify the period, from which country, type of gems etc."

Dolly: "That is fine, but data should be available, Can you name a few research journals."

Jolly: "Social science journals list is available on site http://isidev.nic.in. Followings are important journals, you go through them, and we shall talk tomorrow."

1. Journal of Global Eonomy, Research Centre for Social Sciences, Mumbai
2. Economic and Political Weekly (EPW), Smeeksha Trust, Mumbai
3. Abhigyan — Foundation for Organisational Research & Education (FORE), Delhi
4. Agricultural Situation in India — Department of Agriculture & Co-operation, GOI, Delhi
5. Anvesak — Sardar Patel Institute of Economic & Social Research, Ahmedabad
6. Artha Vijnana — Gokhale Institute of Politics and Economics, Pune
7. Artha Vikas — Department of Economics, Sardar Patel University, Gujarat
8. Asian Economic Review — The Indian Institute of Economics, Hyderabad
9. Chartered Accountant — Institute of Chartered Accountants of India, Delhi
10. Chartered Financial Analyst — The Institute of Chartered Financial Analysts of India, Hyderabad
11. Decision — Indian Institute of Management, Kolkata
12. Demography India — Indian Association for the Study of Population, Delhi
13. Finance India — Indian Institute of Finance, Delhi
14. Foreign Trade Review — Indian Institute of Foreign Trade (IIFT), Delhi
15. Gender, Technology & Development — Gender and Development Studies Centre, Thailand
16. Indian Economic & Social History Review — The Indian Economic and Social History Association (DSE), Delhi
17. Indian Economic Journal — Indian Economic Association, Mumbai
18. Indian Journal of Agriculture Economics — Indian Society of Agricultural Economics, Mumbai
19. Indian Journal of Agricultural Marketing — Indian Society of Agricultural Marketing, Nagpur
20. Indian Journal of Economics — Department of Economics & Commerce, University of Allahabad, Allahabad
21. Indian Journal of Human Development — Institute for Human Development, New Delhi
22. Indian Journal of Industrial Relations — Sri Ram Centre for Industrial Relations and Resources, Delhi
23. Indian Journal of Labour Economics — Indian Society of Labour Economics, Delhi
24. Indian Journal of Political Science — The Indian Political Science Association
25. Indian Journal of Social Work — Tata Institute of Social Work

26. Indian Journal of Training and Development — Indian Society for Training and Development, Delhi
27. Indian Management Studies Journal — Punjab School of Management Studies, Patiala
28. Indian Social Science Review — Indian Council of Social Science Research (ICSSR), Delhi
29. Journal of Environmental Studies and Policy — Tata Energy Research Institute, New Delhi
30. Journal of Family Welfare — Family Planning Association of India Pune
31. Journal of Global Economy — Research Centre for Social Sciences, Mumbai
Journal of Health Management — Indian Institute of Health Management& Research, Jaipur
32. Journal of Higher Education (Discontinued) — University Grants Commission, (UGC), Delhi
33. Journal of Managerial Finance and Research — Institute of Public Enterprises, Hyderabad
34. Journal of Quantitative Economics — The Indian Econometric Society (DSE), Delhi
35. Journal of Rural Development — National Institute of Rural Development (NIRD), Hyderabad
36. Journal of Services Research — Institute for International Management and Technology, Gurgaon
37. Journal of Value Education — National Council of Education Research and Training, Delhi
38. Madhya Pradesh Journal of Social Sciences — Madhya Pradesh Institute of Social Science Research, Ujjain
39. Management Accountant — The Institute of Cost & Works Accountants of India, Kolkata
40. Management and Change — Institute for Integrated Learning & Management, Delhi
41. Margin — National Council of Applied Economic Research (NCAER), Delhi
42. Nagarlok — Indian Institute of Public Administration (IIPA), Delhi
43. Prajnan — National Institute of Bank Management (NIBM), Pune
44. Prashasnika — HCM Rajasthan State Institute of Public Administration, Jaipur
45. Reserve Bank of India Bulletin — Reserve Bank of India (RBI), Mumbai
Reserve Bank of India Occasional Papers — Reserve Bank of India (RBI), Mumbai
46. Review of Development & Change — Madras Institute of Development Studies, Chennai

47. Sarvekshana — National Sample Organisation (NSSO), Delhi Science, Technology and Society — Society for Promotion of S&T Studies, JNU, Delhi
48. Seminar — Romeshraj Trust, Delhi
49. Small Enterprises Development, Management & Extension Journal — National Institute of Small Industry Extension and Training (NISIET), Hyderabad
50. Social Action — Social Action Trust, Indian Social Institute, Delhi
51. Social Change — Council for Social Development, Delhi
52. South Asia Economic Journal — Institute of Policy Studies, Colombo Research and Information System for the Non-Aligned and Other Developing Countries, New Delhi
53. South Asian Survey — Indian Council for South Asian Cooperation, Delhi South India Journal of Social Sciences — A P Academy of Social Science, Visakhapatnam
54. The Journal of Entrepreneurship — Entrepreneurship Development Institute of India, Ahmedabad
55. The ICFAI Journal of Industrial Economics — Institute of Chartered Financial Analysts of India, Hyderabad
56. Urban India — National Institute of Urban Affairs, Delhi
57. Vikalpa — Indian Institute of Management, Ahmedabad
58. Vision — Management Development Institute, Gurgaon
59. Yojana — Ministry of Information & Broadcasting, GOI, Delhi Young Indian — Yuva Bharati Trust, Delhi

CHAPTER

# GENERALIZATION IN RESEARCH

## *Structure*

4.1 Issue of Validity

4.2 Conclusion Validity

4.3 Threats to Conclusion Validity

4.4 Internal Validity

4.5 Threats to Internal Validity

4.6 Construct Validity

4.7 Threats to Construct Validity

4.8 External Validity

4.9 Threats to External Validity

4.10 Theory of Reliability

4.11 Reliability and Validity

4.12 How to Do?

4.13 Study of Consumers' Perceptions about Malls and Traditional Retail Outlets

Management is a process which uses laws from social sciences. A law in social science is a universal generalization about a class of facts. A fact is an observed phenomenon, and observation means it has been seen, heard or otherwise experienced by researcher. A theory is a systematic explanation for the observations that relate to a particular aspect of social life. Concepts are the basic building blocks of theory and are abstract elements representing classes of phenomena. Axioms or postulates are basic assertions assumed to be true. Propositions are conclusions drawn about the relationships among concepts, based on analysis of axioms. Hypotheses are specified expectations about empirical reality which are derived from propositions. Social research involves testing these hypotheses to see if they are true.

All investigations involve specific participants, take place in specific contexts, and involve specific activities, data collections, or manipulations. Investigation or research is of two types-

(i) Applied Research

(ii) Fundamental Research

Applied research is about situation specific; however fundamental research is general and may apply to society in general. Some investigations are intended to have implications beyond specifics. Where there is intent to generalize beyond the specific studies, it is incumbent on the researcher to indicate the individuals, contexts, activities, data collections, and so forth to which the generalization is intended to apply and those to which it may not apply. It is also incumbent on the researcher to provide a justification for the generalization. To justify such generalizations, it is necessary to articulate both the details of the investigation itself and the logic by which the findings of the investigation should apply to the domains intended.

Sometimes the generalization intended is from a sample to a sampling frame (a population or universe). In this case, a logic that could support the generalization is embodied in the sampling theory of generalization. If the investigation is carried out using a probability sample drawn from the population, statistical theory provides guidelines about the uncertainty appropriate for generalizations to the population. This logic involves very strong assumptions about the way in which the sample used in the investigation is chosen, but the validity of this logic depends very little on knowing the specific characteristics of the individuals in the investigation or in the population.

Sometimes the generalization intended is from a sample to a population, but the sample is not a probability sample from that population. In this case, an argument that is similar to the probability sampling argument is used; an argument that involves a claim that the sample is "representative," a non-technical term that usually means that the sample supports the same kind of generalization as a probability sample. Such claims of representativeness are typically supported by evidence that the sample is similar to the population in all important respects.

Generalization that is intended by the researcher should make clear the logic by which the findings of the study should apply within the intended scope of generalization. The logic should provide a clear and persuasive rationale supporting the generalization from the study to the domain to which generalization is intended. The logic should also identify and present evidence that may be necessary to support the **validity** of the claims of generalizability.

## 4.1 Issue of Validity

It is said that measures, samples and designs don't have validity; only propositions inferences or conclusions can be said to be valid. We make lots of different inferences or conclusions while conducting research. Many of these are related to the process of doing research and are not the major hypotheses of the study. Virtually all research, applied or fundamental, involves measurement or observation. Whenever we measure or observe we are concerned with **whether we are measuring what we intend to measure** or with how our observations are influenced by the circumstances in which they are made. We reach conclusions about the quality of our measures conclusions that will play an important role in addressing the broader substantive issues of our study. When we talk about the validity of research, we often refer to these to the many conclusions we reach about the **quality of different parts of our research methodology**.

Undergraduates have many extracurricular recreational activities. Say, one of which is playing cricket. A researcher who wants to measure whether these past-time activities have a negative effect on marks scored by these students, may conduct a survey asking how many students play cricket and then attempt to find a correlation between these two factors, playing cricket and scoring of marks in exam. Because many students may play cricket other than or in addition to recreation (e.g., advance of career in cricket or exercise to keep fit), this research study may prove invalid. Even if a strong correlation was found between playing and average score, playing cricket for career purpose seems to be an invalid measure of recreational activity.

To understand validity and generalization, let us understand that a researcher has two worlds- **one is theory and the other is world of observations**. For instance, theory says people below the age of 25 years educate themselves and prepare for their next social life. Observations are that in a classroom there are boys and girls who are young, unmarried. But in a PGDM classroom, there are also some working people, who are older, married and on leave from office to pursue their educational advancement. The theory goes in the head of the researcher and observations are the real world he faces.

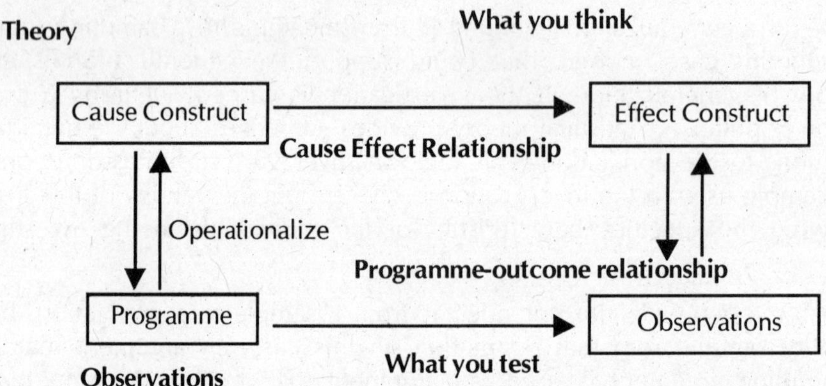


(Adapted from William Trochin)

When we conduct research, we continually go forth and back between these two realms, between what we think about the world and what is going on in it. When we are investigating a cause-effect relationship, we have a theory (implicit or otherwise) of what the cause is (the cause construct). For instance, if we are testing a new educational programme, we have an idea of what it would look like ideally. Similarly, on the effect side, we have an idea of what we are ideally trying to affect and measure (the effect construct). But each of these, the cause and the effect, has to be translated into real things, into a programme or treatment and a measure or observational method. We use the term operationalization to describe the act of translating a construct into its manifestation. In effect, we take our idea and describe it as a series of operations or procedures. Now, instead of it only being an idea in our minds, it becomes a public entity that anyone can look at and examine for themselves.

Now we have parts forming validity.

(1) Conclusion Validity

(2) Internal Validity

(3) Construct Validity

(4) External Validity.

They build on one another. Conclusion validity and internal validity refer to the land of observations that is real world. Construct validity refers to the linkage between bottom and top. External validity is concerned about the range of theory on the top.

Let us assume that we design a new advertisement for a soft drink, name it as 'soft' and we wish to know whether it would attract the customers. 'Soft' is the cause and 'awareness' is the effect. Here are the four validity types and the question each addresses:

**Conclusion Validity:**

Is there a ***relationship*** between the two variables what we are going to study?

In the context of the example we're considering, the question might be worded: in this study, is there a relationship between the 'soft' and consumer 'awareness'? There are several conclusions or inferences we might draw to answer such a question. We can, for example, conclude that there is a relationship. We might conclude that there is a positive relationship. We might infer that there is no relationship. We can assess the conclusion validity of each of these conclusions or inferences.

**Internal Validity:**

*Assuming that there is a relationship in this study;* is the relationship a ***causal*** one?

Just because we find that use of the 'soft' and awareness are correlated, we can't necessarily assume that 'soft' *causes* 'awareness'. There may be some other sources from which consumers may be getting their awareness. When we want to make a claim that our programme or treatment caused the outcomes in our study, we can consider the internal validity of our causal claim.

**Construct Validity:**

*Assuming that there is a causal relationship in this study;* can we claim that the programme reflected well our ***construct*** of the programme and that our measure reflected well our idea of the ***construct*** of the measure?

In simpler terms, did we implement the programme we intended to implement and did we measure the outcome we wanted to measure? In yet other terms, did we operationalize well the ideas of the cause and the effect? When our research is over, we would like to be able to conclude that we did a credible job of operationalizing our constructs, we can assess the construct validity of this conclusion.

**External Validity:**

Assuming that there is a causal relationship in this study between the constructs of the cause and the effect can we **generalize** this effect to other persons, places or times?

We are likely to make some claims that our research findings have implications for other groups and individuals in other settings and at other times. When we do, we can examine the external validity of these claims. Can we generalize that advertisements cause awareness?

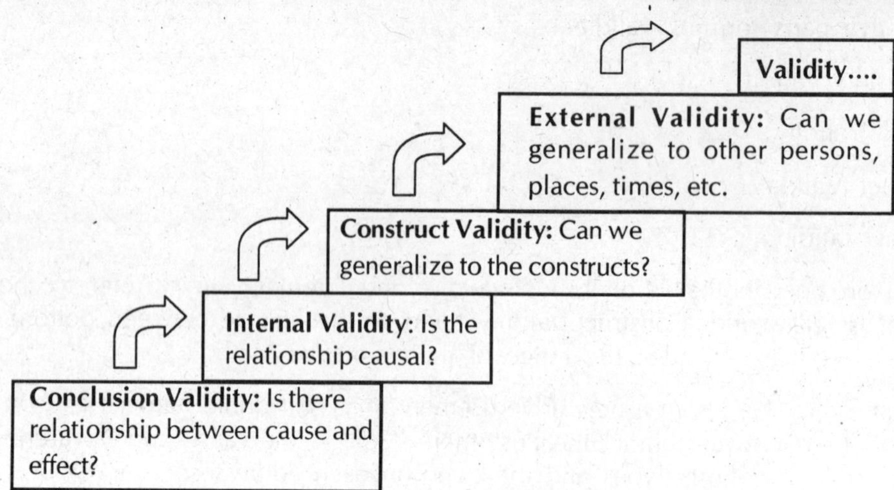


**Source:** William Trochin's 'Research Methods'

Notice how the question that each validity type addresses presupposes an affirmative answer to the previous one. This is what we mean when we say that the validity types build on one another. The figure shows the idea of cumulativeness as a staircase, along with the key question for each validity type.

It starts with Conclusion Validity which means 'is there any relationship between cause and effect'. The next step is Internal Validity which means 'Is the relationship causal'. The next step on the staircase is Construct Validity which means 'Can we generalize to constructs? Next step is External Validity which means 'Can we generalize with other persons, places, time or society in general?'

When we talk about validity, there are many problems. There are always possible threats. For instance, imagine a study examining whether there is a relationship between the amount of training in a specific technology and subsequent rates of use of that technology. Because the interest is in a relationship, it is considered an issue of conclusion validity. Assume that the study is completed and no significant correlation between amount of training and adoption rates is found. On this basis it is concluded that there is no relationship between the two. How could this conclusion be wrong that is, what are the "threats to validity"? For one, it's possible that there isn't sufficient statistical power to detect a relationship even if it exists. Perhaps the sample size is too small or the measure of amount of training is unreliable. Or maybe assumptions of the correlation test are violated given the variables used. Perhaps there were random irrelevancies in the study setting or random heterogeneity in the respondents that increased the variability in the data and made it harder to see the relationship of interest. The inference that there is no relationship will be stronger — have greater conclusion validity — if one can show that these alternative explanations are not credible. The distributions might be examined to see if they conform to assumptions of the statistical test, or analysis conducted to determine whether there is sufficient statistical power.

Let us discuss the terms again in detail.

## 4.2 Conclusion Validity

Of the four types of validity (Conclusion validity, internal validity, construct validity and external validity) conclusion validity is undoubtedly the least considered and most misunderstood. That's probably due to the fact that it was originally labelled as 'statistical' conclusion validity. In many ways, conclusion validity is the most important of the four validity types because it is relevant whenever we are trying to decide if there is a relationship in our observations (and that's one of the most basic aspects of any analysis).

Conclusion validity is the degree to which conclusions we reach about relationships in our data are reasonable.

For instance, if we're doing a study that looks at the relationship between economic condition and expenses of the human beings, we eventually want to reach some conclusion. Based on our data, we may conclude that there is a positive relationship, which means persons with higher income tend to spend more while those with lower income tend to spend less. Conclusion validity is the degree to which the conclusion we reach is credible or believable.

Although conclusion validity was originally thought to be a statistical inference issue, it has become more apparent that it is also relevant in qualitative research. For example, in an observational field study of mobile users, the researcher may, on the basis of field notes, see a pattern that suggests that young people who go to college use mobile phone more for fun. Although this conclusion or inference may be based entirely on impressionistic data, we can ask whether it has conclusion validity, that is, whether it is a reasonable conclusion about a relationship in our observations, college students and use of mobile phones for fun.

When we wish to investigate a relationship, there can be possibly two cases, either there is a relationship in our data or there isn't. We may conclude that there is a relationship when in fact there is not, or we may infer that there isn't a relationship when in fact there is. So, we have to consider all of these possibilities when we talk about conclusion validity.

It's important to realize that conclusion validity is an issue whenever you conclude there is a relationship, even when the relationship is between some programme (or treatment) and some outcome. In other words, conclusion validity also pertains to causal relationships. But **it is different from internal validity**. Conclusion validity is only concerned with a relationship. For instance, in a programme evaluation, we may conclude that there is a positive relationship between our educational programme and achievement test scores, students in the programme get higher scores and students not in the programme get lower ones. Conclusion validity is essentially whether that relationship is a reasonable one or not, given the data. But it is possible that we will conclude that, while there is a relationship between the programme and outcome, the programme didn't cause the outcome. Perhaps some other factor, and not our programme, was responsible for the outcome in this study. For instance, the observed differences in the outcome could be due to the fact that the programme group was smarter than the comparison group to begin with. Our observed post-test differences between these groups could be due to this initial difference and not be the result of our programme. There may be a possibility that some other factor than our programme caused the outcome, is what internal validity is all about. So, it is possible that in a study we can conclude that our programme and outcome are related (conclusion validity) and also conclude that the outcome was caused by some factor other than the programme so we have to say there is no internal validity.

## 4.3 Threats to Conclusion Validity

A threat to conclusion validity is a factor that can lead you to reach an incorrect conclusion about a relationship in your observations. You can essentially make two kinds of errors about relationships:

1. Conclude that there is no relationship when in fact there is.

2. Conclude that there is a relationship when in fact there is not.

Most threats to conclusion validity may be due to the first problem, because it's so hard in most researches to find relationships in our data.

**Finding no relationship when there is one:**

One important threat is **low reliability of measures**. This can be due to many factors including poor question wording, bad instrument design or layout, illegibility of field notes, and so on. (Please note here reliability means dependence or trustworthiness. Reliability in research is something different and needs some clarification, we shall discuss this in the coming sections). The problem relates to **poor reliability of treatment implementation**. If the programme doesn't follow the prescribed procedures or is inconsistently carried out, it will be harder to see relationships between the programme and other factors like the outcomes. Disturbance that is caused by **random irrelevancies in the setting** can also obscure your ability to see a relationship. In a classroom context, the traffic outside the room, disturbances in the hallway and countless other irrelevant events can distract the researcher or the participants. The types of people you have in your study can also make it harder to see relationships. The threat here is due to **random heterogeneity of respondents**. If you have a very diverse group of respondents, they are likely to vary more widely on your measures or observations. Some of their variety may be related to the phenomenon you are looking at, but at least part of it is likely to just constitute individual differences that are irrelevant to the relationship being observed.

All of these threats add variability into the research context and contribute to the "noise" relative to the signal of the relationship you are looking for. But noise is only one part of the problem. We also have to consider the issue of the signal, the true strength of the relationship. There is one broad threat to conclusion validity that tends to subsume or encompass all of the noise-producing factors above and also takes into account the strength of the signal, the amount of information you collect, and the amount of risk you're willing to take in making a decision about whether a relationship exists. This threat is called low statistical power.

**Finding a relationship when there isn't one:**

The researcher usually spends a considerable amount of time analysing the data for relationships. It is important to conduct a thorough analysis, but most people are well aware of the fact that if you play with the data long enough, you can often "turn up" results that support or corroborate your hypotheses. In statistical analysis, we attempt to determine the probability that the finding we get is a "real" one or could have been a "chance" finding. In fact, we often use this probability to decide whether to accept the statistical result as evidence that there is a relationship. In social sciences, researchers often use the rather arbitrary value known as the 0.05 level of significance to decide whether their result is credible or could be considered a "fluke." Essentially, the value 0.05 means that the result you got could be expected to occur by chance at least 5 times out of every 100 times you run the statistical analysis. The probability assumption that underlies most statistical analyses assumes that each analysis is "independent" of the other. But that may not be true when you conduct multiple analyses of the same data. For instance, let's say you conduct 20 statistical tests and for each one you use the 0.05 level criteria for deciding whether you are observing a relationship. For each test, the odds are 5 out of 100 that you will see a relationship even if there isn't one. Odds of 5 out of 100 are equal to the fraction 5/100 which is also equal to 1 out of 20. Now, in this example, you conduct 20 separate analyses. Let's say that you find that of the 20 results, only 1 is statistically significant at the 0.05 level. Does that mean you have found a statistically significant relationship? If you had only done the 1 analysis, you might conclude that you've found a relationship in that result. But if you did 20 analyses, you would expect to find one of them significant by chance alone, even if there is no real relationship in the data. We call this threat to conclusion validity **fishing and the error rate problem**. The basic problem is that you were "fishing" by conducting multiple analyses and treating each one as though it was independent. Instead, when you conduct multiple analyses, you should adjust the error rate (i.e., significance level) to reflect the number of analyses you are doing. The bottom line here is that you are more likely to see a relationship when there isn't one when you keep re-analysing your data and don't take that fishing into account when drawing your conclusions.

### Problems that can lead to either conclusion error

Every analysis is based on a variety of assumptions about the nature of the data, the procedures you use to conduct the analysis, and the match between these two. If you are not sensitive to the assumptions behind your analysis you are likely to draw erroneous conclusions about relationships. In quantitative research we refer to this threat as the **violated assumptions of statistical tests**. For instance, many statistical analyses assume that the data are distributed normally — that the population from which they are drawn would be distributed according to a "normal" or "bell-shaped" curve (Normal distribution has bell-shaped curve, wherein assumption is that mean, mode and median are same). If that assumption is not true for your data and you use that statistical test, you are likely to get an incorrect estimate of the true relationship. And, it's not always possible to predict what type of error you might make, seeing a relationship that isn't there or missing one that is.

### Improving Conclusion Validity

Here are some general guidelines you can follow in designing to improve conclusion validity.

### Guidelines for Improving Conclusion Validity

- **Good Statistical Power**. The rule of thumb in research is that you want statistical power to be greater than 0.8 in value. That is, you want to have at least 80 chances out of 100 to find a relationship when there is one. There are several factors that interact to effect statistical power.

The four components of statistical power are:

1. **sample size**, or the number of units (e.g., people) accessible to the study
2. **effect size**, or the salience of the treatment relative to the noise in measurement
3. **alpha level** ($\alpha$, or significance level), or the odds that the observed result is due to chance
4. **power**, or the odds that you will observe a treatment effect when it occurs

Given values for any three of these components, it is possible to compute the value of the fourth. For instance, you may want to determine what a reasonable sample size would be for a study. If you can make reasonable estimates of the effect size, alpha level and power, it would be simple to compute the sample size.

Some of these components will be more manipulable than others depending on the circumstances of the project. For example, if the project is an evaluation of an educational programme or counselling programme with a specific number of available consumers, the sample size is set or predetermined. Or, if the exposure in a programme is small due to its potential negative side effects, the effect size may consequently be small. The goal is to achieve a balance of the four components that allows the maximum level of power to detect an effect if one exists, given programmatic, logistical or financial constraints on the other components.

To improve conclusion validity, use a larger sample size. Of course, you have to weigh the gain in power against the time and expense of having more participants or gathering more data. The second thing you can do is to increase your risk of making a Type I error — increase the chance that you will find a relationship when it's not there. In practical terms you can do that statistically by raising the alpha level. For instance, instead of using a 0.05 significance level, you might use 0.10. Finally, you can increase the effect size. Since the effect size is a ratio of the signal of the relationship to the noise in the context, there are two broad strategies here. If you increase the dosage of the programme (e.g., increase the hours spent in training or the number of training sessions), it will be easier to see the effect when the treatment is stronger. The other option is to decrease the noise (or, put another way, increase reliability).

- **Good Reliability**. Reliability is related to the idea of noise or "error" that obscures your ability to see a relationship. In general, you can improve reliability by doing a better job of constructing measurement instruments, by increasing the number of questions on a scale or by reducing situational distractions in the measurement context.
- **Good Implementation**. When you are studying the effects of interventions, treatments or programmes, you can improve conclusion validity by assuring good implementation of the procedures.

## 4.4 Internal Validity

**Internal Validity** is the approximate truth about inferences regarding cause-effect or causal relationships. Thus, internal validity is only relevant in studies that try to establish a causal relationship. (Let us repeat time and again — Question of Internal Validity shall arise only after conclusion validity). **Internal validity may not be relevant in most observational or descriptive studies.** But for studies that assess the effects of social programmes or interventions, internal validity is perhaps the primary consideration. Let us come back again to our example of 'soft' and 'awareness'. After ascertaining that there is a relationship between 'soft' and 'awareness', we can advance with internal validity. If there is no conclusion validity, we describe 'soft' and 'awareness' separately. It can be an exploratory. But when we say, there is a relationship; we discuss what the degree of relationship is. It is internal validity. We may like to conclude that our programme or treatment makes a difference. For example, teaching programmes improved the students, advertisement expenditure helped increased revenue, increase in money supply caused inflation, use of pesticides increased yield. But there may be lots of other reasons, other than our programme, why test scores may improve or symptoms may reduce. The key question in internal validity is whether observed changes can be attributed to your programme or intervention (i.e., the cause) and not to other possible causes (sometimes described as "alternative explanations" for the outcome).

One of the things that are most difficult to grasp about internal validity is that it is only relevant to the specific study in question. That is, we can think of internal validity as a "zero generalizability" concern. All that internal validity means is that we have evidence that what we did in the study (i.e., the programme) caused what we observed (i.e., the outcome) to happen. It doesn't tell us whether what we did for the programme was what we wanted to do or whether what we observed was what we wanted to observe, those are construct validity concerns. It is possible to have internal validity in a study and not have construct validity. For instance, imagine a study where we are looking at the effects of a new computerized teaching programme on math performance in first grade students. Imagine that the teaching is unique as it has a heavy computer game component and we think it will really work to improve math performance. Finally, imagine that we were wrong, it turns out that math performance did improve, it had nothing to do with the computer programme. What caused the improvement was the individual attention that the adult tutor gave to the child; the computer programme didn't make any difference. This study would have internal validity because something that we did affected something that we observed, we did cause *something* to happen. But the study would not have construct validity; specifically the label "computer math programme" does not accurately describe the actual cause (perhaps better described as "personal adult attention").

## 4.5 Threats to Internal Validity

For convenience, we divide the threats to validity into three categories.

- Single Group Threat: Criticisms that apply when you are only studying a single group that receives your programme.
- Multiple group threats: Criticisms that are likely to be raised when you have several groups in your study (e.g., a programme and a comparison group).
- Social Threats: Threats that arise because social research is conducted in real-world human contexts where people will react to not only what affects them, but also to what is happening to others around them.

### Single Group Threat

Let us have two groups. First group is not given any treatment; however a test is taken (Post-test). Next we give treatment to the second group we take a Pre-test and after treatment we take a Post-test.

To help make this a bit more concrete, let's imagine that we are studying the effects of a compensatory education programme in mathematics for first grade students on a measure of math performance such as a standardized math achievement test. In the post-only design, we would give the first graders the programme and then give a math achievement post-test. We might choose not to give them a baseline measure because we have reason to believe they have no prior knowledge of the math skills we are teaching. It wouldn't make sense to pre-test them if we expect they would all get a score of zero. In the pre-post design we are not willing to assume that they have no prior knowledge. We measure the baseline in order to determine where the students start out in math achievement. We may hypothesize that the change or gain from pre-test to post-test is due to our special math tutoring programme. This is a *compensatory* programme because it is only given to students who are identified as potentially low in math ability on the basis of some screening mechanism.

With either of these scenarios in mind, consider what would happen if you observe a certain level of post-test math achievement or a change or gain from pre-test to post-test. You want to conclude that the outcome is due to your math programme. But you can be wrong. Here are some of the ways, some of the threats to internal validity that your critics may raise some of the plausible alternative explanations for your observed effect:

- **History Threat:** It's not your math programme that caused the outcome; it's something else, some historical event that occurred. For instance, we know that Astha TV channel teaches math even at the preliminary level. Your programme might not have caused any improvement but group members learnt by viewing a TV channel.
- **Maturation Threat:** The children would have had the exact same outcome even if they had never had your special math training programme. All you are doing is measuring normal maturation or growth in understanding that occurs as part of growing up; your math programme has no effect. This maturation explanation is different from a history threat. In general, if we're talking about a specific event or chain of events that could cause the outcome, we call it a history threat. If we're talking about all of the events that typically transpire in your life over a period of time (without being specific as to which ones are the active causal agents) we call it a maturation threat.
- **Testing Threat:** This threat only occurs in the pre-post design. What if taking the pre-test made some of the children more aware of that kind of math problem, it "primed" them

for the programme so that when you began the math training they were ready for it in a way that they wouldn't have been without the pre-test. This is what is meant by a testing threat, taking the pre-test (not getting your programme) affects how participants do on the post-test.

- **Instrumentation Threat:** Like the testing threat, this one only operates in the pre-test-post-test situation. This may be due to change in test style. In many schools when they have to administer repeated testing they don't use the exact same test but rather give out "alternate forms" of the same tests. Perhaps part or all of any pre-post gain is attributable to the change in instrument, not to your programme. Instrumentation threats are likely especially when the "instrument" is a human observer. The observers may get tired over time or bored with the observations.

- **Mortality Threat:** Mortality is used metaphorically here. It means that people are "dying" with respect to your study. Usually, it means that they are dropping out of the study. What's wrong with that? Let's assume that in our compensatory math tutoring programme we have a non-trivial dropout rate between pre-test and post-test. And, assume that the kids who are dropping out are the low pre-test math achievement test scorers. If you look at the average gain from pre-test to post-test using all of the scores available to you at each occasion, you would include these low pre-test subsequent dropouts in the pre-test and not in the post-test. You'd be dropping out the potential low scorers from the post-test, or, you'd be artificially inflating the post-test average over what it would have been if no students had dropped out. And, you won't necessarily solve this problem by comparing pre-post averages for only those kids who stayed in the study.

- **Regression Threat:** A regression threat, also known as a "regression artefact" or "regression to the mean" is a statistical phenomenon that occurs whenever you have a non-random sample from a population and two measures that are imperfectly correlated. Assume that your two measures are a pre-test and post-test and they are not perfectly correlated. Furthermore, assume that your sample consists of low pre-test scorers. The regression threat means that the pre-test average for the group in your study will appear to increase or improve (relatively to the overall population) even if you don't do anything to them, even if you never give them a treatment.

While there are several ways to rule out threats, one of the most common approaches to ruling out the ones listed above is through your research design. For instance, instead of doing a single group study, you could incorporate a control group. In this scenario, you would have two groups: one receives your programme and the other one doesn't. In fact, the only difference between these groups should be the programme. If that's true, then the control group would experience all the same history and maturation threats, would have the same testing and instrumentation issues, and would have similar rates of mortality and regression to the mean. In other words, a good control group is one of the most effective ways to rule out the single-group threats to internal validity. Of course, when you add a control group, you no longer have a single group design.

## 4.6 Construct Validity

Construct Validity refers to the degree to which inferences can legitimately be made from the operationalizations in your study to the theoretical constructs on which those operationalizations were based. Like external validity, construct validity is related to generalizing. But, where external validity involves generalizing from your study context to other people, places or times, **construct validity involves generalizing from your programme or measures to the *concept* of your programme or measures**. Construct validity seeks agreement between a theoretical concept and a specific measuring device or procedure. For example, a researcher inventing a new IQ test may spend a great deal of time attempting to "define" intelligence in order to reach an acceptable level of construct validity.

To understand whether a piece of research has construct validity, three steps should be followed. First, the theoretical relationships must be specified. Second, the empirical relationships between the measures of the concepts must be examined. Third, the empirical evidence must be interpreted in terms of how it clarifies the construct validity of the particular measure being tested.

There's an awful lot of confusion in the methodological literature that stems from the wide variety of labels that are used to describe the validity of measures. However, we really want to talk about the validity of operationalization. That is, any time you translate a concept or construct into a functioning and operating reality (**the operationalization**), you need to be concerned about how well you did the translation. This issue is as relevant when we are talking about treatments or programmes as it is when we are talking about measures.

Taking the example of sampling, the population of interest in your study is the "construct" and the sample is your operationalization.

If we think of it this way, we are essentially talking about the construct validity of the sampling. Construct validity refers to the general case of translating any construct into an operationalization. Many research books give various types of construct validity. Here is a list of the validity types that are typically mentioned in texts and research papers when talking about the quality of measurement:

## Construct Validity

**(a) Translation validity**

(i) Face validity

(ii) Content validity

**(b) Criterion-related validity**

(i) Predictive validity

(ii) Concurrent validity

(iii) Convergent validity

(iv) Discriminant validity

We know that **Construct validity is the approximate truth of the conclusion that your operationalization accurately reflects its construct**. All of the other terms address this general issue in different ways. In **translation validity**, we focus on whether the operationalization is a good reflection of the construct. This approach is definitional in nature and it assumes we have a good detailed definition of the construct and that we can check the operationalization against it. In **criterion-related validity**, we examine whether the operationalization behaves the way it should, given our theory of the construct. This is a more relational approach to construct validity. It assumes that our operationalization should function in predictable ways in relation to other operationalizations based upon our theory of the construct. Let us assume a population behaves in a typical way that is they take cold milk in the morning, now the sample which I draw will also take cold milk in the morning. (Do you know Indians generally like to take hot milk in the morning? Something like Kellogs' Corn Flakes comes in your mind!).

**(a) Translation validity**

In translation validity we see whether operationalization is good reflection of construct. It has two types – face validity and content validity.

**(i) Face validity**

In **face validity**, we look at the operationalization and see whether "on its face" it seems like a good translation of the construct. This is probably the weakest way to try to demonstrate construct validity. Just because it is weak evidence doesn't mean that it is wrong. We rely on our subjective judgment throughout the research process. This form of judgment won't be very convincing to others.

**(ii) Content validity**

In **content validity**, we check the operationalization against the relevant content domain for the construct. This approach assumes that we have a good detailed description of the content domain. For example, a researcher aims to study mathematical learning and create a survey to test for mathematical skill. If the researcher only tested for multiplication and then drew conclusions from that survey, their study would not show content validity because it excludes other mathematical functions. Although the establishment of content validity for placement-type exams seems relatively straightforward, the process becomes more complex as it moves into the more abstract domain of socio-cultural studies. For example, a researcher needing to measure an attitude like self-esteem must decide what constitutes a relevant domain of content for that attitude. For socio-cultural studies, content validity forces the researchers to define the very domains they are attempting to study.

**(b) Criterion-Related validity**

In **criteria-related validity**, you check the performance of your operationalization against some criterion. How is this different from content validity? In content validity, the criteria are the construct definition itself; it is a direct comparison. In criterion-related validity, we usually make a prediction about how the operationalization will *perform* based on our theory of the construct. The difference among the different criterion-related validity types is in the criteria they use as the standard for judgment.

Criterion-related validity, also referred to as instrumental validity, is used to demonstrate the accuracy of a measure or procedure by comparing it with another measure or procedure which has been demonstrated to be valid. For example, imagine a hands-on driving test has been shown to be an accurate test of driving skills. By comparing the scores on the written driving test with the scores from the hands-on driving test, the written test can be validated by using a criterion related strategy in which the hands-on driving test is compared to the written test.

**(i) Predictive validity**

In **predictive validity**, we assess the ability of operationalization to predict something it should theoretically be able to predict. For instance, we may theorize that a measure of math ability should be able to predict how well a person will do in an engineering-based profession. We can give our measure to experienced engineers and see if there is a high correlation between scores on the measure and their salaries as engineers. A high correlation would provide evidence for predictive validity; it would show that our measure can correctly predict something that we theoretically think it should be able to predict.

**(ii) Concurrent validity**

In **concurrent validity**, we assess the ability of operationalization to distinguish between groups that it should theoretically be able to distinguish between. For example, if we come up with a way of assessing manic-depression, our measure should be able to distinguish between people who are diagnosed manic-depression and those diagnosed paranoid schizophrenic. If we want to assess the concurrent validity of a new measure of empowerment, we may give the measure to both migrant farm workers and to the farm owners, theorizing that our measure should show that the farm owners are higher in empowerment. As in any discriminating test, the results are more powerful if you are able to show that you can discriminate between two groups that are very similar.

**(iii) Convergent validity**

In **convergent validity**, we examine the degree to which the operationalization is similar to other operationalizations that it theoretically should be similar to. For instance, to show the convergent validity of a Head Start programme, we might gather evidence that shows that the programme is similar to other Head Start programmes. Or, to show the convergent validity of a test of arithmetic skills, we might correlate the scores on our test with scores on other tests that purport to measure basic math ability, where high correlations would be evidence of convergent validity.

**(iv) Discriminant validity**

In **discriminant validity**, we examine the degree to which the operationalization is not similar to other operationalizations that it theoretically should not be similar to. For instance, to show the discriminant validity of a Head Start programme, we might gather evidence that shows that the programme is *not* similar to other early childhood programmes that don't label themselves as Head Start programmes. Or, to show the discriminant validity of a test of arithmetic skills, we might correlate the scores on our test with scores on tests that of verbal ability, where *low* correlations would be evidence of discriminant validity.

### Idea of Construct validity

William Trochin writes that construct validity refers to the degree to which inferences can legitimately be made from the operationalizations in your study to the theoretical constructs on which those operationalizations were based. He finds that it helps him to divide the issues into two broad territories that he calls the "land of theory" and the "land of observation." The land of theory is what goes on inside your mind, and your attempt to explain or articulate this to others. It is all of the ideas, theories, hunches and hypotheses that you have about the world. In the land of theory you will find your idea of the programme or treatment as it should be. You will find the idea or construct of the outcomes or measures that you believe you are trying to affect. The land of observation consists of what you see happening in the world around you and the public manifestations of that world. In the land of observation you will find your actual programme or treatment, and your actual measures or observational procedures. Presumably, you have constructed the land of observation based on your theories. You developed the programme to reflect the kind of programme you had in mind. You created the measures to get at what you wanted to get at.

## 4.7 Threats to Construct Validity

Threats refer to plausible rival explanations for the conclusion that the experimenter has drawn, i.e., a competing explanation. In a research study you are likely to reach a conclusion that your programme was a good operationalization of what you wanted and that your measures reflected what you wanted them to reflect. The kinds of questions and issues your critics will raise are threats to construct validity. Following are the threats to construct validity.

1. **Attention and Contact with Participants:** Differential attention across experimental and control groups may be the basis of group differences. It is possible that the difference in the dependent variable is due to the attention given the participants, not because of the characteristics of the "treatment." For instance, Placebo: Substance that has no active pharmacological properties that would be expected to produce change for the problem to which it is applied. A placebo can be a sugar pill, saline solution, or an "active" ingredient which is not helpful for the condition in question. They allow you to control for expectancies across both groups.

2. **Single Operations and Narrow Stimulus Sampling:** Was the intervention as the experimenter conceived it responsible for the outcome or was there a seemingly irrelevant associated feature that caused the change?

3. **Experimenters' expectancies:** Experimenters' beliefs and expectations impact how participants perform. We can hopefully assume it is unintentional. If the one who designed the new treatment is the one administering it, and it turns out to be effective, you should suspect threats to construct validity.

4. **Cues of the Experimental Situation:** It is also known as – **demand characteristics** – sources of influence which come from the experimental situation which could provide a rival explanation for results. They can evoke an expectation for improvement or no improvement.

5. **Inadequate Explication of Constructs:** Failure to adequately explicate a construct may lead to incorrect inferences about the relationship between operation and construct.

6. **Construct Confounding:** Operations usually involve more than one construct, and failure to describe all the constructs may result in incomplete construct inferences.

7. **Mono-Operation Bias:** Any one operationalization of a construct both under-represents the construct of interest and measures irrelevant constructs, complicating inference.

8. **Mono-Method Bias:** When all operationalizations use the same method that method is part of the construct actually studied.

9. **Confounding Constructs with Levels of Constructs:** Inferences about the constructs that best represent study operations may fail to describe the limited levels of the construct that were actually studied.

10. **Treatment Sensitive Factorial Structure:** The structure of a measure may change as a result of treatment; change that may be hidden in the same scoring is always used.

11. **Reactive Self-Report Changes:** Self-reports can be affected by participant motivation to be in a treatment condition, motivation that can change after assignment is made.

12. **Reactivity to the Experimental Situation:** Participants' responses reflect not just treatments and measures but also participants' perceptions of the experimental situation and those perceptions are part of the treatment construct actually tested.

13. **Compensatory Rivalry:** Participants not receiving treatment may be motivated to show they can do as well as those receiving treatment, and this compensatory rivalry must then be included as part of the treatment construct description.

14. **Resentful Demoralization:** Participants not receiving a desirable treatment may be so resentful or demoralized that they may respond more negatively than otherwise and this resentful demoralization must then be included as part of the treatment constructs description.

**12. Treatment Diffusion:** Participants may receive services from a condition to which they were not assigned, making construct descriptions of both conditions more difficult.

## 4.8 External Validity

External validity is related to generalizing. Validity refers to the approximate truth of propositions, inferences, or conclusions. So, external validity refers to the approximate truth of conclusions that involve generalizations. External validity is the degree to which the conclusions in your study would hold for other persons in other places and at other times.

In science there are two major approaches to provide evidence for a generalization.

They are (i) **Sampling Model** (ii) **Proximal Similarity Model**

In the sampling model, we start by identifying the population we would like to generalize to. Then, we draw a fair sample from that population and conduct our research with the sample. Finally, because the sample is representative of the population, we can automatically generalize our results back to the population. There are several problems with this approach. First, perhaps we don't know at the time of our study who we might ultimately like to generalize to. Second, we may not be easily able to draw a fair or representative sample. Third, it's impossible to sample across all times that we might like to generalize.

Second approach to generalizing is the **Proximal Similarity Model**. Under this model, we begin by thinking about different generalizability contexts and developing a theory about which contexts are more like our study and which are less so. For instance, we might imagine several settings that have people who are more similar to the people in our study or people who are less similar. This also holds for times and places. When we place different contexts in terms of their relative similarities, we can call this implicit theoretical a ***gradient of similarity***. Once we have developed this proximal similarity framework, we are able to generalize. We conclude that we can generalize the results of our study to other persons, places or times that are more like (that is, more proximally similar) to our study. Note, we can never generalize with certainty; it is always a question of more or less similar.

## 4.9 Threats to External Validity

A threat to external validity is an explanation of how we may be wrong in making a generalization. For instance, if we conclude that the results of our study (which was done in a specific place, with certain types of people, and at a specific time) can be generalized to another context (for instance, another place, with slightly different people, at a slightly later time). There are three major threats to external validity because there are three ways you could be wrong, they are (i) people, (ii) places or (ii) times. Critics can argue that the results of our study are due to the unusual type of people who were in the study. Or, they can argue that it might only work because of the unusual place we did the study in (perhaps you interviewed mobile phone users who belonged to upper class and your finding about mobile users may be biased and may not be true for public in general). Or, they may suggest that you did your study in a peculiar time. For instance, you surveyed the mobile users when they were mostly free after the term-end examinations.

### Improving External Validity

If your studies are based on the sampling model, draw a good sample from a population. For instance, you should use random selection, if possible, rather than a non-random procedure. And, once selected, you should try to assure that the respondents participate in your study and that you keep your dropout rates low. A second approach would be to use the theory of proximal similarity more effectively. You can describe the ways your contexts and others differ, providing lots of data about the degree of similarity between various groups of people, places, and even times. You may even be able to map out the degree of proximal similarity among various contexts with a methodology like concept mapping. Perhaps the best approach to criticisms of generalizations is simply to show them that they're wrong and do your study in a variety of places, with different people and at different times. That is, your external validity (ability to generalize) will be stronger the more you **replicate** your study.

## 4.10 Theory of Reliability

In general, reliable means dependable or trustworthy. In research, the term "reliable" also means dependable in a general sense, but that's not a precise enough definition. The reason "dependable" is not a good enough description. In may be confused with measurement reliability. Certainly, when we speak of a dependable measure, we mean one that is both reliable and valid. So we have to be a little more precise when we try to define reliability.

In research, the term **reliability means "repeatability" or "consistency"**. A measure is considered reliable if it would give us the same result over and over again assuming that what we are measuring isn't changing.

A company claims that its scooter's mileage is 50 km per litre. You take a test drive and find the mileage as 50. Time and again you test and find the mileage same as 50 with slight variation. Every time we get 50, we say scooter is reliable. Let us say scooter mileage is X and we measure X. If we assume that what we're measuring doesn't change between the time of our first and second observation, we can begin to understand how we get at reliability. While we observe mileage for what we're measuring, we usually think of that mileage as consisting of two parts, the 'true' mileage or actual level for the person on that measure, and the 'error' in measuring it.

$$X_1 = \text{True} + \text{Error}$$

$$X_2 = \text{True} + \text{Error}$$

Let's explore in more detail what it means to say that a measure is "repeatable" or "consistent". We'll begin by defining a measure that we'll arbitrarily label **X**. It might be a person's score on a math achievement test or a measure of severity of illness. It is the value (numerical or otherwise) that we observe in our study. Now, to see how repeatable or consistent an observation is, we can measure it twice. We'll use subscripts to indicate the first and second observation of the same measure. It's important to keep in mind that we observe the **X** score; we never actually see the true (**T**) or error (**e**) scores. For instance, a student may get a score of **80** on a math achievement test. That's the score we observe, an **X** of **80**. But the reality might be that the student is actually better at math than that score indicates. Let's say the student's true math ability is **85** (i.e., **T=85**). That means that the error for that student is **–5**. What does this mean? Well, while the student's true math ability may be **85**, he/she may have had a bad day, may not have had breakfast, may have had an argument, or may have been distracted while taking the test. Factors like these can contribute to errors in measurement that make the student's observed ability appear lower than their true or actual ability.

OK, back to reliability. If our measure, **X**, is reliable, we should find that if we measure or observe it twice on the same persons that the scores are pretty much the same. Because the error scores ($\mathbf{e_1}$ and $\mathbf{e_2}$) have different subscripts indicating that they are different values. But the true score symbol **T** is the same for both observations. What does this mean? That the two observed scores, $\mathbf{X_1}$ and $\mathbf{X_2}$ are related only to the degree that the observations share true score. You should remember that the error score is assumed to be random. Sometimes errors will lead you to perform better on a test than your true ability while at other times it will lead you to score worse.

But the true score, your true ability on that measure, would be the same on both observations (assuming, of course, that your true ability didn't change between the two measurement occasions).

With this in mind, we can now define reliability more precisely. Reliability is a **ratio** or fraction. In layperson terms we might define this ratio as: $\frac{\text{True Level of Meausure}}{\text{The Entire Measure}}$.

The reliability is defined as the proportion of "truth" in our measure and the entire measure. Definition can be restated in terms of a set of observations. The easiest way to do this is to speak of the variance of the scores. Remember that the variance is a measure of the spread or distribution of a *set* of scores. So, we can now state the definition as: (The variance of True score)/(The variance of the measure) or $\frac{\text{Var (T)}}{\text{Var (X)}}$.

We can easily calculate Variance of X, but it is not possible to calculate the variance of T, because we never know what should be true value. Repeating the example of mileage of scooter, our X is 50. But what should be **T** we don't know. Other example, a student score is 80, but true score is 85. How shall we find the true worth of the student? How shall we find the true worth of a scooter? It means it is difficult to find the variance of truth. Therefore it is difficult to find out reliability. However, we can estimate it. We have two observations, $X_1$ and $X_2$. We assume using 'true score theory' that these two observations would be related to each other to the degree that they share true scores. So we calculate the correlation between $X_1$ and $X_2$. with following formula of correlation:

$$\frac{\text{Covariance}(X_1 X_2)}{SD(X_1) * SD(X_2)} \qquad X_1$$

where the 'SD' stands for the standard deviation (which is the square root of the variance). If we look carefully at this equation, we can see that the covariance, which simply measures the "shared" variance between measures, must be an indicator of the variability of the true scores because the true scores in $X_1$ and $X_2$ are the only thing the two observations share. So, the top part is essentially an estimate of var(T) in this context. And, since the bottom part of the equation multiplies the standard deviation of one observation with the standard deviation of the same measure at another time, we would expect that these two values would be the same and that this is essentially the same thing as squaring the standard deviation for either observation. But, the square of the standard deviation is the same thing as the variance of the measure. So, the bottom part of the equation becomes the variance of the measure (or var(X)). The correlation between two observations of the same measure is an estimate of reliability.

In a nut shell, we cannot calculate reliability because we cannot measure the true score component of an observation. But we also know that we can *estimate* the true score component as the covariance between two observations of the same measure. With that in mind, we can estimate the reliability as the correlation between two observations of the same measure. As coefficient of correlation is always between 0 and 1, so the reliability shall also be between 0 and 1. The value of a reliability estimate tells us the proportion of variability in the measure attributable to the true score. A reliability of .5 means that about half of the variance of the observed score is attributable to truth and half is attributable to error. A reliability of .8 means the variability is about 80% true ability and 20% error. And so on.

## 4.11 Reliability and Validity

Reliability and validity are not separate ideas but, in fact, they're related to each other. One of the favourite metaphors for the relationship between reliability is that of the target. Think of the centre of the target as the concept that you are trying to measure. Imagine that for each person you are measuring, you are taking a shot at the target. If you measure the concept perfectly for a person, you are hitting the centre of the target. If you don't, you are missing the centre. The more you are off for that person, the farther you are from the centre. (adapted from William Trochin's Research Methods)

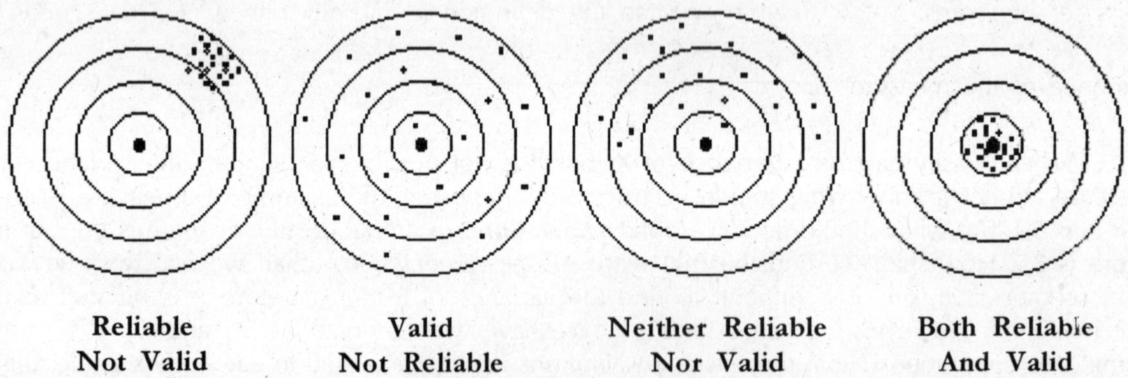


The figure above shows four possible situations. In the first one, you are hitting the target consistently, but you are missing the centre of the target. That is, you are consistently and systematically measuring the wrong value for all respondents. This measure is reliable, but not valid (that is, it's consistent but wrong). The second shows hits that are randomly spread across the target. You seldom hit the centre of the target but, on average, you are getting the right answer for the group (but not very well for individuals). In this case, you get a valid group estimate, but you are inconsistent. Here, you can clearly see that reliability is directly related to the variability of your measure. The third scenario shows a case where your hits are spread across the target and you are consistently missing the centre. Your measure in this case is neither reliable nor valid. Finally, you consistently hit the centre of the target. Your measure is both reliable and valid.

Another way we can think about the relationship between reliability and validity is shown in the figure below. Here, we set up a 2 × 2 table. The columns of the table indicate whether you are trying to measure the same or different concepts. The rows show whether you are using the same or different methods of measurement. Imagine that we have two concepts we would like to measure, student's 'language' and 'math' skill. Furthermore, imagine that we can measure each of these in two ways. First, we can use a written test. Second, we can ask the student's classroom teacher to give us a rating of the student's ability based on their own classroom observation.

| | Concept | |
|---|---|---|
| | **Same** | **Different** |
| Same | **Reliability** English written = English written | **Discriminant** English written = Math written |
| Different | **Convergent** English written = English observed | **Very discriminant** English written = Math observed |

The first cell on the upper left shows the comparison of the English written test score with the English written test score. But how can we compare the same measure with itself? We could do this by estimating the reliability of the written test through a test-retest correlation, parallel forms, or an internal consistency measure. What we are estimating in this cell is the reliability of the measure.

The cell on the lower left shows a comparison of the English written measure with the English teacher observation rating. Because we are trying to measure the same concept, we are looking at convergent validity.

The cell on the upper right shows the comparison of the English written exam with the math written exam. Here, we are comparing two different concepts (English versus math) and so we would expect the relationship to be lower than a comparison of the same concept with itself (e.g., English versus English or math versus math). Thus, we are trying to discriminate between two concepts and we would consider this discriminant validity.

Finally, we have the cell on the lower right. Here, we are comparing the English written exam with the math teacher observation rating. Like the cell on the upper right, we are also trying to compare two different concepts (English versus math) and so this is a discriminant validity estimate. But here, we are also trying to compare two different methods of measurement (written exam versus teacher observation rating). So, we'll call this *very* discriminant to indicate that we would expect the relationship in this cell to be even lower than in the one above it.

When we look at reliability and validity in this way, we see that, rather than being distinct, they actually form a continuum. On one end is the situation where the concepts and methods of measurement are the same (reliability) and on the other is the situation where concepts and methods of measurement are different (*very* discriminant validity).

## 4.12 How to Do?

Jolly Dolly met again.

Dolly: "This appears to be quite confusing but interesting! The term measure is not clear to me."

Jolly: "If possible we shall involve Dada in our discussion, today. But let us understand the term measure. Measurement is the process of observing and recording the observations that are collected as part of a research effort. Measure may be one of your research methods including all your concepts and procedures."

Dolly: "Let us be simple with Validity."

Jolly: "The exact nature of 'validity' is a highly debated topic in both educational and social research, since there is no single or common definition of the term. An account is valid or true if it represents accurately those features of the phenomena, that it is intended to describe, explain or theorise. It may also be called an agreement between two efforts to measure the same thing with different methods. There are two common strands: Firstly, whether the means of measurement are accurate. Secondly, whether they are actually measuring what they are intended to measure."

Dolly: "Let me use a very crude example. Our university has many colleges with courses like Engineering, Medicine, Law, Management, etc., with its total strength more than a lakh. Let it be population. Okay. Now, I think all university students are from upper middle class and like to buy their own books. Let it be theory or general idea. I wish to test it. First I define what I mean with upper middle class and types of books they buy. Now prepare a questionnaire with simple questions asking students their family income and type of books they buy for their study. I cannot go to each and every student. I decide to gather random sample so that each college should have equal chance to represent in my sample. Do you want to say all this is a measure which is going to measure the population?"

Jolly: "Your example is very crude, but it may be good for a beginner to understand."

Dolly: "Now if I wish to measure the intelligence of my class, I prepare a questionnaire. Questionnaire is a measuring tool, but does it really measure what I wish to measure."

Jolly: "Go ahead."

Dolly: "Now if it is simple descriptive study without cause-effect relationship, there is no question of validity. Question of validity should arise when you see relationship. For instance, when I say middle class students buy their own books. Do you say a simple correlation is conclusion validity?

Jolly: "Go ahead! But descriptive studies also have the issue of validity."

Dolly: "Now if we see there is a relationship, we frame a construct to see degree of relationship that is internal validity. Should I say regression is a step to see internal validity? Now in regression I have taken up all the variables properly or not whether my model covers all issues, we may ask whether we have construct validity."

Jolly: "It appears to be okay, but it is better to absorb than to say. 'Validity' is not a unitary concept. There is no single form, construct or concept that can universally be claimed to define or encompass the term. Neither, however, can validity be said to be a discretely identifiable element of any research project, which is capable of being located at multiple and specific stages within the research. The concept of 'validity' defies extrapolation from, or categorisation within, any research project."

Dolly: "In simple words, accuracy is required at every stage of research project; otherwise your results will not be valid, if there is no validity at every step."

Jolly: "You are getting it."

Dolly: "'Validity' is not a singular acid test that can be applied to the research process as a whole. The 'validity' measure can be applied differently depending upon the researcher's beliefs as to what stage of the research process is in need of validation.

Such an approach may perceive validity as referring only to measurement, observers, scores, instruments, relationships between scores or observable variations, rather than to the whole research process."

Jolly: "You are getting intelligent."

Dolly: "I am!"

Jolly: "There are other types of validities also – Descriptive validity, Interpretive validity, Theoretical validity, etc. 'Descriptive validity' is that which is concerned with the initial stage of research, usually involving data gathering. The central issue is factual accuracy in the informational statements that describe what was observed and experienced. Interpretation is essentially couched within the rhetoric that the researcher uses to describe a situation and is mutually constructed between researchers and subjects. Quantitative researchers do much to disassociate themselves from such interpretations, yet these too are inevitable in their categorisations and selection of data. Regardless of the ethical implications of interpreting meaning from the observations of others, other than those that they would necessarily agree with, it is worth noting that an individual may often have no more 'valid' interpretations of their own actions than another might make. 'Theoretical validity' is a more 'abstract' analysis than the 'descriptive' and 'interpretive' 'validities' concerning the 'immediate physical and mental phenomena studied.' Maxwell claims that 'theoretical validity' goes beyond the concrete and descriptive and concerns itself with the constructions that researchers apply to, or develop, during the research."

Dolly: "You want to say question of validity also arises in case of descriptive or exploratory studies. Researcher should also be very careful in qualitative research."

Jolly: "Yes, originally people used to think about these concepts only in quantitative analysis, but it is very important in qualitative studies also. The traditional criteria for 'validity' find their roots in a positivist tradition, and to an extent, positivism has been defined by a systematic theory of 'validity'. Within the positivist terminology, 'validity' was the result and culmination of other empirical conceptions: universal laws, evidence, objectivity, truth, actuality, deduction, reason, fact and mathematical data to name just a few. It is within this tradition and terminology that quantitative research is traditionally defined. Qualitative research, arising out of the post-positivist rejection of a single, static or objective truth, has concerned itself with the meanings and personal experience of individuals, groups and sub-cultures. 'Reality' in qualitative research is concerned with the negotiation of 'truths' through a series of subjective accounts. Whereas quantitative researchers attempt to disassociate themselves as much as possible from the research process, qualitative researchers have come to embrace their involvement and role within the research. For quantitative researchers this involvement would greatly reduce the validity of a test, yet for qualitative researchers denying one's role within research also threatens the validity of the research."

Dolly: "So validity and objectivity are also related."

Jolly: "Yes. Some qualitative researchers have argued that the term validity is not applicable to qualitative research and have at the same time realised the need for some kind of qualifying check or measure for their research. As a result many researchers have espoused their own theories of 'validity' and have often generated or adopted what they consider to be more appropriate terms, such as 'trustworthiness', 'worthy', 'relevant', 'plausible', 'confirmable', 'credible' or 'representative.'

Dolly: "Let us talk something about validity and quantitative analysis."

Jolly: "We shall have to call Dada now."

Dolly: 'Oh yes, he is experienced."

Jolly: "Quantitative research limits itself to what can be measured or quantified and qualitative research attempts to 'pick up the pieces' of the unquantifiable, personal, indepth, descriptive and social aspects of the world. Many of the allegations of invalidity from both sides can be attributed to a failure to recognise the purposes to which each methodology is suited."

Dada joins the discussion.

Dada: "Quantitative research and validity cannot be separated."

Dolly: "What if you have conclusion validity, but no internal validity"?

Dada: "Let me recollect any example which has conclusion validity but no internal validity."

Dolly: "Dada, you may lose your job. I shall give you example of price and demand; they have conclusion validity, but no internal validity."

Dada: "What? Your example is wrong. Dolly, you have not understood the concept. Try to understand when you have relationship between two variables, whether positive or negative, you have conclusion validity and if there is conclusion validity, you will have internal validity. Now price and demand have conclusion validity and then they have internal validity also. Now it may depend to what degree."

Dolly: "But price and demand affect each other."

Dada: "So what, X depends upon Y or Y depends on X, they have internal validity. You know we test the models with F test to see if we have more error term in relationship."

Jolly: "How can we see that our sample is reliable?"

Dada: "Reliability of sample! Surprising! Reliability means repeatability of results. Reliability doesn't mean trustworthiness here. Reliability is concerned with results from measures. If we get the same results from the measure time and again, we can say measure is reliable."

Jolly: "But how can we see whether the sample is trustworthy or not?"

Dada: "You can test it by correlation."

Jolly: "Correlation!!!!"

Dada: "Say we have a population of one lakh. We survey, say, 500 people. We doubt that sample of say 50 from a particular stratum appears to be wrongly selected and/or they may not be telling us the truth. Just correlate the answers from this sample with rest of the observations, if we find there is no or poor correlation between the two samples, we may conclude that samples are not from same population."

Jolly: "Among non-parametric tests — Kendall's coefficient of concordance and Kruskal-Wallis Test, which is better?"

Dada: "Both are good, it depends upon the situation which test you use. This is not the time when we discuss non-parametric tests, we shall learn about it in coming chapters."

Jolly: "But we called you to test your ability."

Dada: "You can test anyone anytime, I am available, but first improve your understanding of the concepts."

Dolly: "I wish to conclude that a researcher will have to be very careful at every stage of research, otherwise the results shall not be accurate."

Dada: "You are right, thanks, see you tomorrow, and read the research work 'Study of Consumers' perceptions about Malls and Traditional Retail Outlets' carried out by Dr. J.K. Sachdeva. The report has already been published in Journal of Global Economy, Volume 4 no. 4. The research work is not complete but the report will tell you how a problem is defined, how primary data is gathered and issues of validity in finding are important."

Research Project 3

## 4.13 Study of Consumers' Perceptions about Malls and Traditional Retail Outlets

J.K. Sachdeva[1] and B.P. Tripathi[2]

### Introduction[3]

Co-operative marketing is not new to India. To get the economies of scale, Indian craftsmen and traders made shrenies or groups of similar products and trade during 6th and 7th centuries, (Romila Thapar, 1966). This was the basis of caste system. The villages during medieval and British period grew with cooperative trade. Co-operative marketing is just an extension and application of the philosophy of co-operation in the area of agricultural marketing. It is a process of marketing through a co-operative society, formed for the producers, by the producers. It seeks to eliminate the middlemen between the producer and the consumer, thus getting the maximum price for their produce (Singh, 2007). Kirana shops are traditional retail outlets in India. However with the advent of new co-operative marketing with modern all-facility malls, there is general perception that retails consumers are getting skewed towards malls and consequently Kirana stores are experiencing tough competition to retain their customers. The ICRIER study (2008), commissioned by the Department of Industrial Policy and Promotion, has said both large stores and neighbourhood Kirana shops can co-exist. Women activist and a politician, Margaret Alva, observed while addressing the silver jubilee celebrations of the FICCI Ladies Organisation (FLO). "The small Kirana shops and establishments run by women are being swept away by the mall culture," (The Hindu Business Line, July 7, 2008).

This paper is an attempt to know consumers' perception of Malls and Kriana stores. Section II reviews the literature. Section III sets objectives and attempts to frame hypotheses. Techniques of data collections and methodology have been explained in Section IV. Data has been analysed in Section V. Section VI concludes with policy suggestions.

### Section 1

### India's Market Reforms

India's market reforms have widely been portrayed as the inevitable consequence of "globalisation" As the reforms were intellectually continued with the liberalisation policies pursued by various past governments; this dispels concern that they were imposed on India by the international financial institutions (IFIs). Also, the reforms were spearheaded by a small group of exceptionally able men who succeeded in winning over the unconvinced through the art of argument and persuasion. This suggests a robust consensus, among policy intellectuals, on not only the need for reform, but also a particular type of (neoliberal) reform, (Mitu, 2008).

The paradigm was seriously questioned in the mid-1960s, when the country was confronted by a looming crisis in agricultural production. Policy-makers were particularly alarmed at this time by India's increasing dependence on American food aid, and seemed prepared to undertake major revisions of the existing agricultural policy regime. The mixed economy was a compromise to adjust the opposing philosophies of right and left, (Mitu 2008).

---

[1] Dr J K SACHDEVA, Professor Head Projects Pillai's Institute of Management Studies and Research, New Panvel, Navi Mumbai and Hon Edtor-in-Chief, Journal of Global Economy, Mumbai.

[2] Prof BRAHM PRAKASH TRIPATHI, Faculty, Indira Institute of Business Management , Mumbai.

[3] The project would not have been completed without the active participation of student committee comprising Vivekanand Education Society, Mumbai and ITM Executive Centre, Mumbai.

Indira Gandhi's return as prime minister in 1980 is viewed as a step forward towards liberalisation. Though she did not come up openly in favour of open market, the market radicals who called for a comprehensive, multi-arena liberalisation of the entire economy, and a clear prioritisation of growth as the chief objective of development, were successful in convincing her in favour of liberalisation. It is this group that is often referred to as the "team" behind the reforms. The thrust of Indira Gandhi's reform lay in relaxing controls on the domestic private sector, which was seen as a route to enhancing growth. Privatisation, trade liberalisation and, more importantly, cutbacks in public investment and social spending were carefully avoided, with political-bureaucratic elites unprepared to abandon equity as an overarching policy objective. A full, multidimensional paradigm shift to neo-liberalism was only one among several market-oriented reform options in the late 1980s. The market radicals' moment of triumph, however, finally arrived in 1991. They were catapulted into commanding positions in the formal government hierarchy, most notably in the prime minister's office (PMO) and the ministries of finance and commerce, (Mitu, 2008).

India's market reformers have drawn strength from a "new breed of entrepreneurs" who, unlike the older generation of family-owned business, are confident in their ability to face global competition without the state's protection. These rising stars of India's "sunrise" industries (information technology, petro-chemicals and engineering) are also said to have developed superior means of communicating their objectives to policy elites through the creation of better, more professionalized institutions – such as the Confederation of Indian Industries (CII) – to represent their interests. The market radicals made common cause with the IFIs in their ambition to defeat opponents of a Washington Consensus style, pro-globalisation model of market reform (Mitu, 2008).

## Growth of Malls in India

As economic reforms were continued by various governments year on year, the economy grew between 8 to 10 per cent which resulted in improvements of income dynamics. These factors along with favourable demographics like increase in spending patterns are driving the consumption demand. Indian Retail Industry is ranked among the ten largest retail markets in the world. India is witnessing an unprecedented consumption boom. The attitudinal shift of the Indian consumer in terms of "Choice Preference", "Value for Money" and the emergence of organized retail formats have transformed the face of Retailing in India. The Indian retail industry is currently estimated to be a US$ 200 billion industry and organized retailing comprises 3 per cent (or) US$6.4 Billion of the retail industry. With a growth over 20 per cent per annum over the last 5 years, organized retailing is projected to reach US$ 23 Billion by 2010, (Singla et al 2007)

Singla et al (2007) comment that India's retail sector is going to transform with a three-year compounded annual growth rate of 46.64 per cent, retail sector is the fastest growing sector in the Indian economy. Traditional markets are transforming themselves in new formats such as departmental stores, hypermarkets, supermarkets and specialty stores. Western-style malls have begun appearing in metros and near metro cities, introducing the Indian consumer to a new shopping experience.

Consumers are attracted to malls because of the presence of well-known anchors, viz. department stores with recognized names. Anchors generate mall traffic that indirectly increases the sales of lesser-known mall stores. Lesser-known stores can free ride off of the reputations of better-known stores. Mall developers internalize these externalities by offering rent subsidies to anchors and by charging rent premiums to other mall tenants.

Eric (1998) estimates that anchors receive rent subsidy of no less than 72 per cent than which non-anchor stores pay. Anchors pay a lower rent per square foot in larger malls (with several department stores) than in smaller malls (with fewer department stores), even though sales per square foot of anchors are the same in the two types of malls. In contrast, the sales and rent per square foot of other mall stores are higher in super-regional malls than in regional malls

## Consumerism and Monetization

The consumer culture has been gripping India, an easy access to credit facility is one of the causes of overspending. This overspending many a time is the reason for the mismanagement of the personal finances and thus creates pressure on investment management of individuals. To investigate the effect of irresponsible use of credit card on compulsive buying among Indian consumers on their personal finances, a survey was conducted by Aggarwal et al (2004). After surveying 250 shoppers in the shopping malls like Shoppers' Stop, Lifestyle, Food World, Q-mart and other retail stores, selected for the study; it was observed that irresponsible use of credit cards facilitates the compulsive buying behaviour that ultimately is the cause for the mismanagement of personal finances, (Aggarwal *et al.,* 2004).

## Reforms and Supply Chains

With the amendment of APMC Act which became the key factor in making organised retailing a viable proposition, direct sourcing of produce by organised retailers from the farmer was possible and this resulted in supply chain getting shrunk considerably by eliminating at least two or even three intermediaries. The rise of organised retailing has shrunk the processed goods supply chain at both the front and back end. At the back end, the amended APMC Act enables the processor to buy produce directly from the farmer, bypassing the mandis. At the front end, the processor can supply goods directly to the retailer's warehouse or to the wholesaler's premises with the intermediate steps of central storage and reliance on the distributors eliminated. Further, the incentive to set up warehouses in particular states to benefit from the differential in sales tax rates will be phased out completely by 2010 and replaced by VAT. Under VAT, all transactions within the state as well as interstate will be taxed at uniform rates, making supply chain shorter and more efficient, (Vijay Kumar *et al.,* 2008).

The traditional retail industry consists of two basic formats: Kirana (Mom and Pop) stores and Pushcart vendors. The kirana stores are (typically) family-owned, small in size (100 sq ft and above), carry a limited number of items, and are run mostly by family members, supplemented with some hired help. There are approximately 12 million such stores in the country with perhaps half of them involved in food retailing. These stores generally cater to the customers within their neighbourhood. The pushcart vendors run their self-owned "mobile stores" and carry, for the most part single or a limited number of items. There is no pushcart vendor census data available but the total number of vendors could be a few million, (Vijay Kumar *et al.,* 2008).

The organised food retailers deploy a number of formats ranging from gigantic hypermarkets at one end of the spectrum to the no-frills discount stores at the other end. They are distinguished by size, number of items carried, pricing strategies and customer segments targeted among others.

There are two main categories of supplying food articles: (1) Farm produce, such as fruits, vegetable, cereals, etc., which are grown and supplied by farms; and (2) processed goods that are supplied by the manufacturing and food processing companies.

In the traditional farm produce supply chain, the trader provides the link between the farmer and the commission agent at a mandi given the distances and the transportation requirements. The commission agent conducts the auction in the mandi with wholesaler as the buyer. Post-auction, the wholesaler provides the link between the mandi and the retailer and at each step, the intermediary marks up the price.

According to Vijay Kumar *et al.,* (2008), the kirana stores can themselves form buying co-operatives to improve their bargaining power. They can also take up the organised sector on their offer to assist in utilising their backend supply chain. The most affected group, namely, traders and commission agents, would have to shift their business strategies and re-orient their business model to the wholesaling or a processing format. They possess sufficient knowledge of the product, supply sources and customers to be able to execute such models. They would still have to join hands with other traders and commission agents. The government can also help with credit and tax benefits, (Vijay Kumar *et al.*, 2008).

## Clustering and Joint Marketing in Retail Trade in USA

Bohlin (2001) observed clustering of stores in Sweden retail trade market for a long time. In the modern age, the reflection of this trend could be observed in the city malls and big shopping centres. The fundamental reason for this phenomenon is thought to be:–

- Economies of scale
- Time and travel cost benefit

Bohlin – (2001) attempted to find other reasons also. It was observed that the stores cluster in an effort to increase their individual visibility among consumers. The underlying presumption is that stores individually reach more consumers for the same marketing expenditure if they cluster. Following may be reasons for clustering:

- If stores cluster at a common geographical location, it's easier for the consumers to remember this address.
- Provides greater opportunity for consumers to compare the stores' competing products and increase the knowledge of product characteristics.
- As there will many products at the same place, consumers feel the risk of mistakes in their choices would be less.
- The marketing cost of achieving the same visibility on it's own would be higher for an individual store if it tried to compete with cluster of stores.

According to CPT (central place theory), the stores cluster because of the cost minimizing behaviour of consumers and profit maximizing behaviour of stores, (Bohlin, 2001).

## Comparative Study of Arab Bazaars and Modern Retail Markets

Lamieri et al (2006) compared two very different market forms: Bazaar, the typical market present in the Arab societies of Northern Africa and Middle East and the common retail markets existing in modern industrial societies, such as the Mall. They observed that in the Mall, standards of measure and weight are formalized and well defined, traded goods are homogeneous and price information is public, since shop retailers use a posted-price mechanism and the transactions are mostly impersonal. On the contrary, in the Bazaar there are not well defined and formalized standards of measure and weight and traded goods are often not homogeneous. Price information is not public, in the sense that retailers do not post prices of products, and the transactions are mostly interpersonal. These characteristics lead to the emergence of the two most peculiar Bazaar institutions: clientelization and bargaining. Clientelization is not simply the emergence of loyalty of some buyers for specific sellers. As in a trading relationship based on interpersonal transaction, clientship between traders is a reciprocal matter, since it ties both the buyer and the seller, one to each other. As clientelization, bargaining usually develops in the presence of economic interpersonal transactions; price setting is the main objective of bargaining and traders.

In the case of the Mall, the price dynamic led to the competitive price, while in the Bazaar, the price dynamics prove that bargaining and clientelization may be effective communicative mechanisms for co-ordinating information among market participants as the Mall institutions.

However, to obtain such result perfect clientelization between traders is required. Eventually, Bazaar institutions proved to affect negatively the stability of the market minimum price, once reached. This drawback sheds light on the information costs of lock-in effects burdening the buyers within stable client relations, (Lamieri et al 2006).

### Economics of Rents

Shopping centres in malls involve, a "business partnership" between the mall owner, mall tenants, and the department stores. The lease agreement between the mall owner and the tenants includes a return to both real estate and business enterprise components. That is, tenants pay for both space (land and building) and to be part of the business enterprise. Jeffery et al (1990) did an empirical test with data provided by Rouse Company. Malls which were surveyed were located in New York. When a shopping mall or major shopping centre is sold, the purchaser acquires land and buildings, fixtures (including those that revert to the owner at the end of any leases), an established name and reputation, an established (but continually evolving) mix of tenants and character or theme, operating agreements with anchor tenants or with major stores on their own "pads" within the area of the shopping centre or mall site, and an operating management staff on site and in place. A successful mall developer/owner has the management expertise to attract anchor tenants who sign operating agreements (agreeing to operate in the mall under their trade name for a specified number of years). Furthermore, the developer/owner creates a balanced tenant mix in the rest of the mall, including certain national tenants with trade names, attracts customers and, through advertising and promotion, creates an image for the mall. All of this ultimately shows up in the market "rental" of mall tenants. This rental includes a return on both realty and non-realty interests.

When the lease is up for renewal, if a tenant has not been successful, his lease may not be renewed. If a tenant has been successful, his lease will be renewed. The mall owner would clearly like to continue to capture some of the going concern value created by the tenant, and can do so by setting a new base rent at a level ***higher*** than would be paid by a new tenant coming into the mall. The tenant will be willing to pay this higher rental because the tenant does not want to leave the mall and lose the going concern value that has been created. With lease renewals for successful tenants, the mall owner is able to capture some of the going concern value being generated by a tenant's business through lease premiums. This results in an aggregate business enterprise value for the mall, (Jeffery et al 1990).

## Section 2

### Objectives of the Study

After going through the literature, the following objectives have been set for further study:

1. To know consumers' perceptions about malls and kirana shops.
2. To study the demographic profile of the urban consumers who visit malls and kirana shops.
3. To find out factors which attract consumers most to malls and kirana shops.

Following hypotheses will be tested:

(a) Younger groups prefer going to malls frequently

(b) Higher income groups frequently go to malls

## Section 3

## Research Methodology

To achieve the objectives, 625 housewives were surveyed in Mumbai with 29 close ended questions and 2 open ended questions. Out of 29 questions 9 were for demographic purposes and 10 with Likert Scale each for malls and kirana shops to know the perceptions of respondents. Entire Mumbai was divided into two parts — Mumbai and Navi Mumbai. Mumbai was further divided into five parts South Mumbai (South of Dadar and Wadala, with 50 samples), Central Suburb (Dadar to Thane with 100 samples), Western Suburbs (Bandra to Virar with 100 samples), Harbour Suburbs (Wadala to Mankhurd with 100 samples) and Thane (with 50 samples) keeping in mind the population concentration. It was further decided that 200 samples would be collected from Navi Mumbai area. Data was collected by students of VES Institute of Management Studies and Research and EMBA students of ITM, Kharghar, Mumbai with convenient sampling frame. Data so collected was edited for any minor missing items with averages, coded, and tabulated for further analysis.

Chi Square test is conducted to test if any consumer group has any preference on demographic basis.

Factor analysis was conducted to reduce the number variables to find out important factors based on coded Likert Scale.

## Section 4

## Analysis and Results

Out of 625 survey forms only 496 were found to be valid with all arrays filled in, except 28 forms where the data was filled with average values.

Table 1 to 5 shows the demographic frequencies of the respondents. Table 1 shows 225 persons out of 496 go to malls once in week However $c^2$ test shows that there is no preference of any income group with frequency of mall visits. Similarly, family income and percentage shopping are not related as per $c^2$ test. Similarly, people frequently visit kirana shops but the visits have nothing to with family income (as shown in Tables 3 and 4). It was further seen that visits to malls is not related to any age group.

**Table 1**

**Number of Respondents Visiting Malls**

| Family Income | Once in Three Months | Once in One Month | Once in A Week | Twice in a Week | Thrice in a Week | Total |
|---|---|---|---|---|---|---|
| Less Than 1.5 lakh | 7 | 12 | 24 | 8 | 7 | 58 |
| 1.5-3 lakhs | 5 | 30 | 73 | 21 | 14 | 143 |
| 3-5 lakhs | 1 | 24 | 60 | 37 | 5 | 127 |
| Greater than 5 lakhs | 2 | 20 | 68 | 53 | 25 | 168 |
| Total | 15 | 86 | 225 | 119 | 51 | 496 |

Table 1 Chi square calculated .000029 statistically not significant (Table value for 12 DF = 21.026)

**Table 2**

**Family Income and Shopping Percentage in Malls**

| Family Income | <20% | 20-40% | 40-60% | 60-80% | 80-100% | Total |
|---|---|---|---|---|---|---|
| Less than ₹ 1.5 lakh | 25 | 10 | 6 | 5 | 12 | 58 |
| 1.5-3 ₹ lakhs | 45 | 48 | 17 | 23 | 10 | 143 |
| 3-5 ₹ lakhs | 41 | 34 | 15 | 21 | 16 | 127 |
| Greater than 5 ₹ lakhs | 40 | 27 | 33 | 31 | 37 | 168 |
| Total | 151 | 119 | 71 | 80 | 75 | 496 |

Table 2 Chi square calculated .00015 and table value 21.026

**Table 3**

**Number of Respondents Visiting Kirana Shops**

| Family Income | Once in Three Months | Once in One Month | Once in a Week | Twice in a Week | Thrice in a Week | Total |
|---|---|---|---|---|---|---|
| Less than ₹ 1.5 Lakh | 4 | 5 | 13 | 10 | 26 | 58 |
| 1.5-3 ₹ lakhs | 13 | 10 | 36 | 33 | 51 | 143 |
| 3-5 ₹ lakhs | 16 | 1 | 31 | 37 | 42 | 127 |
| Greater than 5 ₹ lakhs | 12 | 5 | 50 | 45 | 56 | 168 |
| Total | 45 | 21 | 130 | 125 | 175 | 496 |

(Table 3 Chi square calculated .1158 statistically not significant)

**Table 4**

**Family Income and Shopping Percentage in Kirana Shops**

| Family Income | <20% | 20-40% | 40-60% | 60-80% | 80-100% | Total |
|---|---|---|---|---|---|---|
| Less than ₹ 1.5 lakh | 12 | 8 | 6 | 6 | 26 | 58 |
| 1.5-3 ₹ lakhs | 19 | 25 | 22 | 39 | 38 | 143 |
| 3-5 lakhs | 19 | 20 | 16 | 38 | 34 | 127 |
| Greater than 5 lakhs | 37 | 37 | 35 | 26 | 33 | 168 |
| Total | 87 | 90 | 79 | 109 | 131 | 496 |

Table 4 Chi square calculated .00070 statistically not significant)

**Table 5**

**Age Group Going to Malls**

| Age | Once in Three Months | Once in One Month | Once in A Week | Twice A Week | Thrice in a Week | Total |
|---|---|---|---|---|---|---|
| <21 | 0 | 0 | 3 | 3 | 0 | 6 |
| 21-30 | 11 | 36 | 124 | 64 | 30 | 265 |
| 31-40 | 2 | 17 | 49 | 35 | 12 | 115 |
| 41-50 | 2 | 22 | 30 | 12 | 5 | 71 |
| 50+ | 0 | 12 | 18 | 8 | 1 | 39 |
| Total | 15 | 87 | 224 | 122 | 48 | 496 |

Table 5 Chi square calculated .00000 and table value 21.026

## Consumer Perceptions about Malls

All 496 respondents responded 10 questions each on malls and kirana shops why they like malls and kirana shops. Respondents were asked to give their preference on Likert Scale for each question. Means and standard deviations for malls and kirana shops have been given in table 6 and table 9. Factor analysis are shown in tables 7 and 10.

## Malls

Table 6 depicts the mean, standard deviation and t-values of each question. Highest t-value is for question no. 2 which says "In malls, I have freedom to window shop". Next highest t value is for question number 1 which states that 'In malls, the standard of weights are well defined and price information made public." Mean of question number 9 is negative and statistically insignificant which means in general people feel that there is no home delivery of goods by mall owner. As this question is statistically insignificant we should drop this question for further analysis.

Table 7 shows the results of Factor Analysis of Malls Questions by Principal Axis Factor method. Factor number 1 has eigen value as 2.823 and factor 2 has eigen value. 1.177. Based on eigen value these two factors explain 44% of variation, but sum of squared loadings is only 0.510 for factor two with only 5.6% of the variation. Hence, Factor 1 is significant. After factor one, the slope almost flattens. So, only one factor is taken for further discussion. Factor 1 has three important variables – Question no. 2, 8 and 3 as follows.

1. In malls, I have the freedom to window shop.
2. I like the comforts, ambience and experience in malls.
3. In malls, I am left on my own to make buying decisions and am under no pressure to buy.

The significance of above variables is the confirmation whatever has been shown in table 6. The Factor 1 is being named here as **'Awe factor with freedom."**

**Table 6**

**Descriptive Statistics of Questions for Malls**

| Descriptive Statistics for Malls | | | | |
|---|---|---|---|---|
| | **Mean** | **Std. Deviation** | **Analysis N** | **T-Values** |
| Mall Qno1 | .83 | .906 | 496 | 20.51455 |
| Mall Qno2 | 1.27 | .715 | 496 | 39.71622 |
| Mall Qno3 | 1.08 | .988 | 496 | 24.39428 |
| Mall Qno4 | .35 | 1.268 | 496 | 6.233632 |
| Mall Qno5 | .77 | .952 | 496 | 17.9178 |
| Mall Qno6 | .31 | .920 | 496 | 7.613998 |
| Mall Qno7 | .63 | .983 | 496 | 14.21049 |
| Mall Qno8 | 1.02 | .809 | 496 | 28.0915 |
| Mall Qno9 | -.08 | 1.057 | 496 | -1.61417 |
| Mall Qno10 | .56 | .921 | 496 | 13.54834 |

**Table 7**

**Total Variance of Questions for Malls**

| Total Variance Explained | | | | | | |
|---|---|---|---|---|---|---|
| Factor | Initial Eigen values | | | Extraction Sums of Squared Loadings | | |
| | Total | % of Variance | Cumulative % | Total | % of Variance | Cumulative % |
| 1 | 2.823 | 31.371 | 31.371 | 2.159 | 23.987 | 23.987 |
| 2 | 1.177 | 13.075 | 44.446 | .510 | 5.670 | 29.657 |
| 3 | .966 | 10.732 | 55.178 | | | |
| 4 | .905 | 10.054 | 65.233 | | | |
| 5 | .758 | 8.421 | 73.653 | | | |
| 6 | .682 | 7.582 | 81.235 | | | |
| 7 | .653 | 7.259 | 88.494 | | | |
| 8 | .581 | 6.461 | 94.955 | | | |
| 9 | .454 | 5.045 | 100.000 | | | |

Extraction Method: Principal Axis Factoring.

**Table 8**

**Components of Factors for Malls Factor Matrix[a]**

| | Factor | |
|---|---|---|
| | 1 | 2 |
| Mall Qno2 | .663 | -.404 |
| Mall Qno8 | .604 | |
| Mall Qno3 | .516 | -.218 |
| Mall Qno5 | .488 | .276 |
| Mall Qno10 | .473 | .242 |
| Mall Qno1 | .460 | -.106 |
| Mall Qno7 | .441 | |
| Mall Qno4 | .336 | .314 |
| Mall Qno6 | .326 | .233 |
| Extraction Method: Principal Axis Factoring. | | |
| a. 2 factors extracted. 18 iterations required. | | |

## Kirana Shops

Table 9 describes the means, standard deviation and t-values of questions asked to same kirana shops. The highest t values is for question no.9 ( In kirana shops I the option to buy customized small quantities). Next to that are two questions number 7 and 3 which state that they deliver the grocery at home and grains can be seen and felt before buying.

Questions nos. 6 and 10 have negative means but statistically significant. People feel at kirana shops they do not get new products earlier than we see at malls and salesmen do not explains the features of the products, though the mean values are very minuscule but their statistical significance cannot be ignored.

Table 10 shows the results of factor analysis by Principal Axis Factoring method. As per eignen value two components can be drawn. However, the component number 2 has only 0.906

as sum squares loading and has only 9.06% percentage variance loading, so factor 1 is purposed for further discussion.

Table 10 shows the factor matrix which shows that factor 1 has 4 important variables as question numbers 4, 9, 3 and 5 which state that consumers get personal attention; they can buy customized small quantities; they can feel the products and buy; they can buy a range of products included unbranded. This new component having all four variables has been renamed as **'person customized buying'**.

**Table 9**

**Descriptive Statistics of Questions for Kirana Shops**

| Mean | Std. Deviation | N | t-values | |
|---|---|---|---|---|
| Kirana Qno1 | .20 | .995 | 496 | 4.513726 |
| Kirana Qno2 | .32 | 1.055 | 496 | 6.679834 |
| Kirana Qno3 | .85 | .779 | 496 | 24.20994 |
| Kirana Qno4 | .73 | .948 | 496 | 17.24035 |
| Kirana Qno5 | .14 | .936 | 496 | 3.31105 |
| Kirana Qno6 | -.15 | 1.015 | 496 | -3.31882 |
| Kirana Qno7 | 1.03 | .863 | 496 | 26.69987 |
| Kirana Qno8 | .66 | .927 | 496 | 15.89248 |
| Kirana Qno9 | 1.03 | .708 | 496 | 32.51533 |
| Kirana Qno10 | -.40 | .855 | 495 | -10.4631 |

**Table 10**

**Total Variance of Questions for Kirana Shops**

| Total Variance Explained | | | | | | |
|---|---|---|---|---|---|---|
| Factor | Initial Eigen values | | | Extraction Sums of Squared Loadings | | |
| | Total | % of Variance | Cumulative % | Total | % of Variance | Cumulative % |
| 1 | 3.058 | 30.584 | 30.584 | 2.424 | 24.241 | 24.241 |
| 2 | 1.534 | 15.338 | 45.922 | .906 | 9.061 | 33.302 |
| 3 | .980 | 9.802 | 55.725 | | | |
| 4 | .887 | 8.868 | 64.592 | | | |
| 5 | .755 | 7.548 | 72.140 | | | |
| 6 | .717 | 7.168 | 79.308 | | | |
| 7 | .577 | 5.770 | 85.079 | | | |
| 8 | .542 | 5.417 | 90.496 | | | |
| 9 | .504 | 5.041 | 95.537 | | | |
| 10 | .446 | 4.463 | 100.000 | | | |

Extraction Method: Principal Axis Factoring.

**Table 11**

**Components of factors for Kirana Shops**

| | Factor Matrix[a] | |
|---|---|---|
| | 1 | 2 |
| Kirana Qno4 | .667 | |
| Kirana Qno9 | .579 | –.421 |
| Kirana Qno3 | .550 | –.213 |
| Kirana Qno5 | .521 | .363 |
| Kirana Qno7 | .503 | –.310 |
| Kirana Qno6 | .492 | .461 |
| Kirana Qno8 | .459 | –.123 |
| Kirana Qno1 | .413 | .138 |
| Kirana Qno2 | .373 | .114 |
| Kirana Qno10 | .235 | .436 |
| Extraction Method: Principal Axis Factoring. | | |
| a. 2 factors extracted. 9 iterations required. | | |

## Section 5

### Conclusions

India's market reformers have drawn strength from a "new breed of entrepreneurs" who, unlike the older generation of family-owned business, are confident in their ability to face global competition without the state's protection. The rise of organised retailing has shrunk the processed goods supply chain at both the front and back end. The traditional retail industry consists of two basic formats: Kirana (mom and pop) stores and Pushcart vendors There are two main categories of supplying food articles: (1) Farm produce, such as fruits, vegetable, cereals, etc., which are grown and supplied by farms; and (2) processed goods that are supplied by the manufacturing and food processing companies.

The fundamental reason for clustering of stores takes place due to two main reasons (a) Economies of scale and (b) Time and travel cost benefit

In the case of the malls, the price dynamic leads to the competitive price, while in the Bazaar, the price dynamics prove that bargaining and clientelization. Shopping centres in malls involve, a "business partnership" between the mall owner, mall tenants, and the department stores. The lease agreement between the mall owner and the tenants includes a return to both real estate and business enterprise components which may not allow the benefits of economies scale to consumer.

India is witnessing an unprecedented consumption boom. The economy is growing between 8 to 10 per cent and the resulting improvements in income dynamics along with factors like favourable demographics and spending patterns are driving the consumption demand.

This paper attempted to know the consumers' impressions about malls and kirana shops so as to juxtapose the theory with real life observations. 496 housewives from various areas of Mumbai were surveyed The analysis revealed that all types of people visit malls. There is no specific segment which visits malls. All types of people irrespective of age or income visit malls. People buy from malls as well as from kirana shops. There is no specific pattern. However people go to malls due to Malls' ambience and window shopping freedom. The reduce factor has been named as 'awe factor with freedom'

Consumers get personalized attention at kirana shops and can buy after feeling the products. At kirana shops they can buy a range of products included unbranded. This new component having all four variables has been renamed as **'personal customized buying'**.

A further study is required to know how awe factor is working for malls and personalized customized sales of kirana shops help them to increase their revenue.

## References

Romila Thapar, (1966): *"A History of India", Volume 1*, Penguin publication1966.

Singh, L. P. (2007): 'Co-operative Marketing in India and Aborod':Himalaya Publishing House, Mumbai, 2006.

Mitu Sengupta (2008) : "How the State Changed Its Mind: Power, Politics and the Origins of India's Market Reforms," Economic and Political Weekly, May, 24, 2008.

Bohlin, Nils (2001) : "Clustering and Joint Marketing in Retail Trade", December 4, 2001. http://ideas.repec.org

Lamieri, Marco and Bertacchini, Enrico (2006): "What if Heyek goes shopping in the bazaar" Online at http://mpra.ub.uni-muenchen.de/367/ MPRA Paper No. 367, posted 07. November 2007 link http://ideas.repec.org

Jeffery D Fisher and George H Lentz (1990): " Business Enterprise Value in Shopping Malls, An Empirical Test" Journal of Real Estate Research, Indiana, July, 1990.

Singala Amit and Goyal, Anil Kumar (2007) : "Retail Industry: From Myth to Malls" posted by faculty of ICFAI National College Panipat and Mathura on Indian MBA on March, 19, 2007 (Unpublished).

Eric D Gould (1998) : "Internalizing Externalities: The Pricing of Space in Shopping Malls" in Journal of Law and Economics, University of Chicago Press, 1998.

Aggarwal Anand and Sanjay Fuloria (2004) : "The Effect on Personal Finances due to Irresponsible Use of Credit Cards and Compulsive Buying Behaviour" in ICFAI Journal of Bank Management, Volume III no. 3, August, 2004.

Vijay Kumar, Yogesh Patwari, and Ayush H N (2008): "Organised Food Retailing: A Blessing or a Curse?" in Economic and Political Weekly, May 17, 2008.

...✎...✎...✎

# 5

# CHAPTER

# RESEARCH PLAN

## Structure

After the problem has been defined, the question arises how to carry out the research. The research plan is the main part of a grant application describing a principal investigator's proposed research, stating its importance and how it will be conducted.

The research plan should be written to address the following questions:

What do you intend to do?

Why is the work important?

What has already been done?

How are you going to do the work?

Researcher should know the background and significance of the research problem including the proposed rationale, current state of knowledge and potential contributions and significance of the research to the field. Literature review is very significant. Critically evaluate existing knowledge, including background literature and relevant data. References should reflect an updated knowledge of the field. Specify existing gaps that the project is intended to fill. The preliminary results are important to establish the experience and competence of the applicant to pursue the proposed research project and to provide support for the study hypotheses and research design. The progress report should include a summary of the previous application's specific aims and importance of the findings. Discuss how previous work leads to the current proposal. Emphasize how the previous work demonstrates feasibility of proposed methods. Accuracy and overall presentation are important in figures, tables and graphs.

## 5.1 Research Objectives

Setting objectives is important for any decision maker. It is the starting point of the formal planning process for managers of enterprises and organisations (setting objectives, generating strategies, evaluating strategies, monitoring results and obtaining commitment). The same happens in everyday life at different levels. You strive towards certain big goals in your career, family life, but on a daily basis you constantly set yourself small objectives of a more practical nature such as "I want to finish this difficult job before the end of the week so that I can go on a trip this weekend."

If you don't have any goal to live or work to, you're likely to drift around in a confused state. Setting objectives provides structure, purposiveness, focus, meaning and enables you to measure progress in the right direction or the lack of it.

The same is true for your research. But here there is an extra dimension. Setting objectives, and especially spending enough time to develop well-developed clear and logical objectives, leads to formal hypotheses which form the basis of the analytic phase of your research project. The framework of the analytic phase gives you a widely accepted formal structure to investigate how strong the evidence is in favour of your hypothesis and if the predictions made hold.

Research is an organized investigation of a problem in which there is an attempt to find facts, understand underlying phenomena and to get solution to a problem. To get right solution of a right problem, clearly defined objectives are very important. Clearly defined objectives enlighten the way in which the researcher has to proceed.

A research objective is a clear, concise, declarative statement, which provides direction to investigate the variables. Generally, research objective focus on the ways to measure the variables, such as to identify or describe them. Sometime objectives are directed towards identifying the relationship or difference between two variables. For instance: To establish relationship between market return and stock return during a particular time frame. Or to examine difference in market return and particular stock return during a particular year.

Main problem is sub-divided into sub-problems. The sum total sub-problems is always a main problem. The sub-problems help us define objectives of study. Research objectives are the results sought by the researcher at the end of the research process, i.e., what the researcher will be able to achieve at the end of the research study. The objectives of a research project summarize what is to be achieved by the study. Objective should be closely related to the statement of the problem.

A well-worded objective will be SMART, i.e., Specific, Measurable, Attainable, Realistic, and Time-bound. Research objective should be Relevant, Feasible, Logical, Observable, Unequivocal and Measurable. Objective is a purpose that can be reasonably achieved within the expected time frame and with the available resources.

SMART objectives are:

- **Specific:** states exactly what you need to achieve
- **Measurable:** includes a quality or quantity measure
- **Agreed:** between you and your Reviewer
- **Realistic:** can be challenging but must be achievable
- **Time-bound:** with a clear end date or timescale

Here are some tips for ensuring that your objectives are SMART:

### Specific

Objectives should clearly state what you are expected to achieve, using action verbs to describe what has to be done. For example:

**Not specific:** Encourage more people to join MBA

**Specific:** Increase number of MBA students

**Not specific:** Conduct research

**Specific:** Formulate plans for research on topic X

### Measurable

Objectives should include a quality and/or quantity reference so that you can measure whether or not you have achieved them. For example:

**Not measurable:** Increase membership of the Sports Centre

**Measurable:** Increase membership of the Sports Centre by 10%

**Not measurable:** Formulate plans for research on topic X

**Measurable:** Formulate plans for research on topic X and submit grant application to X Research Council.

### Agreed

Objectives should be agreed between you and your guide, relevant to your job and driven by University strategy and School/Institute/Section plans. Your guide will help ensure that your objectives are relevant and appropriate.

## Realistic

Objectives should be challenging but achievable, i.e., they should not be unrealistic. For example, it might be realistic to plan to lose 10 pounds in weight but it would be unrealistic to plan to lose 10 pounds in one week. Objectives should also take account of the skills, knowledge and resources needed to achieve them. You may need to consider whether you need any training or development (or other support) in order to achieve the objective.

## Time Bound

Objectives should include a time reference, such as a specific deadline. For example:

**Not time-bound:** Increase membership of the Sports Centre by 10%

**Time-bound:** Increase membership of the Sports Centre by 10% over the next six months

**Not time-bound:** Formulate plans for research on topic X and submit grant application to X Research Council

**Time-bound:** Formulate plans for research on topic X and submit grant application to X Research Council by 30th June 2015.

The time reference for other objectives might be in terms of frequency or turnaround time. For example:

**Time-bound:** Once a month, update all library web pages and printed guides.

**Time-bound:** Circulate minutes of Committee Y within five days of the meeting.

If there is a particularly long timescale involved, you may need to break your objective down, identify the steps you need to take to achieve your overall objective and work out how long each step is likely to take so that you can agree a target date.

Each specific objective consists of one infinitive sentence and should be phrased in a way that makes it possible to draw a conclusion from within the scope of the thesis. The more precisely you formulate your specific objectives, the simpler it will be to define the type of study and which method(s) you will use in your further research. You can refine your specific objective by clearly stating if your given action is to understand, analyse or create – in tune with the hierarchy of learning objectives and the key to the assessment of knowledge content as found in for example Bloom's taxonomy. In this way, your specific objectives will signal your level of ambition as well as where you will place the greatest effort in your thesis.

The formulations of objectives organize the study in clearly defined parts or phases. Properly formulated, specific objectives will facilitate the development of research methodology and will help to orient the collection, analysis, interpretation, and utilization of data.

There may be general objectives and specific objectives. General objectives are broad goals to be achieved. The general objectives of the study state what the researcher expects to achieve by the study in general terms. General objectives are usually less in number. Specific objectives are short term and narrow in focus. General objectives can be broken into small logically connected parts to form specific objectives. General objective is met through accomplishing all the specific objective. The specific objectives are more in number and they systematically address various aspects of problem as defined under 'the statement of problem' and key factor that is assumed to influence or causes the problem. They should specify what the researcher will do in the study, where, and for what purpose.

Each specific objective consists of one infinitive sentence and should be phrased in a way that makes it possible to draw a conclusion from within the scope of the thesis. The more precisely you formulate your specific objectives, the simpler it will be to define the type of study and which method you will use in your further research. You can refine your specific objective by clearly stating if your given action is to understand, analyse or create – in tune with the hierarchy of learning objectives and the key to the assessment of knowledge content.

Objectives are usually headed by infinitive verbs such as: To identify, To establish, To describe, To determine, To estimate, To develop, To compare, To analyse and To collect

## Research Objective and Linkage to Further Steps

"Science consists of both knowledge and the process by which this knowledge is created, research. Although research succeeds by building and testing better theories, the process involves constructs, concepts, and activities that are not themselves predictive. Non-predictive constructs serve science as logical devices, memory aids, inspirational prods, incentives to thought, political opinions, personal ideals, half-formed notions, odd beliefs, and unexpressed ideas. These elements are not 'bad' or unscientific. They form a prescientific soup from which each scientist draws inspiration and from which the disciplined human mind has constructed modern science." Peters, Robert Henry (1991), A Critique for Ecology, Cambridge University Press, Cambridge, UK, 366 pp. ISBN 0 521 39588 7 - p. 21

If you carried out an initial problem analysis and critically reviewed relevant literature on the topic, you have come up with a manageable and researchable problem and you have a thorough idea of the current state of knowledge on your research problem. You have done some assessment yourself on the relevance of the problem you want to address and how to cut it into manageable portions, but you relied much on the work of others you found in the literature.

Setting the study objectives basically means that you tell what you are going to do to solve the researchable problem, you explain the purpose of your research, you describe what you hope to achieve with your study, ....

It is closely related with defining your hypothesis or hypotheses. A hypothesis is basically a testable hunch you have; what do you think is true based on what you know so far (i.e., problem analysis and literature review) and stated in a way that you can evaluate the strength of the evidence in favour of it.

There are three distinct steps in your research project: delineating a problem into a researchable problem, literature review and setting study objectives and formulating hypotheses. In reality, it is not possible to draw a clear line between these three steps, hence the up and down arrows in the flowchart are on the right.

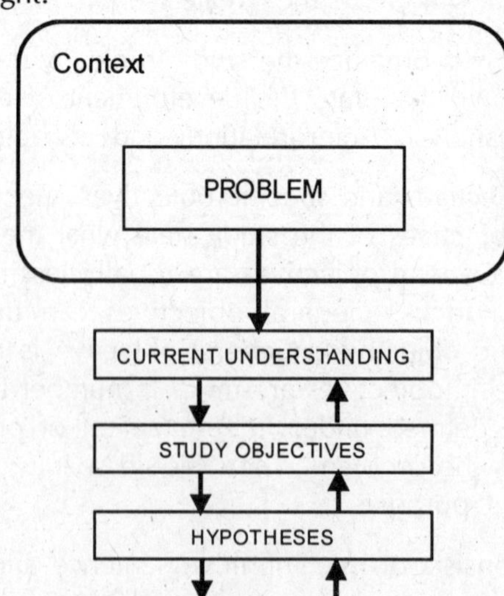

The scientific method can be seen as a hypothetico-deductive method, many people see "the scientific method" and "the hypothetico-deductive method" as being synonyms. Much of the method is based upon the work of Sir Karl Popper.

Since we are now entering the realm of philosophy of science, it means we are at an abstract level and there exist lot of discussion between supporters and opponents of each philosophy. For a majority of research projects however, the hypothetico-deductive method is an appropriate framework for structuring your research process.

According to the philosophy behind the method, scientific research proceeds by formulating a hypothesis that is intended to explain an observation. From this hypothesis, some predictions of further phenomena are deduced and tested. Observations that run contrary to those predicted are taken as a conclusive falsification of the hypothesis, observations which are in agreement with those predicted are taken as corroborating the hypothesis. A simplified flowchart is given below.

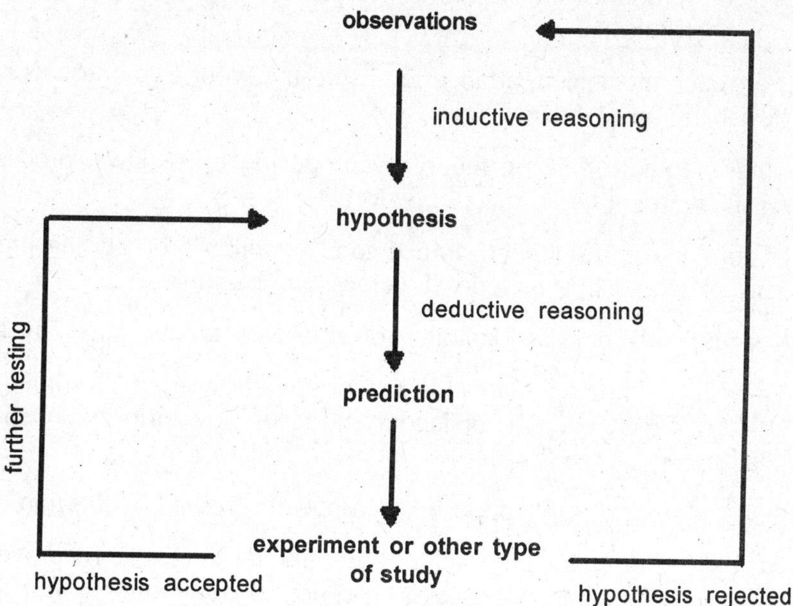


Although the method is called "hypothetico-deductive", we usually use a combination of different ways of reasoning, especially induction (inferring a general law or principle from the observation of particular instances) and deduction (inferring from generals to particulars, as described in chapter 2).

In reality, there is of course no clear distinction between a phase of inductive and deductive reasoning, just as there is no clear distinction between initial problem analysis, reviewing literature and formulating study objectives and hypotheses, as mentioned above.

We can however draw a clear line between what we have been doing until now and what we will do during the rest of your research project. The formal name is the synthetic or private phase. While you think about a perceived problem, your thoughts get shape while being influenced by very many things: existing theory, your knowledge of this theory, your experience, your values and beliefs, your interests, influence from other people such as feedback from your supervisor, personal observations on the perceived problem for instance during field trips or previous work, It is a private struggle during which you constantly switch between synthesising a working hypothesis, critical self-reflection and creativity.

The second phase, the analytic or public phase is much more structured and formal. It starts when your working hypotheses have stabilised into formal hypotheses. You are now ready to set up a study to test your hypothesis against data and publish the results of a critical analysis and interpretation so that other researchers can further evaluate it.

A hypothesis as a hunch the researcher or research team have. You might define it in a more formal way, but basically a hypothesis is nothing more or less than a hunch to solve your research problem.

We are still in the domain of logic and communication although the word hypothesis has a statistical connotation because of the widespread practice of hypothesis testing.

It is not important whether your hypothesis might be proved right or wrong by your study. Your research will be as valuable if it turns out to disprove your hypothesis. Communication of this result will help others to move on. Researchers tend to prefer a hypothesis that turns out correct, partly because of the human preference for winning instead of loosing, but also partly because of the philosophy behind the scientific method. Researchers tend to stick to previous results that have not been falsified.

It is however of much greater importance to ensure that your hypothesis is manageable and being able to be tested by any kind of study.

A good hypothesis adds to existing theory by proposing rules, laws, processes and allows predictions to new situations.

You can often turn a vague statement into a good hypothesis by adding predictions on the how or why. So use sentences that include variations on "because of".

Example of vague statement: "Adoptability of improved fallow varies by gender."

Example of testable hypothesis that adds to current knowledge: "Women find improved fallow less adoptable than men because of labour shortages, low priority for maize production and lack of information."

A null-hypothesis is basically the opposite of a specific research question.

The reason for this lies in philosophy behind the scientific method. To prove that something is true requires an inductive argument. Based on a series of observations, you induct a general statement that the phenomenon is true. There is however a problem with this kind of reasoning because it requires every possible observation to be available, or it requires the assumption that what happens in all possible circumstances not actually observed can be inferred from the cases actually available in the experiment. There is always a possibility that not enough evidence has been obtained and the contrary observation has not yet shown up.

The solution is to use a "falsificationist procedure"; to prove that the opposite is not true. Once an observation has been made that disproves something, this something remains disproved for ever.

Defining a null-hypothesis might have some merit if the study you've set up requires the statistical tool of hypothesis testing. Generally, it is much more informative to define a clear and detailed hypothesis and to evaluate the strength of evidence around it instead of simply proving or disproving the hypothesis.

## 5.2 Research Design

There are many definitions of research design, but no single definition imparts the full range of important aspects.

- Research design constitutes the blueprint for the collection, measurement, and analysis of data.
- Research design aids the researcher in the allocation of limited resources by posing crucial choices in methodology.
- Research design is the plan and structure of investigation so conceived as to obtain answers to research questions. The plan is the overall scheme or programme of the research. It includes an outline of what the investigator will do from writing hypotheses and their operational implications to the final analysis of data.
- Research design expresses both the structure of the research problem—the framework, organization, a configuration of the relationships among variables of a study — and the plan of investigation used to obtain empirical evidence on those relationships.

These definitions differ in detail, but together they give the essentials of **research design:**

- An activity and time based plan.
- A plan always based on the research question.
- A guide for selecting sources and types of information.
- A framework for specifying the relationships among the study's variables.
- A procedural outline for every research activity.

Research design provides the glue that holds the research project together. A design is used to structure the research, to show how all of the major parts of the research project, the samples or groups, measures, treatments or programmes, and methods of assignment, work together to try to address the central research questions. A research design is the arrangement of conditions for collections and analysis of data in a manner that aims at relevance to the research purpose with economy in procedure. In fact research design is the conceptual structure within which research is conducted; it constitutes the blue print for collection, measurement and analysis of data.

Consider the following key questions when designing your research plan:

1. For what purposes is the research being done, i.e., what do you want to be able to decide as a result of the research?
2. Who are the audiences for the information from the research, e.g., funders/bankers, upper management, employees, customers, etc?
3. What kinds of information are needed to make the decisions you need to make and/or to enlighten your intended audiences, e.g., do you need information to really understand a process, the customers who buy certain products, strengths and weaknesses of the product or service or programme, benefits to customers, how the product or service or programme failed some customers and why, etc.?
4. From what sources should the information be collected, e.g., employees, customers, groups of employees or customers, certain documentation, etc.?
5. How can the information be collected in a reasonable fashion, e.g., questionnaires, interviews, examining documentation, observing staff and/or clients in the programme, conducting focus groups among staff and/or clients, etc?
6. When is the information needed (so, by when must it be collected)?
7. What resources are available to collect the information?

8. Will the methods get all of the needed information?
9. What additional methods should and could be used if additional information is needed?
10. Will the information appear as credible to decision-makers, e.g., to bankers, or top management?
11. Will the nature of the audience conform to the methods, e.g., will they fill out questionnaires carefully, engage in interviews or focus groups, let you examine their documentations, etc.?
12. Who can administer the methods now or is training required?
13. How can the information be analysed?

Ideally, the researcher uses a combination of methods, for example, a questionnaire to quickly collect a great deal of information from a lot of people, and then interviews to get more in-depth information from certain respondents to the questionnaires. Perhaps case studies could then be used for more in-depth analysis of unique and notable cases, e.g., those who benefited or not from the programme, those who quit the programme, etc.

## 5.3 Classification of Research Design

A number of different design approaches exist, but, unfortunately, no simple classification system defines all the variations that may be considered. They may be exploratory study, formal study, monitoring, communication study, experimental, Ex-post facto, descriptive, causal, cross sectional, longitudinal, case study, statistical study, field setting, laboratory research, simulation, actual routine, modified routine, etc.

A study may be viewed as exploratory or formal. The essential distinctions between these two options are the degree of structure and the immediate objective of the study. **Exploratory studies tend toward loose structure with the objective of discovering future research tasks.** The immediate purpose of exploration is usually to develop hypotheses or questions for further research. The formal **study begins where the exploration leaves off**; it begins with a hypothesis or research question and involves precise procedures and data source specification. The goal of a formal research design is to test the hypotheses or answer the research questions posed. The exploratory-formal study dichotomy is less precise than some other classifications. All studies have elements of exploration in them, and few studies are completely uncharted.

Method of data collection also differentiates the designs. This classification distinguishes between **monitoring** and **communication** processes. The former includes studies in which the researcher inspects the activities of a subject or the nature of some material without attempting to elicit responses from anyone. Traffic counts at an intersection, license plates recorded in a restaurant parking lot, a search of the library collection, an observation of the actions of a group of decision-makers, are examples of monitoring. In each case the researcher notes and records the information available from observations. In the communication study, the researcher questions the subjects and collects their responses by personal or impersonal means. The collected data may result from (1) interview or telephone conversations. (2) self-administered or self-reported instruments sent through the mail, left in convenient locations, or transmitted electronically or by other means, or (3) instruments presented before and/or after a treatment or stimulus condition in an *experiment*.

In terms of the researcher's ability to manipulate variables, we differentiate between **experimental** and **ex-post facto** designs. In an experiment, the researcher attempts to control and/ or manipulate the variables in the study. It is enough that we can cause variables to be changed or held constant in keeping with our research objectives, Experimental design is appropriate when one wishes to discover whether certain variables produce effects in other variables. Experimentation provides the most powerful support possible for a hypothesis of causation. With an ex-post facto design, investigators have no control over the variables in the sense of being able to manipulate them. They can only report what has happened or what is happening. It is important that the researchers using this design do not influence the variables; to do so is to introduce bias. The researcher is limited to holding factors constant by judicious selection of subjects according to strict sampling procedures and by statistical manipulation of findings.

The essential difference between **descriptive** and **causal** studies lies in their objectives. If the research is concerned *with* finding out *who, what, where, when, or how much,* then the study is descriptive. If it is concerned with learning why—that is, how one variable produces changes in another—it is causal. Research on crime is descriptive when it measures the types of crimes committed, how often, when, where, and by whom. In a causal study, we try to explain relationships among variables—for instance, why the crime rate is higher in city A than city B.

**Cross-sectional** studies are carried out once and represent a snapshot of one point in time. **Longitudinal** studies are repeated over an extended period. The advantage of a longitudinal study is that it can track changes over time. In longitudinal studies of the *panel* variety, the researcher may study the same people over time. In marketing, panels are set up to report consumption data on a variety of products. These data, collected from national samples, provide a major data bank on relative market share, consumer response to new products, and new promotional methods. Other longitudinal studies, such as *cohort groups,* use different subjects for each need measurement. The service industry may have looked at the needs of aging baby boomers by sampling 40- to 45-year-olds in 1990 and 50- to 55- year-olds in 2000. Although each sample would be different, the population of 40 to 50 cohort survivors would remain the same. Some types of information once collected cannot be collected a second time from the same person without the risk of bias. The study of public awareness of an advertising campaign over a six-month period would require different samples for each measurement. While longitudinal research is important, the constraints of budget and time impose the need for cross-section analysis. Some benefits of a longitudinal study can be revealed in a cross-sectional study by adroit questioning about past attitudes, history, and future expectations. Responses to these kinds of questions should be interpreted with care.

The statistical study differs from the case study in several ways. **Statistical studies** are designed for breadth rather than depth. **They attempt to capture a population's characteristics by making inferences from a sample's characteristics**. Hypotheses are tested quantitatively. Generalizations about findings are presented based on the representativeness of the sample and the validity of the design. **Case studies** place more emphasis on a full contextual analysis of fewer events or conditions and their inter-relations. Although hypotheses are often used, the reliance on qualitative data makes support or rejection more difficult. An emphasis on detail provides valuable insight for problem solving, evaluation, and strategy. This detail is secured from multiple sources of information. It allows evidence to be verified and avoids missing data. Although case studies have been maligned as "scientifically worthless" because they do not meet minimal design requirements for comparison, they have a significant scientific role. It is known that important scientific propositions have the form of universals, and a universal can be falsified by a single counter instance. Thus, a single, well-designed case study can provide a major challenge to a theory and provide a source of new hypotheses and constructs simultaneously.

The usefulness of a design may be reduced when people in a disguised study perceive that research is being conducted. **Participants' perceptions** influence the outcomes of the research in subtle ways. Although there is no wide spread evidence of attempts by participants or respondents to please researchers through successful hypothesis guessing or evidence of the prevalence of sabotage, when participants believe that something out of the ordinary is happening, they may behave less naturally. There are three levels of perception:

1. Participants perceive no deviations from everyday routines.
2. Participants perceive deviations, but as unrelated to the researcher.
3. Participants perceive deviations as researcher-induced.

In all research environments and control situations, researchers need to be vigilant to effects that may alter their conclusions. Participant perceptions serve as a reminder to classify one's study by type, to examine validation strengths – and weaknesses, and to be prepared to qualify results accordingly.

### Four Levels of Research Results

There are four levels of information that can be gathered from customers or clients, including getting their: (a) reactions and feelings (feelings are often poor indicators that your service made lasting impact) (b) learning (enhanced attitudes, perceptions or knowledge) (c) changes in skills (applied the learning to enhance behaviours) (d) effectiveness (improved performance because of enhanced behaviours). Usually, the farther your research results get down the list, the more useful is your research results. Unfortunately, it is quite difficult to reliably get information about effectiveness. Still, information about learning and skills is quite useful.

Keeping in mind all above required decisions and information required, one may split the overall research design into four parts:

1. **Sampling design** which deals with the method of selecting items to be observed for the given study.
2. **Observational design** which relates to the conditions under which the observations are to be made.
3. **Statistical design** which concerns with the question of how many items are to be observed and how the information and data gathered are to be analysed.
4. **Operational design** which deals with the technique by which the procedures specified in the sampling, statistical and observational designs can be carried out.

## 5.4 Features of a Good Design

A good design is often characterised by adjectives like flexible, appropriate, efficient, economical, and so on. Generally, **the design which minimises bias and maximises the reliability of the data collected and analysed is considered a good design**. The design which gives the smallest experimental error is supposed to be the best design in many investigations. Similarly, a design which yields maximal information and provides an opportunity for considering many different aspects of a problem is considered most appropriate and efficient design in respect of many research problems. Thus, the question of **good design is related to the purpose or objective of the research problem and also with the nature of the problem to be studied.** A design may be quite suitable in one case, but may be found wanting in one respect or the other in the context of some other research problem. One single design cannot serve the purpose of all types of research problems.

Just to repeat again, a research design appropriate for a particular research problem, usually involves the consideration of the following factors:

(i) the means of obtaining information;

(ii) the availability and skills of the researcher and his staff, if any;

(iii) the objective of the problem to be studied;

(iv) the nature of the problem to be studied; and

(v) the availability of time and money for the research work.

We have already discussed that there are three types of research viz. exploratory, descriptive and causal. In causal studies, some times we perform the experiments.

## 5.5 Experimental Research

As discussed earlier, research can be fundamental or applied. Further research can be classified as **experimental and non-experimental research. Experimental research can be formal or informal.**

Let us discuss **experimental research** and design in causal research

**Experiments** are studies involving intervention by the researcher beyond that required for measurement. The usual intervention is to manipulate some variable in a setting and observe how it affects the subjects being studied (e.g., people or physical entities). The researcher manipulates the independent or explanatory variable and then observes whether the hypothesized dependent variable is affected by the intervention.

It is an attempt by the researcher to maintain control over all factors that may affect the result of an experiment. In doing this, the researcher attempts to determine or predict what may occur. For instance researcher may be interested to find out whether newly developed advertisement will increase the awareness among consumers. Or newly developed teaching pedagogy shall improve the knowledge and intellectual level of the students.

**Experimental Design** – It is a blueprint of the procedure that enables the researcher to test his hypothesis by reaching valid conclusions about relationships between independent and dependent variables. It refers to the conceptual framework within which the experiment is conducted.

Ex-post facto research designs, is where a researcher interviews respondents or observes what is or what has been, also have the potential for discovering causality. The distinction between these methods and experimentation is that the researcher is required to accept the world as it is found whereas an experiment allows the researcher to alter systematically the variables of interest and observe what changes follow.

An outline for the conduct of an experiment is presented as a vehicle to introduce important concepts. The questions of internal and external validity are also examined: Does the experimental treatment determine the observed difference or was some extraneous variable responsible? And how can one generalize the results of the study across times, settings, and persons?

There is at least one **independent variable** (IV) and one **dependent variable** (DV) in a causal relationship. We hypothesize that in some way the IV "causes" the DV to occur.

Let us perform an experiment. Let this be the study of bystanders and thieves. In this experiment, participants are asked to come to an office where they have an opportunity to see a person steal some money from a receptionist's desk. A confederate of the experimenter, of course, does the stealing. The major hypothesis concerned whether people observing a theft will be more likely to report it (1) if they are alone when they observe the crime or (2) if they are in the company of someone else.

The independent or explanatory variable in our example is the state of either being alone when observing the theft ($IV_1$) or being in the company of another person ($IV_2$). The dependent variable was whether the subjects reported observing the crime. The results may suggest that bystanders were more likely to report the theft if they observe it alone rather than in another person's company. On what grounds do the researchers conclude that people who were alone were more likely to report crimes observed than people in the company of others? Three types of evidence form the basis for this conclusion. First, there must be an agreement between independent and dependent variables. The presence or absence of one is associated with the presence or absence of the other. Thus, more reports of the theft (DV) *came* from lone observers ($IV_1$) than from paired observers ($IV_2$).

Second, beyond the correlation of independent and dependent variables, the time order of the occurrence of the variables must be considered. The dependent variable should not precede the independent variable. They may occur almost simultaneously, or the independent variable should occur before the dependent variable. This requirement is of little concern since it is unlikely that people could report a theft before observing it.

The next important support for the conclusion comes when researchers are confident that other extraneous variables did not influence the dependent variable. To ensure that these other variables are not the source of influence, researchers control their ability to confound the planned comparison. Under laboratory conditions, standardized conditions for control can be arranged. The crime observation experiment was carried out in a laboratory set up as an office. The entire event was staged without the observers' knowledge. The receptionist whose money was to be stolen was instructed to speak and act in a specific way. Only the receptionist, the observers, and the "criminal" were in the office. The same process was repeated with each trial of the experiment. While such controls are important, further precautions are needed so that the results achieved reflect only the influence of the independent variable on the dependent variable.

## Advantages of Experiments

The foremost advantage is the researcher's ability to manipulate the independent variable. Consequently, the probability that changes in the dependent variable are a function of that, manipulation increases. Also, a control group serves as a comparison to assess the existence and potency of the manipulation. The second advantage of the experiment is that contamination from extraneous variables can be controlled more effectively than in other designs. This helps the researcher isolate experimental variables and evaluate their impact over time. Third, the convenience and cost of experimentation are superior to other methods. These benefits allow the experimenter opportunistic scheduling of data collection and the flexibility to adjust variables and conditions that evoke extremes not observed under routine circumstances. In addition, the experimenter can assemble combinations of variables for testing rather than having to search for their fortuitous appearance in the study environment. Fourth, replication — repeating an experiment with different subject groups and conditions — leads to the discovery of an average effect of the independent variable across people, situations, and times. Fifth, researchers can use naturally occurring events and, to some extent, field experiments (a study of the dependent variable in actual environmental conditions) to reduce subjects' perceptions of the researcher as a source of intervention or deviation in their everyday lives.

## Disadvantages

The artificiality of the laboratory is arguably the primary disadvantage of the experimental method. Second, generalization from non-probability samples can pose problems despite random assignment. The extent to which a study can be generalized from college students to managers or executives is open to question. And an experiment is unsuccessfully disguised; volunteer subjects are often those with the most interest in the topic. Third, despite the low costs of experimentation, many applications of experimentation far outrun the budgets for other primary data collection methods. Fourth, experimentation is most effectively targeted *at* problems of the present or immediate future. Experimental studies of the past are not feasible, and studies about intentions or predictions are difficult. Finally, management research is often concerned with the study of people. There are limits to the types of manipulation and controls that are ethical:

Following are the steps involved in conducting an experimental study:

(a) Identify and define the problem.

(b) Formulate hypotheses and deduce their consequences.

(c) Construct an experimental design that represents all the elements, conditions, and relations of the consequences. To do this, following are the steps:

1. Select sample of subjects.
2. Group or pair subjects.
3. Identify and control non-experimental factors.
4. Select or construct, and validate instruments to measure outcomes.
5. Conduct pilot study.
6. Determine place, time, and duration of the experiment.

(d) Conduct the experiment.

(e) Compile raw data and reduce to usable form.

(f) Apply an appropriate test of significance.

## Critical Elements of Experimental Design

The critical elements of an experimental research design are follows:

1. Observations or Measures
2. Treatment of Programmes
3. Groups
4. Assignment to groups
5. Time

### 1. Observations or Measures

These are symbolized by an '**O**' in design notation. An **O** can refer to a single measure (e.g., a measure of body weight), a single instrument with multiple items (e.g., a 10-item self-esteem scale), a complex multi-part instrument (e.g., a survey), or a whole battery of tests or measures given out on one occasion. If you need to distinguish among specific measures, you can use subscripts with the **O**, as in $O_1$, $O_2$, and so on.

### 2. Treatments or Programmes

These are symbolized with an '**X**' in design notations. The **X** can refer to a simple intervention (e.g., a one-time surgical technique) or to a complex hodgepodge programme (e.g., an employment training programme). Usually, a no-treatment control or comparison group has no symbol for the treatment. As with observations, you can use subscripts to distinguish different programmes or programme variations.

**3. Groups**

Each group in a design is given its own line in the design structure. If the design notation has three lines, there are three groups in the design.

**4. Assignment to Group**

Assignment to group is designated by a letter at the beginning of each line (i.e., group) that describes how the group was assigned. The major types of assignment are:

- R = random assignment
- N = non-equivalent groups
- C = assignment by cut-off

**5. Time**

Time moves from left to right. Elements that are listed on the left occur before elements that are listed on the right.

Let us see the following notations; we have given a design to our research plan.

$$\mathbf{R} \quad \mathbf{O_1} \quad \mathbf{X} \quad \mathbf{O_{1,2}}$$

$$\mathbf{R} \quad \mathbf{O_1} \qquad \mathbf{O_{1,2}}$$

Here R means random assignment, $O_1$ and $O_2$are observations and X is the treatment. Right side Os are outcomes. As there are two lines, it means there are two groups.

Let us now understand what it means with an example. A management school has developed a new teaching method. We wish to know whether the new method has any effect on students. We divide the class in two groups. Groups are formed at random, so that each student in the class has same probability of being selected in any group. No bias. Now we take the class test of a particular subject. Now these are our observations. We teach the first group with our new method 'X' (i.e., we give treatment to group 1). But second group is not taught. Say after one month's teaching, we again take a class test of that particular subject. Now, we have two groups — one which has been taught with particular method and other which has not been taught. We have pre-treatment and post-treatment results of first group which has been taught. The second group which has not been taught has also given us two outcomes but without teaching. We can compare the results and find out whether there are treatment effects or not.

Types of Research Designs

- Randomized Experimental Design
- Quasi-experimental Design
- Non-experimental Design

If random assignment is used, we call the design a randomized experiment or true experiment. If random assignment is not used, then we have to ask a second question: Does the design use either multiple groups or multiple waves of measurement? If the answer is yes, we would label it a quasi-experimental design. If no, we would call it a non-experimental design. This threefold classification is especially useful for describing the design with respect to **internal validity**. A randomized experiment generally is the strongest of the three designs when your interest is in establishing a cause-effect relationship. A non-experiment is generally the weakest in this respect; it is weak only with respect to internal validity or causal assessment. In fact, the simplest form of non-experiment is a one-shot survey design that consists of nothing but a single observation O. This is probably one of the most common forms of research and, for some research questions, especially descriptive ones, is clearly a strong design. The non-experiment is the weakest with respect to internal validity; it isn't a particularly good method for assessing the cause-effect relationship that you think might exist between a programme and its outcomes. We can show these designs in notations as follows:

| **1. Post-test Only Randomised Experiment** | R | X | O | |
|---|---|---|---|---|
| | R | | O | |
| **2. Pre-Test Post-Test Non-Equivalent** | N | O | X | O |
| **Quasi-Experiment** | N | O | | O |
| **3. Post-test only Non-Experiment** | X | O | | |
| | | O | | |

To illustrate the different types of designs, consider one of each in design notation. The first design is a post-test-only randomized experiment. We can tell it's a randomized experiment because it has an R at the beginning of each line, indicating random assignment. The second design is a pre-post non-equivalent groups quasi-experiment. We know it's not a randomized experiment because random assignment wasn't used. And we know it's not a non-experiment because there are both multiple groups and multiple waves of measurement. That means it must be a quasi-experiment. We add the label "non-equivalent" because in this design we do not explicitly control the assignment and the groups may be non-equivalent or not similar to each other. Finally, we show a post-test-only non-experimental design. You might use this design if you want to study the effects of a natural disaster like a flood or tornado and you want to do so by interviewing survivors. Notice that in this design, you don't have a comparison group (e.g., interview in a town down the road that didn't have the tornado to see what differences the tornado caused) and you don't have multiple waves of measurement (e.g., a pre-tornado level of how people in the ravaged town were doing before the disaster). Even with this type of study we gain lots of valuable information by well-conducted post-disaster interviews. But you may have a hard time establishing which of the things you observed are due to the disaster rather than to other factors like the peculiarities of the town or pre-disaster characteristics.

## 5.6 Essentials of Experimental Research

In experimental design we can manipulate the independent variable. An attempt is made to hold all other variables except the dependent variable constant - *control*. Effect is observed of the manipulation of the independent variable on the dependent variable - *observation*. Experimental control attempts to predict events that will occur in the experimental setting by neutralizing the effects of other factors.

### Methods of Experimental Control

- Physical Control
- Give all subjects equal exposure to the independent variable.
- Controls non-experimental variables that affect the dependent variable

- Selective Control - Manipulate indirectly by selecting in or out variables that cannot be controlled.
- Statistical Control - Variables not conducive to physical or selective manipulation may be controlled by statistical techniques (example: covariance).

### Validity of Experimental Design

**Internal Validity** asks did the experimental treatment make the difference in this specific instance rather than other extraneous variables.

**External Validity** asks to what populations, settings, treatment variables, and measurement variables can this observed effect be generalized?

## Factors Threatening Internal Validity (in experiments)

**History** – The events occurring between the first and second measurements in addition to the experimental variable which might affect the measurement. For *example*, researcher collects gross sales data before and after a 5 day 50% off sale. During the sale a hurricane occurs and results of the study may be affected because of the hurricane, not the sale.

**Maturation** – The process of maturing which takes place in the individual during the duration of the experiment which is not a result of specific events but of simply growing older, growing more tired or similar changes. For example, subjects become tired after completing a training session, and their responses on the Post-test are affected.

**Pre-testing** – The effect created on the second measurement by having a measurement before the experiment. For *example*, subjects take a pre-test and think about some of the items. On the post-test they change to answers they feel are more acceptable. Experimental group learns from the pre-test.

**Measuring Instruments** – Changes in instruments, calibration of instruments, observers, or scorers may cause changes in the measurements. For *example*, interviewers are very careful with their first two or three interviews but on the 4th, 5th, 6th become fatigued and are less careful and make errors.

**Statistical Regression** – Groups are chosen because of extreme scores of measurements; those scores or measurements tend to move toward the mean with repeated measurements even without an experimental variable. For *example*, Managers who are performing poorly are selected for training. Their average post-test scores will be higher than their pre-test scores because of statistical regression, even if no training were given.

**Differential Selection** – Different individuals or groups would have different previous knowledge or ability which would affect the final measurement if not taken into account. For *example*: A group of subjects who have viewed a TV programme is compared with a group which has not. There is no way of knowing that the groups would have been equivalent since they were not randomly assigned to view the TV programme.

**Experimental Mortality** – The loss of subjects from comparison groups could greatly affect the comparisons because of unique characteristics of those subjects. Groups to be compared need to be the same after as before the experiment. For *example*: Over a 6 month experiment aimed to change accounting practices, 12 accountants drop out of the experimental group and none drop out of the control group. Not only is there differential loss in the two groups, but the 12 dropouts may be very different from those who remained in the experimental group.

**Interaction of Factors**, such as Selection Maturation, etc. - Combinations of these factors may interact especially in multiple group comparisons to produce erroneous measurements.

## Factors Threatening External Validity or Generalizability (in Experiments)

**Pre-Testing** – Individuals who were pre-tested might be less or more sensitive to the experimental variable or might have "learned" from the pre-test making them unrepresentative of the population who had not been pre-tested. For *example*: Prior to viewing a film on Environmental Effects of Chemicals, a group of subjects is given a 60 item anti-chemical test. Taking the pre-test may increase the effect of the film. The film may not be effective for a non-pre-tested group.

**Differential Selection** – The selection of the subjects determines how the findings can be generalized. Subjects selected from a small group or one with particular characteristics would limit generalizability. Randomly chosen subjects from the entire population could be generalized to the entire population. For *example*: Researcher, requesting permission to conduct experiment, is turned down by 11 corporations, but the 12$^{th}$ corporation grants permission. The 12$^{th}$ corporation is obviously different than the others because they accepted. Thus subjects in the 12$^{th}$ corporation may be more accepting or sensitive to the treatment.

**Experimental Procedures** – The experimental procedures and arrangements have a certain amount of effect on the subjects in the experimental settings. Generalization to persons not in the experimental setting may be precluded. *For example*: Department heads realize they are being studied, try to guess what the experimenter wants and respond accordingly rather than respond to the treatment.

**Multiple Treatment Interference** – If the subjects are exposed to more than one treatment then the findings could only be generalized to individuals exposed to the same treatments in the same order of presentation. *For example*: A group of CPAs is given training in working with managers followed by training in working with comptrollers. Since training effects cannot be deleted, the first training will affect the second.

## Tools of Experimental Design Used to Control Factors Threatening Validity

**Pre-Test** – The pre-test, or measurement before the experiment begins, can aid control for differential selection by determining the presence or knowledge of the experimental variable before the experiment begins. It can aid control of experimental mortality because the subjects can be removed from the entire comparison by removing their pre-tests. However, pre-tests cause problems by their effect on the second measurement and by causing generalizability problems to a population not pre-tested and those with no experimental arrangements.

**Control Group** – The use of a matched or similar group which is not exposed to the experimental variable can help reduce the effect of History, Maturation, Instrumentation, and Interaction of Factors. The control group is exposed to all conditions of the experiment except the experimental variable.

**Randomization** – Use of random selection procedures for subjects can aid in control of Statistical Regression, Differential Selection, and the Interaction of Factors. It greatly increases generalizability by helping make the groups representative of the populations.

**Additional Groups** – The effects of pre-tests and experimental procedures can be partially controlled through the use of groups which were not pre-tested or exposed to experimental arrangements. They would have to be used in conjunction with other pre-tested groups or other factors jeopardizing validity would be present.

Following table shows the problems of validity and suggests the experimental design to control threat.

The method by which treatments are applied to subjects using tools to control factors jeopardizing validity is the essence of experimental design.

**Tools of Control**

| **Internal Sources** | **Pre-Test/Post-Test** | **Control Group** | **Randomization** | **Additional Groups** |
|---|---|---|---|---|
| History | | X | | |
| Maturation | | X | | |
| Pre-Testing | | | | X |
| Measuring Instrument | | X | | |
| Statistical Regression | | X | X | |
| Differential Selection | X | | X | |
| Experimental Mortality | X | | | |
| Interaction of Factors | | X | X | |
| **External Sources** | | | | |
| Pre-Testing | | | | X |
| Differential Selection | X | | X | |
| Procedures | | | | X |
| Multiple Treatment | | | | |

## Experimental Designs

**Pre-Experimental Design - loose in structure, could be biased**

| **Aim of the Research** | **Name of the Design** | **Notation Paradigm** | **Comments** |
|---|---|---|---|
| To attempt to explain a consequent by an antecedent | One-shot experimental case study | X » O | An approach that prematurely links antecedents and consequences. The least reliable of all experimental approaches. |
| To evaluate the influence of a variable | One group pre-test-post-test | O » X » O | An approach that provides a measure of change but can provide no conclusive results. |
| To determine the influence of a variable on one group and not on another | Static group comparison | Group 1: X » O<br>Group 2: - » O | Weakness lies in no examination of pre-experimental equivalence of groups. Conclusion is reached by comparing the performance of each group to determine the effect of a variable on one of them. |

**True Experimental Design - greater control and refinement, greater control of validity**

| Aim of the Research | Name of the Design | Notation Paradigm | Comments |
|---|---|---|---|
| To study the effect of an influence on a carefully controlled sample | Pre-test-post-test control group | R - - [ O » X » O [ O » - » O | This design has been called "the old workhorse of traditional experimentation." If effectively carried out, this design controls eight threats of internal validity. Data are analysed by analysis of covariance on post-test scores with the pre-test the covariate. |
| To minimize the effect of pre-testing | Solomon four-group design | R - - [ O » X » O [ O » - » O [- » X » O [ - » - » O | This is an extension of the pre-test-post-test control group design and probably the most powerful experimental approach. Data are analysed by analysis of variance on post-test scores. |
| To evaluate a situation that cannot be pre-tested | Post-test only control group | R - - [ X » O [ - » O | An adaptation of the last two groups in the Solomon four-group design. Randomness is critical. Probably, the simplest and best test for significance in this design is the t-test. |

**Quasi-Experimental Design - not randomly selected**

| Aim of the Research | Name of the Design | Notation Paradigm | Comments |
|---|---|---|---|
| To investigate a situation in which random selection and assignment are not possible | Non-randomized control group pre-test-post-test | O » X » O<br>O » - » O | One of the strongest and most widely used quasi-experimental designs. Differs from experimental designs because test and control groups are not equivalent. Comparing pre-test results will indicate degree of equivalency between experimental and control groups. |

| | | | |
|---|---|---|---|
| To determine the influence of a variable introduced only after a series of initial observations and only where one group is available | Time series experiment | O » O » X » O » O | If substantial change follows introduction of the variable, then the variable can be suspect as to the cause of the change. To increase external validity, repeat the experiment in different places under different conditions. |
| To bolster the validity of the above design with the addition of a control group | Control group time series | O » O » X » O » O O » O » - » O » O | A variant of the above design by accompanying it with a parallel set of observations without the introduction of the experimental variable. |
| To control history in time designs with a variant of the above design | Equivalent time-samples | [X1 » O1] »[X0 » O2] » [x1 » O3] | An on-again, off-again design in which the experimental variable is sometimes present, sometimes absent. |

**Correlational and Ex-Post Facto Design**

| Aim of the Research | Name of the Design | Notation Paradigm | Comments |
|---|---|---|---|
| To seek for cause-effect relationships between two sets of data. | Causal-comparative correlational studies. | -» Oa ¥ Ob«- | A very deceptive procedure that requires much insight for its use. Causality cannot be inferred merely because a positive and close correlation ratio exists. |
| To search backward from consequent data for antecedent causes. | Ex-post facto studies. | | This approach is experimentation in reverse. Seldom is proof through data substantiation possible. Logic and inference are the principal tools of this design. |

## 5.7 Basic Principles of Experimental Design

There are three principles of experimental design. They are

1. Principle of Replication
2. Principle of Randomisation
3. Principle of Local Control

According to the Principle of Replication, the experiment should be repeated more than once. Thus, each treatment is applied in many experimental units instead of one. By doing so the statistical accuracy of the experiments is increased. For example, suppose we are to examine the effect of two varieties of rice. For this purpose we may divide the field into two parts and grow one variety in one part and the other variety in the other part. We can then compare the yield of the two parts and draw conclusion on that basis. But if we are to apply the principle of replication to this experiment, then we first divide the field into several parts, grow one variety in half of these parts and the other variety in the remaining parts. We can then collect the data of yield of the two varieties and draw conclusion by comparing the same. The result so obtained will be more reliable in comparison to the conclusion we draw without applying the principle of replication. The entire experiment can even be repeated several times for better results.

The Principle of Randomization provides protection, when we conduct an experiment, against the effect of extraneous factors by randomization. In other words, this principle indicates that we should design or plan the experiment in such a way that the variations caused by extraneous factors can all be combined under the general heading of "chance." For instance, if we grow one variety of rice, say, in the first half of the parts of a field and the other variety is grown in the other half, then it is just possible that the soil fertility may be different in the first half in comparison to the other half. If this is so, our results would not be realistic. In such a situation, we may assign the variety of rice to be grown in different parts of the field on the basis of some random sampling technique, i.e., we may apply randomization principle and protect ourselves against the effects of the extraneous factors (soil fertility differences in the given case). As such, through the application of the principle of randomization, we can have a better estimate of the experimental error.

The Principle of Local Control is another important principle of experimental designs. Under it the extraneous factor, the known source of variability, is made to vary deliberately over as wide a range as necessary, and this needs to be done in such a way that the variability it causes can be measured and hence eliminated from the experimental error. This means that we should plan the experiment in a manner that we can perform a two-way analysis of variance, in which the total variability of the data is divided into three components attributed to treatments (varieties of rice in our case), the extraneous factor (soil fertility in our case) and experimental error. In other words, according to the principle of local control, we first divide the field into several homogeneous parts, known as blocks, and then each such block is divided into parts equal to the number of treatments. Then the treatments are randomly assigned to these parts of a block. Dividing the field into several homogeneous parts is known as 'blocking'. In general, blocks are the levels at which we hold an extraneous factor fixed, so that we can measure its contribution to the total variability of the data by means of a two-way analysis of variance. In brief, through the principle of local control we can eliminate the variability due to extraneous factor(s) from the experimental error.

## 5.8 Formal Experimental Design

Research methodologists have advised four types of formal experimental designs. They are:

1. Completely Randomized Design (C.R. Design)
2. Randomized Block Design ( R.B. Design)
3. Latin Square Design ( L.S. Design)
4. Factorial Design

### 5.8.1 The Completely Randomized Design (CRD):

CRD involves only two principles viz., the principle of replication and the principle of randomization of experimental designs. It is the simplest possible design and its procedure of analysis is also easier. The essential characteristic of the design is that the subjects are randomly assigned to experimental treatments (or vice-versa). For instance, if we have 10 subjects and if we wish to test 5 under treatment A and 5 under treatment B, the randomization process gives every possible group of 5 subjects selected from a set of 10 an equal opportunity of being assigned to treatment A and treatment B. One-way analysis of variance (or one-way ANOVA) is used to analyse such a design. Even unequal replications can also work in this design. It provides maximum number of degrees of freedom to the error. Such a design is generally used when experimental areas happen to be homogeneous, technically, when all the variations due to uncontrolled extraneous factors are included under the heading of chance variation. The CRD is the simplest of all designs. It is equivalent to a t-test when only two treatments are examined. Replications of treatments are assigned completely at random to independent experimental subjects. Adjacent subjects could potentially have the same treatment.

**Sample layout:**

**There are 4 (A-D) treatments with 4 replications (1-4) each.**

A1 B1 C1 A2

D1 A3 D2 C2

B2 D3 C3 B3

C4 A4 B4 D4

**Two group simple randomized experimental design**

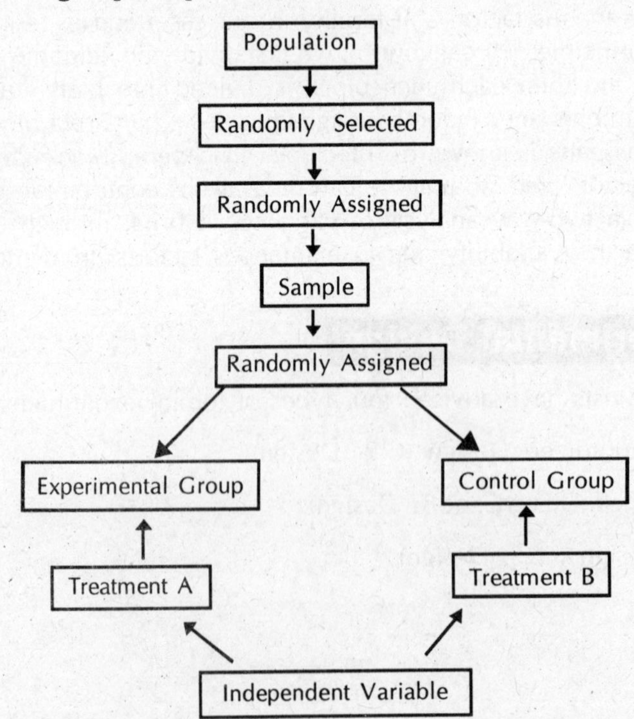

We shall learn more about ANOVA in the concerned chapter. However a sample table is given below:

**ANOVA table format:**

| Source of variation | Degrees of freedom[a] | Sums of squares (SSQ) | Mean square (MS) | F |
|---|---|---|---|---|
| Treatments (*Tr*) | t-1 | $SSQ_{Tr}$ | $SSQ_{Tr}$/(t-1) | $MS_{Tr}$/ $MS_E$ |
| Error (*E*) | t*(r-1) | $SSQ_E$ | $SSQ_E$/(t*(r-1)) | |
| Total (*Tot*) | t*r-1 | $SSQ_{Tot}$ | | |

**[a]where t = number of treatments and r = number of replications per treatment.**

**Sample ANOVA table:**

| Source of variation | Degrees of freedom | Sums of squares (SSQ) | Mean square (MS) | F |
|---|---|---|---|---|
| Treatments | 3 | 80.92 | 26.97 | 9.68a |
| Error | 12 | 33.43 | 2.79 | |
| Total | 15 | 114.35 | | |

**[a]F test with 3,12 degrees of freedom at *P*=0.05 is 3.49**

### 5.8.2 Randomized Block Design

**(R.B. Design):** It is an improvement over the C.R. design. In the R.B. design the principle of local control can be applied along with the other two principles of experimental designs. In the R.B. design, subjects are first divided into groups, known as blocks, such that within each group the subjects are relatively homogeneous in respect to some selected variable. The variable selected for grouping the subjects is one that is believed to be related to the measures to-be obtained in respect of the dependent variable. The number of subjects in a given block would be equal to the number of treatments and one subject in each block would be randomly assigned to each treatment. In general, blocks are the levels at which we hold the extraneous factor fixed, so that its contribution to the total variability of data can be measured. The main feature of the R.B. design is that in this each treatment appears the same number of times in each block. The R.B. design is analysed by the two-way analysis of variance (two-way ANOVA) technique.

The RB is the standard design for agricultural experiments. The field or orchard is divided into units to account for any variation in the field. Treatments are then assigned at random to the subjects in the blocks — once in each block.

Field marks:

- Treatments are assigned at random within blocks of adjacent subjects, each treatment once per block.
- The number of blocks is the number of replications.
- Any treatment can be adjacent to any other treatment, but not to the same treatment within the block.
- Used to control variation in an experiment by accounting for spatial effects.

**Sample Layout:**

There are 4 blocks (I-IV) and 4 treatments (A-D) in this example.

Block I A B C D

Block II D A B C

Block III B D C A

Block IV C A B D

**ANOVA table format:**

| Source of variation | Degrees of freedom[a] | Sums of squares (SSQ) | Mean square (MS) | F |
|---|---|---|---|---|
| Blocks (*B*) | b-1 | $SSQ_B$ | $SSQ_B/(b-1)$ | $MS_B/MS_E$ |
| Treatments (*Tr*) | t-1 | $SSQ_{Tr}$ | $SSQ_{Tr}/(t-1)$ | $MS_{Tr}/MS_E$ |
| Error (*E*) | (t-1)*(b-1) | $SSQ_E$ | $SSQ_E/((t-1)*(b-1))$ | |
| Total (*Tot*) | t*b-1 | $SSQ_{Tot}$ | | |

**[a]where t = number of treatments and b = number of blocks or replications.**

**Sample ANOVA table:**

| Source of variation | Degrees of freedom | Sums of squares (SSQ) | Mean square (MS) | F |
|---|---|---|---|---|
| Blocks | 3 | 26.36 | 8.79 | 1.36[a] |
| Treatments | 3 | 216.23 | 72.08 | 11.19[a] |
| Error | 9 | 57.95 | 6.44 | |
| Total | 15 | 300.54 | | |

**[a]F test with 3,9 degrees of freedom at $P=0.05$ is 3.86**

### 5.8.3 Latin Square Design

It is an experimental design which is again very frequently used in agricultural research and can be used in business research. The conditions under which agricultural investigations are carried out are different from those in other studies for nature plays an important role in agriculture. For instance, an experiment has to be made through which the effects of five different varieties of fertilizers on the yield of a certain crop, say wheat, it to be judged. In such a case, the varying fertility of the soil in different blocks in which the experiment has to be performed must be taken into consideration; otherwise the results obtained may not be very dependable because the output happens to be the effect not only of fertilizers, but it may also be the effect of fertility of soil. Similarly, there may be impact of varying seeds on the yield. To overcome such difficulties, the L.S. design is used when there are two major extraneous factors such as the varying soil fertility and varying seeds.

The merit of this experimental design is that it enables differences in fertility gradients in the field to be eliminated in comparison to the effects of different varieties of fertilizers on the yield of the crop. But this design suffers from one limitation, and it is that although each row and each column represents equally all fertilizer varieties, there may be considerable difference in the row and column means both up and across the field. This, in other words, means that in L.S. design we must assume that there is no interaction between treatments and blocking factors. This defect can, however, be removed by taking the means of rows and columns equal to the field mean by adjusting the results. Another limitation of this design is that it requires number of rows, columns and treatments to be equal. This reduces the utility of the design.

The Latin square design is used where the researcher desires to control the variation in an experiment that is related to rows and columns in the field.

**Field marks:**

- Treatments are assigned at random within rows and columns, with each treatment once per row and once per column.

- There are equal numbers of rows, columns, and treatments.
- Useful where the experimenter desires to control variation in two different directions

**Sample layout:**

There are 4 treatments (A-D) assigned to 4 rows (I-IV) and 4 columns (1-4).

| | | | | |
|---|---|---|---|---|
| Row I | A | B | C | D |
| Row II | C | D | A | B |
| Row III | D | C | B | A |
| Row IV | B | A | D | C |
| Column | 1 | 2 | 3 | 4 |

The analysis of the L.S. design is very similar to the two-way ANOVA technique.

**ANOVA table format:**

| Source of variation | Degrees of freedom[a] | Sums of squares (SSQ) | Mean square (MS) | F |
|---|---|---|---|---|
| Rows (*R*) | r-1 | $SSQ_R$ | $SSQ_R/(r-1)$ | $MS_R/MS_E$ |
| Columns (*C*) | r-1 | $SSQ_C$ | $SSQ_C/(r-1)$ | $MS_C/MS_E$ |
| Treatments (*Tr*) | r-1 | $SSQ_{Tr}$ | $SSQ_{Tr}/(r-1)$ | $MS_{Tr}/MS_E$ |
| Error (*E*) | (r-1)(r-2) | $SSQ_E$ | $SSQ_E/((r-1)(r-2))$ | |
| Total (*Tot*) | $r^2$-1 | $SSQ_{Tot}$ | | |

**[a]where r = number of treatments, rows, and columns.**

**Sample ANOVA table:**

| Source of variation | Degrees of freedom | Sums of squares (SSQ) | Mean square (MS) | F |
|---|---|---|---|---|
| Rows | 3 | 40.77 | 13.59 | 9.68a |
| Columns | 3 | 125.39 | 41.80 | 18.16[a] |
| Treatments | 3 | 160.57 | 53.52 | 23.26[a] |
| Error | 6 | 13.81 | 2.30 | |
| Total | 15 | 340.54 | | |

**[a]F test with 3,6 degrees of freedom at *P*=0.05 is 4.76**

### 5.8.4 Factorial Analysis

Factorial design has several important features. First, it has great flexibility for exploring or enhancing the "signal" (treatment) in our studies. Whenever we are interested in examining treatment variations, factorial designs should be strong candidates as the designs of choice. Second, factorial designs are efficient. Instead of conducting a series of independent studies we are effectively able to combine these studies into one. Finally, factorial designs are the only effective way to examine interaction effects.

A factorial experiment is an experiment whose design consists of two or more factors, each with discrete possible values or "levels", and whose experimental units take on all possible combinations of these levels across all such factors. Such an experiment allows studying the effect of each factor on the response variable, as well as the effects of interactions between factors on the response variable.

For the vast majority of factorial experiments, each factor has only two levels.

If the number of experiments for a full factorial design is too high to be logistically feasible, a fractional factorial design may be done, in which some of the possible combinations (usually at least half) are omitted.

The simplest factorial experiment contains two levels for each of two factors. Suppose an engineer wishes to study the total power used by each of two different motors, A and B, running at each of two different speeds, 2000 or 3000 RPM. The factorial experiment would consist of four experimental units: motor A at 2000 RPM, motor B at 2000 RPM, motor A at 3000 RPM, and motor B at 3000 RPM. Each combination of a single level selected from every factor is present once.

This experiment is an example of a $2^2$ (or $2\times2$) factorial experiment, so named because it considers two levels (the base) for each of two factors (the power or superscript), producing $2^2 = 4$ factorial points.

Designs can involve many independent variables. As a further example, the effects of three input variables can be evaluated in eight experimental conditions shown as the corners of a cube.

This can be conducted with or without replication, depending on its intended purpose and available resources. It will provide the effects of the three independent variables on the dependent variable and possible interactions.

In factorial designs, a **factor** is a major independent variable. A **level** is a subdivision of a **factor**.

**Advantages of** factorial designs are:

- A greater precision can be obtained in estimating the overall main factor effects.
- Interaction between different factors can be explored.
- Additional factors can help to extend validity of conclusions derived.
- Procedure used is General Linear Modelling.

Factors can be analysed either by ANOVA or Multiple Regression. Factorial designs can be of two types:

(1) Simple Factorial Design

(2) Complex Factorial Design

For instance, if the effects of two factors A and B on the output of a process are investigated, and A has 3 levels of intensity (e.g., weak, moderate, and strong presence) while B has 2 levels (weak and strong), then one would need to run 6 treatment combinations to complete the experiment, observing the process output for each of the combinations: weakA-weakB, weakA-strongB, moderateA-weakB, moderateA-strongB, strongA-weakB, strongA-strongB.

The amount of change produced in the process output for a change in the 'level' of a given factor is referred to as the 'main effect' of that factor. Following table shows an example of a simple factorial experiment involving two factors with two levels each. The two levels of each factor may be denoted as 'low' and 'high', which are usually symbolized by '–' and '+' in factorial designs, respectively.

| A Simple 2-Factorial Experiment | | |
|---|---|---|
| | A (–) | A(+) |
| B(–) | 20 | 40 |
| B(+) | 30 | 52 |

The main effect of a factor is basically the 'average' change in the output response as that factor goes from '–' to '+'. Mathematically, this is the average of two numbers: (1) the change in output when the factor goes from low to high level as the other factor stays low, and (2) the change in output when the factor goes from low to high level as the other factor stays high.

In the example in Table, the output of the process is just 20 (lowest output) when both A and B are at their '–' level, while the output is maximum at 52 when both A and B are at their '+' level. The main effect of A is the average of the change in output response when B stays '–' as A goes from '–' to '+', or (40 – 20) = 20, and the change in output response when B stays '+' as A goes from '–' to '+', or (52 – 30) = 22. The main effect of A, therefore, is equal to 21.

Similarly, the main effect of B is the average change in output as it goes from '–' to '+', i.e., the average of 10 and 12, or 11. Thus, the main effect of B in this process is 11. Here, one can see that the factor A exerts a greater influence on the output of process, having a main effect of 21 versus factor B's main effect of only 11.

It must be noted that aside from 'main effects', factors can likewise result in 'interaction effects.' Interaction effects are changes in the process output caused by two or more factors that are interacting with each other. Large interactive effects can make the main effects insignificant, such that it becomes more important for the engineer to pay attention to the interaction of the involved factors than to investigate them individually.

The running of factorial combinations and the mathematical interpretation of the output responses of the process to such combinations is the essence of factorial experiments. It allows an engineer to understand which factors affect his or her process most so that improvements (or corrective actions) may be geared towards these.

## Interaction Effects

If we look at main effects, a factorial design is useful. But, because of the way we combine levels in factorial designs, they also enable us to examine the **interaction effects** that exist between factors. An *interaction effect* exists when differences on one factor depend on the level you are on another factor. It's important to recognize that an interaction is between factors, not levels. We wouldn't say there's an interaction between 4 hours/week and in-class treatment. Instead, we would say that there's an interaction between time and setting, and then we would go on to describe the specific levels involved.

There are three ways you can determine there's an interaction. First, when you run the statistical analysis, the statistical table will report on all main effects and interactions. Second, you know there's an interaction when you can't talk about effect on one factor without mentioning the other factor. if you can say at the end of a study that time in instruction makes a difference, then you know that you have a main effect and not an interaction (because you did not have to mention the setting factor when describing the results for time). On the other hand, when you have an interaction it is impossible to describe your results accurately without mentioning both factors. Graphs can also be helpful to spot interactions.

We shall see more examples in our practical problems in sub-chapter Analysis of Variance in Data Analysis.

## 5.9 How to Do?

Dolly: "I am back. Let me revise before Jolly comes, sometimes he confuses me more. Before starting any research we should clearly define our research problem. Experts can help us define the problem. Reading articles from research journals, books and seminars can also help us define the problem. When in business, issues of products, customers, prices, after sale services, financial, operational and HR issues can have problems. We should be very clear with our problem, what we wish to solve. Research is mainly of three types – descriptive, exploratory and causal. We should take care that in every stage we should be accurate. In causal research issue of validity-conclusion, internal, constructs and external validity- is very important. The measure, we select or design should be reliable and it should repeat the results.

Jolly: "I am also here and listening to you. Issue of validity should also be taken care of in descriptive studies and exploratory studies."

Dolly: "I know, do not disturb me now. What you are talking about is descriptive validity, interpretive validity and theoretical validity."

Jolly: "What do you do after you have defined the problem and decided which type of research you are going to do?"

Dolly: "I cannot forget to review the literature relating to my area of study. This will help me refine my research problem, to update my knowledge what other researchers have done on in this area, what are their findings, what is the gap in their study. I shall be able to frame hypotheses of my study. Literature review also helps me get a bibliography for my study."

Jolly: "Good. What next?"

Dolly: "I shall plan my research. If it is descriptive and exploratory, the main job is to visit the library and gather articles from journals, get books relating to area of my study. But if it is descriptive and empirical I shall have to decide about sampling design, observational design, statistical design and operational design."

Jolly: "Ae Re Wah!"

Dolly: "Listen carefully. This is not just reading, you are to do it practically."

Jolly: "You are telling me! I have already registered myself as research scholar."

Dolly: "Okay, I know. A good design is related to the purpose or objective of the research problem and also with the nature of the problem to be studied."

Jolly: "What we do if it is causal study in applied research."

Dolly: "In business, we some times perform experiments to see the effect of a programme."

Jolly: "How do we do?"

Dolly: " First we select sample of subjects, group or pair of subjects, identify and control non-experimental factors, select or construct, and validate instruments to measure outcomes, conduct pilot study, determine place, time, and duration of the experiment and conduct the experiment. Later, we compile raw data and reduce to usable form and apply an appropriate test of significance. Jolly, what is this significance? Can't we do any research without mathematical work?

Jolly: "We shall learn about significance level in the chapter Data Analysis. Descriptive and exploratory studies are mostly without mathematical calculations, but in descriptive studies descriptive statistics are used. Dear Dolly, we should not be afraid of data analysis. It is interesting and helps us to conclude scientifically."

Dolly: "Don't we criticize scientific methods in social science research."

Jolly: "No, we never criticize any method in business or social science research. We simply say no single method approach can be taken in human studies."

Dolly : "So, in experimental studies we can pre-test and post-test the groups to see the effect of the programme or variation due to external factors.

Jolly: "There are four types of formal....."

Dolly: "They are CR, RCB, LS and FD."

Jolly: "So what is one way Anova?"

Dolly: "Complete randomized designed is tested with one-way ANOVA, it is just to find out the variations in columns, i.e., treatments."

Jolly: "Can you clarify?"

Dolly: "I have three salesmen – Hari, Harpreet and Harish. I send them to various towns like Faridabad, Amritsar, Madurai, and Pune. I record their performance. With One-Way ANOVA, we can see the variation in the performance. The method is used to see only the treatments – Hari, Harpreet and Harish. It is CR design."

Jolly: "What is randomized block design?"

Dolly: "Simple, earlier I wanted to measure the performance of only Hari, Harpreet and Harish. Now, I also want to see the variation due to the places i.e. Faridabad, Amritsar, Madurai and Pune. If I show this data in a matrix, we can find the variations in columns as well as row-variation in salesmen as well as in places. In real life, we may say salesmen have not performed well, but actually they may be very hard working. There may be problems in the field. It is better to know about both."

Jolly: "Latin square design has limitations because we need equal number of treatments and equal number of blocks that is number of columns and rows should be same. Three salesmen are sent to three cities, variation is calculated due to column, rows and salesmen."

Dolly: "This method ignores any interaction factor between salesmen and territory they are sent to. Factorial design is used to find the interaction between territory and salesmen. Hari may have good interaction with Faridabad and Harish may be better attached to Amritsar. Interaction effect is calculated in Factorial design."

Jolly: "I suggest you to start learning data analysis now. Learn One-Way, Two-Way analysis."

Dolly: "Also, give me some good research project to read now."

Jolly: "See you tomorrow, better you prepare abstract of the research project 3, we shall discuss more."

CHAPTER

# DATA COLLECTION

## Structure

## 6.1 Sources of Data

**Data** refers to a collection of natural phenomena descriptors, including the results of experience, observation or experiment, or a set of premises. This may consist of numbers, words, or images, particularly as measurements or observations of a set of variables.

There are two sources of data:

- **Primary Source** and
- **Secondary Source**

Primary source is used to collect initial material during the research process. Primary data is the data that the researcher collects himself using methods such as surveys, direct observations, interviews, as well as logs (objective data sources). Primary data is a reliable way to collect data because the researcher will know where it came from and how it was collected and analysed since he did it himself. Primary sources of information allow the learner to access original and unedited information. A primary source requires the learner to interact with the source and extract information.

Secondary sources are edited primary sources, second-hand versions. They represent thinking of someone else. Secondary data are data that were collected by persons or agencies for purposes other than solving the problem at hand. They are one of the cheapest and easiest means of access to information. Hence, the first thing a researcher should do is to search for secondary data available on the topic. The amount of secondary data is overwhelming, and researchers have to locate and utilize the data that are relevant to their research. Secondary sources take the role of analysing, explaining, and combining the information from the primary source with additional information.

Secondary data analysis is commonly known as second-hand analysis. It is simply the analysis of pre-existing data in a different way or to answer a different question than originally intended. Secondary data analysis utilizes the data that was collected by someone else in order to further a study that you are interested in completing.

In contrast to secondary data, primary data comes from observations made by the researchers themselves. This often creates credibility issues that do not arise with secondary data.

### Uses of Secondary Data

1. Secondary data may actually provide enough information to resolve the problem being investigated.
2. Secondary data can be a valuable source of new ideas that can be explored later through primary research.
3. Secondary data are of use in collecting primary data.
4. Secondary data also help to define the population, select the sample in primary information collection and define the parameters of primary research.
5. Secondary data can also serve as a reference base against which to compare the validity or accuracy of primary data.

### Benefits of Secondary Data

1. The most significant benefit of secondary data is saving in cost and time.
2. This involves very little time, effort and money compared to primary research.

3. Certain research projects may not be feasible for a firm; recourse to secondary data will be the only solution. For example: If a firm needs information on the entire population of some country, it will neither be physically nor financially possible for the company to obtain it.
4. Historical data is always secondary data. If a firm wants to obtain information on something that happened in the past, it cannot conduct primary research to obtain it.
5. In some cases secondary data can be more accurate than primary data. For example, if a company wants information on the sales, profits and so forth, of other companies, it can get more reliable information from government released sources than companies themselves.

## Limitations of Secondary Sources

Despite many potential benefits of secondary data, it has a number of limitations.

1. Problems of fit are likely to occur between the data required for current research and the available data.
2. The researchers have no knowledge of how the data were collected, nor do they have any control over it. Therefore, they do not know anything about its accuracy or its bounds of error.
3. It is also very difficult to evaluate the accuracy of the data already collected.
4. In many cases the secondary data may not be sufficient to meet the data requirement for the research at hand. Secondary data can be outdated, and hence cannot be used in current research.

## Suitability

- The central problem of secondary data which, by definition, was not gathered for purposes of the present research.
- May only partially address the research questions.
- Data definitions, categories, levels of aggregation may differ, if only slightly, from those required; time series may not be continuous.
- Validity of data may vary – government sources are likely to be valid, but company statistics may be unreliable; minutes of meetings may be 'massaged'; newspaper articles adhere to 'journalistic standards' Integration of secondary data with each other and with primary data also an issue.

Common sources of secondary data are social science surveys and data from government agencies, including the Bureau of the Census, the Bureau of Labor Statistics and various other agencies. The data collected are most often collected via survey research methods. Data from experimental studies may also be used.

## 6.2 Sources of Secondary Data

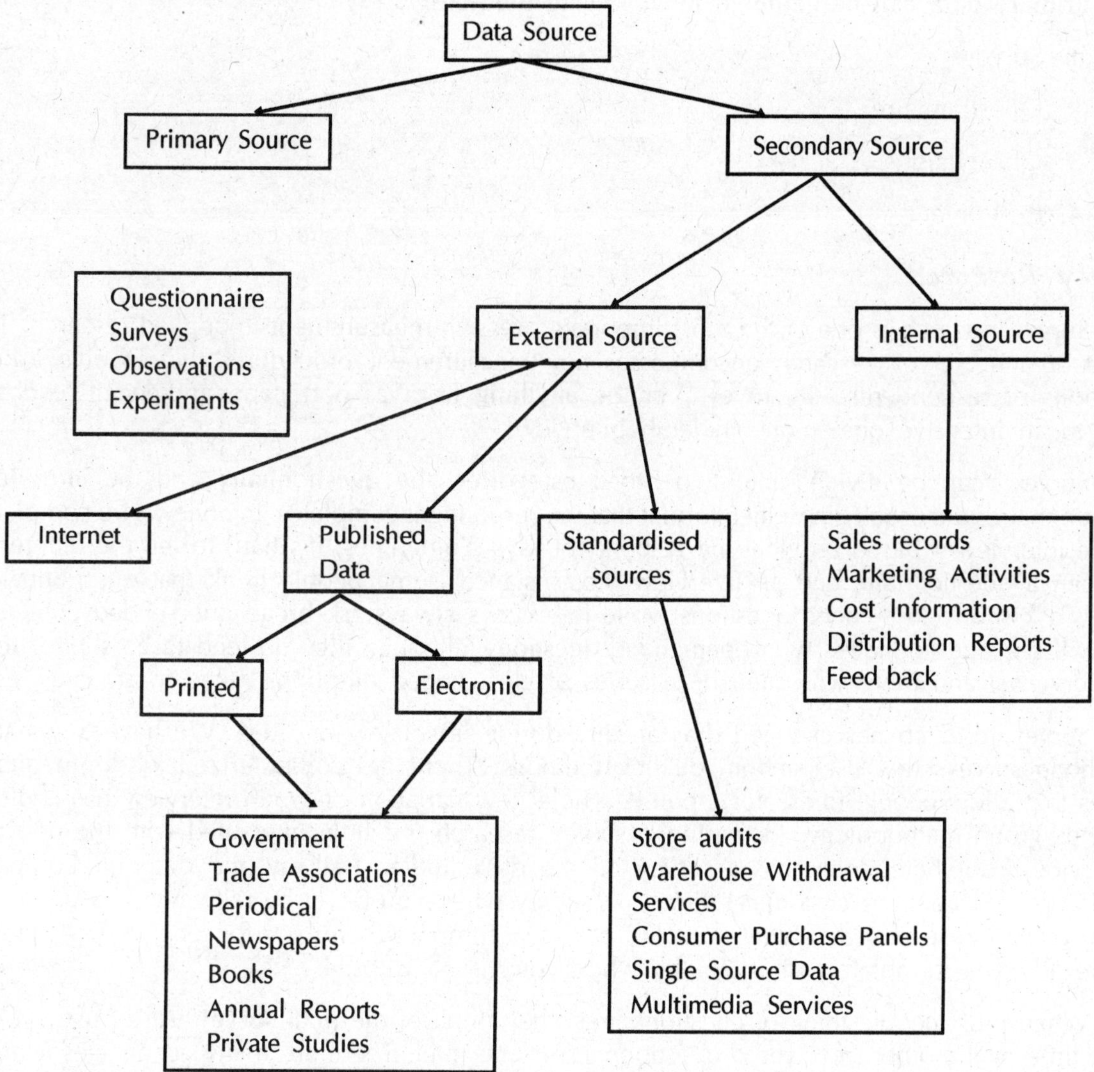


Sources of secondary data from Government:

- Director General of Commercial Intelligence and Statistics, Kolkata
- RBI's Handbook of Statistics on Indian Economy
- RBI Bulletin BOP Statement
- Annual Reports of International Institutions
- Agricultural Statistics at a Glance
- National Sample Surveys

Above is the flow chart which show how data are collected

## 6.3 Sources of Primary Data

**Primary data can be gathered by following methods**

1. Surveys
2. Questionnaire
3. Observations
4. Experiments

### Survey Research

Survey research is one of the most important areas of measurement in applied research. The broad area of survey research encompasses any measurement procedures that involve asking questions of respondents. A "survey" can be anything from a short paper-and-pencil feedback form to an intensive one-on-one in-depth interview.

Surveys can be divided into two broad categories: the **questionnaire** and the **interview**. Questionnaires are usually in written format that the respondent completes. Interviews are completed by the interviewer based on what the respondent says. Sometimes, it's hard to tell the difference between a questionnaire and an interview. For instance, some people think that questionnaires always ask short close-ended questions while interviews always ask broad open-ended ones. But you will see questionnaires with open-ended questions (although they do tend to be shorter than in interviews) and there will often be a series of close-ended questions asked in an interview.

Survey research has changed dramatically during last a few decades. We have automated telephone surveys that use random dialling methods. There are computerized kiosks in public places that allow people to ask for input. A whole new variation of group interview has evolved as focus group methodology. Increasingly, survey research is tightly integrated with the delivery of service. Your hotel room has a survey on the desk. Indian Railway and Catering Company (IRCTC) presents a short customer satisfaction survey when you travel by railways. You get a call for an interview several days after your last call to a computer company for technical assistance. You're asked to complete a short survey when you visit a website.

When most people think of questionnaires, they think of the **mail survey**. All of us have, at some time or the other, received a questionnaire in the mail. There are many advantages to mail surveys. They are relatively inexpensive to administer. You can send the exact same instrument to a wide number of people. They allow the respondents to fill it out at their own convenience. But there are some disadvantages as well. Response rates from mail surveys are often very low. And, mail questionnaires are not the best vehicles for asking for detailed written responses.

A second type is the **group administered questionnaire**. A sample of respondents is brought together and asked to respond to a structured sequence of questions. Traditionally, questionnaires are administered in group settings for convenience. The researcher could give the questionnaire to those who were present and be fairly sure that there would be a high response rate. If the respondents were unclear about the meaning of a question they could ask for clarification. And, there were often organizational settings where it was relatively easy to assemble the group (in a company or business, for instance).

What's the difference between a group administered questionnaire and a group interview or focus group? In the group administered questionnaire, each respondent is *handed an instrument* and asked to complete it while in the room. Each respondent completes an instrument. In the group interview or focus group, the interviewer facilitates the session. People work as a group, listening to each other's comments and answering the questions. Someone takes notes for the entire group; people don't complete an interview individually.

A less familiar type of questionnaire is the **household drop-off** survey. In this approach, a researcher goes to the respondent's home or business and hands the respondent the instrument. In some cases, the respondent is asked to mail it back or the interview returns to pick it up. This approach attempts to blend the advantages of the mail survey and the group administered questionnaire. Like the mail survey, the respondent can work on the instrument in private, when it's convenient. Like the group administered questionnaire, the interviewer makes personal contact with the respondent; they don't just send an impersonal survey instrument. And, the respondent can ask questions about the study and get clarification on what is to be done. Generally, this would be expected to increase the per cent of people who are willing to respond.

## Interviews

Interviews are personal form of research than questionnaires. In the **personal interview**, the interviewer works directly with the respondent. Unlike with mail surveys, the interviewer has the opportunity to probe or ask follow-up questions. And, interviews are generally easier for the respondent, especially if opinions or impressions are sought. Interviews can be very time consuming and they are resource intensive. The interviewer is considered a part of the measurement instrument and interviewers have to be well trained in how to respond to any contingency.

Almost everyone is familiar with the **telephone interview**. Telephone interviews enable a researcher to gather information rapidly. Most of the major public opinion polls that are reported were based on telephone interviews. Like personal interviews, they allow for some personal contact between the interviewer and the respondent. And, they allow the interviewer to ask follow-up questions. But they also have some major disadvantages. Many people don't have publicly-listed telephone numbers. Some don't have telephones. People often don't like the intrusion of a call to their homes. And, telephone interviews have to be relatively short or people will feel imposed upon.

## Sampling Issues

The sample is the actual group you will have to contact in some way. There are several important sampling issues you need to consider when doing survey research – data you wish to collect from samples, their current addresses and their current phone numbers, up to date lists. Can respondents be found? Can your respondents be located? Some people are very busy. Some travel a lot. Some work the night shift. Even if you have an accurate phone or address, you may not be able to locate or make contact with your sample. Who is the respondent? Who is the respondent in your study? Let's say you draw a sample of households in a small city. A household is not a respondent. Do you want to interview a specific individual? Do you want to talk only to the "head of household" (and how is that person defined)? Are you willing to talk to any member of the household? Do you state that you will speak to the first adult member of the household who opens the door? What if that person is unwilling to be interviewed but someone else in the house is willing? How do you deal with multi-family households? Similar problems arise when you sample groups, agencies, or companies. Can you survey any member of the organization? Or, do you only want to speak to the Director of Human Resources? What if the person you would like to interview is unwilling or unable to participate? Do you use another member of the organization? Can all members of population be sampled?

If you have an incomplete list of the population (i.e., sampling frame) you may not be able to sample every member of the population. Lists of various groups are extremely hard to keep up to date. People move or change their names. Even though they are on your sampling frame listing, you may not be able to get to them. And, it's possible they are not even on the list. Are response rates likely to be a problem? Even if you are able to solve all of the other population and sampling problems, you still have to deal with the issue of response rates. Some members of your sample will simply refuse to respond. Others have the best of intentions, but can't seem to find the time to send in your questionnaire by the due date. Still others misplace the instrument or forget about the appointment for an interview. Low response rates are among the most difficult of problems in survey research. They can ruin an otherwise well-designed survey effort. We shall read more sampling issues in the next chapter.

## 6.4 Question Issues

Objectives of your research shall decide what you ask respondents and types of questions that can be asked. Are you going to ask personal questions? Are you going to need to get lots of detail in the responses? Can you anticipate the most frequent or important types of responses and develop reasonable close-ended questions? How complex will the questions be? Sometimes you are dealing with a complex subject or topic. The questions you want to ask are going to have multiple parts. You may need to branch to sub-questions. A screening question may be needed to determine whether the respondent is qualified to answer your question of interest. For instance, you wouldn't want to ask someone their opinions about a specific computer programme without first "screening" them to find out whether they have any experience using the programme. Sometimes you have to screen on several variables (e.g., age, gender, experience). The more complicated the screening, the less likely it is that you can rely on paper-and-pencil instruments without confusing the respondent. Can question sequence be controlled?

Is your survey one where you can construct in advance a reasonable sequence of questions? Or, are you doing an initial exploratory study where you may need to ask lots of follow-up questions that you can't easily anticipate? Will lengthy questions be asked? If your subject matter is complicated, you may need to give the respondent some detailed background for a question. Can you reasonably expect your respondent to sit still long enough in a phone interview to ask your question? Will long response scales be used? If you are asking people about the different computer equipment they use, you may have to have a lengthy response list (CD-ROM drive, floppy drive, mouse, touch pad, modem, network connection, external speakers, etc.). Clearly, it may be difficult to ask about each of these in a short phone interview.

### Bias Issues

People come to the research endeavour with their own sets of biases and prejudices. Sometimes, these biases will be less of a problem but others may give you lot of problems to conclude and findings may not be accurate.

Can social desirability be avoided? Respondents generally want to "look good" in the eyes of others. None of us likes to look like we don't know an answer. We don't want to say anything that would be embarrassing. If you ask people about information that may put them in this kind of position, they may not tell you the truth, or they may "spin" the response so that it makes them look better. This may be more of a problem in an interview situation where they are face-to face or on the phone with a live interviewer.

Can interviewer distortion and subversion be controlled? Interviewers may distort an interview as well. They may not ask questions that make them uncomfortable. They may not listen carefully to respondents on topics for which they have strong opinions. They may make the judgment that they already know what the respondent would say to a question based on their prior responses, even though that may not be true.

Can false respondents be avoided? With mail surveys it may be difficult to know who actually responded. Did the head of household complete the survey or someone else? Did the CEO actually give the responses or instead pass the task off to a subordinate? Is the person you're speaking with on the phone actually who they say they are? At least with personal interviews, you have a reasonable chance of knowing who you are speaking with. In mail surveys or phone interviews, this may not be the case.

### Administrative Issues

Last, but certainly not the least, you have to consider the feasibility of the survey method for your study.

- **Costs:** Cost is often the major determining factor in selecting survey type. You might prefer to do personal interviews, but can't justify the high cost of training and paying for the interviewers. You may prefer to send out an extensive mailing but can't afford the postage to do so.
- **Facilities:** Do you have the facilities (or access to them) to process and manage your study? In phone interviews, do you have well-equipped phone surveying facilities? For focus groups, do you have a comfortable and accessible room to host the group? Do you have the equipment needed to record and transcribe responses?
- **Time:** Some types of surveys take longer than others. Do you need responses immediately (as in an overnight public opinion poll)? Have you budgeted enough time for your study to send out mail surveys and follow-up reminders, and to get the responses back by mail? Have you allowed for enough time to get enough personal interviews to justify that approach?
- **Personnel:** Different types of surveys make different demands of personnel. Interviews require interviewers who are motivated and well-trained. Group administered surveys require people who are trained in group facilitation. Some studies may be in a technical area that requires some degree of expertise in the interviewer.

Clearly, there are lots of issues to consider when you are selecting which type of survey you wish to use in your study. And there is no clear and easy way to make this decision in many contexts. There may not be one approach which is clearly the best. You may have to make tradeoffs of advantages and disadvantages. There is judgment involved. Two expert researchers may, for the very same problem or issue, select entirely different survey methods. But, if you select a method that isn't appropriate or doesn't fit the context, you can doom a study before you even begin designing the instruments or questions themselves.

There are three areas involved in writing a question:

- determining the question content, scope and purpose
- choosing the response format that you use for collecting information from the respondent
- figuring out how to word the question to get at the issue of interest

Finally, once you have your questions written, there is the issue of how best to place them in your survey. You'll see that although there are many aspects of survey construction that are just common sense, if you are not careful you can make critical errors that have dramatic effects on your results.

### 6.4.1 Issues of Measurement and Scale

The level of measurement refers to the relationship among the values that are assigned to the attributes for a variable. The level of measurement helps us to decide how to interpret the data from that variable. When you know that a measure is nominal, then you know that the numerical values are just short codes for the longer names. Second, knowing the level of measurement helps you decide what statistical analysis is appropriate on the values that were assigned. If a measure is nominal, then you know that you would never average the data values or do a t-test on the data.

There are typically four levels of measurement that are defined:

- Nominal
- Ordinal
- Interval
- Ratio

In **nominal** measurement the numerical values just "name" the attribute uniquely. No ordering of the cases is implied. For example, in cricket Sachin has nominal value 10; Saurabh has 99 as the nominal level. It is simply a number like your enrolment number in the class.

In **ordinal** measurement the attributes can be rank-ordered. Here, distances between attributes do not have any meaning. For example, on a survey you may code Educational Attainment as 0 = less than poor; 1 = poor; 2 = satisfactory; 3 = good; 4 = very good; 5 = excellent. In this measure, higher numbers mean *more* education. But is distance from 0 to 1 same as 3 to 4? Of course, it is not. The interval between values is not interpretable in an ordinal measure.

In **interval** measurement the distance between attributes *does* have meaning. For example, when we measure temperature (in Fahrenheit), the distance from 30-40 is same as distance from 70-80. The interval between values is interpretable. Because of this, it makes sense to compute an average of an interval variable, where it doesn't make sense to do so for ordinal scales. But note that in interval measurement ratios don't make any sense - 80 degrees is not twice as hot as 40 degrees (although the attribute value is twice as large).

Finally, in **ratio** measurement there is always an absolute zero that is meaningful. This means that you can construct a meaningful fraction (or ratio) with a ratio variable. Weight is a ratio variable. In applied social research most "count" variables are ratio, for example, the number of clients in past six months. It is meaningful to say that "...we had twice as many clients in the past six months as we did in the previous six months."

There is a hierarchy implied in the level of measurement idea. At lower levels of measurement, assumptions tend to be less restrictive and data analyses tend to be less sensitive. At each level up the hierarchy, the current level includes all the qualities of the one below it and adds something new. In general, it is desirable to have a higher level of measurement (e.g., interval or ratio) rather than a lower one (nominal or ordinal).

Scaling is the branch of measurement that involves the construction of an instrument that associates qualitative constructs with quantitative metric units. Scales are generally divided into two broad categories: uni-dimensional and multidimensional. The uni-dimensional scaling methods were developed in the first half of the twentieth century and are generally named after their inventor. There are three types of uni-dimensional scaling methods:

- Likert or "Summative" Scaling
- Thurstone or Equal-Appearing Interval Scaling
- Guttman or "Cumulative" Scaling

## Likert Scale

As in all scaling methods, the first step is to define what it is you are trying to measure. Because this is a uni-dimensional scaling method, it is assumed that the concept you want to measure is one-dimensional in nature.

Create the set of potential scale items. These should be items that can be rated on a 1-to-5 or 1-to-7 Disagree-Agree response scale. Sometimes you can create the items by yourself based on your intimate understanding of the subject matter. But, more often than not, it's helpful to engage a number of people in the item creation step.

The next step is to have a group of judges (respondents) who rate the items. Usually, you would use a 1-to-5 rating scale where:

1. = strongly unfavourable to the concept
2. = somewhat unfavourable to the concept
3. = undecided
4. = somewhat favourable to the concept
5. = strongly favourable to the concept

Notice that, as in other scaling methods, the judges are not telling you what they believe — they are judging how favourable each item is with respect to the construct of interest.

The next step is to compute the inter-correlations between all pairs of items, based on the ratings of the judges. In making judgements about which item to retain for the final scale there are several analyses you can do:

Throw out any items that have a low correlation with the total (summed) score across all items. You can conduct a t-test of the differences between the mean value for the item for the top and bottom quarter judges.

Higher t-values mean that there is a greater difference between the highest and lowest judges. In more practical terms, items with higher t-values are better discriminators, so you want to keep these items. In the end, you will have to use your judgement about which items are most sensibly retained. You want a relatively small number of items on your final scale (e.g., 10-15) and you want them to have high Item-Total correlations and high discrimination (e.g., high t-values).

All of these odd-numbered scales have a middle value which is often labelled Neutral or Undecided. It is also possible to use a forced-choice response scale with an even number of responses and no middle neutral or undecided choice. In this situation, the respondent is forced to decide whether they lean more towards agreement or disagreement end of the scale for each item.

The final score for the respondent on the scale is the sum of their ratings for all of the items (this is why this is sometimes called a "summated" scale).

Following is the example of Likert Scale. 10 respondents were asked six questions with a scale from 1 to 5. Respondents replied 1 to 5. Followings are the responses. For each question mean and standard deviation has been calculated. Later means of two questions were compared with t test and their powers were found. It is seen question 4 is not relevant and can be dropped if required.

| Respondent | Qno.1 | Qno. 2 | Qno.3 | Qno.4 | Qno.5 | Qno.6 |
|---|---|---|---|---|---|---|
| 1 | 3 | 4 | 2 | 5 | 1 | 5 |
| 2 | 4 | 5 | 2 | 4 | 2 | 4 |
| 3 | 1 | 5 | 5 | 3 | 4 | 3 |
| 4 | 5 | 4 | 4 | 2 | 2 | 2 |
| 5 | 3 | 3 | 3 | 1 | 1 | 4 |
| 6 | 2 | 2 | 1 | 5 | 5 | 5 |
| 7 | 5 | 1 | 5 | 4 | 3 | 2 |
| 8 | 4 | 5 | 2 | 2 | 2 | 1 |
| 9 | 3 | 2 | 5 | 1 | 5 | 5 |
| 10 | 2 | 1 | 1 | 5 | 1 | 5 |
| Mean | 3.2 | 3.2 | 3 | 3.2 | 2.6 | 3.6 |
| S D | 1.3165612 | 1.619328 | 1.632993 | 1.619328 | 1.577621 | 1.505545 |
| T-test power | | 1.00 | | 0.83 | | 0.16 |

Usually Likert Scale is Prepared with zero mean. On either side of 0 are -2, -1 and +1 and +2.

## Guttman Scaling

Guttman scaling is also sometimes known as cumulative scaling or scalogram analysis. The purpose of Guttman scaling is to establish a one-dimensional continuum for a concept you wish to measure. For example, we may like a set of items or statements so that a respondent who agrees with any specific question in the list will also agree with all previous questions. Put more formally, we would like to be able to predict item responses perfectly knowing only the total score for the respondent. For example, imagine a ten-item cumulative scale. If the respondent scores a four, it should mean that he/she agreed with the first four statements. If the respondent scores an eight, it should mean they agreed with the first eight. The object is to find a set of items that perfectly matches this pattern.

We begin by defining the focus for our scale. Let's imagine that you wish to develop a cumulative scale that measures consumer attitudes towards product. You would develop a large set of items that reflect the concept.

Next, we would want to have a group of judges rate the statements or items in terms of how favourable they are to the concept of product. They would give a Yes if the item was favourable towards the product and a No if it is not. Notice that we are not asking the judges whether they personally agree with the statement. Instead, we're asking them to make a judgment about how the statement is related to the construct of interest.

The key to Guttman scaling is in the analysis. We construct a matrix or table that shows the responses of all the respondents on all of the items. We then sort this matrix so that respondents who agree with more statements are listed at the top and those agreeing with fewer are at the bottom. For respondents with the same number of agreements, we sort the statements from left to right from those that most agreed to those that fewest agreed to. We might get a table something like the figure. Notice that the scale is very nearly cumulative when you read from left to right across the columns (items). Specifically if someone agreed with Item 7, they always agreed with Item 2. And, if someone agreed with Item 5, they always agreed with Items 7 and 2. The matrix shows that the cumulativeness of the scale is not perfect, however. While in general, a person agreeing with Item 3 tended to also agree with 5, 7 and 2, there are several exceptions to that rule.

Once you've selected the final scale items, it's relatively simple to administer the scale. You simply present the items and ask the respondent to check items with which they agree.

### Thurstone

Thurstone was one of the first and most productive scaling theorists. He actually invented three different methods for developing a uni-dimensional scale: the method of equal-appearing intervals; the method of successive intervals; and, the method of paired comparisons. The three methods differed in how the scale values for items were constructed, but in all three cases, the resulting scale was rated the same way by respondents.

The method of Equal-Appearing Intervals starts like almost every other scaling method — with the development of the focus for the scaling project. Because this is a uni-dimensional scaling method, we assume that the concept you are trying to scale is reasonably thought of as one-dimensional. The description of this concept should be as clear as possible so that the people who are going to create the statements have a clear idea of what you are trying to measure.

You want to be sure that everyone who is generating statements has some idea of what you are after in this focus command.

For example, you want to know the attributes of a product. Just make some statements about the product and let the judges give grading from 1 to 11 (1 means least favoured attribute while 11 means more favourable).

Please note you DON'T want the participants to tell you what their attitudes towards about the product are whether they would agree with the statements. You want them to rate the "favourableness'" of each statement in terms of an attitude towards product.

The next step is to analyse the rating data. For each statement, you need to compute the Median and the Inter-quartile Range. The median is the value above and below which 50% of the ratings fall. The first quartile (Q1) is the value below which 25% of the cases fall and above which 75% of the cases fall — in other words, the 25th percentile. The median is the 50th percentile. The third quartile, Q3, is the 75th percentile. The Inter-quartile Range is the difference between third and first quartile, or Q3 - Q1. You can compute these values easily with any introductory statistics programme or with most spreadsheet programmes. To facilitate the final selection of items for your scale, you might want to sort the table of medians and Inter-quartile Range in ascending order by Median and, within that, in descending order by Inter-quartile Range. Now, you have to select the final statements for your scale. You should select statements that are at equal intervals across the range of medians. Within each value, you should try to select the statement that has the smallest Inter-quartile Range. This is the statement with the least amount of variability across judges. You don't want the statistical analysis to be the only deciding factor here. Look over the candidate's statements at each level and select the statement that makes the most sense. If you find that the best statistical choice is a confusing statement, select the next best choice.

You now have a scale, a yardstick you can use for measuring attitudes towards product. You can give it to a participant and ask them to agree or disagree with each statement. To get that person's total scale score, you average the scale scores of all the items that person agreed with.

## 6.5 Types of Questions

Survey questions can be divided into two broad types: **structured** and **unstructured**. From an instrument design point of view, the structured questions pose the greater difficulties. From a content perspective, it may actually be more difficult to write good unstructured questions.

### Dichotomous Questions

When a question has two possible responses, we consider it **dichotomous**. Surveys often use dichotomous questions that ask for a Yes/No, True/False or Agree/Disagree response. There are a variety of ways to lay these questions out on a questionnaire:

Please enter your gender Male ☐

Female ☐

Do you believe that the death penalty is ever justified? ___Yes, ____No.

### Questions Based on Level of Measurement

We can also classify questions in terms of their level of measurement. For instance, we may measure occupation using a **nominal** question. Here, the number next to each response has no meaning except as a placeholder for that response. The choice of a "2" for an engineer and a "1" for a doctor is arbitrary — from the numbering system used we can't infer that a lawyer is "twice" something that a truck driver is, for instance

What is your occupation?

1. Doctor
2. Engineer
3. Management Consultant
4. Etc

We may ask respondents to rank order their preferences for prime ministerial candidates using an **ordinal** question:

Rank the candidates in order of preference from best to worst

__________Atal Bihari Bajpai

__________Manmohan Singh

__________Sonia Gandhi

__________Rahul Gandhi

__________L K Advani

We want the respondent to put a 1, 2, 3 or 4 next to the candidate, where 1 is the respondent's first choice. Note that this could get confusing. We may want to state the prompt more explicitly so the respondent knows we want a number from one to 4 (the respondent may check their favourite candidate, or assign higher numbers to candidates they prefer more instead of understanding that we want rank ordering).

We can also construct survey questions that attempt to measure on an **interval** level. One of the most common of these types is the traditional 1-to-5 rating (or 1-to-7, or 1-to-9, etc.). This is sometimes referred to as a **Likert response scale**. Here, we see how we may ask an opinion question on a 1-to-5 bipolar scale (it's called bipolar because there is a neutral point and the two ends of the scale are at opposite positions of the opinion):

**The death penalty is justifiable under some circumstances.**

| 1 | 2 | 3 | 4 | 5 |
|---|---|---|---|---|
| **Strongly disagree** | **disagree** | **neutral** | **agree strongly** | **agree** |

Another interval question uses an approach called the **semantic differential**. Here, an object is assessed by the respondent on a set of bipolar adjective pairs (using 5-point rating scale):

**Please state your opinions on national health insurance on the scale below**

| | very much | some what | neither | some what | very much | |
|---|---|---|---|---|---|---|
| **interesting** | ☐ | ☐ | ☐ | ☐ | ☐ | **boring** |
| **simple** | ☐ | ☐ | ☐ | ☐ | ☐ | **complex** |
| **uncaring** | ☐ | ☐ | ☐ | ☐ | ☐ | **caring** |
| **useful** | ☐ | ☐ | ☐ | ☐ | ☐ | **useless** |

Finally, we can also get at interval measures by using what is called a **cumulative or Guttman scale.** Here, the respondent checks each item with which they agree. The items themselves are constructed so that they are cumulative — if you agree to one, you probably agree to all of the ones above it in the list:

Please check each statement that you agree with:

____ Are you willing to permit immigrants to live in your country?

____ Are you willing to permit immigrants to live in your community?

____ Are you willing to permit immigrants to live in your neighbourhood?

____ Would you be willing to have an immigrant live next door to you?

____ Would you let your child marry an immigrant?

## Filter or Contingency Questions

Sometimes you have to ask the respondent one question in order to determine if they are qualified or experienced enough to answer a subsequent one. This requires using a **filter or contingency question**. For instance, you may want to ask one question if the respondent is married and a different question if they are not. In this case, you would have to construct a filter question to determine whether they've married:

Are you married? ____Yes ____No

If married, how many children do you have?

No child (0), One Child (1), Two Children (2), More than two children (3)

Filter questions can get very complex. Sometimes, you have to have multiple filter questions in order to direct your respondents to the correct subsequent questions. There are a few conventions you should keep in mind when using filters:

- try to avoid having more than three levels (two jumps) for any question

Too many jumps will confuse the respondent and may discourage them from continuing with the survey.

- if only two levels, use graphic to jump (e.g., arrow and box)

The example above shows how you can make effective use of an arrow and box to help direct the respondent to the correct subsequent question.

- if possible, jump to a new page

If you can't fit the response to a filter on a single page, it's probably best to be able to say something like "If YES, please turn to page 4" rather that "If YES, please go to Question 38" because the respondent will generally have an easier time finding a page than a specific question.

## Question Content

For each question in your survey, you should ask yourself how well it addresses the content you are trying to get at. Here are some content-related questions you can ask about your survey questions.

## Is the Question Necessary/Useful?

Examine each question to see if you need to ask it at all and if you need to ask it at the level of detail you currently have.

- Do you need the age of ***each*** child or just the ***number of children under 16***?
- Do you need to ***ask income*** or can you ***estimate***?

### Are Several Questions Needed?

This is the classic problem of the **double-barrelled question**. You should think about splitting each of the following questions into two separate ones. You can often spot these kinds of problems by looking for the conjunction "and" in your question.

- What are your feelings towards African-Americans *and* Hispanic-Americans?
- What do you think of proposed changes in benefits *and* hours?

Another reason you may need more than one question is that the question you ask **does not cover all possibilities**. For instance, if you ask about earnings, the respondent may not mention all income (e.g., dividends, gifts). Or, if you ask the respondents if they're in favour of STAR TV, they may not understand what you're asking generally. They may not be in favour of STAR TV for themselves (they never watch it), but might favour it very much for their children (who watch regularly). You might be better off asking two questions, one for their own viewing and one for other members of their household.

Sometimes you need to ask additional questions because your question **does not give you enough context** to interpret the answer. For instance, if you ask about attitudes towards Catholics, can you interpret this without finding out about their attitudes towards religion in general, or other religious groups?

At times, you need to ask additional questions because your question **does not determine the intensity** of the respondent's attitude or belief. For example, if they say they support public TV, you probably should also ask them whether they ever watch it or if they would be willing to have their tax dollars spent on it. It's one thing for a respondent to tell you they support something. But the intensity of that response is greater if they are willing to back their sentiment of support with their behaviour.

### Do Respondents Have the Needed Information?

Look at each question in your survey to see whether the respondent is likely to have the necessary information to be able to answer the question. For example, let's say you want to ask the question:

Do you know who acted in Hum Panch? People may not have any idea. You must ask did you watch the popular TV serial Hum Panch, then ask who were the lead actors in it?

### Does the Question Need to be More Specific?

Sometimes we ask our questions too generally and the information we obtain is more difficult to interpret. For example, let's say you want to find out respondent's opinions about a specific book. You could ask them

**How well did you like the book?**

On some scale ranging from "Not At All" to "Extremely Well." But what would their response mean? What does it mean to say you liked a book ***very well***? Instead, you might ask questions designed to be more specific like:

**Did you recommend the book to others?**

or

**Did you look for other books by that author?**

### Is Question Sufficiently General?

You can err in the other direction as well by being too specific. For instance, if you ask someone to list the televisions programme they liked best in the past week, you could get a very different answer than if you asked them which show they've enjoyed most over the past year. Perhaps a show they don't usually like had a great episode in the past week, or their show was pre-empted by another programme.

### Is Question Biased or Loaded?

One danger in question-writing is that your own biases and blind-spots may affect the wording. For instance, you might generally be in favour of tax cuts. If you ask a question like:

**What do you see as the benefits of a tax cut?**

you're only asking about one side of the issue. You might get a very different picture of the respondents' positions if you also asked about the disadvantages of tax cuts. The same thing could occur if you are in favour of public welfare and you ask:

**What do you see as the disadvantages of eliminating welfare?**

without also asking about the potential benefits.

### Will Respondent Answer Truthfully?

For each question on your survey, ask yourself whether the respondent will have any difficulty answering the question truthfully. If there is some reason why they may not, consider rewording the question. For instance, some people are sensitive about answering questions about their exact age or income. In this case, you might give them **response brackets** to choose from (e.g., between 30 and 40 years old, between ₹ 50,000 and ₹ 100,000 annual income). Sometimes even bracketed responses won't be enough. Some people do not like to share how much money they give to charitable causes (they may be afraid of being solicited even more). No matter how you word the question, they would not be likely to tell you their contribution rate. But sometimes you can do this by posing the question in terms of a **hypothetical projective respondent** (a little bit like a projective test). In this case, you might get reasonable estimates if you ask the respondent how much money "people you know" typically give in a year to charitable causes. Finally, you can sometimes dispense with asking a question at all if you can obtain the answer unobtrusively (see Unobtrusive Measures). If you are interested in finding out what magazines the respondent reads, you might instead tell them you are collecting magazines for a recycling drive and ask if they have any old ones to donate (of course, you have to consider the ethical implications of such deception!).

## Question Wording

One of the major difficulties in writing good survey questions is getting the wording right. Even slight wording differences can confuse the respondent or lead to incorrect interpretations of the question. Here, I outline some questions you can ask about how you worded each of your survey questions.

### Can the Question be misunderstood?

The survey author has to always be on the lookout for questions that could be misunderstood or confusing. For instance, if you ask a person for their nationality, it might not be clear what you want (Do you want someone from Malaysia to say Malaysian, Asian, or Pacific Islander?). Or, if you ask for marital status, do you want someone to say simply that they are either married or not married? Or, do you want more detail (like divorced, widow/widower, etc.)?

Some terms are just too vague to be useful. For instance, if you ask a question about the "mass media," what do you mean? The newspapers? Radio? Television?

Here's one of my favourites. Let's say you want to know the following:

**What kind of headache remedy do you use?**

Do you want to know what brand name medicine they take? Do you want to know about "home" remedies? Are you asking whether they prefer a pill, capsule or caplet?

### What Assumptions Does the Question Make?

Sometimes we don't stop to consider how a question will appear from the respondent's viewpoint. We don't think about the assumptions behind our questions. For instance, if you ask what social class someone's in, you assume that they know what social class is and that they think of themselves as being in one. In this kind of case, you may need to use a filter question first to determine whether either of these assumptions is true.

### Is the time frame specified?

Whenever you use the words "will", "could", "might", or "may" in a question; you might suspect that the question asks a time-related question. Be sure that, if it does, you have specified the time frame precisely. For instance, you might ask:

**Do you think Congress will cut taxes?**

or something like

**Do you think Congress could successfully resist tax cuts?**

Neither of these questions specifies a time frame.

**How personal is the wording?**

With a change of just a few words, a question can go from being relatively impersonal to probing into your private perspectives. Consider the following three questions, each of which asks about the respondent's satisfaction with working conditions:

**Are working conditions satisfactory or not satisfactory in the plant where you work?**

Do you feel that working conditions are satisfactory or not satisfactory in the plant where you work?

Are you personally satisfied with working conditions in the plant where you work?

The first question is stated from a fairly detached, objective viewpoint. The second asks how you "feel." The last asks whether you are "personally satisfied." Be sure the questions in your survey are at an appropriate level for your context. And, be sure there is consistency in these cross questions in your survey.

**Is the wording too direct?**

There are times when asking a question too directly may be too threatening or disturbing for respondents. For instance, consider a study where you want to discuss battlefield experiences with former soldiers who experienced trauma. Examine the following three question options:

**How did you feel about being in the war?**

**How well did the equipment hold up in the field?**

**How well were new recruits trained?**

The first question may be too direct. For this population it may elicit powerful negative emotions based on their recollections. The second question is a less direct one. It asks about equipment in the field, but, for this population, may also lead the discussion toward more difficult issues to discuss directly. The last question is probably the least direct and least threatening. Bashing the new recruits is standard protocol in almost any social context. The question is likely to get the respondent talking, recounting anecdotes, without eliciting much stress. Of course, all of this may simply be bagging the question. If you are doing a study where the respondents may experience high levels of stress because of the questions you ask, you should reconsider the ethics of doing the study.

## Other Wording Issues

The nuances of language guarantee that the task of the question writer will be endlessly complex. Without trying to generate an exhaustive list, here are a few other questions to keep in mind:

**Does the question contain difficult or unclear terminology?**

**Does the question make each alternative explicit?**

**Is the wording objectionable?**

**Is the wording loaded or slanted?**

## Question Placement

### Decisions about Placement

One of the most difficult tasks facing the survey designer involves the order of questions. Which topics should be introduced early in the survey and which later? If you leave your most important questions until the end, you may find that your respondents are too tired to give them the kind of attention you would like. If you introduce them too early, they may not yet be ready to address the topic, especially if it is a difficult or disturbing one. There are no easy answers to these problems - you have to use your judgment. Whenever you think about question placement, consider the following questions:

**Is the answer influenced by prior questions?**

**Does the question come too early or too late to arouse interest?**

**Does the question receive sufficient attention?**

### The Opening Questions

Just as in other aspects of life, first impressions are important in survey work. The first few questions you ask will determine the tone for the survey, and can help put your respondent at ease. With that in mind, the opening few questions should be easy to answer. You might start with some simple descriptive questions that will get the respondent rolling. You should never begin your survey with sensitive or threatening questions.

### Sensitive Questions

In much of our social research, we have to ask respondents about difficult or uncomfortable subjects. Before asking such questions, you should attempt to develop some trust or rapport with the respondent. Often, preceding the sensitive questions with some easier warm-up ones will help. But, you have to make sure that the sensitive material does not come up abruptly or appear unconnected with the rest of the survey. It is often helpful to have a transition sentence between sections of your instrument to give the respondent some idea of the kinds of questions that are coming. For instance, you might lead into a section on personal material with the transition:

**In this next section of the survey, we'd like to ask you about your personal relationships. Remember, we do not want you to answer any questions if you are uncomfortable doing so.**

### A Checklist of Considerations

There are lots of conventions or rules-of-thumb in the survey design business. Here's a checklist of some of the most important items. You can use this checklist to review your instrument:

**Top of Form**

- start with easy, non-threatening questions
- put more difficult, threatening questions near end
- never start a mail survey with an open-ended question
- for historical demographics, follow chronological order
- ask about one topic at a time
- when switching topics, use a transition

- reduce response set (the tendency of respondent to just keep checking the same response)
- for filter or contingency questions, make a flowchart

**Bottom of Form**

**The Golden Rule**

To put this in more practical terms, you should keep the following in mind:

- Thank the respondent at the beginning for allowing you to conduct your study
- Keep your survey as short as possible — only include what is absolutely necessary
- Be sensitive to the needs of the respondent
- Be alert for any sign that the respondent is uncomfortable
- Thank the respondent at the end for participating
- Assure the respondent that you will send a copy of the final results

## 6.6 Data Mining

Data mining is the process of sorting through large amounts of data and picking out relevant information. It is usually used by business intelligence organizations, and financial analysts, but it is increasingly used in the sciences to extract information from the enormous data sets generated by modern experimental and observational methods. It has been described as "the non-trivial extraction of implicit, previously unknown, and potentially useful information from data" and "the science of extracting useful information from large data sets or databases". Data mining in relation to Enterprise Resource Planning is the statistical and logical analysis of large sets of transaction data, looking for patterns that can aid decision-making.

Traditionally, analysts have performed the task of extracting useful information from recorded data, but the increasing volume of data in modern business and science calls for computer-based approaches. As data sets have grown in size and complexity, there has been a shift away from direct hands-on data analysis toward indirect, automatic data analysis using more complex and sophisticated tools. The modern technologies of computers, networks, and sensors have made data collection and organization much easier. However, the captured data needs to be converted into information and knowledge to become useful. Data mining is the entire process of applying computer-based methodology, including new techniques for knowledge discovery, from data. Data mining identifies trends within data that go beyond simple analysis. Through the use of sophisticated algorithms, users have the ability to identify key attributes of business processes and target opportunities.

Although 'data mining' is a relatively new term, the technology is not. Companies for a long time have used powerful computers to sift through volumes of data such as supermarket scanner data to produce market research reports. Continuous innovations in computer processing power, disk storage, and statistical software are dramatically increasing the accuracy and usefulness of analysis.

The term 'data mining' is often used to apply to the two separate processes of knowledge discovery and prediction. Knowledge discovery provides explicit information that has a readable form and can be understood by a user. Forecasting or predictive modelling provides predictions of future events and may be transparent and readable in some approaches and opaque in others such as neural networks. Moreover, some data mining systems such as neural networks are inherently geared towards prediction and pattern recognition, rather than knowledge discovery.

Metadata, or data about a given data set, are often expressed in a condensed data mineable format, or one that facilitates the practice of data mining. Common examples include executive summaries and scientific abstracts.

Data mining relies on the use of real world data. This data is extremely vulnerable to collinearity precisely because data from the real world may have unknown inter-relations. An unavoidable weakness of data mining is that the critical data that may explain the relationships is never observed. Alternative approaches using an experiment based approach such as Choice Modelling for human generated data may be used. Inherent correlations are either controlled for or removed altogether through the construction of an experimental design.

Recently, there were some efforts to define a standard for data mining, for example the CRISP-DM standard for analysis processes or the Java Data Mining Standard. Independent of these standardization efforts, freely available open-source software systems like Rapid Miner and Weka have become an informal standard for defining data mining processes.

It used to be a lot more difficult to obtain information of what customers were buying and what the trends were but now with new ERP technology all business processes are integrated and it has become very easy to track and analyse exactly what and when consumers are doing. ERP systems make information very easily accessible because so much data is stored within one massive database. Web-based marketers make use of technology known as "cookies" which are small data files stored on your computer that tells them who accessed the site and when.

There are also privacy and human rights concerns associated with data mining, specifically regarding the source of the data analysed. Data mining provides information that would not be available otherwise, and it must be properly interpreted to be useful. When the data collected involves individual people, there are many questions concerning privacy, legality, and ethics. In particular, data mining government or commercial data sets for national security or law enforcement purposes has raised privacy concerns.

Information obtained from data mining can hold things such as what type of products you bought, where do you live, what day of the year did you purchase the product on, and many other pieces of personal information. Many people do not like that all of their buying habits are out there and stored in a massive database for other people to see. These companies that are doing the data mining can use all of this information to their advantage because they will be able to tell with better accuracy what will be the best selling item for a given target market. They will also know things such as when the best time to sell a certain product is and what the best selling features of that product are. With all of this information the companies look for patterns or relationships between the data and buying trends so that they will be able to better predict what will sell the best.

There are companies such as grocery stores that obtain this information by making use of store discount cards that you must sign up for in order to take advantage of their sales. Every time you use these cards it will store what you bought and when in a large database and then that company may do what they please with that information. Some companies will sell the information that they have gathered to third parties. There are also beneficial uses of these store cards because they are able to offer you coupons or discounts based on what products you buy the most.

There are many legitimate uses of data mining. For example, a database of prescription drugs taken by a group of people could be used to find combinations of drugs exhibiting harmful interactions. Since any particular combination may occur in only 1 out of 1000 people, a great deal of data would need to be examined to discover such an interaction. A project involving pharmacies could reduce the number of drug reactions and potentially save lives. Unfortunately, there is also a huge potential for abuse of such a database.

Data mining can also be useful because it can speed up the time to market of certain products, increase product development efficiency, and enables companies to be able to solve issues with products in a faster and more efficient manner.

Data mining in customer relationship management applications can contribute significantly to the bottom line. Rather than contacting a prospect or customer through a call centre or sending mail, only prospects that are predicted to have a high likelihood of responding to an offer are contacted. More sophisticated methods may be used to optimize across campaigns so that we can predict which channel and which offer an individual is most likely to respond to - across all potential offers. Finally, in cases where many people will take an action without an offer, uplift modelling can be used to determine which people will have the greatest increase in responding if given an offer.

By using data mining businesses can identify groups that are less profitable to companies, which could lead to discrimination against certain customers. Many companies will learn which consumers make them the most profit and will start to direct all of their effects into making products for only that target market. This technique could be very beneficial to the company because they are maximizing profit by focusing the efforts on a specific group and not wasting time or resources by selling to a target market that might not return as much value to them. This is good for the firm but if you are a customer that doesn't happen to fall into the target market that they are looking for, then you pretty much get looked over and your needs from a product will most likely not be very important to them.

Businesses employing data mining quickly see a return on investment, but also they recognize that the number of predictive models can quickly become very large. Rather than one model to predict which customers will churn, a business could build a separate model for each region and customer type. Then instead of sending an offer to all people that are likely to churn, it may only want to send offers to customers that will likely take to offer. And finally, it may also want to determine which customers are going to be profitable over a window of time and only send the offers to those that are likely to be profitable. In order to maintain this quantity of models, they need to manage model versions and move to automated data mining.

Data mining can also be helpful to Human Resources in identifying the characteristics of their most successful employees. Information obtained, such as universities attended by highly successful employees, can help HR focus recruiting efforts accordingly. Additionally, Strategic Enterprise Management applications help a company translate corporate-level goals, such as profit and margin share targets, into operational decisions, such as production plans and workforce levels.

Another example of data mining, often called the market basket analysis, relates to its use in retail sales. If a clothing store records the purchases of customers, a data mining system could identify those customers who favour silk shirts over cotton ones. Although some explanations of relationships may be difficult, taking advantage of it is easier. The example deals with association rules within transaction-based data. Not all data are transaction based and logical or in exact rules may also be present within a database.

## 6.7 How to Do?

Jolly and Dolly were together again.

Dolly: "I have gone through the article 'Study of Consumers' Perceptions about Malls and Traditional Retail Outlets, the authors have clearly defined the objectives of study".

Jolly: "Sometimes it may happen, while working additional issues are observed, so objectives are changed while writing the report".

Dolly: "References have been acknowledged, it is a good mix up exploratory and empirical research.

Jolly: "Study is not complete; authors wish to study the result of foot falls at malls."

Dolly: "Can the finding be generalised?"

Jolly: "Yes, it appears to be the case at least in Mumbai. If further research is carried using same tools in other metros, we can generalise for Indian malls".

Dolly: "So, the induction has been gathered by secondary information that literature review, objectives have been set, primary data has been gathered by questionnaire."

Jolly: "Yes, secondary information/data is very useful, it is beneficial. I think beginners should start learning the research process with secondary information/data, the article teaches you the method".

Dolly: "There are two sources of data –Primary source and Secondary source. Primary data can be gathered by surveys, questionnaire, observations and experiments. There are many sources of secondary data. It can be internal and external. External sources can be government sources and private data providers. But I think if I have to collect primary data through questionnaire, I shall have to do lot of practice to write questions."

Jolly: "It is better to show the questionnaire to your friends, teachers and peers and test within your close circle, before actually going to masses".

Dolly: "You mean to say Pilot survey".

Jolly: "Yes, each question should be properly addressed keeping in mind the objectives of the study".

Dolly: "I want to read a project report where questionnaire has been used to gather data".

Jolly: "Dr. Pratibha Desai from Sivaji University, Kolhapur and Prof. S. N. Salawade faculty from Walchand College Solapur, Maharashtara, conducted a research on rural indebtedness and surveyed sugar cane growers to see the causes of their indebtedness and to suggest the measures to reduce indebtedness. They used questionnaire to survey 150 households in a population of 1500 from Chinchali Village of Belgaum district of Karnataka state."

Dolly: "I would like to know what type of questions she asked from the respondents".

Jolly: "It is simple. Interview schedule is given below."

Dolly: "I am thrilled. I shall read it".

Jolly: "See how primary data has been collected and described in the report".

Dolly: "Sometimes we forget the area which is our major concern, Thanks, bye".

**RURAL INDEBTEDNESS: WITH SPECIAL REFERENCE TO SUGARCANE GROWERS OF CHINCHALI VILLAGE IN BELGAUM DISTRICT, "KARNATAKA STATE"**

**Interview Schedule**

1. Name of respondent
2. Land details
   (i) Landholding size
   (ii) Types of land : (a) irrigated (b) dry (rain fed)
3. Major Crop
4. Source of irrigation*
   [Private tube well and public tube well, canal, well, tanks, rivers, rain water and other]
5. Use of Fertilizers, Seeds and Manures
6. Total Expenditure
7. Household Income:
   (i) Total Income
   (ii) Sources of Income
8. Credit Details:
   (i) Do you owe any loan at present? [Y/N]
   (If yes, then move to next question)
   (ii) Amount of loan and sourcewise
   (iii)

| Sr.No | Amount | Source |
|---|---|---|
| | | |
| | | |
| | | |
| | | |

(Moneylenders, banks, co-operatives, friends and relatives and other (Beshi and SHG's)

✦ ✦ ✦

Research Project 4

## 6.8 Rural Indebtedness: With Special Reference to Sugar Cane Growers

Pratibha B.Desai[1] and S.N. Salawade[2]

### Introduction

Increasing rural indebtedness is being recognized as a significant obstacle for rural development. It not only aggravates inequality in the access to socio-economic opportunities but also hinders the growth process in rural areas and creates an inter-generational handicap for participating in democratic processes due to growing distress and shocks to social psyche among the indebted households. The question of agricultural debt in India always had considerable interest and has long been one of the most pressing problems of India. Rural people have been under heavy indebtedness of the village moneylenders and co-operatives and banks and finance. The burden of this debt has been passed one from generation to generation in much as the principal and interest went on increasing. Nearly 65 per cent of population is still living in rural areas with agriculture as its main occupation. Debt has been depicted as a millstone round the neck of the Indian farmer and it also states that the Indian farmer lives in debt and dies in debt. Average of per capita debt for the entire rural population has increased by 27 per cent for agricultural labourers and 36 per cent for farmers.

Sugar cane is a major crop of the village Chinchali. We find about 85% of sugar cane cultivable land. It needs longer investment and expenditure. So for sugar cane cultivation majority of sugar cane growers have taken the loans from institutional and non-intuitional agencies. The sugar cane growers are unable to repay the loans due to continuous crop failure because of flood since three years. So crop failure, higher value of assets, lockout and sickness of co-operative sugar factories and meagre price paid by factories are major reasons for indebtedness of sugar cane growers. Hence, the present study made an attempt to study indebtedness of sugar cane growers of Chinchali village in Belgaum district of Karnataka State.

The agrarian crisis that has rampaged throughout rural India .for the few years has been associated very clearly with the rising burden of indebtedness among farmers. Over 275 farmers have taken their lives between April 1 and September 19 this year in the state. Not only drought prone areas but even irrigated tracts are also experiencing the incidence of suicides. Three years of inadequate rainfall, consequent crop losses due to flood, the fall in price buying the sugar cane by factories and import of sugar from foreign countries are major reasons for increasing indebtedness in the district of Belgaum. Thirteen suicides took place in this district which is less than other districts. But in future the growing indebtedness of sugar cane growers will increase the rate of suicides of sugar cane growers. Therefore, it is necessary to take suitable measures to reduce the indebtedness of sugar cane growers to avoid the suicides. Hence, this present study made an attempt to give the suitable measures to reduce the indebtedness of sugar cane growers.

A number of studies have been undertaken to explain indebtedness. They vary not only in style and temper but also in their major findings. A few important works deserve for reference and review.

**Chandrasekhar C.P. and Ghosh Jayati (2003)** study, deals with a recent report of NSSO on the indebtedness of farmer households. The report provides important information on the extent and nature of cultivation debt. C.P. Chandrasekhar and Ghosh Jayati consider the main result of

[1] Lecturer in Sociology, Sivaji University, Solapur.

[2] Lecturer in Political Science, Walchand College of Arts and Science, Solapur.

this survey and the implications for policy. The major finding of this survey is that the agrarian crisis that has rampaged through Rural India for the past few years has been associated very clearly with the rising burden of indebtedness among farmers.

**P.G.K. Panikar in** his article **'The Burden of Debt in Indian Agriculture'** gave the positive aspects of debt. He said that most writers tend to depict the debt burden as a millstone round the neck of the Indian farmer. But the simple truth that borrowing is not a unique feature of Indian farming has not been adequately appreciated that credit lubricates the engine of production and heightens its efficiency. Author concluded that the attitude of most authors on the subject in this country has been unduly conservative. Hence, author made an attempt to re-examine the question of agrarian debt in India.

**Dhoot Vikas's (2007)** article **"Credit alone can't check rural indebtedness"** deals with measurers that are enough to tackle the problem of rising indebtedness in rural India. He said that credit measures alone will not be enough to tackle the problem of rising indebtedness in rural India improving access to education, health and employment in rural India is an important as improving credit delivery.

**Mohanty Siba Sankar (2007)** in his article entitled with **'An obstacle for Development'** gave major causes for rising indebtedness of Indian farmers. The indebtedness of Indian farmers rose markedly in the 1990's following the turnaround by successive Indian governments to market reforms and the opening up of the Indian economy to foreign investors.

**Parvathi Menon's(2004)** paper entitled with **"From debt to Death"** deals with the major causes of suicides of farmers in Karnataka crop losses caused by three successive years of inadequate rainfall and the diminishing presence of institutional credit force a large number of Karnataka farmers into the debt trap. Some of them choose death as a way-out.

**Dillon G.S. (1999)** paper **'Post-harvest measures to check rural indebtedness'** gave suitable measures to reduce the rural indebtedness. Post-Harvest measures or "value addition" to crops (e.g cereals, pulses, oilseeds, vegetables, flowers, mushroom, milk, eggs and honey) so as to increase the share of profits of the farming community if undertaken can help in the reduction of rural indebtedness.

**Mahajan Vijay (2006)** in his article tries to understand the problem of credit to small farmers and identify possible measures. Moneylenders in India are as old as its villages, agricultural credit co-operative to back a century, commercial banks have been involved in agricultural loans for nearly 30 years old, and reforms in the banking system were triggered a decade back. Yet credit flow to small farmers has remained far below the needs both for crop cultivation and farm equipment as compared to the potential demand. The widespread discontent among farmers has manifested itself in form of a mass voting incumbent government also individual acts of despair such as farmers committing suicide, particularly in Andhra Pradesh.

**Jeromi P.D. (2007)** article entitled with **'Farmers' Indebtedness and Suicides: Impact of Agricultural Trade Liberalization in Kerala"** examines the factors leading to the farm crisis, the rise in indebtedness and various dimensions of farmers' suicide.

By observing many studies we come to the conclusion that there is positive relationship between indebtedness and farmers' suicide. Indebtedness, a huge and growing burden in the rural countryside is the single most conspicuous reason for the mounting number of suicides in the State of Karnataka.

**Objectives**

Following are the major objectives of the present study.

- To find major causes for growing indebtedness of sugar cane growers.
- To understand extent, sources and purposes of indebtedness of sugar cane growers.
- To devise possible measures to reduce indebtedness of sugar cane growers.

**Methodology**

For the present study qualitative methodologies are employed. A case study method is used focusing on a single village, Chinchali, Belgaum District of Karnataka State.

**Source of Data**

Primary as well as secondary data are collected for study. Primary data are collected through interview schedule and observation techniques.

The secondary sources are collected from the books, journals and internet supplementing the village records, co-operatives and banks.

**Area of Study**

A single Chinchali village of Belgaum district of Karnataka State is selected as study area for present study. It is located in North-West part of the Karnataka State.

**Sampling**

For present study both purposive and simple random samplings have been used. A single Chinchali village of Belgaum district of Karnataka State is selected purposefully. With the help of village record total households of village are listed. Out of total households, there are 1500 households of agrarian households listed. Out of 1500 households, 10% households are taken for study, which covers 150 households.

**Extent of Indebtedness**

Nearly half (48.6%) of the farmers' households were reported to be indebted. The incidence of indebtedness was highest in Andhra Pradesh, where more than four-fifths of surveyed farmers were in debt followed by Tamil Nadu with nearly three – fourths of farmers' households reporting indebtedness. 65% of Karnataka and 61% farmers in Maharashtra households were reported to be indebted. Total 68.38% of total households of farmers are indebted in village Chinchali.

**Table No.1**

**Landholding Size of Sample Households of Sugar cane Growers**

| Landholding | Households | Percentage |
|---|---|---|
| Below 2.5 acres | 60 | 40.00% |
| 2.6 to 5 acres | 50 | 33.34% |
| 5.1 to 25 acres | 40 | 26.00% |
| Total | 150 | 26.00% |

Table No: 1 represents the landholding size of sample households of sugar cane growers in Chinchali village out of total respondents majority of respondents, i.e. (40%) have landholding size below 2.5 acres.

**Use Fertilizers, seeds and manures:** Sugar cane requires fertilizers and manures in more proportion as compared to the other crops such as maize average 897.29 kg chemical fertilizer and 6 to 8 trolley organic fertilizer is used. Average expenditure for sugar cane cultivation requires including all expenditure is 16537 rupees per acre. Average production is 50 tons per acre.

**Table No. 2**

**Income Level of Sample Households of Sugar cane Growers**

| Income | Households | Percentage |
|---|---|---|
| Below 25,000/ - | 77 | 35.33% |
| 25,000/- to 50,000/- | 23 | 16.00% |
| 50,000/- to 75,000/- | 25 | 6.00% |
| 75,000/- to 1 Lakh | 15 | 11.33% |
| Above 1 Lakh | 10 | 5.33% |

Table No. 2 represents income level of sample household. Out of total respondents 77 (35.33%) of respondents have income.

**Table No. 3**

**Amount of Loan of Sample Households of Sugar cane Grower**

| Amount of loan (₹) | Households | Percentage |
|---|---|---|
| Below 25,000 | 9 | 6.00 |
| 25,001 to 50,000 | 24 | 16.00 |
| 50,001 to 75,000 | 53 | 35.33 |
| 75,001 to 1 Lakh | 17 | 11.33 |
| Above 1 Lakh | 8 | 5.33 |
| Total | 150 | 100 |

Table No. 3 represents the amount of loan taken by sample households of sugar cane growers out of total respondents majority of respondents, i.e., 53 (35.33%) have taken loans of 50,001 to 75,000 rupees.

**Sources of Credit**: Moneylenders have emerged as the most significant sources of credit for farmers with 29 per cent accessing this source. However institutional sources still remain significant with more than half of farmers accessing government, co-operative societies and banks taken together (NSSO report:2003)

In the case of Chinchali farmer households, most borrowed more from formal institutional agencies than informal agencies.

**Table No. 4**

**Sources of Sample Households of Sugar cane**

| Sources | Households | Percentage |
|---|---|---|
| Moneylenders | 28 | 18.6 |
| Banks | 46 | 44.0 |
| Co-operatives | 23 | 28.6 |
| Friends and Relatives | 4 | 3.3 |
| Other (Beshi and SHGS) | 9 | 5.3 |
| | 150 | 100 |

Table No. 4 represents the sources of credit. Majority of respondents have taken from institutional agencies such as banks and co-operatives.

**Purposes:** It is significant that the dominant cause for taking loans was found to be for productive purposes. The two most important purposes of taking loans were stated to be 'Capital expenditure in farm business, Current Expenditure' in farm business at the all India level. In Karnataka where 68.2 per cent of loans were taken for the productive investment on farms, whether in the form of capital or current expenditure. (NSSO report: 2003).

**Table No. 5**

**Purposes of Loan**

| Purposes | Households | Percentage |
|---|---|---|
| Capital expenditure in farm business | 55 | 36.6 |
| Current expenditure in farm business | 35 | 23.3 |
| Expenditure for non-farm business | 15 | 10.00 |
| Consumption expenditure | 20 | 16.6 |
| Marriages and ceremonies | 10 | 6.6 |
| Education | 5 | 3.3 |
| Medical expenses | 7 | 4.6 |
| Medical expenses | 3 | 2.0 |
| Other | 150 | 100 |

Table No. 4 represents the purposes of loan that is taken by sample households. Out of total respondents, majority of respondents, i.e., 36.6% have taken loan for capital expenditure in farm business.

**Causes**

Several factors contribute to raise rural indebtedness. Some of them are as follows

1. The report of NSSO have suggested that the decline in access to institutional credit has driven more farmers back to potentially more exploitative usurious relations with traditional money lenders or input dealers higher interest rates charged by these informal sources. (NSSO report : 2003)
2. A steady decline in infrastructure investment, droughts, floods and insects infection have contributed to the growth of rural social misery.

3. Due to deregulation, the quality of the seeds has declined.
4. Farmers are getting proper market to sell their agricultural production.
5. Several agricultural commodities have seen a fall in prices in the last three years owing to imports.
6. Cost of cultivation has been raised.
7. Interest rates of moneylenders range from 30 – 50 per cent a year and go upto 60 per cent for short-term loans.
8. Lack of underemployment and employment of rural people.
9. Lack of alternatives for rural people other than agriculture.
10. Indian peasants have faced greater competition due to deregulation of agricultural markets. In 1999, the Bharatiya Janata Party led Indian Federal Government signed pact with the United States to grant US producers import permission for 1,429 agricultural products that were previously prevented from entering the local market. The credit facilities extended by the co-operative societies and formal agencies hardly benefit the small farmers. (Mohanty :1999)
11. The negative impact of globalization on agriculture through the World Trade Organization regime has been already compounded by the rural indebtedness.

Crop failure due to flood and fall in the prices of sugar are major factors for raising the indebtedness of sugar cane growers in the last three years in village Chinchali. The price at which sugar factories are buying has fallen from ₹ 1,500/- per quintal in the year 1992 to ₹ 800/- per quintal. V. Ashok, State Secretary of the Karnataka Rajya Raitha Sangh, told, to "Frontline", the government is now importing sugar at the landed price of ₹ 900/- per quintal which is less than our cost production. (Parvathi Menon: 2007).

**Effects**

Indebtedness, a huge and growing burden in the rural countryside, mostly among the poor farmers is the single most conspicuous reason for the mounting numbers of suicide in the State of Karnataka. Therefore raising indebtedness of sugar cane growers will lead to the suicide of sugar cane growers in the future.

**Measures**

1. The rural debt situation especially for cultivators is grim and requires urgent policy attention. A beginning has been made by UPA Government in terms of increasing the provision of institutional credit to farmers. It is necessary to confront the problems currently affecting the viability of cultivation.
2. Policy intervention must be directed in case of undesirable input use, constantly increasing input costs, volatile crop prices and difficulties in accessing markets.
3. The Govt. agencies must help them in overcoming the problems.
4. It is necessary for the government to undertake surveys periodically related to indebtedness to get the clear picture and feels that rescheduling of agricultural loans is imperative for prompt relief and implementing the "Rural Indebtedness Relief Act".
5. Claiming of outstanding crop loans including interest for small and marginal farmers and postponement of the recovery of the loans for five years in other areas. Fresh loan

should be given in tune with landholding and increased scale of finance to small and marginal farmers.

6. Economic reforms which are implemented by the previous government as the part of the globalization process responsible for crisis in farm sectors. This should be reduced.
7. Agricultural research must be focused on the requirements of these farmers who are in need of support from government.
8. Farmers' indebtedness has many humanitarian and financial implications. Sickness in co-operative credit institutions combined with the unsatisfactory performance of commercial banks has pushed rural indebtedness. This should be reduced.
9. The government has also taken action to supply good quality seeds to farmers at subsidized rates. A medical insurance scheme has been introduced for the farmers and agricultural labourers.
10. Kisan Credit facilities have been extended to all farmers in the State.
11. Such as Self Help Groups, Raythu Mitra Groups (RMGs), through which credit will be extended to farmers.
12. Agricultural diversification is needed.
13. Rather than commercial crops, it is needed to cultivate cereals, pulses, oilseeds, vegetables, flowers and mushroom.
14. To strengthen the rural economy through linking rural production with industry.
15. Cost free skilled oriented education should be provided for minor children and older children should be provided suitable employment.
16. Taking the path of contract farming, between farmers and agri-business firms. (Singh:2004)
17. Appointing the committee to study the problems of farmers.
18. Agro based industrial units should be established.
19. Organizing the farmers themselves to carry out the production, processing and marketing. Elimination of middle man must be made.
20. Marriages of sons and daughters of farmers are conducted free of cost with the help of Gram Panchayat at local level.
21. Primary Health Centre should provide medical service without failing.
22. Lottery, wine shops and other anti-social activities should be controlled.
23. Knowledge based education should be provided.
24. Many farmers spend lot of time and energy to settle their land disputes.
25. Land dispute committee is established under the supervision of the government. Government lawyers' service should be provided to farmers free of cost.
26. Transport facilities should be made available to sell their agricultural goods to the market.
27. To avail of irrigation facilities for marginal farmers as well as small farmers too at low cost.
28. Implementing all the schemes and programme honestly. Real beneficiaries must be found out. Policy implementations need not be influenced by caste, creed and political parties. Increase the farmer-agricultural officer communication.

## Conclusion

Indebtedness, a huge and growing burden in the rural countryside, particularly among the poor farmers is the single factor for agrarian crisis. So rising indebtedness of sugar cane growers in the last years has lead to suicides of the growers. Hence, proper measures should be undertaken to reduce the burden of indebtedness.

## References

Chandershekar C.P. and Ghosh Jayati (2003).'The Burden of Farmers Debt','National News-paper', The Hindu'.

Dhillon G.S. (1999), 'Post Harvest Measures to Check Rural Indebtedness, Journal of Agricultural Tribune.

Dhoot Vikas (2007), 'Credit Alone Cant Check Rural Indebtedness'

Gill Anita and Singh Lakhwinder ( 2006 ), 'Farmers' Suicides and Response of Public Policy', 'Evidence Diagnosis and Alternatives from Punjab', Journal of Economic and Political Weekly.

http://countercurrent.org

Jeromi P.D. (2005), Agricultural Sector in Kerala and Issues Relating to Credit', RBI Staff studies (DEAP), Reserve Bank of India.

Jeromi (2007), 'Farmers Indebtedness and Suicides, Impact of Agricultural Trade Liberalization in Kerala, Journal of Economic and Political Weekly.

Kurup. K.K. (2005), 'Wayanad Karshika Prathisandhi (Agricultural Crisis in Wayanad) , Keraleeya Smarak Samithi, Kozhikode.

Klonner Stephan (2007), Suicide Seeds or Rainfall Shocks?, An analysis of farmers' suicides in North India, International studies at Cornell University.

Mahajan Vijay (2006), Deregulation Rural Credit, Journal of Central Chronicle, Cornell University.

Menon Parvathi, 'From Debt To Death' (2004), National Newspaper, 'The Hindu'.

Mohanty. B.B, Shroff (2004), Farmers' Suicides in Maharashtra, Journal of Economic and Political Weekly.

Mohanty, Sarkar Siba, (2007), Rural Indebtedness in India, An Obstacle for the Development NSSO ( 2005 ), Situation Assessment Survey of Farmers', Indebtedness of Farmers Households NSS 59th Round (Janauary – December 2003, Report No. 498 {58/33/1}, Government of India.

(2006 a), household Borrowings and Repayments in India 2002 – 2003. All India Debt and Investment Survey, 59th Round, Report No. 502, Government of India.

Panikar P.G. (2006), The Burden of Debt in Indian Agriculture, University of Kerala.

Ramoo S.K., 2005, 'Many Factors Behind Farmers' Suicide, National Newspaper, 'The Hindu'.

Speech of Shri. Dharam Singh, Chief Minister of Karnataka (2005), Government of Karnataka.

Shreyas (200 ), Agricultural Crisis and Debt, Suicide in Wayanad, Sultan Bathery, Wayanad, Kerala.

CHAPTER

# SAMPLING TECHNIQUES

## *Structure*

It is not possible to survey the population. It may be time costly or time consuming. Sampling is the process of selecting units (e.g., people, organizations) from a population of interest so that by studying the sample we may fairly generalize our results back to the population from which they were chosen. Let's begin by covering some of the key terms in sampling like "population" and "sampling frame." Then, because some types of sampling rely upon quantitative models, we'll talk about some of the statistical terms used in sampling. Finally, we'll discuss the major distinction between probability and non-probability sampling methods and work through the major types in each.

## 7.1 Sampling Terminology

The major question that motivates sampling in the first place is generalization.

In most research projects we are interested in more than just the people who directly participate in our study. We would like to be able to talk in general terms and not be confined only to the people who are in our study. However, in applied research, there are times when we aren't very concerned about generalizing. It may just be evaluating a programme in a local agency and we don't care whether the programme would work with other people in other places and at other times. In that case, sampling and generalizing may not be of interest. In other cases, we would really like to be able to generalize almost universally. When psychologists do research, they are often interested in developing theories that would hold for all humans. But in most applied social research, we are interested in generalizing to specific groups.

### Population

The group, you wish to generalize to, is often called the **population** in our study. Sample is taken from the group you are interested in generalizing to. Let's imagine that you wish to generalize to urban homeless males between the ages of 20 and 30 in the Karnataka. If that is the population of interest, you are likely to have a tough time to develop a reasonable sampling plan. You are probably not going to find an accurate listing of this population, and even if you did, you would almost certainly not be able to mount a national sample across hundreds of urban areas. So we probably should make a distinction between the population you would like to generalize to, and the population that will be accessible to you. We'll call the former the **theoretical population** and the latter the **accessible population**. In this example, the accessible population may be homeless males between the ages of 30 and 50 in six selected urban areas across the Karnataka.

### Sampling Frame

Once you've identified the theoretical and accessible populations, you have to do one more thing before you can actually draw a sample; you have to get a list of the members of the accessible population. (Or, you have to spell out in detail how you will contact them to assure representativeness). The listing of the accessible population from which you'll draw your sample is called the **sampling frame**. If you are doing a phone survey and selecting names from the telephone directory, the directory is your sampling frame. That wouldn't be a great way to sample because significant sub-portions of the population either don't have a phone or have moved in or out of the area since the last book was printed. Notice that in this case, you may identify the area code and draw a sample simply by randomly dialling numbers. In this case, the sampling frame is not a list per se, but is rather a procedure that you follow as the actual basis for sampling.

## Sample

Finally, you actually draw your sample using one of the many sampling procedures. The **sample** is the group of people who you select to be in your study. The group that actually completes your study is a sub-sample of the sample; it doesn't include non-respondents or dropouts.

People often confuse what is meant by random selection with the idea of random assignment. Randomness means given equal chance for selection, i.e., probability of being selected as sample is equal. **Random *selection*** is how you draw the sample of people for your study from a population. **Random *assignment*** is how you assign the sample that you draw to different groups or treatments in your study.

It is possible to have *both* random selection and assignment in a study. Let's say you drew a random sample of 100 clients from a population list of 1000 current clients of your organization. That is random sampling. Now, let's say you randomly assign 50 of these clients to get some new additional treatment and the other 50 to be controls. That's random assignment.

It is also possible to have *only one of these* (random selection or random assignment) but not the other in a study. For instance, if you do not randomly draw the 100 cases from your list of 1000 but instead just take the first 100 on the list, you do not have random selection. But you could still randomly assign this non-random sample to treatment versus control. Or, you could randomly select 100 from your list of 1000 and then non-randomly (haphazardly) assign them to treatment or control.

Sometimes there is *neither* random selection nor random assignment. In a typical non-equivalent groups design in education you may non-randomly choose two 5th grade classes for your study. This is non-random selection. Then, you may arbitrarily assign one to get the new educational programme and the other to be the control. This is non-random (or non-equivalent) assignment.

Random selection is related to sampling. Therefore, it is most related to the external validity (or generalizability) of your results. We would randomly sample so that our research participants better represent the larger group from which they are drawn. **Random assignment is most related to design.** In fact, when we randomly assign participants to treatments we have, by definition, an experimental design. Therefore, **random assignment is most related to internal validity**. We randomly assign in order to help assure that our treatment groups are similar to each other (i.e., equivalent) prior to the treatment.

## Response

Units of sample supply us with one or more responses. In this sense, a response is a specific measurement value that a sampling unit supplies. For instance a person is asked to choose anything from 1 to 5 and chooses 4 it is a response of '4'.

## Statistics

When we look across the responses that we get for our entire sample, we use a **statistic**. There are a wide variety of statistics we can use - mean, median, mode, and so on.

## Parameter

If you measure the entire population and calculate a value like a mean or average, we don't refer to this as a statistic, we call it a parameter of the population. So statistics is for sample and parameter is for population.

## The Sampling Distribution

Sample statistic is calculated to estimate population parameter. In between the two is sampling distribution. Imagine that instead of just taking a single sample like we do in a typical study, you took three independent samples of the same population. And furthermore, imagine that for each of your three samples, you collected a single response and computed a single statistic, say, mean of the response. Even though all three samples came from the same population, you wouldn't expect to get the exact same statistic from each. They will differ slightly just due to the random or to the natural fluctuations or vagaries of drawing a sample. But you would expect that all three samples would yield a similar statistical estimate because they were drawn from the same population. Imagine that you get an infinite number of samples from the same population and compute the average for each one. If you plot them on a histogram or bar graph you should find that most of them converge on the same central value and that you get fewer and fewer samples that have averages farther away up or down from that central value. In other words, the bar graph will be well described by the bell curve shape that is an indication of a "normal" distribution in statistics. **The distribution of an infinite number of samples of the same size from a population is known as the sampling distribution.** Sampling distribution is rarely constructed.

(Here it is required to explain the difference between frequency and distribution. Frequency of an event is raw data and directly written for the event; however distribution is calculated frequency written for the event.)

When we keep the sampling distribution in mind, we realize that while the statistic we got from our sample is probably near the centre of the sampling distribution (because most of the samples would be there) we could have gotten one of the extreme samples just by the luck of the draw. If we take the average of the sampling distribution — the average of the averages of an infinite number of samples — we would be much closer to the true population average - the parameter of interest. So the average of the sampling distribution is essentially equivalent to the parameter. The standard deviation of the sampling distribution tells us something about how different samples would be distributed. In statistics it is referred to as the standard error. The standard error is the spread of the averages around the average of averages in a sampling distribution.

## Sampling Error

In sampling contexts, the standard error is called **sampling error**. Sampling error gives us some idea of the precision of our statistical estimate. A low sampling error means that we have relatively less variability or range in the sampling distribution. The standard error is also related to the sample size. The greater your sample size, the smaller the standard error. The greater the sample size, the closer your sample is to the actual population itself. If you take a sample that consists of the entire population you actually have no sampling error because you don't have a sample, you have the entire population. In that case, the mean you estimate is the parameter.

## Thumb Rule of Confidence Level

There is a general rule that applies whenever we have a normal or bell-shaped distribution. Start with the average, the centre of the distribution. If you go up and down (i.e., left and right) one standard unit, you will include approximately 68% of the cases in the distribution (i.e., 68% of the area under the curve). If you go up and down two standard units, you will include approximately 95% of the cases. And if you go plus-and-minus three standard units, you will include about 99% of the cases. The same rule holds for both types of distributions, i.e., the raw data and sampling distributions.

At this point, you should appreciate that sampling is a difficult multi-step process and that there are lots of places you can go wrong. In fact, as we move from each step to the next in identifying a sample, there is the possibility of introducing systematic error or **bias**. For instance, even if you are able to identify perfectly the population of interest, you may not have access to all of them. And even if you do, you may not have a complete and accurate enumeration or sampling frame from which to select. And, even if you do, you may not draw the sample correctly or accurately. And, even if you do, they may not all come and they may not all stay. (Do you want to consult Jolly!).

## 7.2 Sampling Methods

In most surveys, access to the entire population is nearly impossible; however, the results from a survey with a carefully selected sample will reflect extremely close results as if provided by the population.

Sampling method therefore is a very important part of the research process. If you have surveyed using an appropriate sampling technique, you can be confident that your results will be generalised to the population in question. If the samples were biased in any way, for example, in a survey for older and younger people, if the selection technique gives older people more of a chance of selection than younger people, it will be inadvisable to make generalizations from the findings.

There are essentiality two types of sampling methods: probability and non-probability sampling.

### (a) Probability Sampling Methods

Probability or random sampling gives all members of the population a known chance of being selected for inclusion in the sample and this does not depend upon previous events in the selection process. In other words, the selection of individuals does not affect the chance of anyone else in the population being selected.

Many statistical techniques assume that a sample was selected on a random basis. There are four basic types of random sampling techniques:

#### (1) Simple Random Sampling

This is the ideal choice as it is a 'perfect' random method. Using this method, individuals are randomly selected from a list of the population and every single individual has an equal chance of selection. This method is ideal, but if it cannot be adopted, and any one of the following alternatives may be chosen if any shortfall in accuracy.

#### (2) Systematic Sampling

Systematic sampling is a frequently used variant of simple random sampling. When performing systematic sampling, every element from the list is selected (this is referred to as the sample interval) from a randomly selected starting point. For example, if we have a listed population of 6000 members and wish to draw a sample of 2000, we would select every 30$^{th}$ (6000 divided by 200) person from the list. In practice, we would randomly select a number between 1 and 30 to act as our starting point.

The one potential problem with this method of sampling concerns the arrangement of elements in the list? If the list is arranged in any kind of order, e.g., if every 30$^{th}$ house is smaller than the others from which the sample is being recruited, there is a possibility that the sample produced could be seriously biased.

### (3) Stratified Sampling

Stratified sampling is a variant on simple random and systematic methods and is used when there are a number of distinct sub-groups, within each of which it is required that there is full representation. A stratified sample is constructed by classifying the population in sub-populations (or strata), based on some well-known characteristics of the population, such as age, gender or socio-economic status. The selection of elements is then made separately from within each stratum, usually by random or systematic sampling methods.

Stratified sampling methods also come in two types – proportionate and disproportionate.

In proportionate sampling, the strata sample sizes are made proportional to the strata population sizes. For example, if the first strata is made up of males, then as there are around 50% of males in the Karnataka population, the male strata will need to represent around 50% of the total sample.

In disproportionate methods, the strata are not sampled according to the population sizes, but higher proportions are selected from some groups and not others. This technique is typically used in a number of distinct situations:

The costs of collecting data may differ from sub-group to sub-group.

We may require more cases in some groups if estimations of population values are likely to be harder to make, i.e., the larger the sample size (up to certain limits); the more accurate any estimation is likely to be.

We expect different response rates from different groups of people. Therefore, the less co-operative groups may be 'over-sampled' to compensate.

### (4) Cluster or Multi-stage Sampling

Cluster sampling is a frequently-used, and usually more practical, random sampling method. It is particularly useful in situations for which no list of the elements within a population is available and therefore cannot be selected directly. As this form of sampling is conducted by randomly selecting sub-groups of the population, possibly in several stages, it should produce results equivalent to a simple random sample.

The sample is generally done by first sampling at the higher level(s) e.g. randomly sampled countries, then sampling from subsequent levels in turn, e.g., within the selected countries sample counties, then within those post-codes, then within those households, until the final stage is reached, at which point the sampling is done in a simple random manner, e.g., sampling people within the selected households. The 'levels' in questions are defined by sub-groups into which it is appropriate to subdivide your population.

Cluster samples are generally used if:

- No list of the population exists.
- Well-defined clusters, which will often be geographic areas, exist.
- A reasonable estimate of the number of elements in each level of clustering can be made.
- Often the total sample size must be fairly large to enable cluster sampling to be used effectively.

### (b) Non-probability Sampling Methods

Non-probability sampling procedures are much less desirable, as they will almost certainly contain sampling biases. Unfortunately, in some circumstances such methods are unavoidable.

In a Market Research context, the most frequently-adopted form of non-probability sampling is known as quota sampling. In some ways this is similar to cluster sampling in that it requires the definition of key sub-groups. The main difference lies in the fact that quotas (i.e., the amount of people to be surveyed) within sub-groups are set beforehand (e.g., 25% of 16-24 yr olds, 30% of 25-34 yr olds, 20% of 35-55 yr olds, and 25% of 56+ yr olds) usually proportions are set to match known population distributions. Interviewers then select respondents according to these criteria rather than at random. Grouping is subjective in nature. It means that only about a proportion of the population has a chance of being selected in a typical quota sampling strategy.

If you are forced into using a non-random method, you must be extremely careful when drawing conclusions. You should always be honest about the sampling technique used and that a non-random approach will probably mean that biases are present within the data. In order to convert the sample to be representative of the true population, you may want to use weighting techniques.

The importance of sampling should not be underestimated, as it determines to whom the results of your research will be applicable. It is important, therefore to give full consideration to the sampling strategy to be used and to select the most appropriate. Only when you have no choice should a non-random method be used.

All too often, researchers succumb to the temptation of generalizing their results to a much broader range of people than those from whom the data was originally gathered. This is poor practice and you should always aim to adopt an appropriate sampling technique. It is better to take advice of experts.

## 7.3 Calculating a Sample Size

What should be the size of sample is a frequently asked question. It is an important question, although unfortunately there is no single answer. In general, the larger the sample size, the more closely your sample data will match that with the population. However in practice, you need to work out how many responses will give you sufficient precision at an affordable cost.

Calculation of an appropriate sample size depends upon a number of factors unique to each survey and it is down to you to make the decision regarding these factors. The three most important are:

- How accurate you wish to be?
- How much confident you are in the results to be?
- What budget you have available?

The temptation is to say all should be as high as possible. The problem is that an increase in either accuracy or confidence (or both) will always require a larger sample and higher budget. Therefore a compromise must be reached and you must work out the degree of inaccuracy and confidence you are prepared to accept.

There are two types of figures that you may wish to estimate in your Market Research project: values such as mean income, mean height, etc., and proportions (the percentage of people who intend to vote for party X). There are slightly different sample size calculations for each:

### 7.3.1 Solved Examples

**For a mean**

The required formula is:

$s = (z/e)^2$

***Where:***

s = the sample size

z = a number relating to the degree of confidence you wish to have in the result. Z is normal variate, its values are available in statistical tables. However as already stated in rule of thumb, 95% confidence is most frequently used and accepted. The value of 'z' should be 2.58 for 99% confidence, 1.96 for 95% confidence, 1.64 for 90% confidence and 1.28 for 80% confidence.

e = the error you are prepared to accept, measured as a proportion of the standard deviation (accuracy)

### Solved Example S-1

Imagine we are estimating mean income, and wish to know what sample size to aim for so that we can be 95% confident in the result. Assuming that we are prepared to accept an error of 10% of the population standard deviation (say, during previous research the standard deviation of income was 8000 and now we are prepared to accept an error of 800 (10%)), we would do the following calculation:

s = (1.96 / 0.1)2

Therefore s = **384.16**

In other words, 385 people should be sampled to meet our criterion.

Because we interviewed a sample and not the whole population (if we had done this we could be 100% confident in our results), we have to be prepared to be less confident and because we based our sample size calculation on the 95% confidence level, we can be confident that amongst the whole population there is a 95% chance that the mean is inside our acceptable error limit. There is of course a 5% chance that the measure is outside this limit. If we wanted to be more confident, we would base our sample size calculation on a 99% confidence level and if we were prepared to accept a lower level of confidence, we would base our calculation on the 90% confidence level.

**For a proportion**

Although we are doing the same thing here, the formula is different:

$s = (z^2(p(1-p))/ e2$

***Where:***

s = the sample size

z = the normal variate for your confidence level or probability you wish to have in your results

p = an estimate of the proportion of people falling into the group in which you are interested in the population

e = the proportion of error we are prepared to accept

## Solved Example S-2

Imagine we are attempting to assess the percentage of voters who will vote for a candidate X. If we assume that we wish to be 99% confident of the result, i.e., z = 2.85 and that we will allow for errors in the region of +/-3%, i.e., e = 0.03. But in terms of an estimate of the proportion of the population who would vote for the candidate (p), if a previous survey had been carried out, we could use the percentage from that survey as an estimate. However, if this were the first survey, we would assume that 50% (i.e., p = 0.05) of people would vote for candidate X and 50% would not. Choosing 50% will provide the most conservative estimate of sample size. If the true percentage were 10%, we will still have an accurate estimate; we will simply have sampled more people than was absolutely necessary. The reverse situation, not having enough data to make reliable estimates, is much less desirable.

$s = 2.58^2(0.5*0.5)/ 0.032$

Therefore **s = 1,849**

This is rather a large sample as it was necessary because we wanted to be 99% sure of the result and desired a very narrow (+/–3%) margin of error. It does, however reveal why many political polls tend to interview between 1,000 and 2,000 people.

## Calculating a Sampling Error

In estimating the accuracy of a sample, there are two critical variables; the size of the sample and the measure being taken. A common mistake about sample size is to assume that accuracy is determined by the proportion of a population included in a sample (e.g., 10% of a population). That is not the case when there is a large population — a sample of 500 drawn from a population of one million will be as accurate as a sample of 500 from a population of five million (assuming both are truly random samples of the respective populations).

The relationship between sampling error, a percentage measure and a sample size can be expressed as a formula.

e = z"(p%(100-p%))/" s

***Where:***

e = sampling error (the proportion of error we are prepared to accept)

s = the sample size

z = the number relating to the degree of confidence you wish to have in the result

p = an estimate of the proportion of people falling into the group in which you are interested in the population.

## Solved Example S-3

Calculate the sample error when sample size is 500, a measure of 20% is aware of a brand (p), at the 95% confidence level.

e = 1.96"(20(80))/ " 500 = 3.5

This means, that based on a sample of 500 we can be 95% sure that the true measure (e.g. of brand awareness) among the whole population from which the sample was drawn will be within +/–3.5% of 20%, i.e., between 16.5% and 23.5%.

## Proportionate Stratified Sampling

### Solved Example S-4

A survey is to be conducted to analyse the behaviour of consumers who make their purchases from general stores situated in a small town. It is planned to conduct stratified sampling for this study. So, the population which consists of different stores is divided into three strata, viz., small, medium and large malls. The total number of stores in the town is 200. The number of stores in the three categories, viz., small, medium, and large are 20, 50 and 130, respectively. If the sample size is 20, determine the number of stores to be sampled from each category.

**Solution:**

We have

Total number of stores in the city, N = 200

Number of small stores, $N_1$ = 20

Number of medium, $N_2$ = 50

Number of large stores, $N_3$ = 130

Total sample size, $n$ = 20

The relationship of proportional stratified sampling is as follows:

$$\frac{n_1}{N_1} = \frac{n_2}{N_2} = \frac{n_3}{N_3} = \frac{n}{N}$$

where $n_1$, $n_2$, $n_3$ are the numbers of stores to be sampled from small, medium and large category.

Therefore $\frac{n}{N}$ = 20/200 = 0.1

$n_1 = \frac{n}{N} * N_1$ = 0.1*20 = 2, similarly $n_2$ = 5 and $n_3$ = 13

## Disproportionalte Stratified Sampling

### Solved Example S-5

The health department of a town wants to study the standard of food quality in eating houses (restaurant). The analyst of the study divided the entire population of the restaurant into restaurants in rural locations, semi-urban locations and urban locations. He found more variation between restaurants in rural locations because of varying kitchen gadgets than the variation between restaurants in semi-urban locations. Same is the case between semi-urban locations and urban locations. The analyst prefers to use disproportionate stratified sampling in which the categories of location represent strata. The total number of restaurants in the town is 1200. The numbers of restaurants in the rural, semi-urban and urban locations are 500, 400 and 300, respectively. The variances of food quality standard of the restaurants in these locations on 0-10 scale are 49, 16 and 4, respectively. If the disproportionate stratified sampling is to be used with the sampling size of 90, determine the number of sampling units for each category of locations.

**Solution:**

As per the statement of the problem, the three different strata are as defined

*Stratum 1:* Locations of restaurant in rural areas.

*Stratum 2:* Locations of restaurant in semi-urban areas.

*Stratum 3:* Locations of restaurant in urban areas.

Size of the population, N = 1200

Size of the stratum 1, $N_1$ = 500

Size of the stratum 2, $N_2$ = 400

Size of the stratum 3, $N_3$ = 300

Variance of the stratum 1, $\sigma_1^2$ = 49

Variance of the stratum 2, $\sigma_2^2$ = 16

Variance of the stratum 3, $\sigma_3^2$ = 4

Sample size, $n$ = 90

**Details of Calculations of Sampling Units of Strata**

| Strata Number | Size of Strata | $q_i = N_i/N$ | $\sigma_i$ | C*D | $n_i = \frac{E}{\sum E} * n$ |
|---|---|---|---|---|---|
| A | B | C | D | E | F |
| 1 | 500 | 0.417 | 7 | 2.916 | 2.916/4.75*90 = 55 |
| 2 | 400 | 0.333 | 4 | 1.333 | 1.333/4.75*90 = 25 |
| 3 | 300 | 0.25 | 2 | .50 | 0.5/4.75*90 = 10 |
| Total | 1200 | | | 4.75 | |

Hence, sample size from each stratum is 55, 25 and 10.

## Sampling Distribution of Mean

**When population is infinite,**

the mean and variance of sampling distribution are given by the formulas

Mean = $\mu$ = same as population mean

Variance = $\frac{\sigma^2}{n}$ where n is the sample size

Standard deviation = $\sqrt{\frac{\sigma^2}{n}} = \frac{\sigma}{\sqrt{n}}$ = standard error of mean

The standard error of the mean represents the deviation of different sample means from the true mean because of sampling error. If this is less then sample means are closer to true mean i.e., population mean.

Standard normal statistic $Z\overline{X} = \dfrac{\overline{X} - \mu}{\sigma / \sqrt{n}}$

**When Population is Finite,**

If the sampling is done with a finite population of size N, we multiply the variance with (N-n)/(N-1) which is called finite population multiplier, because the variance of sampling distribution under finite population is same as under infinite population, except the additional multiplying factor.

Variance of infinite population is $\dfrac{\sigma 2}{n}$

Variance of finite population is $\dfrac{\sigma 2}{n} * \dfrac{N-n}{N-1}$

Standard error $= \dfrac{\sigma}{\sqrt{n}} * \sqrt{\dfrac{N-n}{N-1}}$

**Central Limit Theorem**

If $\overline{X}$ is the mean of a sample of size $n$ taken from a population with mean $\mu$ and known variance $\sigma^2$, then $Z_{\overline{X}}$. *which* is equal to $\dfrac{\overline{X}-\mu}{\sigma/\sqrt{n}}$ will be standard normal distribution when $n$ tends to infinity. This theorem is useful to sample a population when its distribution is unknown or non-normal..

Solved Example:

A non-normal distribution representing the number of trips performed by lorries per week in a coal field has a mean of 100 trips and variance of 121 trips. *A* random sample of 36 Lorries is taken from the non-normal population. What is the probability that the sample mean is greater than 105 trips.

We have

Sample size, $n = 36$

Population mean = 100 trips

Population variance, $\sigma^2 = 121$ trips

Population standard deviation, $\sigma = 11$ trips

Probability when ≥ *105* = ≥ = 2.73

Seeing the normal distribution table Probability (when Z = 2.73) = 0.9968

So when it is greater than 0.9968, shall be as 1 – 0.9968 = 0.0032

Which means probability that sample means shall be greater than 105 is 0.0032

## Other Solved Examples

### Solved Example S-6

The annual sales of dealers of a company follow normal distribution with its mean as ₹ 84 lakh. A random sample of 10 dealers of the company is taken from the normal population. The variance of the annual sales of these 10 dealers is ₹ 64 lakh. Find the probability that the mean annual sales of the sample is

(a) less than ₹ 80 lakh,

(b) more than ₹ 80 lakh.

Sample size, $n = 10$

Mean annual sales of the population, = ₹ 84 lakh

Variance of mean annual sales of the sample, $S^2 =$ ₹ 64 lakh

Standard deviation of the mean annual sales of the sample,

$S =$ ₹ 8 lakh

Please note here population mean is not given and sample variance ($S^2$) is taken as estimate of standard deviation of population variance. As the sample size is less than 30, we take t-stat (instead of Normal Variate Z) with n-1 DF i.e. 10-1 = 9 DF

When X<80 t-stat = (84-80)/(8/Ö10) = 1.58

By seeing the table of t-stat we can see this probability lies between 1.383 and 1.833 at .10 and .0.05significance level with one tail.

Therefore interpolation and extrapolation we get

Probability =0.90 + (1.58 – 1.383)/(1.833 – 1.58)* 0.05 = 0.94

Therefore the probability that X is less than 80 is 94%

(b) When X ñ 80 Probability is 1 – 0.94 = 0.06 i.e. 6%

### Solved Example S-7

The personnel manager of a company feels that 52% of the employees will have enhanced skill after attending the training programme if they are sponsored for an in-house training programme. A sample of records of 49 employees of the company, who attended the training programme. On skill development, reveals that only 24 of them are having enhanced skill after attending the training programme. Find the probability that the sample of employees who attended the training programme have enhanced their skill.

**Solution**: p = 0.52, q = 1-p = 1 – 0.52 = 0.48, $\bar{p}$ = 24/49 = 0.49

Standard deviation of proportion $\sigma_{\bar{p}} = \sqrt{\dfrac{pq}{n}}$ = 0.52*0.48/0.49 = 0.071

Probability = $p = \left( z \geq \dfrac{-p}{\sigma_{\bar{p}}} \right) = 1 - p \left( z \leq \dfrac{\bar{p} - p}{\sigma_{\bar{p}}} \right)$ 1 – P(Zd" [(0.49 – 0.52)/0.071])

= 1 – P (Z d" – 0.42) = 1-(1-P(Zd" 0.42) = .6628

The probabilities that the sample of employees who attended the training programme have enhanced their skills is 66.28%.

### Solved Examples S-8

The manager of a bank feels that 35% of branches will have enhanced yearly collection of deposits after introducing a hike in interest rate. Determine the sample size such that the mean proportion is within plus or minus 0.06 at a confidence level 90%.

*Solution.* Given $p = 0.35$, $q = 1 - p = 0.65$ and confidence level $(1 - \alpha) = 0.9$.

Therefore a= 0.10 and $\alpha/2 = 0.05$. Then, $Z_{\alpha/2} = 1.64$. For the 'desired accuracy, d = 0.06,

We get $n = (Z_{a/2}{}^2\, pq)/D^2 = \dfrac{1.64^2 * 0.35 * 065}{0.06^2} 170$

Therefore the sample size should be 170.

**(To understand the concept of confidence level and Z, students can read 'Testing of Hypothesis' chapter first)**

### 7.3.2 Problems for Practice

1. A random sample of size 49 is taken from a non-normal population. The mean and variance of the population are 30 and 49, respectively. What is the probability that the sample mean is (a) greater than 32, (b) less than 29 and (c) in between 28 and 32?
2. A random sample of size 85 is taken from an infinite normal population, which has its mean and variance as 100 and 225, respectively. What is the probability that the sample mean is greater than 125?
3. Determine the size of the sample for estimating the true weight of the serial containers for the universe with N = 5000, variance of weight is 4 ounce. Estimate should be within 0.8 ounces of the true average weight with 99% probability.
4. A random sample of size 70 is taken from an infinite normal population, which has its mean and variance as 200 and 750, respectively. What is the probability that the sample mean is greater than 205?
5. A random sample of size 66 is taken from a finite normal population of size 900, which has its mean and variance as 95 and 121, respectively. What is the probability that the sample mean is (a) lesser than 92, (b) greater than 98 and (c) in between 85 and 105?
6. A random sample of size 55 is taken from a non-normal population. The mean and variance of the population are 65 and 88, respectively. What is the probability that the sample mean is (a) greater than 70, (b) less than 64 and (c) between 55 and 65?
7. A random sample of 20 customers of a company is taken from a normal population. The mean of the annual purchases made by the customers of the population is ₹ 75 lakh. The variance of the purchases made by customers of the sample is ₹ 121 lakh. Find the probability that the mean annual sales of the sample is (a) less than ₹ 80 lakh, (b) more than ₹ 80 lakh.

8. Two independent samples of students of a programme under distance education are taken from normal populations with the same variance. The size and variance of the first sample are 10 and 104, respectively. The size and variance of marks second sample are 25 and 45, respectively. (a) What is the calculated *F* statistic? (b) What is the probability that the *F* ratio is more than the calculated *F* statistics?

9. Two independent samples of items of vendors are taken from normal population with the same variance. The size of the first sample and the second sample are 13 and 61 respectively. What is the probability that the variance of the first sample is more than 2.5 times that of the second sample?

10. The personnel manager of a company feels that the 45% of the employees will have enhanced skill after the training programme if they are sponsored for an in-housing training programme. A sample of records of 36 employees of the company who attended training programme on skill development reveals that only 25 of them are having enhanced skill after attending the training programme. Find the probability that the sample of who attended the training programme have enhanced their skill.

11. The internal diameter of shafts produced in a machine follows normal distribution with the variance of 225 mm. A random sample of 64 shafts taken from the production has its mean diameter of 100 mm. Find the confidence interval for the diameter of shafts at a significance level of 0.10.

12. The annual income of respondents follows normal distribution. A random sample of 15 respondents is taken. The mean and variance of the annual income of the respondents in the sample are ₹ 3 lakh and ₹ 9 lakh, respectively. Find the confidence interval for the annual income of the respondents at a significance level of 0.05.

13. The finance manager of a company feels that 55% of branches will have enhanced yearly collection of deposits after introducing a hike in interest rate. Determine the sample size such that the mean proportion is within plus or minus 0.05 at a confidence level of 90%.

14. From a packet containing iron nails, 1000 iron nails were taken at random and out of them 100 were found defective. Estimate the percentage of defective iron nails in the packet and assign limits within which the percentage probably lies.

15. A random sample of 200 measurements from an infinite population gave a mean value of 50 and standard deviation of 9. Determine the 95% confidence interval for the mean value of the population.

16. A random sample of 15 dealers of a company is taken from a normal population. The mean of the annual sales of the population is ₹ 50 lakh and the variance of the annual sales of the sample is ₹ 100 lakh, respectively. Find the probability that the mean annual sales of the sample is (a) less than ₹ 55 lakh, (b) more than ₹ 55 lakh.

17. In a big city 325 men out of 600 were found to be smokers. Does this information support the conclusion that majority of men in the city are smokers?

18. A random sample of 400 items gives the mean 4.45 and the variance at 4. Can the sample be regarded as drawn from a normal population mean of 4?

19. Random sample sizes 500 and 400 have means 11.5 and 10.9. Can the samples be regarded as drawn from population of S D 5? Find 99% confidence level limits for the difference of mean.

**20.** A consulting firm wants to decide at 5% significance level if the salaries of construction workers differ between Mumbai and Pune. Average salary of 100 Mumbai workers is ₹ 400 with S D of ₹ 100, while average salary of 75 Pune workers is ₹ 375 with S D of ₹ 80. Is there significant difference between Mumbai and Pune construction workers?

## 7.4 How to Do?

Dolly: "So, selection of sample is very important to get accurate or near accurate result."

Jolly: "To be accurate, we need large samples which will increase the cost of research."

Dolly: "I realize, researchers are always in dilemma to trade off between accuracy and cost. Time is also very important. Sometimes firms want immediate result and they cannot wait. To get accurate result in short time is really challenging."

Jolly: "Research is a challenge and researchers will have always to be on their toes."

Dolly: "Do you want to say research is more challenging than management?"

Jolly: "Off, course management is lame without research."

Dolly: "Are we not landing in areas of debate?"

Jolly: "I agree with you why people prefer specialization in their area. But a researcher is above specialization, you cannot research if you are not specialized in two three areas."

Dolly: "Let us not start a debate. Let me revise — statistic is for sample and parameter is for population. There are two types of sampling procedures – probability sampling and non-probability sampling. Probability sampling includes Simple Random Sampling, Systematic Sampling Stratified Sampling, and Cluster or Multi-stage Sampling. Sample size can be calculated with help of central limit theorem, when it is assumed that population is normally distributed."

Jolly: "Have you gone through the research article 'Rural indebtedness' by Prof Pratibha Desai?"

Dolly: "It is a good descriptive research. 10% of total population has been taken at random."

Jolly: "The results have been generalized to that particular village. The question is — can we generalize the findings to Belgaum district, Maharashtra state or India."

Dolly: "But, there is a question of internal validity. Variables of loans should be related to indebtedness and a degree of cause effect relationship should have been calculated."

Jolly: "Can we not call it finding a gap in research and carry out further research?"

Dolly: "Research is a continuous process. It means research needs funding also."

Jolly: "There are many agencies which fund your research. In India, under Ministry of HRD, there is ICSSR (Indian Council of Social Sciences Research) which get huge funds from the government to fund research activities?"

Dolly: "What is the criterion of funding?"

Jolly: "Leave it."

Dolly: "Do you want me read any other article?

Jolly: "Yes, it is better you start learning basic statistical techniques before that. Prof Gangadhar Sonar and Mr. Ramesh Kundi surveyed some industrial workers to know the relationship of performance and socio-psychological issues. Read to observe how sampling techniques has been used. Also see how chi-square test has been used to find out the relationship."

Dolly: "You mean to say it is descriptive study but degree of conclusion validity has been calculated. What about internal validity?"

Jolly: "That needs further study."

Dolly: "So I should read 'Socio-psychological Correlates with Performance of the Worker in Industry' by Ramesh S. Kundi and Gangadhar B. Sonar."

Jolly: "See you!"

✦ ✦ ✦

Research Project 5

## 7.5 Socio-psychological Correlates with Performance of the Worker in Industry*

**Ramesh S. Kundi[1] and Gangadhar B. Sonar[2]**

**Introduction:**

Performance appraisal is a method of evaluating the behaviour of employees on the work spot, normally including both quantitative and qualitative aspect of job performance. Performance here refers to the degree of accomplishment of the tasks that make up an individual job. It indicates how well an individual is fulfilling the job demand often; but performance is always measured in terms of results and not efforts (Bach, 2002; and Ramsey, 1991). For instance, a student may put a greater effort for preparing for the examination, but may manage to get a poor grade. In this case the effort expended is high but performance is low.

An industry cannot sustain and run without gaining profit. The profit of the industry depends mainly on the sale of the goods and demand for the produced items in the market. The sale and demand for goods depend on their quality. The quality of the goods depends on workers' performance. The performance of worker in production process makes the product qualitative or defective (Hargreaves, 2001; and Pulkingham, 1992). It means the performance of the worker is the prime indicator for the sustainability of any industry. The variation in the performance of employees may bring variations in the existence of industries. Hence, comprehensive understanding of the performance of the employees is very important in the globalised competitive world. There are myriad of factors that affect performance of worker in industries. The socio-cultural, psychological, economical, physical and health, environmental and educational aspects have a bearing on the good or poor performance of the employees (Sewell, 1992; and Townley, 1994).

Workers do not live in seclusion and they have their own external environment. Many industries do not consider the multi-dimensional aspects while appraising the performance of employees. Industry only observes the workers' behaviour and performance within the industry, the outside world is ignored or considered to be irrelevant (Millward and others, 2000). Traditionally, skilled workers are considered not different from machines and they are expected to give the same output. The considerations of socio-psychological aspects of employees are largely neglected which appears to be unreasonable. Such a system of appraisal may lead to injustice or autocratic rule due to biased performance evaluation of the workers in industry. Very few organizations focus on psychological aspect (viewpoint). This article makes an attempt to explore how socio-psychological and economic parameters have a bearing on the performance of the employees. It may help industrial management to improve the performance of workers by knowing some other aspects that may affect performance of workers. This may also help in improving of quality of output. In view of this and to fill up the research gap identified through the detailed review of literature, following objectives have been formulated.

1. To look into general background of the industrial workers;

---

* Already published in Vol 2 no. 3 of Journal of Global Economy. Reprinted with permission from authors and editors of the Journal.

1 MSW student, Walchand College of Arts and Science, Department of Social Work, Walchand Heerachand Marg, Ashok Chowk, Solapur, Maharashtra State, rameshmswhrm@yahoo.com

2 Lecturer, Walchand College of Arts and Science, Department of Social Work, Walchand Heerachand Marg, Ashok Chowk, Solapur, Maharashtra.

2. To know the socio-psychological and economical aspects and their bearing on performance of workers;
3. To understand the working conditions and access performance of workers., and
4. To suggest possible interventions to improve performance of workers.

## Methodology

To satisfy and meet object of study qualitative methodologies along with quantitative techniques were employed. The empirical study has been conducted at the ALSTOM Power Projects India Limited in Shahabad town of Chittapur taluka in Gulbarga district of Karnataka State. With reference to sample, the workers of selected industry are classified into five categories. The categories are A1, A, B, C and D grade workers. From each category it was decided to cover 15 respondents. Due to technical problems and unavailability of workers as per our sample, maintaining uniformity was not possible. However, one or two variations with a cluster of 15 samples in each category was possible. Total of 70 employees based on grades are covered for the study.

Both primary as well as secondary data were collected for the present study. The primary data were collected in face-to-face interviews, observation of workers, supervisors, engineers, managers, personnel department, etc. The secondary data were collected from the industrial reports, journals, and books and from the Internet websites published on performance appraisal by national and international organizations. The data collected from the group of workers was subjected to verification, quantification and coding by referring a coding key. The coded data was entered in a computer for data processing and analysis. The statistical package for social sciences (SPSS) is used to calculate percentile, chi-square, frequency distribution table and cross tabulation.

**Table 1**

**Tools employed to collect data**

| Sr. No. | Respondents | Tools and Techniques Used | Sample |
|---|---|---|---|
| 1. | Industrial Workers | Questionnaire and informal interviews with detailed checklist | 70 Workers |
| 2. | Supervisors | Informal interviews with detailed checklist | Selected Supervisors |
| 3. | Engineers | Informal interviews with detailed checklist | Selected Engineers |
| 4. | Training Officer | Informal interviews with detailed checklist | One |

**Table 2**

**General Background of the Workers**

| Age Distribution | Frequency | Percentage |
|---|---|---|
| 25 to 35 years | 04 | 05.7 |
| 36 to 45 years | 16 | 22.9 |
| 46 to 55 years | 48 | 68.6 |
| 56 years and above | 02 | 02.9 |
| Total | 70 | 100.0 |
| **General Education** | **Frequency** | **Percentage** |
| Up to $10^{th}$ | 52 | 74.3 |

| | | |
|---|---|---|
| Intermediate | 10 | 14.3 |
| Graduation and above | 08 | 11.4 |
| Total | 70 | 100.0 |
| **Technical education** | **Frequency** | **Percentage** |
| I T I | 19 | 27.1 |
| Apprentice training | 23 | 32.9 |
| No technical education | 28 | 40.0 |
| Total | 70 | 100.0 |
| **Religion** | **Frequency** | **Percentage** |
| Hindu | 58 | 82.9 |
| Muslim | 12 | 17.1 |
| Total | 70 | 100.0 |
| **Caste categories** | **Frequency** | **Percentage** |
| SC | 09 | 12.9 |
| ST | 02 | 2.9 |
| BC | 39 | 55.7 |
| OC | 20 | 28.6 |
| Total | 70 | 100.0 |
| **Work Experience** | **Frequency** | **Percentage** |
| 10 to 20 years | 19 | 27.1 |
| 21 to 30 years | 49 | 70.0 |
| 31 to 40 years | 02 | 02.9 |
| Total | 70 | 100.0 |

**Table 3**

**Social Aspects of the Workers**

| **Type of Family** | **Frequency** | **Percentage** |
|---|---|---|
| Joint | 19 | 27.1 |
| Nuclear | 44 | 62.9 |
| Extended | 07 | 10.0 |
| Total | 70 | 100.0 |
| **Dependent members in family** | **Frequency** | **Percentage** |
| 1 to 5 members | 52 | 74.3 |
| 6 to 10 members | 14 | 20.0 |
| 11 and more members | 04 | 05.7 |
| Total | 70 | 100.0 |
| **Social status** | **Frequency** | **Percentage** |
| Good | 47 | 67.1 |
| Moderate | 23 | 32.9 |
| Total | 70 | 100.0 |
| **Interpersonal relations** | **Frequency** | **Percentage** |

| | | |
|---|---|---|
| Good | 35 | 50.0 |
| Moderate | 35 | 50.0 |
| Total | 70 | 100.0 |
| **Association with social organ.** | **Frequency** | **Percentage** |
| Having | 41 | 58.6 |
| Do not have | 29 | 41.4 |
| Total | 70 | 100.0 |
| **Family worries** | **Frequency** | **Percentage** |
| Having | 13 | 18.6 |
| Do not have | 57 | 81.4 |
| Total | 70 | 100.0 |
| **Intergenerational conflicts** | **Frequency** | **Percentage** |
| Having | 02 | 02.9 |
| Do not have | 68 | 97.1 |
| Total | 70 | 100.0 |

## Analysis and Interpretation

Majority of the workers are aged between 46 and 55 years, married, belonging to backward castes and Hindu religion, educated up to 10th standard and completed apprentice training, and have work experience of 21 to 30 years. Most of the workers are living in nuclear families, have 1 to 5 dependent members in the family, have good social status and interpersonal relations with others. They have no intergenerational conflicts. Most workers have association with social organizations and have no worries of the family. Among the employees who have worries are reported as sickness of wife, disability of children, daughter's marriage and education of children.

**Table 4**

**Psychological Aspects of the Workers**

| **Type of hobbies** | **Frequency** | **Percentage** |
|---|---|---|
| Walking | 03 | 04.3 |
| T.V watching | 18 | 25.7 |
| Singing | 03 | 04.3 |
| Paper reading | 11 | 15.7 |
| Listening to music | 05 | 07.1 |
| Photograpy | 01 | 01.4 |
| Have no hobbies | 29 | 41.4 |
| Total | 70 | 100.0 |
| **Having habits** | **Frequency** | **Percentage** |
| Smoking | 14 | 20.0 |
| Tobacco/gutka | 16 | 22.9 |
| Drinking alcohol | 01 | 01.4 |
| Pan-supari | 02 | 02.9 |
| Have no habits | 37 | 52.9 |
| Total | 70 | 100.0 |

| Happy with present life | Frequency | Percentage |
|---|---|---|
| Happy | 48 | 68.6 |
| Unhappy | 22 | 31.4 |
| Total | 70 | 100.0 |
| **Having psychological worries** | **Frequency** | **Percentage** |
| Daughter's marriage | 02 | 02.9 |
| Children's Education | 10 | 14.3 |
| Making property | 01 | 01.4 |
| Regarding family | 05 | 07.1 |
| Have no psychological worries | 52 | 74.3 |
| Total | 70 | 100.0 |

A significant number of the workers have the hobby of watching TV. With reference to habits, they have adopted habits like chewing tobacco and gutka. Generally, addictions interrupt work if they are not satisfied. For many, it is difficult to manage without a habit for a long time because they can't concentrate easily on work and are not able to cope with the workload. Employees get sufficient recreation and are happy with their present life. Employees, who are not happy, mentioned the reasons as financial problems and family tensions.

## Economic Aspects of the Respondents

A good number of the workers have an annual family income between ₹ 80,001 to ₹ 1 lakh. They have a good salary package, as the industry is multinational. They spend ₹ 60,001 to ₹ 80,000 on family expenditures. Employees own land up to 10 acres of dry type, houses of pucca type. All are able to save. Among the employees who have no savings, borrow mostly from a co-operative society and are least satisfied with their salaries as they are unable to balance income and expenditure.

**Table 5**

**Parameters of Performance Appraisal**

| Sr. No. | Indicator of Performance | Measurement of Performance | | | | Total |
|---|---|---|---|---|---|---|
| | | Poor | Satisfactory | Good | Excellent | |
| 01 | Technical knowledge | 10(14.3) | 43(61.4) | 15(21.4) | 2(2.9) | 70(100) |
| 02 | Time management | 14(20.0) | 46(65.7) | 8(11.4) | 2(2.9) | 70(100) |
| 03 | Planning | 16(22.9) | 42(60.00 | 10(14.3) | 2(2.9) | 70(100) |
| 04 | Reporting | 8(11.4) | 46(65.7) | 12(17.1) | 4(5.7) | 70(100) |
| 05 | Communication skill | 12(17.1) | 45(64.3) | 11(15.7) | 2(2.9) | 70(100) |
| 06 | Meeting targets/deadlines | 9(12.9) | 45(64.3) | 14(20.0) | 2(2.9) | 70(100) |
| 07 | Creativity | 22(31.4) | 36(51.4) | 10(14.3) | 2(2.9) | 70(100) |
| 08 | Team working | 5(7.1) | 51(72.9) | 13(18.6) | 1(1.4) | 70(100) |
| 09 | Steadiness | 6(8.6) | 49(70.0) | 14(20.0) | 1(1.4) | 70(100) |
| 10 | Leadership and integrity | 18(25.7) | 42(60.0) | 8(11.4) | 2(2.9) | 70(100) |
| 11 | Adaptability | 9(12.9) | 52(74.3) | 9(12.9) | – | 70(100) |

| 12 | Flexibility | 7(10.0) | 50(71.4) | 11(15.7) | 2(2.9) | 70(100) |
|---|---|---|---|---|---|---|
| 13 | Mobility (the quality of being mobile) | 7(10.0) | 49(70.0) | 12(17.1) | 2(2.9) | 70(100) |
| 14 | Personal appearance and image (discipline) | 2(2.9) | 62(88.6) | 5(7.1) | 1(1.4) | 70(100) |
| 15 | Punctuality (regularity) | 06(08.6) | 49(70.0) | 14(20.0) | 01(01.4) | 70(100) |

**Significance Level: .05**

Table 5 explores parameters of the performance of the employees. Out of 70 workers a very small number of the workers (2%) have excellent performance in all the areas. A good number of the workers, more than one-fifth are good in technical knowledge and steadiness. A majority of the workers, more than three-fifths are good at all the indicators of performance with a slight variation. A considerable number of workers, more than one-fourth, are poor in leadership and integrity, creativity, planning, and time management qualities. If these aspects are poor, the overall performance may get affected.

**Table 6**

**Socio-psychological and Economic Variables Association with Performance of the Workers**

| Sr. No. | Name of the Variable | Chi-square value | Significant level | Result |
|---|---|---|---|---|
| 1 | Education | 11.376 | .050 | Significant |
| 2 | Type of family | 16.853 | .010 | Significant |
| 3 | No. of Independent members | 14.489 | .025 | Significant |
| 4 | Social status | 11.995 | .050 | Significant |
| 5 | Having psychological worries | 15.851 | .030 | Significant |

Table 6 shows the association of socio-psychological and economic variables with performance of the workers. It is clear that the workers who are educated, living in joint family, have more independent members in family, have good social status and have no psychological worries and have good performance in all the areas than their counterparts.

## Conclusion

The present study has made an attempt to understand socio-psychological and economic correlates with performance of the employees. It was carried out in ALSTOM Power Projects India Ltd. (Shahabad) Chittapur taluka of Gulbarga district in Karnataka State. The industry has good reputation in Asia, as it is a multinational company. The salaries that are given to the workers are of a high package as compared to other industries. The facilities provided within and out side the industry are also good.

The workers are technically sound and receive frequent training by the training department in order to update their knowledge to deliver quality of production. They do maintain good quality of products, which is an outcome of good performance of the employees. Overall performance of the workers is observed as more or less good. It is so because majority of the employees have good socio-psychological and economic conditions. Employees who have any one of the problems seem to have bearing on the overall performance.

## Suggestions

(1) The personnel department should take into account of socio-psychological and economic conditions of the employees while making appraisal.

(2) The disciplinary authorities should take a note of the socio-psychological conditions before taking any action with reference to performance of the employees.

(3) The personnel department should have a special section to redress socio psychological and economic problems and counsel the employees with guidance frequently.

(4) Social case work and social group work methods (counselling, guidance, situational corrections, role play, transactional analysis, etc.) may be used effectively by the personnel officer, labour welfare officer while dealing with individuals and groups.

(5) The employees whose performance is affected due to addiction may be treated in de-addiction centres. Further, they may be given intensive counselling to withdraw from such addictions.

(6) The performance appraisal should not be biased with gender, caste, religion, language, domicile, etc. Nothing makes good or bad performance of the Employees; it is only the environment; ability, circumstances and one's own efforts that make a difference.

## Acknowledgements

Thanks are due to Prof. Vilas Bet, HOD, Dr.Channaveer R.M, Lecturer, Department of social work, Walchand College of Arts and Science, Solapur and Dr. B.T. Lawani, Director Bharati Vidyapeeth, Deemed University, Pune for giving valuable comments in finalising this research work.

## References

Bach, S. (2000). 'From Performance Appraisal to Performance Management.' In S. Bach and K. Sisson (eds.), *Personnel Management: A Comprehensive Guide to Theory and Practice in Britain*. Third edition. Oxford: Blackwell.

Hargreaves-Heap, S.P. (2001). 'Expressive Rationality: Is Self-Worth Just Another kind of Preference?' In U. Mäki (ed.), *The Economic World View: Studies in the Ontology of Economics*. Cambridge: Cambridge University Press.

Millward, N., A. Bryson and J. Forth (2000). *All Change at Work?* London: Routledge.

Pulkingham, J. (1992) 'Employment Re-Structuring In The Health Service: Efficiency Initiatives, Working Patterns And Workforce Composition', *Work, Employment and Society*, 6 (3):397-422.

Ramsey, H. (1991) 'Reinventing The Wheel? A Review of the Development of Performance and Employee Involvement', *Human Resource Management Journal*, 4(1):1-22.

Sewell, G., Wilkinson, B. (1992) '"Someone to Watch Over Me": Surveillance, Discipline and 'The Just-in-Time Labour Process', *Sociology*, 26(2):271-290.

Townley, B. (1994) *Reframing Human Resource Management: Power, Ethics, and the Subject at Work*. London: Sage.

CHAPTER

# Qualitative Research

## *Structure*

As already discussed, exploratory research relies on secondary research such as reviewing available literature and/or data, or qualitative approaches such as informal discussions with consumers, employees, management or competitors, and more formal approaches through in-depth interviews, focus groups, projective methods, case studies or pilot studies. The results of exploratory research are not usually useful for decision-making by themselves, but they can provide significant insight into a given situation.

The objectives of exploration may be accomplished with different techniques. Both qualitative and quantitative techniques are applicable, although exploration relies more heavily on **qualitative techniques.** Following are some of the approaches adaptable for exploratory investigations of management questions:

1. Individual depth interviews (usually conversational rather than structured).
2. Participant observation (to perceive firsthand what participants in the setting experience).
3. Films, photographs, and videotape (to capture the life of the group under study).
4. Projective techniques and psychological testing (such as a Thematic Apperception Test, projective measures, games, or role-playing).
5. Case studies (for an indepth contextual analysis of a few events or conditions).
6. Street ethnography (to discover how a cultural sub-group describes and structures its world at the street level).
7. Elite or expert interviewing (for information from influential or well-informed people in an organization or community).
8. Document analysis (to evaluate historical or contemporary confidential or public records, reports, government documents, and opinions).
9. Proxemics and kinesics (to study the use of space and body-motion communication, respectively).

Managers basically do business research to understand how and why things happen. If the manager needs to know only what happened, or how often things happened, quantitative research methodologies would serve the purpose. But to understand the different meanings that people place on their experiences often requires research techniques that delve more deeply into people's hidden interpretations, understandings, and motivations. Qualitative research is designed to tell the researcher how (process) and why (meaning) things happen as they do. **Qualitative research** includes an "array of interpretive techniques which seek to describe, decode, translate, and otherwise come to terms with the meaning, not the frequency, of certain more or less naturally occurring phenomena in the social world.

Qualitative techniques are used both at the data collection and data analysis stages of a research project. At the data collection stage, the array of techniques includes focus groups, individual depth interviews, case studies, ethnography, grounded theory, action research observation. During analysis, the qualitative researcher uses content analysis of written or recorded materials drawn from personal expressions by participants, behavioural observations and debriefing of observers, as well as the study of artefacts and trace evidence from the physical environment. Qualitative research aims to achieve an indepth understanding of a situation, whether it explains why a person entering a particular mall proceeds down each aisle in turn or heads for the rear of the store and chooses alternate aisles thereafter or explains why some advertisements make us laugh and contribute to our commitment to a brand while others generate outrage and boycotts. (Do you remember the advertisement of 'fevicol', each advertisement makes you laugh) Qualitative research draws data from a variety of sources, including the following

- People (individuals or groups)
- Organizations or institutions.
- Texts (published, including virtual ones).
- Settings and environments (visual/sensory and virtual material).
- Objects, artefacts, media products (textual/visual/sensory and virtual material).
- Events and happenings (textual/visual/sensory and virtual material).

## 8.1 The Process of Qualitative Research

The process of developing a qualitative project is similar to the research process. However, there are three key distinctions that affect the research process:

(1) The level of question development in the management-research question hierarchy prior to the commencing of qualitative research, (2) the preparation of the participant prior to the research experience, and (3) the nature and level of data that come from the debriefing of interviewers or observers.

The qualitative researcher starts with an understanding of the manager's problem, but the management research question hierarchy is rarely developed prior to the design of research methodology. Rather, the research is guided by a broader question more similar in structure to the management question.

Much of qualitative research involves the deliberate preparation of the participant, called pre-exercises or **pre-tasking.** This step is important due to the desire to extract detail and meaning from the participant. A variety of creative and mental exercises draw participants' understanding of their own thought processes and ideas to the surface. Some of these include:

- Placing the product or medium for in-home use.
- Having the participants bring visual stimuli (e.g., family photos of areas or rooms in their homes that they hate to clean or have trouble decorating, or a favourite item of clothing).
- Having the participants prepare a visual collage (e.g., taking pictures over several weeks, with a one-time-use camera, of their children's favourite outfits for different purposes or situations or cutting pictures out of magazines that reflect how they feel when using a particular product or brand).
- Having the participants keep detailed diaries of behaviour and perceptions (e.g., a record of their step-by-step experience preparing a meal using a particular product).
- Having the participants draw a picture of an experience (e.g., what they felt like when they last shopped in a particular store).
- Having the participants write a dialog of a hypothetical experience (e.g., how a conversation between the participant and a sales associate would progress when a complaint was not resolved).

Pre-tasking is rarely used in observation studies and is considered a major source of error in quantitative studies. In quantitative research unless a researcher is collecting his or her own data, interviewers or data collectors are rarely involved in the data interpretation or analysis stages. While data collectors contribute to the accuracy of data preparation, their input is rarely, if ever, sought in the development of data interpretations. In qualitative studies, due to the higher level of involvement of both the sponsor and the interviewer/data collector, these parties in the process are often debriefed or interviewed, with their insight adding richness to the interpretation of the data.

Qualitative research involves **non-probability sampling**—where little attempt is made to generate representative sample. Several types of non-probability sampling are common:

***Purposive sampling:*** Researchers choose participants arbitrarily for their unique characteristics or their experiences, attitudes, or perceptions. Conceptual or theoretical categories of participants develop during the interviewing process; researchers seek new participants to challenge emerging patterns.

***Snowball sampling:*** Participants refer researchers to others who have characteristics, experiences, or attitudes similar to or different from their own.

***Convenience sampling:*** Researchers select any readily available individuals as participants.

Following are usual methods of quantitative data collection methods (list is not exhaustive)

1. Interviews
   (a) Individual Indepth interviews
   (b) Group interviews
2. Case studies

When these approaches are combined, seven exploratory techniques emerge with wide applicability for the management researcher:

1. Interviews (Individual and Group Interviews)
2. Secondary data analysis.
3. Experience surveys.
4. FOCUS groups.
5. Two stage design
6. Observation method
7. Case study

## 8.2 Interviews

**The interview** is the primary data collection technique for gathering data in qualitative methodologies. Interviews vary based on the number of people involved during the interview, the level of structure: the proximity of the interviewer to the participant, and the number of interviews conducted during the research.

An interview can be conducted individually (individual depth interview, or IDI) or in groups. The following table differentiates individual and the group interview as a research methodology. Both have a distinct place in qualitative research.

There are three types of Individual interviews

1. Unstructured interview
2. Semi-structured interview and
3. Structured interview

| Individual Interview | Group Interview |
|---|---|
| **Research Objectives**<br>• Explores the individual indepth. Creates case histories through repeated interviews overtime<br>• Test a survey | • Orient the researcher to a field of inquiry and language of the field·<br>• Explores a range of attitude, opinions and behaviour·<br>• Add contextual detail to quantitative findings |
| **Topic Concerns**<br>• Detailed individual experiences, choices, biographies<br>• Sensitive issues that might provoke anxiety | • Issues of public interest·<br>• Issues where little is known or of hypothetical nature |
| **Participants**<br>• High status or elites<br>• Those who have good language skills<br>• Participants whose distinction would inhibit participation. | • Participants whose backgrounds are similar or not so dissimilar as to generate conflict or discomfort. People can articulate the ideas<br>• People who offer a range of positions on issues |

The researcher chooses either an unstructured interview (no specific questions or order of topics to be discussed, with each interview customized to each participant; generally starts with a participant narrative) or a semi-structured interview (generally starts with a few specific questions and then follows individual's tangents of thought with interviewer probes) or a structured interview (often uses a detailed similar to a questionnaire to guide the question order and the specific way the questions are asked but the questions generally remain open-ended). Structured interviews permit more direct comparability of responses; question variability is eliminated and thus answer variability is assumed to be real. Also, in the structured interview, the interviewer's neutrality has been maintained. Most qualitative research relies on the unstructured or semi-structured interview. The unstructured and semi-structured interviews used in qualitative research are distinct from the structured interview in several ways. They rely on developing a dialogue between interviewer and participant, require more interviewer creativity, and use the skill of the interviewer to extract more and a greater variety of data, use interviewer experience and skill to achieve greater clarity and elaboration of answers.

Many interviews are conducted face-to-face, with the obvious benefit of being able to observe and record non-verbal as well as verbal behaviour. An interview, however, can be conducted by phone or online. Phone and online interviews offer the opportunity to conduct more interviews within the same time frame and draw participants from a wider geographic area. These approaches also save the travel expenses of moving trained interviewers to participants, as well as the travel fees associated with bringing participants to a neutral site. Using interviewers who are fresher and more comfortable in conducting an interview — often from their home or office — should increase the quality of the interview. Also, depending on the group from which participants are drawn, there may be insufficient numbers to conduct group interviews in any one market, forcing the use of phone or online techniques.

Interviewing requires a trained interviewer (often called a moderator for group interviews) or the skills gained from experience. These skills include making respondents comfortable, probing for detail without making the respondent feel harassed, remaining neutral while encouraging the participant to talk openly, listening carefully, following a participant's train of thought, and extracting insights from hours of detailed descriptive dialogue. Skilled interviewers learn to use their personal similarities with or differences from their interviewee to mine for information; similarities are used to convey sympathy and understanding, while differences are used to demonstrate eagerness to understand and empathize.

A skilled interviewer must be a "quick-study," someone who can grasp an understanding of an issue without necessarily having prior experience with the product or service or being a technical expert. The interviewer needs to be able to extract information from a willing participant who often is not consciously aware that he or she possesses the information desired. The actual interviewer is usually responsible for generating the interview or discussion guide, the list of topics to be discussed (unstructured interview) or the questions to be asked (semi-structured) and in what order (structured).

In general, then, the interviewer is a consultant with wideranging responsibilities:

- Recommends the topics and questions.
- Controls the interview, but also plans—and may manage—the locations and facilities for the study.
- Proposes the criteria for drawing the sample participants.
- Writes the recruitment screener and may recruit participants. Develops the various pre-tasking exercises.
- Prepares any research tools (e.g., picture sorts or written exercises) to be used during the interview.
- Supervises the transcription process.
- Helps analyse the data and draw insights.

Writes or directs the writing of the client report, including extracting video clips for the oral report.

An **individual depth interview (IDI)** is an interaction between an individual interviewer and a single participant. Individual depth interviews generally take between 20 minutes (telephone interviews) and 2 hours (prescheduled, face-to-face interviews) to complete, depending on the issues or topics of interest and the contact method used. Interviewees are often provided with advance materials via mail, fax, or the Internet. Recently, advances in technology have encouraged the use of detailed visual and auditory aids during interviews, creating methodology known as **computer-assisted personal interviews (CAPIs).** CAPIs often use a structured semi-structured individual depth interview.

Participants for individual depth interviews are usually chosen not because **their opinions are representative of the dominant opinion** but because **their experiences and attitudes will reflect the full scope of the issue under study**. Participants for individual depth interviews also need to be verbally articulate, so that the interviewer may interact with the richness of desired detail. Individual depth interviews are usually recorded (audio and/or video) and transcribed to provide the researcher with the rich detail that the methodology is used for. Interviewers get their personal reactions to participant attitudes, insights, and the quality of the interview. Individual interviews use extensive amounts of interviewer time, in conducting interviews and evaluating them as well as facility time when premises are occupied for interviews. And while some respondents feel more comfortable discussing sensitive topics or sharing their own observations, behaviours, and attitudes with a single person, others are more forthcoming in group situations.

## Group Interviews

A group interview is a data collection method using a single interviewer with more than one research participant. Group interviews can be described by the group's size or its composition. Group interviews vary widely in size: dyads (2 people), triads (3 people), mini-groups (2 to 6 people) small groups (focus groups — 6 to 10 people — unarguably the most well known of group interview techniques), or supergroups (up to 20 people). The smaller groups are usually used when the overall population from which the participants are drawn is small, when the topic or concept list is extensive or technical or when the research calls for greater intimacy. Dyads also are used when the special nature of a friendship or other relationship (e.g., spouses, superior-subordinate, and siblings) is needed to stimulate frank discussion on a sensitive topic. Dyads and triads are also used frequently with young children who have lower levels of articulation or more limited attention spans and are thus more difficult **to** control in large groups. A supergroup is used when a wide range of ideas is needed in a short period of time and when the researcher is willing to sacrifice a significant amount of participant interaction for speed.

In terms of composition, groups can be **heterogeneous** (consisting of different individuals; variety of opinions, backgrounds, actions) or **homogeneous** (consisting of similar individuals; commonality of opinions, backgrounds, actions). Groups also can comprise **experts** (individuals exceptionally knowledgeable about the issues to be discussed) or **non-experts** (those who have at least some desired information but at an unknown level).

Driven by the belief that the data extracted will be richer because of the interaction, group interviews are one of the few research techniques in which the participants are encouraged to interact. However, given time constraints, group interviews permit spending only limited time extracting detail from each participant. This problem is magnified when a group interview is structured to cover numerous questions or topics.

Another drawback of the group interview is the increased difficulty recruiting, arranging, and co-ordinating group discussions. But this aggravation, which can be sub-contracted to a specialist research supplier, is deemed a small price to pay for the insights that often are revealed by group interaction.

Interviewers are tested by the challenge of managing the group's conversation while avoiding interjecting themselves into the group's process. It is also the moderator's job to control the extrovert or dominant personality and ensure meaningful contributions from all others, including the most introverted or private thinkers. When control is not maintained, some members' opinions may be suppressed and valuable insights lost. Sometimes an individual will be more honest with a neutral interviewer than with a group of peers. One example is a group of small-business owners being unwilling to divulge competitive strengths and weaknesses. A skilled researcher can anticipate which topics are more likely to obtain good results with an individual or a group interview.

A group interview's structure and process include moderator interaction with the group and probing of the group to clarify responses. As a result, the moderator may create bias in the results by sending verbal and non – verbal signals that some responses are more favourable than others. The moderator might also direct discussion down paths that are least likely to help the client. Only training, and subsequent experience, can overcome these potential weaknesses of group interviews.

The skilled researcher helps the sponsor determine an appropriate number of group interviews to conduct. The number of groups is determined by:

- The scope of the issues being studied: The broader the issues, the more groups needed.
- The number of distinct market segments of interest: The larger the number and the greater the distinctions, the more groups needed.
- The number of new ideas or insights desired: The larger the number, the more groups needed.
- The level of detail of information: The greater the level of detail, the more groups needed.
- The level of geographic or ethnic distinctions in attitudes or behaviour: The greater these influences, the more groups needed.
- The homogeneity of the groups: The less homogeneity, the more groups needed.

The general rule is: Keep conducting group interviews until no new insights are gained. Often a limited number of groups will suffice, or sometimes the number might grow to 8 or even 12.

Regardless of group composition, it is the moderator who sets the tone of the group. Homogeneous group often discover their similarities early and get along well. But with heterogeneous groups, the moderator must provide the ice-breaker activities that get the participants interacting with each other. As with individual indepth interviews, the moderator is responsible for developing the recruitment screener and the group discussion guide.

## 8.3 Secondary Data Analysis

The first step in an exploratory study is a search of the secondary literature studies made by others for their own purposes. It is inefficient to discover anew through the collection of **primary data** or original research what has already been done and reported at a level sufficient for management to make a decision.

Within secondary data exploration, a researcher should start first with an organization's own data archive. Reports of prior research studies often reveal an extensive amount of historical data or decision-making pattern. By reviewing prior studies, you can identify methodologies that proved successful and unsuccessful. Solution that didn't receive attention in the past due to different environmental circumstances is revealed as potential subject for further study. The researcher needs to avoid duplication in instances when prior collected data can provide sufficient information for resolving the current decision-making dilemma.

The second source of secondary data is published documents prepared by authors outside the sponsor organization. There are tens of thousands of periodicals and hundreds of thousands of books on all aspects of business. Data from secondary sources help us decide what needs to be done and can be a rich source hypotheses.

Special catalogues, subject guides, and electronic indices will help in this search. In many cases you can conduct a secondary search from your home or office using a computer, an Internet gateway.

If you are creative, a search of secondary sources will supply excellent background information as well as many good leads. Yet, if we confine the investigation to obvious subjects in bibliographic sources, we will often miss much of the best information. Suppose the steel industry is interested in estimating a look for over the next 10 years. We can search through the literature under the subjects "steel production" and "steel consumption." However, a search restricted to these two topics misses more than it finds. When a creative search of the steel industry is undertaken, useful information turns up under the following reference headings: mines and minerals; ferrous metals; forecasting; planning; econometrics; consuming industries such as automotive and communications; states where steel is produced, and companies prominent in the industry, such as TATA steel, SAIL etc.

## 8.4 Experience Survey

Published data are a valuable resource, but people do not put their experiences into print. Writing may be proprietary to a given organization and thus unavailable to an outside searcher. Also, internal data archives are rarely well organised, and difficult to locate. Thus, we will profit by seeking information from persons experienced in the area of study, tapping into their collective memories and experiences. When we interview persons in an experience survey, we should seek their ideas about important issues or aspects of the subject and discover what is important across the subject's range of knowledge. The investigative format we use should be flexible enough so that we can explore various avenues that emerge during the interview, for instance, 'what is being done?', 'what has been tried in the past without success?', 'With success?', 'How have things changed?', 'What are the change-producing elements of the situation?', 'Who is involved in decisions and what role does each person play?', 'What problem areas and barriers can be seen?', 'What are the costs of the processes under study?', 'Whom can we count on to assist and/or participate in the research?', 'What are the priority areas?', etc.

The product of such questioning may be a new hypothesis, the discarding of an old one, or information about the practicality of doing the study. Probing may show whether certain facilities are available, what factors need to be controlled and how, and who will co-operate in the study.

Discovery is more easily carried out if the researcher can analyse cases that provide special insight. Typical of exploration, we are less interested in getting a representative cross-section than in getting information from sources that might be insightful. People who may provide insightful information include:

1. Newcomers or recently transferred employees or personnel to this plant from similar plants.
2. Marginal or peripheral individuals-first-line supervisors and lead workers who are often neither management personnel nor workers but some thing in between.
3. Individuals in transition—recently promoted employees who have been transferred to new departments.
4. Deviants and isolates—those in a given group who hold a different position from the majority, as well as workers who are happy with the present situation, highly productive departments and workers, and loners of one sort or another.
5. "Pure" cases or cases that show extreme examples of the conditions under study—the most unproductive departments, the most antagonistic workers, and so forth.
6. Those who fit well and those who do not—the workers who are well established in their organizations versus those who are not, those executives who fully reflect management views and those who do not.
7. Those who represent different positions in the system—unskilled workers, assemblers, superintendents, and so forth.

## 8.5 Focus Groups

A focus **group** is a group of people (typically 6 to 10 participants), led by a trained moderator, who meet for 90 minutes to 2 hours. The facilitator or moderator uses group dynamics principles to focus or guide the group in an exchange of ideas, feelings, and experiences on a specific topic.

In the world of marketing, focus groups are seen as an important tool for acquiring feedback regarding new products, as well as various topics. In particular, focus groups allow companies wishing to develop, package, name, or test market a new product, to discuss, view, and/or test the new product before it is made available to the public. This can provide invaluable information about the potential market acceptance of the product.

In the social sciences and urban planning, focus groups allow interviewers to study people in a more natural setting than a one-to-one interview. In combination with participant observation, they can be used for gaining access to various cultural and social groups, selecting sites to study, sampling of such sites, and raising unexpected issues for exploration. Focus groups have a high apparent validity, since the idea is easy to understand, the results are believable. Also, they are low in cost, one can get results relatively quickly, and they can increase the sample size of a report by talking with several people at once.

Variants of focus groups include:

- **Two-way focus group** — one focus group watches another focus group and discusses the observed interactions and conclusions.
- **Dual moderator focus group** — one moderator ensures the session progresses smoothly, while another ensures that all the topics are covered.
- **Duelling moderator focus group** — two moderators deliberately take opposite sides on the issue under discussion.
- **Respondent moderator focus group** — one or more of the respondents are asked to act as the moderator temporarily.
- **Client participant focus groups** — one or more client representatives participate in the discussion, either covertly or overtly.
- **Mini focus groups** — groups are comprised of 4 or 5 members rather than 8 to 12.
- **Teleconference focus groups** — telephone network is used.
- **Online focus groups** — computers connected via the internet are used.

Traditional focus groups can provide accurate information, and are less expensive than other forms of traditional marketing research. There can be significant costs however: if a product is to be marketed on a nationwide basis, it would be critical to gather respondents from various locales throughout the country since attitudes about a new product may vary due to geographical considerations. This would require a considerable expenditure in travel and lodging expenses. Additionally, the site of a traditional focus group may or may not be in a locale convenient to a specific client, so client representatives may have to incur travel and lodging expenses as well.

The use of focus groups has steadily evolved over time and is becoming increasingly widespread.

How to conduct a focus group

- Select participants to represent the types of users you want to come to the Website. (This is true of all the data-gathering techniques.)
- Decide what you want to learn. (This is also true for other data-gathering techniques.)
- Write a "script" for the moderator to follow. (In usability testing, you write scenarios - tasks - for users to perform. In contextual interviewing, you let the context and the user's work shape the dialogue.)
- Hire a skilled moderator to facilitate the discussion so that everyone participates and the group stays on track. (In the other techniques, you need skilled observers and listeners.)
- Allow the moderator flexibility in using the script. The script usually gives the moderator questions to ask and topics to cover. The moderator may change the order of questions and topics to keep the discussion flowing smoothly. The moderator has to be a good judge of time to decide when to encourage more discussion on a topic and when to move on.
- Tape the sessions and have one or more people take good notes. (This is also true of other data gathering techniques. Good notes are critical to making sense of what you see and hear in all these techniques.)

Focus groups are often unique in research due to the research sponsor's involvement in the process. Most facilities permit the sponsor to observe the group and its dynamics in real time, drawing his or her own insights from the conversations and non-verbal signals he or she observes. Many facilities also allow the client to supply the moderator with new topics or questions that are generated by those observing in real time. This option is generally not available in an individual depth interview, other group interviews, or survey research.

Focus groups typically last about two hours but may run from one to three hours. Facilities usually provide for the group to be isolated from distractions. Thus, the famous, or infamous, mirrored window allows those who are interested to observe the group while they avoid interfering with the group dynamics. Some facilities allow for product preparation and testing, as well as other creative exercises.

Fewer and lengthier focus groups are becoming common. As sessions become longer, activities are needed to bring out deeper feelings, knowledge, and motivations. Besides the creativity sessions that employ projective techniques or involve the participants in writing or drawing sessions, or creating visual compilation, other common activities within focus groups include Free association, Picture sort, Photo sort, Role play, etc.

Focus groups are often used as an exploratory technique but may be a primary methodology. Focus groups are especially valuable in the following scenarios:

- Obtaining general background about a topic or issue.
- Generating research questions to be explored via quantitative methodologies.
- Interpreting previously obtained quantitative results.
- Stimulating new ideas for products and programmes.
- Highlighting areas of opportunity for specific managers to pursue.
- Diagnosing problems that managers need to address.
- Generating impressions and perceptions of brands and product ideas.
- Generating a level of understanding about influences in the participant's world.

Focus groups enable the exploration of surprise information and new ideas. Agendas can be modified as the research team moves on to the next focus group. Even within an existing focus group, an adept facilitator can build on the ideas and insights of previous groups, getting to a greater depth of understanding. However, because they are qualitative devices, with limited sampling accuracy, results from focus groups should not be considered a replacement for quantitative analyses.

If it is difficult to gather participants, you can create Telephone Focus Groups, Online Focus Groups and or Video Conferencing Focus Group. These groups can be formed because of following reasons:

- When it is difficult to recruit desired participants — members of elite groups and hard-to-find respondents such as experts, professionals, physician specialists, high-level executives, and store owners
- When target group members are rare, "low incidence," or widely dispersed geographically—directors of a medical clinic, celebrities, early adopters, and rural practitioners.
- When issues are so sensitive that anonymity is needed but respondents must be from a wide geographical area — people suffering from a contagious disease, people using non-mainstream products, high-income individuals, competitors.
- When you want to conduct only a couple of focus groups but want nationwide representation.

An emerging technique for exploratory research is to approximate group dynamics using e-mail, websites, Usenet newsgroups, or an Internet chat room. It is possible to do "live" voice chats online, reducing or eliminating the cost associated with telephone focus groups. Posting questions to a newsgroup with an interest in the research problem can generate considerable discussion. However, online discussions are not confidential unless they take place on an intranet. Although online forum discussions are unlikely to reflect the average participants, they can be a good way of getting in touch with populations that have special interests. **Online focus groups** have also proved to be effective with teens and young adults, as well as technically employed segments of the market, those essentially comfortable with computer use. They are especially valuable when a computer-based application, such as software or a game, is the topic of group discussion. The technology permits use of visual images of materials (e.g., ads or product concepts) but retains the barrier between the group and the moderator. Online focus groups are a trade-off. What you gain in speed and access you give up in insights extracted from group dynamics, the flexibility to use non-verbal language as a source of data, and the moderator's ability to use physical presence to influence openness and depth of response.

## 8.6 Two-Stage Design

A useful way to design a research study is as a **two-stage design.** With this approach, exploration becomes a separate first stage with limited objectives: (1) clearly defining the research question and (2) developing the research design.

In arguing for a two-stage approach, we recognize that much about the problem is not known but should be known before effort and resources are committed. In these circumstances, one is operating in unknown areas, where it is difficult to predict the problems and costs of the study. Proposals that acknowledge the practicality of this approach are particularly useful when the research budget is inflexible. A limited exploration for a specific, modest cost carries little risk for both sponsor and researcher and often uncovers information that reduces the total research cost.

An exploratory study is finished when the researchers have achieved the following:

- Established the major dimensions of the research task.
- Defined a set of subsidiary investigative questions that can be used as guides to a detailed research design.
- Developed several hypotheses about possible causes of a management dilemma.
- Learned that certain other hypotheses are such remote possibilities that they can be safely ignored in any subsequent study.
- Concluded additional research is not needed or is not feasible.

## 8.7 Descriptive Studies

In contrast to exploratory studies, more formalized studies are typically structured with clearly stated hypotheses or investigative questions. Formal studies serve a variety of research objectives:

- Descriptions of phenomena or characteristics associated with a subject population (the *who, what, when, where, and how of a topic).*
- Estimates of the proportions of a population that have these characteristics.
- Discovery of associations among different variables.

The third study objective is sometimes labelled a *correlational study,* a subset of descriptive studies. A descriptive study may be simple or complex; it may be done in many settings. Whatever the form, a descriptive can just be as demanding of research skills as the causal study, and we should insist on the same high standards for design and execution.

The simplest descriptive study concerns a uni-variate question or hypothesis in which we ask about, or state something about, the size, form, distribution, or existence of a variable. A complex descriptive study may include many variables, their relationship, their interdependence, their distributions, etc.

## 8.8 Case Study

Case study, also referred to as the *case history,* is a powerful research methodology that combines individuals and (sometimes) group interviews with record analysis and observation. Researchers extract information from company brochures, annual reports, sales receipts, and newspaper and magazine articles, along with direct observation (usually done in the participant's "natural" setting), and combine it with interview data from participants. The objective is to obtain multiple perspectives of a single organization, situation, event and process at a point in time or over a period of time. Case study methodology, or the written report from such research project, often called a case analysis or case writeup, can be used to understand particular process of finance, marketing, etc. For example, one study may evaluate new product development processes for similarities, especially the use of outside consultants, ideation techniques, and computer simulation. Another study may examine in detail the purchaser's response to a marketing stimulus like a display. The results of research can be used to experiment with modifications of the new product development process or with display selection and placement processes to generate higher value transactions. The research problem is usually, how and why problem, resulting in a descriptive or explanatory study.

Case study does not use large samples or a rigid protocol to examine a limited number of variables; case study methods involve an in-depth, longitudinal examination of a single instance or event: a case. They provide a systematic way of looking at events, collecting data, analysing information, and reporting the results. As a result the researcher may gain a sharpened understanding of why the instance happened as it did, and what might become important to look at more extensively in future research. Case studies lend themselves to both generating and testing hypotheses.

**Case study** may be defined as a **research strategy**, an empirical inquiry that investigates a phenomenon within its real-life context. Case study research means single and multiple case studies, can include quantitative evidence, relies on multiple sources of evidence and benefits from the prior development of theoretical propositions. Case studies should not be confused with only qualitative research and they can be based on any mix of quantitative and qualitative evidence. Single-subject research provides the statistical framework for making inferences from quantitative case study data. The case study is a research approach, situated between concrete data taking techniques and methodological paradigms.

When selecting a case for a case study, researchers often use information-oriented sampling, as opposed to random sampling. This is because the typical or average case is often not the richest in information. Extreme or typical cases reveal more information because they activate more basic mechanisms and more actors in the situation studied. In addition, from both an understanding-oriented and an action-oriented perspective, it is often more important to clarify the deeper causes behind a given problem and its consequences than to describe the symptoms of the problem and how frequently they occur. Random samples emphasizing representativeness will seldom be able to produce this kind of insight; it is more appropriate to select some few cases chosen for their validity.

## Developing a Case Study

**1. All data about the case is gathered.**

For example, if the study is to highlight a programme's failure with a client, data would be collected about the programme, its processes and the client. Data could result from a combination of methods, including documentation (applications, histories, records, etc.), questionnaires, interviews and observation.

**2. Data is organized into an approach to highlight the focus of the study.**

Data in the case would be organized in a chronological order to portray how the client got into the programme, went through the programme and did not receive effective services.

**3. A case study narrative is developed.**

The narrative is a highly readable story that integrates and summarizes key information around the focus of the case study. The narrative should be complete to the extent that it is the eyes and ears for an outside reader to understand what happened regarding the case. In our example, the narrative might include key demographic information about the client, phases in the programme's process through which the client passed and any major differences noticed about that client during the process, early indicators of failures and key quotes from the client.

**4. The narrative might be validated by review from programme participants.**

For example, the client for whom the programme failed would read the narrative to ensure it fully depicted his or her experience and results.

**5. Case studies might be cross-compared to isolate any themes or patterns.**

For example, various case studies about programme failures might be compared to notice commonalities in these clients' experiences and how they went through the programme. These commonalities might highlight where in the programme the process needs to be strengthened.

Three types of information-oriented cases may be distinguished:

- Extreme or deviant cases
- Critical cases
- Paradigmatic cases.

### Extreme case

The extreme case can be well-suited for getting a point across in an especially dramatic way, which often occurs for well-known case studies.

### Critical case

A critical case can be defined as having strategic importance in relation to the general problem. For example, a researcher wishes to know the impact of Tondon Committee report on working capital advances in banks; he can select a single or multiple banks to study only this particular case.

### Paradigmatic case

A Paradigmatic case may be defined as an exemplar or prototype. Thomas Kuhn has shown that the basic skills, or background practices, of natural scientists are organized in terms of 'exemplars' or 'paradigms' the role of which in the scientific process can be analysed. Similarly, scholars like Clifford Geertz and Michel Foucault have often organized their research around specific cultural paradigms. Kuhn has shown that scientific paradigms cannot be expressed as rules or theories. There exists no predictive theory for how predictive theory comes about. A scientific activity is acknowledged or rejected as good science by how close it is to one or more exemplars; that is, practical prototypes of good scientific work. A paradigmatic case of how scientists do science is precisely such a prototype. It operates as a reference point and may function as a focus for the founding of schools of thought.

### Generalizing from case studies

The case study is effective for generalizing using the type of test that Karl Popper called falsification, which forms part of critical reflexivity. Falsification is one of the most rigorous tests to which a scientific proposition can be subjected: if just one observation does not fit with the proposition it is considered not valid generally and must therefore be either revised or rejected. Popper himself used the now famous example of, "All swans are white," and proposed that just one observation of a single black swan would falsify this proposition and in this way have general significance and stimulate further investigations and theory-building. The case study is well suited for identifying "black swans" because of its in-depth approach: what appears to be "white" often turns out on closer examination to be "black."

For instance, Galileo's rejection of Aristotle's law of gravity was based on a case study selected by information-oriented sampling and not random sampling. The rejection consisted primarily of a conceptual experiment and later on of a practical one. These experiments, with the benefit of hindsight, are self-evident. Nevertheless, Aristotle's incorrect view of gravity dominated scientific inquiry for nearly two thousand years before it was falsified. In his experimental thinking,

Galileo reasoned as follows: If two objects with the same weight are released from the same height at the same time, they will hit the ground simultaneously, having fallen at the same speed. If the two objects are then stuck together into one, this object will have double the weight and will according to the Aristotelian view therefore fall faster than the two individual objects. This conclusion seemed contradictory to Galileo. The only way to avoid the contradiction was to eliminate weight as a determinant factor for acceleration in free fall. Galileo's experimentalism did not involve a large random sample of trials of objects falling from a wide range of randomly selected heights under varying wind conditions, and so on. Rather, it was a matter of a single experiment, that is, a case study.

Galileo's view continued to be subjected to doubt, however, and the Aristotelian view was not finally rejected until half a century later, with the invention of the air pump. The air pump made it possible to conduct the ultimate experiment, known by every pupil, whereby a coin or a piece of lead inside a vacuum tube falls with the same speed as a feather. After this experiment, Aristotle's view could be maintained no longer. What is especially worth noting, however, is that the matter was settled by an individual case due to the clever choice of the extremes of metal and feather. One might call it a critical case, for if Galileo's thesis held for these materials, it could be expected to be valid for all or a large range of materials.. Random and large samples were at no time part of the picture. However, it was Galileo's view that was the subject of doubt as it was not reasonable enough to be Aristotelian view.

Many well-known case study researchers such as Robert E. Stake, Helen Simons, and Robert K. Yin have written about case study research and suggested techniques for organizing and conducting the research successfully. This introduction to case study research draws upon their work and proposes six steps that should be used:

- Determine and define the research questions
- Select the cases and determine data gathering and analysis techniques
- Prepare to collect the data
- Collect data in the field
- Evaluate and analyse the data
- Prepare the report

Although little can be done to combat challenges concerning the generalizability of case studies, most writers suggest that qualitative research should be judged as credible and confirmable as opposed to valid and reliable. Likewise, it has been argued that rather than transplanting statistical, quantitative notions of generalizability and thus finding qualitative research inadequate, it makes more sense to develop an understanding of generalization that is congruent with the basic characteristics of qualitative inquiry. After all, criticizing the case study method for being ungeneralizable is comparable to criticizing a washing machine for not being able to tell the correct time. In other words, it is unjust to criticize a method for not being able to do something which it was never originally designed to do in the first place. To improve generalization and reliability, can use the following techniques:

1. **Prolong the Processes of Data Gathering on Site:** This will help to insure the accuracy of the findings by providing the researcher with more concrete information upon which to formulate interpretations.
2. **Employ the Process of "Triangulation"**: Use a variety of data sources as opposed to relying solely upon one avenue of observation. "Case cluster method," is when a single unit within a larger case is randomly sampled, and that data treated quantitatively. This

cluster profile included an advanced case history of the subject, specific examination and analysis of individual compositions and protocols, and extensive interview sessions...

3. **Conduct Member Checks**: Initiate and maintain an active corroboration on the interpretation of data between the researcher and those who provided the data. In other words, talk to your subjects.
4. **Collect Referential Materials**: Complement the file of materials from the actual site with additional document support. Theoretical research should be done with regards to the creative process, as well as examples of empirical research dealing with the writing of adolescents.
5. **Engage in Peer Consultation**: Prior to composing the final draft of the report, researchers should consult with colleagues in order to establish validity through pooled judgment.

## 8.9 Observation Method

Observation is a scientific inquiry when it is conducted specifically to answer a research question. It is systematically planned and executed, uses proper controls, and provides a reliable and valid account of what happened. The versatility of observation makes it an indispensable primary source method and a supplement for other methods. Many academics have a limited view of observation, relegating it to a minor technique of field data collection. This ignores its potential for forging business decisions and denies its historic stature as a creative means of obtaining primary data.

Besides collecting data visually, observation involves listening, reading, smelling, and touching. Behavioural scientists define observation in terms of animal or human behaviour, but this too is limiting. **Observation** includes the full range of monitoring behavioural and non-behavioural activities and conditions that can be classified roughly as follows:

**Behavioural Observation:**

- Non-verbal analysis
- Linguistic analysis
- Extra-linguistic analysis
- Spatial analysis

**Non-behavioural Observation:**

- Record analysis
- Physical condition analysis
- Physical process analysis

Observation is the only method available to gather certain types of information. The study of records, mechanical processes, and young children, as well as other inarticulate participants, fall into this category. Another value of observation is that we can collect the original data at the time they occur. We need not depend on reports by others. Every respondent filters information no matter how well intentioned he or she is. Forgetting occurs, and there are reasons why the respondent may not want to report fully and fairly. Observation overcomes many of these deficiencies of questioning.

We can secure information that most participants would ignore either because it is so common and expected or because it is not seen as relevant. For example, if you are observing buying activity in a store, there may be conditions important to the research study that the shopper does not notice or consider important. The next advantage of observation is that it alone can capture the whole event as it occurs in its natural environment. Whereas the environment of an experiment may seem contrived to participants, and the number and types of questions limit the range of responses gathered from respondents, observation is less restrictive than most primary collection methods. Also, the limitations on the length of data collection activities imposed by sur-veys or experiments are relaxed for observation. You may be interested in all the conditions surrounding a confrontation at a bargaining session between union and management representatives. These sessions may extend over time, and any effort to study the unfolding of the negotiation is facilitated by observation. Questioning could seldom provide the insight of observation for many aspects of the negotiation process.

Finally, participants seem to accept an observational intrusion better than they respond to questioning. Observation is less demanding of them and normally has a less biasing effect on their behaviour than does questioning. In addition, it is also possible to conduct disguised and unobtrusive observation studies much more easily than disguised questioning.

The observation method has some research limitations. The observer normally must be at the scene of the event when it takes place, yet it is often impossible to predict where and when the event will occur. One way to guard against missing an event is to observe for prolonged periods until it does occur, but this strategy brings up a second disadvantage. Observation is a slow and expensive process that requires either human observers or costly surveillance equipment.

A third limitation of observation is that its most reliable results are restricted to information that can be learned by overt action or surface indicators. To go below the surface, the observer must make inferences. Two observers will probably agree on the nature of various surface events, but the inferences they draw from such data are much more variable.

Fourth, the research environment is more likely suited to subjective assessment and recording of data than to controls and quantification of events. When control is exercised through active intervention by the researchers, their participation may threaten the validity of what is being assessed. Even when sample sizes are small, the observation records can be disproportionately large and difficult to analyse.

Fifth, observation is limited as a way to learn about the past. It is similarly limited as a method by which to learn what is going on in the present at some distant place. It is also difficult to gather information on such topics as intentions, attitudes, opinions or preferences.

## 8.10 Other Qualitative Research Techniques

### 8.10.1 Motivational Research

Motivational Research can be called the psychoanalytic approach. It, in fact, is usually described as the application of techniques from clinical psychology to the advertising and marketing research field. Motivational marketing emerged shortly after World War II and bloomed in the 1950s – an era that witnessed a remarkable wave of prosperity unleashed by pent-up demand for consumer goods. It wove together a number of then-current concepts by:

(a) Shifting the emphasis on the consumer's viewpoint – not the marketer's – as the starting point of all marketing activities.

(b) Modifying psychoanalytic concepts for consumer research.

(c) Adapting clinical or therapy methods to analyse market behaviour.

Depth interviews were free conversations pointed in the general direction of the problem and its various components. The purpose was to cast as wide a net as possible to learn what was on the individual's mind, to determine the kind and quantity of feeling involved and to note if anything in the unguarded conversation contradicts the expressed attitudes.

Products that benefited most from the MR approach were so-called "low-involvement" products that were comparable in price, performance and quality such as soap, gasoline, foods and cigarettes.

An underlying message of canned soup when first introduced was that it is as warm and nutritious as a loving mother's milk. Therefore, women who serve it shouldn't feel guilty for not cooking.

Another reason marketing shifted to MR was that historically, marketing research relied heavily on the direct question survey to explain buying behaviour. Factors such as income, age, education and so forth could only be used to correlate purchasing and sales patterns. This level of information was important, but it usually did not in itself reveal why people buy in terms of the meanings the purchased product or brand had for them.

One of the most significant features of the MR development was that it made researchers realize that they needed new ways of thinking about buyers, consumers and products. New concepts led to investigating factors which hadn't received systematic attention before, and to the use of research approaches relatively new to marketing. MR pointed out the importance of egoistic and social needs as determinants of behaviour, adding them to the physical and economic needs which previously had received the bulk of investigative attention.

In the 1960s, two quantitative approaches came to dominate this new discipline – one based on economics, operations research and statistical inference, the other on the behavioural sciences, centered in schools with powerful social science departments. Both contributed to dissatisfaction with Dichter's theory. Criticism centered on methodological shortcomings, not to mention the improper invasion of people's private thoughts to persuade them to buy things.

Critics also took aim at the MR's tendency to impute sexual motivation to rather prosaic consumer purchases. While the sexual explanations for mundane consumption activities were no doubt interesting, they rarely contained information that marketers really could use, according to critics.

By the end of the 1960s, marketing turned towards more rigorous quantitative research. Proponents of the new "buyer behaviour" school of research that came to dominate marketing turned away from MR.

Despite its generation of eclipse, motivational research is still used by marketers – mostly in advertising agencies -- to gain deeper insights into why consumers behave as they do. The unconscious mind is recognized as an important source of motivation, and some practitioners find value in probing the thoughts of individuals.

Dichter's "depth" interview, in fact, is making a comeback in consumer research. Modified depth interviews are often used in focus groups to elicit ideas for new products and promotional campaigns. Academic researchers acknowledge the historical importance of motivation research as the precursor to lifestyle studies, and deem it once more an acceptable research technique for understanding the consumer.

Newer forms of motivation research are also designed to get at the core truths below a person's surface rationalization. These tools, with snappy names like "Emotional SONAR" and "Emotional Lexicon," are computer-assisted diagnostic tools.

There are four techniques of conducting motivation research:

(a) Non-disguised Structured Techniques.

(b) Non-disguised, Non-structured Techniques.

(c) Disguised Non-structured Techniques.

(d) Disguised structured Techniques.

**(a) Non-disguised Structured Techniques:**

This approach employs a standardized questionnaire to collect data on beliefs, feelings, and attitude from the respondent. For instance

**Single Question Method:**

(I think it is a good product or I think it is a poor product).

**Multiple Questions Method:**

(Numbers of questionnaires asked about the attitude) and Physiological Tests (laboratory tests such as galvanic skin response, eye movement etc. measure attitudes of people towards products) are carried out under this approval.

**(b) Non-disguised, Non-structured Techniques:**

These techniques use a non-standardized questionnaire. The techniques are also called depth interview, qualitative interviews, unstructured interviews, or focussed interviews. All these techniques are designed to gather information on various aspects of human behaviour including the "why" component.

**(c) Disguised, Non-structured Techniques:**

In this approach, the purpose of study is not discussed to respondents unlike above two cases. A list of unstructured questions is used to collect data on consumer's attitudes. This art of using disguised and unstructured method is referred to as "Projective Techniques".

The projective techniques include several tests given to the respondents. They may be asked to give their comments on cartoons, pictures, stories, etc. The stimuli used for this purpose are capable of answering the respondent to a variety of reactions. A number of Projective Techniques, are available to the market researchers for the purpose of analysing "why" part of consumer behaviour.

**Qualitative Techniques:**

(Projective Techniques and Word Association as follows).

The main Projective Techniques are:

**1. Word Association Test:**

The interviewer calls a series of listed words one by one and the respondents quickly replies the first word that enters his mind. The underlying assumption is that by "free associating" with certain stimuli (words). the responses are timed so that those answers which the respondent "response out" are identified.

**2. Sentence Completion:**

Sentence completion test is similar to word association test except that the respondent is required to complete an unfinished sentence.

For example, "I do not use shampoos because......."

"Coffee that is quickly made............ ".

**3. Story Completion:**

In this technique, the respondent is asked to complete a story, end of which is missing. This enables a researcher to find out the almost exact version of images and feelings of people towards a company's product. This helps in finalising the advertising and promotional themes for the product in question.

**4. Research of Ink-blot Tests (or Research Tests):**

Motivation Research employs this famous test. These tests are not in much use in marketing research. The research test expresses in a classic way the rationale behind all projective tests, that is, in filling the missing parts of a vague and incomplete stimulus, the respondent projects himself and his personality into the picture.

A lot of ink is put on the piece of paper and reference is made of company, product, and the respondent is asked to give his viewpoints after interpreting what he sees in the blot before him. The respondent say, "ugly packaging of the product", or "excellent performance of the product". This response will help the seller to finalise his marketing strategies.

**5. Psychographic Technique:**

This includes galvanic skin response, eye movement and eye blink test etc. which uses various instruments with the physiological responses.

**6. Espionage Technique:**

There are two methods in this technique:

(i) **Use of Hidden Recorders:** Such as hidden tape recorders, cameras used to watch consumers as they make purchases or consume items.

(ii) **Rubbish Research:** This is another method of espionage activity. Here, the researcher shifts through the garbage of individuals or groups and record pattern of consumption, waste, and brand preference. It gives most required estimates of consumption of cigarettes, medicines, liquor, magazines, etc.

**(d) Disguised Structured Techniques:**

When we are to measure those attitudes which respondents might not readily and accurately express, we can use disguised structured techniques. The disguised structured questionnaire are easy to administer and code.

Respondents are given questions which they are not likely to be able to answer accurately. In such circumstances, they are compelled to 'guess at' the answers. The respondent's attitude on the subject is assumed to be revealed to the extent and direction in which these guessing errors are committed.

**Uses of Motivation Research:**

1. Motivation Research leads to useful insights and provides inspiration to creative person in the advertising and packing world.
2. Knowledge and measurement of the true attitude of customers help in choosing the best selling appeal for the product and the best way to represent the product in the sales talk, and in determining the appropriateness and weightage of various promotional methods.
3. Motivation Research can help in measuring changes in attitudes, thus advertising research.
4. Knowledge and measurement of attitudes provides us with an imaginative market segmentation tool and also enables estimating market potential of each additional segment.
5. Strategies to position the offer of the company in a particular market segment should be based on the findings of motivation research.

**Limitations of Motivation Research:**

1. Cautions are required to be exercised not only in the application of these techniques but also the resultant data should be analysed and interpreted according to the psychological theory.
2. Originally, these techniques were developed to collect data from a single individual over a period of time. It is not free from drawbacks while we apply these techniques to gather data from a number of individuals.
3. The designing and administering of these techniques need qualified and experimented researchers. Such personnel are not easily available.

### 8.10.2 *Content Analysis*

Content Analysis is described as the scientific study of content of communication. It is the study of the content with reference to the meanings, contexts and intentions contained in messages.

In 1952, Bernard Berelson published Content analysis in Communication Research, which heralded recognition for the technique as a versatile tool for social science and media researchers. Some scholars adopted it for historical and political research as well.

The development of content analysis as a full-fledged scientific method took place during World War II when the U.S. government sponsored a project under the directorship of Harold Lasswell to evaluate enemy propaganda.

Content denotes what is contained and content analysis is the analysis of what is contained in a message. Broadly, content analysis may be seen as a method where the content of the message forms the basis for drawing inferences and conclusions about the content. Content analysis falls in the interface of observation and document analysis. It is defined as a method of observation in the sense that instead of asking people to respond to questions, it "takes the communications that people have produced and asks questions of communications".

Like any other research method, content analysis conforms to three basic principles of scientific method. They are:

1. **Objectivity:** Which means that the analysis is pursued on the basis of explicit rules, which enable different researchers to obtain the same results from the same documents or messages.

2. **Systematic:** The inclusion or exclusion of content is done according to some consistently applied rules whereby the possibility of including only materials which support the researcher's ideas is eliminated.

3. **Generalizability:** The results obtained by the researcher can be applied to other similar situations.

**Purposes of Content analysis**

| | | |
|---|---|---|
| To describe the characteristics of content | What? | • To describe trends in communication content<br>• To relate known characteristics of sources to the messages they produce<br>• To check communication content against standards |
| | How? | • To analyze techniques of persuasion<br>• To analyze style |
| | To whom? | • To relate known characteristics of the audience to messages produced for them<br>• To describe patterns of communication |
| To make inferences about the causes of content | Why? | • To secure political and military intelligence<br>• To analyze psychological traits of individuals<br>• To infer aspects of culture and cultural change<br>• To provide legal evidence |
| | Who? | To answer questions of disputed authorship |
| To make inferences about the effect of content | With what effect? | • To measure readability<br>• To analyze the flow of information<br>• To assess responses to communication |

**What Content Analysis can Do?**

1. It goes beyond the impressionistic observations about the phenomena and can help you make a quantitative expression about the phenomenon, i.e., express it in numbers, in percentages, which will be more specific and objective.

2. It is an unobtrusive research technique useful to study sensitive research topics.

3. It is context-sensitive and therefore can process symbolic meanings of data. Though predominantly seen as a quantitative method, it can effectively capture qualitative content as well. The context-sensitivity of the method will be useful in articulating the qualitative dimensions such as for example, the direction of coverage of news items as favorable or unfavorable.

4. It is a safe method in the sense that if the researcher found that a portion of the necessary information was missing or incorrectly coded, it is possible to return to the text and supplement the missing data. This is not always possible in experimental or survey research.

5. It can deal with large volumes of data. Processing may be laborious but of late computers made the job fairly easy.

6. It is a shoestring methodology, which is typically labour-intensive and requires minimum capital investment.

**Technique of Content Analysis**

More specifically, studies using content analysis usually involve the following six steps:

1. **Formulation of the research question or objectives:** Content analysis is a method for analyzing textual content.

2. **Selection of communication content and sample:** The selection of topic should be one that can be answered by analyzing the appropriate communication content. If the body of content is excessive, then a sample needs to be worked out. Though sampling in content analysis is not so much different from sampling in surveys, because of the unique nature of the source material used in this method, there developed some special sampling techniques for content analysis. Thus, depending upon the nature of the communication content – whether it is a new item, editorial, short story or a TV serial -the sampling techniques differ.

3. **Developing content categories:** Content categories can be defined as compartments or "pigeon holes" with explicitly stated boundaries into which the units of content are coded for analysis. They in fact flow from the research question and should be anchored in a review of relevant literature and related studies. Content categories are constructed in response to the query: What classification would most efficiently yield the data needed to answer the research questions raised? Developing the category system to classify the body of text is the heart of content analysis. Content analysis stands or falls by its categories. Particular studies have been productive to the extent that the categories were clearly formulated and well adapted to the problem and the content. To be useful, every content category must be completely and thoroughly defined, indicating what type of material is and is not to be included.

4. Finalizing units of analysis

5. Preparing a coding schedule, pilot testing and checking inter-coder reliabilities

6. Analyzing the collected data

"Content analysis stands or falls by its categories. Particular studies have been productive to the extent that the categories were clearly formulated and well adapted to the problem and the content". To be useful, every content category must be completely and thoroughly defined, indicating what type of material is and is not to be included. Such definitions in most of the cases should be written down before coding begins. These form the operational definitions of categories. Categories must be mutually exclusive so that a word, a paragraph or a theme belongs in one and only one category. Also, the categories must be exhaustive so that all units examined fit in an appropriate category. Sometimes, a 'miscellaneous or residual category' is added for units that occur rarely or are uncodable for other reasons. There are two kinds of units of analysis. (1) Recording units, and (2) Context units. The recording unit is the specific segment of content in which the occurrence of a reference/fact is counted or the unit can be broken down so that reference/facts can be placed in different categories. For example, if it is a single word say 'democracy', the number of times the word appears can be counted. Similarly, a sentence, or a paragraph, a news item or an article containing a symbol or a theme, or a group of facts can also be a unit. Thus, a news item containing a group of facts can be coded in different categories. Defining categories and preparing coding schedule for the analysis and coding of content are simultaneous steps. A coding schedule resembles a survey questionnaire and contains different dimensions of the communication content to be coded. Next, piloting the coding schedule is a crucial step before launching the full-scale content analysis. Test coding of a small sample of the material to be analyzed helps reveal inconsistencies and inadequacies in the category construction. The definition of the research problem gives direction to data analysis, the patterns to be examined, and the relationships to be explored. As in the case of analysis of survey data, the starting point can be the description of the profile of the main categories such as for example characteristics and types of content by period, actors, and so on. One important development in content analysis is the use of computers in data analysis. Computer programmes like the "General Inquirer" can identify within a body of text, those words and phrases that belong to specified categories. Content analysis is a useful research technique for analyzing large bodies of text. It offers objective guidelines in the coding of the text and to draw inferences from the data. It helps in the coding of the text according to systematic and objective rules and in drawing inferences from the data. A successful content analysis study is the outcome of a series of good decisions. The process starts from the point of deciding whether the method is suitable to study the research topic under question. After clearly setting out the objectives of the study, the researcher proceeds to make decisions relating to units of analysis, developing content categories, sample and the sampling period. Orienting coders, checking inter-coder reliabilities and selecting appropriate statistical designs for presenting results are some of the essential tasks, which add rigor to the study.

Example: Content analysis. Assuming you have read news papers from 2001 to 2015 regarding farmers' suicide in India. You can represent your content analysis as follows:

| | |
|---|---|
| Due to burden of heavy loans | 55% |
| Due to tension from daughter's marriage and daughter | 15% |
| Crops failure due to bad monsoon | 15% |
| Bad habit of drinking | 5% |
| Gambling | 5% |
| Troubling family life | 5% |
| **Total** | **100%** |

### 8.10.3 Projective Technique

Researchers have given various descriptions of this technique. Projective Techniques are indirect and unstructured methods of investigation which have been developed by the psychologists and use projection of respondents for inferring about underline motives, urges or intentions which cannot be secure through direct questioning as the respondent either resists to reveal them or is unable to figure out himself. These techniques are useful in giving respondents opportunities to express their attitudes without personal embarrassment. These techniques help the respondents to project their own attitude and feelings unconsciously on the subject under study. Thus, Projective Techniques play an important role in motivational researches or in attitude surveys.

A focus group moderator's guide will often include group exercises or facilitation techniques as alternative approaches to direct questioning. While many of these alternative tactics are not unique to the group discussion method, and are also used in in-depth inter-college view research, they have become a popular device in focus groups, especially, in the marketing research field. These alternative approaches can be broadly categorized as either enabling or projective techniques, the difference being whether the moderator's intent is to simply modify a direct question to make it easier for group participants to express their opinions (enabling techniques) or delve into participants' less conscious, less rational, less socially-acceptable feelings by way of indirect exercises (projective techniques). Examples of enabling techniques are: sentence completion – e.g., "When I think of my favourite foods, I think of _____." or "The best thing about the new city transit system is _____."; word association – e.g., asking prospective college students, "What is the first word you think of when I say, 'first day of college'?" or asking hospital administrators, "When I say 'patient care', what is the first word or words that come to mind?"; and storytelling – e.g., "Tell me a story about the last time you made something for dinner using leftovers."

Projective techniques serve to depersonalize the discussion by moving away from direct questions specific to the research topic and instead ask participants to project their feelings by imagining the thoughts of others, role playing, and describing visual stimuli (such as images). Completing thought bubbles on a cartoon drawing depicting genderless characters, and selecting from a stack of photographs the images that best represent how participants feel about a topic are just two examples of projective techniques.

The use of projective techniques is especially rampant among marketing researchers who increasingly (with the growing capabilities of online research) devise new variations of projective exercises. However, from a quality-design perspective, the use of projective techniques can be problematic and begs the question of whether or how much projective techniques bring added value to the group discussion. While enabling techniques are extensions of direct questioning that fall within the researcher's natural skill set, the indirect method of projective exercises drifts into the little-known realm, among many social science researchers, of clinical psychology. Regardless of whether focus group participants are given the opportunity to explain their own interpretation of their thought bubble, drawing, or picture sort – or whether the interpretation is left for the researcher – the inherent subjectivity of the meanings that are ultimately associated with participants' output threatens the validity of these techniques.

The credibility of qualitative research data partially rests on knowing what is being measured, yet the short duration of a focus group session - and the moderator's limited depth of knowledge about the participants – may make true interpretations of the data (and linkages back to the research objectives) from projective techniques a challenge. What, for example, has the researcher measured from a collage exercise resulting in a collection of seemingly unrelated images from each of 10 group participants? The moderator can investigate each participant's interpretation of their "artwork" but the reality is that the focus group moderator does not have the capability of knowing whether the collage exercise tapped into an unconscious realization important to the research objectives, or knowing if the exercise measured aspects of the participant related to (for example) motivations, cultural background, or social awareness.

To maximize the credibility of focus group data stemming from the use of enabling and projective techniques, researchers must carefully select which techniques to use based on their ability to interpret the results in conjunction with the in-session time the moderator will be able to give to these exercises. For instance, the researcher might opt for a smaller discussion format, such as dyads and triads, in order to accommodate the necessary time to complete a projective technique, such as a picture sort, including a thorough examination of each participant's reasons for the photographs he or she selected as well as those that were rejected. The careful use of these techniques will not only enhance data credibility but also increase the overall quality of the research by allowing the researcher to perform necessary verification procedures (such as triangulation) in the analysis phase. (Source: www.researchreview.com)

## Important Projective Techniques

1. Word Association Test.
2. Completion Test.
3. Construction Techniques
4. Expression Techniques

1. **Word Association Test:** An individual is given a clue or hint and asked to respond to the first thing that comes to mind. The association can take the shape of a picture or a word. There can be many interpretations of the same thing. A list of words is given and you don't know in which word they are most interested. The interviewer records the responses which reveal the inner feeling of the respondents. The frequency with which

any word is given a response and the amount of time that elapses before the response is given are important for the researcher. For example, out of 50 respondents, 20 people associate the word "Fair" with "Complexion".

2. **Completion Test:** In this, the respondents are asked to complete an incomplete sentence or story. The completion will reflect their attitude and state of mind.
3. **Construction Test:** This is more or less like completion test. They can give you a picture and you are asked to write a story about it. The initial structure is limited and not detailed like the completion test. For example, 2 cartoons are given and a dialogue is to be written.
4. **Expression Techniques:** In this, the people are asked to express the feeling or attitude of other people.

**Disadvantages of Projective Techniques**

1. Highly trained interviewers and skilled interpreters are needed.
2. Interpreters bias can be there.
3. It is a costly method.
4. The respondent selected may not be representative of the entire population.

## 8.11 Qualitative versus Quantitative Research

Qualitative research methodologies have roots in a variety of disciplines, including anthropology, psychology, linguistics, communication, economics, and semiotics. Historically, qualitative methodologies have been available much longer, some as early as the 19th century, than the quantitative tools marketers rely on so heavily. Possibly because of their origins, qualitative methods don't enjoy the unqualified endorsement of upper management. Many senior managers maintain that qualitative data are too subjective and are susceptible to human error and bias in data collection and interpretation. They believe such research provides an unstable foundation for expensive and critical business decisions. The fact that results cannot be generalized from a qualitative study to a larger population is considered a fundamental weakness. Increasingly, however, managers are returning to these techniques as quantitative techniques fall short of providing the insights needed to make those ever-more-expensive business decisions. Managers deal with the issue of trustworthiness of qualitative data through exacting methodology:

- Carefully using literature searches to build probing questions.
- Thoroughly justifying the methodology or combination of methodologies chosen.
- Executing the chosen methodology in its natural setting (field study) rather than a highly controlled setting (laboratory).
- Choosing sample participants for relevance to the breadth of the issue rather than how well they represent the target population.
- Developing and including questions that reveal the exceptions to a rule or theory.
- Carefully structuring the data analysis.
- Comparing data across multiple sources and different contexts.
- Conducting peer-researcher debriefing on results for added clarity, additional insights, and reduced bias.

On the other hand quantitative **research** attempts precise measurement of something. In business research, quantitative methodologies usually measure consumer behaviour, knowledge, opinions, or attitudes. Such methodologies answer questions related to how much, how often, how many, when, and who. While the survey is not the only methodology of the quantitative researcher, it is considered a dominant one.

The purpose of qualitative research is based on "researcher immersion in the phenomenon to be studied gathering data which provide a detailed description of events, situations and interaction between people things, providing depth and detail. Quantitative research is often used for theory testing, requiring the researcher maintain a distance from the research so as not to bias the results. Qualitative research — times labelled as *interpretive research* because it seeks to develop understanding through detailed description, often builds theory but rarely tests it.

Besides the purpose of the research, this process sets up several key distinctions between qualitative and quantitative research, as shown below (adopted from 'Cooper and Schindler, 2006).

| **Research Agenda** | **Qualitative** | **Quantitative** |
|---|---|---|
| Focus | Understand and interpret | Describe, explain and predict |
| Involvement | High as researcher is participant and catalyst | Researcher keeps himself away to reduce bias |
| Purpose | In-depth understanding, theory building | Describe, predict and test theory |
| Sample design | Non-probability, purposive | Probability |
| **Sample size** | **Small** | **Large** |
| Research design | May evolve during research<br>Often uses multiple methods<br>Consistency is not expected<br>Longitudinal approach | Pre-determined<br>One method or mixed methods<br>Consistency is critical<br>Cross sectional or longitudinal |
| Participants | They need to be explained the process or purpose | No preparation desired to avoid bias |
| Data Type | Verbal or pictorial description | Data is reduced to numerical codes |
| Data analysis | Primarily non-quantitative –human coding and analysis<br>Always ongoing during the research process<br>Distinction between facts and judgment less clear | Statistical and mathematical methods dominate.<br>May be ongoing<br>Maintains clear distinction between facts and judgment |
| Insights and meanings | Deeper level of understanding is the norm; determined by type and quantity of free-response questions<br>Researchers, participants interaction need insights | Limited by the opportunity to probe respondents; quantity of the original data instrumental.<br>Insights follow data collection and data entry with a limitation to interview partcipants |

Unlike the case with quantitative data, both the researcher and research sponsor often have more significant involvement in collecting and interpreting qualitative data. The researcher may serve as a participant or a catalyst, as a participant observer, or as a group interview moderator. The research sponsor may observe with close circuit televisions and, influence interview questions, and add interpretations and insights during the process. By contrast, with large quantitative studies researcher who interprets the data and draws conclusions from it is rarely the data collector and often has no contact at all with the participant. Since researchers are immersed in the participant's world, any knowledge they gain can be used to adjust the data extracted from the next participant. In quantitative research, identical data are desired from all participants, so evolution of methodology is not acceptable.

Quantitative data often consist of participant responses that are coded, categorized, and reduced to numbers so that these data may be manipulated for statistical analysis. One objective is the quantitative tally of events or opinions, *called frequency of response*. Qualitative data are all about texts. Detailed descriptions of events, situations, and interactions, either verbal or visual, constitute the data. Data may be contained within the transcriptions of interviews or video focus groups, as well as in notes taken during those interactions. By definition they generate reams of words that need to be coded and analysed by humans for meaning.

Qualitative studies with their smaller sample sizes offer an opportunity for faster turnaround of findings. While speed should never be the primary reason for choosing a methodology, qualitative data may be especially useful to support a low-risk decision that must be made quickly.

## 8.12 Merging Qualitative and Quantitative Methodologies

**Triangulation** is the term used to describe the combining of several qualitative methods or combining qualitative with quantitative methods. Triangulation is the application and combination of several research methodologies in the study of the same phenomenon.

- It can be employed in both quantitative (validation) and qualitative (inquiry) studies.
- It is a method-appropriate strategy of founding the credibility of qualitative analyses.
- It becomes an alternative to traditional criteria like reliability and validity
- It is the preferred line in the social sciences

By combining multiple observers, theories, methods, and empirical materials, researchers can hope to overcome the weakness or intrinsic biases and the problems that come from single method, single-observer, and single-theory studies.

Qualitative studies may be combined with quantitative ones to increase the perceived quality of the research, especially when a quantitative study follows a qualitative one and provides validation for the qualitative findings. Four strategies for combining methodologies are common in marketing research:

1. Qualitative and quantitative studies can be conducted simultaneously.
2. A qualitative study can be ongoing while multiple waves of quantitative studies are done, measuring changes in behavior and attitudes over time.
3. A qualitative study can precede a quantitative study, and a second qualitative study thon might follow the quantitative study, seeking more clarification.
4. A quantitative study can precede a qualitative study.

## 8.13 How to Do?

Dolly: "Something has been repeated in the chapter what has already been discussed."

Jolly: "See, we discussed literature review, descriptive studies and exploratory studies in earlier chapters. Qualitative studies are exploratory in nature. However when the methods of data, we may also call it information, are individual interviews, group interviews, focus group discussion, observations, case studies, etc, the discussion is mostly qualitative. Quantitative data is rarely discussed. In case studies we use secondary data, but in other studies quantitative data does not take any dominance. However in observations frequencies are observed."

Dolly: "You mean to say we learn by experience and observation."

Jolly: "If qualitative data is corroborated with quantitative data analysis, the findings can be valid."

Dolly: "In MBA curriculum, many students go for a summer job, what should they do."

Jolly: "They can work on their projects in two ways –one experience survey and second a case study."

Dolly: "Suppose if I go to Axis Bank for a summer job?"

Jolly: "You see, you can have a specific problem which you can address – for instance treasury procedures of bank, but your main objective should be to learn about organization structure, branch network, branch operations, top-middle level strategies, finance of the bank, marketing strategies, HR policies, operational controls, management controls."

Dolly: "You mean to say I should study it as a case, with experience and I can also work on specific problem."

Jolly: "Yes"

Dolly: "I wish to read a case study report."

Jolly: "Advanced researchers take up a problem and study with a case; some times they may not take other issues and may leave it on the readers to study."

Dolly: "For instance".

Jolly: "Dr. Mrs. Gunmala Suri from University Business School, Punjab University, Chandigarh has analysed Quality Management with a case study of Verka. Verka is a small town in District Amritsar, Punjab. It has a milk plant. Verka milk plant supplies milk to near by areas and butter and pure ghee to all over India. The case has been published in Journal of Global Economy, Volume 4 no.2"

Dolly: "Yes, I want to read it."

Jolly: "Go ahead which is our project no 6."

✦ ✦ ✦

Research Project 6

## 8.14 Paving The Way For Business Quality With Integrated Business Innovations: A Case Study of Verka

Dr Gunmala Suri[1]

### Introduction

In today's highly competitive business environment, customer satisfaction level is a single most factor which measures the fitness level of a business organization. Best quality at lowest cost is a hallmark for every entrepreneur in all spheres of activities they perform and all products and services they deliver; Taylor (2003).

There is no choice left other than sustaining excellence by making Total Quality happen not only for survival of the organization but also for the survival of individuals. Question now is how? Answer lies in TQM — Total Quality Management; Paton (1994).

TQM is not a fixed destiny. It is a continuous journey towards excellence. A strong foundation based on Quality Assurance system in any organization is a must for TQM; Stratton (1993). This is essential to adopt a systematic approach towards regular setting of higher goals of improvements and achieving them continually; Tari (2004).

Installation and maintenance of an internationally recognized ISO: 9000 Quality Assurance system at all the prime production shops of an organization is a first step for its journey toward excellence. This system provides a structured platform for continuous improvement based on Deming's PDCA cycle; Sun (2000).

To do things that you alone can do best requires a high degree of creativity and innovation. It requires a culture where failure is not punished but it is treated as one step towards success. Such quality culture has to be fostered and nurtured in an organization. Only then improvements will take place at a faster pace to match with the changing needs of the customer; Fullerton (2001).

### Quality Assurance System

Organizations that prepare themselves to endure the test of time, maintain cutting edge on a clearly laid down vision, policy and strategies. The vision guides and communicates with the organization's people ensuring steadfast commitment to their own aspiration for determining a constancy of purpose; Byrne (1997). Vision therefore stipulates a process of communication, which builds trust and enables permeation of clear and consistent values through the rank and file of the organization.

In order to explore various aspects of international competitiveness MILKFED has identified **seven key dimensions** (popularly known as 7Cs) that are as follows:

1. Consistent quality
2. Committed delivery
3. Customized product-mix

[1] Faculty, University Business School, Punjab University, Chandigarh.

4. Contemporary products
5. Competitive price
6. Complaint price
7. Complaint settlement
8. Culture of customer service

## Core Values

The path of vision is lit up by the four core values, which are embedded in every activity by the people. These Core Values are:

- Customer satisfaction
- Concern for people
- Consistent profitability
- Commitment to excellence

To meet the expectations of the customers regarding better quality products at a competitive price and faster delivery is formulating a suitable Quality Policy; Stratton (1993).

## Quality Policy

1. Attaining market leadership through enhancing customer satisfaction.
2. Achieving continual improvement in productivity, quality and saleability of products.
3. Active involvement of all people in achieving objectives and targets.
4. Adherence to a quality management system based on ISO: 9001:2000 and its periodic review for continued effectiveness.

## Quality Objectives

In order to achieve highest level of customer satisfaction, MILKFED has set an organizational level Quality objective in line with its Quality policy. The quality objective is set to enhance customer satisfaction through-

1. Improvement in productivity and product quality.
2. Skill enhancement of people and
3. Reviewing market trends.

The organizational level Quality objective is further broken into department level objectives and targets for achieving improvements. Against each departmental objective and target a detailed action plan is made and implemented. The status of fulfilment of the action plan is reviewed periodically at different levels.

## Quality Management at MILKFED:

MILKFED is using various quality management tools and techniques namely 5S activities, Kaizen Activities, Brainstorming, PERT, CPM, PDCA Cycle, Failure Mode Effect analysis, Control Chart and Histograms.

In respect of quality, the Federation has established new milestones and received certification under ISO: 9001:2000 and HACCP: 15000. Quality milk is collected from producers by trained staff after inspection or testing. Incentives are paid to milk producers based on testing. The aim is to provide remunerative prices to milk producers directly by avoiding middle men and manufacture and supply of best quality of milk. The ISO certification has enhanced the national and international competitiveness of Milk Plant, which is the first Dairy Plant in the country to have got ISO-9002 certification. Recently MILKFED has received the ISO/HACCP certification as per IS/ISO 9002 and IS 15000, which are also first integrated certificates awarded by BIS.

## TQM and JIT Manufacturing

Implementing JIT system requires implementation of a TQM system, where quality of the part produced by each piece of equipment is known. JIT is the next logical step in the TQM process; Prajogo (2006). The various steps that are part of the JIT system is essentially parts of the TQM and include:

1. Cutting lot sizes
2. Cutting setup times
3. Total quality management
4. Flexibility of manufacturing
5. Withdrawing buffer inventories
6. Simplifying buying practices

## TQM Model at MILKFED

TQM model at MILKFED rests on three pillars, namely the Total Employees Involvement (TEI), Just-In-Time (JIT), and Total Quality Control (TQC), encompassing all these is continuous improvement involving Kaizen and Small Group Activities.

There has been a paradigm shift in the people's involvement where employees are treated as partners A.S. Mishra, Manager Quality Control says, "If we are to stop at participation alone, TQM will stop just before that." Collaboration according to him will have to be induced slowly into the system. This ownership in involvement is much more meaningful than ownership is brought about by communication, training, respect for each other and openness. He feels that it is important to make every employee a happy member of the organization. This is the crux of people's involvement.

At MILKFED it has been significant that increases in productivity have been achieved by merging incentives into salary. By giving recognition, rewards and responsibilities to the workmen, there has been a continuous individual improvement. The TEI also helped evolve work culture, work ethics, improved housekeeping and formation of teams for improvement activities.

MILKFED has undergone a sea change with regard to housekeeping, workers involvement and work culture through Kaizen and small group activities (SGAs) Workers, who in the past were idle have now, occupied positions as partners. Each worker has been trained in multiple-functions. They clean; they set machine times and are responsible in handling and maintenance of machines.

JIT as generally perceived is the supply of parts for the producing. But Mishra says that "In our TQM model it is something much beyond. The first thing which he points out is to expose and eliminate waste. The next thing is to find the requirements of the customer (be it internal or external) and expose them so that they can be tackled. There is emphasis on cost reduction through waste elimination explains Mishra because the customer will always choose the product which has the lowest unit cost. The results of JIT he says "have been mind-boggling. The manufacturing system has become flexible, inventories have been reduced, and vendors have been benefited."

## About Organization: MILKFED-PUNJAB

The Punjab State Co-operative Milk Producers' Federation Limited popularly known as MILKFED Punjab came into existence in 1973 with a twin objective of providing remunerative milk market to Milk Producers in the State by value addition, marketing of produce and to provide technical inputs to milk producers for enhancement of milk production.

The Federation was registered much earlier, but it took shape in the 1983 when all milk plants of the erstwhile Punjab Dairy Development Corporation Limited were handed over to Co-operative sector and the entire State of Punjab was covered under Operation Flood to give farmers a better deal and customers better products. The set up is a three tier system, Milk Producers Co-operative Societies at the village level, Milk Unions at District level and Federation as an Apex Body at State level.

## The Umbrella Brand

Verka products are available in a number of retail outlets across states of Punjab, Himachal, Haryana and Chandigarh through its strong distribution network. The network follows an umbrella branding strategy. Verka is a common brand for most product categories produced by various unions: liquid milk, milk powders, cheese, sweets, ice creams and condensed milk. By insisting on an umbrella brand, MILKFED not only skilfully avoided inter-union conflicts but also created an opportunity for the union members to co-operate in developing products.

## Working Environment

The manufacturing process is labour intensive. As in any team concept, rewards and incentives are linked to team output. MILKFED profits are distributed amongst the milk producers. Every Friday, between 10:00 a.m. and 11:00 a.m., all employees at Verka meet at the nearest office, department, branch or depot to discuss their quality concerns.

## Brand Extension

Changing times brought new trends, needs, tastes and hopes. Verka dynamic as ever, too acquired newer forms. Consumers could have their own pick as Verka came up with varied varieties of cheese like the Processed Cheese, Cheese Spread, and cheese singles. And there were milk powders like Dairy Whitener, Skimmed Milk Powder and Infant Milk Powder. Health Drinks like Verka Vigor, Verka Lassi, Sweetened Flavored Milk and a mango drink called Raseela. Then there were Curd and a whole lot of different flavours of Ice Creams. Milk had never meant so much before.

The process of organizing societies at villages started in Punjab as early as 1978. By the end of March, 2005 there were 6104 functional Dairy Co-operative Societies (DCS). Efforts were made to strengthen the existing DCS and to revitalize the defunct/closed Societies. Average milk procurement during 2004-05 was 7.81 lacs kg per day as compared to 7.45 lacs kg in 2003-04. As a step to bring transparency in Milk Procurement at the village level and accuracy in the milk payment system and to boost the confidence of the Milk Producer Farmers, MILKFED has installed around 1000 Automatic Milk Collection Centres and 1035 Electronic Milko Testers at village level Dairy Co-operative Societies.

The Federation is providing technical input services like veterinary Health Care, Artificial Insemination services, prophylactic vaccination, supply of balanced Cattle Feeds and quality

Fodder Seeds to the specific target group (Milk Producers Co-operative Society's Members) at their door steps with a view to enhance milk production at low cost.

MILKFED assisted District Co-operative Milk Unions perform large number of inseminations, serving societies through single and cluster artificial insemination centres.

Acquiring and application of best technologies in breed improvements is the key to improve the animal production and helping in raising the milk producers' income. MILKFED continued to assist dairy co-operatives in the state in animal breeding, feeding and health care.

MILKFED has it own Sperm Station at Khanna (District Ludhiana) for production of excellent quality of Frozen Semen. MILKFED'S Sperm Station has recently been awarded IS/ISO:9001-2000 Certification by B.I.S. MILKFED Punjab has become the first Co-operative Sector organization in Northern India to get International Quality Management Certificated for its Sperm Station for providing Frozen Semen of elite bulls of Cattle and Buffaloes of International Standards.

Government of Punjab has identified Dairy Sector as thrust area for rural development. Recently MILKFED Punjab has signed Memorandum of understanding (MOU) with State Bank of India, State Bank of Patiala and Oriental Bank of Commerce for providing loans up to ₹ 50,000 without any collateral security to Milk Producers farmers for purchase of milch cattle on soft terms and low rate of interest.

MILKFED has started production of various types of Cattle Feeds at its Cattle Feed Plants as per the requirement of the milk producers viz ISI-Typer-II, High Energy & By-Pass protein Cattle Feeds. Federation has introduced Buffalo feed which has rich FAT contents and meets the nutritional requirements of Buffaloes.

Cattle Feed Plants are producing mineral mixture as per ISI specifications with a view to provide good quality mineral mixture at reasonable rates to dairy Farmers. MILKFED has established Urea Molasses of Lick Brick Plant of 5 M.Ts. per day capacity at Cattle Feed Plant, Bhattian which is catering to the needs of dairy farmers throughout Punjab. Earlier the Urea Molasses Bricks were produced by hot process and now to decrease the cost of UMB it has been modified to produce by cold process. Both Cattle Feed Plants have obtained ISO certification to ensure best quality of Cattle Feeds.

Considering the shortage and non-availability of quality fodder seeds, MILKFED, Punjab in the year 1984 started its own Fodder Seed production and distribution programme. It has established an automatic Seed processing Plant at Bassi Pathana, Distt. Fatehgarh Sahib. It has a capacity to process fodder seed at a rate of 2 M.Ts per hour.

## Women Dairy Project

MILKFED Punjab with a view to empower rural women has undertaken Women Dairy Project in six districts namely Hoshiarpur, Ropar, Patiala, Jalandhar, Ludhiana and Amritsar under Support to Training & Employment Programme (STEP) at an outlay of ₹ 8.37 crores with 90% grant from Govt. of India. Under these 390 Women Dairy Co-operative Societies have been organized having 19,980 women beneficiary members. STEP constitutes scheme for providing support services in organizing the Co-operative Societies for sustainable functioning. The process is coupled with creating awareness campaigns for member women concerning management of the societies, enhancement of milk production by providing breeding, feeding and managerial services to the beneficiaries.

MILKFED is serving nationwide consumers through its network of regional offices and strong distribution channels. MILKFED markets a wide range of products which include liquid Milk, Skimmed Milk Powder, Whole Milk Powder, Ghee, Butter, various types of Cheese, Tetra-pack Lassi, SFM, Ice Cream, Milk in variants of Standard, Toned, Double Toned and Panjabi Premium

Milk etc. under the brand name of VERKA. Verka is brand leader in milk powders particularly in northern and eastern sectors and SMP marketed by Milkfed commands a premium price over powders manufactured by competitors.

Federation exported milk products to the tune of ₹ 11.42 crore against export of ₹ 6.98 crore during the year. Milkfed has established its ghee market in Middle East. Verka ghee reaches all the Emirates and is available almost in all the super markets. The penetration is so deep that Verka ghee is available in far off labour camp. MILKFED Punjab ventured into the manufacture of Indian Sweets during different festivals. Tremendous response from customers was received and the quality of sweets marketed was highly appreciated by the consumers.

## Adoption of Information Technology

Computerization in MILKFED was started during 1987-88 with the installation of two Main Frame Computer Systems one at Milk Union, Jalandhar and other at MILKFED Head Office to process the data of Milk Unions. With the introduction of Personal Computer during 1992-93, the data processing was decentralized at Milk Union level. The activities like Milk Billing, Payroll, Financial Accounting, Marketing of Liquid Milk, Sale of products through Dealers and Milk Bars and different C.I.S. reports to Govt have been computerized. Keeping pace with changing technology SAP based ERP was implemented at Milk Union, Ropar in 2002.

MILKFED is catering to the need of unions in software development and providing training to staff in the operation of applications software and computer packages. The window based office automation package is being used in MILKFED and Milk Unions for routine office work. Computers have been inter-linked under Local Area Network at MILKFED Head Office and Milk Union, Ropar, Jalandhar, Ludhiana and Amristar.

E-Mail facility has been provided at all locations. Milk fed has launched its website and is receiving large number of trade enquiries from the buyers through its web site.

## Milk Plant Mohali - Symbol of White Revolution

The Ropar District is one of the smallest districts of Punjab forming only 4.3% of the total area of the State. About 40% of its area is sub-mountainous and not very conducive for dairying because of scarcity of green fodder. Despite all these bottlenecks, Milk Union Ropar District commenced its operations in the year 1979. Milk Plant Mohali of Ropar Union is now one of the best plants in Co-operative sector.

The salient points of its performance are summarized as under:

1. **Functional Societies:** Total 856 societies have membership of 45144 Milk Producers functioning at present. Of this, 110 societies are from Fatehgarh Sahib Distt., 75 from Patiala Distt. and remaining 671 societies fall in Ropar Distt.

2. **Financial Status of Societies:** Almost all the societies affiliated to this plant are running in profit and distribute their earning among the members in the form of bonus.

3. **Capacity Utilization of Plant:** During the year 2004-05, average 202% installed handling capacity of the plant per day has been utilized and during the year 2005-06 average 203% handling capacity has been utilized per day manned with 532 employees.

4. **ISO Certification:** In the field of Quality, this Plant has established new milestones and received certification under ISO: 9001: 2000 and HACCP: 15000.

## Conclusion

### (a) Quality Certification

India is a signatory to WTO Agreement on sanitary and phytosanitary (SPS) making it obligatory to adopt the standards, guideline and recommendations issued by Codex Alimentations Commission, which advocates of HACCP.

The Indian standard on Food Hygiene Hazard Analysis and Critical control point (HACCP) – system and guidelines for its application, IS: 15000:1998 is technically equivalent to the codex document on the subject. For food industry in India, adoption of HACCP has become imperative to reach global standards, demonstrate compliance to regulations and customer requirements for providing safe food to millions.

### Bureau of Indian Standards (BIS) Offers Two Certifications to the Food Industry

(a) Food Safely Management System Certification (HACCP) against IS: 15000: 1998.

(b) HACCP integrated with quality Management Certification provides for twin certification of Management System IS/ISO 9001: 2000 and certification of HACCP against IS 15000: 1998 through one audit and under one certificate.

During the post liberalization period, MILKFED in order to keep pace with an all-round development, decided to go in for certification of various Milk Plants and Cattle Feed Plants under International standards. Milk Plant, Ludhiana was the first Dairy Plant in the country to get ISO-9002 certificate. Thereafter, with the introduction of HACCP, decision was taken that besides taking certification for Milk Plant, Ludhiana all other plants will take joint certificate under ISO-9002 and IS-15000 (HACCP). Eight Milk Plants and two Cattle Feed Plants have already got this certification.

### (b) Dairy Co-operative Movement

A recent decision of the district co-operative milk unions in Punjab to sell milk under a single brand VERKA will definitely strengthen the co-operative dairy sectors.

This welcome development provides a competitive edge in today's market-driven economy. Before consolidation, the unions were selling their own brands in their respective territories. This was despite the fact that a national brand like Amul was available to them. At a time when there was a need to strengthen the common works brand in the wake of foray into production of various value-added products, the unions' passionate clinging to their local brands defied business logic.

In recent years, co-operatives have not been able to do effective marketing of their products as compared to big players due to their inability to generate adequate resources for advertisements, publicity events, and the like.

As a result, the co-operatives are always on the look out for cost effective methods to prune their expenditure on publicity, while remaining competitive at the same time by canalizing their resources into other needful areas.

Consolidation under a single brand led to a significant decline in the publicity expenses incurred by each union. This will enhance appeal as a unified brand with a clear identity that the customer can relate to.

Further consolidation of the brand provided clear identity of the strengths of co-operatives to customers. It is a perfect marketing tool to propagate the co-operative concept as a viable business strategy for the benefit of the consumers.

Despite co-operatives making immense progress in all fields, brand building has been a neglected area. Brand-building and consolidation, and highlighting the ways in which co-operative products are different from private sector products, are needed if co-operatives are to emerge as competitive business units.

Despite brand consolidation, MILKFED must take all necessary steps to ensure quality. Quality has been the trademark which has enabled it to build a strong customer base. The quality has to be standardized and strictly maintained. MILKFED must re-evaluate and devise effective strategies in this regard. Its ability to work on these lines will determine its competitiveness as compared to other private players.

The dairy sector has played a big role in building the image of the co-operative sector in recent times. The decision of the district unions to forge unity through a single brand definitely provides a new direction to the co-operative dairy sector. This will mould public opinion towards co-operatives in a more favourable way.

## References

Byrne, J. A. (1997). "Management Theory-or Fad of the Month?", *Business Week* , June 23, pp. 47.

Fullerton RR, McWatters CS. The production performance benefits from JIT implementation. Journal of Operations Management 2001;19:81–96.

Paton, S. M. (1994). "Is TQM Dead?", *Quality Digest*, April, pp. 24-28. Stratton, B. (1993). "Why You Can't Link Quality Improvement to Financial Performance",*Quality Progress*, February, pp. 5.

Prajogo I. Daniel, Sohal S. Amrik. (2006). "The relationship between organization strategy, total quality management (TQM), and organization performance—the mediating role of TQM". *Journal of Operational Research*, 168, 35-50.

Stratton, B. (1993). "Why You Can't Link Quality Improvement to Financial Performance",*Quality Progress*, February, pp. 5.

Sun, H. 2000. Total quality management, ISO 9000 certification and performance improvement. International Journal of Quality & Reliability Management 17, no. 2: 168-179.

Tari Jose Juan, and Sabater Vincente. (2004). "Quality tools and techniques: Are they necessary of quality management?" *Int. J. Production Economics*. 92, 267-280.

Taylor, W. A., and G. H. Wright. 2003. A longitudinal study of TQM implementation: Factors influencing success and failure. Omega 31: 97-111.

http://milkfed.nic.in/mark.htm

http://milkfed.nic.in/verka.htm

CHAPTER

# Quantitative Analysis

## Structure

The most difficult part in research is to define the research problem, develop and implement a sampling plan, conceptualize, operationalize and test your measures, and develop a design structure. The next step is to analyse data.

The data analysis involves three major steps, done roughly in this order:

(i) Transforming, editing, coding and organizing the data for analysis (Data Preparation)

(ii) Describing the data (Descriptive Statistics)

(iii) Testing Hypotheses and Models (Inferential Statistics)

Data Preparation involves checking and editing the data; checking the data for accuracy; tabulating the data; entering the data into the computer, if required; transforming the data; and developing and documenting a database structure that integrates the various measures.

Descriptive Statistics are used to describe the basic features of the data in a study. They provide simple summaries about the sample and the measures. Together with simple graphic analysis, they form the basis of virtually every quantitative analysis of data. With descriptive statistics you are simply describing what is, what the data shows.

Inferential Statistics investigate questions, models and hypotheses. We use descriptive statistics simply to describe what's going on in our data. But in case of inferential statistics we try to infer from the sample data what the population thinks or to make judgments of the probability that an observed difference between groups is a dependable one or one that might have happened by chance in this study. Usually, the researcher links each of the inferential analyses to specific research questions or hypotheses that were raised in the introduction, or notes any models that were tested that emerged as part of the analysis.

We come back again to our term validity. Of the four types of validity (internal validity, construct validity, external validity and conclusion validity) conclusion validity is undoubtedly the least considered and most misunderstood because it was earlier termed as 'statistical' conclusion validity and statistics scares off most of the students.

Conclusion validity is the degree to which conclusions we reach about relationships in our data are reasonable. For instance, if we wish to study the relationship between income and consumption, we eventually want to reach some conclusion. Based on our data, we may conclude that there is a positive relationship that persons with higher income tend to consume more. Conclusion validity is the degree to which the conclusion we reach is credible or believable.

Although conclusion validity was originally thought to be a statistical inference issue, it has become more apparent that it is also relevant in qualitative research. Whenever you investigate a relationship, you essentially have two possible conclusions – either there is a relationship in your data or there isn't. In either case, you may be wrong in your conclusion. You may conclude that there is a relationship when in fact there is not, or you may infer that there isn't a relationship when in fact there is. So, we have to consider all of these possibilities when we talk about conclusion validity.

It's important to realize that conclusion validity is an issue whenever you conclude there is a relationship, even when the relationship is between some programme (or treatment) and some outcome. In other words, conclusion validity also pertains to causal relationships. To differentiate between conclusion validity and internal validity which is also involved with causal relationships, we shall have to understand that conclusion validity is only concerned with whether there is a relationship. For instance, in income and consumption relationship we conclude that with rise in income consumption rises. Conclusion validity is essential whether that relationship is a reasonable one or not, given the data. But it is possible that we will conclude that, while there is a relationship between the income and consumption, the income didn't cause the consumption. Perhaps some other factor, and not income, was responsible for the rise in consumption. For instance, the observed differences in the consumption could be due to the fact families were wealthy or some other reasons. This issue, the possibility that some other factor than income caused consumption, is what internal validity is all about. So, it is possible that in a study we can conclude that income and consumption are related (conclusion validity) and also conclude that the consumption was caused by some factor other than the income (i.e., we don't have internal validity).

One major problem is that it is often hard to see a relationship because our measures or observations have low reliability – they are too weak relative to all of the 'noise' in the environment. Another issue is that the relationship we are looking for may be a weak one and seeing it is a bit like looking for a needle in the haystack. Sometimes the problem is that we just didn't collect enough information to see the relationship even if it is there. To explain the internal validity and external validity let us see the following function:

Consumption = f (income)

Can income be the only factor causing consumption, we think that wealthy persons also consume more so consumption = f (income, wealth) but here income and wealth are also correlated (issue of autocorrelation has been discussed in chapter regression), but we may raise our doubts in internal validity. But age is also an important factor which may cause more consumption, so there are many threats to internal and conclusions validity. All of these problems are related to the idea of statistical power.

## Data Preparation

When quantitative or qualitative data is gathered, it may have many errors. A few questions might not have been answered. Other questions may have errors in writing. Further a few responses have to be coded. For instance, if you ask somebody's age, age say from 5 to 65. It will be difficult to analyze with such a big range. You need to create a range say between 5 to 25, 25-55 and above 55. Further, you can code 5 to 25 as 1, 25-55 as 2 and above 55 as 3. Errors are removed through editing and coding is done to simplify data ranges for analysis.

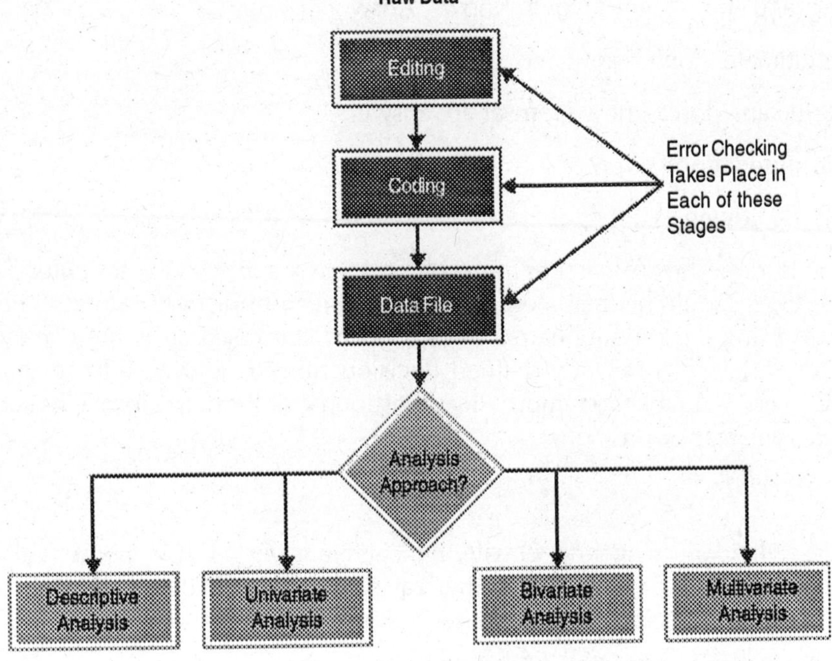

## Editing

Editing is the process of checking and adjusting responses in the completed questionnaires for omissions, legibility, and consistency and readying them for coding and storage.

1. **Field Editing:** Preliminary editing is done by a field supervisor on the same day as the interview to catch technical omissions, check legibility of handwriting, and clarify responses that are logically or conceptually inconsistent. If you are researcher and surveyor, you can edit the data there and then at the time of interview.

2. **In-house Editing:** Editing is performed by a central office staff; often done more rigorously than field editing.

    1. For consistency between and among responses
    2. For completeness in responses – to reduce effects of item non-response
    3. To better utilize questions answered out of order
    4. To facilitate the coding process

## Editing for Completeness

- **Item Non-response:** The technical term for an unanswered question on an otherwise complete questionnaire resulting in missing data.
- **Plug Value:** An answer that an editor "plugs in" to replace blanks or missing values so as to permit data analysis; choice of value is based on a predetermined decision rule.
- **Impute:** To fill in a missing data point through the use of a statistical algorithm that provides a best guess for the missing response based on available information.
- Facilitating the Coding Process
- Data Clean-up
    - Checking written responses for any stray marks, remove unwanted marks
- Editing and Tabulating "Don't Know" Answers
    - Legitimate don't know (no opinion)
    - Reluctant don't know (refusal to answer)
    - Confused don't know (does not understand)
- Pitfalls of Editing

As editing is done by researcher himself, it allows subjectivity to enter into the editing process. Data editors should be intelligent, experienced, and objective. Failing to have a systematic procedure for assessing the questionnaires developed by the research analyst, may lead to biased results. An editor should have clearly defined decision rules to follow. Editing during the pre-test stage can prove very valuable for improving questionnaire format, identifying poor instructions or inappropriate question wording.

## Coding

The process of identifying and classifying each answer with a numerical score or other character symbol is called coding. The numerical score or symbol is called a code, and serves as a rule for interpreting, classifying, and recording data. Identifying responses with codes is necessary if data is to be processed by computer.

Coded data is often stored electronically in the form of a data matrix – a rectangular arrangement of the data into rows (representing cases) and columns (representing variables)

The data matrix is organized into fields, records, and files:

**Field:** A collection of characters that represents a single type of data

**Record:** A collection of related fields, i.e., fields related to the same case (or respondent)

**File:** A collection of related records, i.e., records related to the same sample.

**Key Issues in Coding**

Pre-coding Fixed Alternative Questions (FAQs) – Writing codes for FAQs on the questionnaire before the data collection.

**Coding Open-ended Questions – A 3-stage Process:**

(a) Perform a test tabulation, (b) Devise a coding scheme, (c) Code all responses

**Two Rules for Code Construction are:**

Coding categories should be exhaustive. Coding categories should be mutually exclusive and independent

**Maintaining a Code Book** – A book that identifies each variable in a study, the variable's description, code name, and position in the data matrix.

**Production Coding** – The physical activity of transferring the data from the questionnaire or data collection form [to the computer] after the data has been collected. Sometimes done through a coding sheet – ruled paper drawn to mimic the data matrix.

Sometimes, editing and coding is combined.

**Example of Likert Scale Coding:** If you have asked question on Likert scale, as strongly agree, agree, neutral, disagree and strongly disagree, code it as +2, +1, 0, –1 and –2. It is easy to analyze data.

## 9.1 Basic Statistical Techniques

The number of people we speak to during quantitative business research projects can often run into thousands. Inevitably, this can result in very large sets of data. The human brain is limited in its capacity to deal with rapid incoming information, and when faced with large groups of numbers, most people cannot normally hold them all in their minds at once. It is difficult to make any conclusions by simply looking at the data in its raw state; therefore it is useful to glean some kind of overall picture or summary of what is going on. The main purpose of statistics is to accurately summarise the data into easily interpretable fewer numbers. Some of the simplest statistics are described below

- Average (Mean)
- Median and Mode
- Measures of Dispersion
- The range
- The mean deviation
- The standard deviation

### Average (or mean)

Once research data has been collected, a good starting point is to tabulate the data to find numbers of respondents' answers to each question, for example the number of items sold at a particular supermarket each week. However with large data sets, this could result in numerous sheets of data and could be difficult to take in and mentally summarise. The next step would be to get an indication of the 'normal' or 'usual' number of items sold from the supermarket each week. These figures are called averages and the researcher may say: on average about 600 items are sold each week from the supermarket. Notice the word about is used as you may not expect exactly 600 items to be sold every week, but that there would be some variation around the figure of 600. For example if the research spanned a four – week period, there may have been 535 items sold in the first week, 692 in the second week, 550 in the third week and 623 in the fourth week.

The average figure is calculated as:

The average = (535+692+550+623)/4 = 600

The average is one kind of descriptive statistic, which indicates a 'typical' or 'central' figure for a group of numbers. It is officially called a 'measure of central tendency'.

### Median and Mode

On the whole, when numbers in a particular group cluster closely around the central value, the mean is a good way of indicating the 'typical' score, i.e. it is truly representative of the numbers. If, however, the numbers are very widely spread, are very unevenly distributed, or contain extreme values, e.g. 9, 10, 13, 17, 23, 30, 45; or a hundred values of 10 and one value of 50 then the mean can be misleading, and other measures of central tendency such as the median or the mode should be used instead.

### Median

If you have a set of values, and wish to obtain a figure which represents the central point, then a sensible way of doing this may be to arrange the numbers in order of size and pick the number which falls in the middle as being of typical value. For example, if we had seven apples weighing 120g, 100g, 200g, 80g, 130g, 160g and 140g, if we arrange them in order of size, we get 80g, 100g, 120g, 130g, 140g, 160g and 200g. The value in the middle i.e. the fourth from the end weighs 130g, our median value.

If, however, there are eight apples, we shall take the weight of apples four and five as our two central numbers, and find the halfway point between them. For example, if the two central numbers were 140g and 180g, the median would be 160g i.e. you can find this mid point by adding the two numbers in question and then dividing by two, that is, by finding their average (or mean).

### Advantages of the median are:

- If one of the extreme values changes (and often in experiments it is the extreme values which are least reliable), then the median remains unaltered, whereas the mean would be affected hugely.
- If a set of numbers has a lop-sided pattern – if for example, most of the scores are small, several medium sized, but only one or two high – then the median may again be more appropriate than the mean, as its value will be close to the majority of numbers.

### The disadvantages of the median are:

- If you have a large set of numbers, it would be time consuming to place each in order of size

- If one of the numbers near the middle of the distribution moves even slightly, then the median would alter, unlike the mean, which is relatively unaffected by change in one of the central numbers.

## Mode

It is simply the value in any set of scores that occurs most often – or is the most 'popular'. Take the following set of numbers: 5, 6, 7, 8, 8, 8, 9, 10, 10, 12. As the number 8 occurs most often (three times), 8 is the mode of these set of numbers. If one of the 8s vanished, we would be left with two 8s and two 10s. In this case, there would be two modes of values 8 and 10 and this is known as bimodal. An example of a bimodal distribution is the height of six children in a nursery all aged 2 years. They are 40, 40, 40, 40, 80, 80, 80. Although the mean is 60, this figure is not a good indication of the height of any single child in the nursery aged 2 years. We would be far better off knowing that there are two modes of values 40 and 80.

If on the other hand the numbers were 5, 6, 7, 8, 9, 10, in which there is no single number that occurs more than once, there is no mode as all the numbers appear with the same frequency.

## Advantages of the mode

The mode can be a very useful statistic. One of its main assets is that it can be used to indicate a 'normal' or 'usual' figure. It is exactly opposite to the mean in this respect, as the modal value must be a commonly occurring figure. Often the value of a mean is a number with a decimal point, and sometimes may not remotely resemble any of the values in the data set – as in the nursery children. Often people use the mode as an average as in the 'average person', the figure quoted being the usual or typical value, and quite often will not be the mean.

The mode is also a useful descriptive statistic when the numbers in a distribution are not evenly spread around a central value (as is the median). Such a lop-sided distribution is called a 'skewed' distribution.

## Disadvantages of the mode are:

Firstly and sadly, the mode is hardly ever used, due to its instability as it can swing wildly through the whole set of numbers. Take the numbers 1, 1, 6, 7, 8, 10. The mode here is 1, which is not a very representative figure of the group as a whole. However, if we change the score of 1 to a 10, the mode shifts right to the other end of the scale. Thus a single number change can alter the mode dramatically. This is in great contrast to the mean (average) and the medium, where number changes can take place and leave them virtually unaffected.

If a distribution of numbers has more than two modes, and with large sets of numbers, it might be possible to have many modes – then the modal values themselves could need summarising, and so the usefulness of the mode as a descriptive statistic begins to dwindle.

## Measures of Dispersion

Another type of descriptive statistic is used to qualify the word about as in the sentence 'on average about 600 items are sold each week from the supermarket'. There are between 535 and 692 items sold. If there were 440 items sold in the first week, 589 sold in the second week, 670 sold in the third week and 701 sold in the fourth week, the average number of items sold over the period would also be 600.

However, the word about signifies that there maybe, and are, large departures of actual items sold from the averages for each type of dog food. Used by itself, the word about is far too vague, and we need some means of giving more details about the variation. The solution is to use one of the descriptive statistic known as the measure of spread; these simply indicate just how much the word 'about' means for a particular set of figures, and indicates how widely scattered the numbers are. If one of these measures is used together with one of the averages, then the two summary numbers together will give an extremely concise and useful description of the particular distribution. There are three commonly used measures of dispersion.

### The Range

The range tells you over how many numbers altogether a distribution is spread. It is easily obtained by subtracting the smallest score from the largest. For example, if I find that various kinds of potatoes for sale in several greengrocers' shops are priced at 10p, 25p, 12p, 8p, 14p, 14p, 14p, 24p and 15p per lb, the range for these prices would be 25p-8p = 17p.

The problem with the range is that extreme value has a very big effect on the descriptive statistic and outliers may cause distributions which overall look very different to have similar ranges. Clearly then, the range can only be used sensibly as a descriptive statistic when all the scores are fairly well bunched together.

### The Mean Deviation

The mean deviation is a number that indicates how much, on average, the scores in a distribution differ from a central point, the mean. Suppose you take the numbers 8, 9, 10, 11, 12. The mean is 10 and the range is 4. The number 8 is 2 points away from the mean, and so is the number 12. Numbers 9 and 11 are both 1 point away from the mean, and 10, the remaining number in the set is the mean, so does not differ at all. Listing these differences, you get 2 + 1 + 0 + 1 + 2 = 6. There are 5 numbers in the group and so you can say that the average (mean) amount they all vary from the mean is 6 divided by 5 i.e. 1.2 points. The differences, 2, 1, 0, etc., which were obtained are called deviations. The larger the mean deviation is, the more spread out the scores in the distribution are. Given the calculation of the mean deviation is based on all the numbers in a distribution; it is a much more stable statistic than the range, which is only based on two of them.

### The Standard Deviation

When we calculated the mean deviation (above), we did not take into account the fact that some numbers are higher than the mean and some are lower, i.e. our true deviations should have been –2, –1, 0, +1, +2. However, if we add these together, our total would be zero, so we ignored the signs for this reason. Ignoring signs is not especially pleasing to mathematicians because the mean deviation is a very simple figure without any powerful mathematical properties, it is rarely used as a measure of dispersions. The preferred measure, known as the standard deviation is used far more often, usually in conjunction with the mean and the range.

In principle, the standard deviation (often shortened to 'SD' or $\sigma$) is very similar to the mean deviation. It summarises an average distance of all the scores from the mean of a particular set. But it is calculated in a slightly different manner.

As just discussed, if we take into account the signs (+ or –) of the deviations from the mean, the mean deviation will always be zero. There is, however, a solution to the problem. If you multiply two negative numbers together, you get a positive result. The same applies to squaring a negative number (multiplying the number by itself).

Now suppose you have the set of deviations –2, –1, 0, +1, +2; these equal zero when added together, or 6 when the signs are ignored. If instead of adding the deviations, you square each one you get +4, +1, 0, +1, +4 for the squared deviations, and all are positive numbers. Now you need to add these numbers and find their mean, just as you did with the mean deviation calculations. You should get 10, divided by 5, to obtain the value 2. The figure 10 is called the sum of squares, and 2, the mean of the sum of squares is called the variance. Notice that 2 is not the standard deviation. As we squared all the differences, the figure 2 must be 'unsquared' (find its square root), to bring it back in perspective. In this case, the square root of 2 is 1.4142. This then is the standard deviation. This is slightly higher than the figure 1.2 which was calculated as the mean deviation for the same set of numbers.

A slight complication with the standard deviation is the use of N (the number of scores in the particular set). The majority of quantitative Business Research Methodologies involve taking a sample from a population, however because this is only a sample, some error will inevitably occur in the results. The sensible way to compensate for this is to make an allowance for it in the calculation of the standard deviation. Some statistical books tell us to divide the sum of squares by N-1 instead of N i.e., dividing by a smaller number will give a larger variance, and hence a larger standard deviation, which compensates for the margin of error in taking a sample. Thus a formula for the standard deviation involving N-1 rather than N is preferred whenever we are working with samples rather than a set of scores which is absolutely complete (a population). This issue is called degree of freedom (DF), we shall discuss more in coming chapters.

### 9.1.1 Solved Examples

### Solved Example S-1

**From the following data, calculate Median:**

| Marks | No. of students |
|---|---|
| Below10 | 10 |
| 10-20 | 20 |
| 20-30 | 30 |
| 30-40 | 50 |
| 40-50 | 40 |
| Above 50 | 30 |

**Solution:**

| Marks | No. of students | Cumulative Frequency |
|---|---|---|
| Below 10 | 10 | 10 |
| 10-20 | 20 | 30 |
| 20-30 | 30 | 60 |
| 30-40 | 50 | 110 |
| 40-50 | 40 | 150 |
| Above 50 | 30 | 180 |

Median = 180/2 = $90^{th}$ item

Since cumulative frequency 90 corresponds to the class 30-40, therefore median class is 30-40.

Therefore median can be calculated with formula

$$\text{Median} = L + \frac{N/2 - cf}{f} * i = 30 + \frac{90 - 60}{50} * 10 = 36$$

**Solved Example S-2**

From the following data, calculate Mode:

| Marks X | No. of students (f) |
|---|---|
| 1-10 | 10 |
| 11-20 | 20 |
| 21-30 | 30 |
| 31-40 | 50 |
| 41-50 | 40 |
| 51-60 | 30 |

**Solution:**

Assume classes are inclusive:

| Marks X | No. of students (f) |
|---|---|
| 0.5-10.5 | 10 |
| 10.5-20.5 | 20 |
| 20.5-30.5 | 30 |
| 30.5-40.5 | 50 |
| 40.5-50.5 | 40 |
| 50.5-60.5 | 30 |

As maximum frequency is 50, so modal class is 30.5-40.5.

$$\text{Mode} = L + \frac{f_1 - f_2}{2f_1 - f_0 - f_2} * i = 305 + \frac{50 - 30}{2*50 - 30 - 40} * 10 = 37.17$$

Where $f_1$ is modal class frequency and $f_0$ is frequency before model class and $f_2$ follows

**Solved Example S-3**

From the following data, calculate Standard Deviation, Coefficient of Variation.

| Marks X | No. of students (f) |
|---|---|
| 1-10 | 10 |
| 11-20 | 20 |
| 21-30 | 30 |
| 31-40 | 50 |
| 41-50 | 40 |
| 51-60 | 30 |

**Solution:**

| Marks X | Mid point m | No. of students f | fm | X-35 = x | $fx^2$ |
|---|---|---|---|---|---|
| 1-10 | 5 | 10 | 50 | -30 | 9000 |
| 11-20 | 15 | 20 | 300 | -20 | 8000 |
| 21-30 | 25 | 30 | 750 | -10 | 30000 |
| 31-40 | 35 | 50 | 1750 | 0 | 0 |
| 41-50 | 45 | 40 | 1800 | 10 | 4000 |
| 51-60 | 55 | 30 | 1650 | 20 | 12000 |
| | | N = 180 | $\Sigma fm$ = 6300 | | $\Sigma fx^2$ = 36000 |

$\overline{X}$ = 35

Standard deviation

$$\text{Coefficient of variation} = (\sigma) = \sqrt{\frac{\Sigma fx^2}{N}} = \sqrt{\frac{36000}{180}} = \sqrt{200} = 14.142$$

$$= (CV) = \frac{\sigma}{X} * 100 = 14.142/35 * 100 = 40.4$$

Variance = $14.14^2$ = 200

**Solved Example S-4**

From the following data, calculate first four moments about mean, standard deviation, Skewness and Kurtosis on moments.

| Marks X | No. of students (f) |
|---|---|
| 1-10 | 10 |
| 11-20 | 20 |
| 21-30 | 30 |
| 31-40 | 50 |
| 41-50 | 40 |
| 51-60 | 30 |

**Solution:**

Calculation of first four moments

| Marks X | Mid point m | No. Of students f | fm | (m-35)/10 = x | fx | fx² | fx³ | fx⁴ |
|---|---|---|---|---|---|---|---|---|
| 1-10 | 5 | 10 | 50 | -3 | -30 | 90 | -270 | 810 |
| 11-20 | 15 | 20 | 300 | -2 | -20 | 80 | -160 | 320 |
| 21-30 | 25 | 30 | 750 | -10 | -100 | 300 | -300 | 300 |
| 31-40 | 35 | 40 | 1750 | 0 | 0 | 0 | 0 | 0 |
| 41-50 | 45 | 30 | 1800 | 1 | 10 | 40 | 40 | 40 |
| 51-60 | 55 | 30 | 1650 | 2 | 20 | 120 | 240 | 480 |
| | | N = 180 | Σfm = 6300 | | Σ fx = 0 | Σ fx² = 360 | Σ fx³ = -180 | Σ fx⁴ = 1680 |

$\mu_1 = \Sigma fx/N * i = 0/180*10 = 0$

$\mu_2 = \Sigma fx^2/N * i = 360/180*10^2 = 200$

$\mu_3 = \Sigma fx^3/N * i = -180/180*10^3 = 1000$

$\mu_4 = \Sigma fx^4/N * i = 1680/180*10^4 = 93,333,33$

Standard deviation based on second moment

$$\sigma = \sqrt{\mu_2} = \sqrt{200} = 14.142$$

Calculation of skewness based on second and third moment

$$\text{Skewness} = \frac{\mu_3^2}{\mu_2^3} = \frac{(-1000)^2}{(200)^3} = .125 \text{ It is positively skewed}$$

$$\text{Kurtosis} = \frac{\mu_4}{\mu_2^2} = \frac{93333}{(200)^2} = 2.333$$

Since Kurtosis is less than three, the distribution is less curved than normal curve.

### 9.1.2 Problems for Practice

1. The mean annual R&D expenditure of 150 firms in an industrial estate is ₹ 60 lakh. The mean annual R&D expenditure of the large-scale industries in that estate is ₹ 70 lakh and that of the medium-scale industries is Rs. 55 lakh. Find the number of large-scale industries and the number of medium-scale industries in that estate. (Hint: Let number of large scale industries be X, therefore medium are 150-X. Now total expenditure 150*60 = X*70+(150-X)*55. Find the value of X)

2. The demand of a product is estimated using the four-year moving average method, which is nothing but the weighted arithmetic mean method. The demand in units of the years 1999, 2000, 2001 and 2002 are 300, 350, 400 and 325, respectively. The corresponding weights are 1, 2, 3 and 4, respectively. Find the demand for the year 2003.

3. Beta Incorporation has introduced a performance appraisal system in which there are five different factors for evaluating each employee at managerial position. Employees are rated on 0-10 scale for all the factors. The scheme of weights for the factors are as shown below:

| Factor | A | B | C | D | E |
|---|---|---|---|---|---|
| Weight | 3 | 1 | 2 | 4 | 2 |

If an employee is rated with 8, 7, 6, 9 and 5 points for the factors A, B, C, D and E, respectively, find the overall weighted rating of the employee.

4. The growth rate of the demand of a product during the last four years, 1999, 2000, 2001 and 2002 when compared to the demand of the base year 1998 are 15%, 20%, 25% and 30%, respectively. Find the average growth rate of the demand of the product.

5. The kilometre per litre given by a new vehicle on five different occasions are 50 km/hr, 60 km/hr, 55 km/hr, 60 km/hr and 45 km/hr. Find the average kilometre per litre given by the new vehicle.

6. The distribution of number of shares applied to the recently concluded equity issue of an automobile company is shown as follows:

| No. of shares applied for | No. of applications | No. of shares applied for | No. of applications |
|---|---|---|---|
| 50-100 | 500 | 300-350 | 850 |
| 100-150 | 1500 | 350-400 | 760 |
| 150-200 | 1800 | 400-450 | 600 |
| 200-250 | 1600 | 450-500 | 400 |
| 250-300 | 1000 | | |

Compute the average deviation as well as coefficient of average deviation for the number of shares applied.

7. Find the coefficient of skewness of the following data:

| Age in years | No. of employees | Age in years | No. of employees |
|---|---|---|---|
| 22-26 | 30 | 38-42 | 70 |
| 26-30 | 50 | 42-46 | 60 |
| 30-34 | 70 | 46-50 | 40 |
| 34-38 | 80 | 50-54 | 30 |

8. The first four moments of distribution about X = 4, are 1, 4, 10 and 45. Obtain the various characteristics of distribution on the basis of information given. Comment on the nature of distribution.

9. Given below is the information relating to marks in Statistics (X) and marks in Accountancy (Y) obtained by the students of a class

Covariance between X and Y = 144

Second moment of X about 20 = 244

First moment of X about 20 = 10

Arithmetic mean of Y = 45

Correlation coefficient between X and Y = 0.75

Calculate coefficient of variation of marks of statistics and that of accountancy in which subject the performance of students is more consistent.

10. Find the coefficient of skewness from the following information:

Difference of two quartiles = 8 Mode = 11

Sum of two quartiles = 22 Mean = 8

## 9.2 Testing of Hypothesis

There are four inter-related components that influence the conclusions. For instance, you hear an announcement at railway station that all trains are running on time. But when observed during a particular hour, it was found that 5 trains out of 10 trains were late. Was sample size okay? How much were the station authorities confident of their statement? All issues need proper study.

The four components that influence conclusions are:

- **sample size**, or the number of units (e.g., people) accessible to the study
- **effect size**, or the salience of the treatment relative to the noise in measurement
- **alpha level** ($\alpha$, or significance level), or the odds that the observed result is due to chance
- **power**, or the odds that you will observe a treatment effect when it occurs

Given values for any three of these components, it is possible to compute the value of the fourth. As discussed in chapter 7, for instance, you may want to determine what a reasonable sample size would be for a study. If you make reasonable estimates of the effect size, alpha level and power, it would be simple to compute the sample size.

Some of these components are more manipulable than others depending on the circumstances of the project. For example, if the project is an evaluation of an educational programme or counselling programme with a specific number of available consumers, the sample size is set or predetermined. Or, if the drug dosage in a programme has to be small due to its potential negative side effects, the effect size may consequently be small. The goal is to achieve a balance of the four components that allows the maximum level of power to detect an effect if one exists, given programmatic, logistical or financial constraints on the other components.

A statement of prediction is called hypothesis. It is a tentative statement which needs to be verified. It is an intelligent guess for your objectives. We have two types of hypotheses – one Null Hypothesis (labelled $H_0$) and other Alternate hypothesis (labelled $H_1$). For instance

**$H_0$: Income Effect = 0**

**$H_1$: Income Effect ≠ 0**

The null hypothesis is so termed because it usually refers to the "no difference" or "no effect" case. Usually in management research we expect that our treatments and programmes will make a difference. So, typically, our theory is described in the alternative hypothesis. α, or significance level is a chance you can take while confidence level (β) is power behind your statement. $\alpha = 1-\beta$, for instance, if one can take a chance of 5% for his statement; it means he is 95% confident to his statement.

### 9.2.1 Type I and Type II error

Two types of errors can be expected when you accept or reject your hypothesis — Type 1 error and Type II error. You make a Type I error when you reject Null Hypothesis when it is true. You make Type II error when you reject Alternate hypothesis when actually it is true.

You have to be careful about interpreting the meaning of these terms. When we talk about *higher* α-levels, we mean that we are *increasing* the chance of a Type I Error. Therefore, a *lower* α-level actually means that you are conducting a *more rigorous* test. We should keep it in mind that if α is lower, the power is lower; higher the α, higher the power. With lower the α, the less likely it is that you will make a Type I Error (i.e., reject the null when it's true); however, when lower the α, the more "rigorous" the test is. An α of .01 (compared with .05 or .10) means the researcher is being relatively careful, he is only willing to risk being wrong 1 in 100 times in rejecting the null when it's true (i.e., saying there's an effect when there really isn't).

### Probability and Normal Distribution in Testing of Hypothesis

Probability distribution is classified as either discrete or continuous. A discrete probability is allowed to take on only a limited number of values. For instance, the probability that you were born in a given month is discrete since there are only twelve months in a year and there are only twelve possible values.

In continuous probability distribution, the variable under consideration is allowed to take any value within a given range. Continuous distributions are convenient ways to represent discrete distributions that have many possible outcomes, all very close to each other. For instance, you wish to find out the level of pollution in variety of streams which have been affected by effluent, you will see some streams may be clears, other highly polluted, you can represent the pollution with a range. A very important continuous probability distribution is normal distribution. In normal distribution, mean, median and mode have same value, which means data is spread equally with its means which can be shown with the help of bell shaped figure, at centre of it mean; mode give the height while median which is also at the same level of mode and means depicts that half of the observations are on the left side while other half are on the right side.

A value, x, from a normal distribution specified by a mean of μ and a standard deviation of σ can be converted to a corresponding value, z, in a standard normal distribution with the transformation $z=(x-\mu)/\sigma$. And, of course, in reverse, any value from α standard normal graph, say z, can be converted to a corresponding value on a normal distribution with a mean of μ and a standard deviation of σ by the formula $x=\mu+z*\sigma$. Remember that the standard normal distribution has a mean of 0 and a standard deviation of 1 — i.e., ($\mu=0$, $\sigma=1$). We usually say x is normally distributed ($x \sim N(\mu,\sigma)$).

The ability to carry out this transformation is very important since we can do all our analysis with the standard normal distribution and then apply the results to ***every*** other normal distribution, including the one that is actually of interest. For example, to draw a normal curve with a mean of 10 and a standard deviation of 2 ($\mu=10$, $\sigma=2$), we would draw the standard normal distribution and just re-label the axis. The figure below is the standard normal curve and mean, $\mu=10$ is shown at the middle while area from centre is measured in standard deviation and in our case $\sigma=2$.

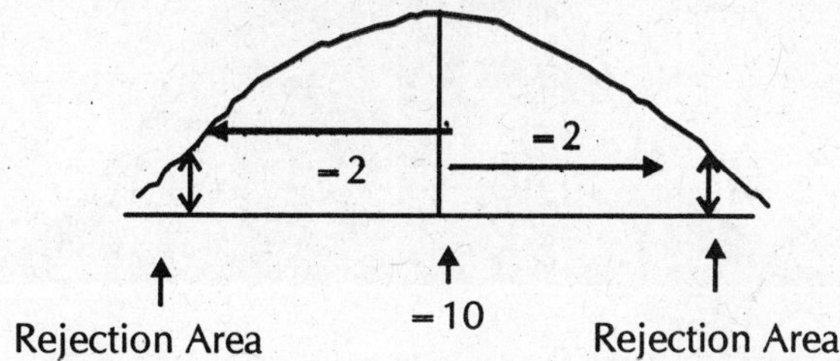


Each value along the x-axis represents that many standard deviations from the mean. Note for the standard normal distribution, mean is zero and standard deviation is 1. The 1 (or -1) is one standard deviation from the mean. Similarly, the 3 (or -3) is three standard deviations from the mean.

Exactly as in the case of the standard normal distribution, the numbers on the x-axis represent the standard deviations from the mean. Since the mean is 10 and the standard deviation is 2, one standard deviation from the mean ($\pm 1\sigma$) yields the values 12 and 8 ($10 \pm 1*2$). Similarly, $\pm 3\sigma$ yields the values 4 and 16.

Area around the mean is measured in standard deviations and staticians have calculated the area of the bell shaped figure when mean is zero and standard deviation is one (denoted by N ~ (0,1) which means normally distributed with mean zero and standard deviation one). 'z' is calculated in terms of standard deviations that is how far an observation is away from mean in terms of standard deviations. Z is calculated with formula

$$Z = \frac{x-\mu}{\sigma}$$

Where x is observation while μ is mean and σ is standard deviation. Normal area table showing probability and Z are given at the end of this book.

To test the hypothesis relating to means, comparisons of means and proportions we use normal distributions.

## Two Tail Test

When you expect that observation can fall in any direction of mean, we may say that there is equal probability of getting observation on both sides of the mean.

In a one-tailed test, the critical region will have just one part. If our sample value lies in this region, we reject the null hypothesis in favour of the alternative.

Suppose we are looking for a definite decrease. Then the critical region will be to the left. Note, however, that in the one-tailed test the value of the parameter can be as high as you like.

### One Tail Test

When you expect that observation can fall only on one side of the mean, we use one tail only

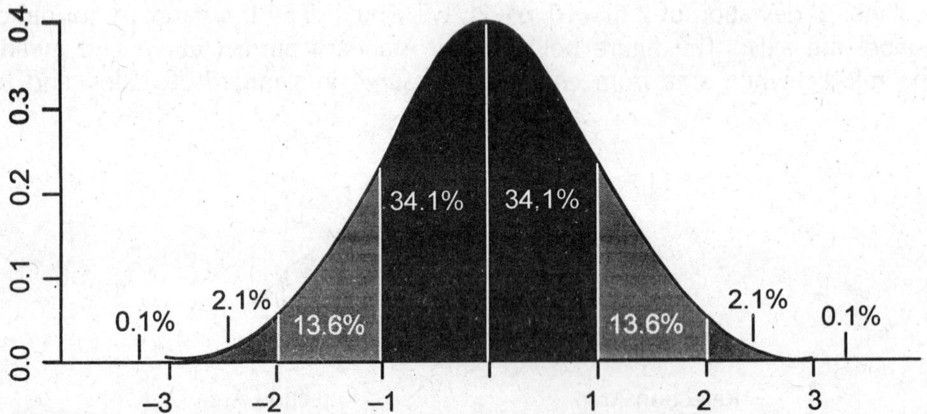


As we have already discussed in chapter 7, (rule of thumb), about 68% of values drawn from a normal distribution are within one standard deviation $\sigma > 0$ away from the mean $\mu$; about 95% of the values are within two standard deviations and about 99.7% lie within three standard deviations. This is known as the "68-95-99.7 rule" or the "empirical rule."

In a one-tailed test, the critical region will have just one part. If our sample value lies in this region, we reject the null hypothesis in favour of the alternative.

Suppose we are looking for a definite decrease. Then the critical region will be to the left. Note, however, that in the one-tailed test the value of the parameter can be as high as you like.

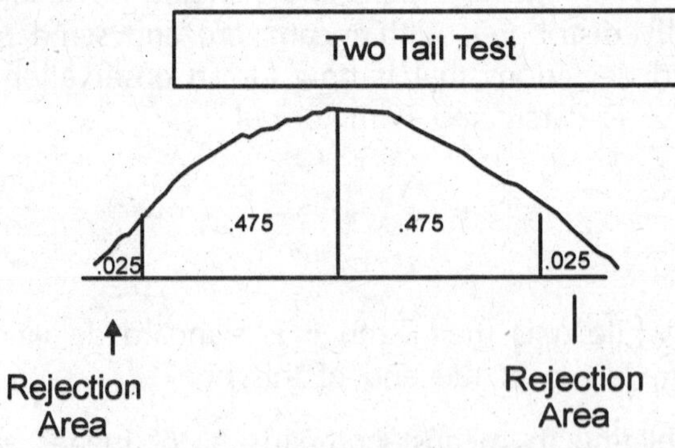

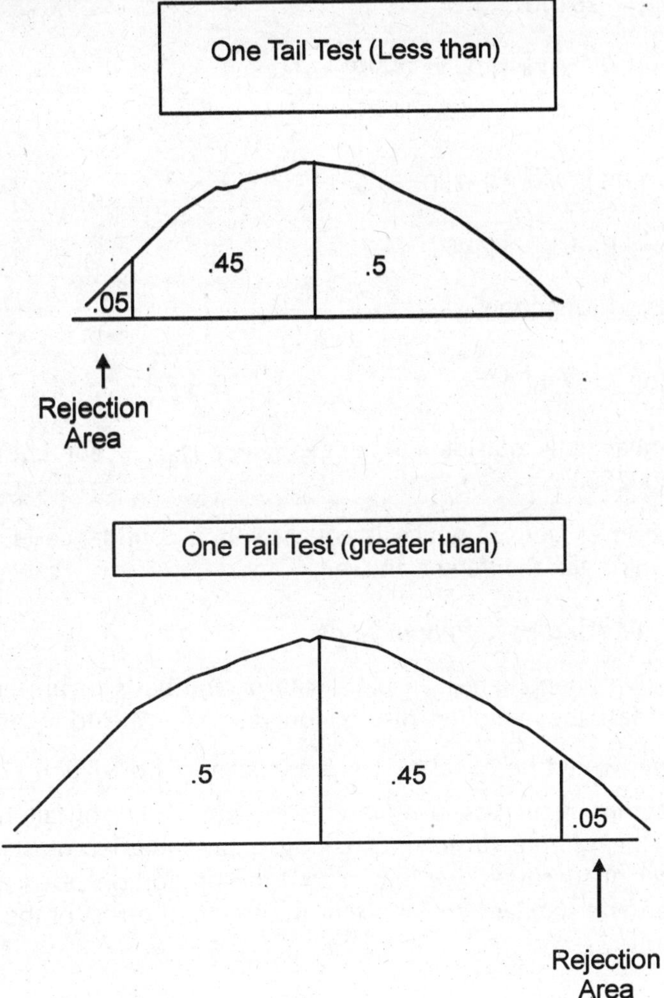


**Solved Example S-1**

Sports and media magnate Ned Sterner is interested in purchasing the Atlanta Stalwarts, if he can be reasonably certain that operating the team will not be too costly. He figures that average attendance would have to be about 28,500 fans per game to make the purchase attractive to him. Ned randomly chooses 64 home games over the past 4 years and finds from figures reported in Sporting Reviews that average attendance at these games was 26,100. A study he commissioned the last time he purchased a team showed that the population standard deviation for attendance at similar events had been quite stable for the past 10 years at about 6,000 fans. Using 2 standard errors as the decision criterion, should Ned purchase the Stalwarts? Can you think of any reason(s) why your conclusion might not be valid?

**Solution:**

Frame the hypothesis

$H_0$: $\mu = 28500$

$H_1$ : $\mu = 28500$

Population mean $\mu = 28500$

Sample mean $\overline{X}$ = 26100

Standard Deviation of sample $\sigma$ = 6000

n = 64

$\sigma_{\overline{X}} = \sigma/\sqrt{n} = 6000/\sqrt{64} = 750$

2 SD = 2*750 = 1500

$\overline{X}_U = 28500+1500 = 30000$

$\overline{X}_L = 28500-1500 = 27000$

As the sample mean falls outside the range, reject $H_0$, accept $H_1$ which mean average attendance is less than 28000.

As the confidence level is 2 SD which is equal to 95% confidence level, if we increase the confidence level, we may get a different answer.

### 9.2.2 Hypothesis Testing of Proportions

In case of qualitative phenomena, we have data on the basis of presence or absence of an attribute(s). With such data the sampling distribution may take the form of binomial probability distribution whose mean would be equal to $n \bullet p$ and standard deviation equal to $\sqrt{npq}$, where $p$ represents the probability of success, $q$ represents the probability of failure such that p + q = 1 and $n$, the size of the sample. Instead of taking mean number of successes and standard deviation of the number of successes, we may record the proportion of successes in each sample in which case the mean and standard deviation (or the standard error) of the sampling distribution may be obtained as follows:

Mean proportion of successes = np and standard deviation of the proportion of successes

$$= \sqrt{\frac{p.q}{n}}$$

In n is large, the binômial distribution tends to become normal distribution, and as such for j proportion testing purposes we make use of the test statistic z as under:

$$\frac{p-q}{\sqrt{\frac{p.q}{n}}}$$

For testing of proportion, we formulate $H_0$ and $H_1$ and construct rejection region, with normal approximation of the binomial distribution, for a predetermined level of significance and may judge the significance of the observed sample result.

**Solved Example S-2**

An automobile manufacturer claims that a particular model gets 28 miles to the gallon. The Environmental Protection Agency, using a sample of 49 automobiles of this model, finds the sample mean to be 26.8 miles per gallon. From previous studies, the population standard deviation is known to be five miles per gallon. Could we reasonably expect (within 2 standard errors) that we could select such a sample if indeed the population mean is actually 28 miles per gallon?

Frame the hypothesis

$H_0$: $\mu$ = 28

$H_1$ : $\mu$ # 28

Population mean $\mu$ = 28

Sample mean $\overline{X}$ = 26.8

Standard Deviation of sample $\sigma$ = 5

n = 49

$\sigma_{\overline{X}} = \sigma/\sqrt{n} = 5/\sqrt{49} = 5/7$

2 SD = 2*5/7 = 1.43

$\overline{X}_V$ = 28 + 1.43 = 29.43

$\overline{X}_L$ = 28-1.43 = 26.57

As the sample mean (26.8) falls outside the range, accept $H_0$, reject $H_1$ which means average mileage equal to 28 miles per gallon.

### 9.2.3 Hypothesis Testing of Difference between Means

To test the difference of means of two populations or samples, we should need to know the means of two samples, their standard deviations and sample size. It is hypothesized that there is no difference i.e. $\mu_1 - \mu_2 = 0$ (in case of population) $\overline{X}_1 - \overline{X}_2 = 0$ (in case of samples) Joint standard deviation is taken as $\sqrt{\frac{\sigma_1^2}{n^1} + \frac{\sigma_2^2}{n^2}}$ in case of population and if population standard deviation is not known we take sample standard deviation as population standard deviation.

### 9.2.3.1 Solved Examples

**Solved Example S-1**

Intelligence test on two groups of boys and girls gave the following results:

| | Mean | S.D. | N |
|---|---|---|---|
| Girls | 61 | 2 | 64 |
| Boys | 60 | 4 | 100 |

Is there a significant difference in the mean scores obtained by boys and girls at 5% level?

**Solution:**

Null Hypothesis $H_0 : \mu_1 - \mu_2 = 0$

Alternate Hypothesis $H_1 : \mu_1$ # $\mu_2$

$$\text{S. D.}_{(\overline{X}^1 - \overline{X}^2)} = \sqrt{\frac{\sigma_1^2}{n^1} + \frac{\sigma_2^2}{n^2}} = \sqrt{\frac{4}{64} + \frac{16}{100}} = 0.4716$$

At 5% significance level normal variate z = 1.96, hence range is

Upper range = $X_U$ = 0 + 1.96*0.4716= + 0.9243

Lower Range = $X_L$ = 0 – 1.96*0.4716 = – 0.9243

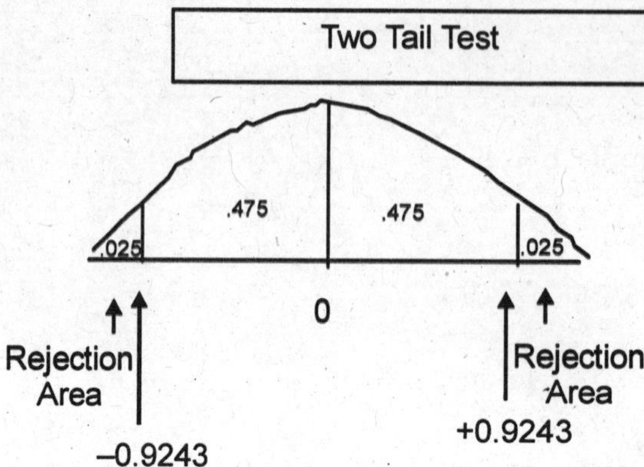


Now actual difference is = 61 – 60 = 1, this difference falls outside the accepted area, so null Hypothesis is rejected and alternate Hypothesis $H_1$ is accepted which means there is significance difference.

Alternatively $|z| = \frac{61-60}{0.4716}$ = 2.12 which also means that as absolute value of z is greater than tabulated value of 1.96, hence reject $H_0$ and accept $H_1$

### 9.2.3.2 Problems for Practice

1. A sample of 400 male students is found to have a mean height 67.47 inches. Can it be regarded as a sample from a large population with mean height 67.39 inches and standard 1.30 inches? Test at 5% level of significance.
2. The mean produce of wheat of a sample of 100 fields is 200 lbs. per acre with a standard deviation of 10 lbs. Another sample of 150 fields gives the mean of 220 lbs. with a standard deviation of 12 lbs. Can the two samples be considered to have been taken from the same population whose standard deviation is 11 lbs? Use 5 per cent level of significance.
3. A simple random sampling survey in respect of monthly earnings of semi-skilled workers in two cities gives the following statistical information. Test the hypothesis at 5 per cent level that there is no difference between monthly earnings of workers in the two cities.

| City | Mean monthly earnings (₹) | Standard deviation of sample data of monthly earnings (₹) | Size of Sample |
|---|---|---|---|
| A | 695 | 40 | 200 |
| B | 710 | 60 | 175 |

4. A sample of sales in similar shops in two towns are taken for a new product with the following results:

| Town | Mean Sales | Variance | Sample size |
|---|---|---|---|
| A | 5 | 5 | 5 |
| B | 7 | 3 | 7 |

Is there any evidence of difference in sales in the two towns? Use 5 per cent level of significance *to test* this difference between the means of two samples.

5. A group of seven-week-old chickens reared on a high protein diet weigh 12, 15, 11, 16, 14, 14 and 16 ounces; a second group of five chickens, similarly treated except that they receive a low protein diet, weigh 8, 10, 14, 10 and 13 ounces. Test at 5 per cent level whether there is significant evidence that additional protein has increased the weight of the chickens. Use assumed mean (or $A_1$) = 10 for the sample of 7 and assumed mean (or $A_2$) = 8 for the sample of 5 chickens in your calculations.

6. A drug research experimental unit is testing two drugs newly developed to reduce blood pressure levels. The drugs are administered to two different sets of animals. In group one, 350 of 600 animals tested respond to drug one and in group two, 260 of 500 animals tested respond to drug two. The research unit wants to test whether there is a difference between the efficacies of the said two drugs at 5 per cent level of significance. How will you deal with this problem?

7. At a certain date in a large city 400 out of a random sample of 500 men were found to be smokers. After the tax on tobacco had been heavily increased, another random sample of 600 men in the same city included 400 smokers. Was the observed decrease in the proportion of smokers significant? Test at 5 per cent level of significance.

8. In two large populations, there are 35% and 30% respectively fair haired people. Is this difference likely to be revealed by simple sample of 1500 and 1000 respectively from the two populations?

9. A large corporation uses thousands of light bulbs every year. The brand that has been used in the past has an average life of 1000 hours with a standard deviation of 100 hours. A new brand is offered to the corporation at a price far lower than one they are paying for the old brand. It is decided that they will switch to the new brand unless it is proved with a level of significance of 5% that the new brand has smaller average life than the old brand. A random sample of 100 new brand bulbs is tested yielding an observed sample mean of 985 hours. Assuming that the standard deviation of the new brand is the same as that of the old brand, (a) What conclusion should be drawn and what decision should be made?, b) What is the probability of accepting the new brand if it has the mean life of 950 hours?

10. An examination was given to two classes, each consisting of 49 students. In the first class, the mean marks were 74 with a standard deviation of 8; in the second class, the mean marks were 78 with a standard deviation of 9. Is it reasonable to regard the two classes as having been obtained from two normal populations with equal means? Test your hypothesis at 5% and 1% level of significance.

11. The daily sales of a product in different shops follow normal distribution. The targeted mean of the daily sales of the product and their variance in the population are ₹ 10,000 and ₹ 2,500, respectively. The sales manager of the company which produces the product feels that the sale of the product has improved in the recent past. A random sample of 49 shops is taken from the normal population for which the mean daily sales

is found to be ₹ 9,600. Check whether the sale of the product in different shops has really improved at a significance level of 0.05.

12. The annual sales of small scale industries in an industrial estate follow normal distribution. The targeted mean of the annual sales of the industries of the population is ₹ 75 lakhs. The variance of the annual sales of the industries of the population is ₹ 400 lakhs. The director of the industry department feels that the performance of the industries has not changed from the population mean in the recent past. A random sample of 49 industries is taken from the normal population for which the mean annual sales is found to be ₹ 70 lakhs. Check whether the sale of the industries has not changed from ₹ 75 lakhs at a significance level of 0.05.

13. The weight of cement bags produced by ABC Cement Company follows normal distribution whose population is finite and its size is 1000. The expected mean of the weight of the cement bags for sales of this population is 65 kg and its variance is unknown. The sales manager of the firm claims that the mean weight of the cement is significantly more than the expected mean weight of the population. So, the manager of XYZ Construction Company who places an order for cement bags with XYZ Cement Company has selected a random sample of 64 bags and its mean and variance are found to be 62 kg and 2.25 kg, respectively. Verify the intuition of the sales manager of the cement company at a significance level of 0.05.

14. The monthly income of respondents in a survey follows normal distribution with finite population size of 1000. The expected mean of the monthly income of the respondents of the population is ₹ 8,000. The variance of the monthly income of the respondents of the population is ₹ 3,00,000. The researcher feels that the mean monthly income of the respondents has declined from the expected mean of ₹ 8,000 in the recent past. A random sample of 64 respondents is taken from the normal population for which the mean monthly income is found to be ₹ 8,750. Check whether the mean monthly income has declined from the expected mean of ₹ 8,000 at a significance level of 0.01.

15. The production manager of an automobile company is convinced that the reduction in standard times for the employees working in its assembly line will improve the productivity of the line. But the quality manager has a contradicting view, because such reduction will decrease the proportion of the number of assemblies passing out of the assembly line which are free from missing components. Before introducing the new standard times, the quality manager ascertained through a study that 90% of the assemblies coming out of the assembly line will be free from missing components. After introducing the new standard times for the employees in the assembly line, it is found that out of a sample of 60 assemblies which passed out of the assembly line, 57 assemblies are free from missing components. Check the view of the quality manager at a significance level of 0.01.

16. The weight of a drug produced by Alpha Pharmaceutical Company follows normal distribution whose population is infinite. The specified mean of the weight of the drug of this population is 100 mg and its variance is unknown. The quality engineer of the firm claims that the mean weight of the drugs does not differ significantly from the specified mean weight of the population. So, the purchase manager of Beta hospital who places an order for that drug with the Alpha Pharmaceutical Company has selected a random sample of 36 drugs. The mean and variance of the sample are found to be 99% mg and 25 mg, respectively. Verify the intuition of the quality manager of Alpha Pharmaceutical Company at a significance level of 0.01.

17. The supplier of electrical motors to a washing machine company claims that the mean time between failures of the motors is at most 90 days. The quality manager of the washing machine company wants to test the claim of the vendor. Hence, he has taken a sample of 25 motors whose mean time between failures and its variance are found to be 93 days and 16 days, respectively. Verify the claim of the vendor at a significance level of 0.05.

18. The weight of costly catalyst electrodes purchased by a chemical company follows normal distribution. The sales manager of the vendor firm claims that the mean weight of the electrodes is 200 gm. The quality manager of the chemical company wants to verify this claim. So, he has taken a sample of 20 electrodes. The mean and the variance of the electrodes in .the sample are found to be 205 gm and 81 gm, respectively. Verify the claim of the sales manager at a significance level of 0.10.

19. The personnel manager of a firm is recruiting its graduate trainees through two consultancy agencies. The performance index (0-10 scale) of the trainees from each consultancy agency follows normal distribution. The variance of the performance index of the trainees selected through a Consultancy Agency X is 12 and that of the trainees selected through another Consultancy Agency Y is 6. The manager feels that the mean performance index of the trainees selected through the Consultancy Agency X is less than that of the trainees selected through the Consultancy Agency Y. To test his intuition, he has drawn a sample of 64 trainees selected through the Consultancy Agency X and their mean performance index is found to be 8. Similarly, he has drawn a sample of 81 trainees selected through the Consultancy Agency Y and their mean performance index is found to be 6.5. Test the intuition of the manager at a significance level of 0.01.

20. The sales representative of a pharmaceutical company claims that a new drug for a disease cures 95% of the cases. When it is administered by a doctor to 100 patients, it cured only 90 patients. Check the claim of the sales representative at a significance level of 0.05.

21. The number of defective pieces of an item produced by Machine-X as well as Machine-Y follows binomial distribution. The quality manager of the firm buying the item believes that the proportion of the number of defective pieces in the lot produced by the Machine-X is less than the proportion of the number of defective pieces in the lot produced by the Machine-Y. So, the quality assistant under him selected a sample of 100 pieces from the production of the Machine-X and found that the number of defective pieces in it is 10. Similarly, he selected a sample of 90 pieces from the production of the Machine-Y and found that the number of defective pieces in it is 6. Check the intuition of the quality manager at the significance level of 0.10.

22. The number of credit card holders of a bank in two different cities (City X and City-Y) settling their excess withdrawal amounts in time without attracting interest follows binomial distribution. The manager (collections) of the bank feels that the proportion of the number of such credit card holders in the City-X is not different from the proportion of the number of such credit card holders in the City-Y. To test his intuition, a sample of 200 credit card holders is taken from the City-X and it is found that 160 of them are settling their excess withdrawal amounts in time without interest. Similarly, a sample of 180 credit card holders is taken from the City Y and it is found that 150 of them are settling their excess withdrawal amounts in time without attracting interest. Check the intuition of the sales manager at a significance level of 0.05.

23. The daily demand of a product seems to follow uniform distribution. The observed frequency of daily demand values are summarized in the following table:

| Demand (Units) | 25 | 26 | 27 | 28 | 29 | 30 | 31 | 32 | 33 | 34 |
|---|---|---|---|---|---|---|---|---|---|---|
| Observed Frequency | 18 | 15 | 12 | 15 | 11 | 14 | 17 | 15 | 19 | 14 |

Check whether the given data follow uniform distribution at significance level of 0.01 (Hint: Total of observed frequency = 150. Expected frequency (E) = 150/10 = 15. Calculate $\chi^2$ by formula $(O-E)^2/E$. Find the total chi-square and compare with tabulated value).

## 9.3 How to Do?

Dolly: "Now we are in the midway of learning the research process."

Jolly: "Yes, after defining the problem, decide the objectives of your study. Review the literature. Frame the hypotheses. Gather the data. Analyse the data. Test the hypotheses"

Dolly: "If it is descriptive study, no need to test the hypothesis"

Jolly: "Who says? Even in descriptive studies hypotheses are tested. You can test your means and proportions. You can also compare two means."

Dolly: "Yesterday, you told me read "Quality Management with a case study of Verka." Author has not tested any hypotheses."

Jolly: "You can test hypotheses in a case study also. Here author had no such objectives or hypothesis to be tested."

Dolly: "I understand, but there are many issues. The author first reviewed the literature to define terminologies of quality and its management. Then author described seven key dimensions which MILKFED has adopted. Author further describes how quality improvement process is carried out in MILKFED. But can there not be a better way to study this case. I feel the author should have attempted to see cause effect relationship. It is the quality which attracts customers, which in turn may increase revenue and profit. What is the opportunity cost of quality? I feel the report lacks descriptive validity and theoretical validity. The report gives us good information but not knowledge as there is no conclusion, internal or external validity also."

Jolly: "Do not be highly negative. When you write a report for a journal, there is always time and space constraint. Within limited words authors have to write the article and it is not possible to cover everything, the report you read is a good mix-up of exploratory, descriptive and a case study."

Dolly: "I agree, author has attempted to study the quality and its qualitative effects. But I feel it should have been a mix up of both qualitative as well as quantitative analysis."

Jolly: "I know you are getting intelligent, but appreciate the case study."

Dolly: "I wish to read an article wherein there is both qualitative as well as quantitative analysis."

Jolly: "But you need to learn many quantitative techniques like ANOVA, regression, chi-square, non-parametric tests."

Dolly: "See, we have another subject like 'Basic Statistics', 'Business Maths' etc. There also we are learning these techniques. There are some areas in management studies which overlap. So we are getting good practice. I wish to read how quantitative analysis is carried out practically."

Jolly: "I have a good collection of project reports. I shall suggest you to read a simple report with a simple quantitative analysis."

Dolly: "Is it possible that we learn everything but they do not ask in the exam."

Jolly: "You are leaving the track. Research Methodology is not the subject to be tested only for exam purpose. It is the way how you decide in your professional life. Do not just learn for the exam purpose; learn to be a good researcher"

Dolly: "Okay, tell me which project report should I read."

Jolly: "There is a small report written by Dr. J K SACHDEVA about the Exports of live-stock and allied products. The report is based on secondary data. You are to see how data has been collected, how compounded growth rate has been calculated and how market share has been calculated. You can call it a blend of descriptive study and empirical study with quantitative analysis."

Dolly: "Okay I shall read and like a panellist I shall write my comments."

Jolly: "Good, go ahead."

✦ ✦ ✦

Research Project 7

## 9.4 Exports of Livestock and Allied Products

By J.K. SACHDEVA[1]

### Introduction

Export-led agricultural growth can be a basis for overall development of a country. This also facilitates the establishment of requisite infrastructure in the country as market environment forces for the same. One of the main objectives of the governments' export policy is to maximise agricultural exports in order to earn foreign exchange. It also seeks to provide remunerative prices to the farmers while ensuring adequate availability of essential commodities to the domestic consumers at reasonable prices (Rajeswar Rao, 2002). The new Exim Policy (2002-2007) announced by ministry of commerce is beneficial to the farmers as it makes exports free, easy and rewarding for them.

Traditional exports of cereals and other primary commodities have been hit hard by low international prices during the last ten years (Chand, 2003 and Gulati, 2003). There is a consensus that agriculture should be diversified beyond the traditional primary exports. Being value added products, exports of livestock and products of animal origin form a significant part of total export of agriculture pool. Analysis of trends in supply to buyers can help devise strategies to increase exports.

This paper analyses the exports of livestock and allied products to principal groups of countries in the light of world trade. The direction of trade has been analysed to explore the areas where exports can be given a further boost.

### Issues Relating to Trade in Livestock and Allied Products

There are four important issues which need attention. They are (a) lack of studies especially the analysis of direction of trade, (b) effect of globalisation after the establishment of WTO on exports of livestock and allied products, (c) lack of infrastructure facilities to enhance export of livestock products and (d) Sanitary and Phyto sanitary restrictions used as NTB (Non Tariff Barrier).

Considering the importance attached to the livestock sector, a number of studies on market structure, nature of demand and supply in the domestic and international markets for milk and milk products, meat and other animal by-products are conducted. Some private and public agencies have undertaken studies. But these studies are not accessible to public or made available for wider professional audience. They are found in purely technical or industry specific journals (George, 1995).

Tewari (1995) found (prior to WTO establishment, 1995) that while Indian export of livestock and livestock products had grown faster than the rates at which total Asian or world exports of these products were rising, their imports into India had grown at a rate lower than the rates of Asia and the world. There was a marked increase of share in total export of livestock products in Asia and the world. She opined that situation would further improve if more emphasis was laid on producing more of value added products of international quality standards and aggressive marketing strategies are adopted.

---

1 Dr. J K Sachdeva, Hon Editor, Journal of Global Economy. Author is obliged to his guide Professor C. S. Murthy, Senior Fellow, CESS, Hyderabad, for his guidance. The article has already been published in Volume 1 no. 1 of Journal of Global Economy, Jan, 2005 issue. Reprinted with permission from management of Research Centre for Social Sciences.

Gill *et al.* (1995) suggested that the non-descript breed of animals (like buffaloes) could be used for meat purposes and export to foreign lands. This would go a long way in lessening the mounting pressure of animals on scarce land resources. If export of animals is encouraged through policy instruments, the earnings from livestock could be enhanced to a great extent.

Parekh (1997) and Kondaiah (1997) analysed the prospects of dairy products and meat and meat preparations respectively. According to them India can direct its exports to SAARC countries and the Middle East. Milk product prices have doubled in the SAARC region. Pakistan imports huge quantity of milk products i.e., milk powder. Middle East countries import 1200 tonnes of cheese daily. However, Pandey (1995) observes that inadequate market infrastructure, more particularly unregulated and unorganised markets for livestock and its products inhibit the growth of this enterprise. Due to lack of appropriate price policies, share of the producer in consumer rupee is also very small.

With the signing of WTO agreements, exports of developing countries to developed world has started increasing as it is very difficult for the developed countries to impose quantitative restrictions or place high tariff. They, however, can take recourse to non-tariff measures, mainly on the ground of quality. Gulati (2003) feels that necessary regulations are required for food and environment safety, but developed countries may use them as NTBs.

The quality and safety of food products cannot be ascertained by sheer physical inspection. It involves usage of sophisticated and advanced technology. Sometimes dangerous toxins, at low level, are difficult to detect at early stages. Due to these factors, free-market economy cannot solve the problems of food quality. Therefore, along with AoA two other agreements, namely, the Agreement on Sanitary and Phytosanitary Measures (SPS) and Technical Barriers to Trade (TBT), aim to address these concerns (Jaiswal, 2003).

The benefits of trade liberalisation in the agriculture sector achieved by the Uruguay Round negotiations could be undermined by the protectionist use of SPS. An effective way to overcome a number of the problems faced by developing countries is to introduce certain amendments to the legal text to ensure that the risk of using SPS measures as a border protection instrument is minimised. Some provisions of SPS do not take adequate account of circumstances as well as trade interests of developing countries. There is a consensus (Vyas, 1999; Gulati, 2003; Jaiswal 2003) that regulations should be harmonised, aligned and simplified. There should be increased length of time between the routine notification of a new SPS measure and its application. There also needs a revision of the format of notifications so that they routinely contain more information on the nature of the proposed SPS measure. Steps should also be taken to make producers, traders and exporters aware of the health and safety standards imposed by different countries.

Kondaiah (1997) listed the constraints affecting meat exports as livestock disease situation, abattoir facilities, conditions of slaughter houses, some social groups against meat exports, lack of grading and inspection system in meat trade and lack of pragmatic slaughter policies.

## Data and Methodology

Four groups of commodities — (1) Live animals, (2) meat and meat preparations, (3) milk and milk products and (4) eggs, honey and other products of animal origin – have been selected for the analysis. Harmonised system of nomenclature classifies the commodities on the basis of origin, use, functions and trade. Live animals have been classified in chapter 1 which includes live horses, asses, mules, hinnies, bovine animals, swine, sheep, goat, live poultry (fowls, ducks, geese, turkeys and guinea fowls) and other live animals. Second select group of commodities are meat and meat preparations which includes meat and edible offal of all animals, fresh, chilled, salted in brine or dried. Other two groups comprise, 1, milk and milk products that include milk, cream, whey, buttermilk, yogurt, cheese and curd, 2, birds' eggs in shell, yolks dried or cooked, natural honey and edible products of animal origin, (Customs Tariff Act, 1975, 2002-03 issue GOI publication and UN Comtrade Database Notes).

Exports of select groups of commodities over 10 years have been analysed from the period 1993-1994 to 2002-2003 (in short 1993 to 2002). Importers of Indian products have been arranged in 5 groups — SAARC includes Bangladesh, Bhutan, Maldives, Nepal, Pakistan, and Sri Lanka. Middle East Group includes UAE, Saudi Arabia, Kuwait, Yemen, Bahrain, Turkey, Qatar, Lebanon, Iran, Iraq, and Israel. High Income Asian Countries (HIAC) includes Japan, Singapore, South Korea, Taiwan, China, Hong Kong, Thailand, Indonesia, Malaysia and Philippines. High Income Other Countries (HIOC) include Australia, Austria, Belgium, Canada, Denmark, Germany, Iceland, Ireland, Israel, Netherlands, Portugal, Spain, Switzerland, UK and USA, Rest of World is the fifth group. No country has been repeated in any group.

Raw data of individual countries and commodities have been taken from UN Comtrade Database, CMIE September 2003 issue, RBI Hand Book of Statistics and Agriculture Situation in Brief. Growth of the select commodities have been calculated by using growth model Ln (y) = a +b*time, where 'b' is exponential growth and Compound Growth Rate (CGR) = (Antilog (b) -1)*100. Percentage share of select commodities' exports to different group of countries have been calculated and growth has been arrived at.

A reference has been made to worlds' top exporters and importers during the year 2002 to get a comparative view with Indian exports. Total imports of the select group of commodities have also been calculated and CGR calculated.

## Direction of Export

India's exports of total agricultural and allied products have grown at compounded growth rate (CGR) of 3.57% from US $ 4027.5 in 1993 to US $ 6428.5 in 2002. But the CGR after 1995 (i.e. after the establishment WTO) is negative 1.54%. While the total agricultural exports recorded negative growth, exports of livestock and allied products recorded growth rates in excess of 7.83% between 1995 and 2002.

## Live Animals

In the year 2002, total world trade of live animals was 8.6 billion dollars. The top importers were USA (2.159 billion dollars), Italy (1.37 Billion dollars), UK (523.6 million dollars), Saudi Arabia (511.7 million dollars) and Germany (445.9 million dollars). Top exporters were Canada (1.593 Billion dollars), France (1.537 Billion dollars), USA (641.9 million Dollars), Australia (635.08 million Dollars) and Netherlands (631.9 million Dollars). The import-export figures of Canada and USA indicate that there is a good business of re-export. Live animals are exported from Canada to USA and processing takes place in USA from where they are exported as it is or as meat preparations.

Compared to world trade, exports of Indian live animals is very miniscule, yet it has grown at CGR of 1.04% (Table 1). CGR after 1995 is 9.47%. Major importers of Indian live animals are Bangladesh, Sri Lanka, Kazakhstan, Malaysia and Nepal. During the referred ten-year period exports of live animals to SAARC and Middle East countries is reducing at CGR of 1.76% and 24.06% respectively (Table 2). However, exports of animals to High Income Asian Countries (HIAC) cannot be analysed due to negligible export value, but exports to high income other countries (HIOC) and rest of world are rising at CGR of 29.81% and 57.46% respectively (Table 2), latter is statistically significant at 1% level. Table 3 shows the growth of per cent share to select group of countries. Increase in share to high income countries is compensating the loss in share of SAARC and Middle East countries. India also imports animals from Nepal, USA, UK, Denmark and France, but this import is negligible.

## Meat and Meat Preparations

Total world export of meat and meat preparations in the year 2002 was 40.04 billion US dollars. The top exporters were USA (5.9 billion US D), Netherlands (3.7 billion US D), Australia (3.2 billion US D), Denmark (3.13 billion US dollars) and Canada (2.792 billion dollars). Major importers were Japan (6.7 billion US D), USA (3.9 billion US D), Germany (3.4 billion dollars), UK (3.3 billion US D) and Italy (2.97 billion dollars). The figures of developed countries again indicate their involvement in re-export business.

India's total exports of meat and meat preparations have grown at the rate of 10.03% which is statistically significant at 1% level (Table 1). CGR after 1995 is 7.26%. Major importers of meat and meat preparations are Malaysia, Philippines, UAE, Egypt and Jordan. CGR of exports to HIAC and ROW are 9.38% and 21.91% respectively and statistically significant at 1% level. Growth to Middle East countries is only 2.70%. In table 3, it is seen that share of total exports of meat and meat products are increasing with HIOC and ROW while same is reducing with SAARC and Middle East countries. India also imports meat and meat preparations in a small quantity mainly from Netherlands, Denmark, Germany, Ireland and Australia.

## Milk and Milk Preparations

World's total export in the year 2002 was 23.6 billion dollars. Top exporters were Germany (3.7 billion US dollars), France (3.6 billion US D), Netherlands (3.2 billion US D) and Belgium (1.7 billion US D). Top world importers were Germany (3.0 billion US D), Italy (2.3 billion US D), Belgium (1.8 billion US D), France (1.75 billion US D) and Netherlands (1.73 billion US D). These figures reiterate that developed countries re-export these commodities and earn good foreign exchange.

India's total exports of milk and milk products have grown at CGR of 23.58% during the referred period. This growth is statistically significant at 5% level. CGR between 1995 to 2002 is 56.04% which is statistically significant at 1% level. Major importer of Indian milk and milk products are Bangladesh, Yemen, UAE, Nepal, and Singapore. Milk and milk products have shown better growth to all select groups of countries. Though growth to SAARC (26.50%), Middle East (24.47%), HIAC (35.86%), HIOC (19.56) and ROW (36.66%) are statistically not significant but this high growth is very considerable as Indian Milk products are capturing a good market share all over the world. Share of exports to HIAC and ROW is increasing while to other group of countries it is stagnant. India also imports milk and milk products from New Zealand, France, Australia, Denmark and USA.

**Table 1**

**Exports of Total Agricultural Commodities and Livestock and Products Exports**

**(All figures in US $ million)**

| Years | TOTAL AGRIC - ULTURE | HSN 01 (LIVE ANIMALS) | HSN 02 (MEAT AND MEAT PREPARATIONS) | HSN 0401 to 0406 (MILK AND MILK PRODUCTS) | HSN 0407 to 0410 EGGS, (HONEY AND OTHERS) |
|---|---|---|---|---|---|
| a | b | c | d | e | f |
| 1993 | 4027.5 | 1.46 | 109.65 | 3.67 | 3.20 |
| 1994 | 4226.1 | 0.85 | 125.67 | 12.25 | 2.60 |
| 1995 | 6081.9 | 2.59 | 183.61 | 7.84 | 7.25 |
| 1996 | 6868.5 | 1.95 | 195.13 | 3.45 | 29.68 |
| 1997 | 6634.2 | 0.36 | 213.81 | 3.89 | 27.54 |

| | | | | | |
|---|---|---|---|---|---|
| 1998 | 6033.1 | 1.13 | 183.47 | 4.13 | 18.01 |
| 1999 | 5614.9 | 1.02 | 184.82 | 11.26 | 15.86 |
| 2000 | 5982.9 | 1.70 | 323.83 | 22.66 | 23.61 |
| 2001 | 5921.3 | 1.92 | 250.73 | 40.27 | 34.45 |
| 2002 | 6428.5 | 1.29 | 279.19 | 26.17 | 47.19 |
| CGR | 3.57 | 1.04 | 10.03* | 23.58** | 32.07* |
| CGR between 1995-2002 | –1.54 | 9.47 | 7.26 | 56.04* | 7.83 |

Source of Raw data: UN Comtrade Database, CMIE Sept, 2003 issue.
* Statistically significant at 5% level ** Statistically significant at 10% level.

## Eggs, Honey and Other Products of Animal Origin

Last group of commodities is poultry eggs, honey and other products of animal origin. Total world trade in year 2002 was 2.1 billion US D. During this year major exporting countries were Netherlands (383 million US D), USA (158.2 Million US D) Germany (178.9 Million US D), France (150 million US D) and China (139 million US D). Top importers were Germany (469.9 million US D), China, Hong Kong SAR (203 million US D), USA (213 million US D), and France (126.5 million US D). These figures reiterate that developed countries re-export the imported commodities, as it is or after value additions.

**Table 2**

**Growth of Exports to Select Group of Countries**

| Products | SAARC | MIDDLE EAST | HIAC | HIOC | ROW |
|---|---|---|---|---|---|
| HSN 01 (LIVE ANIMALS) | –1.76 | –24.06 | N.C. | 29.81 | 57.46 * |
| HSN 02 (MEAT AND MEAT PREPARATIONS) | 8.85 | 2.70 | 9.38* | 24.06 | 21.91 * |
| HSN 0401 TO 0406 (MILK AND MILK PRODUCTS) | 26.50 | 24.47 | 35.86 | 19.56 | 36.66 |
| HSN 0407 to 0410 (EGGS, HONEY AND OTHERS) | 10.61 | 29.53 | 109.80 * | 56.74 | 25.17 * |

* Statistically significant at 5% level ** Statistically significant at 10% level.

**Table 3**

**Growth of Per cent Share of Total Exports to Select Group of Countries**

| Products | SAARC | MIDDLE EAST | HIAC | HIOC | ROW |
|---|---|---|---|---|---|
| HSN 01 (LIVE ANIMALS) | –2.76 | –24.84 * | 123.96 | 28.48 | 56.03 * |
| HSN 02 (MEAT AND MEAT PREPARATIONS) | –1.07 | –6.66 | –0.58 | 12.76 | 10.80 |

| HSN 0401 TO 0406 (MILK AND MILK PRODUCTS) | 2.36 | 0.72 | 9.94 | -3.25 | 10.58 |
|---|---|---|---|---|---|
| HSN 0407 to 0410 (EGGS, HONEY AND OTHERS) | -16.25 | -1.92 | 58.85 | 18.68 | -5.22 |

* Statistically significant at 5% level

CGR of India's export is 32.07% which is consistent as it is statistically significant at 1% level. CGR between 1995 and 2002 is 7.83%. Growth to all select groups of countries is more than 10% but the growth to HIAC and ROW are statistically significant. Share of total export is increasing to all High Income countries but reducing with Middle East and SAARC countries after 1993. India exports these products to UAE, Germany, Oman, Japan, Saudi Arabia, Belgium, Bangladesh, Kuwait and Denmark. India also imports these commodities from UK, USA and Netherlands, but the value so far is very small.

Exports do not show the actual picture of terms of trade until imports are analysed simultaneously. Table 4 shows the imports of the select group of commodities. Imports of milk and milk products and poultry products are growing at CGR of 7.70% and 66.15% respectively. During this period of globalisation after the establishment of WTO, no country can deny market access. Rising imports can be due to urban demand which may be due to high demonstration effect of consumers and promotional techniques used by producers.

**Table 4**

**Imports Into India (Values in US $ Million)**

| Years | HSN 01 (LIVE ANIMALS) | HSN 02 (MEAT AND MEAT PREPARATIONS) | HSN 0401 to 0406 (MILK AND MILK PRODUCTS) | HSN 0407 to 0410 EGGS, (HONEY AND OTHERS) |
|---|---|---|---|---|
| 1993 | 0.83 | 0.02 | 5.64 | 0.01 |
| 1994 | 1.00 | 0.00 | 9.79 | 0.23 |
| 1995 | 1.04 | 0.00 | 18.75 | 0.20 |
| 1996 | 0.83 | 0.00 | 1.48 | 0.11 |
| 1997 | 0.75 | 0.06 | 8.04 | 0.03 |
| 1998 | 0.35 | 0.01 | 10.07 | 0.04 |
| 1999 | 0.43 | 0.06 | 41.61 | 0.17 |
| 2000 | 0.30 | 0.10 | 10.70 | 1.22 |
| 2001 | 0.36 | 0.12 | 6.86 | 1.47 |
| 2002 | 0.75 | 0.08 | 12.67 | 4.75 |
| CGR | -9.78 | 1.31 | 7.70 | 66.15 ** |

** Statistically significant at 10% level.

## Conclusions

India's exports of all select commodities are very small compared to world trade but this also indicates the potential for Indian exporters to enter into huge market of livestock and allied products. There is considerable growth in the exports of live animals, meat and meat preparations, milk and milk preparations and eggs, honey and other products. Share of these products is growing faster than the total agricultural exports. There is a considerable growth of exports to High Income countries, both Asian and others than other group of countries. India is losing business with traditional partners in SAARC and Middle East, especially the trade of meat and meat preparations, eggs etc. But the loss is compensated by exports to High Income countries. After the establishment of WTO, exports of milk and milk products are growing to all group of countries, but efforts should be made to bring consistency in growth. Indian exporters should compete with rivals with aggressive marketing in SAARC and Gulf countries. India should improve its infrastructure and should take the strategic advantage being in the centre of the world. India can import these commodities and re-export after some value addition. Indian products especially the milk and milk products, egg preparations, honey, etc. should be promoted domestically among urban classes. These products should compete with international products in promotion, presentation and pricing so that they are as popular as imported. The comparison of CGR during the periods 1993-2002 and 1996-2002 clearly shows that there is good increase of Indian exports to developed countries, but there is a need to maintain the consistency in trade.

WTO has opened more gates due to market access pressure but has also paved the way for more competition. The major problem is that Sanitary and Phytosanitary restrictions which are used as NTBs. Indian exporters should be well versed with standards and improve their quality. Infrastructure facilities like transportation, freezing, canning and packing should be increased to enhance export of livestock and allied products.

## References

Gandhi, Vasant P and Mani Gyanendera (1995): "Are Livestock Products Rising in Importance" "A Study of the Growth and Behaviour of their Consumption in India," in Indian Journal of Agricultural Economics Vol 50 No. 3, July-Sept 1995.

George P.S. (1996): "Dairying and Livestock Economy of India – A Review" in Indian Journal of Agricultural Economics Vol 51 No. 1 and 2, Jan-June 1996.

Gill G.S., Chamak J.S. and Satpal Singh (1995): "An Empirical Investigation into Behaviour of Prices and Export Potentials of Buffaloes in Punjab" in Indian Journal of Agricultural Economics Vol 50 No. 3, July-Sept 1995.

Gulati, Ashok (2003) : "India" in Merlinda D Ingco (ed) "Agriculture Trade, WTO in South Asia", World Bank, Washington D.C. 2003.

Jaiswal, Anand Kumar (2003): "WTO Agreement on SPS Strategic Implications" in EPW, Vol XXXVIII no. 45 Nov 8 – 14, 2003.

Kondaiah, N (1997): "Exports of Meat and Meat Products – Prospects and Constraints" in "Promotion of Agricultural Exports – Role of Financial Institutions", Indian Institute of Foreign Trade, New Delhi (1997).

Pandey, U.K. (1995): "The Livestock Economy of India – a Profile" in Indian Journal of Agricultural Economics Vol 50 No. 3, July-Sept 1995.

Parekh J.V. (1997): "Export Prospects For Dairy Products in "Promotion Of Agricultural Exports – Role Of Financial Institutions", Indian Institute of Foreign Trade, New Delhi (1997).

Rajeswar Rao J (2002): "Indian agricultural exports during tenth five years plan 2002-2007 and beyond – strategies to overcome constraints and enhance competitiveness" in Agricultural Situation in India, August 2002.

Rao K.V. (1997): "Technical Appraisal of Export Oriented Live Stock Projects" in " Promotion Of Agricultural Exports – Role of Financial Institutions", Indian Institute of Foreign Trade, New Delhi (1997).

Tewari, Kanchan (1995): "India's Trade Experience in Livestock and Livestock Products" in Indian Journal of Agricultural Economics Vol 50 No. 3, July-Sept 1995.

Vyas V S (1999): "Agricultural Trade Policy and Export Strategy" in *EPW* March *27-April 2, 1999.*

## 9.5 Analysis of Variance

Earlier in chapter 'Research Plan' we learnt that there are four types formal experimental designs. They are

1. Completely randomized design (C.R. Design)
2. Randomized block design (R.B. Design)
3. Latin square design (L. S. Design)
4. Factorial design

Analysis of Variance (ANOVA) is used to compare the means of two or more populations. The analysis of variance was developed by R. A. Fisher. Decomposing of total variability into its components is called ANOVA. The essence of ANOVA is that the total amount of variation in a set of data is broken down into two types, that amount which can be attributed to chance and that amount which can be attributed to specified causes. There may be variations between samples and also within sample items. ANOVA consists in splitting the variance for analytic purpose. In the early stages of its evolution, it was mainly used in agricultural research. As such, the terminology used in analysis of variance with agricultural terms such as blocks (meaning land) and treatments (meaning varieties of seeds and fertilizers or methods of cultivation). In course of time, the technique of analysis of variance began to be used in other spheres too. Today, it is widely used in many different fields. For example, in manufacturing industries, quality control engineers can use it to compare the production from different assembly lines or different plants.

### Assumptions of Analysis of Variance

Before we discuss the procedure of carrying out an analysis of variance, it is necessary to know the assumptions implicit in its use. There are three assumptions:

1. The data are quantitative in nature and are normally distributed. In case of nominal or ordinal data where results are given in percentages or ranks, analysis of variance should not be carried out. If the data are not exactly normally distributed but are close to a normal distribution, analysis of variance still gives good results. One should ensure that data are not highly skewed.
2. The second assumption is that the samples are drawn from the population randomly and independently. In case of an experimental design, the treatments must be assigned to test units by means of some randomising device. In case this assumption does not hold, inferences drawn from ANOVA will not be valid.
3. The third assumption is homogeneity of variance, which means that the variances of the population from which samples have been drawn are equal. In order to combine the variances within the groups into a single within-group source of variation (SSW), this assumption must be satisfied. However, non-compliance of this assumption may not seriously affect the inferences based on the F distribution provided that the sample from each group is of equal size. When the distribution is highly skewed and population variances are not approximately equal, then ANOVA should not be used. A non-parametric technique known as the *Kruskal-Wallis test,* can be used.

Let us learn the technique of ANOVA

### 9.5.1 One-Way ANOVA

**For Completely Randomized design**

#### 9.5.1.1 Solved Examples

#### Solved Example S-1

The following table gives the sales revenue of three salesmen taken on five occasions. Test at 5% level whether there is any difference between the performances of three salesmen

| | Salesmen (Sales in lakhs) | | |
|---|---|---|---|
| **Observations** | **A** | **B** | **C** |
| 1 | 5 | 3 | 10 |
| 2 | 6 | 5 | 13 |
| 3 | 8 | 2 | 7 |
| 4 | 1 | 10 | 13 |
| 5 | 5 | 0 | 17 |

**Solution:**

Before learning the solution, let us learn some of the terminology.

In the table $Y_{ij}$ is the *ith* sales data of j salesman. Salesman is the factor which has effect on the response variable $Y_{ij}$. Let it be factor A. 'a' is the number of salesmen of the company. This is also known as number of levels/treatments of the factor A. 'n' is the number of data under each salesman. This is also known as replications under each factor A.

In an experiment, if a specific set of treatment of a factor is selected with certainty, then the factor is termed as a fixed factor. Under such situation, the inference of the analysis is applied to only the set of treatment of that factor.

The effect of the treatments of the fixed factor A on the response variable is given by the formula

Effect of fixed factor $A = \dfrac{\sum_{j=1}^{n} A_j}{a-1}$

In an experiment, if a set of treatment of a factor is selected randomly from among available treatments, then factor is termed as a random factor. Under such situation, the inference of the analysis of the experiment can be generalised to all the treatments of that factor.

Variance component of random factor A = $\sigma_A^2$

The model of this situation is $Y_{ij} = \mu + A_j + e_{ij}$

Where $\mu$ is the overall mean of the sales revenue, $A_j$ is the effect of jth treatment of Factor A on response variable $Y_{ij}$ and $e_{ij}$ is the random error associated with ith replication of jth treatment.

Now in our problem

Null Hypothesis $H_0 : T_1 = T_2 = T_3$

Alternate Hypothesis $H_1$: Treatment means are not equal for at least one pair of the treatment means.

The relationship between the different sums of squares of this model is as follows:

Total sum of squares = (Sum of squares of treatment) + (sum of squares of errors)

$$SS_{(Total)} = SS_{(Treatment)} + SS_{(Error)}$$

$$SS_{(Total)} = \sum_{i=1}^{n} \sum_{j=1}^{a} Y_{ij}^2 - ..\frac{Y^2..}{N}$$

$$SS_{(Treatment)} = \Sigma \frac{Y_{.j}^2}{n} - \frac{Y_{..}^2}{N}$$

$$SS_{(Error)} = SS_{(Total)} - SS_{(Treatment)}$$

Our problem with columns total is reproduced below

| Observations | Salesmen (Sales in lakhs) | | |
|---|---|---|---|
| | A | B | C |
| 1 | 5 | 3 | 10 |
| 2 | 6 | 5 | 13 |
| 3 | 8 | 2 | 7 |
| 4 | 1 | 10 | 13 |
| 5 | 5 | 0 | 17 |
| Total | 25 | 20 | 60 |

**Grand total = 25+20+60 = 105**

| Observations | Salesmen (Sales in lakhs) | | | | | |
|---|---|---|---|---|---|---|
| | A | $Y_A^2$ | B | $Y_B^2$ | C | $Y_C^2$ |
| 1 | 5 | **25** | 3 | **9** | 10 | **100** |
| 2 | 6 | **36** | 5 | **25** | 13 | **169** |
| 3 | 8 | **64** | 2 | **4** | 7 | **49** |
| 4 | 1 | **1** | 10 | **100** | 13 | **169** |
| 5 | 5 | **25** | 0 | **0** | 17 | **289** |
| Total | 25 | **151** | 20 | **138** | 60 | **776** |

$\frac{Y_{..}^2}{N}$ is also called correction factor.

$$\frac{Y_{..}^2}{N} = (25+20+60)^2/15 = 735$$

$$SS_{(Total)} = \sum_{i=1}^{n} \sum_{j=1}^{a} Y_{ij}^2 - ..\frac{Y^2..}{N} = (151+138+776)-735 = 330$$

$$SS_{(Treatment)} = \Sigma \frac{Y_{.j}^2}{n} - \frac{Y_{..}^2}{N} = \frac{25^2}{5} + \frac{20^2}{5} + \frac{60^2}{5} - 735 = 190$$

$SS_{(Error)} = SS_{(Total)} - SS_{(Treatment)} = 330\text{-}190 = 140$

| Sources of variance | SS | DF | Mean | Computed F | Tabulated F |
|---|---|---|---|---|---|
| $SS_{(treatment)}$ or Between Samples | 190 | c-1 = 3-1 = 2 | 190/2 = 95 | MSS/MSE =95/11.67 = 8.14 | 3.88 |
| $SS_{(Error)}$ or Within samples | 140 | n-c = 15-3 = 12 | 140/12 = 11.67 | | |
| SS Total | 330 | n-1 = 15-1 = 14 | | | |

Tabulated value of F for 5% significance level and 2 numerator DF and 12 denominator DF = $(F_{2,12,0.5})$ = 3.88. Since the computed value is greater than the tabulated value, we reject $H_0$ and accept $H_1$ and conclude that there is a significant difference in the variance. Hence average sales revenue of one of the salesmen is different.

### Solved Problem S-2

A company has deputed four different batches (A, B, C and D) of its employees to four different training programmes which aims to train them with negotiation skills. Each batch consists of five employees with same qualification and experience. After training programme, company conducted a test and employees scored marks as per following table. Perform ANOVA to check whether there is any significant difference between the training programmes of A, B, C and D by assuming a significance level of 5%.

| | Scores of Batches with training programmes | | | |
|---|---|---|---|---|
| Employees | A | B | C | D |
| 1 | 80 | 70 | 65 | 90 |
| 2 | 90 | 60 | 50 | 89 |
| 3 | 96 | 55 | 58 | 85 |
| 4 | 85 | 85 | 55 | 95 |
| 5 | 70 | 90 | 40 | 80 |

**Solution:**

This is one-way ANOVA just to find the difference in batches
Table is again produced with column totals

| | Scores of Batches with training programmes | | | |
|---|---|---|---|---|
| Employees | A | B | C | D |
| 1 | 80 | 70 | 65 | 90 |
| 2 | 90 | 60 | 50 | 89 |
| 3 | 96 | 55 | 58 | 85 |
| 4 | 85 | 85 | 55 | 95 |
| 5 | 70 | 90 | 40 | 80 |
| Total | 421 | 360 | 268 | 439 |

$Y_{..} = SS\ Y_{ij} = 1488$

$$SS_{(Total)} = 80^2+90^2+96^2+85^2+.......+95^2+80^2 - \frac{1488^2}{20} = 5368.8$$

$SS_{(Treatment)} = (421^2+360^2+268^2+439^2)/5 - \quad = 3570$

$SS_{(Error)} = 5368.8 - 3570 = 1798.8$

**ANOVA TABLE**

| Sources of variance | SS | DF | Mean | Computed F | Tabulated F |
|---|---|---|---|---|---|
| $SS_{(treatment)}$ or Between Samples | 3570 | c-1= 4-1= 3 | 3570/3 = 1190 | MSS/MSE =1190/112.43 = 10.58 | 3.24 |
| $SS_{(Error)}$ or Within samples | 1798.8 | n-c = 20-4 =16 | 1798.8/16 = 112.43 | | |
| SS Total | 5368.8 | n-1 = 20-1=19 | | | |

Tabulated value of F for 5% significance level and 3 numerator DF and 16 denominator DF = $(F_{3,16,0.5})$= 3.24. Since the computed value is greater than the tabulated value, we reject $H_0$ and accept $H_1$ and conclude that there is a significant difference in the variance. This means that there is a significant difference in terms of scores between batches trained under various programmes.

### 9.5.2 Two-Way ANOVA

#### Randomized Complete Block Design (Two-Way ANOVA)

In this type of design both treatment and blocks are examined. For instance in the above example, we checked difference in batches (treatment). Here we have to check difference between batches (treatment) as well as employees (blocks).

The relationship between different sums of squares of this model is as follows:

Total sum of Squares = (Sum of Squares of blocks) + (Sum of Square of Treatment)+ (Sum of Square of Errors)

$SS_{(Total)} = SS_{(Blocks)} + SS_{(Treatment)} + SS_{(Error)}$

#### 9.5.2.1 Solved Examples

A company has appointed four salesmen A, B, C and D and has observed their sales in three seasons- summer, winter and monsoon. The figures in (₹ lakhs) are given in the following table

| | Salesmen | | | |
|---|---|---|---|---|
| Seasons | A | B | C | D |
| Summer | 36 | 36 | 21 | 35 |
| Winter | 28 | 29 | 31 | 32 |
| Monsoon | 26 | 28 | 29 | 29 |

Perform ANOVA to check whether there is any significant between sales of salesmen or between sales during different season at 5% level.

**Solution**: We shall give solution by three methods

First as explained above finding SS of original data

Second by coding of data

Third by computer software MS Excel

**First method**

Let us reproduce the table with row and column total

| | Salesmen | | | | |
|---|---|---|---|---|---|
| **Seasons** | **A** | **B** | **C** | **D** | **Total** |
| Summer | 36 | 36 | 21 | 35 | 128 |
| Winter | 28 | 29 | 31 | 32 | 120 |
| Monsoon | 26 | 28 | 29 | 29 | 112 |
| Total | 90 | 93 | 81 | 96 | 360 |

Hypothesis in respect of seasons:

$H_0$: There is no difference in the means of sales in seasons.

$H_1$: Sale is different in at least one of the seasons

Hypothesis in respect of salesmen

$H_0$: There is no difference in the means of sales by salesmen

$H_1$: Sale is different at least by one of the salesmen

Correction Factor: $\frac{Y_{..}^2}{N} = 360^2/12 = 10800$

Sum of Squares between salesmen $= 90^2/3 + 93^2/3 + 81^2/3 + 96^2/3 - 360^2/12 = 42$

Sum of Squares between seasons $= 128^2/4 + 120^2/4 + 112^2/4 = 32$

Total Sum of squares $= 36^2 + 36^2 + 21^2 + 35^2 + 28^2 ....... + 29^2 - 360^2/12 = 210$

We can also use second method 'coding'. Just observe the data; all figures are near to 30. Let us subtract 30 from each figure our coded table shall be as follows:

| | Salesmen | | | | |
|---|---|---|---|---|---|
| **Seasons** | **A** | **B** | **C** | **D** | **Total** |
| Summer | 6 | 6 | –9 | 5 | 8 |
| Winter | –2 | –1 | 1 | 2 | 0 |
| Monsoon | –4 | –2 | –1 | –1 | –8 |
| Total | 0 | 3 | –9 | 6 | 0 |

So Correction Factor: $\frac{Y_{..}^2}{N} = 0^2/12 = 0$

Sum of Squares between salesmen $= 0^2/3 + 3^2/3 + (-9)^2/3 + 6^2/3 - 0^2/12 = 42$

Sum of Squares between seasons $= 8^2/4 + 0^2/4 + (-8)^2/4 = 32$

Total Sum of squares $= 6^2 + 6^2 + (-9)^2 + 5^2 + (-2)^2 ...... + (-1)^2 - 0^2/12 = 210$

**ANOVA TABLE**

| Sources of variance | SS | DF | Mean | Computed F | Tabulated F |
|---|---|---|---|---|---|
| SS $_{(treatment)}$ or Between Salesmen | 42 | c-1 = 4-1 = 3 | 42/3 = 14 | MSS/MSE = 14/22.67 = .62 | 4.76 |
| SS $_{(Blocks)}$ or Between Seasons | 32 | (r-1) = 3-1 = 2 | 32/2 = 16 | MSB/MSE =16/22.67 = .71 | 5.14 |
| SS $_{(Error)}$ or Residuals | 136 | (c-1)*(r-1) = 3*2 = 6 | 136/6 = 22.67 | | |
| SS Total | 210 | n-1 = 20-1 = 19 | | | |

Tabulated $F_{(3,6,\ 05)}$ = 4.76 while $F_{(2,6,\ 05)}$ = 5.14,

In case of salesmen computed F is less than tabulated value, hence accept $H_0$

In case of seasons computed F is less than tabulated value hence accept $H_0$

In both the cases we have accepted $H_0$, there is no difference either between salesmen, nor between seasons.

**Solution with MS Excel**

Enter data in excel spreadsheet

Go to tools

Select data analysis

Select ANOVA without replication

Input range of data

Select Output range in on the same sheet you will get

| 36 | 36 | 21 | 35 |
|---|---|---|---|
| 28 | 29 | 31 | 32 |
| 26 | 28 | 29 | 29 |

**Anova: Two-Factor Without Replication**

| SUMMARY | Count | Sum | Average | Variance |
|---|---|---|---|---|
| Row 1 | 4 | 128 | 32 | 54 |
| Row 2 | 4 | 120 | 30 | 3.333333 |
| Row 3 | 4 | 112 | 28 | 2 |
| | | | | |
| Column 1 | 3 | 90 | 30 | 28 |
| Column 2 | 3 | 93 | 31 | 19 |
| Column 3 | 3 | 81 | 27 | 28 |
| Column 4 | 3 | 96 | 32 | 9 |

**ANOVA**

| Source of Variation | SS | df | MS | F | P-value | F crit |
|---|---|---|---|---|---|---|
| Rows | 32 | 2 | 16 | 0.705882 | 0.530504 | 5.143249 |
| Columns | 42 | 3 | 14 | 0.617647 | 0.628574 | 4.757055 |
| Error | 136 | 6 | 22.66667 | | | |
| | | | | | | |
| Total | 210 | 11 | | | | |

## 9.5.3 Latin Square Design

Both **One-way** ANOVA (C.R. Design) and Two-way ANOVA (R.B. design) have some problems. There is no homogeneity of assignments of treatments to blocks. In Latin square design homogeneity in case of assignments is introduced.

See the table below:

| | W1 | W2 | W3 | W4 |
|---|---|---|---|---|
| S1 | A1 | D2 | B1 | C1 |
| S2 | B2 | C4 | A2 | D3 |
| S3 | C3 | A3 | D4 | B4 |
| S4 | D1 | B3 | C2 | A4 |
| | | | | |

Here there are four salesmen. They are assigned the area S1,S2, S3, and S4. We record their performance for four weeks. Please note there can be variance due to salesmen, due to area and due to weeks.

So Latin square has the following model

$$SS_{(Total)} = SS_{(Rows)} + SS_{(Treatments)} + SS_{(Columns)} + SS_{(errors)}$$

We shall have to solve the problem originally as two way ANOVA and then rearrange the assignment and find the variations due to treatment.

### 9.5.3.1 Solved Examples

A company assigns four salesmen to four areas and records their sales performance of four weeks as below

| | W1 | W2 | W3 | W4 |
|---|---|---|---|---|
| S1 | A = 23 | D = 40 | B = 30 | C = 35 |
| S2 | B = 20 | C = 45 | A = 34 | D = 40 |
| S3 | C = 25 | A = 45 | D = 34 | B = 20 |
| S4 | D = 28 | B = 30 | C = 29 | A = 34 |

Calculate at 5% significance level whether there is any difference between salesmen, between areas and/or between weeks.

**Solution:**

Hypotheses can be framed as follows:

In case of salesmen:

$H_0 = T_1 = T_2 = T_3 = T_4$

$H_1$ = Treatments means are not equal, at least any one of them is different

In case of area

$H_0 = S_1 = S_2 = S_3 = S_4$

$H_1$ = Area means are not equal, at least any one of them is different

In case of period

$H_0 = W_1 = W_2 = W_3 = W_4$

$H_1$ = Period means are not equal, at least any one of them is different

Table is being reproduced with totals

| | W1 | W2 | W3 | W4 | Total |
|---|---|---|---|---|---|
| S1 | A = 23 | D = 40 | B = 30 | C = 35 | 128 |
| S2 | B = 20 | C = 45 | A = 34 | D = 40 | 139 |
| S3 | C = 25 | A = 45 | D = 34 | B = 20 | 124 |
| S4 | D = 28 | B = 30 | C = 29 | A = 34 | 121 |
| Total | 96 | 160 | 127 | 129 | 512 |

$SS_{(Total)} = 23^2 + 40^2 + 30^2 + \ldots\ldots + 34^2 - 512^2/16 = 938$

$SS_{(Area)} = ¼\ (128^2 + 139^2 + 124^2 + 121^2) - 512^2/16 = 46.5$

$SS_{(Weeks)} = ¼\ (96^2 + 160^2 + 127^2 + 129^2) - 512^2/16 = 512.5$

Now rearrange the table as per salesmen and variation due to salesmen

| A | B | C | D | Total | |
|---|---|---|---|---|---|
| S1 | A = 23 | B = 30 | C = 35 | D = 40 | . |
| S2 | A = 34 | B = 20 | C = 45 | D = 40 | . |
| S3 | A = 45 | B = 20 | C = 25 | D = 34 | . |
| S4 | A = 34 | B = 30 | C = 29 | D = 28 | . |
| Total | 136 | 100 | 134 | 142 | 512 |

$SS_{(Salesmen)} = ¼\ (136^2 + 100^2 + 134^2 + 142^2) - 512^2/16 = 270$

$SS_{(Errors)} = SS_{(Total)} - SS_{(Area)} - SS_{(Weeks)} - SS_{(Salesmen)}$

$SS_{(Errors)} = 938 - 46.5 - 270 - 512.5 = 109$

## ANOVA TABLE

| Sources of variance | SS | DF | Mean | Computed F | Tabulated F |
|---|---|---|---|---|---|
| $SS_{(treatment)}$ or Between Salesmen | 270 | c–1 = 4–1 = 3 | 270/3 = 90 | MSS/MSE = 90/18.17 = 4.95 | 4.76 |
| $SS_{(rows)}$ or Between areas | 46.5 | (r–1) = 4–1 = 3 | 46.5/3 = 15.5 | MSS/MSE = 15.5/18.17 = 0.85 | 4.76 |

| | | | | | |
|---|---|---|---|---|---|
| SS $_{(columns)}$ or Between period | 512.5 | c–1 = 4–1 = 3 | 512.5/3 = 170.83 | MSS/MSE = 170.83/18.17 = 9.40 | 4.76 |
| SS $_{(Error)}$ or Residuals | 109 | = 6 | 109/6 = 18.17 | | |
| SS Total | 938 | n–1 = 16–1 = 15 | | | |

Tabulated $F_{(3,6,\ 05)}$ = 4.76

In case of salesmen computed F is more than tabulated value, hence accept $H_1$ (which means at least one of the salesman is different.

In case of rows computed F is less than tabulated value hence accept $H_0$ (which means there is no difference between areas).

In case of columns, computed F is more than the tabulated value reject $H_0$ (which means any one of the period has some difference).

### 9.5.4 Factorial Design Analysis

In this design we calculate the interaction between columns and rows.

$$SS_{(Interaction)} = SS_{(Sub\text{-}totals)} - SS_{(Rows)} - SS_{(Columns)}$$

$$SS_{(error)} = SS_{(Total)} - SS_{(Sub\text{-}totals)} - SS_{(Rows)} - SS_{(Columns)} - SS_{(Interaction)}$$

#### 9.5.4.1 Solved Examples

See the example below

**Solved Example**: The sales manager of ABC wants to study the effect of sales regions as well as salesmen on quarterly sales revenue. So, he has designed a factorial experiment involving two factors as shown in Table, with two replications for each experimental combination:

Quarterly Sales of ABC company

| | | Salesman (B) ₹ in lakhs | | | |
|---|---|---|---|---|---|
| | | **1** | **2** | **3** | **4** |
| Sales Area (A) | East | 65 | 30 | 50 | 20 |
| | | 70 | 35 | 65 | 40 |
| | West | 30 | 60 | 20 | 50 |
| | | 35 | 55 | 25 | 40 |

As per this design each salesman is assigned to each region for two different quarters. Perform ANOVA and check the following at the significance level of 0.05.

(a) Whether there is a significant difference in terms of sales revenue between sales regions

(b) Whether there is a significant difference in terms of sales revenue between salesmen.

(c) Whether there is a significant difference in terms of sales revenue between different combinations of sales region and salesman.

**Solution:**

Data is again being reproduced with rows total and columns total

Quarterly Sales of ABC company

| Sales Area (A) | | Salesman (B) ₹ in lakhs | | | | |
|---|---|---|---|---|---|---|
| | | 1 | 2 | 3 | 4 | Total |
| | East | 65<br>70 | 30<br>35 | 50<br>65 | 20<br>40 | 375 |
| | West | 30<br>35 | 60<br>55 | 20<br>25 | 50<br>40 | 315 |
| Total | | 200 | 180 | 160 | 150 | 690 |

This problem has two factors, namely sales region (A) and salesman (B). The number of treatments for the factor A is 2 ($A_1$ and $A_2$) and that of the factor B is 4 ($B_1$, $B_2$, $B_3$ and $B_4$). The number of replications for each of the eight experimental combinations ($A_1B_1$, $A_1B_2$, $A_1B_3$, $A_1B_4$, $A_2B_1$, $A_2B_2$, $A_2B_3$ and $A_2B_4$) is 2.

Hypothesis with respect to treatment of the factor A:

Null hypothesis, $H_0$: $A_1 = A_2 = \ldots = A_a$

Alternate hypothesis, $H_1$: Treatment means are not equal for at least one pair of the treatment means of the factor A.

Hypothesis with respect to treatment of the factor B:

Null hypothesis, $H_0$: $B_1 = B_2 = B_3 = \ldots = B_b$

Alternate hypothesis, $H_1$: Treatment means are not equal for at least one pair of the treatment means of the factor B.

Hypothesis with respect to interaction component, AB

Null hypothesis, $H_0$: $A_1B_2 = A_1B_2 = A_1B_3 = \ldots A_2B_4$

Alternate hypothesis, $H_1$: Interaction means are not equal for at least one pair of interaction means.

The generalized model of the factorial design is as follows:

$$SS_{(Total)} = \sum_{i=1}^{a}\sum_{j=1}^{b}\sum_{k=1}^{n} Y_{ijk}^2 - \frac{Y_{..}^2}{N}$$

$$= (65)^2 + (30)^2 + (50)^2 + (20)^2 + (70)^2 + \ldots..(40)^2 - \frac{(690)^2}{16} = 4093.75$$

Where $Y_{ijk}$ is the individual observation and $Y_{..}$ (= 690) is total of all observations.

$$SS_{(Rows)} = \sum\frac{Y_i^2}{bn} - \frac{Y^2}{N} = \frac{(375)^2 + (315)^2}{8} - \frac{(690)^2}{16} = 225$$

$$SS_{(Columns)} = \Sigma \frac{Y_{.j.}^2}{an} - \frac{Y_{..}^2}{N} = \frac{200^2 + 180^2 + 160^2 + 150^2}{4} - \frac{690^2}{16} = 368.75$$

$$SS_{(Sub\text{-}totals)} = \sum_{i=1}^{a} \sum_{j=1}^{b} \frac{Y_{ij.}^2}{n} - \frac{Y_{..}^2}{N} =$$

$$\frac{(65+70)^2 + (30+35)^2 + (50+65)^2 + (20+40)^2 + \ldots\ldots + (20+25)^2 + (50+40)^2}{2} - \frac{690^2}{16} = 3668.75$$

$$SS_{(Interaction)} = SS_{(Sub\text{-}totals)} - SS_{(Rows)} - SS_{(Columns)} = 3668.75 - 225 - 368.75 = 3075$$

$$SS_{(error)} = SS_{(Total)} - SS_{(Sub\text{-}totals)} - SS_{(Rows)} - SS_{(Columns)} - SS_{(Interaction)}$$

$$= 4093.75 - 225 - 368.75 - 3075 = 425$$

**Generalized Results in Factorial Design (ANOVA Format)**

| Sources of Variation | DF | Sum of squares | Mean SS | F Ratio |
|---|---|---|---|---|
| Between Rows | a-1 | $SS_{(Rows)}$ | $SS_{(Rows)}/(a-1)$ | $\frac{MSS_{Rows}}{MSS_{Error}}$ |
| Between Columns | b-1 | $SS_{(Columns)}$ | $SS_{(Columns)}/(b-1)$ | $\frac{MSS_{Columns}}{MSS_{Error}}$ |
| Between Rows x Columns | (a-1)(b-1) | $SS_{(Interaction)}$ | $SS_{(Interaction)}/(a-1)(b-1)$ | |
| Error | ab(n-1) | $SS_{(error)}$ | $SS_{(error)}/(ab(n-1)$ | |
| **Total** | **abn-1** | $SS_{(Total)}$ | | |

**ANOVA for given problem**

| Sources of Variation | DF | Sum of squares | Mean SS | F Ratio |
|---|---|---|---|---|
| Between Rows | 1 | 225 | 225/1 = 225 | 225/53.13 = 4.24 |
| Between Columns | 3 | 368.75 | 368.7/3 = 122.92 | 122.92/53.13 = 2.31 |
| Between Rows x Columns | 3 | 3075 | 3075/3 = 1025 | 1025/53.13 = 19.29 |
| Error | 8 | 425 | 425/8 = 53.13 | |
| Total | 15 | 4093.75 | | |

The value of the calculated F ratio for the factor *A* is 4.24, whereas its table value with the significance level of 0.05 and degrees of freedom (1, 8) is 5.32. The calculated ratio for the factor *B* is 2.31, whereas its table value with the significance level of 0.05 and degrees of freedom (3, 8) is 4.07. The calculated ratio for the interaction *AB* is 19.29, whereas its table value with the significance level of 0.05 and degrees of freedom (3, 8) is 4.07.

Hence in case of Factor A, $H_0$ should be accepted, which means there is no significant difference in terms of sales between different regions.

In case of Factor B, $H_0$ should be accepted, which means there is no significant difference in terms of sales between different salesmen.

In case of Factor AB, $H_1$ should be accepted which means that there is a significant difference in quarterly sales because of the interaction between the factor 'sales region' and the factor 'salesman'. Alternatively, this means that the interaction between 'sales region' and 'salesman' has significant effect on quarterly sales.

### 9.5.5 ANOCOVA

### ANALYSIS OF COVARIANCE (ANOCOVA)

It is assumed in experimental design that the results observed may be attributed to the treatment variable and to no other causal circumstances. However, this may not be true. For instance, in classroom teaching programme, it is not the only teaching which increases the knowledge of students, but also other factors like his background, family influence, exposure to media. These influences cannot be controlled through experimental designs. For instance, the researcher studying one independent variable, X, may wish to control the influence of some uncontrolled variable (sometimes called the covariate or the concomitant variables), Z, which is known to be correlated with the dependent variable, Y, then he should use the technique of analysis of covariance for a valid evaluation of the outcome of the experiment. While applying the ANOCOVA technique, the influence of uncontrolled variable is usually removed by simple linear regression method and the residual sums of squares are used to provide variance estimates which in turn are used to make tests of significance. In other words, covariance analysis consists in subtracting from each individual score (Y) that portion of it Y′ that is predictable from uncontrolled variable (Z) and then computing the usual analysis of variance on the resulting (Y-Y′)s, of course making the due adjustment to the degrees of freedom because of the fact that estimation using regression method required loss of degrees of freedom.

#### 9.5.5.1 Solved Examples

The following are paired observation for the three groups concerning an experiment involving three methods of teaching on a single class. X represents the initial measurement of achievement in a subject and Y is the final measurement after subjects have been taught. 12 pupils were assigned at random to 3 groups of 4 pupils each, one group from one method as shown in table. After applying the technique of analysis of covariance for applying the experimental results, state whether teaching methods differ significantly at 5% level. Also calculate adjusted means on Y.

| Method A to Group 1 | | Method B to Group 2 | | Method C to Group 3 | |
|---|---|---|---|---|---|
| X | Y | X | Y | X | Y |
| 33 | 20 | 35 | 31 | 15 | 15 |
| 40 | 32 | 50 | 45 | 10 | 20 |
| 40 | 22 | 10 | 5 | 5 | 10 |
| 32 | 24 | 50 | 33 | 35 | 15 |

**Solution:**

| | Group 1 | | Group II | | Group III | |
|---|---|---|---|---|---|---|
| | X | Y | X | Y | X | Y |
| | 33 | 20 | 35 | 31 | 15 | 15 |
| | 40 | 32 | 50 | 45 | 10 | 20 |
| | 40 | 22 | 10 | 5 | 5 | 10 |

| | 32 | 24 | 50 | 33 | 35 | 15 |
|---|---|---|---|---|---|---|
| Total | 145 | 98 | 145 | 114 | 65 | 60 |
| Mean | 36.25 | 24.5 | 36.25 | 28.5 | 16.25 | 15 |
| General Mean | For X= | 29.58333 | For Y= | 22.66667 | | |
| N =15 | | | | | | |
| Sum X | 145+145+65 = | | 355 | | | |

| $X^2$ (I) | $Y^2$ (I) | XY (I) | $X^2$ (II) | $Y^2$ (II) | XY (II) | $X^2$ (III) | $Y^2$ (III) | XY (III) |
|---|---|---|---|---|---|---|---|---|
| 1089 | 400 | 660 | 1225 | 961 | 1085 | 225 | 225 | 225 |
| 1600 | 1024 | 1280 | 2500 | 2025 | 2250 | 100 | 400 | 200 |
| 1600 | 484 | 880 | 100 | 25 | 50 | 25 | 100 | 50 |
| 1024 | 576 | 768 | 2500 | 1089 | 1650 | 1225 | 225 | 525 |
| Sum = | | | | | | | | |
| 5313 | 2484 | 3588 | 6325 | 4100 | 5035 | 1575 | 950 | 1000 |
| $\Sigma X^2$ = | $\Sigma Y^2$ = | $\Sigma XY$ = | | | | | | |
| 13213 | 7534 | 9623 | | | | | | |

Correction Factor for X = $(\Sigma X^2)/N = 10502.08$

Sum Y=98+114+60 = 272

Correction Factor for Y = $(\Sigma Y^2)/N = 6165.333$

Correction Factor for XY = $(\Sigma X\ \Sigma Y)/N = 8046.667$

Hence Total SS for X = ΣX2- correction factor for X =2710.917

SS between X = $(145^2/4+145^2/4+65^2/4)$ – correction factor for X=1066.667

SS within X = Total SS for X – SS between X =1644.25

Total SS for Y= $\Sigma Y^2$ – correction factor for Y = 1368.667

SS between Y = $(98^2/4+114^2/4+60^2/4)$ – correction factor for Y= 384.6667

SS within Y= Total SS for Y – SS between Y = 984

Total sum of product of XY = ΣXY – correction factor of XY= 1576.333

SS between for XY= {(145*98)/4+(145*114)/4+(65*60)/4} – correction factor= 613.3333

SS within XY= Total sum of XY-SS between XY= 963

ANOVA table for X, Y and XY

| Source | DF | SS for X | SS for Y | SS for XY |
|---|---|---|---|---|
| Between | 2 | 1066.667 | 384.6667 | 613.3333 |
| Within $E_{XX}, E_{YY}$ | 9 | 1644.25 | 984 | 963 |
| Total | 11 | 2710.917 | 1368.667 | 1576.333 |

| Adjusted total SS= | $Sum_{XX}$ – $(Sum_{XY})^2/(Sum_{YY})$= | 895.4076 | |
|---|---|---|---|
| Adjusted SS within group = | $E_{XX}$ – $(E_{XY})^2/(E_{YY})$= | 701.8018 | |
| Adjusted SS between groups= | Total SS-Adjusted SS within group | | 193.6057 |

ANOVA Table for adjusted X

| **Source** | **DF** | **SS** | **MS** | **F ratio** |
|---|---|---|---|---|
| Between groups | 2 | 193.6057 | 96.80287 | 1.241413 |
| Within groups | 9 | 701.8018 | 77.97798 | |
| Total | 11 | 895.4076 | | |

At 5% level tabulated value for F is 4.26 with 2 DF as numerator and 9 DF as denominator at 5% level, as calculated value is less than table value it can be inferred that F ratio is not significant which means difference in groups is insignificant.

Adjusted means on X

| Regression coefficient for X on Y = b = | $E_{XY}/E_{YY}$= | 963/984= | 0.978659 |
|---|---|---|---|

| Deviation of intial means in case of Y | | Means of X | |
|---|---|---|---|
| Group 1 | 1.833333 | 36.25 | |
| Group 2 | 5.833333 | 36.25 | |
| Group 3 | –7.66667 | 16.25 | |
| Adjusted means for | | (mean x) - b*(deviation of Y from general mean) | |
| Group 1 | =(36.24)-.0.978*(1.88)= | 34.45579 | |
| Group 2 | = 36.25-.97*(5.8)= | 30.54116 | |
| Group 3 | = (16)-.978*(–7.667)= | 23.75305 | |

**Another example of ANOCOVA**

Following are the paired observations for three experimental groups.

Y is the covariate variable. Calculate the adjusted total within groups and between groups, sum of squares on X and test the significant differences between the adjusted means on X by using the appropriate F-ratio. Also calculate the adjusted means on X.

**Solution**

| **Method A to Group 1** | | **Method B to Group 2** | | **Method C to Group 3** | |
|---|---|---|---|---|---|
| X | Y | X | Y | X | Y |
| 7 | 2 | 15 | 8 | 30 | 15 |
| 6 | 5 | 24 | 12 | 35 | 16 |
| 9 | 7 | 25 | 15 | 32 | 20 |
| 15 | 9 | 19 | 18 | 38 | 24 |
| 12 | 10 | 31 | 19 | 40 | 30 |

| | Group 1 | | Group II | | Group III | |
|---|---|---|---|---|---|---|
| | X | Y | X | Y | X | Y |
| | 7 | 2 | 15 | 8 | 30 | 15 |
| | 6 | 5 | 24 | 12 | 35 | 16 |
| | 9 | 7 | 25 | 15 | 32 | 20 |
| | 15 | 9 | 19 | 18 | 38 | 24 |
| | 12 | 10 | 31 | 19 | 40 | 30 |
| Total | 49 | 33 | 114 | 72 | 175 | 105 |
| Mean | 9.8 | 6.6 | 22.8 | 14.4 | 35 | 21 |
| General Mean | For X= | 22.53333 | For Y= | 14 | | |
| N =15 | | | | | | |
| Sum X | 49+114+75 = | | 338 | | | |

| $X^2$ | $Y^2$ | XY | $X^2$ | $Y^2$ | XY | $X^2$ | $Y^2$ | XY |
|---|---|---|---|---|---|---|---|---|
| 49 | 4 | 14 | 225 | 64 | 120 | 900 | 225 | 450 |
| 36 | 25 | 30 | 576 | 144 | 288 | 1225 | 256 | 560 |
| 81 | 49 | 63 | 625 | 225 | 375 | 1024 | 400 | 640 |
| 225 | 81 | 135 | 361 | 324 | 342 | 1444 | 576 | 912 |
| 144 | 100 | 120 | 961 | 361 | 589 | 1600 | 900 | 1200 |
| 535 | 259 | 362 | 2748 | 1118 | 1714 | 6193 | 2357 | 3762 |
| $\Sigma X^2$ = | $\Sigma Y^2$ = | $\Sigma XY$ = | | | | | | |
| 9476 | 3734 | 5838 | | | | | | |

Correction Factor for X = $(\Sigma X^2)/N$ = 7616.267

Sum Y = 33+72+105 = 210

Correction Factor for Y = $(\Sigma Y^2)/N$ = 2940

Correction Factor for XY = $(\Sigma X\ \Sigma Y)/N$ = 4732

Hence Total SS for X = ΣX2- correction factor for X = 1859.733

SS between X = $(49^2/5+114^2/5+175^2/5)$ – correction factor for X=1588.133

SS within X = Total SS for X – SS between X = 271.6

Total SS for X = $\Sigma Y^2$ – correction factor for Y = 794

SS between Y = $(33^2/5+72^2/5+105^2/5)$ – correction factor for Y = 519.6

SS within Y = Total SS for Y – SS between Y = 274.4

Total sum of product of XY = ΣXY – correction factor of XY = 1106

SS between for XY = {(49*33)/5+(114*72)/5+(175*105)/5} – correction factor = 908

SS within XY = Total sum of XY-SS between XY = 198

ANOVA table for X, Y and XY

| Source | DF | SS for X | SS for Y | SS for XY |
|---|---|---|---|---|
| Between | 2 | 1588.133 | 519.6 | 908 |
| Within $E_{XX}, E_{YY}$ | 12 | 271.6 | 274.4 | 198 |
| Total | 14 | 1859.733 | 794 | 1106 |

Adjusted total SS = $Sum_{XX} - (Sum_{XY})^2/(Sum_{YY})$ = 319.1338

Adjusted SS within group = $E_{XX} - (E_{XY})^2/(E_{YY})$ = 128.7283

Adjusted SS between groups = Total SS-Adjusted SS within group 190.4056

ANOVA Table for adjusted X

| Source | DF | SS | MS | F ratio |
|---|---|---|---|---|
| Between groups | 2 | 190.4056 | 95.20278 | 8.135202 |
| Within groups | 11 | 128.7283 | 11.70257 | |
| Total | 13 | 319.1338 | | |

At 5% level tabulated value for F is 3.98 with 2 DF as numerator and 11 DF as denominator at 5% level, as calculated value is greater than table value it can be inferred that F ratio is significant which means difference in groups is significant.

Adjusted means on X

| | | | |
|---|---|---|---|
| Regression coefficient for X on Y = b | $= E_{XY}/E_{YY} =$ | 198/274.4 = | 0.721574 |

Deviation of intial means in case of Y Means of X

| | | |
|---|---|---|
| Group 1 | -7.4 | 9.8 |
| Group 2 | 0.4 | 22.8 |
| Group 3 | 7 | 35 |

Adjusted means for (mean x) - b*(deviation of Y from general mean)

| | | |
|---|---|---|
| Group 1 | = (9.8)-.72*(-7.4) = | 15.13965 |
| Group 2 | = 22.8-.72*(0.4) = | 22.51137 |
| Group 3 | = (35)-.72*(7) = | 29.94898 |

### 9.5.5.2 Problems for Practice

1. A stock market analyst wants to study the impact of the type of company on the quarterly averages of the earnings per share (EPS). So, he collected four quarterly averages of EPS data of four different companies during the last financial year from 'capital market', which is summarized as follows:

| | Company | | | |
|---|---|---|---|---|
| | $C_1$ | $C_2$ | $C_3$ | $C_4$ |
| Replications | 12 | 16 | 25 | 13 |
| | 8 | 18 | 15 | 8 |
| | 16 | 10 | 22 | 20 |
| | 19 | 11 | 9 | 5 |

Check whether there is significant difference between different companies in terms of EPS at a significance level of 5%.

2. An experiment was run to determine whether four specific intervals of patrolling (in minutes) by a quality inspector affect the number of acceptable parts produced per hour in a machine. The corresponding data for four different periods with four replications are shown as:

| | Period of Inspection | | | |
|---|---|---|---|---|
| **Replications** | **30 mins** | **45 mins** | **60 mins** | **75 mins** |
| 1. | 50 | 30 | 40 | 35 |
| 2. | 25 | 60 | 12 | 10 |
| 3. | 40 | 20 | 30 | 48 |
| 4. | 23 | 38 | 39 | 25 |

3. An agriculturalist wants to study the effect of four different fertilizers on the yield (in tons) of a specific crop. Because there might be variability from one plot to another plot, he decides to use the randomized complete block design. The corresponding data are presented as in the following table:

| | Fertilizers | | | |
|---|---|---|---|---|
| | **Sodium Nitrate** | **Potassium Phosphate** | **Organic Manure** | **Mixed Salts** |
| Plots | 100 | 150 | 120 | 70 |
| | 80 | 70 | 110 | 100 |
| | 68 | 90 | 85 | 78 |
| | 125 | 138 | 60 | 124 |

(a) Write the corresponding model. Check whether each component of the model has any effect on the yield of the crop at a significance level of 1%.

4. The R&D Manager of an automobile company wishes to study the effect of the tyre brand on the tread loss (in millimetre) of tyres. Four different tyres of four different brands (A, B, C and D) are fitted at four different positions of four different cars, because there might be variability from one car to another car as well as from one position to another position, which is a Latin square design. The data as per this design are presented as:

| | Car | | | |
|---|---|---|---|---|
| **Position** | **1** | **2** | **3** | **4** |
| 1. | A = 8 | B = 7 | C = 1 | D = 7 |
| 2. | B = 11 | C = 2 | D = 7 | A = 8 |
| 3. | C = 6 | D = 8 | A = 6 | B = 6 |
| 4. | D = 4 | A = 2 | B = 3 | C = 8 |

(a) Write the corresponding model.

(b) Check whether each component of the model has any effect on the tread loss of tyres at a significance level of 5%.

5. The director of a School of Management wants to study the effect of 'faculty' on the average performance (0-10 scale) of the participants of a training programme. Five different faculty members (A, B, C, D and E) were assigned to five different subjects of the training programmes conducted for five different batches, because there might be variability from one subject to another subject as well as from one batch to another batch, which is a Latin square design. The data as per this design are given as follows:

| | Batch | | | | |
|---|---|---|---|---|---|
| **Subject** | **1** | **2** | **3** | **4** | |
| 1. | A = 10 | B = 6 | C = 6 | D = 6 | E = 8 |
| 2. | B = 7 | C = 6 | D = 5 | E = 1 | A = 4 |
| 3. | C = 5 | D = 3 | E = 3 | A = 2 | B = 1 |
| 4. | D = 6 | E = 4 | A = 1 | B = 2 | C = 5 |
| 5. | E = 4 | A = 2 | B = 3 | C = 8 | D = 9 |

(a) Write the corresponding model.

(b) Check whether each component of the model has effect on the performance of the batches at a significance level of 5%.

6. The sales manager of a leading textile showroom at Chennai wishes to study the opinion of its customers on its service quality in a 0-10 scale. In this experiment, the nature of profession as well as the monthly income levels of the customers are taken as fixed factors. Two different customers have been sampled under each experimental combination and the corresponding ratings are as shown below:

| | | **Doctor** | **Engineer** | **Lawyer** | **Others** |
|---|---|---|---|---|---|
| Income Level | < ₹ 10000 | 3 | 3 | 8 | 10 |
| | | 1 | 8 | 2 | 9 |
| | > ₹ 10000 | 3 | 10 | 9 | 2 |
| | | 7 | 4 | 7 | 8 |

(a) Write the model of this factorial experiment.

(b) Check the significance of each of the components of the model at the significance level of 0.05.

7. The sales manager of Devi Engineering Works wants to study the effect of salesman as well as sales region on its quarterly sales revenue (in lakhs of rupees). He designed a factorial experiment involving two factors, as shown in the following table, with two replications for each experimental combination. The factor sales region (factor *A)* is considered to be a fixed factor and the factor salesman (factor *B)* is considered to a random factor. As per this design, each salesman is assigned to each sales region for two different quarters.

| | | Salesman (B) | | | |
|---|---|---|---|---|---|
| | | 1 | 2 | 3 | 4 |
| **Sales Region (A)** | **North** | 10 | 10 | 20 | 5 |
| | | 5 | 15 | 35 | 20 |
| | **South** | 9 | 40 | 5 | 30 |
| | | 15 | 35 | 8 | 20 |

Perform ANOVA and check the following at the significance level of 0.05. (a) (i) Whether there is any significant difference in terms of sales revenue between salesmen. (ii) Whether there is any significant difference in terms of sales revenue between sales regions. (iii) Whether there is any significant difference in terms of sales revenue between different combinations of salesman and sales region. (b) If the factor *A* and the factor *B* are assumed to be random factors, comment on the results of ANOVA.

8. Test the following observations with two-way ANOVA.

| | TEACHING METHOD | | | |
|---|---|---|---|---|
| **Student's Performance in Exam** | **A** | **B** | **C** | **D** |
| P | 20 | 8 | 14 | 20 |
| Q | 16 | 10 | 16 | 16 |
| R | 18 | 12 | 18 | 18 |
| S | 15 | 16 | 20 | 14 |

9. Test the following observation with two – way ANOVA.

| SALESMEN | | | | |
|---|---|---|---|---|
| AREA | A | B | C | D |
| P | 10 | 15 | 14 | 20 |
| Q | 20 | 18 | 16 | 16 |
| R | 30 | 16 | 18 | 18 |
| S | 40 | 12 | 20 | 14 |

10. Test the following observation with Latin Square design when the sales are recorded on weekly basis also in area.

| | SALESMEN | | | |
|---|---|---|---|---|
| **AREA** | **A** | **B** | **C** | **D** |
| P | 10 (W1) | 15 (W2) | 14 (W3) | 20 (W4) |
| Q | 20 (W2) | 18 (W3) | 16 (W4) | 16 (W1) |
| R | 30 (W3) | 16 (W4) | 18 (W1) | 18 (W2) |
| S | 40 (W4) | 12 (W1) | 20 (W2) | 14 (W3) |

## 9.6 Chi-Square Test

### 9.6.1 Relation Between Test Stats

Before we start Chi-Square Test procedure, let us understand the relation among 'Z', 'T-stat', 'F' and $\chi^2$. We shall have to understand some of the theorems. The t, $\chi^2$ and F are intimately related to normal variate Z. Damodar Gujrati (in his book Basic Econometrics) refers 'Introduction to the Theory of Statistics' by Mood et al., (1974) and writes following theorems:

**Theorem 4.1:** If $Z_1$, $Z_2$, $Z_3$.....$Z_n$ are normally and independently distributed random variables such that $Z_i \sim N(\mu_I, \sigma_i^2)$, then sum $Z = \Sigma k_i Z_i$ where $k_i$ are constant and not all zeros is also distributed normally with mean $\Sigma k_i \mu_I$ and variance $\Sigma k_i^2\sigma_i^2$ where $\mu$ is the mean value.

For example if $Z_1$, and $Z_2$ are normally distributed as $Z_1 \sim N(10\ 2)$ and $Z_2 \sim N(8\ 1.5)$ and say linear combination is $Z = 0.8\ Z_1$ and $0.2\ Z_2$. Now Z is also normally and independently distributed with mean 0.8(10) and 0.2(8) = 9.6 and variance $.8^2(2) + 0.2^2(1.5) = 1.34$, i.e. $Z \sim N\ (9.6,\ 1.34)$.

**Theorem 4.3:** 1: If $Z_1$, $Z_2$, $Z_3$.....$Z_n$ are normally and independently distributed random variables such that $Z_i \sim N(\mu_I, \sigma_i^2)$, such that $Z_i \sim N(0\ 1)$, i.e. standardized normal variate, then $\Sigma Z_i^2 = Z_1^2 + Z_2^2 + Z_3^2 + .....Z_n^2$ follows chi-square distribution with n DF. Symbolically $\Sigma Z_i^2 \sim \chi_n^2$ where n denotes DF.

**Theorem 4.4:** If $Z_1$, $Z_2$, $Z_3$.....$Z_n$ are independenly distributed random variables each following $\chi^2$ distribution, then the sum $S\ Z_i = Z_1 + Z_2 + Z_3 + .....Z_n$ also follows chi-square distribution with $k = \Sigma k_i$ DF.

**Theorem 4.5:** If $Z_1$, is normally and independenly distributed random variables such that $Z_i \sim N(\mu_I, \sigma_i^2)$, and another variable $Z_2$ follows chi-square distribution with k DF and is independent of $Z_1$, then the variable defined is

$$t = \frac{Z_1}{\sqrt{Z_2}/\sqrt{k}} \quad \frac{Z_1\sqrt{k}}{\sqrt{Z_2}}$$

It follows Student's t distribution with k DF.

**Theorem 4.6:** If $Z_1$ and $Z_2$ are independently distributed chi-square variable

$$F = \frac{Z_1/k_1}{Z_2/k_2} \sim F_{k1,\ k2}$$

It has F distribution with $k_1$ and $k_2$ degrees of freedom where $k_1$ is known as numerator degree of freedom while $k_2$ is known denominator degree of freedom.

**Theorem 4.7:** The square of t (student' t stat) with k DF has an F distribution with $k_1 = 1$DF in numerator and $k_2 = k$ DF in the denominator, that is

$$F_{1,k} = t_k^2$$

Students can check these theorems by observaing stat values from tables. For instance at 5% significance level (or 95% confidence level) Z = 1.96. If we square it i.e. $Z^2 = 1.96^2 = 3.841$. Now check the chi-square table. At 1DF at 5% level $\chi^2 = 3.814$.

### 9.6.2 Chi-Square

A **chi-square test** (also **chi-squared** or $\chi^2$ **test**) is a test in which the test statistic has a chi-square distribution when the null hypothesis is true, or any in which the probability distribution of the test statistic (assuming the null hypothesis is true) can be made to approximate a chi-square distribution as closely as desired by making the sample size large enough. There are many forms of chi-square test. Pearson's chi-square test is also known as the chi-square goodness-of-fit test or chi-square test for independence. Yates' chi-square test is also known as Yates' correction for continuity. $\chi^2$ test as a non-parametric test, but is very popular. It is used as a parametric test also.

Pearson's chi-square ($\chi^2$) test is the best-known of several chi-square tests whose results are evaluated by reference to the chi-square distribution. Its properties were first investigated by Karl Pearson.

It tests a null hypothesis that the frequency distribution of certain events observed in a sample is consistent with a particular theoretical distribution. The events considered must be mutually exclusive and have total probability 1.

The first step in the chi-square test is to calculate the chi-square statistic. The chi-square statistic is calculated by finding the difference between each observed and theoretical frequency for each possible outcome, squaring them, dividing each by the theoretical frequency, and taking the sum of the results.

$$\chi^2 = \sum_{i=1}^{n} \frac{(O_i - E_i)^2}{E_i}$$

where

$O_i$ = an observed frequency;

$E_i$ = an expected (theoretical) frequency, asserted by the null hypothesis;

$n$ = the number of possible outcomes of each event.

The computed chi-square statistic is compared with tabulated value of chi-square (with confidence level and degree of freedom). DF can be calculated as (r-1)*(c-1) where r is number of rows and c is number columns.

For example, to test the hypothesis that a random sample of 100 people has been drawn from a population in which men and women are equal in frequency, the observed number of men and women would be compared to the theoretical frequencies of 50 men and 50 women. If there were 45 men in the sample and 55 women, then

| | **Men** | **Women** |
|---|---|---|
| Observed | 45 | 55 |
| Expected | 50 | 50 |

$$\chi^2 = \frac{(45-50)^2}{50} + \frac{(55-50)^2}{50} = 1$$

If the null hypothesis is true (i.e., men and women are chosen with equal probability in the sample), the test statistic will be drawn from a chi-square distribution with one degree of freedom. Though one might expect two degrees of freedom (one each for the men and women), we must take into account that the total number of men and women is constrained (100), and thus there is only one degree of freedom (2 – 1). Alternatively, if the male count is known the female count is determined, and vice-versa. Tabulated value for 1 DF at 5% level is 3.841. As computed value is less than tabulated value we can infer that there is consistency in data and is normally distributed.

### 9.6.2.1 Solved Examples

### Solved Problem S-1

A total of 1600 families were selected at random in a city to test the belief that high income families usually send their children to public schools and low income families often send their children to government schools. The following results were obtained.

| | Schools | | |
|---|---|---|---|
| **Income** | **Public** | **Government** | **Total** |
| Low | 494 | 506 | 1000 |
| High | 162 | 438 | 600 |
| Total | 656 | 944 | 1600 |

Test whether income and type of school are independent

**Solution:**

$H_0$: Income and choice of school are not related.

$H_1$: Income and choice of school are related.

To calculate the expected value we should apply the formula as

(Row Total × Column Total)/Grand Total

Degree of Freedom shall be (r–1) × (c–1). = (2–1) *(2–1) = 1

| Observation | Observed Value | Expected Value | $\chi^2 = (O-E)^2/E$ |
|---|---|---|---|
| Row 1 (Public) | 494 | 1000*656/1600 = 410 | $(494 - 410)^2/410 = 17.21$ |
| Row 1 (Government) | 506 | 1000*944/1600 = 590 | $(506 - 590)^2/590 = 11.96$ |
| Row 2 (Public) | 162 | 600*656/1600 = 246 | $(162 - 246)^2/246 = 28.68$ |
| Row 3 (Government) | 438 | 600*944/1600 = 354 | $(438 - 354)^2/354 = 19.93$ |

Total $\chi^2 = 17.21 + 11.96 + 28.68 + 19.93 = 77.78$

The critical value of $\chi^2$ for 1DF at 5% level is 3.841. As the calculated value of $\chi^2$ is greater than critical value. $H_0$ is rejected. $H_1$ is accepted. There is relationship of income and choice of school.

### Solved Problem S-2

A survey of 200 firms found the following evidence regarding profitability and market share. Do you find that data below gives you significant evidence to conclude that market share and profitability are related. Test the hypothesis at 0.01 level of significance.

| | Market share | | | |
|---|---|---|---|---|
| Profitability | Upto 10% | 11-25% | >25% | Total |
| Low | 36 | 14 | 16 | 66 |
| Medium | 26 | 22 | 16 | 64 |
| High | 16 | 24 | 30 | 70 |
| Total | 78 | 60 | 62 | 200 |

**Solution:**

$H_0$: Market share and profitability are not related.

$H_1$: Market share and profitability are related.

| Observation | Observed Value | Expected Value | $\chi^2$ = (O-E)²/E |
|---|---|---|---|
| Low (upto 10%) | 36 | 66*78/200=25.74 | (36-25.74)²/25.74= 4.09 |
| Low (11-25%) | 14 | 19.80 | 1.699 |
| Low (>25%) | 16 | 20.46 | 0.972 |
| Medium(up to 10%) | 26 | 24.96 | 0.043 |
| Medium (11-25%) | 22 | 19.20 | 0.048 |
| Medium (>25%) | 16 | 19.84 | 0.743 |
| High (up to 10%) | 16 | 17.30 | 4.677 |
| High (11-25%) | 24 | 21.00 | 0.429 |
| High (>25%) | 30 | 21.70 | 3.175 |

Total $\chi^2$ = 4.09+0.972+0.043+0.048+0.743+4.677+0.429+3.175 = 16.246

DF = (3-1)* (3-1) = 4

The critical value of $\chi^2$ for 4DF at 1% level is 13.277. As the calculated value of $\chi^2$ is greater than critical value. $H_0$ is rejected. $H_1$ is accepted. There is relationship of market share and profitability.

**Solved Example S-3**

The sales manager of a showroom feels that the daily demand of a product follows uniform distribution. The observed frequencies of demand values are given in the table below. Check whether the given data follows uniform distribution at a significance level of 0.05

| | Demand and frequency | | | | | | | | | |
|---|---|---|---|---|---|---|---|---|---|---|
| Demand (Units) | 30 | 31 | 32 | 33 | 34 | 35 | 36 | 37 | 38 | 39 |
| Observed Frequency | 13 | 10 | 7 | 10 | 6 | 9 | 12 | 10 | 14 | 9 |

**Solution**

$H_0$: The given data follows uniform distribution.

$H_1$: The given data do not follow uniform distribution.

The total observed frequencies = 100

Number of demand values = 10

Expected frequency for each demand value = 100/10 = 10

The details of chi-square values are given in the table

| | Calculations of Chi-square value | | | |
|---|---|---|---|---|
| Sr. No. | Demand Value | Observed Frequency | Expected Frequency | $\chi^2$ |
| 1 | 30 | 13 | 10 | $(13-10)^2/10 =$ 0.9 |
| 2 | 31 | 10 | 10 | 0.0 |
| 3 | 32 | 7 | 10 | 0.9 |
| 4 | 33 | 10 | 10 | 0.0 |
| 5 | 34 | 6 | 10 | 1.6 |
| 6 | 35 | 9 | 10 | 0.1 |
| 7 | 36 | 12 | 10 | 0.4 |
| 8 | 37 | 10 | 10 | 0.0 |
| 9 | 38 | 14 | 10 | 1.6 |
| 10 | 39 | 9 | 10 | 0.1 |

Total $\chi^2$ = 5.6

The tabulated chi-square value with 9 DF at 5% significance level is 16.919. Since the calculated value is less than tabulated value accept $H_0$, reject $H_1$, which means given data follows uniform distribution.

## Solved Example S-4

A certain chemical plant processes sea water to collect sodium chloride and magnesium. From scientific analysis sea water is known to contain sodium chloride, magnesium and other elements in the ratio of 62:4:34. A sample of 200 tons of sea water resulted in 130 tons of sodium chloride and 6 tons of magnesium. Are these data consistent with the significant level of 5%?

**Solution:**

$H_0$: The given data is consistent

$H_1$: The given data is not consistent.

Observed value in 200 tonnes

| Salts | Observed Quantity | Expected Quantity | $\chi^2$ |
|---|---|---|---|
| Sodium | 130 | 124 | $(130-124)^2/124$ =0.2903 |
| Magnesium | 6 | 8 | $(6-8)^2/8$ = 0.5 |
| Others | 64 | 68 | $(64-68)^2/68$ = 0.2352 |

Total $\chi^2$ = 1.0255

The tabulated value of chi-square for 2 DF at 5% level is 5.991.

Since the calculated value is less than tabulated value accept $H_0$, reject $H_1$, which means given data is consistent.

## Solved Example S-5

Eight coins were tossed 256 times and the following results were obtained:

| Number of heads | 0 | 1 | 2 | 3 | 4 | 5 | 6 | 7 | 8 |
|---|---|---|---|---|---|---|---|---|---|
| Frequency | 2 | 6 | 30 | 52 | 67 | 56 | 32 | 10 | 1 |

Test whether coins are biased using $\chi^2$ test.

**Solution:**

$H_0$: Coins are not biased

$H_1$: Coins are not biased.

Getting of a head has the probability as 0.5, and the probability distribution can be calculated by binomial theorem as there are only two outcomes – head and tail.

| No. of heads | Observed frequency | Expected frequency | O-E | $\chi^2$ |
|---|---|---|---|---|
| 0 | 2 | ${}^8C_0\left(\frac{1}{2}\right)^0\left(\frac{1}{2}\right)^8 * 256 = 1$ | 1 | 1.00 |
| 1 | 6 | ${}^8C_1\left(\frac{1}{2}\right)^1\left(\frac{1}{2}\right)^7 * 256 = 8$ | -2 | 0.50 |
| 2 | 30 | ${}^8C_2\left(\frac{1}{2}\right)^2\left(\frac{1}{2}\right)^6 * 256 = 28$ | 2 | 0.14 |
| 3 | 52 | ${}^8C_3\left(\frac{1}{2}\right)^3\left(\frac{1}{2}\right)^5 * 256 = 56$ | –4 | 0.29 |
| 4 | 67 | ${}^8C_4\left(\frac{1}{2}\right)^4\left(\frac{1}{2}\right)^4 * 256 = 70$ | –3 | 0.13 |
| 5 | 56 | ${}^8C_5\left(\frac{1}{2}\right)^5\left(\frac{1}{2}\right)^3 * 256 = 56$ | 0 | 0.00 |
| 6 | 32 | ${}^8C_6\left(\frac{1}{2}\right)^6\left(\frac{1}{2}\right)^2 * 256 = 28$ | 4 | 0.57 |
| 7 | 10 | ${}^8C_7\left(\frac{1}{2}\right)^7\left(\frac{1}{2}\right)^1 * 256 = 8$ | 2 | 0.50 |
| 8 | 1 | ${}^8C_8\left(\frac{1}{2}\right)^8\left(\frac{1}{2}\right)^0 * 256 = 1$ | 0 | 0.00 |
| Sum $x^2$ | | | | 3.13 |

Degree of freedom = 9 – 1 = 8

The tabulated value of $\chi^2$ with 9 DF at 5% significance level is 15.507

Since the calculated value is is less than tabulated value accept $H_0$, reject $H_1$, which means given data is consistent which means coins are not biased.

### 9.6.3 Yates Correction

Yates has suggested a correction for continuity in $\chi^2$ value calculated in connection with a (2 × 2) table, particularly when cell frequencies are small (since no cell frequency should be less than 5 in any case, through 10 is better) and $\chi^2$ is just on the significance level. The correction suggested by Yates is popularly known as Yates' correction. It involves the reduction of the deviation of observed from expected frequencies which of course reduces the value of $\chi^2$. The rule for correction is to adjust the observed frequency in each cell of a (2 × 2) table in such a way as to reduce the deviation of the observed from the expected frequency for that cell by 0.5, but this adjustment is made in all the cells without disturbing the marginal totals. The formula for finding the value of $\chi^2$ after applying Yates' correction can be stated thus:

$$\chi^2 \text{ (corrected)} = \sum \frac{[|O - E| - 0.5]^2}{E}$$

The following information is obtained concerning an investigation of 50 ordinary shops of small size:

| | Shops | | |
|---|---|---|---|
| | **In towns (a)** | **In villages (b)** | **Total** |
| Run by Men (A) | 17 | 18 | 35 |
| Run by Women (B) | 3 | 12 | 15 |
| Total | 20 | 30 | 50 |

Can it be inferred that shop run by women are relatively more in vaillages than in towns, use $\chi^2$ with Yates correction.

**Solution:**

$H_0$: Everything is normal i.e. there is no bias with women or men in town or villages

$H_1$: Women run shops are more in villages.

Calculation of $\chi^2$ with Yates correction

| Observation | Observed Value | Expected | $\chi^2$ (corrected) |
|---|---|---|---|
| Aa | 17 | (20*35)/50 = 14 | (\|17–14\|–0.5)²/14= 0.446 |
| Ab | 18 | (30*35)/50 = 21 | 0.298 |
| Ba | 3 | (20*15)/50 = 6 | 1.04 |
| Bb | 12 | (30*15)/50 = 9 | 0.694 |
| Sum $x^2$ | | | 2.478 |

Degree of Freedom = (r-1)(c-1) = (2-1)*(2-1) = 1

The tabulated value of $\chi^2$ with 1 DF at 5% significance level is 3.841

Since the calculated value is less than tabulated value accept $H_0$, reject $H_1$, which means given data does not show that women run more shops in rural area.

### 9.6.3.1 Problems for Practice

1. The daily demand of a product seems to follow uniform distribution. The observed frequency of daily demand values are given below. Check whether the given data follow uniform distribution at significance level of 1%, 5% and 10%

| | Demand and frequency | | | | | | | | | |
|---|---|---|---|---|---|---|---|---|---|---|
| Demand (Units) | 25 | 26 | 27 | 28 | 29 | 30 | 31 | 32 | 33 | 34 |
| Observed Frequency | 18 | 15 | 12 | 15 | 11 | 14 | 17 | 15 | 19 | 14 |

2. 200 digits were chosen at random from a set of tables. The frequencies of the digits were:

| Digit | 0 | 1 | 2 | 3 | 4 | 5 | 6 | 7 | 8 | 9 |
|---|---|---|---|---|---|---|---|---|---|---|
| Frequency | 18 | 19 | 23 | 21 | 16 | 25 | 22 | 20 | 21 | 15 |

Calculate $x^2$ and test whether data is uniformly distributed.

3. On the basis of information given below about the treatment of 200 patients suffering from a disease, state whether the new treatment is comparatively superior to the conventional treatment.

| | No of patients | |
|---|---|---|
| Treatment | Favourable Response | No response |
| New | 60 | 20 |
| Conventional | 70 | 50 |

4. Find the value of Chi-square applying Yates' correction to the following data:

| | Passed | Failed | Total |
|---|---|---|---|
| Day classes/Evening classes | 104 | 2066 | 3070 |
| Total | 14 | 86 | 100 |

Also state whether the association, if any, between passing in the examination and studying in day classes is significant using Chi-square test.

5. 1000 babies were born during a certain week in a city of which 600 were boys and 400 girls. Use test to examine the correctness of the hypothesis that the sex-ratio is 1: 1 in newly born babies.

6. The percentage of smokers in a certain city was 90. A random sample of 100 persons was selected in which 85 persons were found to be smokers. Is the sample proportion significantly different from the proportion of smokers in the city? Answer on the basis of Chi-square test.

7. A college is running postgraduate classes in five subjects with equal number of students. The total number of absentees in these five classes is 75. Test the hypothesis that these classes are alike in absenteeism if the actual absentees in each are as follows:

History = 19

Philosophy = 18

Economics = 15

Commerce = 12

Chemistry = 11

8. The number of automobile accidents per week in a certain community were as follows:

12, 8, 20, 2, 14, 10, 15, 6, 9, 4

Are these frequencies in agreement with the belief that accident conditions were the same during the 10 weeks period under consideration?

9. A group of 150 college students were asked to indicate their most liked film star from among six different well known film actors, viz., A, *B*, *C*, *D*, *E* and *F* in order to ascertain their relative popularity. The observed frequency data were as follows:

| Actors | A | B | C | D | E | F | Total |
|---|---|---|---|---|---|---|---|
| Frequencies | 24 | 20 | 32 | 25 | 28 | 21 | 150 |

Test at 5% whether all actors are equally popular.

10. A marketing researcher interested in the business publication reading habits of purchasing agents has assembled the following data:

| Business Publication Preferences | (First Choice Mentions) |
|---|---|
| Business Publication | Frequency of first choice |
| A | 35 |
| B | 30 |
| C | 45 |
| D | 55 |

Test the null hypothesis (a = 0.05) that there are no differences among frequencies of first choice of tested publications.

## 9.7 How to Do?

Jolly and Dolly started their discussion again at dining table.

Dolly: "I have gone through the research project 'Exports of Livestock and allied products'. Though it is a descriptive study it explores a lot. It has only two objectives -1 Exports to groups of countries and 2 to explore the areas where exports can be given a boost. Literature has been reviewed, but it is limited. Data has been gathered on HSN basis. Countries have been grouped on the basis of income. Compounded growth rate has been calculated by log-linear method. But, no hypothesis has been tested."

Jolly: "Wrong, at each stage hypotheses have been tested. To see whether growth rate is statistically significant or not, for instance in equation Ln (y) = a +b*time, it has been tested whether b = 0 or b # 0."

Dolly: "But it has not been written anywhere"

Jolly: "Dear, please read regression thoroughly. There is a method to write regression equation. Usually researchers write t-stat values below the parameters and show the significance with the help of stars (*). For instance

$$Y = 30 + 0.7\ X\ (2.8715^{**})$$

$$n = 20,\ R^2 = 0.95,\ F = 8.7$$

This is a hypothetical regression equation, which means b is statistically significant at 5% level.

Dolly: "But there is no chi-square or ANOVA in the project."

Jolly: "You can read more projects where these techniques have been used. Dr. M. Dhanabhakyam and K.R. Vijayasanthi from Bharathiar University, Coimbatore surveyed 50 textile workers to see factors influencing HRD climate in textile industry. The report is very interesting and researchers use techniques like ANOVA and Chi-Square. Please note it is an applied research".

Dolly: "You are really great. I do not understand from where you find such great scholars."

Jolly: "I am not great. Great are researchers who work hard. Read the report and discuss among your friends."

Dolly: I always have problems which framimg hypotheses.

Jolly: Keep in mind while framing hypotheses that null hypotheses should be normal. It should not have association, attachment or abnormality.

Dolly: "Next time I shall call some of friends to discuss the issues in the report 'Human Resources Development Climate in Textile Industries' by Dr. Dhanabhakayam and K.R. Vijayasanthi."

Jolly: "Yes, I shall see your friends."

Dolly: "Do not try to be over-smart before my friends?"

Jolly: "Okay, I shall only try to impress them."

Dolly: "Good night"

✦ ✦ ✦

Research Project 8

## 9.8 Human Resource Development Climate in Textiles Industries

M. Dhanabhakyam[1] and K.R.Vijaysanthi[2]

### Introduction

#### Meaning of Human Resource

Human Resource is the actual workforce, including sometimes the potential workforce, of an organisation. Another meaning of the term Human Resource is the contribution to an employing organisation, which its workforce could provide in efforts, skill and knowledge etc. Human Resource and Human Labour are two terms closely associated with each other; both are contributory processes in production of any organisation. Generally these terms have close links with economics. In the terms of political economy and economics, human resources are labelled as labour, one of three components of production. In the corporate world the term conveys its traditional meaning.

#### Definitions of Human Resources

- The health, strength, talent, education and skills that human can use to produce goods and services.
- Labour used as an input into the production process.
- People's intellectual and physical abilities.

#### Human Resources Development

Human Resource Development (HRD) is a system of developing in a continuous and planned way the competencies of individual employees, dyadic groups, teams and the total organization to achieve organizational objectives. It attempts at the maximization of congruence between individuals and organization and develops the organization culture in which superior - subordinate relationships, teamwork and collaboration among various organizational units become strong. Prof. Rao has defined HRD as follows:

#### Role of Human Resource Development

- Effective management and utilisation of people.
- Enhancement of proficiencies that improve individual and organisational achievement.
- Fortifying the modernization, talent, and resilience essential to boost competitiveness.

The role of HRD is to enhance the talent of labourers and executives, design the plan and allocate the work, evaluate and examine performance of workforce. The HRD is also supposed to keep itself abreast of modern technology and trade and then augment the talent and knowledge of human capital by employing the obtained knowledge. HRD can conduct training and workshop/ seminars to impart this knowledge. The combined effect of HRD will create an atmosphere wherein productivity will be increased, cost and wastage will be checked, labour and staff will

[1] Lecturer, Department of Commerce, Bharathiar University, Coimbatore – 46.

[2] M. Phil Research Scholar, Department of Commerce, Bharathiar University, Coimbatore – 46.

• The article has already been published in Volume 3 No. 2 of Journal of Global Economy, April, 2007 issue. Reprinted with permission from authors and management of Journal of Global Economy.

be right sized. By harmonizing training and development, career development and organization development, HRD improves individual effectiveness.

**HRD Practices**

The following HRD practices may be developed, implemented and practiced for the better working in every organisation to meet the global requirements. They are given as follows:

- Investing in Human Resource Development
- Performance Appraisal
- Staff Training
- Promoting Participatory Process in HRD
- Management Development
- Career Planning and Development

**Organizational Climate**

'Motivation' development is also an aim of HRD. Motivation means the desire to work or put in work effort. It is a commitment to the job, work and organisation. An employee motivation is influenced by the organisation climate and a healthy organisation climate is required for utilizing and enhancing employee competencies. HRD should also aim at building healthy climate, where the free expression of ideas, opinion and suggestions are encouraged. This leads to en efficient learning platform, capacity building of the team members, decentralization of decision-making, feeling of ownership, accountability, homely environment and good working climate.

HRD climate is an integral part of general organizational climate. Organization climate is the summary percentage, which people have about an organization. It is a global expression of what the organization is, organizational climate is the manifestation of the attitudes of organizational members toward the organization itself. An organization tends to attract and keep people who fit its climate so that it's patterns are perpetuated at least to some extent.

An HRD climate or culture is essential for developing human resources. The HRD climate can be characterized as consisting of the following:

- Openness or freedom to express one's ideas and opinions
- Collaborative attitudes or team spirit
- Trust
- Authenticity as correlation between words and actions
- Pro-actions or encouraging some degree of initiative and risk takings by employees
- Autonomy or a certain degree of freedom of action for each individual
- An interest in confronting issues and solving them rather than hiding them.

Such climate can be developed through various HRD instruments. Chief executives should facilitate the development of an HRD and effectiveness of the HRD instruments will help greatly in the implementation of HRD system

### Textile Industry

Textile Industry is providing one of the most basic needs of people and holds importance; maintaining sustained growth for improving quality of life. It has a unique position as a self-reliant industry, from the production of raw materials to the delivery of finished products, with substantial value-addition at each stage of processing; it is a major contribution to the country's economy. Its vast potential for creation of employment opportunities in the agricultural, industrial, organised and decentralised sectors and rural and urban areas, particularly for women and the disadvantaged is noteworthy.

The textile policy of 2000 aims at achieving the target of textile and apparel exports of US $ 50 billion by 2010 of which the share of garments will be US $ 25 billion. The main markets for Indian textiles and apparels are USA, UAE, UK, Germany, France, Italy, Russia, Canada, Bangladesh and Japan. The main objective of the textile policy 2000 is to provide cloth of acceptable quality at reasonable prices for the vast majority of the population of the country, to increasingly contribute to the provision of sustainable employment and the economic growth of the nation; and to compete with confidence for an increasing share of the global market.

### Current Scenario

Developing countries with both textile and clothing capacity may be able to prosper in the new competitive environment after the textile quota regime of quantitative import restrictions under the multi-fibre arrangement (MFA) came to an end on 1st January, 2005 under the World Trade Organisation (WTO) Agreement on Textiles and Clothing.

### Textile Industry in India

The textile industry plays a crucial role in the Indian economy. The presence of textile sector can be felt through its share of contribution to the industrial output, employment generation and the export earnings of the country. Currently, it contributes about 14 per cent to industrial production, 4 per cent to the GDP and 16 per cent to the country's export earnings. The textile sector is the second largest provider of employment after agriculture and provides employment to about 35 million people. The major sectors forming part of the textile industry include the organized Cotton/Man Made Fibre Textile Mill Industry, Man made fibre/ filament yarn industry, the decentralized powerloom sector, woollen textile industry, silk industry, handloom industry, handicraft industry, jute industry and textile exports.

### Exports of Textiles

The textile products continue to play an important role in total export basket of the country. The exports of textiles (including handicrafts, jute and coir) formed 24.6% of total exports in 2001-2002, however this percentage decreased to 16.24% during 2004-05. The textile exports recorded a growth of 15.3% in 2002-2003 and 8.7% in 2003-2004. During 2004-05, textile exports were US$ 13,039.00 million, recording a decline of 3.4% as compared to the corresponding period of previous year. However, during April-November 2005, the textile exports have shown a growth of 8.2% as compared to the corresponding period of previous year.

Textile production played a crucial part in the American industrial revolution, the establishment of organized labour, and the technological development of this country. Once, textile production was simple enough that the entire process could and did take place in the home. Now, textiles represent a complex network of inter-related industries that produce fiber, spin yarns, fabricate cloth, and dye, finish, print, and manufactured goods.

## Statement of the Problem

HRD climate or culture is essential for developing human resources. It is not determined by a single factor. It depends upon number of factors such as experience, promotion, supervision, working condition, welfare facilities, co-worker relation etc. The factors of HRD climate may differ from person to person even in the same industry due to the personal characters, needs, attitudes, desires, problems, etc., may differ from individual to individual. Here problem means common problem such as a low wages, lack of job security, less intensives, family problem, etc. These problems are faced by employees in almost all industries. The firm may control the problems by way of taking effective steps. This study is undertaken to study the Human Resource Development climate and give suggestions to management to improve the HRD climate.

### Scope of the Study

HRD is vital to any organization, by which the management can make the workers achieve the desired organizational goals. The main aim or need of the study to know HRD in Textile Industries. When an employee is made to develop his skill, the target will be achieved quickly. The study clearly portrays the human resource development in the company and where it needs to improve. The study has been made with the help of interview schedule including personal data with OCTAPAC (Openness, Confrontation, Trust, Autonomy, Pro-action, Authenticity, Collaboration) culture, general climate HRD mechanisms. The recommendations have been given wherever the HRD needed improvement.

### Objectives of the Study

1. To study the factors which influence the HRD climate in Textile Industries.
2. To study the employees perception regarding the HRD climate in Textile Industries.
3. To provide suggestions to the organization to improve Human Resource Development climate.

### Hypotheses

- There is no relationship between age of the respondents and education of the respondents.
- There is no relationship between experience of the respondents and income of the respondents.
- There is no relationship between income of the respondents and educational level of the respondents.
- There is no relationship between experience of the respondents and age group level of the respondents.

### Methodology

This study is to know development of human resource by the company, it aims at portraying accurately the characteristics of a particular group or situation and it is geared to the solution of specific problems by the discovery of relevant variables. In any study accuracy and precaution are the fundamental factors which are to be emphasized. Therefore, to test the validity and reliability of the study a pre-test was done.

This is an empirical study based on survey method. Data for the study was collected by both primary and secondary sources. Primary data was obtained mainly from the employees. ***Interview schedule*** was used to collect primary data. Secondary data was obtained through company magazines and from personnel departments of the organizations.

## Sample Design

***Non-probability sampling technique*** has been followed to collect data for this study. Sample size is 50 respondents. The samples in this study are taken from workers of all the departments of the organization.

## Tools Used

Particulars were collected using interview schedule. In interview schedules the nature, purpose and meaning of the questions was explained. Whenever respondents felt any doubt with regard to any questions, it was classified by the enumerators. Following statistical techniques were used for analysis:

1. Chi-square Analysis
2. Analysis of Variance
3. Scaling Techniques

## Chi-Square Analysis

The chi-square test is one of the simplest and most widely used non-parametric tests in statistical work. The quantity chi-square describes the magnitude of the discrepancy between theory and observation. It is defined as O refers to the Observed Frequencies, E refers to the Expected Frequencies. In this study, the chi-square test is performed between personal factors and other factors and were tested at 5% significance level.

## Analysis of Variance

Analysis of variance to test for the significance of the difference between more than two sample means and to make inferences about whether our samples are drawn from the populations having the same mean. The "Analysis of Variance" procedure or "F-test" is used in such problems where we want to test for the significance of the difference among more than two sample means.

## Scaling Technique

The schedule was developed using *5 point Likert-type* Scale. Each question has 5 options they are

1. Almost always true
2. Mostly true
3. Sometimes true
4. Rarely true
5. Not at all true

Points allotted are as follows:

| Scale | Points |
|---|---|
| Almost always True | 5 |
| Mostly True | 4 |
| Sometimes True | 3 |
| Rarely True | 2 |
| Not at all True | 1 |

By means of the above scale, points are allotted and using this, total points are calculated and analysed.

After calculating the points, the attitude of employees are as follows:

| Scale | Points |
|---|---|
| 0-100 | Not at all True |
| 101-200 | Rarely True |
| 201-300 | Sometimes True |
| 301-400 | Mostly True |
| 401-500 | Almost always True |

## Limitation of the Study

1. The respondents looked at the researcher suspiciously thinking that the researchers had been sent by the management.
2. Sample size is restricted to 50.
3. Personal bias of the respondents may affect the project.

## Analysis and Interpretation

### Socio-Economic Characteristics

**1. Table Showing Age Group of the Respondents**

| S.No. | Age | Respondents | Percentage of respondents |
|---|---|---|---|
| 1. | 18-25 | 15 | 30 |
| 2. | 26-33 | 25 | 50 |
| 3. | 34-41 | 8 | 16 |
| 4. | Above 42 | 2 | 4 |
| | **Total** | **50** | **100** |

The above table reveals that 30% of the respondents come under 18-25 years, 50% are 26-33 years, 16% are 34-41 years and only 4% of the respondents are above 42 years old. The majority of the workers fall under the age group of 26-33. It is the age group where the employees can work efficiently and effectively.

**2. Experience of the Respondents**

| S.No. | Experience | Respondents | Percentage of respondents |
|---|---|---|---|
| 1. | Below 3 years | 8 | 16 |
| 2. | 3-6 years | 24 | 48 |
| 3. | 7-10 years | 18 | 28 |
| 4. | Above 10 years | - | - |
| | **Total** | **50** | **100** |

The above table indicates that 16% of the respondents are having below 3 years experience, 48% are having 3-6 years and 28% of the respondents are having 7-10 years experience. Nobody is having experience above 10 years. It shows that the employees with 10 years experience and above are not with the company, though the company was started in the year 1979. It indirectly shows the negative labour turnover of the company. This may be due to poor pay package or amenities provided by the company.

**3. Table Showing the Educational Background of the Respondents**

| S.No. | Educational Status | Respondents | Percentage of respondents |
|---|---|---|---|
| 1. | Below 8th Std | 7 | 14 |
| 2. | 8th – 10th Std | 10 | 20 |
| 3. | 11th – 12th Std | 28 | 56 |
| 4. | Above 12th Std | 5 | 10 |
| | **Total** | **50** | **100** |

Out of 50 respondents 56% of the respondents have studied between 11th - 12th Standard and 20% of the respondents' educational status is between 8th - 10th Standard, 14% of the respondents are below 8th Standard and 10% of the respondents are qualified for above 12th Standard. The company requires technical knowledge rather than education. That is why 56% of the respondents are under the category of 11th - 12th Standard.

**4. Table Showing Interest of Senior Officers in Helping Juniors**

| Sr. No. | Properties | Respondents | Percentage of respondents |
|---|---|---|---|
| 1. | Almost Always true | 5 | 10 |
| 2. | Mostly true | 12 | 24 |
| 3. | Sometimes true | 22 | 44 |
| 4. | Rarely true | 8 | 16 |
| 5. | Not at all true | 3 | 6 |
| | **Total** | **50** | **100** |

The above table exhibits the income levels of the respondents. Out of 50 respondents 10% of the respondents earn below ₹ 1000. 36% of the respondents are earnings ₹ 2000 and more per month.

**Chi-square Value – Age and Education of the respondents**

**Null Hypothesis:** There is no significant relationship between age of the respondent and education of the respondents.

**Alternative Hypothesis:** There is significant relationship between age of the respondents and education of the respondents.

**Chi-square Value – Age and Education of the Respondents**

| Personnel Factor | Chi-square | Degrees of freedom | Table value | S/NS |
|---|---|---|---|---|
| Education | 140.17 | 9 | 16.919 | S |

Since the calculated value (140.17) is more than the table value (16.919), null hypothesis is rejected. To conclude, there is a significant relationship between age of the respondents and education level of the respondents.

## Chi-square Value – Experience and Income of the Respondents

**Null Hypothesis:** There is no significant relationship between experience and income of the respondents.

**Alternative Hypothesis:** There is significant relationship between experience and income of the respondents.

| Personnel Factor | Chi-square | Degrees of freedom | Table value | S/NS |
|---|---|---|---|---|
| Income | 85.714 | 6 | 12.592 | S |

**Chi-square Value – Experience and Income of the Respondents**

Since the calculated value (85.714) is more than the table value (12.592), null hypothesis is rejected. To conclude, there is a significant relationship between experience of the respondents and income level of the respondents.

## Analysis of Variance

### Income and Educational Level of the Respondents

**Null Hypothesis:** There is no significant relationship between income of the respondents and educational level of the respondents.

**Alternative Hypothesis:** There is a significant relationship between income of the respondents and educational level of the respondents.

**Income and Educational Level of the Respondents**

| Score | Sum of Square | Difference | Mean Square | F |
|---|---|---|---|---|
| Between groups | 34.087 | 3 | 11.362 | 47.983 |
| Within groups | 10.893 | 46 | 0.237 | |
| Total | 44.980 | 49 | | |

It is derived from the above table that the calculated value (47.983) is more than the table value (2.76). Hence, the null hypothesis was rejected. It is concluded that there is a significant relationship between income of the respondents and educational level of the respondents.

### Age Group and Experience of the Respondents

**Null Hypothesis:** There is no significant relationship between age group of the respondents and experience level of the respondents.

**Alternative Hypothesis:** There is significant relationship between age group of the respondents and experience level of the respondents.

**Age Group and Experience of the Respondents**

| Score | Sum of Square | Difference | Mean Square | F |
|---|---|---|---|---|
| Between groups | 17.862 | 2 | 8.931 | 32.392 |
| Within groups | 12.958 | 47 | 0.276 | |
| Total | 30.820 | 49 | | |

It is derived from the above table that the calculated value (32.392) is more than the table value (3.15). Hence, the null hypothesis was rejected. It is concluded that there is a significant relationship between age group of the respondents and experience level of the respondents.

## Scaling Technique

### 1. Table Showing Treatment of Human Resource

| S.No. | Properties | Respondents | Percentage of respondents |
|---|---|---|---|
| 1. | Almost always true | 7 | 14 |
| 2. | Mostly true | 18 | 36 |
| 3. | Sometimes true | 20 | 40 |
| 4. | Rarely true | 4 | 8 |
| 5. | Not at all true | 1 | 2 |
| | **Total** | **50** | **100** |

40% of the respondents feel it's sometimes true that their top management believes human resource is an important resource and is to be treated more humanely, 36% of the respondents find it mostly true, 14% of the respondents find it almost always true, 8% of the respondents feel it's rarely true and 2% of the respondents find it not at all true.

Total points = 354. The respondents feel that it is mostly true that the top management believes human resource is an important resource and it is treated more humanely.

### 2. Table Showing Development of Subordinates by Superior

| S.No. | Properties | Respondents | Percentage of respondents |
|---|---|---|---|
| 1. | Almost always true | 4 | 8 |
| 2. | Mostly true | 25 | 50 |
| 3. | Sometimes true | 13 | 26 |
| 4. | Rarely true | 6 | 12 |
| 5. | Not at all true | 2 | 4 |
| | **Total** | **50** | **100** |

It is clear from the above table that 50% of the respondents find it mostly true that their managers consider development of subordinates as an important part of their job, 26% of the respondents say it's sometimes true, 13% of the respondents are for rarely true, 8% of the respondents are almost always true and 4% of the respondents are not at all true.

Total points = 346. The respondents feel that it is mostly true that the development of subordinates is seen as an important part of their job by the managers.

### 3. Table Showing Personnel Policies

| S.No. | Properties | Respondents | Percentage of respondents |
|---|---|---|---|
| 1. | Almost always true | 3 | 6 |
| 2. | Mostly true | 20 | 40 |
| 3. | Sometimes true | 20 | 40 |
| 4. | Rarely true | 7 | 14 |
| 5. | Not at all true | - | - |
| | **Total** | **50** | **100** |

The above table shows that 40% of the respondents are for mostly true that personnel policies in their organization facilitate employee development, 40% of the respondents feel it's sometimes true, 14% of the respondents are rarely true and 6% of the respondents are almost always true.

Total points = 378. This implies it is mostly true for the respondents, that the personnel policies in this organization facilitate employee development.

**4. Table Showing Interest of Senior Officers in Helping Juniors**

| S.No. | Properties | Respondents | Percentage of respondents |
|---|---|---|---|
| 1. | Almost always true | 5 | 10 |
| 2. | Mostly true | 12 | 24 |
| 3. | Sometimes true | 22 | 44 |
| 4. | Rarely true | 8 | 16 |
| 5. | Not at all true | 3 | 6 |
| | **Total** | **50** | **100** |

The above table depicts that 44% of the respondents are for sometimes true that their senior officers take active interest in their juniors and help them learn their job, 24% of the respondents find it mostly true and 16% of the respondents are for rarely true, 10% of the respondents are for almost always true, 6% of the respondents are not at all true.

Total points = 316. It is concluded that the senior officer take active interest in their juniors and helping in learning their job is mostly true.

**5. Table Showing Helping Tendency to Acquire Competence**

| S.No. | Properties | Respondents | Percentage of respondents |
|---|---|---|---|
| 1. | Almost always true | 6 | 12 |
| 2. | Mostly true | 11 | 22 |
| 3. | Sometimes true | 21 | 42 |
| 4. | Rarely true | 11 | 22 |
| 5. | Not at all true | 1 | 2 |
| | **Total** | **50** | **100** |

Out of 100 respondents, 42% are for sometimes true that when they lack competence in doing their jobs they are helped to acquire competence rather than being left unattended. 22% of them are mostly true, 22% of the respondents are rarely true, 12% of the respondents are almost always true and 2% of respondents are not at all true.

Total points = 320. This depicts that people lacking competence in doing their jobs are helped to acquire competence rather than being left unattended is mostly true.

**6. Table Showing Change and Development of Employee at Any Stage**

| S.No. | Properties | Respondents | Percentage of respondents |
|---|---|---|---|
| 1. | Almost always true | 7 | 14 |
| 2. | Mostly true | 16 | 32 |
| 3. | Sometimes true | 15 | 30 |

| | | | |
|---|---|---|---|
| 4. | Rarely true | 10 | 20 |
| 5. | Not at all true | 2 | 4 |
| | **Total** | **50** | **100** |

The above table indicates that 32% of the respondents are for mostly true that their managers believe that employee behaviour can be changed and people can be changed and developed at any stage of their life, 30% of the respondents are for sometimes true, 20% of the respondents are rarely true, 14% of the respondents says almost always true and 4% of the respondents are not at all true.

Total points = 332. The respondents accept that the managers in the organization believe that employee behaviour can be changed, people can be developed at any stage of their life is mostly true.

**7. Table Showing Helpfulness of People to Each Other**

| S.No. | Properties | Respondents | Percentage of respondents |
|---|---|---|---|
| 1. | Almost always true | 15 | 30 |
| 2. | Mostly true | 13 | 26 |
| 3. | Sometimes true | 14 | 24 |
| 4. | Rarely true | 8 | 16 |
| 5. | Not at all true | 2 | 4 |
| | **Total** | **50** | **100** |

The above table reveals that 30% of the respondents are almost always true that people in this organization are helpful to each other, 26% of the respondents are mostly true, 24% of the respondents are sometimes true, 16% of the respondents are rarely true, 4% of the respondents are not at all true.

Total points = 362. It is concluded that people is this organization are helpful to each other is mostly true.

**8. Table Showing Discussion of Personal Problems with Supervisors**

| S.No. | Properties | Respondents | Percentage of respondents |
|---|---|---|---|
| 1. | Almost always true | 4 | 8 |
| 2. | Mostly true | 16 | 32 |
| 3. | Sometimes true | 18 | 36 |
| 4. | Rarely true | 11 | 22 |
| 5. | Not at all true | 1 | 2 |
| | **Total** | **50** | **100** |

Out of 100 respondents, 36% of the respondents feel it is sometimes true that they don't hesitate to discuss their personal problems with their supervisor, 32% of them are for mostly true, 22% of the them for rarely true, 8% of them are almost always true and 2% of them are not at all true.

Total points = 322. It is found that the respondents have accepted, it is mostly true that employees in the organization are very informal and do not hestitate to discuss their personal problems with their supervisors.

**9. Table Showing Psychological Climate of Employees Development**

| S.No. | Properties | Respondents | Percentage of respondents |
|---|---|---|---|
| 1. | Almost always true | 4 | 8 |
| 2. | Mostly true | 11 | 22 |
| 3. | Sometimes true | 15 | 30 |
| 4. | Rarely true | 16 | 32 |
| 5. | Not at all true | 4 | 8 |
| | **Total** | **50** | **100** |

The above table reveals that 32% of the respondents are for rarely true that the psychological climate in this organization is conducive and employees are interested in developing themselves by acquiring new knowledge and skills, 30% of the respondents are for sometimes true, 22% of the respondents are for mostly true, 8% of the respondents are for almost always true and 8% of the respondents are for not at all true.

Total points = 290. The respondents said it is some times true that the psychological climate in this organization is very conducive to any employee who is interested in developing himself by acquiring new knowledge and skills.

**10. Table Showing Identification and Utilization of Employee Potentials by Top Management**

| S.No. | Properties | Respondents | Percentage of respondents |
|---|---|---|---|
| 1. | Almost always true | 4 | 8 |
| 2. | Mostly true | 16 | 32 |
| 3. | Sometimes true | 22 | 44 |
| 4. | Rarely true | 6 | 12 |
| 5. | Not at all true | 2 | 4 |
| | **Total** | **50** | **100** |

The above table reveals that 44% of the respondents feel its sometimes true that their top management makes efforts to identify and utilize the potential of the employees, 32% of the respondents are for mostly true, 12% of the respondents are for rarely true, 8% of the respondents are for almost always true and 4% of the respondents are not at all true.

Total points = 328. It is mostly true that the top management makes efforts to identify and utilize the potential of the employees.

**11. Table Showing Promotional Decisions**

| S.No. | Properties | Respondents | Percentage of respondents |
|---|---|---|---|
| 1. | Almost always true | 6 | 12 |
| 2. | Mostly true | 16 | 32 |
| 3. | Sometimes true | 19 | 38 |
| 4. | Rarely true | 7 | 14 |
| 5. | Not at all true | 2 | 4 |
| | **Total** | **50** | **100** |

The above table shows that 38% of the respondents find it sometime true that promotional decisions are based on suitability of the promotee rather than favouritism, 32% of the respondents feel mostly true, 14% of the respondents feel rarely true, 12% of the respondents are almost always true and 4% of the respondents are not at all true.

Total points = 334. It details that it is mostly true that the promotion decisions are based on the suitability of the promotee rather than on favouritism.

**12. Table Showing Mechanisms for Reward for Work by Employees**

| S.No. | Properties | Respondents | Percentage of respondents |
|---|---|---|---|
| 1. | Almost always true | 5 | 10 |
| 2. | Mostly true | 15 | 30 |
| 3. | Sometimes true | 18 | 36 |
| 4. | Rarely true | 10 | 20 |
| 5. | Not at all true | 2 | 4 |
| | **Total** | **50** | **100** |

The above table shows that 36% of the respondents find it sometimes true that there are mechanisms to reward good work done or any contribution made by the employee, 30% of the respondents are for mostly true, 20% of the respondents are for rarely true, 9% of the respondents are for almost always true and 4% of the respondents are not at all true.

Total points = 322. It is mostly true that there are mechanisms in these organizations to reward any of the good work done by employees.

**13. Table Showing Fixed Mental Impression**

| S.No. | Properties | Respondents | Percentage of respondents |
|---|---|---|---|
| 1. | Almost always true | 4 | 8 |
| 2. | Mostly true | 16 | 32 |
| 3. | Sometimes true | 15 | 30 |
| 4. | Rarely true | 12 | 24 |
| 5. | Not at all true | 3 | 6 |
| | **Total** | **50** | **100** |

It is clear from the above table that 32% of the respondents are mostly true that people in their organization do not have any fixed mental impression about each other, 30% of the respondents are sometimes true, 24% of the respondents are rarely true, 8% of the respondents are almost always true and 6% of the respondents are not at all true.

Total points = 312. It is mostly true, that the people in this organization do not have any fixed mental impressions about each other.

### 14. Table Showing Communication of Weakness to Employees

| S.No. | Properties | Respondents | Percentage of respondents |
|---|---|---|---|
| 1. | Almost always true | 4 | 8 |
| 2. | Mostly true | 25 | 50 |
| 3. | Sometimes true | 11 | 22 |
| 4. | Rarely true | 7 | 14 |
| 5. | Not at all true | 3 | 6 |
| | **Total** | **50** | **100** |

The above table shows that 50% of the respondents are mostly true, that weakness of employees should be communicated to them in a non-threatening way, 22% of the respondents are sometimes true, 14% of the respondents are rarely true, 8% of the respondents are almost always true and 6% of the respondents are not at all true.

Total points = 346. It depicts that the weakness of the employees are communicated to them in a non-threatening way is mostly true.

### 15. Table Showing the Result of Training Programmes

| S.No. | Properties | Respondents | Percentage of respondents |
|---|---|---|---|
| 1. | Almost always true | 3 | 6 |
| 2. | Mostly true | 14 | 28 |
| 3. | Sometimes true | 23 | 46 |
| 4. | Rarely true | 9 | 18 |
| 5. | Not at all true | 1 | 2 |
| | **Total** | **50** | **100** |

The above table exhibits that 46% of the respondents are sometimes true that when they are sponsored for training they take it seriously and try to learn from the programme they attend, 28% of the respondents are mostly true, 18% of the respondents are rarely true, 6% of the respondents are almost always true and 2% of the respondents are not at all true.

Total points = 318. The respondents said it is mostly true that when the employees are sponsored for training, they take it seriously and try to learn from the programme they attend.

### 16. Table Showing Performance Appraisal Reports

| S.No. | Properties | Respondents | Percentage of respondents |
|---|---|---|---|
| 1. | Almost always true | 3 | 6 |
| 2. | Mostly true | 15 | 30 |
| 3. | Sometimes true | 19 | 38 |
| 4. | Rarely true | 11 | 22 |
| 5. | Not at all true | 2 | 4 |
| | **Total** | **50** | **100** |

The above table reveals that 38% of the respondents says that it is sometimes true that performance appraisals reports is based on objective assessment and adequate information, 30% of the respondents says that it is mostly true, 22% of the respondents says that it is rarely true, 6% of the respondents say that it is almost true and 4% of the respondents says that it is not at all true.

Total points = 312. The respondents have accepted that the performance appraisal reports in our organization are based on objectives assessment and adequate information is mostly true.

**17. Table Showing Opportunities Given After Training**

| S.No. | Properties | Respondents | Percentage of respondents |
|---|---|---|---|
| 1. | Almost always true | 3 | 6 |
| 2. | Mostly true | 16 | 32 |
| 3. | Sometimes true | 22 | 44 |
| 4. | Rarely true | 7 | 14 |
| 5. | Not at all true | 2 | 4 |
| | **Total** | **50** | **100** |

The above table shows that 44% of the respondents say that the opportunities given for training is not always true but only sometimes true. Seniors delegate authority to their subordinates, they treat this as an opportunity for their development, 32% of the respondents are mostly true, 14% of the respondents are rarely true, 6% of the respondents are almost always true and 4% of the respondents are not at all true.

Total points = 322. It shows, the respondents agree that when seniors delegate authority to juniors, they use it as an opportunity for development is mostly true.

**18. Table Showing Team Spirit in the Organization**

| S.No. | Properties | Respondents | Percentage of respondents |
|---|---|---|---|
| 1. | Almost always true | 5 | 10 |
| 2. | Mostly true | 16 | 32 |
| 3. | Sometimes true | 20 | 40 |
| 4. | Rarely true | 7 | 14 |
| 5. | Not at all true | 2 | 4 |
| | **Total** | **50** | **100** |

The table exhibits that 40% of the respondents are sometimes true that the team spirit is of high order in their organization and 32% of the respondents are mostly true and 14% of the respondents are rarely true and 10% of them are almost always true and 4% of the respondents are not at all true.

Total points = 330. The respondents have said mostly true that the team spirit is of high order is this organization.

**19. Table Showing Career Opportunities by Senior Officers**

| S.No. | Properties | Respondents | Percentage of respondents |
|---|---|---|---|
| 1. | Almost always true | 4 | 8 |
| 2. | Mostly true | 15 | 30 |
| 3. | Sometimes true | 19 | 38 |
| 4. | Rarely true | 10 | 20 |
| 5. | Not at all true | 2 | 4 |
| | **Total** | **50** | **100** |

The above table exhibits 38% of the respondents are sometimes true that senior officers in their organization point out career opportunities to juniors and 30% of them find mostly true and 20% of the respondents says rarely true, 8% of the respondents are almost always true and 4% of the respondents are not at all true.

Total points = 318. It is mostly true that the senior officers in the organization point out career opportunities to juniors.

**20. Table Showing Future Plans in Development of Employee**

| S.No. | Properties | Respondents | Percentage of respondents |
|---|---|---|---|
| 1. | Almost always true | 4 | 8 |
| 2. | Mostly true | 15 | 30 |
| 3. | Sometimes true | 19 | 38 |
| 4. | Rarely true | 11 | 22 |
| 5. | Not at all true | 1 | 2 |
| | **Total** | **50** | **100** |

Mostly 38% of the respondents are sometimes true that the organization's future plans are made known to the managerial staff to help them develop their juniors and prepare them for the future and 30% of them say mostly true and 22% of them are rarely true and 8% of them are almost always true and 2% of them are not at all true.

Total points = 320. It is concluded that the organization's future plans are made known to the managerial staff to help them develop their juniors and prepare them for the future is mostly true.

**21. Table Showing Employee Welfare**

| S.No. | Properties | Respondents | Percentage of respondents |
|---|---|---|---|
| 1. | Almost always true | 5 | 10 |
| 2. | Mostly true | 17 | 34 |
| 3. | Sometimes true | 18 | 36 |
| 4. | Rarely true | 9 | 18 |
| 5. | Not at all true | 1 | 2 |
| | **Total** | **50** | **100** |

The above table reveals that 36% of the respondents are sometimes true that their organization ensures their welfare to such an extent that they can save a lot of their mental energy for work purpose and 34% of them say mostly true and 18% of them are rarely true and 10% of say almost always true and 2% of the respondents are not at all true.

Total points = 332. The respondents have said it is mostly true that this organization ensures employee welfare to such an extent that the employees can save a lot of their mental energy for work purposes.

**22. Table Showing Job Rotation**

| S.No. | Properties | Respondents | Percentage of respondents |
|---|---|---|---|
| 1. | Almost always true | 5 | 10 |
| 2. | Mostly true | 12 | 24 |
| 3. | Sometimes true | 17 | 34 |
| 4. | Rarely true | 12 | 24 |
| 5. | Not at all true | 4 | 8 |
| | **Total** | **50** | **100** |

The above table informs that 34% of the respondents are sometimes true that job rotation in their organization facilitates their development and 24% of the respondents are mostly true and 24% of the respondents are rarely true and 10% of the respondents are almost always true and 8% of the respondents are not at all true.

Total points = 304. The respondents have appreciated that it is mostly true that the job rotation in this organization facilitates employees development.

## Conclusion

The study portrays the HRD prevailing in Textile Ltd. It is found from the study that there is a development of human resource, but still more concentration should be put on development. When employee skills are developed, it can be used for achieving the desired target.

It can be concluded that Textile Ltd. too have HRM practices that can be characterized by informality and flexibility. Having understood the constraints and opportunities of Textile Ltd. with respect to nature of business and style if managing its operation, it is suggested to formalize a sound performance appraisal system that can be used to motivate better performers and link their performance with monetary benefits so that the unit as well as employees gain substantially from such as intervention. The researcher hopes that this project will serve as a practical guides and contribute to further research and implementation.

## Suggestions

1. The senior officers should take interest in helping the juniors learning their job.
2. When employees lack competence, they should be helped to acquire competence rather than unattended.
3. Employees should be encouraged to discuss their personal problems with supervisors.
4. The top management should take measures to identify and utilize the potential of employees.
5. Seniors should guide juniors and prepare them for the future.

6. Promotional policies should be based on suitability.
7. Supervising officers should take care to appreciate good work done by employees.
8. When employees make mistakes, the supervisor shall treat it with understanding and make them learn from such mistakes.
9. The organization should provide training on genuine needs.
10. Employees should be given opportunities to try out what they have learnt from training.
11. Superiors should delegate authority, which will develop managerial ability of the employees.
12. Carrier opportunities should be provided.
13. Employee welfare should save mental energy of employees for work purposes.

## Bibliography

1. T.V. Rao, "Designing Integrated Human Resource Development Systems", Handbook for group facilitators, California University Associates, 1995.
2. J.J. Famularo, Handbook of personnel forms, Records and Reports, New York : Mc Graw-Hill, 1982, p.133
3. Thomas J. Peters and Robert H. Waterman, In Search of Excellence, New York : Harper K. Row, 1982, p.8
4. Yoder, D., Personnel Management and Industrial Relations, New Delhi: Prentice Hall of India Pvt. Ltd., 1972.
5. T.V. Rao, "Human Resource Development", Present and Future in ATIRA, 1986 & Reading in HRD.
6. Dr. C.B. Mamoria, Personal Development.
7. Ashok Kumar, Human Resource System.
8. R.S. Dwivedi, Management of Human Resource.
9. D. Yuvaraj, Human Resource Development.
10. T.V. Rao and E. Abraham – HRD Climate in Organization.
11. C.R. Kothari, Research Methodology.

## 9.9 Regression

### 9.9.1 Establishing a Cause-Effect Relationship

Generally, there are three criteria that should be met before we can say that we have evidence for a causal relationship:

- **Temporal Precedence**

First, cause should have happened ***before*** effect. It is easier to say than logically explained. We never hear that effect happened before the cause. Consider a classic example from economics: inflation causes unemployment. It certainly appears plausible that as inflation increases, more employers find that in order to meet costs they have to lay off employees. So it seems that inflation caused for unemployment. But both inflation and employment rates are occurring together on an ongoing basis. But let us see the other side of it. If there is an increase in employment, people have more money in their hands, we may have more demand for goods, which would tend to drive up the prices at least until supply can catch up. So it is difficult to see the cause and the effect, inflation or unemployment. These types of cyclical situations involving ongoing processes that interact that both may cause and, in turn, be affected by the other. This makes it very hard to establish a causal relationship in this situation.

- **Covariation of the Cause and Effect**

Before we show that we have a *causal* relationship we shall have to show that we have some type of relationship. For instance, consider the syllogism:

if X then Y

if not X then not Y

If we observe that whenever X is present, Y is also present, and whenever X is absent, Y is too, then you have demonstrated that there is a relationship between X and Y. See another example, advertisement causes consumer awareness. Or, in colloquial terms: if you give a programme you observe the outcome but if you don't give the programme you don't observe the outcome. This provides evidence that the programme and outcome are related. Now this syllogism doesn't provide evidence that the programme caused the outcome. Perhaps there was some other factor present with the programme that caused the outcome, rather than the programme. The relationships described so far are rather simple binary relationships. Sometimes we want to know whether different amounts of the programme lead to different amounts of the outcome – a continuous relationship:

if more of the programme then more of the outcome

if less of the programme then less of the outcome

- **No Plausible Alternative Explanations**

Now there's a relationship doesn't mean it's a causal one. It's possible that there is some other variable or factor that is causing the outcome. This is sometimes referred to as the "third variable" or "missing variable" problem and it's at the heart of the issue of internal validity. You will have to look at the threats to internal validity, each one describes a type of alternative explanation.

Let's consider a simple single group threat to internal validity, a *history* threat. Let's assume we measure our programme group before they start the programme (to establish a baseline), we give them the programme, and then you measure their performance afterwards in a post-test. You see a marked improvement in their performance which you would like to infer is caused by your programme. One of the plausible alternative explanations is that you have a history threat - it's not your programme that caused the gain but some other specific historical event, something happened between pre-test and post-test. One of the simplest ways to rule this out would be to incorporate the use of a control group, a group that is comparable to your programme group with the only difference being that they didn't receive the programme.

In most applied social research that involves evaluating programmes, temporal precedence is not a difficult criterion to meet because you administer the programme before you measure effects. And, establishing covariation is relatively simple because you have some control over the programme and can set things up so that you have some people who get it and some who don't (if X and if not X). Typically the most difficult criterion to meet is the third- ruling out alternative explanations for the observed effect. That is why research design is such an important issue and why it is intimately linked to the idea of internal validity.

### 9.9.2 Linear Regression

**Regression analysis** is a technique used for the modelling and analysis of numerical data consisting of values of a dependent variable (response variable) and of one or more independent variables (explanatory variables). For instance revenue has increased or decreased with advertisement. Revenue is dependent variable and advertisement exposure or expenditure is independent variable. The dependent variable in the ***regression equation*** is modelled as a function of the independent variables, corresponding parameters ("constants"), and an *error term*. For instance Y depends upon X but it has constant and errors also. The error term is treated as a ***random variable***. It represents unexplained variation in the dependent variable. The parameters are estimated so as to give a "best fit" of the data. Most commonly the best fit is evaluated by using the least squares method, but other criteria are also used.

When functions are established on priory assumptions which are based on theory, we may call it models. For instance consumption is the functions of income C= f(Y), we call it a model as both income (Y) and consumption (C) are based on a theory. Data modelling can be used without there being any knowledge about the underlying processes that have generated the data; in this case the model is an empirical model. Moreover, in modelling knowledge of the probability distribution of the errors is not required. Regression analysis requires assumptions to be made regarding probability distribution of the errors. Statistical tests are made on the basis of these assumptions. In regression analysis the term "model" embraces both the function used to model the data and the assumptions concerning probability distributions.

Regression can be used for prediction (including forecasting of time-series data), inference, hypothesis testing, and modelling of causal relationships. These uses of regression rely heavily on the underlying assumptions being satisfied. Regression analysis has been criticized as being misused for these purposes in many cases where the appropriate assumptions cannot be verified to hold. One factor contributing to the misuse of regression is that it can take considerably more skill to critique a model than to fit a model.

**Linear regression** is a form of regression analysis in which observational data are modelled by a function which is a linear combination of the model parameters and depends on one or more independent variables. In simple linear regression the model function represents a straight line. The results of data fitting are subject to statistical analysis.

The data consist of n values taken from observations (dependent or response variable), *Y*. the dependent variable is subject to error. This error is assumed to be random variable, with a mean of zero. The independent variable (explanatory variable), *X*, is assumed to be error-free. If this is not so, there may be problems which needs to be rectified with various econometric techniques. The independent variables are also called regressors, exogenous variables, input variables and predictor variables. In simple linear regression the data model is written as

$$Y = \beta_0 + \beta_1 X + e$$

or

$$\hat{Y} = \beta_0 + \beta_1 X$$

where e is an observational error. $\beta_0$ (intercept) and $\beta_1$ (slope) are the parameters of the model. $\hat{Y}$ is the estimated Y.

Unless otherwise stated it is assumed that the observational errors are uncorrelated and belong to a normal distribution. This, or another assumption, is used when performing statistical tests on the regression results. An equivalent formulation of simple linear regression that explicitly shows the linear regression as a model of conditional expectation can be given as

$E(y|x) = \alpha + \beta x$

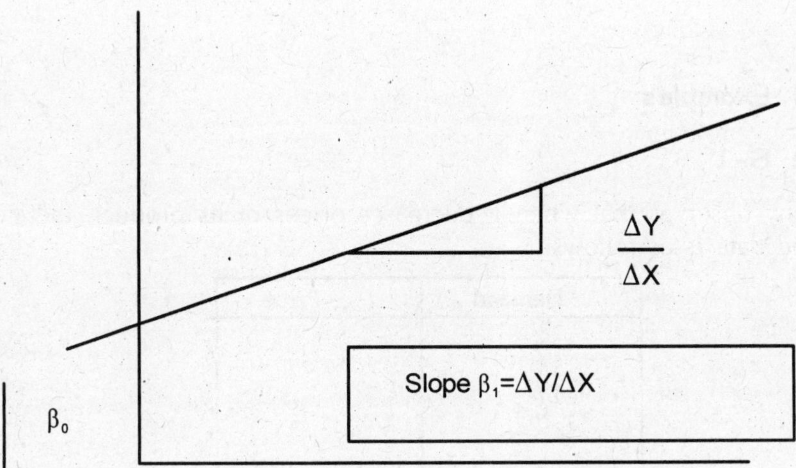


A **trend line** represents a trend, the long-term movement in time series data after other components have been accounted for. It tells whether a particular data set (say GDP, oil prices or stock prices) have increased or decreased over the period of time. A trend line could simply be drawn by eye through a set of data points, but more properly their position and slope is calculated using statistical techniques like **linear regression**. Trend lines typically are straight lines, although some variations use higher degree poiynomials depending on the degree of curvature desired in the line.

Trend lines are sometimes used in business analysis to show changes in data over time. This has the advantage of being simple. Trend lines are often used to argue that a particular action or event (such as training, or an advertising campaign) caused observed changes at a point in time. This is a simple technique, and does not require a control group, experimental design, or a sophisticated analysis technique. However, it suffers from a lack of scientific validity in cases where other potential changes can affect the data.

Staticians have suggested many methods to frame regression equation. The purpose of these formulas is to minimise the stochastic error.

$\beta_0$ is called intecept and $\beta_1$ is called slope. Slope means change in Y divided by change in X. It can also be termed as tangent of the angle opposite to perpendicular, if we show change in Y and X with a right angle triangle.

In regression, Normal Equations are written as follows

$\Sigma Y = n\beta_0 + \beta_1 \Sigma X$ .................. (1)

$\Sigma XY = \beta_0 \Sigma X + \beta_1 \Sigma X^2$ ...............(2)

If we calculate $\Sigma Y$, $\Sigma X$, $\Sigma XY$ and $\Sigma X^2$ we can find $\beta_0$, $\beta_1$

The other method is to find $\beta_1$ and then $\beta_0$ as follows

$$\beta_1 = \frac{\Sigma xy}{\Sigma x^2}$$

$\beta_0 = \bar{Y} - \beta_1 * \bar{X}$

Please note the difference between 'x' and 'X' or 'y' and 'Y'. Here x means $X-\bar{X}$ while y $= Y-\bar{Y}$

### 9.9.2.1 Solved Examples

#### Solved Example S-1

Say a company observes that when it decreases prices of its product, there is increase in sales. The observed data is as follows:

| Demand | Price |
|---|---|
| 28 | 8 |
| 33 | 7 |
| 38 | 6 |
| 47 | 5 |
| 52 | 4 |
| 56 | 3 |
| 61 | 2 |

Fit a regression equation and test the significance of slope and model. Also find goodness of fit.

**Solution:**

Let demand be Y and price be X

| | Demand(Y) | Price(X) | ΣXY | $\Sigma X^2$ |
|---|---|---|---|---|
| | 28 | 8 | 224 | 64 |
| | 33 | 7 | 231 | 49 |
| | 38 | 6 | 228 | 36 |
| | 47 | 5 | 235 | 25 |
| | 52 | 4 | 208 | 16 |
| | 56 | 3 | 168 | 9 |
| | 61 | 2 | 122 | 4 |
| ΣY | 315 | | | |
| ΣX | | 35 | | |
| ΣXY | | | 1416 | |
| $\Sigma X^2$ | | | | 203 |

The normal equations are

$315 = 7\,\beta_0 + 35\,\beta_1$ .................. (1)

$1416 = 35\beta_0 + 203\,\beta_1$ ..............(2)

By solving the above equation $\beta_0 = 73.39$ and $\beta_1 = -5.6$

The regression eqaution is

$\hat{Y} = 73.39 - 5.678X$

or

$Y = 73.39 - 5.678X + e$

We can also find out $\beta_1$ by

$$\beta_1 = \frac{\Sigma xy}{\Sigma x^2}$$

| | Y | X | $y = Y-\overline{Y}$ | $x = X-\overline{X}$ | xy | $x^2$ |
|---|---|---|---|---|---|---|
| | 28 | 8 | −17 | 3 | −51 | 9 |
| | 33 | 7 | −12 | 2 | −24 | 4 |
| | 38 | 6 | −7 | 1 | −7 | 1 |
| | 47 | 5 | 2 | 0 | 0 | 0 |
| | 52 | 4 | 7 | −1 | −7 | 1 |
| | 56 | 3 | 11 | −2 | −22 | 4 |
| | 61 | 2 | 16 | −3 | −48 | 9 |
| | | | | | | |
| Mean Y, X | 45 | 5 | 0 | 0 | −159 | 28 |

Please note 'x' is small and is deviation of X from its mean, similarly y is small and is deviation of Y from its mean.

$$\beta_1 = \frac{\Sigma xy}{\Sigma x^2} = \frac{-159}{28} = 5.678$$

$\beta_0 = 45 - 5.678 * 5 = 73.39$

Hence regression equation is

$\hat{Y} = 73.39 - 5.678X$

or

$Y = 73.39 - 5.678X + e$

Now error is $Y - \hat{Y}$

| Y | X | $\hat{Y}$ | Error | Square of error |
|---|---|---|---|---|
| 28 | 8 | 27.966 | 0.034 | 0.001156 |
| 33 | 7 | 33.644 | −0.644 | 0.414736 |
| 38 | 6 | 39.322 | −1.322 | 1.747684 |
| 47 | 5 | 45 | 2 | 4 |
| 52 | 4 | 50.678 | 1.322 | 1.747684 |
| 56 | 3 | 56.356 | −0.356 | 0.126736 |
| 61 | 2 | 62.034 | −1.034 | 1.069156 |
| Sum | | | 0 | 9.107152 |

$\Sigma e^2 = 9.1071$

(Let us understand the concept of DF, before continueing further)

### 9.9.3 Degree of Freedom (Concept)

Here we need to know about degree of freedom (DF). In simple words we do not have freedom to certain results, as they are not original results. Some results affect the results. For instance, if we wish to know the deviation from mean we use mean to find out the deviation. Mean is the first result and mean deviation is the second result. Hence, we lose one degree of freedom. Similarly in a single variable regression equation, error is calculated after two results – one $\beta_0$ (which is also called intercept) and $\beta_1$ (which is also called slope).

So in the above example degree of freedom (DF) for error is n-2 i.e. 5

$$\text{So variance of error} = \sigma_e^2 = \Sigma e^2/n\text{-}2 = \frac{9.1071}{5} = 1.8214$$

Let us now hypothesize

$H_0$: $\beta_1 \neq 0$ (which means slope is almost flat, though it may show some negative or positive figure)

$H_1$: $\beta_1$ 0 (which means slope is statistcally significant)

Standard Error of $\beta_1$ is found by formula

$$\text{S. E. of } \beta_1 = \sqrt{\frac{\sigma_e^2}{\Sigma x^2}} = \sqrt{\frac{1.8214}{28}} = 0.255$$

$$\text{T-stat for } \beta_1 = \frac{\beta_1}{\text{S.E of } \beta_1} = -5.678/0.255 = -22.2666$$

Now tablulated t for 5 degrees of freedom at 5% level = 2.571 (with two tails)

As computed t is more than tabulated t, we reject $H_0$ and accept $H_1$ which means $\beta_1$ is statistically significant at 5% level.

Another test for regression is **goodness of fit, i.e., $R^2$**

$$R^2 = \frac{ESS}{TSS}$$

ESS is explained sum of square due to regression and TSS is total sum of square.

TSS = ESS + RSS

Total sum of square = Estimated Sum of Square + Residual Sum of Square

To understand, we know

$$Y = \hat{Y} + e$$

Subtracting $\overline{Y}$ from both sides

$$y - \overline{y} = \hat{y} - \overline{y} + e$$

This can be written in the form of deviation as follows

$$y = \hat{y} + e$$

Taking summation and square of both sides

We have

$y^2 \quad \hat{y}^2 \quad e^2$..........(a)

TSS = ESS + RSS

Further we know

$\hat{y} = \beta_0 + \beta_1 X$

and

$\bar{y} = \beta_0 + \beta_1 \bar{X}$

therefore

$\hat{y} - \bar{y} = \beta_1 X - \beta_1 \bar{X}$

$\hat{y} = \beta_1 X$

Taking summation and square of both sides

$\Sigma \hat{y} = \beta_1^2 \Sigma x^2$

Now

TSS = ESS + RSS

$TSS = \beta_1^2 \Sigma x^2 + \Sigma e^2 = (5.678)^2 * 28 + 9.1071 = 911.818$

$R^2 = \frac{ESS}{TSS} = (902.\ 711)/911.818 = .99$

This means 99% of Y is explained by X. $R^2$ is considered good if it is more than .80.

The next test of regression is F Test.

$$F = \frac{\text{Mean ESS}}{\text{Mean RSS}}$$

Mean ESS = (ESS)/1 = 902.711/1 = 902.711

Mean RSS = (RSS)/n-2 = 9.1071/5 = 1.8214

Computed F = 902.711/1.8214 = 495.61

Tabulated value for F with 5% DF and numerator DF with 1 and denominator DF as 5 is

$F_{1,5,\ 5\%} = 6.61.$

As computed F value is more than tabulated value, overall model is statistically significant at 5% level.

Thus we can evaluate the model by three tests

1. T-test for slope
2. $R^2$ for goodness of fit
3. F test for overall significance of model

(Students interested to know more about regression must read a good book on econometrics)

### 9.9.4 Use of Computer (Regression)

The above calculations can be done on Excel spreadsheet, if your computer MS OFFICE has add-in tools.

In Excel spreadsheet write values in cells, There shall be two columns —one for Y and other for X. Go to tools, select data analysis. A window shall appear. Select Regression. In input Y range entre Y cell range. In input X range entre X cell range.

Output can be on the same sheet or separate sheet. You can plot and get charts for residuals and estimated Y. With Ok you will get following results.

| SUMMARY OUTPUT | | | | | |
|---|---|---|---|---|---|
| | | | | | |
| Regression Statistics | | | | | |
| Multiple R | 0.994995 | | | | |
| R Square | 0.990014 | | | | |
| Adjusted R Square | 0.988017 | | | | |
| Standard Error | 1.349603 | | | | |
| Observations | 7 | | | | |
| | | | | | |
| ANOVA | | | | | |
| df SS | MS | F | Significance F | | |
| Regression | 1 | 902.8929 | 902.8929 | 495.7059 | 3.4E-06 |
| Residual | 5 | 9.107143 | 1.821429 | | |
| Total | 6 | 912 | | | |
| | | | | | |
| | Coefficients | Standard Error | t Stat | P-value | Lower 95% |
| Intercept | 73.39286 | 1.373492 | 53.43524 | 4.34E-08 | 69.86219 |
| X Variable 1 | -5.67857 | 0.255051 | -22.2645 | 3.4E-06 | -6.3342 |
| RESIDUAL OUTPUT | | | | | |
| | | | | | |
| Observation | Predicted Y | Residuals | | | |
| 1 | 27.96429 | 0.035714 | | | |
| 2 | 33.64286 | -0.64286 | | | |
| 3 | 39.32143 | -1.32143 | | | |
| 4 | 45 | 2 | | | |
| 5 | 50.67857 | 1.321429 | | | |
| 6 | 56.35714 | -0.35714 | | | |
| 7 | 62.03571 | -1.03571 | | | |

We are not discussing multiple R, adjusted $R^2$ etc.

## Solved Example S-2

Your company sales from 2001 to 2007 are as follows. Fit a regression model. Find sales in year 2010. Is year on year sale coefficient significant? Find the goodness of fit. Find the overall significance of model. Also find the compounded growth rate and find its significance.

| Year | Sales |
|---|---|
| 1 | 10 |
| 2 | 15 |
| 3 | 14 |
| 4 | 9 |
| 5 | 10 |
| 6 | 18 |

**Solution:**

| | Y | X | $y = Y - \bar{Y}$ | $\chi = X - \bar{X}$ | xy | $\chi^2$ |
|---|---|---|---|---|---|---|
| | 10 | 1 | –4 | –3 | 12 | 9 |
| | 15 | 2 | 1 | –2 | –2 | 4 |
| | 14 | 3 | 0 | –1 | 0 | 1 |
| | 9 | 4 | –5 | 0 | 0 | 0 |
| | 10 | 5 | –4 | 1 | –4 | 1 |
| | 18 | 6 | 4 | 2 | 8 | 4 |
| | 22 | 7 | 8 | 3 | 24 | 9 |
| | | | | | | |
| **Mean Y,X** | 14 | 4 | 0 | 0 | 38 | 28 |

Please note 'x' is small and is deviation of X from its mean, similarly y is small and is deviation of Y from its mean.

$$\beta_1 = \frac{\sum xy}{\sum x^2} = \frac{38}{28} = 1.357$$

$$\beta_0 = 14 - 1.3571 * 4 = 8.571$$

Hence, regression equation is

$$\hat{Y} = 8.571 + 1.3571X_i$$

or

$$Y = 8.571 + 1.3571X_i + e$$

Sales in year 2010

In year 2010, X shall be 10.

$$Y = 8.571 + 1.3571*10 = 22.142$$

By Excel the results are

| SUMMARY OUTPUT | | | | | |
|---|---|---|---|---|---|
| | | | | | |
| Regression Statistics | | | | | |
| Multiple R | 0.611315 | | | | |
| R Square | 0.373706 | | | | |
| Adjusted R Square | 0.248447 | | | | |
| Standard Error | 4.157609 | | | | |
| Observations | 7 | | | | |
| | | | | | |
| ANOVA | | | | | |
| | df | SS | MS | F | Significance F |
| Regression | 1 | 51.57143 | 51.57143 | 2.983471 | 0.144699 |
| Residual | 5 | 86.42857 | 17.28571 | | |
| Total | 6 | 138 | | | |
| | | | | | |
| | Coefficients | Standard Error | t Stat | P-value | Lower 95% |
| Intercept | 8.571429 | 3.513821 | 2.439347 | 0.058701 | –0.46112 |
| X Variable 1 | 1.357143 | 0.785714 | 1.727273 | 0.144699 | –0.6626 |

Now the model can be rewritten as

$$\hat{Y} = 8.571 + 1.3571X_i$$

$$(1.7272)$$

$n = 7$ $R^2 = .37$ $F = 2.9834$

Results

$R^2$ is very low, so Goodness of Fit is very low, only 37% of Y is explained by X. $\beta_1$ is statistically not significant at 5% level. So year on year sale does not depend much on time. Overall model is not siginificant as computed F is less than tabulated F at 5% level.

Students should note how regression results are written. T-stat values are written below parameters. N, $R^2$ and F should be written below regression equation.

### 9.9.5 How to Find Compounded Growth Rate?

To find the compounded growth rate we shall have to use formula:

$$Y_t = Y_0 * (1+g)^t$$

Where g is compounded growth rate in fractions, t is the the number of observations or number of years, $Y_0$ is the beginning of the sales. This is the same formula which you used to find amount with compounded interest at your school level.

If we take log of both sides, we get,

$$\text{Log } Y_t = \text{Log } Y_0 + t \log (1+g)$$

Now we can regress and find (1+g). Take anti-log of (1+g), subtract 1, you will get g in fraction. Multiply by 100 and you will get percentage compounded growth rate.

| Y | X | Log Y | X | ΣXY | $\Sigma X^2$ |
|---|---|---|---|---|---|
| 10 | 1 | 2.302585 | 1 | 2.302585 | 1 |
| 15 | 2 | 2.70805 | 2 | 5.4161 | 4 |
| 14 | 3 | 2.639057 | 3 | 7.917172 | 9 |
| 9 | 4 | 2.197225 | 4 | 8.788898 | 16 |
| 10 | 5 | 2.302585 | 5 | 11.51293 | 25 |
| 18 | 6 | 2.890372 | 6 | 17.34223 | 36 |
| 22 | 7 | 3.091042 | 7 | 21.6373 | 49 |
| | ΣY | 18.13092 | | | |
| | ΣX | | 28 | | |
| | ΣXY | | | 74.91721 | |
| | $\Sigma X^2$ | | | | 140 |

The normal equations are

$18.1309 = 7\ \beta_0 + 28\ \beta_1$ .................. (1)

$74.9172 = 28\beta_0 + 140\ \beta_1$ ...............(2)

By solving the above equation $\beta_0 = 2.24$and $\beta_1 = 0.85$

By taking anti-log of 0.85 and substracting 1 we shall get 0.089 which is equal to 8.9%. Now the trend shows that the growth rate is 8.9%. But you will have to test whether this growth rate is statistically significant or not. Let us see Excel result.

| **SUMMARY OUTPUT** | | | | | |
|---|---|---|---|---|---|
| | | | | | |
| Regression Statistics | | | | | |
| Multiple R | 0.549714 | | | | |
| R Square | 0.302186 | | | | |
| Adjusted R Square | 0.162623 | | | | |
| Standard Error | 0.307404 | | | | |
| Observations | 7 | | | | |
| | | | | | |
| **ANOVA** | | | | | |
| | df | SS | MS | F | Significance F |
| Regression | 1 | 0.204609 | 0.204609 | 2.165231 | 0.201135 |
| Residual | 5 | 0.472487 | 0.094497 | | |
| Total | 6 | 0.677096 | | | |
| | | | | | |
| | Coefficients | Standard Error | t Stat | P-value | Lower 95% |
| Intercept | 2.248196 | 0.259804 | 8.653426 | 0.000341 | 1.580349 |
| X Variable 1 | 0.085484 | 0.058094 | 1.471472 | 0.201135 | -0.06385 |

Computed t stat for $\beta_1$ is 1.47 which is statistically not significant at 5% level. F is 2.1652 which is also less than tabulated value at 5% level. So model does not fit well. Other factors, not time, play the major role on year to year sale.

### 9.9.6 Multiple Regression

#### Formulas for Multiple Regression

**In case of two independent variables:**

$$\hat{\beta}_0 = \overline{Y} - \hat{\beta}_1 X_1 - \hat{\beta}_2 - X_2$$

$$\overline{\beta}_1 = \frac{(\Sigma x^1 y)(\Sigma x_2^2) - (\Sigma x^2 y)(\Sigma x_2^1 x^2)}{(\Sigma x_1^2)(\Sigma x_2^2) - (\Sigma x^1 x^2)}$$

$$\hat{\beta}_2 = \frac{(\Sigma x^2 y)(\Sigma x_1^2) - (\Sigma x^1 y)(\Sigma x_2^1 x^2)}{(\Sigma x_1^2)(\Sigma x_2^2) - (\Sigma x^1 x^2)}$$

$$\text{Variance of } \hat{\beta}_1 = \frac{\Sigma x_2^2}{(\Sigma x_1^2)(\Sigma x_2^2) - (\Sigma x^1 x^2)^2} * \sigma_\mu^2$$

$$\text{Variance of } \hat{\beta}_2 = \frac{\Sigma x_1^2}{(\Sigma x_1^2)(\Sigma x_2^2) - (\Sigma x^1 x^2)^2} * \sigma_\mu^2$$

$$\text{Where } \sigma^2{}_u = \frac{\Sigma e^2}{n-3}$$

$$\Sigma e^2 - \Sigma y^2(1 - R^2)$$

### 9.9.7 Issues in Regression

**Assumptions of Regression Models**

1. The relationship between the dependent variable Y and the independent variable(s) X are linear. This does not mean that the independent variable cannot be a non-linear relationship (like log(X), $X^2$) but the parameters must be linear.
2. Var(X) > 0. Without multiple X values in the sample we have no way to show that there is a relationship between the Y and the X variables.
3. The mean of the error terms, given the independent variable X, is zero. $E(\varepsilon i \mid Xi) = 0$. Here we are assuming that on average, our X variables are on our regression line.
4. The variance of the error terms are constant. $Var(\varepsilon i \mid Xi) = \sigma^2$, the variance does not change with different samples. This is known as homoscedastic errors, and means the X terms are equally scattered above and below the regression line through out the line.
5. The error terms are independently distributed so that their Covariance = 0. This is known as serial independence.
6. The number of observations is greater than the number of estimators. so that regression has enough degrees of freedom for test results.
7. The error terms are normally distributed amongst the estimated X variable.

$\epsilon_i \; N(O, \sigma^2) \Rightarrow \epsilon_i \; N(\alpha + \beta X_i, \sigma^2)$

When any of the assumption is wrong, our results may either be wrong or biased.

Auto-correlation, auto-regression, unit root, multi-collinearity and heteroscedasticity are some of the problems which can affect our results.

## Auto-correlation

In any time series containing non-random patterns of behaviour, it is likely that any particular item in the series is related in some fashion to other items in the same series. If there is a consistent relationship between entries in the series, e.g., the 5$^{th}$ item is like the 1st, the 6th is like the 2$^{nd}$, and so on, then it should be possible to use information about the relationship to forecast future values of the series, i.e., the 33$^{rd}$ item should be like the 29$^{th}$. In this case we may say that the series has some ability to forecast itself because of auto-correlation (or self-correlation) among values within the series. Students can read a good book on econometrics for further study.

## Multi-collinearity

**Multi-collinearity** refers to a situation in which two or more explanatory variables in a multiple regression model are highly correlated. We have perfect multi-collinearity if the correlation between two independent variables is equal to 1 or –1. In practice, we rarely face perfect multi-collinearity in a data set. More commonly, the issue of multicollinearity arises when there is a high degree of correlation (either positive or negative) between two or more independent variables.

Mathematically, a set of variables is collinear if there exists one or more linear relationships among the variables. For example, we may have:

$$\lambda_1 X_{1i} + \lambda_2 X_{2i} + \ldots + \lambda_k X_{ki} = 0$$

where $\lambda_i$ are constants and $X_i$ are explanatory variables. We can explore the issue caused by multi-collinearity by examining the parameter estimates for the parameters of the multiple regression equation.

In the presence of multi-collinearity, the estimate of one variable's impact on Y while controlling the others tends to be less precise than if predictors were un-correlated with one another. The usual interpretation of a regression coefficient is that it provides an estimate of the effect of a one unit change in an independent variable, $X_1$, holding the other variables constant. If $X_1$ is highly correlated with another independent variable, $X_2$, in the given data set, then we only have observations for which $X_1$ and $X_2$ have a particular relationship (either positive or negative). We don't have observations for which $X_1$ changes independently of $X_2$, so we have an imprecise estimate of the effect of independent changes in $X_1$.

## Auto-regression

The values of a times series of data at particular points in time are highly correlated with the value which preceedes and succeed them. Dependent variable is a function of itself at the previous moment of period or time. The most often seen form of the equation is a linear form:

$$y_t = b_0 + \sum_{i-1}^{p} b_i y_{t-i} + e_t$$

A first-order auto-regressive model is concerned with only the correlation between consecutive values in a series.

$$y_t = b_0 + b_1 y_{t-1} + e_t$$

A second-order autoregressive model considers the effect of relationship between consecutive values in a series as well as the correlation between values two periods apart.

$$y_t = b_0 + b_1 y_{t-1} + b_2 y_{t-2} + e_t$$

### Heteroscedasticity

In a regression, a sequence or a vector of random variables is **heteroscedastic** if the random variables have different variances. The complementary concept is called homoscedacity. The term means "differing variance". One of the assumptions of regression model is that the error term has a constant variance. This will be true if the observations of the error term are assumed to be drawn from identical distributions. Heteroscedasticity is a violation of this assumption.

For example, the error term could vary or increase with each observation, something that is often the case with cross-sectional or time series measurements. With the advent of robust standard errors allowing us to do inference without specifying the conditional second moment of error term, testing conditional homoscedasticity is not as important as in the past. Heteroscedasticity does not cause OLS coefficient estimates to be biased. However, the variance (and, thus, standard errors) of the coefficients tends to be underestimated, inflating t-scores and sometimes making insignificant variables appear to be statistically significant.

#### 9.9.7.1 Problems for Practice

1. The following data relate to training and performance of salesmen employed in a company.

| Salesman | Hours of Training (X) | Performance (Average weekly sales in '000 rupees (Y) |
|---|---|---|
| 1 | 20 | 44 |
| 2 | 5 | 22 |
| 3 | 10 | 25 |
| 4 | 13 | 32 |
| 5 | 12 | 27 |

Fit a regression line to the above data. Find out the weekly sales that are likely to be attained by a salesman who is given 16 hours of training. Check goodness of fit.

2. For 10 observations on Price (X) and Supply (Y), the following data were obtained
$\Sigma X = 130$, $\Sigma Y = 220$, $\Sigma X^2 = 2288$, $\Sigma Y^2 = 5506$, $\Sigma XY = 3467$,
Fit a linear regression of Y on X and estimate the supply when price is 25 units.

3. Fit a regression line of consumption (C) and income (Y) on the basis of the following data:

| C ('000 ₹) | 90 | 95 | 100 | 105 | 106 |
|---|---|---|---|---|---|
| Y ('000 ₹) | 100 | 110 | 120 | 130 | 140 |

Estimate consumption when income is ₹ 1,50,000.

4. A company manufactures different types of electrical appliances. It has been using < advertising its products. The following table shows the amounts of radio time (X, in min and the number of electrical appliances sold (Y) over the last seven weeks.

| X | 25 | 18 | 32 | 21 | 35 | 28 | 30 |
|---|---|---|---|---|---|---|---|
| Y | 16 | 11 | 20 | 15 | 26 | 32 | 20 |

(a) Fit a regression of Y on X.

(b) What will be the value of Y when X is 27?

5. To investigate the relationship between the level of advertising in local newspapers and the level of sales, the marketing manager of a national firm in the consumer-products field applies different amounts of advertising in 10 randomly selected geographic areas. The following table indicates the level of advertising and the level of sales for the relevant time period in the 10 areas.

| **Area** | **Level of Advertising ('000 ₹)** | **Level of Sales ('000 ₹)** |
|---|---|---|
| 1 | 10.5 | 17.3 |
| 2 | 6.0 | 14.0 |
| 3 | 8.7 | 19.1 |
| 4 | 9.3 | 14,5 |
| 5 | 11.8 | 20.0 |
| 6 | 7.5 | 16.3 |
| 7 | 15.0 | 23.8 |
| 8 | 6.3 | 14.0 |
| 9 | 8.5 | 17.3 |
| 10 | 5.4 | 13.3 |

6. A firm that sells office supplies wants to expand. The head of the firm wants to know what sales volume can be expected in various market areas. Regression analysis with sales as the dependent variable, is suggested. It is decided that effective buying income would be the independent variable. A sample of 15 trade areas in which the firm now does business gives the following results in lakh of rupees.

Sum of $X$= 1385 Sum of $Y$= 83.6

Sum of X * $Y$= 10917.6 Sum of $X$ squares = 179661

Sum of $Y$ squares = 681.32

(i) Develop the equation that best describes the relationship between effective income and sales.

(ii) For a trade area with an effective buying income of 115, what is the estimated amount of sales?

(iii) What is the correlation coefficient for these data? Is it an appropriate measure that enables the manager to determine the proportion of variability in sales explained by the effective buying income? Explain.

7. From the following data estimate the regression of Y on $X_1$ and $X_2$. Prepare the ANOVA table to test the overall significance of the model. (Data in deviation form)

| | y | $x_1$ | $x_2$ |
|---|---|---|---|
| y | 66042.269 | 74778.346 | 4250.9 |
| $x_1$ | - | 84855.096 | 4796.0 |
| $x_2$ | | | 280 |

$\overline{Y} = 367.693, \quad \overline{X}_1 = 402.760, \quad \overline{X}_2 = 8.0, \; n = 15$

8. Given $\hat{Y} = 53.1603 + 0.7266 X_1 + 2.7363 X_2$

$\qquad\qquad\qquad\qquad (0.0487) \qquad (0.8486)$

$n = 5$, d.f. $= 12$, $R^2 = 0.9988$, $\overline{R}^2 = 0.9986$

Evaluate the model and interpret the results.

9. A company has the sales pattern (in units) during 1995 to 2002 as shown below:

| Year | Sales in lakhs |
|---|---|
| 1995 | 15 |
| 1996 | 19 |
| 1997 | 27 |
| 1998 | 35 |
| 1999 | 45 |
| 2000 | 56 |
| 2001 | 70 |
| 2002 | 86 |

(a) Fit a linear regression for the data.

(b) Compute the sales forecast for the year 2005.

10. The results of a survey on the sales of a product Y as function time period X are summarised as below:

| | X | Y |
|---|---|---|
| Mean | 40 | 125 |
| Standard Deviation | 2.5 | 16 |
| Coefficient of Correlation | | .85 |

(a) Fit the regression line Y on X and estimate the value of Y when X is 45.

(b) Fit the regression line X on Y and estimate the value of X when Y is 135.

11. The rate of return (in percentage) of a product as a function of R&D expenditure (in lakhs of rupees) and annual advertising expenditure (in lakhs of rupees) for the past 7 years are summarized below:

| **Rate of return (Y)** | **R&D expenditure (Xi)** | **Annual advertising expenditure (Xz)** |
|---|---|---|
| 12 | 12 | 30 |
| 15 | 16 | 50 |
| 14 | 18 | 65 |
| 18 | 20 | 75 |
| 17 | 18 | 80 |
| 15 | 25 | 95 |
| 20 | 30 | 105 |

Design a regression model to forecast the rate of return of the product.

## 9.10 How to Do?

Jolly and Dolly arranged a small get – together at their residence and called their friends –Nina, Mala, Gauri, Kavita, Poonam and Sunder.

Nina: "Research Methodology is a good subject, but I have still many doubts."

Jolly: "Relax, have a cup of tea with snacks and we shall clear your doubts."

Mala: "When you talk about quality in research, you mean to say we should have validity at every step."

Gauri: "Of course, defining the problems, deciding the objectives, framing hypothesis, reviewing the literature, collecting data, making models, and drawing inferences, all need meticulous handling."

Kavita: "Do we have any short-cut?"

Poonam: "Short-cut, of what?"

Jolly: "If you wish to be effective and efficient, there is no short-cut. To be effective and efficient, you need not know only communication skills, selling skills, negotiation skills, operational skills, financial skills, but also to find out ways to develop them. Research can never be short-cut. Research is all to develop them."

Sunder: "We have just gone through the report 'HRD climate in Textile industry' by Dr. Dhanbhakyam and K.R. Vijayasanthi. I am doing my specialization in HR, I loved this report. Authors after defining the terms of HRD system, discuss why HRD system is important in textile industry. The industry is growing with exports. They further say that the factors of HRD climate may differ from person to person even in the same industry due to the personal characters, needs, attitudes, desires, problems etc., may differ from individual to individual here problem means common problem such as a low wages, lack of job security, less intensives, family problem, etc. These problems are faced by employees in almost all industries. The firm may control the problems by way of taking effective steps. The present study is undertaken to study the Human Resource Development climate and give suggestions to management to improve the HRD climate. Okay."

Dolly: "The authors' objectives are to find out factors which influence HRD climate and to study the employees' perception about HRD system."

Poonam: "But do the hypotheses which they framed to find out the relationship between age, income, education, experience etc. have anything with factors. Are they not in a hurry to frame hypotheses?"

Kavita: "No, they are just at the beginning and wish to establish conclusion validity. They have no objectives to go for internal validity and construct validity. They just want to test their conclusion validity."

Sunder: "Okay, their sample size is very small, which will create problems for generalizing."

Jolly: "Oh, yes, but they have explained the limitations, their other limitation is that responses may be biased as the respondents thought that the interviewers had been sent by management. So question of validity arises. But we cannot get 100%

validity in human sciences. These are not natural sciences like physics, chemistry or biology."

Poonam: "Do you think we should go with ahead such limitations."

Jolly: "Of course, but before drawing inferences, we should keep our limitations in mind. External validity and interpretive validity will also have limitations."

Sunder: "Don't you think sampling techniques is not random and they have taken non-probability sampling. For instance 80% of the respondents are young people, while 64% are experienced for less than 6 years."

Kavita: "Do you think the statements like 'It is the age group where the employees can work effiectively and efficiently' are valid statements. I am not an expert researcher but researchers should avoid such generalization."

Jolly: "I agree with you, but sometimes researchers propose for further studies while creating such gaps."

Poonam: "They perform Chi-square test to see the relationship between age and education. And they have found that there is a significant relationship between age and education and also between experience and income."

Nina: "The authors again retest the means of age, education, income and experiences with ANOVA tests."

Dolly: "Then on 10 – point scale, they ask the respondents about management policies on HR."

Gauri "But tell me, are the conclusions based on findings? Are the suggestions based on conclusions?"

Nina: "Authors have clearly written 'The researcher hopes that this project will serve as a practical guide and contribute to further research and implementation'."

Dolly: "But what are the factors, which influence the culture, we are still unable to grasp."

Sunder: "The work lacks descriptive and predictive validity. On causal front, it lacks conclusion, internal, constructs and external validity."

Jolly: "We should not conclude so early, but this is a fact that the project is incomplete and needs further study, and cause and effect should be clear."

Dolly: "We need to study an article where researcher takes care of validity."

Jolly: "Are you experienced to study?"

Kavita: "What do you understand about yourself?"

Jolly: "I was just joking."

Kavita: "No, jokes with me. Be serious."

Sunder: "What a meeting! All serious talks, no jokes!"

Dolly: "One of my friends says 'if you just copy from an article, it is called 'copying', but if you copy from 10 books, it is called research."

Guari: "Who is he?"

Dolly: "What do you mean?"

| | |
|---|---|
| Jolly: | "I give you one article written by Dr. R.K. Mandal from Itanagar." |
| Dolly: | "Oh, yes, he is a researcher known all over India." |
| Jolly: | "He has written an article 'Variation of Output With the Variation of Anticipated and Unanticipated Money Supply in India 1950 – 91 *(Under Rational Expectations)*. Read the article and observe how regression models have been used to verify which part of money supply is responsible for the observed variation in output level." |
| Kavita: | "All of us shall read the research project and analyse it." |
| Jolly: | "Thanks come again, bye" |

✦ ✦ ✦

Research Project 9

# 9. 11 Variation of Output With the Variation of Anticipated and Un-anticipated Money Supply in India 1950 – 91

**(Under Rational Expectations)**

**Ram Krishna Mandal**[1]

## INTRODUCTION

It has been examined that output level has responded to money supply over the time period 1950-1991. This money supply has two parts: the anticipated and unanticipated. Consequently, we face an immediate question – which part of money supply is responsible for the observed variation in output level? This paper seeks to address this issue. Now, anticipated money supply and unanticipated money supply are to be sought first and then we see their relationships with the variation output level.

S.A.Ozga says, "Expectations Proper" is attitudes, dispositions or states of mind which determine our behaviour or at least accompany it. The precision of expectations depends on the quality and nature of information available and the model through which the information set is processed. The agent has very limited set of information. In such case 'Adaptive Expectations' are very suitable where future value of a variable is related to a set of some past values. This constitutes the heart of 'Rational Expectations Process'. Sargent and Wallace, therefore, hold, "Expectations about a variable are said to be rational if they depend, in the proper way, on the same things, that economic theory says actually determine the variable".

Under Adaptive Expectations Model, expectations are directly related to past observations. The empirical estimation of expected money supply under 'Adaptive Expectations Model may be explained through the estimation of the following money supply equation.

$$M_t = \alpha + \beta_1 M_{t-1} + \beta_2 M_{t-2} + \dots\dots\dots + \beta_k M_{t-k} + W_t$$

where $W_t \sim i\ i\ d\ N\ (o, \delta^2_w)$ and

$\beta_1, \beta_2, \dots\dots, \beta_k$ obey BLU properties,

$M_t$ = money supply at time, t

$M_{t-1}$ = money supply at time, t–1 and so on.

J. F. Muth developed the concept of Rational Expectations as an alternative to Adaptive Expectations in 1961. Expectations are rational when they coincide with forecasts derived from the relevant economic theory. In 1973, Sargent repeated exactly the idea of Muth to describe 'Rational Expectations.

Several models have been specified in Macroeconomics for capturing anticipated money supply. The essence of these models is that, while specifying the money supply equation, the two-way linkage between money and income must be given due weightages. Sims has done extensive work on such relationship along the line of 'Granger Causality'. The following model, as suggested by Dornbusch, has been used for estimation.

---

1 Dr. Ram Krishna Mandal, S.G. Lecturer in Economics, Dera Natung Govt. College, Itanagar, Arunachal Pradesh

• The article has already been published in Vol 2 no. 4 of Journal of Global Economy, Dec, 2006 issue. Reprinted with permission from author and editors of Journal.

$$M_t = \alpha + \beta Y_{t-1} + \lambda_1 M_{t-1} + \lambda_2 M_{t-2} + \ldots\ldots\ldots + \lambda_k M_{t-k} + V_t$$

where $V_t \sim$ i i d N $(o, \delta^2{}_v)$ and

$Y_t$ = (log) output level (G.N.P) at time, t

$M_t$ = (log) money supply at time, t and so on.

Here, the exact number of lagged money regressors (i.e., the value of k) is determined through estimation.

**Table 1**

**Data**

| Year | Y (in billions of ₹) | M2 (in billions of ₹) |
|---|---|---|
| 1950 | 95.4 | 21.64 |
| 1951 | 94.4 | 21.07 |
| 1952 | 97.5 | 20.60 |
| 1953 | 104.5 | 21.09 |
| 1954 | 96.8 | 22.66 |
| 1955 | 102.6 | 25.26 |
| 1956 | 118.2 | 27.12 |
| 1957 | 119.9 | 29.87 |
| 1958 | 134.4 | 32.90 |
| 1959 | 139.8 | 36.94 |
| 1960 | 149.5 | 38.92 |
| 1961 | 158.8 | 40.17 |
| 1962 | 169.9 | 44.03 |
| 1963 | 195.4 | 48.69 |
| 1964 | 229.0 | 53.27 |
| 1965 | 239.5 | 59.07 |
| 1966 | 274.3 | 65.69 |
| 1967 | 320.4 | 71.84 |
| 1968 | 330.2 | 78.68 |
| 1969 | 365.8 | 89.32 |
| 1970 | 399.8 | 100.1 |
| 1971 | 430.7 | 117.1 |
| 1972 | 475.6 | 135.2 |
| 1973 | 586.2 | 161.5 |
| 1974 | 693.0 | 181.3 |
| 1975 | 738.3 | 206.7 |
| 1976 | 799.7 | 257.4 |

| | | |
|---|---|---|
| 1977 | 896.2 | 306.7 |
| 1978 | 975.9 | 371.5 |
| 1979 | 1077.0 | 437.4 |
| 1980 | 1362.0 | 506.9 |
| 1981 | 1595.0 | 595.3 |
| 1982 | 1769.0 | 697.7 |
| 1983 | 2063.0 | 815.6 |
| 1984 | 2281 | 962.3 |
| 1985 | 2603 | 1125 |
| 1986 | 2911 | 1326 |
| 1987 | 3306 | 1505 |
| 1988 | 3921 | 1825 |
| 1989 | 4483 | 2112 |
| 1990 | 5240 | 2430 |
| 1991 | 6027 | 2875 |

**Source :** IFS - Year Book, 1979, 1988 and Sept. 1993.

## First Model

Among several alternative models the best fit one is sought.

$M_t = \alpha + \beta M_{t-1} + \varepsilon_t$ is found best fit one. Now we consider this model to find out anticipated money ($M^e_t$) and unanticipated money ($UM_t$) supply at time, t, $\alpha$ and $\beta$ are OLS estimators with BLU properties and $\varepsilon_t$ is used for unanticipated money supply.

The estimated model (GLS) is as follows:

Mt= 0.016380 + 0.7218 M t-1 ........................ (1)

(0.005103) (0.090562)

[3.2099] [7.9702]

R2 = 0.6257038 D.F. = 38 F* = 63.524 D.W. = 2.47.

From the equation (1), it appears that

(i) the equation is good fit since R2 = 0.625 and the joint estimation is significant at 5% level since F* = 63.524;

(ii) both the regression constant (a) and regression coefficient (b) are significant at 5% level; and

(iii) the equation is free from auto-correlation since D.W.[9] = 2.47.

The estimated model is best fit one among the alternative estimated models shown in Note 10.

## Findings & Implications of the Estimated model:

The estimated model (i) is found to be free from auto-correlation. So, given the vectors for Mt-1, vector of unbiased forecast (one period) can be generated from the equation. These forecasts are nothing but the fitted values for Mt. Again Mt = E $[M_t / I_{t-1}]$ where $\{I_{t-1}\} = [M_{t-1}]$. Therefore, the vector for Mt represents the vector for rationally anticipated (expected) money supply. This part of the money supply is predictable on the basis of $M_{t-1}$. Any decision/ activity of the monetary authority which affects b will immediately be known to the market participants. This they do through 'Signal Extraction' from the flow of information.

It may again be noted that

$M_t = M_t + \varepsilon_t$ where $\varepsilon_t \sim$ i i d N $(0, \sigma\varepsilon^2)$.

$\varepsilon_t$ is the surprise or random part of $M_t$. Market participants cannot guess or predict it. At best, the participants know that

$E(\varepsilon_t) = 0$

and $\text{cov}(M_t, \varepsilon_t) = 0$

The estimated equation delineates an AR (I) process for money supply. The vector for Mt can now be used as the vector for 'anticipated money supply' ($M^e_t$). Similarly, vector for et can be used for 'un-anticipated money supply' ($UM_t$). Consequently, it becomes possible for us to investigate the effects of change in anticipated and unanticipated money supplies on output level in Indian Economy over the period concerned. The data set for $M^e_t$ and $UM_t$ are shown in Table 2.

Rational expectationists like Sargent, Lucas and N. Wallace hold that change in money supply, if it is already anticipated by the agents, affects only inflation but it has no effect on real output and employment. This is the famous **"Invariance Proposition"** put forth by the rational expectationists. This proposition asserts that any predictable part of money supply would have no effect on output, employment or any other real variables in the economy. Only unpredictable money supply changes can affect output level, employment or any other real variables in the economy. The introduction of rational expectatioins to a macroeconomic model affects dramatically the ability of a government or a Central Bank to control economic policy. In presence of rational expectations, real variables (such as relative prices, unemployment rate and real output) are independent of changes in the Anticipated Monetary Policy. Rational expectationists like Sargent, Lucas and N. Wallace hold that change in money supply, if it is already anticipated by the agents, affects only inflation but it has no effect on real output and employment. This is the famous "Invariance Proposition" put forth by the rational expectationists. This proposition asserts that any predictable part of money supply would have no effect on output, employment or any other real variables in the economy. Only unpredictable money supply changes can affect output level, employment or any other real variables in the economy.

**Table 2**

**Anticipated (Met) and Unanticipated (UMt) Parts of Money Supply**

| Year (in billion of ₹) | $M_te$ (in billion of ₹) | $UM_t$ |
|---|---|---|
| 1951 | 1.366 | –0.04218 |
| 1952 | 1.354 | –0.03987 |
| 1953 | 1.344 | –0.01978 |
| 1954 | 1.354 | 0.001016 |
| 1955 | 1.386 | 0.01610 |
| 1956 | 1.435 | –0.001328 |
| 1957 | 1.466 | 0.008856 |
| 1958 | 1.509 | 0.007872 |
| 1959 | 1.552 | 0.01502 |
| 1960 | 1.604 | –0.01384 |
| 1961 | 1.627 | –0.02343 |
| 1962 | 1.641 | 0.002412 |
| 1963 | 1.682 | 0.005070 |
| 1964 | 1.727 | –0.0005678 |
| 1965 | 1.767 | 0.004212 |
| 1966 | 1.81 | 30.004293 |
| 1967 | 1.861 | –0.004264 |
| 1968 | 1.90 | –0.004577 |
| 1969 | 1.941 | 0.01009 |
| 1970 | 1.998 | 0.002651 |
| 1971 | 2.048 | 0.02067 |
| 1972 | 2.118 | 0.01258 |
| 1973 | 2.1820 | 0.02605 |
| 1974 | 2.261 | –0.003163 |
| 1975 | 2.313 | 0.002529 |
| 1976 | 2.371 | 0.03904 |
| 1977 | 2.469 | 0.01766 |
| 1978 | 2.547 | 0.02277 |
| 1979 | 2.633 | 0.003192 |
| 1980 | 2.705 | –0.0004592 |
| 1981 | 2.771 | 0.003457 |
| 1982 | 2.843 | 0.0009479 |
| 1983 | 2.914 | –0.002053 |
| 1984 | 2.983 | 0.0001767 |

| | | |
|---|---|---|
| 1985 | 3.057 | –0.005698 |
| 1986 | 3.126 | –0.003768 |
| 1987 | 3.20 | –0.02213 |
| 1988 | 3.256 | 0.00513 |
| 1989 | 3.342 | –0.01735 |
| 1990 | 3.407 | –0.02151 |
| 1991 | 3.470 | –0.01090 |

**Note:** The data set on $M^e_t$ and $UM_t$ are presented upon log- transformation. These add up to total money supply (stationary). Stationary in the total money supply is ensured through First Differencing. This accounts for the beginning of the data set at 1951.

**Second Model**

The idea of 'Invariance Proposition' can be clearly explained following Lucas. Let real output level (yt)[10] be regressed on anticipated money supply (Mte) and unanticipated money supply (UMt). Such that the idea of 'Invariance Proposition' can be clearly explained following Lucas. Let real output level (yt)[38] be regressed on anticipated money supply (Mte) and unanticipated money supply (UMt). Such that

$Y_t = Y_p + \beta_1 M_t e + \beta_2 UM_t + V_t$

$Y_t = Y_p + M_t e + UM_t + V_t$ ............................ (6.1)

Here Yp is the capacity or existing output level.

So $Y_t - Y_p = \beta_1 M_t e + \beta_2 UM_t + V t$

or, $y_t = \beta_1 M te + \beta_2 UM_t + V_t$

or, $y_t = M_t e + UM_t + V_t$ ........................... (6.2)

where yt[13] represents the variation in output around its capacity level. The 'Invariance Proposition' holds that $\beta_1 = 0$ and $\beta_2 \neq 0$. Thus, output fluctuates randomly around the existing (or capacity) level (Yp) following unanticipated fluctuations in the money stock only.

where yt represents the variation in output around its capacity level. The 'Invariance Proposition'holds that 0 and = 0. Thus output fluctuates randomly around the existing (or capacity) level (Yp) following unanticipated fluctuations in the money stock only. We seek to examine whether such invariance proposition holds in context of Indian Economy or not.

## Estimation and Findings:

The GLS estimation of the model[14] is

wt = 0.226598 + 0.65303Mte + 0.10351UMt ............... (2)

(0.0141688) (0.12864) (0.48192)

[15.9927] [50.761] [0.2536]

R2 = 0.603523 D.F. = 37

F* = 8.065 D.W. = 1.99

It is observed from the equation that

(i) the equation is good fit at 1% level since F* = 8.065 ;

(ii) the equation is free from auto-correlation since D.W.[11] = 1.99;

(iii) the regression constant ($\alpha$); and the regression coefficient ($\beta_1$) are significant even at 5% level and

(iv) the other regression coefficient ($\hat{\beta}_2$) is not significant even at 1% level.

These findings have several implications. First, $\hat{\beta}_1 > 0$ is significant and $\hat{\beta}_2$ is insignificant even at 1% level. It, therefore, appears that output variation around its capacity levels is mainly due to the changes in anticipated part of money supply. Output level seems to rise above its capacity level when money supply is anticipated to rise. Similarly, output level seems to have gone down below its capacity level (Yp) in response to an anticipated fall in money supply.

Second, $\hat{\beta}_2$ is not significant even at 1% level. It indicates that surprise part of money supply variation has no bearing on output variation over the period concerned (1950-91).

Third, $\hat{\beta}_1 > 0$ and insignificant $\hat{\beta}_2$[12] bear no testimony to the 'Invariance Proposition' as put forth by the rational expectationists.

Fourth, $\hat{\beta}_1 > 0$ indicates that any monetary policy which is designed to affect the anticipated part of money supply can affect output level. It may be noted that monetary policy formulations, which affect money supply, can only control the anticipated part of money supply. Consequently, monetary policy seems to have a significant role in Indian Economy over the period of study.

Any counter cyclical or pro-cyclical monetary policies designed to control money supply is systematic and, therefore, known to market participants. That is why, the market participants take due note of these policy parameters while forming their anticipation for money supply. $\beta 1 > 0$ indicates that changes in these policy parameters might have significant bearing on output variation around its capacity level over the period concerned (1950-91). To see the effect of Mte and $UM_t$ on output graphically, we may consider the following Graph–1 and Graph–2.

**GRAPH 1**

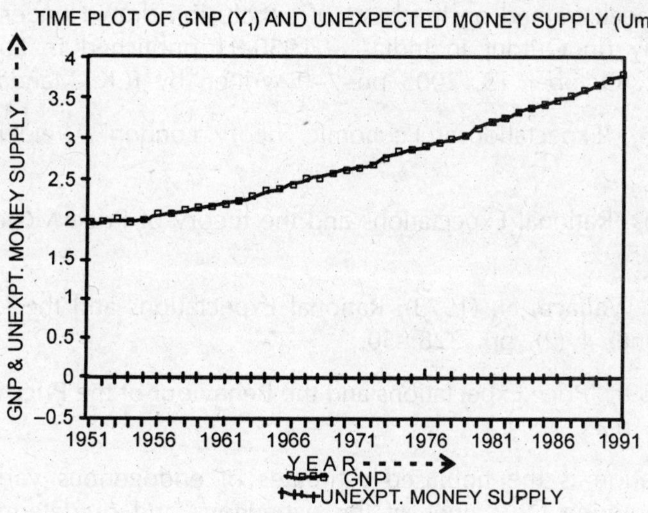


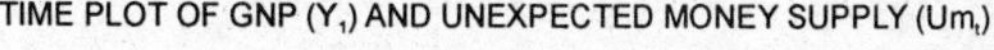


**GRAPH 2**

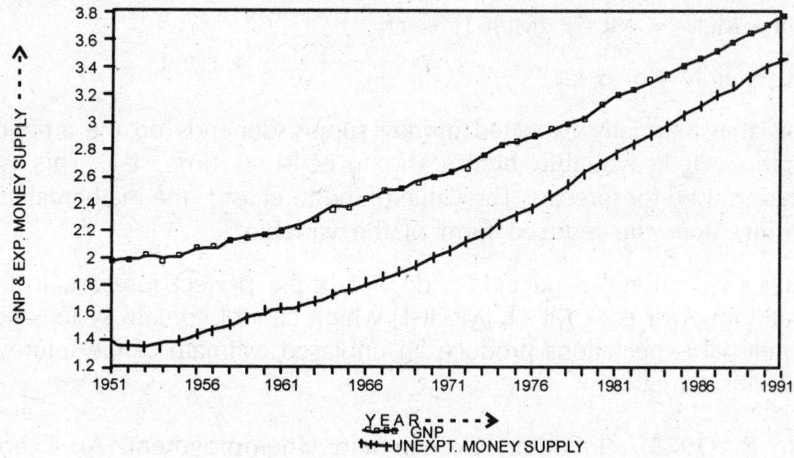


The graph 1 represents both the GNP and expected money supply. It is observed that variation in GNP is in conformity with that in expected money supply over the period concerned. The graph 2 represents that variation in GNP is in no way related to that in unexpected money supply.

## Some Relevant Issues

The long period may be considered as a time span with heterogeneous process of growth. Growth of output and that of money supply have been varying overtime within this long period. Consequently, the overall picture which we have obtained from the use of historical data set of output and money supply (anticipated and unanticipated) over the period 1950 – 1991 may have summarized the relations over different individual sub-periods. This needs further investigation into the response of output level to the changes in anticipated and unanticipated parts of money supply over shorter homogeneous sub-periods.

## References and Notes

1. This article has been framed on the basis of conclusion drawn under the article, "Effect of Money Supply on Output in India" – 1950-91 published in Southern Economist, Vol. 44, No. 12, October 15, 2005 pp.-7–9 written by R.K. Mandal.


2. Ozga, S. A. (1965), "Expectations in Economic Theory, London", Weidenfeld and Nicolson, p. 23.

3. Muth, J.F. (1961), "Rational Expectations and the theory of Price Movements", E.C. (July) 29(3), pp. 315-35.

4. Sargent, T.J. and Wallace, N. (1973), Rational Expectations and the Dynamics of Hyper Inflation, IER (June) 4 (2), pp. 328 -50.

5. Solow, R.M. (1969), "Price Expectations and the Behaviour of the Price Level", Manchester University Press, p.4.


6. Rational expectation is the unbiased estimates of endogenous variable in which all information concerning the values of the exogenous and predetermined variables are known and used for the prediction. Let Met and Mt be the expected and actual money supply at period, t. Let It-1 be the set of information available at the end of the period, t-1. Then rational expectations imply the following two assumptions.

   (1) $E [ Mt /It\text{-}1] = M^e_t$

   and (2) $Mt - Met = Mt - E [Mt/It\text{-}1] = \varepsilon t$

   where $\varepsilon t \sim iidN ( o, \sigma t2 )$

   (i) states that rationally expected money supply depends on the amount of relevant information, It-1 available before the forecast at time, t-1. This is conditional expectation used for forecast. The value of the forecast is the mathematical expectation that results from the reduced form of the variable.

   (ii) states that rational expectations do not imply perfect forecast. Instead, it allows for a random error et = Mt - E [Mt/ It-1] which cannot contain systematic component. Thus, rational expectations produce an unbiased estimate of the future values of the endogenous variable.


7. Dornbusch, R. (1975), "Inflation, Growth and Unemployment: An Expository Frame Work" (Mimeograph).

8. Sims, C.A. (1972), "Money, Income and Causality:" The American Economic Review, Vol. LXII, No.4, pp. 540-552.


9. D.W. Statistics = 2.47. So 4 – D.W. = 4 – 2.47 = 1.53, indicates the absence of A.C. in the estimated equation (1).

10. Alternative Estimated Models:

    (i) $m_t = \alpha + \beta m_{t-1} + v_t$ : $m_t = -1.5598 + 1.1714 m_{t-1}$ (OLS)

    (3.0876) (0.0041816)

    [–0.5052] [280.12]

    D.F = 39 $R^2 = 0.9995$ F* = 78467 D.W. = 2.87

(ii) $\log m_t = \alpha + \beta \log m_{t-1} + v_t$ : $M_t = -0.0043823 + 1.0261 M_{t-1}$ (OLS)

i.e. $M_t = \alpha + \beta \log M_{t-1} + v_t$ (0.008844) (0.00039337)

[-0.4955] [260.85]

D.F = 39 $R^2 = 0.99942$ $F^* = 68044$ D.W. = 0.845

[Small scripts for the variables represent the data set without any transformation used for the variables concerned. Both the estimated models (i) and (ii) with non-stationary data set suffer from A.C., hence, rejected]

(iii) $m_t = \alpha + \beta_1 m_{t-1} + \beta_2 y_{t-1} + u_t$ : $m_t = -6.1284 + 1.114 m_{t-1} + 0.028292 y_{t-1}$ (OLS)

(3.6519 (0.027216) (0.013276)

[-1.6782] [40.931] [2.1311] D.F = 38

$R^2 = 0.9995$ $F^* = 42792$ D.W. = 2.83

(iv) $\log m_t = \alpha + \beta_1 \log m_{t-1} + \beta_2 \log y_{t-1} + u_t$ : $M_t = -0.1303 + 0.9082 M_{t-1} + 0.1416 Y_{t-1}$ (OLS)

i.e. $M_t = \alpha + \beta_1 M_{t-1} + \beta_2 Y_{t-1} + v_t$

(0.068441) (0.063697) (0.076346)

[-1.9044] [14.257] [1.8550]

D.F = 38 $R^2 = 0.9994$ $F^* = 36153$ D.W. = 0.898

(v) $M'_t = \alpha + \beta_1 M'_{t-1} + \beta_2 Y'_{t-1} + v'_t$ : $M'_t = 0.01610 + 0.7125 M'_{t-1} + 0.17441 Y'_{t-1}$ (GLS)

(0.005391) (0.1049) (0.095244)

[2.9865] [6.7893] [0.1831]

D.F = 37 $R^2 = 0.62603$ $F^* = 30.97$ D.W. = 2.47

[Both the estimated models (iii) and (iv) with non-stationary data set suffer from A.C. The estimated model (v) with stationary data set shows that the co-efficient $\beta_2$ is insignificant even at 1% level. Hence, these estimated models are rejected.]

11. D.W. Statistics = 1.99. So 4 – D.W. = 4 – 1.99 = 2.01, indicates the absence of A.C. in the estimated equation (2).

12. In order to confirm $\beta_2$ being insignificant, the equation (4) is further estimated with the following modification where $UM_t$ is the only independent variable:

$y_t = \delta + \beta_2 UM_t + w_t$

The GLS estimation of the equation is

$y_t = -0.0041209 + 0.086891 UM_t$

(0.0039412) (0.2623)

[-1.0456] [0.3311]

$R^2$ = 0.0032132 D.F. = 37

F* = 0.1096 D.W. = 1.52

It is observed that,

(i) the estimated equation is not good fit since $R^2$ and F* are very small;

(ii) the equation is free from auto-correlation at 1% level;

(iii) $\beta_2$ is not significant even at 1% level.

This further indicates that unanticipated money supply bears no effect on the variation of output around its capacity level ($Y_p$) over the period concerned (1950-91).

13. Here $y_t = Y_t - Y_p$. However, $Y_p$ is proxies through Y (mean).

14. The OLS estimation of the equation (2), we get $w_t$ = –1.8339 + 0.8324 Mte + 0.8404UMt

(0.017988) (0.0078116) + (0.3272)

[-101.95] [106.55] [2.5685]

D.F = 38 $R^2$ = 0.9966

F* = 5678.8 D.W. = 0.5062

This is an alternative OLS estimation of non-stationary data set of the equation (2).

It is observed that the regression constant (α) and the regression coefficient ($\beta_1$ and $\beta_2$) are significant even at 5% level; the equation is good fit since $R^2$ = 0.996 and F* = 5678; and the equation suffers from A.C. at 5% level. So the equation is not considered for the analysis in our study.

## 9.12 Non-Parametric Tests

A statistical test is a formal technique, based on some probability distribution, for arriving at a decision about the validity of an assertion or hypothesis. The test technique makes use of one or more values obtained from sample data to arrive at a probability statement about the hypothesis. It is generally assumed that all practical data follow normal distribution. Under such situations, **one** can estimate the parameters such as mean, variance, etc., and use the standard tests which have been discussed in earlier chapter. Hence, they are known as ***parametric*** tests. The normality of the population distribution forms the basis for making statistical inferences about the sample drawn from the population. But no such assumptions are made in case of non-parametric tests.

In some situations, the practical data may be non-normal and/or it may not be possible to estimate the parameter(s) of the data. The tests which are used for such situations are called *non-parametric* tests. Since these tests are based on the data which are free from distribution and parameter, these tests are known as non-parametric tests.

The non-parametric tests can be used even for nominal data like qualitative data and ordinal data like ranked data. These tests require less calculation, because there is no need to compute parameters. Also, these tests can be applied to very small samples, more specifically during pilot studies in market research.

In a statistical test, two kinds of assertions are involved viz., an assertion directly related to the purpose of investigation and other assertions to make a probability statement. The former is an assertion to be tested and is technically called a hypothesis, whereas the set of all other assertions is called the model. When we apply a test (to test the hypothesis) without a model, it is known as distribution-free test, or the non-parametric test. Non-parametric tests do not make an assumption about the parameters of the population and thus do not make use of the parameters of the distribution. In other words, under non-parametric or distribution-free tests we do not assume that a particular distribution is applicable, or that a certain value is attached to a parameter of the population. For instance, while testing the two training methods, say *A* and *B*, for determining the superiority of one over the other, if we do not assume that the scores of the trainees are normally distributed or that the mean score of all trainees taking method *A* would be a certain value, then the testing method is known as a distribution-free or non-parametric method. In fact, there is a growing use of such tests in situations when the normality assumption is open to doubt. As a result many distribution-free tests have been developed that do not depend on the shape of the distribution or deal with the parameters of the underlying population.

Inference about the population can be made by the non-parametric tests when the assumptions of the standard methods cannot be satisfied, since the non-parametric tests involve no or less restricting assumptions when compared to the parametric tests.

There are many non-parametric tests, however, following are considered important and discussed in this chapter:

(i) One-sample sign test,

(ii) Two-sample sign test,

(iii) Rank correlation,

(iv) Test of a hypothesis concerning variation in the given data i.e., test analogous to ANOVA viz., Kruskal-Wallis test,

(v) Tests of randomness of a sample based on the theory of runs viz., one sample runs test,

(vi) Test of hypothesis to determine if categorical data shows dependency or if two classifications are independent viz., the chi-square test, (which has already been discussed. It is used as parametric test as it is used to make comparison between theoretical populations and actual data when categories are used).

### 9.12.1 Sign Tests

The sign test is one of the easiest parametric tests. Its name comes from the fact that it is based on the direction of the plus or minus signs of observations in a sample and not on their numerical magnitudes. The sign test may be one of the following two types:

(a) One-sample sign test;

(b) Two-sample sign test.

#### One-sample Sign Test

This one-sample sign test is applied to a situation where a sample is taken from a population which has a continuous symmetrical distribution and known to be non-normal such that the probability of having a sample value less than the mean value as well as the probability of having a sample value more than the mean value *(p)* is 1/2. It will be difficult to verify the symmetry of the distribution when the sample size is small. Hence, under such situation, it is better to formulate the hypotheses using its median (m). Here, based on the hypothesized 'population mean' (when the sample size is large), 'population median' (when the sample size is small), each sample observation will be classified into either plus (+) or minus (–). After counting the total pluses, a hypothesis is tested whether proportion is same or more. Let us see the example below:

## Solved Example

A salesman visits 11 retail stores at random and time spent on each store in minutes are 13, 12, 17, 10, 9, 8, 15, 14, 11, 14, 8. Using sign test at 5% level of significance to test the hypothesis that the salesman spends 15 minutes in a store against the alternate hypothesis that he spends less than 15 minutes in a store.

**Solution:** To test the null hypothesis $\mu_{H0} = 15$ against the alternate hypothesis $\mu_{H1} < 15$, we replace + sign for values more than 15, - sign for values less than 15 and ignore the values which have 15 as value, we get as follows:

–,–,+,–,–,–,–,–,–,–.

Now we can test the proportion that one plus sign out of ten trials supports the null hypothesis that $p = ½$ or $p < ½$. The probability of one or fewer successes with n=10 trials can be worked with binomial distribution as follows:

$$^{10}C_1\ p^1q^9 + {}^{10}C_0\ p^0\ q^{10} = 10\ (1/2)^1(1/2)^9 + 1(1/2)^0(1/2)^{10}$$

$$= 0.010+0.001 = 0.011$$

Since this value is less than 5% significance level, we reject null hypothesis and conclude that the salesman spends less than 15 minutes in a store.

Alternate to the above binomial distribution we can also use normal distribution as follows.

Standard deviation of expected proportion $\sigma_p = \sqrt{\frac{pq}{n}} = \sqrt{\frac{\frac{1}{2}*\frac{1}{2}}{10}} = 0.1581$

Using one tail test, (because less than is the alternate hypothesis) we have probability of 0.45 on the left side of normal distribution, so t stat for 8 DF = 1.859, so expected proportion is

$p_L = ½-1.859*0.1581= 0.214$, which is the lower limit of acceptance. As our proportion is only $1/10 = 0.1$, so we reject hypothesis that $p = 1/2$, rather say $p<1/2$

## Another Example

The weight of a drug produced by a Pharmaceutical Company follows non-normal distribution. The specified weight of the drug of this population is 100 mg. Any excess weight of the drug will lead to side reactions. The quality engineer of the firm claims that the weight of the drug is not greater than the specified mean weight of the population. So, the purchase manager of a Hospital who places an order for that drug with the Pharmaceutical Company has selected a random sample of 36 drugs and their weights.

| | | | | | | | | |
|---|---|---|---|---|---|---|---|---|
| 101 | 102 | 95 | 103 | 96 | 103 | 101 | 103 | 105 |
| 99 | 100 | 99 | 102 | 104 | 102 | 108 | 102 | 101 |
| 91 | 95 | 98 | 101 | 109 | 103 | 102 | 109 | 106 |

Verify the intuition of the quality manager of Alpha Pharmaceutical Company that the weight of the drugs is 100 mg ($H_0$: $\mu = 100$), against the alternate hypothesis ($H_1$: $\mu > 100$), using sign test at a significance level of 0.05.

**Solution:**

By taking + sign for more than 100 and – sign for less than 100 and ignoring 100, we have

| | | | | | | | | |
|---|---|---|---|---|---|---|---|---|
| + | + | – | + | – | + | + | + | + |
| – | 0 | – | + | + | + | + | + | + |
| – | – | – | + | + | + | + | + | + |
| – | – | – | + | + | + | + | – | + |

No. of pluses = 24

No. minus = 11

Since n is more than 30, we can use Z as normal variate.

Standard deviation of expected proportion $\sigma_p = \sqrt{\frac{pq}{n}} = \sqrt{\frac{\frac{1}{2}*\frac{1}{2}}{35}} = 0.084$

Using one tail test, (because greater than is the alternate hypothesis) we have probability of 0.45 on the left side of normal distribution, so z = 1.65, so expected proportion is

$P_U$ = ½ + 1.64*0.084 = 0.638 which is the upper limit of acceptance of null hypothesis. As our proportion is only 24/35 = 0.69, so we reject null hypothesis that is p=1/2, rather say p >1/2 i.e drug quantity is more than 100 mg.

## Two Sample Sign Test

Before placement, 2 students were examined on 30 counts and scored following grades, check at 1% significance level whether X is better than Y.

X = 1, 0, 2, 3, 1, 0, 2, 2, 3, 0, 1, 1, 4, 1, 2, 1, 3, 5, 2, 1, 3, 2, 4, 1, 3, 2, 0, 2, 4, 2

Y = 0, 0, 1, 0, 2, 0, 0, 1, 1, 2, 0, 1, 2, 1, 1, 0, 2, 2, 6, 0 , 2, 3, 0, 2, 1, 0, 1, 0, 1, 0

**Solution:**

Compare X and Y, if X > Y, write + else -, ignore if they are equal

X = 1, 0, 2, 3, 1, 0, 2, 2, 3, 0, 1, 1, 4, 1, 2, 1, 3, 5, 2, 1, 3, 2, 4, 1, 3, 2, 0, 2, 4, 2

Y = 0, 0, 1, 0, 2, 0, 0, 1, 1, 2, 0, 1, 2, 1, 1,0, 2, 2 ,6 ,0 ,2 ,3 ,0 ,2 ,1 ,0 ,1 ,0 ,1, 0

+ 0 + + – 0 + + + – + 0 + 0 + + + + – + + – + – – + + – + ++

Total Number of + signs = 20

Total Number of – signs = 6

Total sample size = 26

The observed proportion of pluses is 20/26 = 0.769

Since n is less than 30, we can use t-stat

Standard deviation of expected proportion $\sigma_p = \sqrt{\frac{pq}{n}} = \sqrt{\frac{\frac{1}{2} * \frac{1}{2}}{26}} = 0.0981$

Using one tail test, (because greater than is the alternate hypothesis) we have probability of 0.49 on the right side of t-stat, so t for 25 DF at .01 = 2.485, so expected proportion (upper limit) is

$P_U$ = ½ + 2.485*0.0981 = 0.744 which is the upper limit of acceptance of null hypothesis. As our proportion is 20/36 = 0.769, so we reject null hypothesis and accept H, i.e., both students not are equal.

### 9.12.2 Kolmogorov-Smirnov Test

Kolmogorov-Smirnov (K-S) test is similar to the chi-square test as discussed in earlier chapter to do goodness of fit of a given set of data to an assumed distribution. This test is more powerful for small samples whereas the chi-square test is suited for large samples.

The combination of hypotheses used in this test is as:

$H_0$: The given set of observations follows the assumed distribution.

$H_1$: The given set of observations does not follow the assumed distribution.

In K-S test, the values of the observed cumulative distribution of the random variable in a given situation are compared with the corresponding values of the theoretical cumulative distribution of the random variable and their absolute differences are calculated. Then, the maximum of these absolute differences is treated as the calculated statistic of K-S test, namely $D_{cal}$ which is given by the following formula:

$$D_{cal} = \max|OF_i - EF_i|$$

where $OF_i$ is the observed cumulative probability for the ith value of the random variable *X*, $EF_i$ is the expected cumulative probability for the ith value of the random variable *X*, from the theoretical distribution.

For a given significance level *(a)* and the sample size, the theoretical value of *D* can be obtained from K-S, D tables. This theoretical value of *D* is distribution-free, as it is a function of the significance level *(α)* and the sample size *(n)*.

The Kolmogorov-Smirnov test is a one-tailed test. Hence, if the calculated value of *D* is more than the theoretical value of *D* for a given significance level, then reject the null hypothesis; otherwise, accept the null hypothesis.

**Solved Example**

The GD-PI score of the MBA entrance in a college was found to be as follows, check whether the given data follows uniform distribution using Kolmogorov-Smirnov test at 5% significance level.

| GD-PI score | Frequency |
|---|---|
| 41 | 2 |
| 42 | 3 |
| 43 | 1 |
| 44 | 4 |
| 45 | 2 |
| 46 | 2 |
| 47 | 4 |
| 48 | 2 |
| 49 | 4 |
| 50 | 1 |

**Solution:**

$H_0$: The given set of observations follows the assumed distribution.

$H_1$: The given set of observations does not follow the assumed distribution.

Total observed frequencies = 25

Number of observations $X_i$ = 10

Expected frequency for each $X_i$ = 25/10 = 2.5

Expected probability for each $X_i$ = 2.5/25 = 0.1

| GD-PI Score | Observed Frequency | Observed Probability | Expected Probability | Observed Cumulative Probability (OF) | Expected Cumulative Probability (EF) | D = \|OF-OE\| |
|---|---|---|---|---|---|---|
| 41 | 2 | 0.08 | 0.10 | 0.08 | 0.10 | 0.02 |
| 42 | 3 | 0.12 | 0.10 | 0.20 | 0.20 | 0.00 |
| 43 | 1 | 0.04 | 0.10 | 0.24 | 0.30 | 0.06 |
| 44 | 4 | 0.16 | 0.10 | 0.40 | 0.40 | 0.00 |
| 45 | 2 | 0.08 | 0.10 | 0.48 | 0.50 | 0.02 |
| 46 | 2 | 0.08 | 0.10 | 0.56 | 0.60 | 0.04 |
| 47 | 4 | 0.16 | 0.10 | 0.72 | 0.70 | 0.02 |
| 48 | 2 | 0.08 | 0.10 | 0.80 | 0.80 | 0.00 |
| 49 | 4 | 0.16 | 0.10 | 0.96 | 0.90 | 0.06 |
| 50 | 1 | 0.04 | 0.10 | 1.00 | 1.00 | 0.00 |

The maximum value of $D_{cal}$ = 0.06 which is either 43 or 49. The table value $D_n$ for sample size 25 at significance level of 5% is 0.27.

Since the calculated value is less than table value hence, accept $H_0$, which means given data follow normal distribution.

### 9.12.3 Run Test for Randomness

Consider the example of arrivals of customers at a food bazaar of a mall. The store manager wants to verify whether the gender of the arriving customers is random.

An example sequence of arriving customers is shown as below, in which M means male and F means female.

MM FFF MMM FFF M F MMMM FF

In this sequence of customers, the number of male customers is 10 and the number of female customers is 9.

In this context, a run is defined as a sequence which consists of repeated occurrence of a particular symbol and the immediate preceding and succeeding symbols are different from the symbol in it or no other symbol on either side.

Though the proportion of the number of male customers and that of the female customers is almost same in this example, here the objective is to test about the randomness of the occurrence of runs at a given significance level, $\alpha$.

Let $n_1$ be the frequency of occurrence of a particular symbol in the whole stream of symbols, $n_2$ be the frequency of occurrence of another symbol in the whole stream of symbols and $r$ be the number of runs.

If $n_1$ as well as $n_2$ is less than or equal to 20, then the sample is treated as a small sample. If either $n_1$ or $n_2$, or both is/are larger than 20, then the sample is treated as a larger sample.

The combination of hypotheses for the run test of randomness is:

$H_0$ : The occurrence of the runs in the given stream of symbols is random.

$H_1$: The occurrence of the runs in the given stream of symbols is not random.

For such Run Tests, statisticians have made the tables. If the sample size is small, (less than 20) find the small critical value and large critical values. If the observed r value is less than or equal to the smaller critical value, or more than or equal to the larger critical value for the given combination of $n_1$ and $n_2$ at the given significance level ($\alpha$), then reject the null hypothesis; otherwise, accept the null hypothesis.

**Example**

Consider the example stated earlier as reproduced below:

The manager of a mall store wants to verify whether the gender of the arriving customers is random.

Check the randomness of gender of the arriving customers at a significance level of 0.05.

MMFFFMMMFFFMFMMMMFF

**Solution:**

The given stream of arrivals of male and female customers is as shown below with underscoring to represent different runs:

MM FFF MMM FFF M F MMMM FF

Frequency of occurrence of M, $n_1$ = 10

Frequency of occurrence of F, $n_2$ = 9

Number of runs, = 8

Significance level, a = 0.05

Since both $n_1$ and $n_2$ are less than 20, the sample of the problem is to be treated as small.

Now, consider

$H_0$: The occurrence of the runs of the given stream of symbols (M, F) is random.

$H_1$: The occurrence of the runs of the given stream of symbols (M, F) is not random.

From Annexure table, the smaller critical value, and the larger critical value for the given combination of $n_1$ (10) and $n_2$ (9) at a significance level of 0.05 are 5 and 16, respectively.

Since the calculated number of runs, $r_{cal}$ (8), is not less than the smaller critical value (5) as well as not greater than the larger critical value (16), accept the null hypothesis.

Thus the occurrences of the sub-streams of M and F are random.

## When Sample is Large

As stated earlier, if $n_1$ or $n_2$ or both is/are more than 20, then the sample is treated as a large sample. Under such situation, one can approximate the sampling distribution of r to normal distribution with the following mean and variance:

$$\text{Mean of r } (\mu) = \frac{2n_1n_2}{n_1+n_2}+1$$

$$\text{Variance of r } (\sigma^2) = \frac{2n_1n_2(2_{n2}-{n1}-{n2})}{(n_1+n_2)^2({n1}+{n2}-1)}$$

The formula for the standard normal statistic to test the significance of *r* is as shown below:

$$Z=\frac{r-\mu}{\sigma}$$

It is a two-tailed test. Hence, the values of table $-Z_{\alpha/2}$ and $z_{\alpha/2}$ , define the left critical value and right critical value of *r*. If the calculated Z value is in between $-Z_{\alpha/2}$ and $z_{\alpha/2}$, then accept the null hypothesis; otherwise reject the null hypothesis.

## Solved Example

The manager of a mall store wants to verify whether the gender of the arriving customers is random.

Check the randomness of gender of the arriving customers at a significance level of 0.05.

MM FF MMMMMM FF MMM F MMM FF MM FF MM FFF M FF MMM FF MM

The given stream of arrivals of male and female customers is as shown below with underscoring to represent different runs:

MM FF MMMMMM FF MMM F MMM FF MM FF MM FFF M FF MMM FF MM

Frequency of occurrence of M, $n_1$ = 24

Frequency of occurrence of F, $n_2$ = 16

Number of runs = 17

Significance level, *a* = 0.05

Since $n_1$ is more than 20, sample of problem is large.

$H_0$: The occurrence of the runs of the given stream of symbols (M, F) is random.

$H_1$: The occurrence of the runs of the given stream of symbols (M, F) is not random.

$$\text{Mean of } r\ (\mu) = \frac{2n_1n_2}{n_1+n_2}+1 = (2*24*16)/(26+14)+1 = 20.2$$

$$\text{Variance of } r\ (\sigma^2) = \frac{2n_1n_2(2n_1n_2-n_1-n_2)}{(n_1 \quad n_2)^2(n_1 \quad n_2-1)}$$

$= \{(2*24*16)(2*24*16\text{-}24\text{-}16)\}/\{(24+16)^2(24+16\text{-}1)\}$

$= 8.96$

Standard Deviation $= \sigma = 2.993$

The formula for the standard normal statistic to test the significance of $r$ is as shown below:

$$z = \frac{r-\mu}{\sigma} = (17-20.2)/2.99\ 3 = -1.069$$

For two tail test value of Z for 5% significance level is -1.96 and +1.96, since the calculated value falls within range, hence accept $H_0$ which means male and female are random.

### 9.12.4 Mann-Whitney U Test

**The** Mann-Whitney *U* **test (also called the Mann-Whitney-Wilcoxon (MWW),** Wilcoxon **rank-sum test**, or **Wilcoxon-Mann-Whitney test)** is a non-parametric test for assessing whether two samples of observations come from the same distribution. The null hypothesis is that the two samples are drawn from a single population, and therefore that their probability distributions are equal. It requires the two samples to be independent, and the observations to be ordinal or continuous measurements, i.e. one can at least say, of any two observations, which is the greater. In a less general formulation, the Wilcoxon-Mann-Whitney two-sample test may be thought of as testing the null hypothesis that the probability of an observation from one population exceeding an observation from the second population is 0.5. This formulation requires the additional assumption that the distributions of the two populations are identical except for possibly a shift (i.e., $f_1(x) = f_2(x + ä)$). Another alternative interpretation is that the test assesses whether the Hodges-Lehmann estimate of the difference in central tendency between the two populations is zero. The Hodges-Lehmann estimate for this two-sample problem is the median of all possible differences between an observation in the first sample and an observation in the second sample. It is commonly thought that the MWW test, tests for differences in medians but this is not strictly true.

The test involves the calculation of a statistic, usually called *U*, whose distribution under the null hypothesis is known. In the case of small samples, the distribution is tabulated, but for samples above 20 there is a good approximation using the normal distribution. Some books tabulate statistics equivalent to *U*, such as the sum of ranks in one of the samples.

The *U* test is included in most modern statistical packages. It is also easily calculated by hand, especially for small samples. There are two ways of doing this.

For small samples a direct method is recommended. It is very quick, and gives an insight into the meaning of the *U* statistic.

1. Choose the sample for which the ranks seem to be smaller (The only reason to do this is to make computation easier). Call this "sample 1," and call the other sample "sample 2."
2. Taking each observation in sample 2, count the number of observations in sample 1 that are smaller than it (count a half for any that are equal to it).
3. The total of these counts is $U$.

For larger samples, a formula can be used:

1. Arrange all the observations into a single ranked series. That is, rank all the observations without regard to which sample they are in.
2. Add up the ranks in sample 1. The sum of ranks in sample 2 follows by calculation, since the sum of all the ranks equals $N(N + 1)/2$ where $N$ is the total number of observations.
3. "U" is then given by:

$$U = n_1n_2 + (n_1(n_1+1))/2 - R_1$$

where $n_1$ is the two sample size for sample 1, and $R_1$ is the sum of the ranks in sample 1

$$m_U = (n_1n_2)/2$$

$$s_U^2 = (n_1n_2)(n_1+n_2+1)/12$$

$$Z_U = (U - m_U)/s_U$$

The null hypothesis of this test is:

$H_0$: Two samples are drawn from different populations having the same distribution.

A suitable alternate hypothesis ($H_1$) can be assumed as per the reality and it may be one of the following:

$H_1$: Population 1 is stochastically larger than population 2 (greater than type).Under this case, if the calculated $Z_U$ is less than -Za, then reject $H_0$; otherwise accept $H_0$.

OR

$H_2$: Population 1 is stochastically lesser than population 2 (smaller than type). Under this case, if the calculated $Z_U$ is more than $Z_\alpha$, then reject $H_0$; otherwise accept $H_0$.

OR

$H_3$ : Population 1 stochastically differs from population 2 (not equal to type). Under this case, if the calculated $Z_U$ is less than $-Z_\alpha$or more than $+ Z_\alpha$, then reject $H_0$; otherwise accept $H_0$.

**Solved Example:**

In a marketing company, the performance indices of a randomly selected sample of salesmen of each of its two branches located in different cities are summarized below. Check whether the two samples are drawn from identical populations against the alternate hypothesis that the first population is stochastically larger than the second population at a significance level of 0.05.

| Performance of Employees | | | |
|---|---|---|---|
| **Branch 1** | **Branch 2** | **Branch 1** | **Branch 2** |
| 87 | 78 | 91 | 83 |
| 76 | 55 | 68 | 97 |
| 57 | 92 | 73 | 53 |
| 50 | 71 | 79 | 89 |
| 43 | 25 | 59 | 74 |
| 73 | 62 | 50 | 30 |
| 40 | 45 | 35 | 54 |
| 90 | 77 | 82 | 32 |
| 75 | 34 | 73 | - |
| 85 | 50 | 66 | - |

**Solution:**

The number of programmers from the Branch-1 $n_1$ = 20. The number of programmers from the Branch-2, $n_2$ = 18. Significance level, $\alpha$ - 0.05. The combination of hypotheses for the problem situation is:

$H_0$: Two samples are drawn from different populations having the same distribution.

$H_1$: The mean performance ratings of the salesmen from the population of the Branch- 1 is stochastically larger than that of the programmers from the population of the Branch-2.

**Rule for decision-making:** Under this case, if the calculated $Z_v$ is more than table value, reject $H_0$; otherwise accept $H_0$.

**The pooled rank is shown below**

| Branch | Index | Rank | Branch | Index | Rank |
|---|---|---|---|---|---|
| 2 | 25 | 1 | 2 | 71 | 20 |
| 2 | 30 | 2 | 1 | 73 | 21 |
| 2 | 32 | 3 | 1 | 73 | 22 |
| 2 | 34 | 4 | 1 | 73 | 23 |
| 1 | 35 | 5 | 2 | 74 | 24 |
| 1 | 40 | 6 | 1 | 75 | 25 |
| 1 | 43 | 7 | 1 | 76 | 26 |
| 2 | 45 | 8 | 2 | 77 | 27 |
| 1 | 50 | 9 | 2 | 78 | 28 |
| 1 | 50 | 10 | 1 | 79 | 29 |
| 2 | 50 | 11 | 1 | 82 | 30 |
| 2 | 53 | 12 | 2 | 83 | 31 |
| 2 | 54 | 13 | 1 | 85 | 32 |
| 2 | 55 | 14 | 1 | 87 | 33 |
| 1 | 57 | 15 | 2 | 89 | 34 |
| 1 | 59 | 16 | 1 | 90 | 35 |

| 2 | 62 | 17 | 1 | 91 | 36 |
|---|---|---|---|---|---|
| 1 | 66 | 18 | 2 | 92 | 37 |
| 1 | 68 | 19 | 2 | 97 | 38 |

The observation 50 and 73 are repeated three times hence their ranks shall be their mean rank, for 50 it is (9+10+11)/3 = 10 and for 73 it is (21+22+23)/3 = 22

Rank of sample –1 = 5, 6, 7,10, 10,15, 16, 18, 19, 22, 22, 22, 25, 26, 29, 30, 32, 33, 35, 36

Sum of rank of sample 1 = $R_1$ = 418

Rank of sample 2 = 1, 2, 3, 4, 8, 10, 12, 13, 14, 17, 20, 24, 27, 28, 31, 34, 37, 38

Sum of rank of sample 2 = 323

$U = n_1n_2 + (n_1(n_1+1))/2 - R_1 = 20*18 + (20*21)/2 - 418 = 152$

where $n_1$ is the sample size for sample 1, and $R_1$ is the sum of the ranks in sample 1

$\mu_U = (n_1n_2)/2 = 20*18/2 = 180$

$\sigma_U^2 = (n_1n_2)(n_1+n_2+1)/12 = 20*18*(20+18+1)/12 = 1170$

$\sigma_U = (U - \mu_U)/\sigma_U$

$Z_U = (U - \mu_U)/\sigma_U = (152-180)/34.21 = -0.819$

The standard normal value for Z at 5% significance level at 1% level is 1.64, since calculated value is less than 1.64, we accept $H_0$ which means two samples are drawn from population having identical distribution.

### 9.12.5 Kendall's *Coefficient* of Concordance

Kendall's Coefficient of Concordance is an important non-parametric measure of relationship. Symbolically it is represented as W. It is used for determining the degree of association among several sets of ranking of objects or individuals. When there are only two sets of rankings of objects, Spearman's coefficient of correlation is worked out, but Kendall's coefficient of concordance *(W)* is considered an appropriate measure of studying the degree of association among three or more sets of rankings. This descriptive measure of the agreement has special applications in providing a standard method of ordering objects according to consensus when we do not have an objective order of the objects.

The basis of Kendall's coefficient of concordance is to imagine how the given data would look if there were no agreement among the several sets of rankings, and then to imagine how it would look if there were perfect agreement among the several sets. For instance, in case of, say, four interviewers interviewing six job applicants and assigning rank order on suitability for employment, if there is observed perfect agreement amongst the interviewers, then one applicant would be assigned rank 1 by all the four and the sum of his ranks would be 1 + 1 + 1 + 1= 4. Another applicant would be assigned a rank 2 by all four and the sum of his ranks will be 2 + 2 + 2 + 2 = 8. The sum of ranks for the six applicants would be 4, 8, 12, 16, 20 and 24 (not necessarily in this very order). In general, when perfect agreement exists among ranks assigned by *k* judges to *N* objects, the rank sums are *k*, *2k*, 3k, ... *Nk*. The, total sum of ranks for *k* judges is *kN(N* + l)/2 and the mean rank sum *is k(N* + l)/ 2. The degree of agreement between judges reflects itself in the variation in the rank sums. When all judges agree, this sum is a maximum. Disagreement between judges reflects itself in a reduction in the variation of rank sums. For maximum disagreement, the rank sums will tend to be more or less equal. This provides the basis for the definition of a coefficient of concordance. When perfect agreement exists between judges, *W* equals to 1. When maximum disagreement exists, *W* equals to 0. It may be noted that *W* does not take negative values because of the fact that with more than two judges complete disagreement cannot take place. Thus, coefficient of concordance (W) is an index of divergence of the actual agreement shown in the data from the perfect agreement.

The procedure for computing and interpreting Kendall's coefficient of concordance *(W)* is as follows:

(a) All the objects, *N*, should be ranked by all *k* judges in the usual fashion and this information may be put in the form of a *k* by N matrix;

(b) For each object determine the sum of ranks ($R_j$) assigned by all the *k* judges;

(c) Determine $\overline{R}_j$ and then obtain the value of *s* as under:

$$s = (\overline{R}_j - \overline{R}_j)$$

(d) Work out the value of *W* using the following formula:

$$W = \frac{s}{\frac{1}{12}k^2(N^3 - N)}$$

Where tied ranks occur, the average method of assigning ranks be adopted i.e., assign to each member the average rank which the tied observations occupy. If the ties are not numerous, we may compute W as stated above without making any adjustment in the formula; but if the ties are numerous, a correction factor is calculated for each set of ranks. This correction factor is given as:

$$T = \frac{\Sigma(t^3 - t)}{12}$$

where $t$ = number of observations in a group tied for a given rank.

A correction factor *T* is calculated for each of the *k* sets of ranks and these are added together over the *k* sets to obtain $\Sigma T$ and formula for W changes as follows:

$$W = \frac{s}{\frac{1}{12}k^2(N^3 - N) - k\Sigma T}$$

If sample size is less than 7, W is compared with tables given by statistician, otherwise $\chi^2$ value for judging W's significance.

**Solved Example:**

Eight individuals have been assigned ranks by four judges at a certain competition as shown below. Is there significant agreement in ranking assigned by different judges? Test at 5% level. Also point out the best estimate of true rankings.

| | Individuals | | | | | | | |
|---|---|---|---|---|---|---|---|---|
| **Judges** | A | B | C | D | E | F | G | H |
| Judge 1 | 1 | 3 | 2 | 5 | 7 | 4 | 6 | 8 |
| Judge 2 | 2 | 4 | 1 | 3 | 7 | 5 | 6 | 8 |
| Judge 3 | 3 | 4 | 1 | 2 | 7 | 6 | 5 | 8 |
| Judge 4 | 1 | 2 | 5 | 4 | 6 | 3 | 7 | 8 |

**Solution:**

With four judges and seven individuals let us first find s.

| | Individuals | | | | | | | |
|---|---|---|---|---|---|---|---|---|
| **Judges** | A | B | C | D | E | F | G | H |
| Judge 1 | 1 | 3 | 2 | 5 | 7 | 4 | 6 | 8 |
| Judge 2 | 2 | 4 | 1 | 3 | 7 | 5 | 6 | 8 |
| Judge 3 | 3 | 4 | 1 | 2 | 7 | 6 | 5 | 8 |
| Judge 4 | 1 | 2 | 5 | 4 | 6 | 3 | 7 | 8 |
| Sum of Ranks ($R_j$) | 7 | 13 | 9 | 14 | 27 | 18 | 24 | 32 |
| s = $(R_j - \overline{R_j})^2$ | 121 | 25 | 81 | 16 | 81 | 0 | 36 | 196 |

$\Sigma R_j = 7+13+9+14+27+18+24+32 = 144$

$\overline{R_j} = 144/8 = 18$

First calculation is $(7-18)^2 = 121$

$$s = \Sigma(R_j - \overline{R}_j) = 556$$

$$W = \frac{S}{\frac{1}{12}k^2(N^3 - N)} = \frac{556}{\frac{1}{12}4^2(8^3 - 8)} = 556/672 = 0.827$$

As N is larger than 7, we shall calculate the value of $\chi^2$ as follows

$\chi^2 = k(N\text{-}1)*W = 4*7*0.827 = 23.167$

Table value of $c^2$ for (8-1) = 7 DF at 5% significance level is 14.067

As calculated value is higher than tabulated value we can reject the null hypothesis that there is a difference among judges. As such we can infer that W is significant at 5% level.

As already stated W lies between 0 and 1. When it is 0 there is no agreement between judges but at 1 judges are perfectly in agreement. When W is 0.827, it is near to 1 and have been tested by $c^2$.

### 9.12.6 Kruskal-Wallis Test (H Test)

The Kruskal-Wallis one-way analysis of variance by ranks is again a non-parametric method for testing equality of population medians among groups. Intuitively, it is identical to a one-way analysis of variance with the data replaced by their ranks. It is an extension of the Mann-Whitney U test to 3 or more groups.

Since it is a non-parametric method, the Kruskal-Wallis test does not assume a normal population, unlike the analogous one-way analysis of variance. However, the test does assume an identically-shaped distribution for each group, except for any difference in medians. H follows chi-square distribution with K-1 degrees of freedom.

Rank all data from all groups together; i.e., rank the data from 1 to N ignoring group membership. Assign any tied values the average of the ranks they would have received had they not been tied. H statistic is given as:

$$H = \frac{12}{N(N-1)} \Sigma \frac{R_j^2}{n_j} - 3(N+1)$$

Where $R_j$ is the sum the ranks of the sample j, $n_j$ is the sample j, N is the size of pooled data.

If the value of H is more than the table chi-square value, then reject the null hypothesis; otherwise accept the null hypothesis.

## Solved Example

The production volume of units assembled by three different operators (A, B and C) during 9 shifts are summarized below. Check whether there is significant difference between the production volumes of units assembled by the three operators using Kruskal-Wallis test at a significance level of 0.05.

| | Production Volume of Units Assembled | | |
|---|---|---|---|
| Shift No. | A | B | C |
| 1 | 29 | 30 | 26 |
| 2 | 34 | 21 | 36 |
| 3 | 34 | 23 | 41 |
| 4 | 20 | 25 | 48 |
| 5 | 32 | 44 | 27 |
| 6 | 45 | 37 | 39 |
| 7 | 42 | 34 | 28 |
| 8 | 24 | 19 | 46 |
| 9 | 35 | 38 | 15 |

**Solution:**

Total N = n1 + n2 + n3 = 9 + 9 + 9 = 27

Hypothesis

$H_0$: There is no significant difference in productions by operators

$H_1$: There is a significant difference

Ranking of pooled observations

| Sample No. | Observations | Rank | Sample | Observations | Rank |
|---|---|---|---|---|---|
| 3 | 15 | 1 | 2 | 38 | 20 |
| 2 | 19 | 2 | 3 | 39 | 21 |
| 1 | 20 | 3 | 3 | 41 | 22 |

| | | | | | |
|---|---|---|---|---|---|
| 2 | 21 | 4 | 1 | 42 | 23 |
| 2 | 23 | 5 | 2 | 44 | 24 |
| 1 | 24 | 6 | 1 | 45 | 25 |
| 2 | 25 | 7 | 3 | 46 | 26 |
| 3 | 26 | 8 | 3 | 48 | 27 |
| 3 | 27 | 9 | | | |
| 3 | 28 | 10 | | | |
| 1 | 29 | 11 | | | |
| 2 | 30 | 12 | | | |
| 1 | 32 | 13 | | | |
| 1 | **34** | 14 | | | |
| 1 | **34** | 15 | | | |
| 2 | **34** | 16 | | | |
| 1 | 35 | 17 | | | |
| 3 | 36 | 18 | | | |
| 2 | 37 | 19 | | | |

The observation 34 is repeated three times, hence its revised rank shall be (14 + 15 + 16)/3 = 15,

Sum of Ranks of sample 1 = 3+6+11+13+15+15+17+23+25 = 128

Sum of Ranks of sample 2 = 2+4+5+7+12+15+19+20+24 = 108

Sum of Ranks of sample 3 = 1+8+9+10+18+21+22+26+27 = 142

$$H = \frac{12}{N(N-1)}\Sigma\frac{R_j^2}{n_j} - 3(N+1) = \frac{12}{27(27-1)}\Sigma\frac{128^2}{9} + \frac{108^2}{9} + \frac{142^2}{9} - 3(27+1)$$

= 1.03

The table value of chi-square with 2 DF at 5% significance level is 5.991. Since calculated value of H is less than tabulated value of $x^2$, accept null hypothesis.

There is no significant difference between the production of three operators.

### 9.12.7 Jarque-Bera Test

**The** Jarque-Bera test **is a goodness-of-fit measure of departure from normality, based on the sample kurtosis and skewness. The test statistic *JB* is defined as:**

$$JB = \frac{n}{6}(S^2 + \frac{(K-3)^2}{4})$$

where $n$ is the number of observations (or degrees of freedom in general); $S$ is the sample skewness, $K$ is the sample kurtosis, defined as

$$S = \frac{\mu_3}{\sigma_3} = \frac{\mu_3}{(\sigma^2)^{3/2}} = \frac{\frac{1}{n}\Sigma(x-\overline{x})^3}{\frac{1}{n}\Sigma\left((x-\overline{x})^2\right)^{3/2}}$$

$$K = \frac{\mu_4}{\sigma^4} = \frac{\mu_4}{(\sigma^2)^2} = \frac{\frac{1}{n}\Sigma(x-\overline{x})^4}{\frac{1}{n}\Sigma\left((x-\overline{x})^2\right)^2}$$

where $\mu_3$ and $\mu_4$ are the third and fourth central moments, respectively, $\overline{X}$ is the sample mean, and $\sigma^2$ is the second central moment, the variance.

The statistic *JB* has an asymptotic chi-square distribution with two degrees of freedom and can be used to test the null hypothesis that the data are from a normal distribution. The null hypothesis is a joint hypothesis of the skewness being zero and the excess kurtosis being 0, since samples from a normal distribution have an expected skewness of 0 and an expected excess kurtosis of 0. As the definition of *JB* shows, any deviation from this increases the JB statistic.

### 9.12.8 Remarks on Non-parametric Tests

Parametric tests need populations to be normal, samples to be independent and standard deviation of population to be known, however, some of the conditions are not met. We use non-parametric methods when we do not know parameters of population. They are easier to explain and easier to understand. This is the reason why such tests have become popular. But researchers do not prefer such tests as they are usually less efficient and powerful as they are based on no assumption and we all know that the less one assumes, the less one can infer from a set of data. These tests are mostly used to find out whether samples are from the population which is distribution free or not. Questions of validity (internal validity, construct validity and external validity) shall remain unanswered and many debatable issues shall arise.

#### 9.12.8.1 Problems for Practice

1. The following are the numbers of tickets issued by two counter clerks on 20 days:
   By first man: 7,10,14,12,6,9,11,13,7,6,10,8,14,8,12,11,9,8,10 and 15.

   By second man: 10,13,14,11,10,7,15,11,10,9,8,12,16,10,10,14,10,12,8 and 14.

Use the sign test at 1% level of significance to test the null hypothesis that on the average the two counter issue equal number of tickets against the alternative hypothesis that on the average the second issues more tickets than the first one.

2. A housing contractor plans to build a large number of brick homes in the coming year. Two brick manufacturing concerns have given him nearly identical rates for supplying the bricks. But before placing his order, he wants to apply a test at 5% level of significance. The nature of the test is to subject each sampled brick to a force of 900 pounds. The test is performed on 8 bricks randomly chosen from a day's production of concern A and on the same number of bricks randomly chosen from a day's production of concern *B*. The results were as follows:

Of the 8 bricks from concern A, two were broken and of the 8 bricks from concern B five were broken. On the basis of these test results, determine whether the contractor should place order with concern A or with concern *B* if he prefers significantly stronger bricks.

3. Suppose that the breaking test described in problem 2 above is modified so that each brick is subjected to an increasing force until it breaks. The force applied at the time the brick breaks (calling it the breaking point) is recorded as under:

| | Breaking-points | | | | | | |
|---|---|---|---|---|---|---|---|
| Bricks of concern A | 880, | 950,990, | 975 | 895, | 1030, | 1025 | 1010 |
| Bricks of concern B | 915, | 790,905, | 900, | 890, | 825, | 810 | 885. |

On the basis of the above test results, determine whether the contractor should place order for bricks with concern A or with concern B (You should answer using U test or Wilcoxon-Mann-Whitney test).

4. The following are the kilometres per gallon which a test driver got for ten tankfuls each of three kinds of gasoline:

A 30, 41,34,43,33,34,38,26,29,36

B 39,28,39,29,30,31,44,43,40,33

C 29,41,26,36,41,43,38,38,35,40.

Use the Kruskal-Wallis test at the significance level of 0.05 to test the null hypothesis that there is no difference in the average kilometre yield of the three types of gasoline.

5. The following are the number of students absent from a college on 24 consecutive days:

29,25,31,28,30,28,33,31,35,29,31,33,35,28,36,30,33,26,30,28,32,31,38 and 27. Test for randomness at 1% level of significance.

6. The following arrangement indicates whether 25 consecutive persons interviewed by a social scientist are for (F) or against (A) an increase in the number of crimes in a certain locality:

F, F, F, F, F, F, A, F, F, F, F, F, A, F, F, F, F, A, A, F, F, F, F, F, F.

Test whether this arrangement of A's and F's may be regarded as random at 5% as well as at 10% level of significance.

7. The production rate of spindles produced in a machine follows non-normal distribution. The production manager feels that the production rate of the machine is not different from 75 spindles per hour. To test his intuition, the quality assistant of the shop has selected a random sample of 36 different hourly productions which are as shown below:

| | | | | | | | | |
|---|---|---|---|---|---|---|---|---|
| 67 | 70 | 76 | 85 | 60 | 66 | 80 | 85 | 77 |
| 79 | 80 | 89 | 82 | 74 | 82 | 98 | 82 | 71 |
| 81 | 85 | 78 | 71 | 89 | 83 | 82 | 89 | 86 |
| 72 | 87 | 89 | 78 | 75 | 74 | 73 | 89 | 88 |

Check the intuition of the production manager using sign test at a significance level of 0.05.

8. At a toll gate, 9 randomly selected inter-arrival times (in seconds) are found to be 40, 90, 120, 300, 250, 130, 60, 90 and 100. Check whether the inter-arrival time is 130 seconds ($H_0$: $m$ = 130) as against the alternate hypothesis ($H_1$ : $m >$ 130) using sign test at a significance level of 0.01.

9. The volume of syrup in capsule form produced in a Pharmaceutical Company follows non-normal distribution. The specified volume of the syrup in the capsule of this population is 10 ml. Any excess volume of the syrup will lead to side reactions. The quality engineer of the

firm claims that the volume of the syrup in the capsule is not greater than the specified mean volume of the population. So, the purchase manager of a Hospital who places an order for that capsule with the Pharmaceutical Company has selected a random sample of 32 capsules and their volumes are as given below:

| | | | | | | | |
|---|---|---|---|---|---|---|---|
| 9 | 8 | 10 | 7 | 11 | 12 | 9 | 9.5 |
| 8.5 | 9.9 | 10 | 9 | 6 | 7 | 8 | 8 |
| 9 | 11 | 10 | 9 | 8 | 7 | 9 | 8 |
| 7 | 9.5 | 11 | 13 | 14 | 11 | 8 | 8 |

Verify the intuition of the quality manager of Pharmaceutical Company that the volume of the syrup in the capsule is 10 ml (H0 : $\mu$ = 10), as against the alternate hypothesis H1 > 10 using sign test at a significance level of 0.10.

10. The annual revenue (in lakhs of rupees) of small scale industries in a state follows non-normal distribution. The researcher feels that the annual revenue of the small scale industries is not different from ₹ 150 lakhs. To test his intuition, he has selected a random sample of 32 small scale industries and their annual revenues are as shown below:

| | | | | | | | |
|---|---|---|---|---|---|---|---|
| 170 | 100 | 160 | 150 | 100 | 160 | 100 | 150 |
| 190 | 100 | 190 | 120 | 140 | 120 | 180 | 120 |
| 110 | 150 | 180 | 110 | 190 | 130 | 120 | 190 |
| 120 | 170 | 190 | 180 | 150 | 140 | 130 | 190 |

Check the intuition of the researcher using sign test at a significance level of 0.05

11. The gender of arrival of applicants at a passport office is summarized below in terms of M (male) and F (female). Verify whether the gender of the arriving applicants is random at a significance level of 0.05.

M M M F F M M F F F M M M F F M M M M

12. The monthly production in tons of cement produced in 12 randomly selected cement plants before and after introducing sales tax concession is summarized below. Check whether the monthly production of cement in these plants improved after tax concession using the sign test at a significance level of 1%.

| **Plants** | **Before** | **After** | **Plants** | **Before** | **After** |
|---|---|---|---|---|---|
| 1 | 7 | 9 | 7 | 12 | 18 |
| 2 | 15 | 18 | 8 | 16 | 21 |
| 3 | 6 | 5 | 9 | 10 | 16 |
| 4 | 15 | 19 | 10 | 11 | 14 |
| 5 | 12 | 20 | 11 | 13 | 14 |

13. In a survey, the number of respondents covered by two enumerators during randomly selected days is summarized below. Check with Mann-Whitney U test at significance level of 1% that two samples are drawn from identical population:

| Plants | Before | After | Plants | Before | After |
|---|---|---|---|---|---|
| 1 | 24 | 30 | 8 | 13 | 16 |
| 2 | 17 | 20 | 9 | 22 | 21 |
| 3 | 34 | 15 | 10 | 28 | 8 |
| 4 | 28 | 22 | 11 | 27 | 22 |
| 5 | 15 | 31 | 12 | 15 | 14 |
| 6 | 35 | 24 | 13 | 13 | 16 |
| 7 | 25 | 12 | 14 | 17 | - |

14. A stock market analyst wants to study the impact of the type of company on the quarterly averages of EPS. So he collected four quarterly averages of EPS data of four different companies during the financial year from NSE website. Check whether there is a significance between the quarterly averages of EPS of the four companies. Use Kruskal-Wallis test at 5% level.

| | Companies | | | |
|---|---|---|---|---|
| | **C1** | **C2** | **C3** | **C4** |
| Replications | 12 | 16 | 25 | 13 |
| | 8 | 18 | 15 | 8 |
| | 16 | 10 | 22 | 20 |
| | 19 | 11 | 9 | 5 |

## 9.13 How to Do?

Dolly: "My God, last project report was really esoteric. I have read Dr. R. K. Mandal's paper 'Variation of Output with variation of anticipated and Unanticipated Money Supply in India'. Until and unless you are well versed with economic terms, research methodology and constructs, you cannot appreciate the report written by the author."

Jolly: "You are right; reader should have good knowledge of the subject. Researcher should also try to demystify the terms."

Dolly: "Here if you are not aware of the terms like 'Money Supply', 'types of money', 'anticipated' and 'unanticipated money supply', 'GNP' and 'variations', as a researcher you cannot construct the models and as a reader also you cannot enjoy the write-up."

Jolly: "The author has reviewed the literature concerning expectations. He has quoted S.A. Ozga and explained what expectations are and how they are related to economic theory. He emphasizes that expectations are directly related to past observations."

Dolly: "With this he explains how adaptive explanations model explains the money supply. How past performance or money supply in the past is going to effect the present money supply. Is it not sounding like Augmented Dickey Fuller Model?"

Jolly: "Now, you are talking like a matured researcher comparing the models. However, please note every model has some specific issues, but can be generalized for other places and time."

Dolly: "So time and again, issue of quality in research will arise."

Jolly: "Of course, a good researcher shall take care of validity at every stage."

Dolly: "In simple words, author views that past money supply effects future money supply which may be called anticipated money supply while the estimated errors are unanticipated money supply."

Jolly: "This will be a very unprocessed derivation of the result, anyway, carry on."

Dolly: "The author in the second model uses both anticipated and unanticipated money as independent variable and Output (GNP) is dependent variable."

Jolly: "In simple words, yes."

Dolly: "So findings are GNP is related to anticipated money supply and not with unanticipated money supply."

Jolly: "But there are many issues like time variability and external issues. For instance in the final model $R^2$ is .60 which means the model explains only 60% of output. It means there are some other factors which explain the output. Second model is based on historical data and with time there are pushes and pulls or cyclic effects in economy, there may be variations due to time."

Dolly: "So there is gap in study, yes author has also emphasized 'This needs further investigation into the response of output level to the changes in anticipated and unanticipated parts of money supply over shorter homogeneous sub-periods'."

Jolly: "The author has used other models and given at the foot note."

Dolly: "But I have understood very important point – one should work hard on a problem."

Jolly: "To construct the models properly, you should read, read and read."

Dolly: Also see the numerical style of refrences."

Jolly: Usually, there are two types of refrences – Haward style, other numerical."

Dolly: "Now, let us talk about non-parametric test."

Jolly: "Researchers do not prefer such tests as they are usually less efficient and powerful as they are based on no assumption and we all know that the less one assumes, the less one can infer from a set of data. These tests are mostly used to find out whether samples are from the population which is distribution free or not. Questions of validity (internal validity, construct validity and external validity) shall remain unanswered and many debatable issues shall arise."

Dolly: "You want to say, non-parametric tests are useless."

Jolly: "No, no. They are very useful in applied research. Sometimes you do not know anything about population, you will have to get some idea about the population or see whether population is normally distributed or non-normal. Non-parametric tests are helpful in applied research. They are very helpful in business research which is mostly applied."

Dolly: "But most of the tests are based on testing of proportion and ANOVA."

Jolly: "But you should not use them alone. Construct the model with parametric models so as to increase its validity."

Dolly: "Can you give me another article where I can read cause-effect relation thoroughly?"

| | |
|---|---|
| Jolly: | "Yes, Professor Neerav Nagar, formerly with St. Francis Institute of Management and Research, Mumbai, has worked on a project 'Drivers of Shareholders' value.' Here author discusses Economic Value Added and Market Value Added and attempts to find what shareholders expect." |
| Dolly: | "So it is finance." |
| Jolly: | "Dear, we have divided the management into specialization for sake of our convenience. Researcher should have basic knowledge of all and then work on area of his liking." |
| Dolly: | "I shall read the report, then we shall discuss tomorrow." |

✦ ✦ ✦

Research Project 10

## 9.14 Drivers of Shareholders' Value

**Neerav Nagar**[1]

"Economic Value Added measures the profitability of a company after taking into account the cost of all capital. It is the post-tax return on capital employed (adjusted for the tax shield on debt) less the cost of capital employed. Companies which earn higher returns than cost of capital create value. Companies which earn lower returns than cost of capital are deemed destroyers of shareholder value." Infosys's Annual Report (FY 2005-06)

### Introduction

The most important objective of Financial Management is the maximization of shareholders' value. After reading this, the first question which comes to our mind is that how do shareholders know that the company to whom they have entrusted their hard earned money is efficiently utilizing it and thus, creating value for them. We have always read the annual reports of the companies to find out information about their 'top line' and 'bottom line'. We also have various financial ratios for our aid like Return on Capital Employed (ROCE), Return on Net Worth (RONW), Earning per Share (EPS), Dividend per Share (DPS) etc.

In 1890, Alfred Marshall introduced the concept of Residual Income, which can be arrived at by subtracting the charge for the capital employed from the operating profit. In the beginning of the 1990s, Stern Stewart & Co. came out with a modified way of calculating Residual Income suggesting accounting changes with respect to depreciation, inventory, research and development expenditure etc., for arriving at the figures of operating profit and capital employed. With this, the term – Economic Value Added (EVA) was introduced on which the firm has the copyright.

Many studies have been carried out to find out whether these measures really contribute to the shareholders' wealth. However, since EVA was introduced as an indicator for shareholders' wealth maximization, it has been a focal point for majority of the studies. Also, many Indian companies like Infosys, Hindustan Lever, Tata Steel, Godrej etc. have adopted EVA and are mentioning about it in their annual reports.

This paper is another attempt to find out whether EVA really explains the value accretion for the shareholders. Are we better off by removing the focus from EVA and concentrating on traditional measures like ROCE, RONW, EPS, DPS etc.?

#### Objective

The primary objective of this paper is to find out what drives the shareholders' value. The study has been conducted to find out the correlation of the measures like ROCE, RONW, EPS, DPS, Cash Flow from Operations and Economic Value Added with Market Value Added (MVA).

#### EVA and MVA

As the introductory paragraph of this paper suggests, EVA is the surplus profit after accounting for all the expenses including the cost of capital. We have always looked at the figures of Profit after Tax to find out whether a company is performing well or not. However, what we forget is that the shareholders invest money in a company in expectation of some return. So, the basis for

1. Formerly, Lecturer (Finance), St. Francis Institute of Management and Research, Mt. Poinsur, S.V.P. Road, Borivali (West), Mumbai – 400103

evaluation should be whether the company has earned over and above the minimum required rate of return by the investors. If there is surplus after accounting for this opportunity cost of equity, the company is creating value for its shareholders. If not, then it is destroying value. In other words, value is created when return earned by the firm is more than its cost of capital or firm invests in the projects with positive NPV.

EVA can be calculated through any one of the following methods:

- Profit after Tax – (Cost of Equity*Net Worth)
- Operating Profit after Tax – (Weighted Average Cost of Capital*Capital Employed)
- (Return on Capital Employed – (Weighted Average Cost of Capital*Capital Employed)

As JHvH de Wat (2005) puts it, EVA is an internal measure of performance that determines MVA, which is an external measure of performance.

MVA can be calculated by subtracting Capital Employed from the Market Value of the firm. Another variant is subtracting Net Worth from the Market Capitalization of the firm. MVA states the value addition at a particular point of time, hence it is a stock variable where as EVA is a flow variable.

A company can be an EVA and/or MVA positive company by:

- Increasing revenue
- Reducing operating costs
- Efficient utilization of assets
- Raising funds at cheaper cost

**Literature Review**

Stewart (1991) had carried out a research to find out the relationship between EVA and MVA. This study was done by taking average EVA values for the years 1987 and 1988 of 613 companies in USA and then comparing them with their MVA values for 1988. The study found an $r^2$ of 97% between the EVA and MVA values for the companies with positive EVA while this correlation was insignificant for the companies with negative EVA values. Finegan (1991) took a sample of 450 companies in USA and found that average values of EVA could explain 61% of the variance in MVA whereas the similar figure was 44% between the change in EVA and change in MVA. He also observed that this $r^2$ was 47% between ROCE and MVA. Dodd and Chen (1992) found ROA as a better driver of shares returns as compared to EVA.

Stern (1993) found out that EVA is the best measure that drives the shareholders' value with an $r^2$ of 50% with MVA. The next important driver was ROE with an $r^2$ of 25% with MVA. Lehn and Makhija (1996) also studied the relationship of share returns with ROE, ROA, Return on Sales (ROS), EVA, MVA and CEO turnover. Correlation was found to be highest in case of EVA, however, CEO turnover also affected the shares returns. O'Byrne (1996) used measures like capitalized EVA (EVA divided by the cost of capital), NOPAT and free cash flows and correlated them with market value divided by the invested capital. He found NOPAT as a better indicator with an $r^2$ of 33% compared with 31% in case of EVA. However, changes in EVA values explained 74% of the changes in market value over a period of 10 years. Uyemara and others (1996) studied MVA's correlation with EVA, Net Income, EPS, ROE, and ROA over a period of 10 years. $r^2$ was highest in case of EVA (40%) followed by ROA (13%). It was least in case of EPS.

Grant's (1996 and 1997) study of 983 companies showed that of Standardized EVA (EVA divided by Capital) had an $r^2$ of 32% with Standardized MVA (MVA divided by Capital). The data taken was for the year 1993 and he also found that the correlation was higher for positive EVA companies. Milunovich and Tsuei (1996) studied the correlation between EVA and MVA in the US information technology industry for the period 1990-95 and found an $r^2$ of 42%. EPS was judged as the second best measure with an $r^2$ of 34%. Kramer and Pushner (1997) established that lagged levels of NOPAT explained MVA better as compared to EVA. This correlation was found higher even when changes in NOPAT were correlated with changes in MVA. According to Biddle and others (1999), Net Income was found to be the best measure to explain share returns. Majority of these studies were focused on US companies. Griffith (2004) concluded that an investor or analyst using EVA or MVA measures to forecast performance would have experienced significant losses. Ferguson and others (2005) also doubted that adopting EVA improves stock performance.

JHvH de Wet (2005) analyzed the database of 89 South African companies and observed that the Standardized Cash Flow from Operations (CFO divided by the Invested Capital in the beginning) had an $r^2$ of 38% with the Standardized MVA (MVA divided by the Invested Capital in the beginning), which was found to be the best driver as compared to the Standardized EVA (EVA divided by the Invested Capital in the beginning), ROA, ROE, EPS and DPS. He also observed that correlation of EPS and DPS with MVA was insignificant and thus questioned the logic of using EPS and DPS for valuing the shares. Roji George (2005) analyzed the data of 21 Indian banks for the period 1999-2003 and concluded that there is a positive relationship between EVA and productivity and negative relationship between EVA and NPA.

**Research Method**

This analysis was carried out over a period of 10 years on 25 companies which form part of BSE Sensex. Though Sensex comprises 30 companies, 5 companies were eliminated because of the inadequate information available as these companies were listed post 2001 while the study period was April 1997 – March 2006. The reason for choosing companies from Sensex was its reliability in terms of the selection of the companies as only those companies are selected which have a listing history of at least 3 months with sufficient trading frequency. This helps in efficient discovery of price which in turn helps in calculating an accurate value of MVA, Beta and the Cost of Equity.

The regression analysis was done to establish the relationship of MVA with EVA, ROCE, RONW, EPS, DPS and Cash Flow from Operations.

Different measures which were used for the analysis were:

- Standardized Market Value Added (Std. MVA), which is MVA/Avg. Net Worth
- Standardized Economic Value Added (Std. EVA), which is EVA/Avg. Net Worth
- Return on Capital Employed (ROCE)
- Return on Net Worth (RONW)
- Earning per Share (EPS)
- Dividend per Share (DPS)
- Standardized Cash Flow from Operations (Std. CFO), which is CFO/Avg. Capital Employed

Database used was CMIE's Prowess and Business Beacon from where the values of Avg. Market Capitalization, Avg. Capital Employed, Avg. Net Worth, risk-free return, market return, beta, profit after tax (net of non-recurring transactions), ROCE, RONW, EPS, number of outstanding equity shares, dividends paid and cash flow from operations were taken.

MVA was calculated by subtracting Avg. Net Worth from Avg. Market Capitalization. Value of debt was ignored while calculating MVA because India still doesn't have a well developed corporate debt market which would have created problems in terms of availability as well as the reliability of the data.

EVA was calculated as follows:

EVA = Profit after Tax – (Cost of Equity*Avg. Net Worth)

where, Profit after Tax was net of non-recurring transactions.

Cost of Equity was calculated using the Capital Asset Pricing Model, where:

Cost of Equity = Risk-free return + Beta*Market Risk Premium

For calculating risk-free return, average of maximum and minimum yield on 364-days Treasury bill has been used. Beta values have been taken from BSE website and Prowess. Market risk premium has been taken as 7% for the period 2002-05 and 8% for the period 1996-2001, as representative figures being used by some of the companies in Sensex.

**Research Results**

Results of the regression analysis (each with a single variable) are tabulated as follows:

| | Standardized EVA | ROCE | RONW | EPS | DPS | Standardized CFO |
|---|---|---|---|---|---|---|
| r | 0.53 | 0.36 | 0.59 | 0.02 | -0.02 | 0.16 |
| $r^2$ | 28.57 | 12.92 | 34.79 | 0.04 | 0.03 | 2.7 |
| Standard Error | 7.18 | 7.93 | 6.86 | 8.49 | 8.49 | 8.38 |

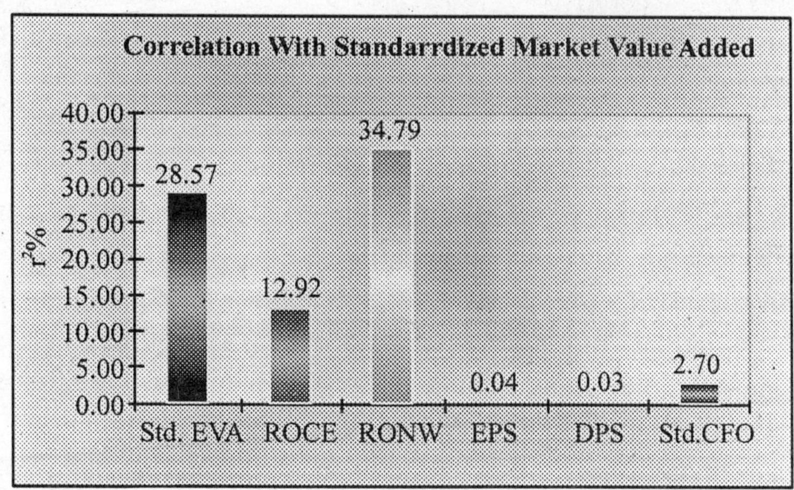


Analysis establishes that RONW has the strongest correlation **(0.59)** with Std. MVA with an $r^2$ of **34.79%**. Standardized EVA comes second with an $r^2$ of **28.57%** followed by ROCE ($r^2$ of **12.92%**). Much sought after ratios like EPS and DPS have shown insignificant correlation.

## Conclusion

The regression analysis suggests that RONW is the most important variable which explains 34.79% of the variance in MVA, which is not a surprise since shareholders should value an enterprise, based on the returns what they are getting on their invested money, which proves that it doesn't matter whether the company retains or distributed its earnings, so long it is being utilized for productive purposes.

EVA values do have an impact on the MVA of the companies. It takes into account the opportunity cost of capital and it is proved that increase in EVA does add value for the shareholders. ROCE also has some impact, however, EPS, DPS and Std. Cash Flow from Operations have shown insignificant relationship.

Thus Return on Net Worth and Economic Value Added emerge as strong drivers of the shareholders' value.

## References

Biddle, G.C., Bowen, R.M. & Wallace, J.S., "Evidence on EVA," *Journal of Applied Corporate Finance*, Summer 1999, pp. 69-79.

Damodaran, Aswath, *Corporate Finance (Theory and Practice)*, John Wiley and Sons Inc., 2nd edition, pp. 812-822.

Dodd, J.L. & Chen, S., "EVA: A new panacea?," *B & E review*, July – September 1996, pp. 26-28

Durant, Michael W., "Economic Value Added: The Invisible Hand at Work," *Credit Research Foundation*.

Ferguson, Robert, Rentzler, Joel and Yu, Susana, "Does EVA improve stock performance profitability?," *Journal of Applied Finance*, Fall/Winter 2005, pp. 101-113.

Grant, J.L., "Foundations of Economic Value Added," 1997, *New Hope: Frank & Fabozzi.*

Grant, J.L., "Foundations of EVA for investment managers," *The Journal of Portfolio Management,* Fall 1996, pp. 41-45.

Griffith, John M., "The True Value of EVA," *Journal of Applied Finance*, Fall/Winter 2004, Vol. 14, Issue 2, pp. 25-29.

Kramer, J.K. and Pushner, G., "An empirical analysis of Economic Value Added as a proxy for Market Value Added," *Financial Practice and Education*, Spring/Summer 1997, pp. 41-49.

Kramer, J.K. and Peters, J.R., "Economic Value Added and Cost of Capital," *Journal of Applied Corporate Finance*.

Lehn, K. and Makhija, A.K., "EVA and MVA as performance measures and signals for strategic change," *Strategy & Leadership*, May/June 1996, pp 34-38.

Weaver, Samuel C, "Measuring Economic Value Added: A Survey of the Practices of EVA Proponents," *Journal of Applied Finance*, 2001, Vol. 11, Issue 1, p. 50.

Wet, JHvH de, "EVA versus traditional accounting measures of performance as drivers of shareholder value – A comparative analysis," *Meditari Accountancy Research*, Vol. 13, No. 2, 2005, pp. 1-16.

**Websites:**

www.sternstewart.com

ww.financeadvisor.com

## 9.15 Multivariate Data Analysis

Multivariate Data Analysis refers to any statistical technique used to analyze data that arises from more than one dependable variable. It is easy to analyse data when dependent variable is one. It is a complex task when there are more than one dependent variable and/or these variables are interdependent. Multivariate analysis methods are typically used for consumer and market research, Quality control and quality assurance across a range of industries such as food and beverage, paint, pharmaceuticals, chemicals, and telecommunications, process optimization and process control, research and development.

Multivariate techniques possess the ability to analyse complex data. Accordingly in most of the applied and behavioural researches, we generally resort to multivariate analysis techniques for realistic results. Besides being a tool for analyzing the data, multivariate techniques also help in various types of decision-making. For example, take the case of MBA entrance examination wherein a number of tests are administered to candidates, and the candidates scoring high total marks based on many subjects are admitted. This system, though apparently fair, may at times be biased in favour of some subjects with the larger standard deviations. Multivariate techniques may be appropriately used in such situations for developing norms as to who should be admitted in MBA. We may also cite an example from medical field. Many medical examinations such as blood pressure and cholesterol tests are administered to patients. Each of the results of such examinations has significance of its own, but it is also important to consider relationships between different test results or results of the same tests at different occasions in order to draw proper diagnostic conclusions and to determine an appropriate therapy. Multivariate techniques can assist us in such a situation. In view of all this, we can state that if the researcher is interested in making probability statements on the basis of sampled multiple measurements, then the best strategy of data analysis is to use some suitable multivariate statistical technique.

Multivariate techniques transform a mass of observations into a smaller number of composite scores in such a way that they may reflect as much information as possible contained in the raw data obtained concerning a research study. Thus, the main contribution of these techniques is in arranging a large amount of complex information involved in the real data into a simplified visible form. Mathematically, multivariate techniques consist in forming a linear composite vector in a vector subspace, which can be represented in terms of projection of a vector onto certain specified subspaces.

For better appreciation and understanding of multivariate techniques, one must be familiar with fundamental concepts of linear algebra, vector spaces, orthogonal and oblique projections and univariate analysis. Even then before applying multivariate techniques for meaningful results, one must consider the nature and structure of the data and the real aim of the analysis. We should also not forget that multivariate techniques do involve several complex mathematical computations and as such can be utilized largely with the availability of computer facility.

### 9.15.1 Classification of Multivariate Techniques

Today, there exist a great variety of multivariate techniques which can be conveniently classified into two broad categories viz., dependence methods and interdependence methods. If some of the involved variables are dependent upon others, we have dependence methods; but in case they are not dependent on others, we have interdependence methods. Two more questions are relevant for understanding the nature of multivariate techniques. Firstly, in case some variables are dependent, the question is how many variables are dependent? The other question is, whether the data are metric or non-metric? This means whether the data are quantitative, collected on interval or ratio scale, or whether the data are qualitative, collected on nominal or ordinal scale. The technique to be used for a given situation depends upon the answers to all these very questions. We have two types of multivariate techniques: one type for data containing both dependent and independent variables, and the other type for data containing several variables without dependency relationship. In the former category are included techniques like multiple regression analysis, multiple discriminant analysis, multivariate analysis of variance and canonical analysis, whereas in the latter category we put techniques like factor analysis, cluster analysis, multidimensional scaling or MDS (both metric and non-metric) and the latent structure analysis.

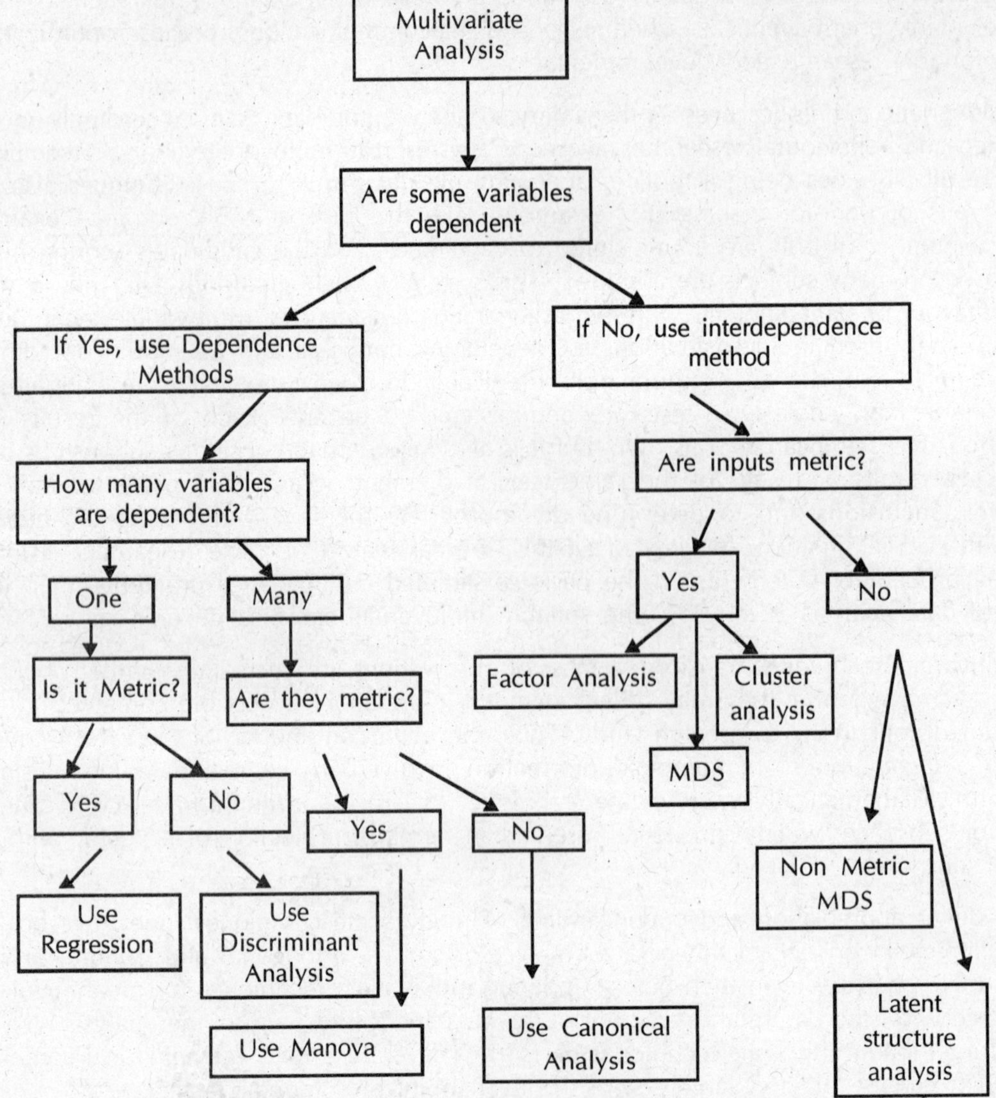


Keeping in mind the syllabus of Indian Universities, following techniques have been discussed in this book. Basics of these techniques have been explained in this chapter. Some complicated issues have been discussed in chapter 'Use of Computer Software in Research'.

Following techniques have been discussed in this chapter

- Discriminant Analysis
- Factor Analysis
- Cluster Analysis
- Multi-Dimensional Scaling

## 9.15.2 Discriminant Analysis

The discriminant analysis aims at studying the effect of two or more predictor variables on certain evaluation criterion. Usually the evaluation criterion is categorised into two groups, they may be good or bad, like or dislike, successful or unsuccessful, etc.

**For example**

- While grouping investment alternatives based on rate of return, the criterion of the rate of return will be categorized into 'good' or 'bad'.
- While grouping sales regions based on their sales potential, the criterion of sales potential will be categorized into good or bad.
- While grouping CEOs of companies based on their overall managerial skills from the point of view of organizational productivity, the criterion will be 'successful' or 'unsuccessful'.
- While grouping R&D projects based on their successful completion, the criterion will be 'successful' or 'unsuccessful'.
- While grouping salesmen in terms of meeting sales target, the criterion will be 'successful' or 'unsuccessful'.
- While grouping products by consumers in terms of their flavour, the criterion will be 'like' or 'dislike'.
- While grouping executives in a company in terms of their leadership qualities, the criterion will be 'like' or 'dislike'.
- While grouping employees after a training programme in terms of their enhanced skills, the criterion will be above expected level or below expected level.
- While grouping the performance of educational institutions in terms of their achievements, the criterion will be 'above expected level' or 'below expected level'.

The researcher is usually interested to know whether the predictor variables discriminate among the groups. More specifically, it is necessary to identify the predictor variable (independent variable) which is more important when compared to the other predictor variable(s). Such analysis is called *discriminant* analysis.

The different stages of the discriminant analysis are as listed below:

- Designing a discriminant function like the one shown below:

  $Y = aX_1 + bX_2$

  where $Y$ is the linear composite representing the discriminant function, $X_1$ and $X_2$ are the predictor variables (independent variables) which are having effect on the evaluation criterion of the problem of interest.

  (Student should note so far we have taken Xs as independent variables and Y as dependent variable. However, in this case Xs are predictor variables. Y is composite of the two.)

- Finding the discriminant ratio *(K)* and determining the variables which account for inter-group differences in terms of group means.

  This ratio is the maximum possible ratio between the 'variability between groups' and the 'variability within groups'.

- Finding the critical value which can be used to include a new data set (i.e. new combination of instances for the predictor variables) into its appropriate group.
- Testing the null hypothesis, $H_0$: The group means are equal in importance, against the alternate hypothesis, $H_1$: The group means are not equal in importance, using *F* test at a given significance level, α.

### 9.15.2.1 Solved Example

The director of State health department wants to do discriminant analysis concerning the effect of two factors, namely yearly spending on infrastructures of the restaurant ($X_1$) and yearly spending on employees training on food preparation on grading the restaurants. He has collected data for 12 years from a restaurant and submitted to a committee. The committee awarded grades as 'below average i.e. 0' and 'above average i.e. 1'.

1. Design the discriminant function $Y = aX_1 + bX_2$
2. Compute the discriminant ratio, K and identify the variable which is more important in relation to the other variable.
3. Validate the discriminant function using the given data by forming groups based on the critical discriminant score.
4. Test whether the group means are equal in importance of at a significance level of 5%.

| Year | Grade | Expenses on Infrastructure $X_1$ | Expenses on training $X_2$ |
|---|---|---|---|
| 1 | 0 | 3 | 2 |
| 2 | 0 | 4 | 5 |
| 3 | 1 | 10 | 7 |
| 4 | 0 | 5 | 4 |
| 5 | 0 | 6 | 6 |
| 6 | 1 | 11 | 4 |
| 7 | 0 | 7 | 4 |
| 8 | 1 | 12 | 5 |
| 9 | 0 | 8 | 7 |
| 10 | 0 | 9 | 5 |
| 11 | 1 | 13 | 6 |
| 12 | 1 | 14 | 9 |

**Solution:**

$H_0$: Group means are equal in importance

$H_1$: Group means are not equal in importance

**Summary of means of $X_1$ and $X_2$ for each group**

| Group | Year | Grade | Infrastructure $X_1$ | Training $X_2$ |
|---|---|---|---|---|
| G1 | 1 | 0 | 3 | 2 |
| | 2 | 0 | 4 | 5 |
| | 4 | 0 | 5 | 4 |
| | 5 | 0 | 6 | 6 |
| | 7 | 0 | 7 | 4 |

| | | | | |
|---|---|---|---|---|
| | 9 | 0 | 8 | 7 |
| | 10 | 0 | 9 | 5 |
| Total of '0' | | | 42 | 33 |
| Mean of '0' | | | 6 | 4.714286 |

| Group | Year | Grade | Infrastructure $X_1$ | Training $X_2$ |
|---|---|---|---|---|
| G2 | 3 | 1 | 10 | 7 |
| | 6 | 1 | 11 | 4 |
| | 8 | 1 | 12 | 5 |
| | 11 | 1 | 13 | 6 |
| | 12 | 1 | 14 | 9 |
| | | | | |
| Total of '1' | | | 60 | 31 |
| Mean of '1' | | | 12 | 6.2 |
| | | | | |
| Grand mean | | 8.5 | 5.333333 | |

**Calculation of necessary results to solve normal equations**

| Group | Year | Grade | Infrastructure $X_1$ | Training $X_2$ | $X_1^2$ | $X_2^2$ | $X_1 * X_2$ |
|---|---|---|---|---|---|---|---|
| G1 | 1 | 0 | 3 | 2 | 9 | 4 | 6 |
| | 2 | 0 | 4 | 5 | 16 | 25 | 20 |
| | 4 | 0 | 5 | 4 | 25 | 16 | 20 |
| | 5 | 0 | 6 | 6 | 36 | 36 | 36 |
| | 7 | 0 | 7 | 4 | 49 | 16 | 28 |
| | 9 | 0 | 8 | 7 | 64 | 49 | 56 |
| | 10 | 0 | 9 | 5 | 81 | 25 | 45 |
| Total of '0' | | | 42 | 33 | 280 | 171 | 211 |
| Mean of '0' | | | 6 | 4.714286 | | | |
| n = | | 7 | | | | | |

| Group | Year | Grade | Infrastructure $X_1$ | Training $X_2$ | $X_1^2$ | $X_2^2$ | $X_1 * X_2$ |
|---|---|---|---|---|---|---|---|
| G2 | 3 | 1 | 10 | 7 | 100 | 49 | 70 |
| | 6 | 1 | 11 | 4 | 121 | 16 | 44 |
| | 8 | 1 | 12 | 5 | 144 | 25 | 60 |
| | 11 | 1 | 13 | 6 | 169 | 36 | 78 |
| | 12 | 1 | 14 | 9 | 196 | 81 | 126 |
| | | | | | | | |
| Total of '1' | | 60 | 31 | 730 | 207 | 378 | |
| Mean of '1' | | 12 | 6.2 | | | | |
| n = | | 5 | | | | | |
| Grand mean | | 8.5 | 5.333333 | | | | |

| | | Below | Above | Total |
|---|---|---|---|---|
| $\Sigma(X_1-\overline{X}_1)^2=\Sigma X_1^2-n\overline{X}_1^2=$ | | 28 | 10 | 38 |
| $\Sigma(X_2-\overline{X}_2)^2=\Sigma X_2^2-n\overline{X}_2^2=$ | | 15.42857143 | 14.8 | 30.22857143 |
| $\Sigma(X_1-\overline{X}_1)(X_2-\overline{X}_2^2)=\Sigma X_1X_2-n\overline{X}_1\overline{X}_2=$ | | 13 | 6 | 19 |

Let the linear composite discriminant function be $Y = aX_1+bX_2$

Normal Equations are

$$a\Sigma(X_1-\overline{X}_1)^2+b\Sigma(X_1-\overline{X}_1)(X_2-\overline{X}_2)=\overline{X}_{1(G2)}-\overline{X}_{1(G1)}$$

$$a\Sigma(X_1-\overline{X}_1)(X_2-\overline{X}_2)+b\Sigma(X_2-\overline{X}_2)^2=\overline{X}_{2(G2)}-\overline{X}_{2(G1)}$$

$38a+19b = 12-6 = 6$

$19a+30.22b = 6.2-4.714 = 1.485$

Solution to the above equations are

$a = 0.19157$

$b = -0.077877$

$Y = 0.19157X_1 - 0.077877X_2$

Computation of discriminant ratio, K and identification of the variable which is more important.

$\overline{Y}_{below}$ $a\overline{X}_1$ $b\overline{X}_2 = 0.8221345$

$\overline{Y}_{above}$ $a\overline{X}_1$ $b\overline{X}_2 = 1.880126229$

$\overline{Y}_{Grand\ Mean}$ $a\overline{X}_1$ $b\overline{X}_2 = 1.2629644$

| Group | Year | Grade | Infrastructure $X_1$ | Training $X_2$ | Discriminant Score S1 | $(S1\text{-}St1)^2$ |
|---|---|---|---|---|---|---|
| G1 | 1 | 0 | 3 | 4 | 0.2911 | 0.2603 |
| | 2 | 0 | 4 | 5 | 0.4124 | 0.1512 |
| | 4 | 0 | 5 | 4 | 0.6799 | 0.0147 |
| | 5 | 0 | 6 | 6 | 0.7282 | 0.0053 |
| | 7 | 0 | 7 | 4 | 1.0687 | 0.0715 |
| | 9 | 0 | 8 | 7 | 1.0440 | 0.0589 |

| | 10 | 0 | 9 | 5 | 1.3845 | 0.3402 |
|---|---|---|---|---|---|---|
| | | | Total | | 5.6088 | 0.9022 |
| | | | Mean (St1) | | 0.8013 | |

| Group | Year | Grade | Infrastructure $X_1$ | Interface events $X_2$ | Discriminant Score S2 | $(S2\text{-}St2)^2$ |
|---|---|---|---|---|---|---|
| G2 | 3 | 1 | 10 | 7 | 1.4328 | 0.2133 |
| | 6 | 1 | 11 | 4 | 1.8464 | 0.0023 |
| | 8 | 1 | 12 | 5 | 1.9678 | 0.0053 |
| | 11 | 1 | 13 | 6 | 2.0892 | 0.0378 |
| | 12 | 1 | 14 | 8 | 2.1375 | 0.0589 |
| | | | Total | | 9.4737 | 0.3177 |
| | | | Mean (St2) | | 1.8947 | |
| | | | | | | |
| | | | | | | |
| | | Grand Total of discriminant score= | | 15.0825 | | |
| | | Grand Mean of Discriminant score S= | | 1.256876685 | | |

The variability between Groups (VBG) is computed =

$V_{BG}$ = n1(MeanS1- S)$^2$ + n2(Mean S2-S)$^2$ = 7(0.8013-1.25687)$^2$ + 5(1.8947-1.25687) = 3.487419

The variability within Groups (VBG) is computed = $V_{WG}$= S(S1- S)$^2$+S( S2-S)$^2$ = + 0.9022+ 0.3177 = 1.22

K = (VBG)/(VWG) = 2.86

This is the maximum possible ratio between 'the variability between groups' and 'the variability within groups'. This means that if the variable $X_2$ is suppressed in the discriminant function, then the revised value of the discriminant ratio will be less than the previous value. In the discriminant function, $Y = 0.19157X_1 - 0.077877X_2$ the coefficient of $X_2$ has negative sign which indicates that the variable $X_1$ (spending on infrastructure) is more important than the variable $X_2$ (spending on training).

The discriminant function can be validated based on the grand mean of the discriminant scores which is known as the critical discriminant score. If the discriminant score of a data set is less than the critical discriminant score (1.2065), include that data set into group corresponding to 'Below' category; otherwise, include that data set into 'Above' category. As per these guidelines, the classification of the twelve data sets of the given problem is shown in Table below. One can notice that the discriminant function has grouped all the years into their original category as given in the problem except the year 10 which now falls in above category.

**Classification of data set based on critical discriminant score**

| Below, 0 | Above, 1 |
|---|---|
| 1 | 10 |
| 2 | 3 |
| 4 | 6 |
| 5 | 8 |
| 7 | 11 |
| 9 | 12 |

Testing whether the group means are equal in importance at a significance level of 5%

The formula to compute *F* is as shown below:

$$F = \frac{n_1 n_2 (n_1 + n_2 - m - 1)}{m(n_1 + n_2)(n_1 \_ n_2 - 2)} * D^2$$

Where m is the number of predictor variables (in this case it is 2)

$$D^2 = (n_1 + n_2 - 2)\{a(\overline{X_{1(G2)}} - \overline{X_{1(G1)}}) + b(\overline{X_{2(G2)}} - (\overline{X_{2(G2)}})\}$$

$$= (7+5\text{-}2)\ (0.19157\ {*}5.8 + 0.0778{*}1.2) = 10.5779$$

and F = 13.88

DF are as follows: numerator as m and denominator as $(n_1 + n_2 - m - 1)$, i.e., 2 and 9

Table value for $F_{2,9,\ 0.5}$ = 4.26

As calculated F value is more than table value we reject $H_0$ and accept $H_1$ which means group means are not equal in importance.

Based on $H_1$ and discriminant function, it is clear that spending on infrastructure is important than training employees.

The above calculations can be done on SPSS which shall be shown in chapter on 'Use of Computer Software in Research.

### 9.15.3 Factor Analysis

Let us start directly with an example. Your company manufactures toilet soap. You survey some consumers with following attributes and ask them grade these attributes between 0 to 10. The attributes are:

1. Packing paper
2. Packing design
3. Size of soap
4. Weight of soap
5. Colour of soap
6. Reaction to skin

7. Quality
8. Lather formation
9. Dissolvability
10. Price,

etc.

After you get data, you may be confused what consumer wants in general. You wish to know whether consumer wants brand, packing, quality or price. They are all dependent variables, but important factors (like brand, packaging, quality or price) are not known.

Factor analysis is intended to grouping the original input variables into factors which underlie the input variables. Each factor will account for one or more input variables. Theoretically, the total number of factors in the factor analysis is equal the total number of input variables. But, after performing factor analysis, the total number of factors in the study can be reduced by dropping the insignificant factors based on certain criterion.

## Factor Analysis in Marketing

The basic steps are:

- Identify the salient attributes consumers use to evaluate products in this category.
- Use quantitative marketing research techniques (such as surveys) to collect data from a sample of potential customers concerning their ratings of all the product attributes.
- Input the data into a statistical programme and run the factor analysis procedure. The computer will yield a set of underlying attributes (or factors).
- Use these factors to construct perceptual maps and other product positioning devices.

Factor analysis is an interdependence technique. The complete set of interdependent relationships are examined. There is no specification of either dependent variables, independent variables, or causality. Factor analysis assumes that all the rating data on different attributes can be reduced down to a few important dimensions. This reduction is possible because the attributes are related. The rating given to any one attribute is partially the result of the influence of other attributes. The statistical algorithm deconstructs the rating (called a raw score) into its various components, and reconstructs the partial scores into underlying factor scores. The degree of correlation between the initial raw score and the final factor score is called a ***factor loading***. There are two approaches to factor analysis: "principal component analysis" (the total variance in the data is considered); and "common factor analysis" (the common variance is considered).

**Factor analysis** is used to explain variability among observed variables in terms of fewer unobserved variables called **factors**. The observed variables are modelled as linear combinations of the factors, plus "error" terms. The information gained about the interdependencies can be used later to reduce the set of variables in a dataset. Factor analysis originated in psychometrics, and is used in behavioural sciences, social sciences, marketing, product management, operations research, and other applied sciences that deal with large quantities of data. The two methods are related, but distinct, though factor analysis becomes essentially equivalent to principal components analysis if the "errors" in the factor analysis model are assumed to have the same variance.

Note that principal component analysis and common factor analysis differ in terms of their conceptual underpinnings. The factors produced by principal component analysis are conceptualized as being linear combinations of the variables whereas the factors produced by common factor analysis are conceptualized as being latent variables. Computationally, the only difference is that the diagonal of the relationships matrix is replaced with communalities (the variance accounted for by more than one variable) in common factor analysis. This has the result of making the factor scores indeterminate and thus differ depending on the method used to compute them whereas those produced by principal components analysis are not dependent on the method of computation. Although there have been heated debates over the merits of the two methods, a number of leading statisticians have concluded that in practice there is little difference which makes sense since the computations are quite similar despite the differing conceptual bases, especially for datasets where communalities are high and/or there are many variables, reducing the influence of the diagonal of the relationship matrix on the final result.

The use of principal components in a semantic space can vary somewhat because the components may only "predict" but not "map" to the vector space. This produces a statistical principal component use where the most salient words or themes represent the preferred basis.

Before the advent of computer, researcher used to analyse factors manually by Centroid Method. The Centroid method maximises the sum of absolute loadings. In this method, the coefficients of terms in the linear composite of each factor will be either +1 or –1. This method is less cumbersome when compared to other methods. We shall use Centroid method in this chapter. Principal component method shall be discussed in chapter 'Use of computer software in Research'.

Factor analysis involves many terminologies which are presented below for understanding of the related techniques.

### Correlation coefficient matrix

It is the matrix of correlation coefficients of the original observations between different pairs of input variables.

### Factor loadings, $L_i$ (j)

It is a matrix representing the correlation between different combinations of variables and factors. $L_i(j)$ is the factor loading of the variable; on the factor *i*, where i = 1, 2, 3, ..., *n* and *j* = 1, 2, 3, ..., *n*.

### Communality, $h_i^2$

It is the sum of squares of the factor loadings of the variable *i* on all factors.

$$h_i^2 = \Sigma L_i^2$$

### Eigenvalue

It is the sum of squares of the factor loadings of all variables on a factor.

Eigenvalue of the factor $j = \Sigma L_{ij}^2$

The sum of the eigenvalues of all factors (if no factor is dropped) is equal to the sum of the communalities of all variables.

### Rotation

After obtaining factor loadings, one should examine whether the factor loading matrix possesses simple structure. If a factor loading matrix has a simple structure, it is easy to make interpretations about the factors. If there is no simple structure, then the n-dimensional space of the factors should be rotated by an angle such that the factor loadings are revised to have a simple structure which will simplify the process of interpretation of the factors. Such rotation is called *rotation of factors*.

A simple structure means that each variable has very high factor loading (as high as 1) on one of the factors and very low factor loading (as low as 0) on other factors. The communalities of each variable before and after factor rotation will be the same.

The popular methods of rotation of factors are *varimax* method and *promax* method. Varimax method of factor rotation employs orthogonality between different pairs of factor axes. This means that the angles between different pairs of factors axes are 90° even after rotation. The promax method employs oblique rotation. This means that the angles between different pairs of factors axes are not 90° after rotation. Both the techniques aim at better interpretations.

## Significant Number of Factors

As explained earlier, the main objective of the factor analysis is to group the given set of input variables into minimal number factors with the maximum capability of "extracting information with the reduced set of factors".

There are certain criteria to determine the number of factors to be retained for future study which are, as explained below:

**Minimum eigenvalue criterion:** If the eigenvalue (sum of squares of the factor loadings of all variables on a factor) of a factor is more than or equal to 1, then that factor is to be retained; otherwise, that factor is to be dropped.

**Scree plot criterion:** As per this criterion, plot the eigenvalues of the factors by taking the factor number on *X-axis* and the eigenvalues on Y-axis. Then, identify the factor number at which the slope of the line connecting the points changes from steep to a gradual trailing off towards the right of the identified factor number. Such change in slope in the graph is known as *scree* and the point is known as *scree point.* The factors which are marked up to the scree point from the origin are to be retained for future study and all the factors to the right of the scree point are to be dropped from the study.

## Factor Scores

Though a factor is not visible like an original input variable, it is still a variable which can be used to find the scores for respondents. At the initial stage, the respondents assign scores for the variables. After performing factor analysis, each factor assigns a score for each respondent. Such scores are called *factor scores.*

The expression to compute the factor score of a respondent by the factor *k* is shown below. By substituting the standardized values of the input variables assigned by a respondent in this expression, the factor score of that respondent can be obtained:

$$F_k = w_{1k}X_1 + w_{2k}X_2 + w_{3k}X_3 \ldots\ldots\ldots + wn_kX_n$$

Where $wn_k$ is the weight of the input variable $X_i$ in the linear composite of factor.

## Centroid Method

- Input the data matrix *of m* × *n* size, where *m* is the number of sets of observations and *n* is the number of characteristics (variables).
- Find *n* x *n* correlation coefficient matrix ( say $R_1$) summarizing the correlation coefficient for each pair of the variables. Each diagonal value of the correlation coefficient/matrix is assumed as 1, as the respective variable is correlated to itself.
- If any of the correlation is negative, perform reflection, i.e., write its absolute value and note the column for which reflection was made.

- Find the total of each column ($S_j$). Find the grand total from the sum of each column total (say it is $T = \Sigma S_j$). Find the root of T.
- Divide each $S_j$ by $\sqrt{T}$.
- Now reverse the reflection, i.e., Columns where reflections have been made in earlier steps should be converted to negative.
- These are the loadings of the first factor.
- Now find the cross product matrix starting with first loading and multiplying with itself and then next loading. In this way we shall have m×n matrix again.
- Subtract this cross product matrix from first matrix ($R_1$). Now the cross product matrix is ($R_2$). Perform the steps till we find factors we need to find.

### 9.15.3.1 Solved Example

The general manager of a restaurant designed a questionnaire to study the customer's feedback about its restaurant and in turn he is interested to know what his customers in general wish. He wishes to identify factors of his study. He identifies six variables which are listed below:

1. Food hygiene (X1)
2. Menu items (X2)
3. Service quality (X3)
4. Food quality (X4)
5. Ambience (X5)
6. Price (X6)

So the company administered questionnaire to 10 respondents who responded the above questionnaire variable on 0-10 scale. The score 0 means low rating while 10 means high rating. Survey data is placed below and find the three factors which can represent the variables in study.

| Respondents | X1 | X2 | X3 | X4 | X5 | X6 |
|---|---|---|---|---|---|---|
| 1 | 4 | 6 | 7 | 7 | 0 | 0 |
| 2 | 4 | 4 | 6 | 8 | 2 | 1 |
| 3 | 4 | 1 | 6 | 5 | 1 | 2 |
| 4 | 1 | 2 | 6 | 3 | 2 | 3 |
| 5 | 4 | 3 | 5 | 5 | 2 | 3 |
| 6 | 4 | 4 | 6 | 8 | 2 | 3 |
| 7 | 3 | 3 | 0 | 9 | 1 | 3 |
| 8 | 7 | 7 | 6 | 9 | 9 | 2 |
| 9 | 4 | 3 | 1 | 8 | 1 | 2 |
| 10 | 5 | 4 | 2 | 3 | 1 | 0 |

**Solution:**

| Respondents | X1 | X2 | X3 | X4 | X5 | X6 |
|---|---|---|---|---|---|---|
| 1 | 4 | 6 | 7 | 7 | 0 | 0 |
| 2 | 4 | 4 | 6 | 8 | 2 | 1 |
| 3 | 4 | 1 | 6 | 5 | 1 | 2 |
| 4 | 1 | 2 | 6 | 3 | 2 | 3 |
| 5 | 4 | 3 | 5 | 5 | 2 | 3 |
| 6 | 4 | 4 | 6 | 8 | 2 | 3 |
| 7 | 3 | 3 | 0 | 9 | 1 | 3 |
| 8 | 7 | 7 | 6 | 9 | 9 | 2 |
| 9 | 4 | 3 | 1 | 8 | 1 | 2 |
| 10 | 5 | 4 | 2 | 3 | 1 | 0 |

Observations = m = 10

Number of variables = n = 6

Number of factors = F = 3

Initialize factor f = 1

Correlation matrix First matrix R1

| | X1 | X2 | X3 | X4 | X5 | X6 |
|---|---|---|---|---|---|---|
| X1 | 1 | 0.674919 | 0.059496 | 0.385297 | 0.622513 | –0.37354 |
| X2 | 0.674919 | 1 | 0.238422 | 0.474039 | 0.557693 | –0.43594 |
| X3 | 0.059496 | 0.238422 | 1 | –0.12417 | 0.255734 | –0.0926 |
| X4 | 0.385297 | 0.474039 | –0.12417 | 1 | 0.333128 | 0.139927 |
| X5 | 0.622513 | 0.557693 | 0.255734 | 0.333128 | 1 | 0.188243 |
| X6 | –0.37354 | –0.43594 | –0.0926 | 0.139927 | 0.188243 | 1 |

Since variable X6 is negative, the weights of variables are 1,1,1,1,1,–1

Correlation matrix First matrix R1' with reflections on variable 6

| | X1 | X2 | X3 | X4 | X5 | X6 |
|---|---|---|---|---|---|---|
| X1 | 1 | 0.674919 | 0.059496 | 0.385297 | 0.622513 | 0.373544 |
| X2 | 0.674919 | 1 | 0.238422 | 0.474039 | 0.557693 | 0.435943 |
| X3 | 0.059496 | 0.238422 | 1 | 0.12417 | 0.255734 | 0.092602 |
| X4 | 0.385297 | 0.474039 | 0.12417 | 1 | 0.333128 | 0.139927 |
| X5 | 0.622513 | 0.557693 | 0.255734 | 0.333128 | 1 | 0.188243 |
| X6 | 0.373544 | 0.435943 | 0.092602 | 0.139927 | 0.188243 | 1 |
| Total Sj | 3.115769 | 3.381017 | 1.770424 | 2.456561 | 2.957311 | 2.23026 |

Grand Total T = ΣSj = 15.91134

$\sqrt{T}$ = 3.988902

Calculations to Determine Loading Values of factors and variable X6 has been changed back to negative.

| Total Sj | Uli=Sj/ | Lj | |
|---|---|---|---|
| 3.115769 | 0.781109 | 0.781109 | A |
| 3.381017 | 0.847606 | 0.847606 | B |
| 1.770424 | 0.443837 | 0.443837 | C |
| 2.456561 | 0.615849 | 0.615849 | D |
| 2.957311 | 0.741385 | 0.741385 | E |
| 2.23026 | 0.559116 | –0.55912 | F |

Cross Product Matrix P2 (This has been calculated first multiplying A to all (A, B, C, D, E and F), then B to all etc.

| | X1 | X2 | X3 | X4 | X5 | X6 |
|---|---|---|---|---|---|---|
| X1 | 0.610132 | 0.662073 | 0.346686 | 0.481045 | 0.579102 | –0.43673 |
| X2 | 0.662073 | 0.718436 | 0.376199 | 0.521997 | 0.628402 | –0.47391 |
| X3 | 0.346686 | 0.376199 | 0.196992 | 0.273337 | 0.329054 | –0.24816 |
| X4 | 0.481045 | 0.521997 | 0.273337 | 0.37927 | 0.456581 | –0.34433 |
| X5 | 0.579102 | 0.628402 | 0.329054 | 0.456581 | 0.549651 | –0.41452 |
| X6 | –0.43673 | –0.47391 | –0.24816 | –0.34433 | –0.41452 | 0.312611 |

Residuals Matrix (R2) - subtracting P2 from R1

| | X1 | X2 | X3 | X4 | X5 | X6 |
|---|---|---|---|---|---|---|
| X1 | 0.390 | 0.013 | –0.287 | –0.096 | 0.043 | 0.063 |
| X2 | 0.013 | 0.282 | –0.138 | –0.048 | –0.071 | 0.038 |
| X3 | –0.287 | –0.138 | 0.803 | –0.398 | –0.073 | 0.156 |
| X4 | –0.096 | –0.048 | –0.398 | 0.621 | –0.123 | 0.484 |
| X5 | 0.043 | –0.071 | –0.073 | –0.123 | 0.450 | 0.603 |
| X6 | 0.063 | 0.038 | 0.156 | 0.484 | 0.603 | 0.687 |

Since variable X3,X4 are negative, the weights of variables are 1,1,-1,-1,1,1

Reflection Matrix R2' by converting negative values to positive

Residuals Matrix (R2) - subtracting P2 from R1

| | X1 | X2 | X3 | X4 | X5 | X6 |
|---|---|---|---|---|---|---|
| X1 | 0.390 | 0.013 | 0.287 | 0.096 | 0.043 | 0.063 |
| X2 | 0.013 | 0.282 | 0.138 | 0.048 | 0.071 | 0.038 |
| X3 | 0.287 | 0.138 | 0.803 | 0.398 | 0.073 | 0.156 |
| X4 | 0.096 | 0.048 | 0.398 | 0.621 | 0.123 | 0.484 |
| X5 | 0.043 | 0.071 | 0.073 | 0.123 | 0.450 | 0.603 |
| X6 | 0,063 | 0.038 | 0.156 | 0.484 | 0.603 | 0.687 |
| Total Sj | 0.892 | 0.589 | 1.854 | 1.770 | 1.364 | 2.031 |

Grand Total T= 8.500

=2.915512

Calculations to Determine Loading Values of factors with change in sign for variable X3,X4

| Total Sj | $Uli = Sj/T^{0.05}$ | Lj |
|---|---|---|
| 0.892 | 0.306035 | 0.306035 |
| 0.589 | 0.201962 | 0.201962 |
| 1.854 | 0.636032 | −0.63603 |
| 1.770 | 0.606979 | −0.60698 |
| 1.364 | 0.467844 | 0.467844 |
| 2.031 | 0.69666 | 0.69666 |

Cross Product Matrix P3

| | X1 | X2 | X3 | X4 | X5 | X6 |
|---|---|---|---|---|---|---|
| X1 | 0.094 | 0.062 | −0.195 | −0.186 | 0.143 | 0.213 |
| X2 | 0.062 | 0.041 | −0.128 | −0.123 | 0.094 | 0.141 |
| X3 | −0.195 | −0.128 | 0.405 | 0.386 | −0.298 | −0.443 |
| X4 | −0.186 | −0.123 | 0.386 | 0.368 | −0.284 | −0.423 |
| X5 | 0.143 | 0.094 | −0.298 | −0.284 | 0.219 | 0.326 |
| X6 | 0.213 | 0.141 | −0.443 | −0.423 | 0.326 | 0.485 |

Residual matrix R3

| | X1 | X2 | X3 | X4 | X5 | X6 |
|---|---|---|---|---|---|---|
| X1 | 0.296 | −0.049 | −0.093 | 0.090 | −0.100 | −0.150 |
| X2 | −0.049 | 0.241 | −0.009 | 0.075 | −0.165 | −0.103 |
| X3 | −0.093 | −0.009 | 0.398 | −0.784 | 0.224 | 0.599 |
| X4 | 0.090 | 0.075 | −0.784 | 0.252 | 0.161 | 0.907 |
| X5 | −0.100 | −0.165 | 0.224 | 0.161 | 0.231 | 0.277 |
| X6 | −0.150 | −0.103 | 0.599 | 0.907 | 0.277 | 0.202 |

Since variable X2,X3,X5 and X6 are negative, the weights of variables are 1,−1,−1,1,−1,−1

Residual matrix with reflections

| | X1 | X2 | X3 | X4 | X5 | X6 |
|---|---|---|---|---|---|---|
| X1 | 0.296 | 0.049 | 0.093 | 0.090 | 0.100 | 0.150 |
| X2 | 0.049 | 0.241 | 0.009 | 0.075 | 0.165 | 0.103 |
| X3 | 0.093 | 0.009 | 0.398 | 0.784 | 0.224 | 0.599 |
| X4 | 0.090 | 0.075 | 0.784 | 0.252 | 0.161 | 0.907 |
| X5 | 0.100 | 0.165 | 0.224 | 0.161 | 0.231 | 0.277 |
| X6 | 0.150 | 0.103 | 0.599 | 0.907 | 0.277 | 0.202 |
| Total Sj | 0.778 | 0.642 | 2.107 | 2.268 | 1.158 | 2.237 |

Grand Total T = 9.189

=3.031418

Calculations to Determine Loading Values of Factors

| Total Sj | $Uli = Sj/T^{0.05}$ | Lj |
|---|---|---|
| 0.778 | 0.256482 | 0.256482 |
| 0.642 | 0.211655 | –0.21166 |
| 2.107 | 0.694987 | –0.69499 |
| 2.268 | 0.748212 | 0.748212 |
| 1.158 | 0.382009 | –0.38201 |
| 2.237 | 0.738072 | –0.73807 |

Factor Loading

| | F1 | F2 | F3 | Communality = $h^2$ |
|---|---|---|---|---|
| X1 | 0.781109 | 0.306035 | 0.256482 | 0.769572 |
| X2 | 0.847606 | 0.201962 | –0.21166 | 0.804022 |
| X3 | 0.443837 | –0.63603 | –0.69499 | 1.084535 |
| X4 | 0.615849 | –0.60698 | 0.748212 | 1.307515 |
| X5 | 0.741385 | 0.467844 | –0.38201 | 0.91446 |
| X6 | –0.55912 | 0.69666 | –0.73807 | 1.342696 |
| Eigenvalue | 2.767091 | 1.611619 | 1.844091 | 6.222801 |
| | | | | |
| Proportion of | 0.46 | 0.27 | 0.31 | |
| Total variance = | | | | |
| Proportion | 0.44467 | 0.258986 | 0.2963441 | |
| of common variance | | | | |
| | | | | |
| Absolute Highest value of factors | | | | |
| | | | | |
| X1 | ***0.78111*** | 0.306035 | 0.256482 | |
| X2 | ***0.84761*** | 0.201962 | –0.21166 | |
| X3 | 0.443837 | –0.63603 | ***–0.695*** | |
| X4 | ***0.61585*** | –0.60698 | 0.748212 | |
| X5 | ***0.74138*** | 0.467844 | –0.38201 | |
| X6 | –0.55912 | ***0.69666*** | –0.73807 | |
| | | | | |
| | | | | |
| Assignment Factors | | | | |
| F1 | F2 | F3 | | |
| X1 | X6 | X3 | | |
| X2 | | | | |
| X4 | | | | |

| X5 | | | | |
|---|---|---|---|---|
| | | | | |
| | Proportion of | Total variance = | Proportion | |
| | F1 | 0.46 | | 0.44 |
| | F2 | 0.27 | | 0.26 |
| | F3 | 0.31 | | 0.30 |

Assignment of factors

Factor F1 = Food hygeniety (X1), Menu items (X2), Food quality (X4), Ambience (X5)

which has propotion of 46% this factor can be named as 'Food factor' the owner should concentrate on food

Factor F2 = Price (X6) which has proportion of 27%, Food Price

Factor 3 =Service quality (X3) which has a proption of 31%.

## Principal Component Analysis

This method maximises the sum of squares of loadings of each factor. This is a popular method which determines loadings of variables on different factors by using standard normal values of the observations of original values.

PCA is mathematically defined as an orthogonal linear transformation that transforms the data to a new co-ordinate system such that the greatest variance by any projection of the data comes to lie on the first co-ordinate (called the first principal component), the second greatest variance on the second co-ordinate, and so on. PCA is theoretically the optimum transform for a given data in least square terms.

PCA can be used for dimensionality reduction in a data set by retaining those characteristics of the data set that contribute most to its variance, by keeping lower-order principal components and ignoring higher-order ones. Such low-order components often contain the "most important" aspects of the data. However, depending on the application this may not always be the case.

PCA is theoretically the optimal linear scheme, in terms of least mean square error, for compressing a set of high dimensional vectors into a set of lower dimensional vectors and then reconstructing the original set. It is a non-parametric analysis and the answer is unique and independent of any hypothesis about data probability distribution. However, the latter two properties are regarded as weakness as well as strength, in that being non-parametric, no prior knowledge can be incorporated and that PCA compressions often incur loss of information.

As this method needs lot of calculation and iterations are made to converge data, we shall discuss the procedure in chapter 'Use of Computer in research'.

## 9.15.4 Cluster Analysis

Cluster analysis aims at grouping of persons/objects/occasions into unknown number of groups such that the members of each group are having similar characteristics.

**Clustering** is the classification of objects into different groups, or more precisely, the partitioning of a data set into subsets (clusters), so that the data in each subset (ideally) share some common trait -- often proximity according to some defined distance measure. Data clustering is a common technique for statistical data analysis, which is used in many fields, including machine learning, data mining, pattern recognition, image analysis and bioinformatics. The computational task of classifying the data set into *k* clusters is often referred to as ***k*-clustering**.

Besides the term data clustering (or just clustering), there are a number of terms with similar meanings, including cluster analysis, automatic classification, numerical taxonomy, and typological analysis.

The different techniques of cluster analysis form groups such that the similarity among the members within each group is maximized. The cluster algorithms are classified into *hierarchical* clustering algorithms and *non-hierarchical* clustering algorithms.

## Market Research

Cluster analysis is widely used in market research when working with multivariate data from surveys and test panels. Market researchers use cluster analysis to partition the general population of consumers into market segments and to better understand the relationships between different groups of existing consumers or potential customers.

- Segmenting the market and determining target markets
- Product positioning
- New product development
- Selecting test markets

## Distance Measure

An important step in any clustering is to select a distance measure, which will determine how the *similarity* of two elements is calculated. This will influence the shape of the clusters, as some elements may be close to one another according to one distance and further away according to another. For example, in a 2-dimensional space, the distance between the point (x=1, y=0) and the origin (x=0, y=0) is always 1 according to the usual norms, but the distance between the point (x=1, y=1) and the origin can be 2, $\sqrt{2}$ or 1 if you take respectively the 1-norm, 2 norm or infinity-norm distance.

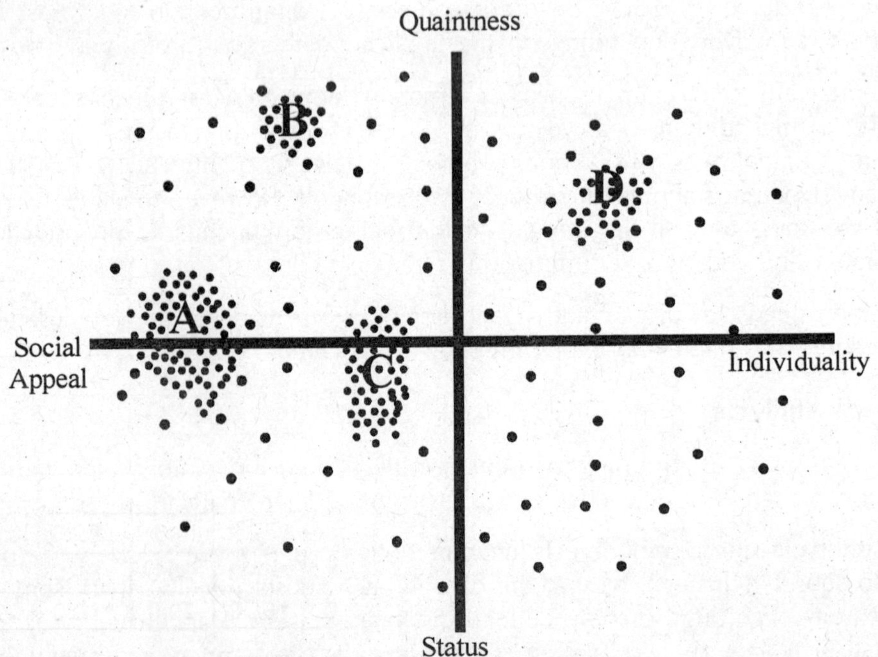

We can take the example of vacation tourists. Three clusters or market segments can be identified. They are the: (1) The demanders – they want exceptional service and expect to be pampered; (2) The escapists – they want to get away and just relax; (3) The educationists – they want to see new things, go to museums, go on a safari, or experience new cultures.

Cluster analysis, like factor analysis and multi – dimensional scaling, is an interdependence technique: it makes no distinction between dependent and independent variables. The entire set of interdependent relationships is examined. It is similar to multi – dimensional scaling in that both examine inter-object similarity by examining the complete set of interdependent relationships. The difference is that multi – dimensional scaling identifies underlying dimensions, while cluster analysis identifies clusters. **Cluster analysis is the obverse of factor analysis. Whereas factor analysis reduces the number of variables by grouping them into a smaller set of factors, cluster analysis reduces the number of observations or cases by grouping them into a smaller set of clusters.**

The basic procedure is:

1. Formulate the problem – select the variables that you wish to apply the clustering technique.
2. Select a distance measure – various ways of computing distance:
   - Squared Euclidean distance – the square root of the sum of the squared differences in value for each variable
   - Manhattan distance – the sum of the absolute differences in value for any variable
   - Chebychev distance – the maximum absolute difference in values for any variable
   - Mahalanobis (or correlation) distance – this measure uses the correlation coefficients between the observations and uses that as a measure to cluster them. This is an important measure since it is unit invariant (can literally compare apples to oranges).
3. Select a clustering procedure.
4. Decide on the number of clusters.
5. Map and interpret clusters – draw conclusions – illustrative techniques like perceptual maps, icicle plots, and dendrograms are useful.
6. Assess reliability and validity – various methods:
   - repeat analysis but use different distance measure
   - repeat analysis but use different clustering technique
   - split the data randomly into two halves and analyze each part separately
   - repeat analysis several times, deleting one variable each time
   - repeat analysis several times, using a different order each time

## Clustering Procedures

There are several types of clustering methods:

- **Hierarchical Clustering:** Hierarchical clustering builds (agglomerative), or breaks up (divisive), a hierarchy of clusters. The traditional representation of this hierarchy is a tree (called a dendrogram), with individual elements at one end and a single cluster containing every element at the other. Agglomerative algorithms begin at the top of the tree, whereas divisive algorithms begin at the root.

- **Non-Hierarchical Clustering** (also called k-means clustering) first determine a cluster centre, then group all objects that are within a certain distance.
- **Sequential Threshold Method** – first determine a cluster centre, then group all objects that are within a pre-determined threshold from the centre - one cluster is created at a time.
- **Parallel Threshold Method** – simultaneously several cluster centres are determined, then objects that are within a pre-determined threshold from the centres are grouped.
- **Optimizing Partitioning Method** – first a non-hierarchical procedure is run, then objects are reassigned so as to optimize an overall criterion.

Let us understand in detail.

## Hierarchical Clustering

Objects are organized into an hierarchical structure as part of the procedure.

- **Divisive Clustering** – start by treating all objects as if they are part of a single large cluster, then divide the cluster into smaller and smaller clusters.
- **Agglomerative clustering** – start by treating each object as a separate cluster, then group them into bigger and bigger cluster.
- **Centroid Methods** – clusters are generated that maximize the distance between the centres of clusters (a centroid is the mean value for all the objects in the cluster).
- **Variance Methods** – clusters are generated that minimize the within-cluster variance.
- **Ward's Procedure** – clusters are generated that minimize the squared Euclidean distance to the center mean between them (also called the nearest neighbour rule)
- **Complete Linkage Method** – cluster objects based on the maximum distance between them (also called the furthest neighbour rule).
- **Average Linkage Method** – cluster objects based on the average distance between all pairs of objects (one member of the pair must be from a different cluster).

Cutting the tree at a given height will give a clustering at a selected precision. In the following example, cutting after the second row will yield clusters {a} {b c} {d e} {f}. Cutting after the third row will yield clusters {a} {b c} {d e f}, which is a coarser clustering, with a smaller number of larger clusters.

The diagram below illustrates the results of a survey that studied drinkers' perceptions of spirits (alcohol). Each point represents the results from one respondent. The research indicates there are four clusters in this market.

## Agglomerative Hierarchical Clustering

For example, suppose this data is to be clustered, and the Euclidean distance is the distance metric.

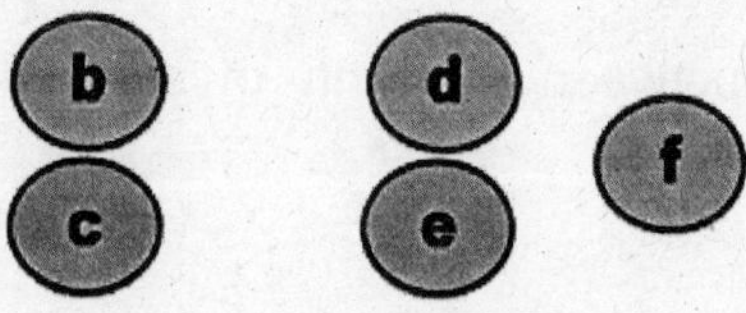


Raw data

The hierarchical clustering dendrogram would be as such:

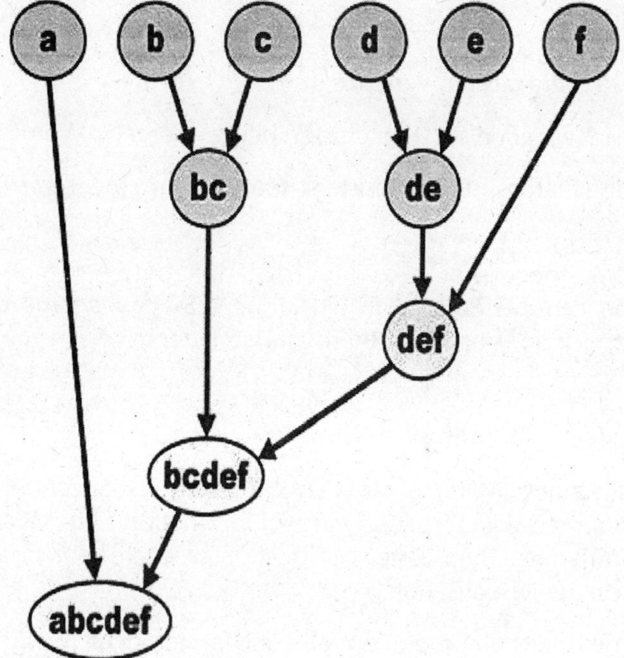


## Traditional Representation

This method builds the hierarchy from the individual elements by progressively merging clusters. In our example, we have six elements {a} {b} {c} {d} {e} and {f}. The first step is to determine which elements to merge in a cluster. Usually, we want to take the two closest elements, according to the chosen distance.

Optionally, one can also construct a distance matrix at this stage, where the number in the *i*-th row *j*-th column is the distance between the *i*-th and *j*-th elements. Then, as clustering progresses, rows and columns are merged as the clusters are merged and the distances updated. This is a common way to implement this type of clustering, and has the benefit of catching distances between clusters. A simple agglomerative clustering algorithm is described in the single linkage clustering page; it can easily be adapted to different types of linkage.

Suppose we have merged the two closest elements *b* and *c*, we now have the following clusters {*a*}, {*b*, *c*}, {*d*}, {*e*} and {*f*}, and want to merge them further. To do that, we need to take the distance between {a} and {b c}, and therefore define the distance between two clusters. Usually the distance between two clusters *A* and *B* is one of the following:

- The maximum distance between elements of each cluster (also called complete linkage clustering):

$$\max\{d(x,y): x \in A, y \in B\}$$

- The minimum distance between elements of each cluster (also called single linkage clustering):

$$\min\{d(x,y): x \in A, y \in B\}$$

- The mean distance between elements of each cluster (also called average linkage clustering, used e.g. in UPGMA):

$$\frac{1}{|A| \cdot |B|} \sum_{x \in A} \sum_{y \in B} d(x,y)$$

- The sum of all intra-cluster variance
- The increase in variance for the cluster being merged (Ward's criterion)
- The probability that candidate clusters spawn from the same distribution function (V-linkage)

Each agglomeration occurs at a greater distance between clusters than the previous agglomeration, and one can decide to stop clustering either when the clusters are too far apart to be merged (distance criterion) or when there is a sufficiently small number of clusters (number criterion).

### 9.15.5 Multidimensional Scaling

**Multidimensional Scaling (MDS)** is often used in data visualization for exploring similarities or dissimilarities in data. MDS is a special case of ordination. An MDS algorithm starts with a matrix of item–item similarities, then assigns a location of each item in a low-dimensional space, suitable for graphing or 3D visualisation.

MDS is used to measure human perceptions and preferences towards some stimuli (objects), like products, organizations, places, events, brands, etc., and position them in a perceptual space. The scale value of each stimulus may be in the form of either metric or non-metric. The metric data are interval-scaled or ratio-scaled, whereas the non-metric data are ordinal-scaled. The input as well as output of fully metric form of MDS is ratio-scaled. This means that the output data are either multiple or linear functions of input data. Similarly, the input as well as output of fully non-metric form of MDS is ordinal-scaled. This means that the input as well as output is rank ordered. The input and output of non-metric form of MDS are ordinal-scaled and interval-scaled, respectively.

There are several steps in conducting MDS research:

1. **Formulating the Problem** – You will have to decide what type of variables you wish to analyse and also decide how many variables are to be used. More than 20 is cumbersome. Less than 8 (4 pairs) will not give valid results. You will have to keep in mind the purpose of study.

2. **Obtaining Input Data** – Respondents are asked a series of questions. For each product pair they are asked to rate similarity (usually on a 7 – point Likert scale from very similar to very dissimilar). The first question could be for Coca Cola and Pepsi for example, the next for Coca Cola and Fanta, the next for Pepsi and Fanta, the next for Fanta and Thums Up, etc. The number of questions is a function of the number of brands and can be calculated as Q = *N*(*N* " 1) / 2 where Q is the number of questions and N is the number of brands. This approach is referred to as the "Perception data: direct approach". There are two other approaches. There is the "Perception data: derived approach" in which products are decomposed into attributes which are rated on a semantic differential scale. The other is the "Preference data approach" in which respondents are asked their preference rather than similarity.

3. **Running the MDS Statistical Programme** – Software for running the procedure is available in most of the better statistical applications programmes. Often there is a choice between Metric MDS (which deals with interval or ratio level data), and Non-metric MDS (which deals with ordinal data). The researchers must decide on the number of dimensions they want the computer to create. The more dimensions, the better the statistical fit, but the more difficult it is to interpret the results.

4. **Mapping the Results and Defining the Dimensions** – The statistical programme (or a related module) will map the results. The map will plot each product (usually in two dimensional space). The proximity of products to each other indicate either how similar they are or how preferred they are, depending on which approach was used. The dimensions must be labelled by the researcher. This requires subjective judgement and is often very challenging. Perceptual mapping may be helpful.

5. **Test the Results for Reliability and Validity** – Compute R-squared to determine what proportion of variance of the scaled data can be accounted for by the MDS procedure. An R-square of .6 is considered the minimum acceptable level. Other possible tests are Kruskal's Stress, split data tests, data stability tests (i.e., eliminating one brand), and test-retest reliability.

**Perceptual Mapping** is a graphics technique used by marketers that attempts to visually display the perceptions of customers or potential customers. Typically the position of a product, product line, brand, or company is displayed relative to their competition.

Perceptual maps can have any number of dimensions but the most common is two dimensions. Any more is a challenge to draw and confusing to interpret. The perceptual map below shows consumer perceptions of various automobiles on the two dimensions of sportiness/conservative and classy/affordable. This sample of consumers felt Porsche was the sportiest and classiest of the cars in the study (top right corner). They felt Plymouth was most practical and conservative (bottom left corner).

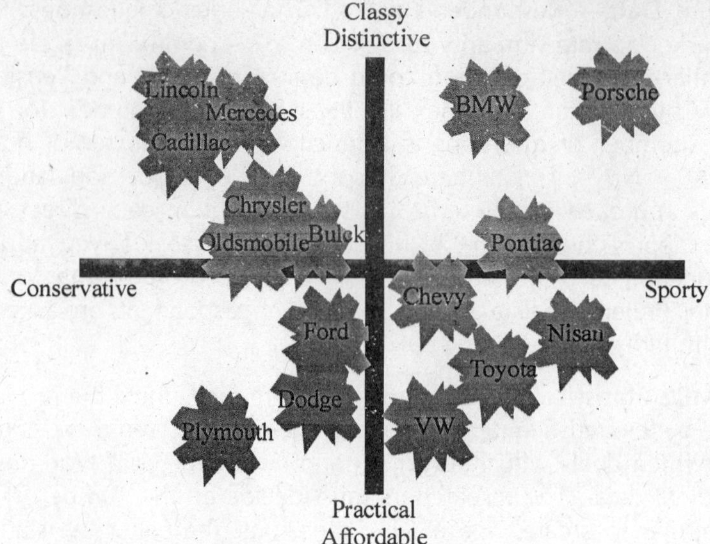


**Perceptual Map of Competing Products**

Cars that are positioned close to each other are seen as similar on the relevant dimensions by the consumer. For example consumers see Buick, Chrysler, and Oldsmobile as similar. They are close competitors and form a competitive grouping. A company considering the introduction of a new model will look for an area on the map free from competitors. Some perceptual maps use different size circles to indicate the sales volume or market share of the various competing products.

We shall discuss more with examples in chapter 'Use of Computer Software in Research'.

### 9.15.5.1 Problems For Practice

**(Students should solve the problems after reading the next chapter and should use computer software for calculations and interpret the results.)**

1. The performance standard of employees as a function of their age ($X_1$,) and family size ($X_2$) is classified into 'Above average' and 'Below average'. The data on 10 different employees in a company are presented in the following table:

| Employee | Standard | $X_1$ (in Hours) | $X_2$ (%) |
|---|---|---|---|
| 1 | Good | 24 | 5 |
| 2 | Good | 12 | 8 |
| 3 | Bad | 36 | 4 |
| 4 | Bad | 12 | 0 |
| 5 | Bad | 36 | 3 |
| 6 | Good | 36 | 10 |
| 7 | Good | 24 | 3 |
| 8 | Bad | 48 | 4 |
| 9 | Bad | 96 | 5 |
| 10 | Good | 36 | 12 |

(i) Design the discriminant function $Y = aX_1 + bX_2$ (ii) Compute the discriminant ratio K and identify the variable which is more important in relation to the other. Test whether group means are equal in importance at a significance level of 5%.

2. In a survey on a product, data on three variables have been collected, as shown in the following table:

| | Variable | | |
|---|---|---|---|
| Respondent | $X_1$ | $X_2$ | $X_3$ |
| 1 | 5 | 7 | 8 |
| 2 | 3 | 3 | 5 |
| 3 | 3 | 1 | 5 |
| 4 | 1 | 1 | 5 |
| 5 | 3 | 2 | 4 |
| 6 | 3 | 3 | 5 |
| 7 | 2 | 2 | 1 |
| 8 | 6 | 6 | 5 |
| 9 | 4 | 2 | 1 |
| 10 | 4 | 3 | 2 |

Perform factor analysis using centroid method to identify two factors which can represent the variables of the study. Also analyse by using computer software using Principal Component Analysis.

3. Find the proportion of total variance as well as common variance for each factors:

| | Variable | | |
|---|---|---|---|
| Respondent | $X_1$ | $X_2$ | $X_3$ |
| 1 | 8 | 3 | 5 |
| 2 | 6 | 1 | 7 |
| 3 | 6 | 1 | 7 |
| 4 | 4 | 7 | 6 |
| 5 | 9 | 5 | 8 |
| 6 | 4 | 4 | 1 |
| 7 | 8 | 1 | 5 |
| 8 | 8 | 2 | 7 |
| 9 | 7 | 2 | 4 |
| 10 | 1 | 3 | 9 |

4. The factor loading matrix in a factor analysis with 6 variables and two factors, shown in the following table:

| | Factors | |
|---|---|---|
| Variable (i) | 1 | 2 |
| 1 | –0.875 | –0.350 |
| 2 | –0.840 | –0.400 |
| 3 | 0.610 | –0.700 |
| 4 | 0.600 | –0.650 |
| 5 | 0.625 | –0.475 |
| 6 | –0.825 | –0.450 |

Plot the factor loadings on a two-dimensional plane ($F_1$-$F_2$ plane) and find the revised factors loadings using the varimax factor rotation method.

5. In a survey, the monthly income (in thousands of rupees) and monthly purchases of health care products (in hundreds of rupees) of respondents are summarized in the following table:

| Respondent | Monthly income | Monthly purchase |
|---|---|---|
| 1 | 12 | 5 |
| 2 | 19 | 8 |
| 3 | 14 | 6 |
| 4 | 15 | 9 |
| 5 | 18 | 7 |
| 6 | 10 | 2 |

(a) Cluster the employees using agglomerative hierarchical clustering method with distance measure.

(b) Draw a dendrogram and find the clusters using distance measure.

6. The annual labour welfare fund (lakhs of rupees) and the corresponding annual production (in Crores of rupees) for the past 8 years of a company are presented below:

| Year | Annual Labour Fund | |
|---|---|---|
| I | $X_i$ | Annual Production |
| 1 | 8 | 18 |
| 2 | 10 | 28 |
| 3 | 12 | 35 |
| 4 | 14 | 45 |
| 5 | 16 | 50 |
| 6 | 18 | 70 |
| 7 | 20 | 85 |
| 8 | 22 | 95 |

**Regress and test results**

7. A district industries centre has collected data summarizing the number of industries in the district under each combination of R&D expenditure (in lakhs of rupees) and annual sales (in crores of rupees), as shown below:

| Annual sales (crores of ₹) | R&D expenditure (in lakhs of ₹) | | |
|---|---|---|---|
| | 10-30 | 30-50 | 50-70 |
| 10-14 | 3 | 6 | 2 |
| 14-18 | 6 | 8 | 3 |
| 18-22 | 4 | 8 | 9 |
| 22-26 | 2 | 4 | 7 |

Find the correlation coefficient of this grouped data.

8. The preference ratings of 10 brands of washing machine by two judges are shown below:

| Brand | Rating by judge-1 | Rating by judge-2 | Brand | Rating by judge-1 | Rating by Judge-2 |
|---|---|---|---|---|---|
| **1** | 1 | 3 | **6** | 6 | 7 |
| **2** | 2 | 5 | **7** | 7 | 8 |
| **3** | 3 | 6 | **8** | 8 | 10 |
| **4** | 4 | 2 | **9** | 9 | 1 |
| **5** | 5 | 4 | **10** | 10 | 9 |

Find the rank correlation between the preference ratings assigned by the ji different brands of washing machines. Also, test the significance of the correlation at a significance level of 0.05.

9. The demand values of a product over the past 10 years are summarized below:

| Year (t) | Demand in lakhs | Year (t) | Demand in lakhs |
|---|---|---|---|
| 1 | 40 | 6 | 75 |
| 2 | 45 | 7 | 87 |
| 3 | 52 | 10 | 90 |
| 4 | 60 | 9 | 95 |
| 5 | 68 | 10 | 110 |

Find the auto-correlation coefficients with one-year lag ($r_1$), two-year lag ($r_2$) and three-year lag ($r_3$).

## 9.16 How to Do?

Dolly: "I have read Prof Neerav Nagar's article 'Drivers of Shareholders' Value'. It is a nice and good paper. Objectives are very clear. Variables have been explained well in research methodology. Literature has been reviewed. All statements are properly authenticated with proper references. But there is a problem. Research methodology does not explain the construct properly."

Jolly: "What do you mean?"

Dolly: "The author says that relationship has been calculated by regression. But actually it appears variables have only been correlated and goodness of fit of correlation 'r' has been found by calculating $r^2$."

Jolly: "Now, you are becoming highly critical."

Dolly: "No, I am not an expert researcher. But I feel if the researcher does not write the methodology properly, readers can draw their own inferences."

Jolly: "I agree with you but in this case it is clear that correlation has been calculated between individual variables, however the significance of the correlations needs testing."

Dolly: "I think there is a gap and we should study further."

Jolly: "We can find a gap in every study which provokes us for further study."

Dolly: "We are criticizing the researchers openly. Don't you think they will mind it?"

Jolly: "No, dear. A researcher cannot be narrow-minded. The first lesson of research is that research is not carried out for self-enlightenment. Research must be shared with others. When you are open in public you are exposed both to appreciations and unappreciation. Purity in gold is the result of continuous heating. Researcher becomes great only after criticism."

Dolly: "The findings in the paper are purely based on calculations."

Jolly: "The project report has all the qualities of a good research."

Dolly: "What about multivariate analysis?"

Jolly: "Mostly multivariate analysis techniques are used in applied research"

Dolly: "Can we get a good research report on discriminant analysis, factor analysis, cluster analysis etc?"

Jolly: "See, all these analyses are used on specific issues. The results are beneficial only to the company for which the research is carried out."

Dolly: "You mean to say, issue of external validity may arise."

Jolly: "Though, you may find some research reports in good journals, but discussion is only short-lived."

Dolly: "Can we read some article where multivariate analysis has been used."

Jolly: "Of course, Prof A.M. Suresh, Prof K.G. Raja and Mrs. S Vijayalakhsmi faculty members from Graduate Department of Management Studies, Dayanand Sagar College of Management and Information Technology, Bangalore have worked on 'Changes in Indian Garment Industry due to dismantling of Trade Quotas – An Empirical Study'. The article has already been published in Vol 1 no. 3 of Journal of Global Economy"

Dolly: "I shall read it along with my friends."

Jolly: "Discuss positively."

Dolly: "See you tomorrow."

✦ ✦ ✦

Research Project 11

# 9.17 Changes in Indian Garment Industry Due to Dismantling of Trade Quotas – An Empirical Study

**Prof.A.M.Suresh[1], Mr. K.G.[2] Raja and Mrs. S. Vijayalakshmi[3]**

## 1. INTRODUCTION

Textile industry is an important and emerging sector for both the global and Indian economy. India has many of the ingredients conducive to a thriving textile industry, which incidentally is one of the oldest organized industries in India. In a country of growing population like India, the textiles production both in terms of quality and quantity has to keep pace with the preferences and trends of consumers. On the supply side, the textile industry in India accounts for 20 per cent of industrial production and is next to agriculture in providing employment. The textile industry plays a vital role in the Indian economy, both with regard to employment generation and earning foreign exchange. Textile sector employs lakhs of workers and also contributes significantly to the national economy through inland and export sales. Table 1 gives the share of India's exports in the world market for the last decade.

**Table 1**
**Export of Apparel: World & India (figure in US $ billion)**

| Year | World Exports | India's Share | India's Share % |
|---|---|---|---|
| 1990 | 108.13 | 2.53 | 2.34 |
| 1995 | 158.34 | 4.11 | 2.60 |
| 2000 | 193.26 | 5.48 | 2.79 |
| 2001 | 193.26 | 5.05 | 2.61 |
| 2002 | 206.38 | 5.53 | 2.68 |

Source: Compendium of International Textile Statistics, 2004

## 2.The History of International Trade in Textiles and Clothing

### 2.1 Multi Fibre Agreement (MFA) 1974-1994[1]

Multi Fibre Agreement (MFA) provided a legal framework under which developed countries could impose quotas on their imports from the more competitive developing countries under bilateral agreements. The system derogated from the general principles of the General Agreement on Trade and Tariff (GATT), the predecessor of the WTO, which requires all signatories to treat all their trading partners on a basis of equality. The Multi Fibre Agreement (MFA) therefore can be considered as form of protectionism, given that it discriminated against the exports of developing countries, many of who are highly dependent on the textile and garment sectors an important engine of economic development. The Multi Fibre Agreement was a major departure from the basic GATT rules and particularly the principle of non-discrimination.

1. Head of Department
2. Faculty Member
3. Faculty Member, Postgraduate Department of Management Studies, Dayanand Sagar College of Management and Information Technology, Savige Malleswara Hills, Kumaraswami, Layout Bangalore-78.

• The article has already been published in general of global economy volume 3, No. 1, reprinted with permission from author and editors.

Table 2

Quota Phase out Schedule

| Step | Percentage of products to be brought under GATT (including removal of any quotas) | Percentage of products to be brought under GATT (including removal of any quotas) |
|---|---|---|
| Step 1:1 Jan 1995 (to 31 Dec 1997) | 16% (minimum, taking 1990 imports as base) | 6.96% per year |
| Step 2:1 Jan 1998 (to 31 Dec 2001) | 17% | 8.7% per year |
| Step 3:1 Jan 2002 (to 31 Dec 2004) | 18% | 11.05% per year |
| Step 4:1 Jan 2005 Full integration into GATT (and final elimination of quotas). Agreement on Textiles and Clothing terminates. | 49% (maximum) | No quotas left |

**Source:** wto.org

On 1 January, 1995 it was replaced by the WTO Agreement on Textiles and Clothing, which sets out a transitional process for the ultimate removal of these quotas. Since 1 January, 1995, international textiles and clothing trade has been going through fundamental change under the 10-year transitional programme of the WTO's Agreement on Textiles and Clothing (ATC). Under the Agreement, WTO Members have committed themselves to remove the quotas by 1 January, 2005 by integrating the sector fully into GATT rules. Table 2 gives quota phase out plan.

## 2.2 The WTO Agreement on Textiles and Clothing (ATC) 1995-2004

The Agreement on Textile and Clothing (ATC) is a transitional tool that will be used in place of the Multi Fibre Agreement (MFA) until January 1, 2005. The Agreement on Textile and Clothing (ATC) has number of defining features. Some of these are;

(a) The product coverage, basically encompassing yarns, fabrics, made-up textile products and clothing;

(b) A programme for the progressive integration of these textile and clothing products into GATT 1994 rules;

(c) A liberalization process to progressively enlarge existing quotas (until they are removed) by increasing annual growth rates at each stage;

(d) A special safeguard mechanism to deal with new cases of serious damage or threat thereof to domestic producers during the transition period;

(e) Establishment of a Textiles Monitoring Body ("TMB") to supervise the implementation of the Agreement and ensure that the rules are faithfully followed; and

4. www.wto.org

(f) Other provisions, including rules on circumvention of the quotas, their administration, treatment of non-MFA restrictions, and commitments undertaken elsewhere under the WTO's agreements and procedures affecting this sector.

The ATC calls for a progressive phasing out of all the MFA restrictions and other discriminatory measures in a period of 10 years. In contrast to the MFA, the ATC is applicable to all members of the WTO.

## 2. Review of Literature

All studies indicate that Asia will experience the greatest changes in the distribution of production. The most extreme impact study foresee that China, which currently holds about one-fifth of the global apparel market, might have a 150% increase in their overall textile and clothing exports[1] or nearly 50 per cent of the world market after MFA phaseouts[2]. These assumptions are based both on the very high utilisation of many quotas by China and its production capacities. According to estimates, India and Pakistan may lose market share to China, but could compensate through shares taken from other (mostly smaller) suppliers if domestic structural reforms are undertaken. Table 3 gives us a picture of the key players in the world textile market and their core competencies and weaknesses.

A Study says India will not be able to make the most of quota-free world because there are too many loose threads in its textiles strategy[1]. In the post-ATC era, if the Indian textile and clothing industry is to remain competitive, it has to maintain quality, consistency and commitment to tight delivery schedules, production; technological and marketing strategies are needed to maintain a competitive edge[2].

**Table 3**

**Post quota phase-out scenario**

| Key countries/regions | Key positives | Key negatives |
|---|---|---|
| China | Efficient, low cost, vertically integrated | Growth at the cost of profits |
| India, Pakistan | Vertically integrated, low cost | Lacks economies of support scale and infrastructure |
| Mexico (NAFTA), Turkey | Proximity to market, duty and quota free | Lack China and India's degree of competitiveness |
| ASEAN (Vietnam, Cambodia, Indonesia) | Cheap labour | No other cost or locational advantage |
| AGOA (African) countries, Bangladesh | Quota and tariff free, cheap labour | Lacks integration and China and India's degree of competitiveness |
| Hong Kong, Korea, Taiwan<br>USA and EU | Trading hubs – proximity to China<br>Non-quota barriers likely to prove irritant to imports | No cost advantage, protected currently by quotas<br>US$ 400 bn trade loss likely over 10 years |

**Source** - Industry, I-SEC Research

[1] Joseph François and Dean Spinanger, Greater China's Accession to the WTO, December 2001.

[2] Ianchovichina E. and W. Martin, 2001, Trade Liberalization in China's Accession to the WTO, World Bank, June 2001.

A recent study[1] says that even big companies like Raymond and Arvind Mills are building factories that are just a tenth in size compared to those in China. The largest factory of India's largest garment exporter, Gokuldas Images has just 1000 sewing machines while even a medium-sized Chinese factory boasts of 2000 machines. The Chinese companies were ready 2 years before and when the quota regime was phased out, the China's share of export shot up from 9% in 2001 to 45% in 2003, since they had spare capacity waiting. An industry analyst feels that the sector would need an investment of at least $6 billion to $7 billion in the next four years, which is more than the current size of the industry. The existing players will not be able to make up this entire investment, hence now there exists wide opportunities available for new companies to make fresh investments in this sector.

## 3. Research Problem

The biggest challenge for the Indian industry in the next few years will be the dismantling of MFA trade quotas after almost four decades of restrictions. With the dismantling of Multi Fibre Agreement (MFA), trade in textile and garment will be a free for all affairs. There are both positive and negative implications of this. Removal of quotas will create new opportunities for Indian textile in international market. To reap the benefits of phasing out of quota system, Indian textile has to be internationally competitive, productive and efficient and it should be fast in responding to changes in consumer preferences. However, with termination of quotas the garment exporting countries will be competing intensively with each other for market share without the protection of a bilateral quota system. Hence the researchers found the need to understand the impact of quotas on Indian garment industry in the post quota scenario.

## 4. Research Design

For the purpose of the study, target population was identified as all middle and top-level employees of garment export firms of Bangalore city. The sample population consisted of 50 top and middle level employees of the 12 garments export firms of Bangalore. A structured questionnaire was constructed. The draft was pre-tested and in the light of the outcome of the pretest, the questionnaire was revised and finalized. The questionnaire consisted of 2 parts. Part 1 consisted of background details of the respondents. Part 2 consisted of questions related to the impact of quota phase out on Indian export firms. 50 questionnaires were administered to the respondents and all the questionnaires were returned. This yielded 100% response rate.

## 5. Results and Discussions

All the top and middle level employees of various textile mills were interviewed through a structured questionnaire to understand their opinions towards quota free system. The responses were analyzed to arrive at mean scores. These scores were ascertained after giving weightages 5, 4, 3, 2, 1 to answers like strongly agree, agree, neutral, disagree, and strongly disagree. The results are shown in table 4.

Earlier Studies revealed that removal of quotas would create new opportunities for Indian garment sector. The respondents of the present study also feel quota phase out will provide lot of opportunities for long-term investments. This is ranked first with a mean score of 4.200. There is a consensus that with termination of quotas the garment exporting countries will be competing intensively with each other for market share without the protection of a bilateral quota system. The respondents feel that heavy competition from the neighbouring counties will be the biggest challenge for the garment sector due to phasing out of quota system with a mean score of 4.16.

**Table 4**

**Changes in the Garment Sector due to Phasing out of the Quota System**

| Factors | Mean | Std. Deviation | Sig (one tailed) |
|---|---|---|---|
| Increase in productivity | 3.8400 | .99714 | 0.00** |
| Increase in quality standards | 3.8800 | .84853 | 0.00** |
| Increased customer satisfaction | 3.2400 | 1.04119 | 0.107 |
| Effective marketing/sales and cost control | 3.4800 | 1.18218 | 0.06* |
| Fast delivery and service | 3.7600 | 1.09842 | 0.00** |
| Better planning and merchandising | 3.4600 | .95212 | 0.050* |
| Modernization in the industry | 3.6600 | 1.06157 | 0.00** |
| Product diversification | 4.0000 | .85714 | 0.00** |
| Opportunities for long-term investments. | 4.2000 | .75593 | 0.00** |
| Increased market access to non-quota countries | 3.7000 | 1.03510 | 0.00** |
| Unique selling advantage for industry | 3.9000 | 1.09265 | 0.00** |
| Increased popularity of cotton | 3.6400 | 1.10213 | 0.00** |
| Heavy competition from the neighbouring countries | 4.1600 | .91160 | 0.00** |
| Price wars | 3.5600 | .95105 | 0.00** |

- Significant at .05, ** Significant at .01
- **Source:** Primary Data

Executives have agreed that dismantling of trade quotas will lead to product diversifications (4.00), increase in productivity (3.88), improvement in quality standards (3.84),fast delivery and service, (3.70), modernization in the industry (3.66).

Executives are not sure whether dismantling of trade quotas would lead to increased customer satisfaction (3.24), better planning and merchandizing (3.46), effective marketing and sales control (3.48).

**The respondents have also felt that the quota phase out will provide unique selling opportunities (3.90) and result in increased market access to non-quota countries (3.76) and popularity of cotton (3.64).**

## Inter Correlations Between Variables

An important aspect of the study was to identify the relationship between the variables. Correlation analysis can assist to identify the association between the variables that define the post quota scenario. Thus it was decided to conduct correlation analysis in the present study. Correlation analysis was applied for all the 14 variables to understand the relationship between each variable with respect to all other variables. The results are presented in Table no 5. For many combinations the correlation is not significant. Only few variables have significant relationships. There are high-level correlations for modernization of the industry and better planning and merchandizing (.64), popularity of cotton and unique selling advantage for industry (.56), price wars and heavy competition with the neighbouring countries (.55).

1. Too little, too late, 15th November edition, Business World by Latha Jishnu.
2. Phaseout Will Bring Both Opportunities And Challenges- September 23rd, 2004 edition of Financial Express, by Sarika Gupta.
3. The big factories are coming, Mr.T.Surendra, Business World, Nov 15th, 2004.

## Cluster Analysis

Cluster analysis is a set of techniques for grouping similar objects or people. Cluster analysis starts with an undifferentiated group of people, events, or objects and attempts to reorganize them into homogeneous subgroups. Three groups were clearly identified using K- means cluster analysis. Table 6 indicates the means for all the 14 variables in clusters 1, 2, and 3. Figure 1 gives the cluster profile plots.

## Cluster Interpretation

Interpreting the clusters involves examining the cluster mean values. Analysis of the mean values (see Table 6) for each clusters results in the following interpretation of clusters.

Cluster 1 with 22 cases show strong agreements for most of the changes and show slight disagreement towards increased customer satisfaction and fast delivery and service. Overall this cluster is optimistic about post quota scenario.

Cluster 2 with 11 cases show strong agreements for opportunities for long-term investments. The cluster shows strong disagreement towards marketing/sales control and modernization in the industry. It can be inferred that this cluster is not optimistic about post quota scenario.

Cluster 3 with 17 cases show strong agreements towards increase in productivity, unique-selling advantage for industry and heavy competition from the neighbouring countries. Overall this cluster is cautiòus about post-quota scenario.

The variables in cluster profile plots are ordered by the *F* ratios. The vertical line under each cluster number indicates the grand mean across all data. A variable mean within each cluster is marked by a dot. The horizontal lines indicate one standard deviation above or below the mean. Cluster 1 has above average means of Increase in quality standards, gross domestic product, life expectancy, literacy, and urbanization, and spend considerable money on health care and the military, while the means of their birth rates, infant mortality rates, and birth-to-death ratios are low. The opposite is true for cluster 2.

**Table 5**
**Inter Correlations**

| 1 | | 2 | 3 | 4 | 5 | 6 | 7 | 8 | 9 | 10 | 11 | 12 | 13 |
|---|---|---|---|---|---|---|---|---|---|---|---|---|---|
| 2 | -0.24 | | | | | | | | | | | | |
| 3 | -0.31* | -0.08 | | | | | | | | | | | |
| 4 | 0.27 | 0.24 | -0.27 | | | | | | | | | | |
| 5 | 0.20 | -0.03 | -0.16 | 0.09 | | | | | | | | | |
| 6 | -0.32* | 0.47** | 0.05 | 0.12 | 0.08 | | | | | | | | |
| 7 | -0.18 | 0.45** | -0.01 | 0.23 | -0.03 | 0.64** | | | | | | | |
| 8 | -0.14 | 0.22 | -0.09 | -0.16 | 0.02 | 0.25 | 0.24 | | | | | | |
| 9 | -0.03 | 0.00 | -0.24 | 0.11 | 0.18 | 0.32 | 0.16 | 0.22 | | | | | |
| 10 | -0.20 | 0.37* | -0.15 | 0.35* | 0.04 | 0.47** | 0.42** | 0.23 | 0.39* | | | | |
| 11 | 0.02 | 0.20 | -0.12 | 0.27* | -0.12 | 0.08 | 0.16 | 0.24 | -0.17 | 0.00 | | | |
| 12 | -0.10 | 0.23 | -0.08 | 0.29* | -0.24 | 0.35 | 0.32* | 0.13 | -0.01 | 0.24 | 0.56** | | |
| 13 | 0.16 | 0.18 | 0.00 | 0.45** | 0.08 | 0.07 | 0.22 | 0.20 | -0.10 | -0.07 | 0.50** | 0.30* | |
| 14 | -0.22 | 0.31* | 0.02 | 0.33* | -0.04 | 0.40** | 0.25 | 0.15 | -0.07 | 0.07 | 0.31* | 0.46** | 0.55** |

* Correlation is significant at the 0.05 level (2-tailed).

** Correlation is significant at the 0.01 level (2-tailed).

**Table 6**
**Cluster Analysis**

| Variables | Cluster 1 | Cluster 2 | Cluster 3 | F ratio |
|---|---|---|---|---|
| | (22 cases) | (11 cases) | (17 cases) | |
| Increase in productivity | 3.55 | 3.55 | 4.41 | 4.91** |
| Increase in quality standards | 4.32 | 3.27 | 3.71 | 7.80** |
| Increased customer satisfaction | 3.27 | 3.73 | 2.88 | 2.34* |
| Effective marketing/sales and cost control | 4.09 | 1.91 | 3.71 | 26.39** |
| Fast delivery and Service | 3.64 | 3.91 | 3.82 | .26 |
| Better planning and merchandising | 4.09 | 3.00 | 2.94 | 12.79** |
| Modernization in the industry | 4.45 | 2.82 | 3.18 | 20.39** |
| Product diversification | 4.18 | 3.91 | 3.82 | .914 |
| Opportunities for long-term investments. | 4.41 | 4.36 | 3.82 | 3.54* |
| Increased market access to non-quota countries | 4.23 | 3.27 | 3.29 | 6.17** |
| Unique selling advantage for industry | 4.18 | 2.82 | 4.24 | 9.25** |
| Increased popularity of cotton | 4.36 | 2.64 | 3.35 | 15.88** |
| Heavy competition from the neighbouring countries | 4.45 | 3.09 | 4.47 | 15.40** |
| **Price wars** | **4.14** | **2.73** | **3.35** | **12.84**** |

## Cluster Profile Plots

1

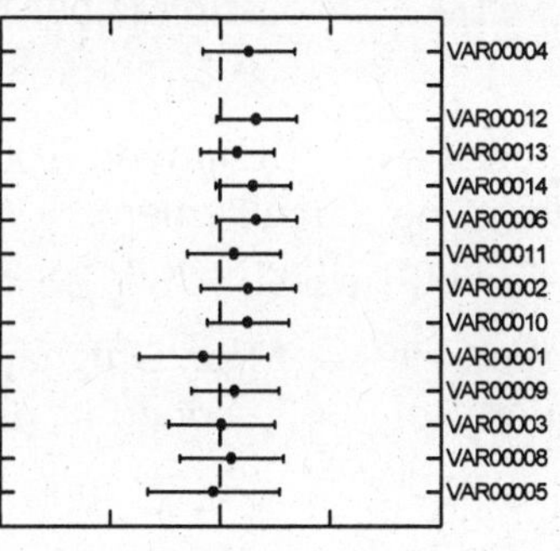


2

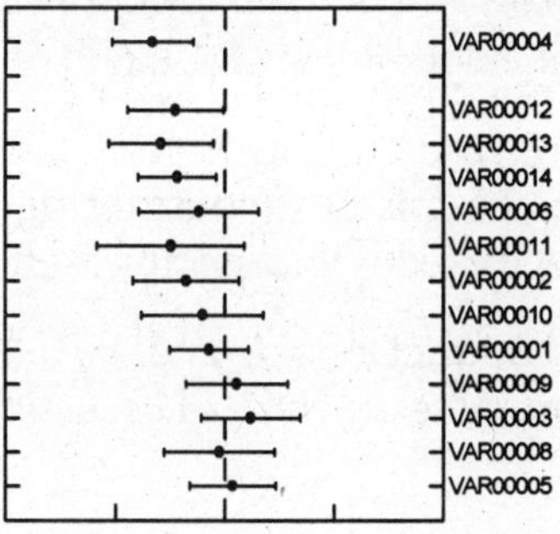


3

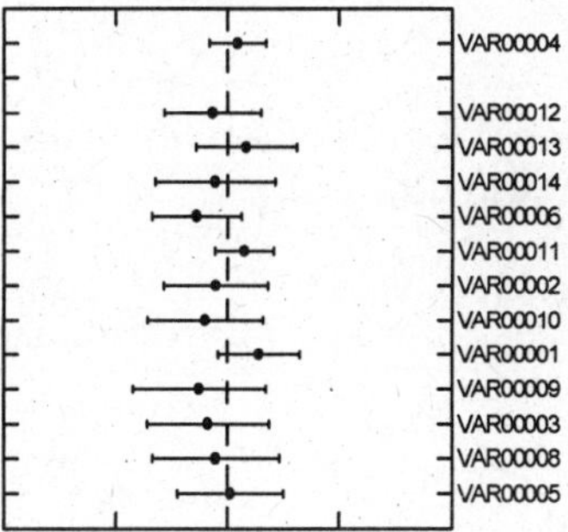

## 7. Conclusions

The present research focused on identifying the opportunities and challenges posed by post quota phase out scenario. This scenario opens up innumerable opportunities as the quota constraints are completely removed. This includes opportunity for long-term investments, and expansion of the market. As the protection of the bilateral quota system is removed, it is also likely that there will be intensified competition and pressure on prices.

Phasing out of the quota system in the year 2005 will be beneficial to Indian exporters as it provides opportunities for growth in the garment sector and opportunities for long-term investments. Phase out of quota system also poses number of challenges to Indian exporters such as heavy competition, need for on time delivery and need to increase quality and productivity. Exporters can exploit mentioned opportunities only if these challenges are effectively taken care of.

## References

Audet, D., 2003. "Structural Adjustment in Textiles and Clothing," Working Party of the Trade Committee (2003)/13. Paris: OECD.

Bach, C.F., B. Dimaranan, T. Hertel, and W. Martin, 2000. "Market Growth, Structural Change, and the Gains from the Uruguay Round." *Review of International Economics* 8(2): 295-310.

Bora, B., L., Cernat and A. Turrini, 2002. "Duty and Quota-Free Access for LDCs: Further Evidence from CGE Modelling," Policy Issues in International Trade and Commodities Study Series n°14, Geneva: UNCTAD.

Chadha, R., S. Pohit, R.M. Stern, and A.V. Deardorff, 1999. "Phasing out the Multi-fibre Arrangement: Implications for India." Paper presented at the Second Annual Conference on Global Economic Analysis, Copenhagen.

Diao, X., and A. Somwaru, 2001. "Impact of MFA Phase out on the World Economy: An Intertemporal, Global General Equilibrium Analysis," TMD Discussion Paper No. 79, Washington, D.C.: International Food Policy Research Institute.

Fouquin, M., P. Morand, R. Avisse, G. Minvielle, and P. Dumont, 2002. "Mondialisation et Régionalisation : Le Cas des Industries du Textile et de l'Habillement." Working Paper 2002-08. Paris: Centre d'Etudes Prospectives et d'Informations Internationales.

Francois, J.F., B. McDonald, and H. Nordström, 1994. "The Uruguay Round: A Global General Equilibrium Assessment," Discussion Paper No. 1067, London: Centre for Economic Policy Research.

Francois, J.F., and D. Spinanger, 2002. "Greater China's Accession to the WTO: Implications for International Trade/Production and for Hong Kong." Paper presented at the Fifth Annual Conference on Global Economic Analysis, Taipei, Taiwan.

Harrison, G.W., T.F. Rutherford, and D.G. Tarr, 1997. "Quantifying the Uruguay Round," *Economic Journal* 107: 1405-1430.

Ianchovichina E. and W. Martin, 2001. "Trade Liberalization in China's Accession to the WTO", Working Paper, Washington, D.C.: The World Bank.

Kathuria, S., and A. Bhardwaj, 1998. "Export Quotas and Policy Constraints in the Indian Textile and Garment Industries," Working Paper, Washington, D.C.: The World Bank.

CHAPTER

# REPORT WRITING

## *Structure*

## 10.1 Writing a Good Report

In earlier chapters, we defined problems, planned our research, reviewed literature, designed the experiments, collected data, analysed data, made inferences from data, tested our hypotheses and concluded. Now at the end we are to write a report. A report which the readers should understand what you have done and what are your findings.

Writing up your research report may be one of the most difficult. Developing a good, effective and concise report is an art form in itself. And, in many research projects you will need to write multiple reports that present the results at different levels of detail for different audiences.

There are several general considerations to keep in mind when generating a report:

♦ **The Audience**

Reader is very important to whom we are going to present our report. Reports will differ considerably depending on whether the audience will want or require technical detail, whether they are looking for a summary of results, or whether they are about to examine your research in a research exam.

♦ **The Story**

Every research project has at least one major "story" in it. Sometimes the story centres on a specific research finding. Sometimes it is based on a methodological problem or challenge. When you write your report, you should attempt to tell the "story" to your reader. Even in very formal journal articles where you will be required to be concise and detailed at the same time, a good "storyline" can help make an otherwise very dull report interesting to the reader.

The hardest part of telling the story in your research is finding the story in the first place. You might have worked hard for weeks, months or years. You've been worrying about sampling response, struggling with operationalizing your measures, dealing with the details of design, and wrestling with the data analysis. You were introvert, now while writing the report you will have to be extrovert and you have to try to view your research from your audience's perspective. You may have to let go of some of the details that you obsessed so much about and leave them out of the write up or bury them in technical appendices or tables.

♦ **Formatting Considerations**

If you are writing your report for publishing in the journal, you should be aware that every journal requires articles that you follow specific formatting guidelines. Thinking of writing a book, again, every publisher will require specific formatting. If you are writing your thesis or dissertation, keep it in mind every university has very strict policies about formatting and style. There are legendary stories that circulate among graduate students about the dissertation that was rejected because the page margins were a quarter inch off or the figures weren't labelled correctly.

## 10.2 Critical Elements of a Report

The following are the elements or criteria that you must typically address in a research paper. There are no hard and fast rules, however, a general research format should have the following if it has a causal hypothesis.

### I. Introduction

**Statement of the problem:** The general problem area is stated clearly and unambiguously. The importance and significance of the problem area is discussed.

## II. Objectives of the Study

1. **Statement of causal relationship:** The cause-effect relationship to be studied is stated clearly and is sensibly related to the problem area.
2. **Statement of constructs:** Each key construct in the research/evaluation project is explained (minimally, both the cause and effect). The explanations are readily understandable without any jargon to an intelligent reader.
3. **Literature citations and review:** The literature cited is from reputable and appropriate sources (e.g., professional journals, books and not Time, Newsweek, Outlook, India Today etc.) and you have a minimum of five references. The literature is condensed in an intelligent fashion with only the most relevant information included. Citations are in the correct format.
4. **Statement of hypothesis:** The hypothesis (or hypotheses) is clearly stated and is specific about what is predicted. The relationship of the hypothesis to both the problem statement and literature review is readily understood from reading the text.

## III. Research Methodology

**(a) Sample section:**

1. **Sampling procedure specifications:** The procedure for selecting units for the study is described and is appropriate. The author states which sampling method is used and why. The population and sampling frame are described. In an evaluation, the programme participants are frequently self-selected (i.e., volunteers) and, if so, should be described as such.
2. **Sample description:** The sample is described accurately and is appropriate. Problems in contacting and measuring the sample are anticipated.
3. **External validity considerations:** Generalizability from the sample to the sampling frame and population is considered.

**(b) Measurement section:**

1. **Measures:** Each outcome measurement construct is described briefly (a minimum of two outcome constructs is required). For each construct, the measure or measures are described briefly and an appropriate citation and reference is included (unless you created the measure). You describe briefly the measure you constructed and provide the entire measure in an Appendix. The measures which are used are relevant to the hypotheses of the study and are included in those hypotheses. Wherever possible, multiple measures of the same construct are used.
2. **Construction of measures:** For questionnaires, tests and interviews: Questions are clearly worded, specific, appropriate for the population and follow in a logical fashion. The standards for good questions are followed. For archival data: original data collection procedures are adequately described and indices (i.e., combinations of individual measures) are constructed correctly. For scales, you must describe briefly which scaling procedure you used and how you implemented it. For qualitative measures, the procedures for collecting the measures are described in detail.
3. **Reliability and validity:** You must address both the reliability and validity of all of your measures. For reliability, you must specify what estimation procedure(s) you used. For validity, you must explain how you assessed construct validity. Wherever possible, you

should minimally address both convergent and discriminant validity. The procedures which are used to examine reliability and validity are appropriate for the measures.

**(c) Design and procedures section:**

1. **Design:** The design is clearly presented in both notational and text form. The design is appropriate for the problem and addresses the hypothesis.
2. **Internal validity:** Threats to internal validity and how they are addressed by the design are discussed. Any threats to internal validity which are not well controlled are also considered.
3. **Description of procedures:** An overview of how the study will be conducted is included. The sequence of events is described and is appropriate to the design. Sufficient information is included so that the essential features of the study could be replicated by a reader.

### IV. Results

1. **Statement of Results:** The results are stated concisely and are plausible for the research described.
2. **Tables:** The tables are correctly formatted and accurately and concisely presents part of the analysis.
3. **Figures:** The figure(s) is clearly designed and accurately describes a relevant aspect of the results.

### V. Conclusions, Abstract and Reference Sections

1. **Implications of the study:** Assuming the expected results are obtained, the implications of these results are discussed. The author mentions briefly any remaining problems which are anticipated in the study.
2. **Abstract:** The abstract is 125 words or less and presents a concise picture of the proposed research. Major constructs and hypotheses are included. The abstract is the first section of the paper. See the format sheet for more details.
3. **References:** All citations are included in the correct format and are appropriate for the study described.

## 10.3 Stylistic Elements

**I. Professional Writing**

First person and sex-stereotyped forms are avoided. Material is presented in an unbiased and unemotional (e.g., no "feelings" about things), but not necessarily uninteresting, fashion.

**II. Parallel Construction**

Tense is kept parallel within and between sentences (as appropriate).

**III. Sentence Structure**

Sentence structure and punctuation are correct. Incomplete and run-on sentences are avoided.

**IV. Spelling and Word Usage**

Spelling and use of words are appropriate. Words are capitalized and abbreviated correctly.

**V. General Style**

The document is neatly produced and reads well. The format for the document has been correctly followed.

## 10.4 Formatting

### Overview

The instructions provided here are for a research article or a research report.

All sections of the paper should be typed, double-spaced on white A4 size paper with margins set to as top 2cm, bottom 2cm, right 2cm and left 4cm. Every page must have a header in the upper right corner with the running header right-justified on the top line and the page number right-justified and double-spaced on the line below it. The paper must have all the sections in the order given below, following the specifications outlined for each section (all page numbers are approximate):

- Title Page
- Abstract (on a separate single page)
- The Body (no page breaks between sections in the body)
  - ♦ Introduction (2-3 pages)
  - ♦ Methods (7-10 pages)
    - ➤ Sample (1 page)
    - ➤ Measures (2-3 pages)
    - ➤ Design (2-3 pages)
    - ➤ Procedures (2-3 pages)
  - ♦ Results (2-3 pages)
  - ♦ Conclusions (1-2 pages)
- References
- Tables (one to a page)
- Figures (one to a page)
- Appendices

### Title Page

On separate lines and centered, the title page has the title of the study, the author's name, and the institutional affiliation. At the bottom of the title page you should have the words (in caps) RUNNING HEADER: followed by a short identifying title (2-4 words) for the study. This running header should also appear on the top right of every page of the paper.

### Abstract

The abstract is limited to one page, double-spaced. At the top of the page, centered, you should have the word **'Abstract'**. The abstract itself should be written in paragraph form and should be a concise summary of the entire paper including: the problem; major hypotheses;

sample and population; a brief description of the measures; the name of the design or a short description (no design notation here); the major results; and, the major conclusions. Obviously, to fit this all on one page you will have to be very concise.

## Body

The first page of the body of the paper should have, centered, the complete title of the study.

## Introduction

The first section in the body is the introduction. There is no heading that says 'Introduction,' you simply begin the paper in paragraph form following the title. Every introduction will have the following (roughly in this order): a statement of the problem being addressed; a statement of the cause-effect relationship being studied; a description of the major constructs involved; a brief review of relevant literature (including citations); and a statement of hypotheses. The entire section should be in paragraph form with the possible exception of the hypotheses, which may be indented.

## Methods

The next section of the paper has four subsections: Sample; Measures; Design; and Procedure. The Methods section should begin immediately after the introduction (no page break) and should have the centered title 'Methods'. Each of the four sub-sections should have an underlined left justified section heading.

## Sampling

This section should describe the population of interest, the sampling frame, the method for selecting the sample, and the sample itself. A brief discussion of external validity is appropriate here, that is, you should state the degree to which you believe results will be generalizable from your sample to the population.

## Measures

This section should include a brief description of your constructs and all measures that will be used to operationalize them. You may present short instruments in their entirety in this section. If you have more lengthy instruments you may present some "typical" questions to give the reader a sense of what you will be doing (and include the full measure in an Appendix). You may include any instruments in full in appendices rather than in the body. Appendices should be labelled by letter. (e.g., 'Appendix A') and cited appropriately in the body of the text. For pre-existing instruments you should cite any relevant information about reliability and validity if it is available. For all instruments, you should briefly state how you will determine reliability and validity, report the results and discuss. For reliability, you must describe the methods you used and report results. A brief discussion of how you have addressed construct validity is essential. In general, you should try to demonstrate both convergent and discriminant validity. You must discuss the evidence in support of the validity of your measures.

## Design

You should state the name of the design that is used and tell whether it is a true or quasi-experiment, non-equivalent group design, and so on. You should also present the design structure in X and O notation (this should be indented and centered, not put into a sentence). You should also include a discussion of internal validity that describes the major likely threats in your study and how the design accounts for them, if at all. Be your own study critic here and provide enough information to show that you understand the threats to validity, whether you've been able to account for them all in the design or not.

### Procedures

Generally, this section ties together the sampling, measurement and research design. In this section you should briefly describe the overall plan of the research, the sequence of events from beginning to end (including sampling, measurement, and use of groups in designs), how participants will be notified and how their confidentiality will be protected (where relevant). An essential part of this subsection is a description of the programme or independent variable that you are studying.

### Results

The heading for this section is centered with upper and lower case letters. You should indicate concisely what results you found in this research. Your results don't have to confirm your hypotheses. In fact, the common experience in social research is the finding of no effect.

### Conclusions

Here you should describe the conclusions you reach (assuming you got the results described in the Results section above). You should relate these conclusions back to the level of the construct and the general problem area which you described in the Introduction section. You should also discuss the overall strength of the research proposed (e.g., general discussion of the strong and weak validity areas) and should present some suggestions for possible future research which would be sensible based on the results of this work.

### References

There are really two parts to a reference citation. First, there is the way you cite the item in the text when you are discussing it. Second, there is the way you list the complete reference in the reference section at the back of the report.

#### Reference Citations in the Text of Your Paper

Cited references appear in the text of your paper and are a way of giving credit to the source of the information or quote you have used in your paper. They generally consist of the following bits of information:

The author's last name, unless first initials are needed to distinguish between two authors with the same last name. If there are six or more authors, the first author is listed followed by the term, *et al.,* and then the year of the publication is given in parenthesis. Year of publication in parenthesis. Page numbers are given with a quotation or when only a specific part of a source was used.

"To be or not to be" (Shakespeare, 1660, p. 241)

### One Work by One Author:

Rogers (1994) compared reaction times...

### One Work by Multiple Authors:

Wasserstein, Zappulla, Rosen, Gerstman and Rock (1994) [first time you cite in text]

Wasserstein et al. (1994) found [subsequent times you cite in text]

### Reference List in Reference Section

There are a wide variety of reference citation formats. Before submitting any research report you should check to see which type of format is considered acceptable for that context. If there is no official format requirement then the most sensible thing is for you to select one approach and implement it consistently (there's nothing worse than a reference list with a variety of formats). Here, I'll illustrate by example some of the major reference items and how they might be cited in the reference section.

The References lists all the articles, books and other sources used in the research and preparation of the paper and cited with a parenthetical (textual) citation in the text. These items are entered in alphabetical order according to the authors' last names; if a source does not have an author, alphabetize according to the first word of the title, disregarding the articles "a", "an", and "the" if they are the first word in the title.

### EXAMPLES BOOK BY ONE AUTHOR:

Jones, T. (1940). My life on the road. New York: Doubleday.

### BOOK BY TWO AUTHORS:

Williams, A., & Wilson, J. (1962). New ways with chicken. New York: Harcourt.

### BOOK BY THREE OR MORE AUTHORS:

Smith, J., Jones, J., & Williams, S. (1976). Common names. Chicago: University of Chicago Press.

### BOOK WITH NO GIVEN AUTHOR OR EDITOR:

Handbook of Korea (4th ed.). (1982). Seoul: Korean Overseas Information, Ministry of Culture & Information.

### TWO OR MORE BOOKS BY THE SAME AUTHOR:

Oates, J.C. (1990). Because it is bitter, and because it is my heart. New York: Dutton.

Oates, J.C. (1993). Foxfire: Confessions of a girl gang. New York: Dutton.

Entries by the same author are arranged chronologically by the year of publication, the earliest first. References with the same first author and different second and subsequent authors are listed alphabetically by the surname of the second author, then by the surname of the third author. References with the same authors in the same order are entered chronologically by year of publication, the earliest first. References by the same author (or by the same two or more authors in identical order) with the same publication date are listed alphabetically by the first word of the title following the date; lower case letters (a, b, c, etc.) are included after the year, within the parentheses.

### BOOK BY A CORPORATE (GROUP) AUTHOR:

President's Commission on Higher Education (1977). Higher education for American democracy. Washington, D.C.: U.S. Government Printing Office.

### BOOK WITH AN EDITOR:

Bloom, H. (Ed.). (1988). James Joyce's Dubliners. New York: Chelsea House.

### A TRANSLATION:

Dostoevsky, F. (1964). Crime and Punishment (J. Coulson Trans.). New York: Norton. (Original work published 1866).

## AN ARTICLE OR READING IN A COLLECTION OF PIECES BY SEVERAL AUTHORS (ANTHOLOGY):

O'Connor, M.F. (1975). Everything that rises must converge. In J.R. Knott, Jr. & C.R. Raeske (Eds.), Mirrors: An introduction to literature (2nd ed., pp. 58-67). San Francisco: Canfield.

## EDITION OF A BOOK:

Tortora, G.J., Funke, B.R., & Case, C.L. (1989). Microbiology: An introduction (3rd ed.). Redwood City, CA: Benjamin/Cummings.

## DIAGNOSTIC AND STATISTICAL MANUAL OF MENTAL DISORDERS:

American Psychiatric Association, (1994). Diagnostic and statistical manual of mental disorders (4th ed.). Washington, D.C.: Author.

## A WORK IN SEVERAL VOLUMES:

Churchill, W.S. (1957). A history of the English speaking peoples: Vol. 3. The Age of Revolution. New York: Dodd, Mead.

## ENCYCLOPEDIA OR DICTIONARY:

Cockrell, D. (1980). Beatles. In The new Grove dictionary of music and musicians (6th ed., Vol. 2, pp. 321-322). London: Macmillan.

## ARTICLE FROM A WEEKLY MAGAZINE:

Jones, W. (1970, August 14). Todays's kids. Newsweek, 76, 10-15.

## ARTICLE FROM A MONTHLY MAGAZINE:

Howe, I. (1968, September). James Baldwin: At ease in apocalypse. Harper's, 237, 92-100.

## ARTICLE FROM A NEWSPAPER:

Brody, J.E. (1976, October 10). Multiple cancers termed on increase. New York Times (national ed.). p. A37.

## ARTICLE FROM A SCHOLARLY ACADEMIC OR PROFESSIONAL JOURNAL:

Barber, B.K. (1994). Cultural, family, and personal contexts of parent-adolescent conflict. Journal of Marriage and the Family, 56, 375-386.

## GOVERNMENT PUBLICATION:

U.S. Department of Labor. Bureau of Labor Statistics, (1980). Productivity. Washington, D.C.: U.S. Government Printing Office.

## PAMPHLET OR BROCHURE:

Research and Training Center on Independent Living, (1993). Guidelines for reporting and writing about people with disabilities. (4th ed.) [Brochure]. Lawrence, KS: Author.

## 10.5 How to Do?

Dolly: "So we have come to concluding part of our learning."

Jolly: "Who says?"

Dolly: "No, we are still to learn use of computer in research, and then it is the end?"

Jolly: "No dear, you are wrong. This is the beginning. You have just been acquainted with methodology with some research projects, now it is going to be beginning from your side. If somebody teaches you how clutch, accelerator and brakes are used in car, will you be able to drive the car? Until and unless you drive the car first under guidance and then yourself, you will not become a good driver."

Dolly: "You are discouraging me."

Jolly: "No, you have simply learnt the techniques of methodology. You are to use these techniques to solve the problems of your organization."

Dolly: "Yes, it is very simple. Count1, define the problem. 2. Review the literature. 3. Set your objectives 4. Frame Hypotheses. 5. Design the research 6. Collect information and data 7. Frame the constructs or models. 7 Analyse the data 8. Interpret the results. 9 Write a good report. It is easy."

Jolly: "You may have to go back to step 6 through 1. You will have to redefine your problems, sub-problems, objectives and hypotheses at every stage; this may be due to non-availability of data or design may have some problems due to constructs or constructs may have more external factors than internal and so on."

Dolly: "Then there may be hundreds of constructs, models, designs and procedures. To test these there may be hundreds of techniques. In my library I have seen a book '100 tests' in statistics."

Jolly: "So don't you think this is the beginning?"

Dolly: "Yes, I will have to start now. The best place is to spend time in library and search more and more research books and journals."

Jolly: "The beginners should start with literature review. Go on reading the research articles relating to the topic of your interest. Prepare the abstracts. Adjust the abstracts in this way so that they are logically related."

Dolly: "Then I can take some secondary data relating to my topic and analyse."

Jolly: "Beginners should start with secondary data."

Dolly: "Primary data collection should be done under some experts; otherwise you will waste money and time."

Jolly: "Go ahead."

Dolly: "But don't you think we should read more papers and discuss."

Jolly: "I have some more articles, but they should be discussed in the class."

Dolly: "What should we discuss in the class?"

Jolly: "Mainly you should see what the problem is. What are the objectives of the study? How data has been collected? How data has been analysed? Discuss research methodology in the class."

Dolly: "We have a discussion group in the class."

Jolly: "Good, I wish you and your team best of luck."

...✎...✎...✎

CHAPTER

# USE OF COMPUTER SOFTWARE IN DATA ANALYSIS

## *Structure*

In the chapter 'Quantitative Analysis', we have discussed how ANOVA and regression can be done MS Excel. In this chapter we shall learn how to use SPSS (Statistical Package for Social Sciences) to calculate ANOVA, to regress, Discriminant Analysis, Factor Analysis, Cluster Analysis and MDS. Students should note that there are certain outcomes which need further study on the topics. We are limiting ourselves to our syllabus.

## 11.1 Regression

Linear regression is used to model the value of a dependent scale variable based on its linear relationship to one or more predictors. The linear regression model assumes that there is a linear, or "straight line," relationship between the dependent variable and each predictor. This relationship is described in the following formula.

$$Y = b_0 + b_1X_1 + b_2X_2 + b_3 X_3 + e$$

The model is linear because increasing the value of the jth predictor by 1 unit increases the value of the dependent by bj units. Note that $b_0$ is the intercept, the model-predicted value of the dependent variable when the value of every predictor is equal to 0.

For the purpose of testing hypotheses about the values of model parameters, the linear regression model also assumes the following:

- The error term has a normal distribution with a mean of 0.
- The variance of the error term is constant across cases and independent of the variables in the model. An error term with non-constant variance is said to be heteroscedastic.
- The value of the error term for a given case is independent of the values of the variables in the model and of the values of the error term for other cases.

Let us assume the following hypothetical data, say Y is demand in lakhs, X1 is the price of the commodity and X2 is the income level of consumers. We are to fit a regression equation and test parameters from various points.

We have already learnt the regression procedure by MS Excel. Now let us learn by SPSS. Start SPSS from your window programme. Text editor will open as like a spreadsheet. Fill in the data.

| Y | X1 | X2 |
|---|---|---|
| 25 | 8 | 10 |
| 28 | 7 | 12 |
| 31 | 6 | 14 |
| 34 | 5 | 17 |
| 36 | 4 | 20 |
| 38 | 3 | 22 |

You can change the variable names to Y, X1 and X2.

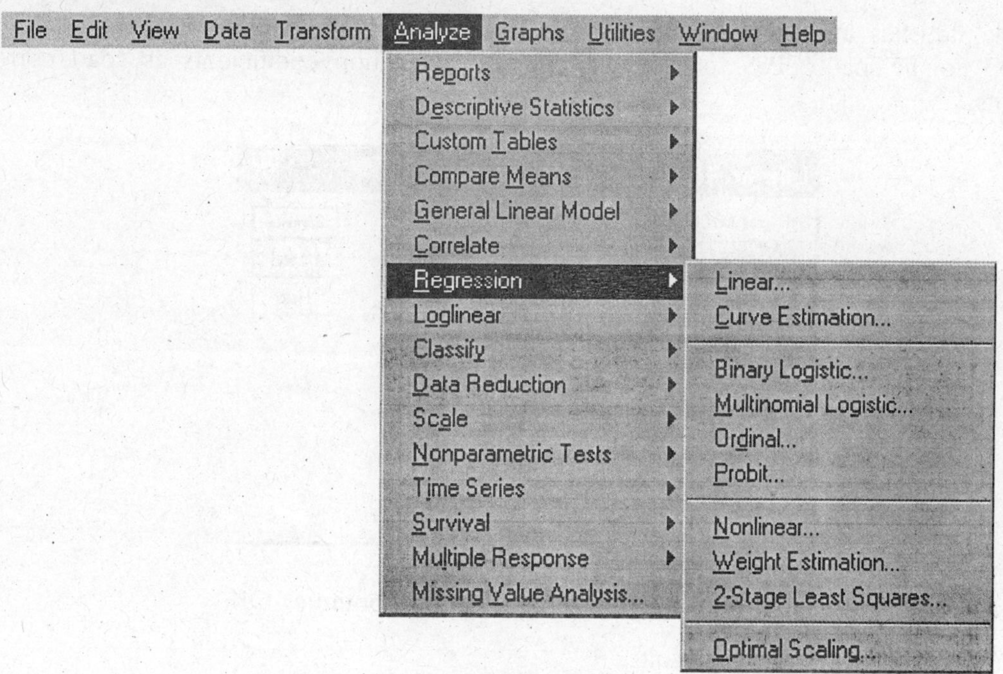


To run a linear regression analysis, from the menus choose:

Analyze

Regression

Linear...

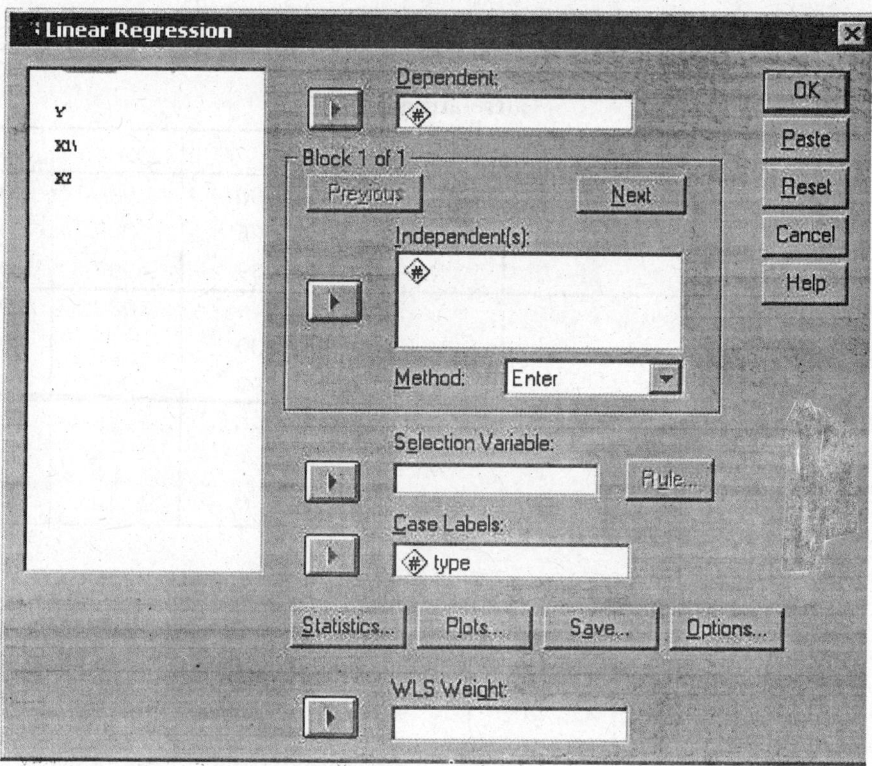


Enter Y in Dependent Variable array and X1 and X2 in independent variable.

Click Statistics and select Estimates, Confidence intervals, Model fit and Part & partial correlation coefficients. SPSS refers to semipartial correlation coefficients as "part correlation coefficients."

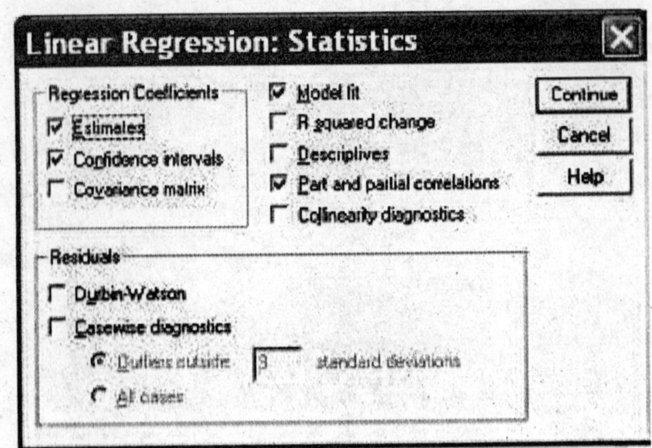


To test auto correlation click Durbin Watson also. Continue, OK.

You will get the following results.

**Regression**

**Descriptive Statistics**

| | Mean | Std. Deviation | N |
|---|---|---|---|
| Y | 32.0000 | 4.93964 | 6 |
| X1 | 5.5000 | 1.87083 | 6 |
| X2 | 15.8333 | 4.66548 | 6 |

**Correlations**

| | | Y | X1 | X2 |
|---|---|---|---|---|
| Pearson Correlation | Y | 1.000 | –.996 | .989 |
| | X1 | –.996 | 1.000 | –.997 |
| | X2 | .989 | –.997 | 1.000 |
| Sig. (1-tailed) | Y | . | .000 | .000 |
| | X1 | .000 | . | .000 |
| | X2 | .000 | .000 | . |
| N | Y | 6 | 6 | 6 |
| | X1 | 6 | 6 | 6 |
| | X2 | 6 | 6 | 6 |

**Variables Entered/Removed[b]**

| Model | Variables Entered | Variables Removed | Method |
|---|---|---|---|
| 1 | X2, X1[a] | . | Enter |

a. All requested variables entered.

b. Dependent Variable: Y

**Model Summary[b]**

| Model | R | R Square | Adjusted R Square | Std. Error of the Estimate | Durbin-Watson |
|---|---|---|---|---|---|
| 1 | .996a | .992 | .987 | .55345 | 1.430 |

a. Predictors: (Constant), X2, X1
b. Dependent Variable: Y

**ANOVA[b]**

| Model | | Sum of Squares | df | Mean Square | F | Sig. |
|---|---|---|---|---|---|---|
| 1 | Regression | 121.081 | 2 | 60.541 | 197.647 | .001[a] |
| | Residual | .919 | 3 | .306 | | |
| | Total | 122.000 | 5 | | | |

a. Predictors: (Constant), X2, X1
b. Dependent Variable: Y

**Coefficients[a]**

| | | Unstandardized Coefficients | | Standardized Coefficients | | |
|---|---|---|---|---|---|---|
| Model | | B | Std. Error | Beta | t | Sig. |
| 1 | (Constant) | 60.811 | 19.466 | | 3.124 | .052 |
| | X1 | –3.838 | 1.644 | –1.454 | –2.334 | .102 |
| | X2 | –.486 | .659 | –.459 | –.738 | .514 |

a. Dependent Variable: Y

**Residuals Statistics[a]**

| | Minimum | Maximum | Mean | Std. Deviation | N |
|---|---|---|---|---|---|
| Predicted Value | 25.2432 | 38.5946 | 32.0000 | 4.92100 | 6 |
| Residual | –.59459 | .64865 | .00000 | .42870 | 6 |
| Std. Predicted Value | –1.373 | 1.340 | .000 | 1.000 | 6 |
| Std. Residual | –1.074 | 1.172 | .000 | .775 | 6 |

a. Dependent Variable: Y

## Interpretations

The first table gives the descriptive statistics. It give means and standard deviation of Y, X1 and X2. Second table gives the correlation between Y and X1, X1 and X2, and X2 and Y.

The next table give $R^2$, adjusted $R^2$. Durbin Watson (if it is between 2 and -2) tells us that there is auto-regression.

The ANOVA table tests the acceptability of the model from a statistical perspective.

The Regression row displays information about the variation accounted for by your model.

The Residual row displays information about the variation that is not accounted for by your model.

Coefficient table gives constant ($b_0$) and coefficients of X1 and X2. (i.e. $b_1$ and $b_2$)

Hence our equation is

$$Y = 60.81 - 3.838X1 - 0.486X2$$

T values of $b_1$ and $b_2$ are given as –2.334 and –.738. We can compare with table values and shall see they are not statistically significant.

## 11.2 Discriminant Analysis

The discriminant model has the following assumptions:

- The predictors are not highly correlated with each other.
- The mean and variance of a given predictor are not correlated.
- The correlation between two predictors is constant across groups.
- The values of each predictor have a normal distribution.

Let us start with example, if you are a loan officer at a bank, you want to be able to identify characteristics that are indicative of people who are likely to default on loans, and you want to use those characteristics to identify good and bad credit risks. You have data of 25 customers with age, current employment age, Family income, Debt/Income Ratio and you also know whether they have already defaulted. By discriminant analysis we shall try to find out what are the chances that they will default. Data for 25 clients is as follows.

| Age | Year with Current Employer | Family income | Debt/Income Ratio | Whether previously Defaulted |
|---|---|---|---|---|
| 41 | 17 | 176 | 9.3 | 1 |
| 27 | 10 | 31 | 17.3 | 0 |
| 40 | 15 | 55 | 5.5 | 0 |
| 41 | 15 | 120 | 2.9 | 0 |
| 24 | 2 | 28 | 17.3 | 1 |
| 41 | 5 | 25 | 10.2 | 0 |
| 39 | 20 | 67 | 30.6 | 0 |
| 43 | 12 | 38 | 3.6 | 0 |
| 24 | 3 | 19 | 24.4 | 1 |
| 36 | 0 | 25 | 19.7 | 0 |
| 27 | 0 | 16 | 1.7 | 0 |
| 25 | 4 | 23 | 5.2 | 0 |
| 52 | 24 | 64 | 10 | 0 |
| 37 | 6 | 29 | 16.3 | 0 |
| 48 | 22 | 100 | 9.1 | 0 |
| 36 | 9 | 49 | 8.6 | 1 |
| 36 | 13 | 41 | 16.4 | 1 |
| 43 | 23 | 72 | 7.6 | 0 |
| 39 | 6 | 61 | 5.7 | 0 |
| 41 | 0 | 26 | 1.7 | 0 |
| 39 | 22 | 52 | 3.2 | 0 |
| 47 | 17 | 43 | 5.6 | 0 |
| 28 | 3 | 26 | 10 | 0 |
| 29 | 8 | 27 | 9.8 | 0 |
| 21 | 1 | 16 | 18 | 1 |

Load the above data on SPSS editor.

Setting the random seed allows you to replicate the random selection of cases in this analysis.

To set the random seed, from the menus choose:

Transform

Random Number Seed...

Select Set seed to and type 9191972 in the text box.

Click OK.

To create the selection variable for validation, from the menus choose:

Transform

Compute...

Type validate in the Target Variable text box.

Type rv.bernoulli(0.7) in the Numeric Expression text box.

This sets the values of validate to be randomly generated Bernoulli variates with probability parameter 0.7.

To perform the computation only for previous customers, click If.

Select Include if case satisfies condition.

Type MISSING(default) = 0 as the conditional expression.

This ensures that validate is only computed for cases with non-missing values for default; that is, for customers who previously received loans.

Click Continue.

Click OK in the Compute Variable dialog box.

Approximately 70 per cent of the customers previously given loans will have a validate value of 1. These customers will be used to create the discriminant function. The remaining customers who were previously given loans will be used to validate the model results.

To run the discriminant analysis, from the menus choose:

Analyze

Classify

Discriminant...

Select Previously defaulted as the grouping variable.

Select Age, Years with current employer, family income Debt to income ratio (x100), as the independent variables.

Select validate as the selection variable.

Select Previously defaulted and click Define Range.

Type 0 as the minimum.

Type 1 as the maximum.

Click Continue.

Select validate and click Value in the Discriminant Analysis dialog box.

Type 1 as the value for selection variable.

Click Continue.

Click Statistics in the Discriminant Analysis dialog box.

Select Means, Univariate ANOVAs, and Box's M in the Descriptives group.

Select Fisher's and Unstandardized in the Function Coefficients group.

Select Within-groups correlation in the Matrices group.

Click Continue.

Click Classify in the Discriminant Analysis dialog box.

Select Summary table and Leave-one-out classification.

Click Continue.

Click Save in the Discriminant Analysis dialog box.

Select Predicted group membership and Probabilities of group membership.

Click Continue.

Click OK in the Discriminant Analysis dialog box.

These selections produce a discriminant model based on Years with current employer, Family income Debt to income ratio (x100).

The classification functions are used to assign cases to groups.

Click OK and you will get following result

**Discriminant**

**Analysis Case Processing Summary**

| **Unweighted** | **Cases** | **N** | **Per cent** |
|---|---|---|---|
| Valid | | 14 | 56.0 |
| Excluded | Missing or out-of-range group codes | 0 | .0 |
| | At least one missing discriminating variable | 0 | 0 |
| | Both missing or out-of-range group codes and at least one missing discriminating variable | 0 | 0 |
| | Unselected | 11 | 44.0 |
| | Total | 11 | 44.0 |
| Total | | 25 | 100.0 |

**Group Statistics**

| Previously defaulted | | Mean | Std. Deviation | Valid N (listwise) | |
|---|---|---|---|---|---|
| | | | | Unweighted | Weighted |
| No | Age in years | 38.2727 | 8.67284 | 11 | 11.000 |
| | Years with current employer | 12.7273 | 8.41535 | 11 | 11.000 |
| | Household income | 54.2727 | 32.90012 | 11 | 11.000 |
| | Debt to income ratio (x 100) | 9.0455 | 8.46468 | 11 | 11.000 |
| Yes | Age in years | 28.0000 | 6.92820 | 3 | 3.000 |
| | Years with current employer | 4.6667 | 3.78594 | 3 | 3.000 |
| | Household income in thousands | 32.0000 | 15.39480 | 3 | 3.000 |
| | Debt to income ratio (x 100) | 16.7667 | 7.91349 | 3 | 3.000 |
| Total | Age in years | 36.0714 | 9.18581 | 14 | 14.000 |
| | Years with current employer | 11.0000 | 8.27415 | 14 | 14.000 |
| | Household income in thousands | 49.5000 | 30.96835 | 14 | 14.000 |
| | Debt to income ratio (x 100) | 10.7000 | 8.69253 | 14 | 14.000 |

**Tests of Equality of Group Means**

| | Wilks' Lambda | F | df1 | df2 | sig. |
|---|---|---|---|---|---|
| Age in years | .773 | 3.519 | 1 | 12 | .085 |
| Years with current employer | .828 | 2.494 | 1 | 12 | .140 |
| Household income in thousands | .906 | 1.242 | 1 | 12 | .287 |
| Debt to income ratio (x 100) | .857 | 2.003 | 1 | 12 | .182 |

**Pooled Within-Groups Matrices**

| | | Age in years current | Years with income in | Household income ratio thousands | Debt to employer (x 100) |
|---|---|---|---|---|---|
| Correlation | Age in years | 1.000 | .728 | .622 | –.088 |
| | Years with current employer | .728 | 1.000 | .650 | .219 |
| | Household income in thousands | .622 | .650 | 1.000 | –.033 |
| | Debt to income ratio (x 100) | –.088 | .219 | –.033 | 1.000 |

## Analysis 1

### Box's Test of Equality of Covariance Matrices

**Log Determinants**

| Previously defaulted | Rank | Log Determinant |
|---|---|---|
| No | 4 | 18.305 |
| Yes | .[a] | .[b] |
| Pooled within-groups | 4 | 17.865 |

The ranks and natural logarithms of determinants printed are those of the group covariance matrices.

a. Rank < 3

b. Too few cases to be non-singular

**Test Results[a]**

Tests null hypothesis of equal population covariance matrices.

a. No test can be performed with fewer than two non-singular group covariance matrices.

### Summary of Canonical Discriminant Functions

**Eigenvalues**

| Function | Eigenvalue | % of variance | Cumulative% | Canonial Correlation |
|---|---|---|---|---|
| 1 | .509a | 100.0 | 100.0 | .581 |

a. First 1 cannonical discriminant functions were used in the analysis.

**Wilk's Lambda**

| Test of Function(s) | Wilks' Lambda | Chi-square | df | Sig. |
|---|---|---|---|---|
| 1 | .663 | 4.116 | 4 | .391 |

**Standardized Canonical Discriminant Function Coefficients**

| | Function 1 |
|---|---|
| Age in years | .329 |
| Years with current employer | .710 |
| Household income in thousands | –.239 |
| Debt to income ratio (x 100) | –.707 |

**Structure Matrix**

| | Function 1 |
|---|---|
| Age in years | .759 |
| Years with current employer | .639 |
| Debt to income ratio (x 100) | –.573 |
| Household income in thousands | .451 |

Pooled within-groups correlations between discriminating variables and standardized canonical discriminant functions Variables ordered by absolute size of correlation within function.

**Canonical Discriminant function Coefficients**

| | Function 1 |
|---|---|
| Age in years | .039 |
| Years with current employer | .091 |
| Household income in thousands | –.008 |
| Debt to income ratio (x 100) | –.084 |
| (Constant) | –1.118 |

Unstandardized coefficients

**Functions at Group Centroids**

| Previously defaulted | Function 1 |
|---|---|
| No | .345 |
| Yes | –1.265 |

Understandardized canonical discriminant functions evaluated at group means

## Classification Statistics

**Classification Processing Summary**

| | | |
|---|---|---|
| Processed | | 25 |
| Excluded | Missing or out-of-range group codes | 0 |
| | At least one missing discriminating variable | 0 |
| Used in Output | | 25 |

**Prior Probabilities for Groups**

| Previously defaulted | Prior | Cases Used in Analysis | |
|---|---|---|---|
| | | Unweighted | Weighted |
| No | .500 | 11 | 11.000 |
| Yes | .500 | 3 | 3.000 |
| Total | 1.000 | 14 | 14.000 |

**Classification Function Coefficients**

| | Previously defaulted | |
|---|---|---|
| | No | Yes |
| Age in years | 1.047 | .984 |
| Years with current employer | –.686 | –.832 |
| Household income in thousands | –.004 | .009 |
| Debt to income ratio (x 100) | .361 | .497 |
| (Constant) | –17.897 | –16.837 |

Fisher linear discriminant functions

**Classification Result[b,c,d]**

| | | | Previously defaulted | Predicted Group Membership | | Total |
|---|---|---|---|---|---|---|
| | | | | No | Yes | |
| Cases Selected | Original | Count | No | 9 | 2 | 11 |
| | | | Yes | 1 | 2 | 3 |
| | | % | No | 81.8 | 18.2 | 100.0 |
| | | | Yes | 33.3 | 66.7 | 100.0 |
| | Cross-validated[a] | Count | No | 6 | 5 | 11 |
| | | | Yes | 1 | 2 | 3 |
| | | % | No | 54.5 | 45.5 | 100.0 |
| | | | Yes | 33.3 | 66.7 | 100.0 |
| Cases Not Selected | Original | Count | No | 5 | 3 | 8 |
| | | | Yes | 2 | 1 | 3 |
| | | % | No | 62.5 | 37.5 | 100.0 |
| | | | Yes | 66.7 | 33.3 | 100.0 |

(a) Cross validation is done only for those cases in the analysi. In cross validation, each case is classified by the functions derived from all cases other than that case.

(b) 78.6% of selected original grouped cases correctly classified.

(c) 54.5% of unselected original grouped case correctly classified.

(d) 57.1% of selected cross-validate grouped cases correctly classified.

There is a separate function for each group. For each case, a classification score is computed for each function. The discriminant model assigns the case to the group whose classification function obtained the highest score.

The coefficients for age and years with current employer are smaller for the Yes classification function, which means that customers who are younger, have worked more with the same employer are less likely to default.

Similarly, customers with greater debt are more likely to default.

The within-groups correlation matrix shows the correlations between the predictors.

The age and working with same employer have good correlation. Family income and debt are least correlated.

The group statistics table reveals a potentially more serious problem. For all four predictors, larger group means are associated with larger group standard deviations.

Box's M tests the assumption of equality of covariances across groups.

Log determinants are a measure of the variability of the groups. Larger log determinants correspond to more variable groups. Large differences in log determinants indicate groups that have different covariance matrices.

Wilks' lambda is another measure of a variable's potential. Smaller values indicate the variable is better at discriminating between groups.

Wilks' lambda is a measure of how well each function separates cases into groups. It is equal to the proportion of the total variance in the discriminant scores not explained by differences among the groups. Smaller values of Wilks' lambda indicate greater discriminatory ability of the function.

The standardized coefficients allow you to compare variables measured on different scales. Coefficients with large absolute values correspond to variables with greater discriminating ability.

The eigenvalues table provides information about the relative efficacy of each discriminant function.

The associated chi-square statistic tests the hypothesis that the means of the functions listed are equal across groups. The small significance value indicates that the discriminant function does better than chance at separating the groups.

The classification table shows the practical results of using the discriminant model.

Reader can recheck the results by changing to other classification methods given in the software.

## 11.3 Factor Analysis

Factor Analysis is primarily used for data reduction or structure detection.

- The purpose of data reduction is to remove redundant (highly correlated) variables from the data file, perhaps replacing the entire data file with a smaller number of uncorrelated variables.
- The purpose of structure detection is to examine the underlying (or latent) relationships between the variables.

The Factor Analysis procedure has several extraction methods for constructing a solution.

**For Data Reduction:** The principal components method of extraction begins by finding a linear combination of variables (a component) that accounts for as much variation in the original variables as possible. It then finds another component that accounts for as much of the remaining variation as possible and is uncorrelated with the previous component, continuing in this way until there are as many components as original variables. Usually, a few components will account for most of the variation and these components can be used to replace the original variables. This method is most often used to reduce the number of variables in the data file.

**For Structure Detection:** Other Factor Analysis extraction methods go one step further by adding the assumption that some of the variability in the data cannot be explained by the components (usually called factors in other extraction methods). As a result, the total variance explained by the solution is smaller; however, the addition of this structure to the factor model makes these methods ideal for examining relationships between the variables.

With any extraction method, the two questions that a good solution should try to answer are "How many components (factors) are needed to represent the variables?" and "What do these components represent?"

Let us start with the same example as we took in chapter 9.

The general manager of a restaurant designed a questionnaire to study the customers' feedback about its restaurant and in turn he is interested to know what his customers in general wish. He wishes to identify factors of his study. He identifies six variables which are listed below:

1. Food hygiene (X1)
2. Menu items (X2)
3. Service quality (X3)

4. Food quality (X4)
5. Ambience (X5)
6. Price (X6)

So the company administered questionnaire to 10 respondents who responded the above questionnaire variable on 0-10 scale. The score 0 means low rating while 10 means high rating. Survey data is placed below and find the three factors which can represent the variables in study.

| Respondents | X1 | X2 | X3 | X4 | X5 | X6 |
|---|---|---|---|---|---|---|
| 1 | 4 | 6 | 7 | 7 | 0 | 0 |
| 2 | 4 | 4 | 6 | 8 | 2 | 1 |
| 3 | 4 | 1 | 6 | 5 | 1 | 2 |
| 4 | 1 | 2 | 6 | 3 | 2 | 3 |
| 5 | 4 | 3 | 5 | 5 | 2 | 3 |
| 6 | 4 | 4 | 6 | 8 | 2 | 3 |
| 7 | 3 | 3 | 0 | 9 | 1 | 3 |
| 8 | 7 | 7 | 6 | 9 | 9 | 2 |
| 9 | 4 | 3 | 1 | 8 | 1 | 2 |
| 10 | 5 | 4 | 2 | 3 | 1 | 0 |

To run a principal components factor analysis, from the menus choose:

Analyze

Data Reduction

Factor...

Select the variables X1 through X6

Click Extraction.

Select Analyse by Correlation matrix

(If you want you can select scree plot, this will give the chart depicting factor loadings)

Continue

Select Rotation

None

Continue

(If you wish you can recheck by rotation by varimax)

Select Save as variables and Display factor score coefficient matrix.

Click Continue.

Click OK in the Factor Analysis dialog box.

These selections produce a solution using principal components extraction, which are not rotated by any method. Components with eigenvalues greater than 1 are saved to the working file. You will get following results.

## Factor Analysis

**Correlation Matrix**

| | | X1 | X2 | X3 | X4 | X5 | X6 |
|---|---|---|---|---|---|---|---|
| Correlation | X1 | 1.000 | .675 | .059 | .385 | .623 | –.374 |
| | X2 | .675 | 1.000 | .238 | .474 | .558 | –.0436 |
| | X3 | .059 | .238 | 1.000 | –.124 | .256 | –.093 |
| | X4 | .385 | .474 | –.124 | 1.000 | .333 | .140 |
| | X5 | .623 | .558 | .256 | .333 | 1.000 | .188 |
| | X6 | –.374 | –.436 | –.093 | .140 | .188 | 1.000 |

**KMO and Bartlett's Test**

| | | |
|---|---|---|
| Kaiser-Meyer-Olkin Measure of Sampling Adequency. | | .417 |
| Bartlett's Test of Sphericity | Approx. Chi-Square | 17.975 |
| | df | 15 |
| | Sig. | .264 |

**Communalities**

| | Initial | Extraction |
|---|---|---|
| X1 | 1.000 | .796 |
| X2 | 1.000 | .847 |
| X3 | 1.000 | .880 |
| X4 | 1.000 | .723 |
| X5 | 1.000 | .836 |
| X6 | 1.000 | .972 |

Extraction Method: Principal Component Analysis

**Total Variance Explained**

| | Initial Eigenvalues | | | Extraction Sums of Squared Loadings | | |
|---|---|---|---|---|---|---|
| Component | Total | % of Variance | Cumulative % | Total | % of Variance | Cumulative % |
| 1 | 2.642 | 44.040 | 44.040 | 2.642 | 44.040 | 44.040 |
| 2 | 1.318 | 21.966 | 66.006 | 1.318 | 21.966 | 66.006 |
| 3 | 1.093 | 18.216 | 84.221 | 1.093 | 18.216 | 84.221 |
| 4 | .598 | 9.961 | 94.182 | | | |
| 5 | .256 | 4.266 | 98.448 | | | |
| 6 | .093 | 1.552 | 100.000 | | | |

Extraction Method: Principal Component Analysis.

**Component Matrix[a]**

| | Component | | |
|---|---|---|---|
| | 1 | 2 | 3 |
| X2 | .902 | –.170 | –.060 |
| X1 | .873 | –.083 | –.163 |
| X5 | .757 | .365 | .360 |
| X4 | .572 | .535 | –.329 |
| X6 | –.317 | .874 | .327 |
| X3 | .255 | –.313 | .847 |

Extraction Method: Principal Component Analysis.

a. 3 components extracted.

Communalities indicate the amount of variance in each variable that is accounted for.

Initial communalities are estimates of the variance in each variable accounted for by all components or factors. For principal components extraction, this is always equal to 1.0 for correlation analyses.

Extraction communalities are estimates of the variance in each variable accounted for by the components. The communalities in the table are all high, which indicates that the extracted components represent the variables well. If any communalities are very low in a principal components extraction, you may need to extract another component.

The variance explained by the initial solution, extracted components and rotated components is displayed. The first section of the table shows the Initial Eigenvalues.

The Total column gives the eigenvalue, or amount of variance in the original variables accounted for by each component.

The % of Variance column gives the ratio, expressed as a percentage, of the variance accounted for by each component to the total variance in all of the variables.

The Cumulative % column gives the percentage of variance accounted for by the first n components. For example, the cumulative percentage for the second component is the sum of the percentage of variance for the first and second components.

For the initial solution, there are as many components as variables and in a correlation analysis, the sum of the eigenvalues equals the number of components. You have requested that eigenvalues greater than 1 be extracted, so the first three principal components form the extracted solution.

Further results have explained in chapter 9

## 11.4 Cluster Analysis

Hierarchical cluster analysis (HCA) is an exploratory tool designed to reveal natural groupings (or clusters) within a data set that would otherwise not be apparent. It is most useful when you want to cluster a small number (less than a few hundred) of objects.

The objects in hierarchical cluster analysis can be cases or variables, depending on whether you want to classify cases or examine relationships between the variables.

Hierarchical cluster analysis begins by separating each object into a cluster by itself. At each stage of the analysis, the criterion by which objects are separated is relaxed in order to link the two most similar clusters until all of the objects are joined in a complete classification tree.

The basic criterion for any clustering is distance. Objects that are near each other should belong to the same cluster and objects that are far from each other should belong to different clusters. For a given set of data, the clusters that are constructed depend on your specification of the following parameters:

- Cluster method defines the rules for cluster formation. For example, when calculating the distance between two clusters, you can use the pair of nearest objects between clusters or the pair of furthest objects, or a compromise between these methods.

- Measure defines the formula for calculating distance. For example, the Euclidean distance measure calculates the distance as a "straight line" between two clusters. Interval measures assume that the variables are scale; count measures assume that they are discrete numeric; and binary measures assume that they take only two values.
- Standardization allows you to equalize the effect of variables measured on different scales.

Let us start directly with an example. HR department has received the CV of 10 employees. The following table shows their present salary, experience and their sex. You are to group them into cluster for their selection in particular departments.

| Candidate | Salary | Experience | Sex |
|---|---|---|---|
| Ram | 30000 | 32 | 0 |
| Maya | 35000 | 27 | 1 |
| Hari | 38000 | 24 | 0 |
| Gauri | 38000 | 38 | 1 |
| Mala | 15000 | 11 | 1 |
| Kavita | 35000 | 26 | 1 |
| Sita | 29000 | 28 | 1 |
| Geeta | 39000 | 18 | 1 |
| Jagdish | 27000 | 22 | 0 |
| Deepa | 40000 | 24 | 1 |

Load the data in SPSS editor.

To run the cluster analysis, from the menus choose:

Analyze

Classify

Hierarchical Cluster...

Click Plots.

Select Dendrogram.

Select None in the Icicle group.

Click Continue.

Click Method in the Hierarchical Cluster Analysis dialog box.

Select nearest neighbour as the cluster method.

Select Z scores as the standardization in the Transform Values group.

Click Continue.

Click OK in the Hierarchical Cluster Analysis group.

You will get the following results.

## Cluster

**Case Processing Summary a,b**

| Cases | | | | | |
|---|---|---|---|---|---|
| Valid | | Missing | | Total | |
| N | Per cent | N | Per cent | N | Per cent |
| 10 | 100.0 | 0 | .0 | 10 | 100.0 |

a. Squared Euclidean Distance used

b. Average Linkage (Between Groups)

## Average Linkage (Between Groups)

**Agglomeration Schedule**

| Stage | Cluster Combined | | Coefficients | Stage Cluster First Appears | | Next Stage |
|---|---|---|---|---|---|---|
| | Cluster 1 | Cluster 2 | | Cluster 1 | Cluster 2 | |
| 1 | 2 | 6 | 1.000 | 0 | 0 | 7 |
| 2 | 3 | 4 | 197.000 | 0 | 0 | 5 |
| 3 | 1 | 7 | 1000017.00 | 0 | 0 | 6 |
| 4 | 8 | 10 | 1000036.00 | 0 | 0 | 5 |
| 5 | 3 | 8 | 2500158.50 | 2 | 4 | 7 |
| 6 | 1 | 9 | 6500068.50 | 3 | 0 | 8 |
| 7 | 2 | 3 | 14750054.8 | 1 | 5 | 8 |
| 8 | 1 | 2 | 83166721.7 | 6 | 7 | 9 |
| 9 | 1 | 5 | 402666939 | 8 | 0 | 0 |

Vertical Icicle

| Number of clusters | Case | | | | | | | | | | | | | | | | | | |
|---|---|---|---|---|---|---|---|---|---|---|---|---|---|---|---|---|---|---|---|
| | 5: Mala | | 10: Deepa | | 8: Geeta | | 4: Gauri | | 3: Hari | | 6: Kavita | | 2: Maya | | 9: Jagdish | | 7: Sita | | 1: Ram |
| 1 | X | X | X | X | X | X | X | X | X | X | X | X | X | X | X | X | X | X | X |
| 2 | X | | X | X | X | X | X | X | X | X | X | X | X | X | X | X | X | X | X |
| 3 | X | | X | X | X | X | X | X | X | X | X | X | X | | X | X | X | X | X |
| 4 | X | | X | X | X | X | X | X | X | | X | X | X | | X | X | X | X | X |
| 5 | X | | X | X | X | X | X | X | X | | X | X | X | | X | | X | X | X |
| 6 | X | | X | X | X | | X | X | X | | X | X | X | | X | | X | X | X |
| 7 | X | | X | | X | | X | X | X | | X | X | X | | X | | X | X | X |
| 8 | X | | X | | X | | X | X | X | | X | X | X | | X | | X | | X |
| 9 | X | | X | | X | | X | | X | | X | X | X | | X | | X | | X |

## Dendrogram

* * * * * * H I E R A R C H I C A L C L U S T E R A N A L Y S I S * * * * * *

From the dendogram it is clear Mala forms a separate group. Parsing the classification tree to determine the number of clusters is a subjective process. Generally, you begin by looking for "gaps" between joinings along the horizontal axis.

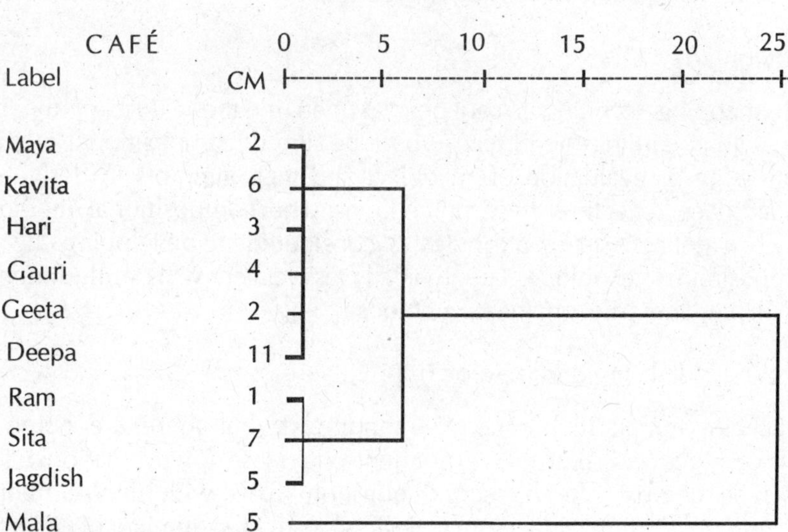


## 11.5 Multidimensional Scaling

Multidimensional scaling (MDS) is a series of techniques that helps the analyst to identify key dimensions underlying respondents' evaluations of objects. It is often used in Marketing to identify key dimensions underlying customer evaluations of products, services or companies.

Once the data is in hand, multidimensional scaling can help determine:

- what dimensions respondents use when evaluating objects
- how many dimensions they may use in a particular situation
- the relative importance of each dimension, and
- how the objects are related perceptually

The purpose of MDS is to transform consumer judgments of similarity or preference (eg. preference for stores or brands) into distances represented in multidimensional space. The resulting perceptual maps show the relative positioning of all objects.

Multidimensional scaling is based on the comparison of objects. Any object (product, service, image, etc.) can be thought of as having both perceived and objective dimensions. For example, a firm may see their new model of lawnmower as having two colour options (red versus green) and a 24-inch blade. These are the objective dimensions. Customers may or may not see these attributes. Customers may also perceive the lawnmower as expensive-looking or fragile, and these are the perceived dimensions.

- The dimensions perceived by customers may not coincide with (or even include) the objective dimensions assumed by the researcher.
- The evaluations of the dimensions may not be independent and may not agree. For example, one soft drink may be judged sweeter than another because the first has a fruitier aroma, although both contain the same amount of sugar.

Perceptual mapping, and multidimensional scaling in particular, is most appropriate for achieving two objectives:

1. As an exploratory technique to identify unrecognized dimensions affecting behaviour
2. As a means of obtaining comparative evaluations of objects when the specific bases of comparison are unknown or undefinable

## Research Design of MDS

Perceptual mapping techniques can be classified by the nature of the responses obtained from the individual concerning the object. One type, the decompositional method, measures only the overall impression or evaluation of an object and then attempts to derive spatial positions in multidimensional space reflecting these perceptions. The compositional method is an alternative method in which a defined set of attributes is considered in developing the similarity between objects. Decompositional techniques are typically associated with multidimensional scaling and so our focus will be primarily on these methods.

## Objects: Their Number and Selection

An implicit assumption in perceptual mapping is that there are common characteristics, either objective or perceived, that the respondent could use for evaluations. Therefore, it is vital that the objects be comparable. A second question deals with the number of objects to be evaluated. The researcher must balance two desires: a smaller number of objects to ease the effort on the part of the respondent versus the required number of objects to obtain a stable multidimensional solution. A suggested guideline for stable solutions is to have more than four times as many objects as dimensions desired.

## Collection of Similarity or Preference Data

The primary distinction among multidimensional scaling programmes is the type of data (qualitative or quantitative) used to represent similarity and preferences. For many of the data collection methods, either quantitative (ratings) or qualitative (rankings) data may be collected.

## Similarities Data

When collecting similarities data, the researcher is trying to determine which items are the most similar to each other and which are the most dissimilar. Three procedures commonly used to obtain respondents' perceptions of similarities are outlined below:

- Comparison of Paired Objects: By far the most widely used method of obtaining similarity judgments, the respondent is asked simply to rank or rate the similarity of all pairs of objects.
- Confusion Data: The pairing (or "confusing") of stimulus I with stimulus J is taken to indicate similarity. Also known as subjective clustering, the typical procedure for gathering these data is to place the objects whose similarity is to be measured on small cards, either descriptively or with pictures. The respondent is asked to sort the cards into stacks so that all the cards in a stack represent similar candy bars. The data result is an aggregate similarities matrix similar to a cross-tabulation table.
- Derived Measures: These measures of similarity are typically based on scores given to stimuli by respondents. For example, subjects are asked to evaluate 3 stimuli (Pepsi, Coke and Allsport) on 2 semantic differential scales (Sweet to Tart, Light Tasting to Heavy). The 2 × 3 matrix could be evaluated for each respondent to create similarity measures.

There are several assumptions made with derived measures that make it the least desirable in meeting the "spirit" of MDS – that the evaluation of objects be made with minimal influence by the researcher.

## Preference Data

Preference implies that stimuli should be judged in terms of dominance relationships – that is, stimuli are ordered in terms of the preference for some property. The two most common procedures for obtaining preference data are outlined below:

- Direct Ranking: Each respondent ranks the objects from most preferred to least preferred, as in the following example:

  Rank from most preferred (1) to least preferred (4)

  ____ Candy Bar A

  ____ Candy Bar B

  ____ Candy Bar C

  ____ Candy Bar D

- Paired Comparisons: A respondent is presented with all possible pairs and asked to indicate which member of each pair is preferred, as in this example:

  Please circle the preferred candy bar in each pair:

  A B

  A C

  A D

  B C

  B D

  C D

Let us take the example

Following table shows hypothetical data about 10 cars where the consumers have been asked to find dissimilarity among ten cars and award 0-15 scale 0 for most similar and 15 for least similar.

| | Maruti 800 | Alto | Santro | Zen | Indica V2 | WagonR | Fordlkon | Accent | Indigo | Esteem |
|---|---|---|---|---|---|---|---|---|---|---|
| Maruti800 | 0 | 2 | 5 | 8 | 8 | 9 | 10 | 11 | 11 | 12 |
| Alto | 3 | 0 | 7 | 9 | 9 | 10 | 11 | 10 | 11 | 13 |
| Santro | 5 | 5 | 0 | 3 | 2 | 2 | 5 | 7 | 8 | 9 |
| Zen | 8 | 5 | 1 | 0 | 2 | 1 | 7 | 7 | 8 | 10 |
| IndicaV2 | 8 | 7 | 1 | 2 | 0 | 2 | 5 | 8 | 3 | 11 |
| WagonR | 9 | 5 | 2 | 1 | 3 | 0 | 5 | 5 | 5 | 9 |
| Fordlkon | 10 | 8 | 7 | 5 | 5 | 5 | 0 | 3 | 3 | 4 |
| Accent | 11 | 9 | 8 | 6 | 7 | 6 | 3 | 0 | 3 | 3 |
| Indigo | 11 | 9 | 5 | 3 | 8 | 10 | 2 | 2 | 0 | 3 |
| Esteem | 12 | 10 | 10 | 6 | 5 | 10 | 1 | 3 | 1 | 0 |

Data was addressed to SPSS editor

Analyse

Scale

Multidimensional scale

Select

Create distances from data

Measure

Select Interval and Euclidean Distance

Continue

Select Option

Select display

Group plots

Individual subject plots

Continue

You will get the following results

See the Euclidean distance plot how Alto and Maruti800 are near to each other and Zen, Wagon R, Santro and IndicaV2 form a group.

We use and approach a **stress measure**, which indicates the proportion of the variance of the **disparities** not accounted for by the MDS model. This measurement varies according to the type of commonly used measure for determining a model's goodness of fit, and is provided in SPSS. Stress is minimized when the objects are placed in a configuration so that the distances between the objects best match the original distances. A problem found in using stress, however, is analogous to that of R2 in multiple regression in that stress always improves with increased dimensions. A trade-off must then be made between fit of the solution and the number of dimensions. We can plot the stress value against the number of factors to help us determine the optimal number of dimensions, in a similar technique to using a Scree Plot in Factor Analysis. We can also use an R2 measure as an **index of fit**, indicating the proportion of variance of the disparities accounted for by the MDS procedure.

## Proximities

**Case Processing Summary(a)**

| Cases | | | | | |
|---|---|---|---|---|---|
| Valid | | Missing | | Total | |
| N | Per cent | N | Per cent | N | Per cent |
| 10 | 100.0% | 0 | .0% | 10 | 100.0% |

a Euclidean Distance used

## Alscal

Alscal Procedure Options

**Data Options-**

| | |
|---|---|
| Number of Rows (Observations/Matrix). | 10 |
| Number of Columns (Variables) . . . | 10 |
| Number of Matrices . . . . . . | 1 |
| Measurement Level . . . . . . . | Ordinal |
| Data Matrix Shape . . . . . . . | Symmetric |
| Type . . . . . . . . . . . . | Dissimilarity |
| Approach to Ties . . . . . . . | Leave Tied |
| Conditionality . . . . . . . . | Matrix |
| Data Cut off at . . . . . . . . . | 000000 |

**Model Options-**

| | |
|---|---|
| Model . . . . . . . . . . . | Euclid |
| Maximum Dimensionality . . . . . | 2 |
| Minimum Dimensionality . . . . . | 2 |
| Negative Weights . . . . . . . | Not Permitted |

**Output Options-**

| | |
|---|---|
| Job Option Header . . . . . . . | Printed |
| Data Matrices . . . . . . . . | Printed |
| Configurations and Transformations . | Plotted |
| Output Dataset . . . . . . . . | Not Created |
| Initial Stimulus Co-ordinates . . . | Computed |

**Algorithmic Options-**

| | |
|---|---|
| Maximum Iterations . . . . . . . | 30 |
| Convergence Criterion . . . . . . | 00100 |
| Minimum S-stress . . . . . . . . | 00500 |
| Missing Data Estimated by . . . . | Ulbounds |
| Tiestore . . . . . . . . . . . | 45 |

**Raw (unscaled) Data for Subject 1**

| | 1 | 2 | 3 | 4 | 5 |
|---|---|---|---|---|---|
| 1 | .000 | | | | |
| 2 | 7.416 | .000 | | | |
| 3 | 16.462 | 12.728 | .000 | | |
| 4 | 20.445 | 16.031 | 7.280 | .000 | |

| | | | | | |
|---|---|---|---|---|---|
| 5 | 18.547 | 15.067 | 7.681 | 6.325 | .000 |
| 6 | 18.974 | 15.588 | 8.185 | 8.367 | 6.782 |
| 7 | 23.580 | 20.567 | 17.059 | 12.083 | 12.806 |
| 8 | 22.869 | 19.849 | 18.055 | 13.304 | 14.866 |
| 9 | 24.290 | 21.424 | 18.028 | 12.884 | 14.071 |
| 10 | 24.104 | 23.022 | 23.108 | 18.947 | 19.209 |
| | 6 | 7 | 8 | 9 | 10 |
| 6 | .000 | | | | |
| 7 | 16.125 | .000 | | | |
| 8 | 16.703 | 6.083 | .000 | | |
| 9 | 17.607 | 5.292 | 6.708 | .000 | |
| 10 | 21.656 | 10.149 | 8.246 | 10.050 | .000 |

Iteration history for the 2 dimensional solution (in squared distances)

**Young's S-stress formula 1 is used.**

| Iteration | S-stress | Improvement |
|---|---|---|
| 1 | .02314 | .00640 |
| 2 | .01674 | .00231 |
| 3 | .01443 | .00089 |
| 4 | .01354 | .001000 |

Iterations stopped because S-stress improvement is less than Stress and squared correlation (RSQ) in distances RSQ values are the proportion of variance of the scaled data (disparities) in the partition (row, matrix, or entire data) which is accounted for by their corresponding distances. Stress values are Kruskal's stress formula 1.

For. matrix

Stress = .02979 RSQ = .99573

Configuration derived in 2 dimensions

**Stimulus Co-ordinates**

**Dimension**

| **Stimulus Number** | **Stimulus Name** | **1** | **2** |
|---|---|---|---|
| 1 | Maruti800 | 1.7454 | –1.3439 |
| 2 | Alto | 1.4871 | –.7069 |
| 3 | Santro | .9672 | .7444 |
| 4 | Zen | .1194 | .8286 |
| 5 | IndicaV2 | .3108 | .7165 |
| 6 | WagonR | .6780 | .9511 |
| 7 | FordIkon | –1.1749 | .0914 |
| 8 | Accent | –1.1859 | –.3024 |
| 9 | Indigo | –1.3357 | .0232 |
| 10 | Esteem | –1.6114 | –1.0021 |

Optimally scaled data (disparities) for subject 1

| | **1** | **2** | **3** | **4** | **5** |
|---|---|---|---|---|---|
| 1 | .000 | | | | |
| 2 | .663 | .000 | | | |
| 3 | 2.229 | 1.542 | .000 | | |
| 4 | 2.714 | 2.049 | .663 | .000 | |
| 5 | 2.511 | 1.846 | .663 | .320 | .000 |
| 6 | 2.531 | 1.846 | .663 | .706 | .436 |
| 7 | 3.254 | 2.779 | 2.234 | 1.489 | 1.612 |
| 8 | 3.111 | 2.703 | 2.404 | 1.727 | 1.811 |
| 9 | 3.372 | 2.916 | 2.404 | 1.663 | 1.786 |
| 10 | 3.372 | 3.112 | 3.114 | 2.519 | 2.578 |
| | 6 | 7 | 8 | 9 | 10 |
| 6 | .000 | | | | |
| 7 | 2.049 | .000 | | | |
| 8 | 2.234 | .320 | .000 | | |
| 9 | 2.234 | .175 | .358 | .000 | |
| 10 | 3.009 | 1.177 | .706 | 1.062 | .000 |

**Derived Stimulus Configuration**
**Euclidean distance model**

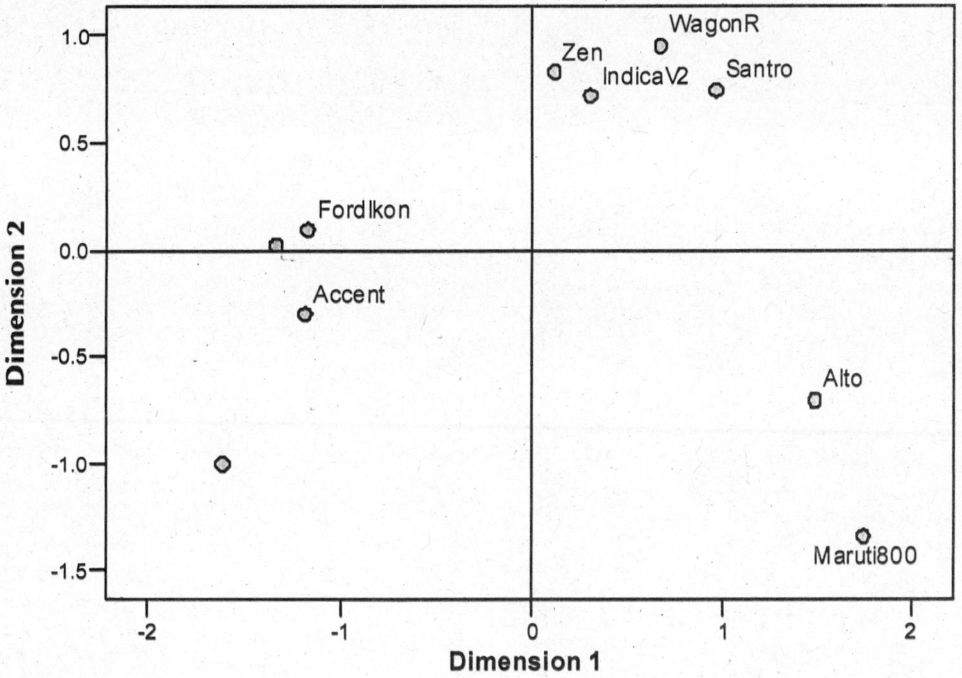

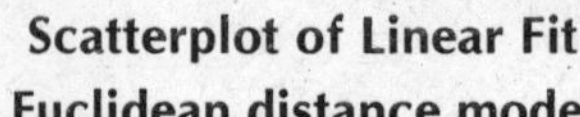
Scatterplot of Linear Fit
Euclidean distance model

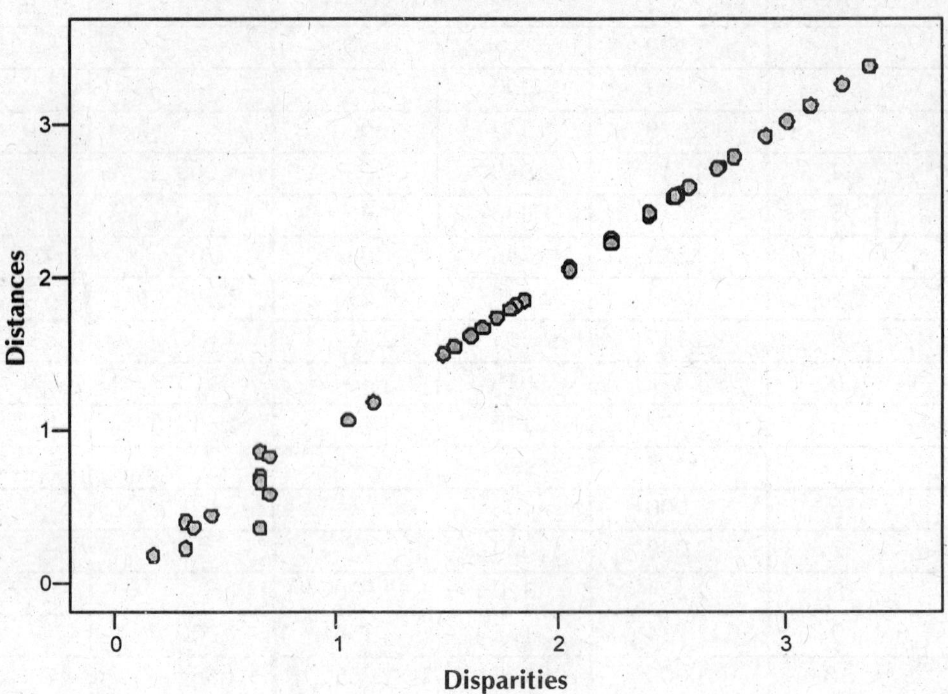
Distances
0
1
2
3
0
1
2
3
Disparities

CHAPTER

# More Sample Research Projects

## Structure

Research Project 12

# 12.1 A Case Study on Financial Performance of Centurion Bank and Bank of Punjab – In Pre and Post Merger Period

P. Chellasamy[1] and J. Udhaya Kumar[2]

## Introduction

Over the past decade, the banking industry has experienced an unprecedented level of consolidation as mergers and acquisitions among large financial institutions have taken place at record levels. To a large extent, this consolidation is based on a belief that gains can accrue through expense reduction, increased market power, reduced earnings volatility and scale and scope economies. Whether or not bank mergers actually achieve the expected performance gains is the critical question. If consolidation does, in fact, lead to value gains, then shareholder wealth can be increased. On the other hand, if consolidating entities does not lead to the promised positive effects, then mergers may lead to a less profitable and valuable banking industry.

Merger and acquisitions have been considered as a strategy for fast track technology led companies. In the current, rapidly changing environment and in the era of systemic innovation, where technology is embedded in people and process well planned mergers and acquisitions are recognized as critical for the fast track technology companies' success and even for their survival.

Merger is a combination of two or more companies where by acquirer company acquires all the assets and liabilities of acquiree company. The acquiree company loses its identity.

Sec 2(1B) of the Income Tax Act 1961 defines the term amalgamation. Amalgamation in relation to companies means the merger of one or more companies with another company or the merger of two or more companies to form one company.

Merger and acquisition is looked upon as an immediate mode for external growth. This phenomena has been prevailing both in the developed and developing economies. But it is gaining more prominence in the present globalizing world. The banking sector which plays a very vital role in the economic development of India have been witnessing tremendous change.

The various players in the banking arena have already begun to feel the heat of the intense competition. Merger and acquisition is one among the various modes of restructuring restored by banks to ensure a better growth prospect.

Some of the reasons for this growing tendency of adopting merger and acquisition tactics are due to the increasing needs to achieve economies of large scale, brand building, expanding branch network over a geographical area. It is believed that by undergoing such merger and acquisition deals banks will enable them to emerge stronger, increase their earning capacity and strengthen their capital base.

Currently foreign banks have been permitted to buy stakes up to 74% in the Indian banks. This adds more oil to the spreading fire because foreign banks would consider merger and acquisition as a quick method of inorganic growth. In order to expand their presence in the Indian scenario they would join hands with other Indian banks. Such a deal would enable it to have a collective strength while doing banking business.

1 Dr. P. Chellasamy Lecturer in Commerce, Department of Commerce, Bharathiar University, Coimbatore- 46

2 J. Udhaya Kumar, M.phil Scholar, Department of Commerce, Bharathiar University, Coimbatore- 46

Merger of commercial banks provide a very rare opportunity for examining whether the merger has been successful or not, most of the attempts would either concentrate on anticipated economics or they have been conducted on a macro level. Independent micro level analysis is, therefore, necessary to examine the various aspects of merger. Accordingly Centurion Bank — Bank of Punjab merger has been opted for a case study. It has been intentionally selected as this deal has been the recent merger (i.e.) one year deal between two private sector banks.

## Benefits of Merger

**Growth:** One of the fundamental motives that entice mergers is impulsive growth. Organizations that intend to expand need to choose between organic growth or acquisitions driven growth. Since the former is very slow, steady and relatively consumes more time the latter is preferred by firms which are dynamic and ready to capitalize on opportunities.

**Synergy:** Synergy is a phenomenon where 2 + 2 –> 5; this translates into the ability of a business combination to be more profitable than the sum of the profits of the individual firms that were combined. It may be in the form of revenue enhancement or cost reduction.

**Managerial efficiency:** Some acquisitions are motivated by the belief that the acquirer's management can better manage the target's resources. In such cases, the value of the target firm will rise under the management control of the acquirer.

**Strategic:** The strategic reasons could differ on a case-to-case basis and a deal to the other. At times, if the two firms have complimentary business interests, mergers may result in consolidating their position in the market.

**Market entry:** Firms that are cash rich use acquisition as a strategy to enter into new market or new territory on which they can build their platform.

**Tax shields:** This plays a significant role in acquisition if the distressed firm has accumulated losses and unclaimed depreciation benefits on their books. Such acquisitions can eliminate the acquiring firms' liability by benefiting from a merger with these firms.

## Bank of Punjab

Established in 1989, in pursuance of The Bank of Punjab Act 1989 and was given the status of scheduled bank in 1994. Bank of Punjab is operating since April 1995 when its first branch was opened in Chandigarh. By March 1996, its deposit base was ₹ 2342.17 Crores. In 4 years, the annual growth rose to ₹ 3244.76 which was 200%. Bank of Punjab is the first bank to focus on retail banking and to introduce fax banking and telebanking for its customers. It has a tie up with Master Card International for its MAESTERO, SWADHAN and CIRRUS International card network. It has set up 'Dr. Inderjit Singh Institute of Banking and Insurance Management' at Gurgaon, near Delhi, to provide ideal learning environment for banks' professionals. The Bank of Punjab is working as a scheduled commercial bank with its network of 266 branches at all major business centres in the country. The Bank provides all types of banking services such as Deposit in Local Currency, Client Deposit in Foreign Currency, Remittances, and Advances to Business, Trade, Industry and Agriculture. The Bank of Punjab has indeed entered a new era of science to the nation under experience and professional hands of its management. The Bank of Punjab plays a vital role in the national economy through mobilization of promoting savings and providing funds for investments. Attractive rates of profit on all types of deposits, opening of Foreign Currency Accounts and handling of Foreign Exchange business such as Imports, Exports and Remittances, Financing, Trade and Industry for working capital requirements and money market operations are some facilities being provided by the Bank. As agriculture is considered as the backbone of our economy the Bank of Punjab has introduced "Kissan Dost Agriculture Finance Scheme" to small farmers.

## Centurion Bank of Punjab

Private Banks are taking to the consolidation route in a big way. Bank of Punjab (BoP) and Centurion Bank (CB) have been merged to form Centurion Bank of Punjab (CBP). RBI has approved merger of Centurion Bank and Bank of Punjab effective from October 1, 2005. The merger is at a swap ratio 9:4 and the combined bank is called Centurion Bank of Punjab. The merger of the banks will have a presence of 240 branches and extension counters, 386 ATMs, about 2.2 million customers. As on March 2005, the net worth of the combined entity is Rs 696 crore and the capital adequacy ratio is 16.1 per cent in the private sector, nearly 30 banks are operating. The top five control nearly 65% of the assets. Most of these private sector banks are profitable and have adequate capital and technology edge.

Due to intensifying competition, access to low-cost deposits is critical for growth. Therefore, size and geographical reach becomes the key for smaller banks. The choice before smaller private banks is to merge and form bigger and viable entities or merge into a big private sector bank. The proposed merger of Bank of Punjab and Centurion Bank is sure to encourage other private sector banks to go for the M&A road for consolidation. Centurion Bank of Punjab is a new generation private sector bank offering a wide spectrum of retail, SME and corporate banking products and services. It has been among the earliest banks to offer a technology-enabled customer interface that provides easy access and superior customer service. The shares of the bank are listed on the major stock exchanges in India and also on the Luxembourg Stock Exchange.

## Highlights of the Merger — Centurion Bank and Bank of Punjab

1. Bank of Punjab will be merged into Centurion Bank.
2. New entity will be named 'Centurion Bank of Punjab'
3. Centurion Bank's chairman Rana Talwar will take over as the chairman of the merged entity.
4. Centurion Bank's MD Shailendra Bhandari will be the MD of the merged entity.
5. KPMG India Pvt. Ltd. and NM Raiji & Co. are the independent valuers and Ambit Corporate Finance was the sole investment banker to the transaction.
6. Swap ratio has been fixed at 4:9, that is, for every four shares of ₹ 10 of Bank of Punjab, its shareholders would receive nine shares of ₹ 1 of Centurion Bank.
7. There has been no cash transaction in the course of the merger; it has been settled through the swap of shares.
8. There will no downsizing via the voluntary retirement scheme.

## Share Holding Pattern of Centurion Bank of Punjab

After the merger the share holding of Bank of Punjab (BoP) promoters will shrink to 5%.The family of Darshanjit Singh which promoted BoP currently holds 15.62%, while associates hold another 11.40%. The promoter stake will now fall down to around 5% and for associate that would be 7-8%. The major stakeholder of the Centurion Bank, Bank of Muscat's stake will fall to 20.5% from 25.91%, Keppel's stake will be at 9% from current level of 11.33% and Rana Talwar's saber capital will have a stake of 4.4% as against 5.61%. The promoters of the BoP and major stakeholders of Centurion Bank will have a combine stake of around 42% in the merged entity- Centurion Bank of Punjab.

## Gains from the Merger

Combined entity the Punjab-Centurion Bank would be among the top 10 private sector banks in the country. Merged entity would benefit from the fact that Centurion Bank had recently written of its bad loans against equity. Branch network of the two banks will complement each other. The combined entity will have a nationwide reach. Centurion Bank is strong in South India, Maharashtra and Goa whereas Bank of Punjab is strong in Punjab, Haryana and Delhi. While Centurion Bank has 82 per cent of its business coming from retail, Bank of Punjab is strong in the Small and Medium Enterprises (SMEs) segment and agricultural sector. The book value of the bank would also go up to around ₹ 300 crore. The higher book value should help the combine entity to mobilize funds at lower rate. The combined bank will be full-service commercial bank with a strong presence in the Retail, SME and Agricultural segments.

## Methodology

The researcher has depended heavily on secondary data. Data has been gathered from the annual reports of Centurion Bank and Bank of Punjab for a period of 2004-2005 to 2005-2006. The whole evaluation is based on the principle that if one plus one gives a figure greater than two then the variable under study has resulted in synergy. In other words the study adopts a before and after approach for evaluating the merger's impact. Accordingly an attempt has been made to analyze, several financial tools have been used namely Comparative financial statements, Profitability ratio, Business income ratio, Deposit mobilization ratio, Working fund ratio, Operating Performance ratio, Returns ratio, Capital adequacy ratio, Resource deployed ratio.

## Comparative Balance Sheet

Comparative balance sheet can be used for comparing assets and liabilities of two different periods in order to find out any increase or decrease in those items. Thus in a single balance sheet the emphasis is on present position, it is on change in the comparative balance sheet.

**Table 1**

**Comparative Balance Sheet**

(₹ in crores)

| Source of funds | Pre-merger | Post-merger (average) | Increase/decrease (in amount) | Increase/decrease (in percentage) |
|---|---|---|---|---|
| Capital | 103.16 | 140.83 | 37.67 | 36.51 |
| Reserve & surplus | 223.23 | 790.37 | 567.14 | 254.06 |
| Deposits | 3918.59 | 9399.64 | 5481.05 | 139.87 |
| Borrowing | 183.58 | 266.57 | 82.99 | 45.20 |
| Other liabilities & provisions | 240.73 | 732.78 | 492.05 | 204.39 |
| TOTAL | 4669.29 | 11330.19 | 6660.90 | 142.60 |
| **Application of funds** | | | | |
| Cash& bank balances | 521.59 | 1046.04 | 524.45 | 100.50 |
| Investments | 1441.16 | 2922.83 | 1481.67 | 102.81 |
| Advances & loans | 2305.46 | 6533.44 | 4227.98 | 183.38 |
| Receivables | 239.68 | 250.99 | 16.95 | 7.24 |
| Fixed assets | 161.40 | 197.41 | 36.01 | 22.30 |
| TOTAL | 4669.29 | 11330.19 | 6660.90 | 142.60 |

**Source:** Compiled from the annual reports of Centurion Bank and Bank of Punjab.

The above table shows the comparative balance sheet of Centurion Bank of Punjab before merger and after merger. After the merger deposits have increased by ₹ 5481.05 crores. Cash and bank balances have also increased by ₹ 524.5 crores. The overall financial position of the Centurion Bank of Punjab is good after the merger.

## Comparative Income Statement

The income statement discloses net profit or net loss on account of operations. A comparative income statement will show the absolute figures for two or more periods, the absolute change from one period to another and if, desired, the change in terms of percentages. Since the two periods are shown side by side, the reader can quickly ascertain whether interest income has increased or decreased, whether interest expenses have increased or decreased etc., thus comparative income statement will be helpful in deriving meaning full conclusions.

**Table 2**
**Comparative Income Statement**

**(₹ in crores)**

| Income | Pre-merger | Post-merger (average) | Increase/decrease (in amount) | Increase/decrease (in percentage) |
|---|---|---|---|---|
| Interest income | 241.86 | 608.04 | 366.81 | 151.60 |
| Investment income | 81.53 | 179.90 | 98.37 | 120.65 |
| Others | 70.88 | 231.91 | 161.03 | 227.18 |
| Other income | 18.7 | 15.34 | –3.36 | –17.96 |
| Non-recurring income | 63.4 | 186.66 | 123.26 | 194.40 |
| **Total income** | 476.37 | 1220.94 | 754.57 | 158.30 |
| **Expenditure** | | | | |
| Interest expended | 180.94 | 404.43 | 223.49 | 123.50 |
| Personnel cost | 35.84 | 142.40 | 106.56 | 297.30 |
| Provision for contingencies | 77.59 | 172.40 | 94.81 | 122.10 |
| Insurance premium | 3.57 | 9.40 | 5.83 | 163.30 |
| Other expenses | 153.23 | 334.19 | 180.96 | 118.09 |
| **Total expenditure** | 451.17 | 1062.82 | 611.65 | 135.50 |
| Profit/loss | | | | |
| PBDT | 16.44 | 159.00 | 142.56 | 861.70 |
| DEP | 30.21 | 51.48 | 21.27 | 70.40 |
| PBT | 13.77 | 107.52 | 93.75 | 680.80 |
| TAX PROVISION | 4.29 | 19.72 | 15.43 | 359.60 |
| PAT | 18.065 | 87.80 | 69.73 | 385.90 |

**Source:** Compiled from the annual reports of Centurion Bank and Bank of Punjab.

The comparative income statement is presented in the Table no. 2. This statement reveals that there has been increase in interest income in ₹ 366.81 crores. While the total expenditure has increased proportionately by ₹ 1062.82 crores, thereby resulting in an increase of profit of ₹ 142.56 crores. The bank needs to look in to the cause of increase in expenditure and control the same. The profit before tax also increased by ₹ 93.75 crores after the merger. It reveals that the profitability of the Centurion Bank of Punjab has improved after the merger.

## Profitability

Profit is the ultimate aim of any business. And the future of the business depends upon the profitability. Here the Spread-Burden model has been adapted to measure banks profitability. Where spread which denotes the difference between interest income and interest expense. Burden implies difference between non-interest income and non-interest expense and profit margin refers to the profit earned by the banks before making provisions and contingencies. Return denotes to earning before interest and tax.

**Table 3**
**Profitability Ratios**

**(Percentage)**

| Item | Combined pre-merger (average) | Post-merger |
|---|---|---|
| Spread/total income | 12 | 16.6 |
| Burden/total income | -9.3 | -3.6 |
| Profit margin/total income | 13.35 | 22.9 |
| Return on total asset | 0.83 | 1.39 |
| Return on investment | 2.6 | 5.43 |

**Source:** Compiled from the annual reports of Centurion Bank and Bank of Punjab.

The above Table no.3 which depicts that before the merger spread average ratio is 12 per cent but after the merger the spread is increased to 16.6 per cent profitability ratio was only 3.8 per cent of the total income. Profit margin also increased to 22.9 per cent after the merger. So we can say that profitability position of the Centurion Bank of Punjab is good.

## Total Income

Income refers to the streams of revenue of a business. Bank may generate income from the activities directly related to its activities or other activities. Since it assumes great importance it has been chosen as a variable for measuring the impact of merger. The Table No.4 shows the business income ratios of merged banks.

**Table 4**
**Business Income Ratios of Merged Banks**

**(Percentage)**

| Item | Combined pre-merger (average) | Post-merger |
|---|---|---|
| Interest income/total income | 50.65 | 49.76 |
| Interest expenses/total income | 38 | 33 |
| Non-interest income/total income | 49 | 50 |
| Non-interest expenses/total income | 58.6 | 53.8 |

**Source:** Compiled from the annual reports of Centurion Bank and Bank of Punjab.

The above Table shows that before the merger of the banks, average income ratios ranged between 38 and 58.6 per cent. After the merger, the bank's income ratios ranged between 33 per cent and 53.8 per cent. The non-interest income is 53.8 per cent and interest expenses is 33 per cent, the non-interest expenses and interest expenses have reduced, so the business income ratio after the merger is satisfactory.

## Deposit Mobilization Efficiency

Deposits are an important source of finance for all banks. In this era of globalization there is intense competition among banks in mobilizing deposits. In the private sector, remuneration of bank officials depends upon the targets of deposits raised by them. Thus deposits being an important component for a bank it is taken as a variable for measurement. Here deposit mix refers to the ratio of total of current and saving deposits to total deposits. The Table no 5 shows the deposit mobilization efficiency of the merged banks.

**Table 5**
**Deposit Mobilization Ratios**

**(Percentage)**

| Item | Combined pre-merger (average) | Post-merger |
|---|---|---|
| Investment to deposit | 37.25 | 31.09 |
| Deposit mix | 38.10 | 38.75 |
| Operating expenses/total deposit | 3.13 | 4.30 |
| Income/deposit | 12.25 | 12.93 |
| Total deposit/total liabilities | 83.35 | 82.61 |
| Demand deposits/total deposits | 16.32 | 15.21 |
| Saving deposit/total deposit | 21.72 | 23.51 |
| Time deposit/total deposit | 61.93 | 61.27 |

**Source:** Compiled from the annual reports of Centurion Bank and Bank of Punjab.

The Table no.5 depicts that before the merger the average deposit mobilization ratios were between 83.35 per cent and 3.13 per cent. After the merger of the bank's deposit mix has increased to 38.75. Saving deposit also increased to 23.5 per cent. So there is increase in deposits after the merger.

## Working Fund

Working fund refers to that capital which is required for financing the activities during the operating cycle. Working capital has assumed such significance that it is now being taught as a discipline in various universities. Here working fund refers to total of all assets.

**Table 6**
**Working Fund Ratio**

**(Percentage)**

| Item | Combined pre-merger (average) | Post-merger |
|---|---|---|
| Interest income/working fund | 5.66 | 7.74 |
| Non-interest income/working fund | 4.90 | 5.40 |
| Interest expended/borrowing & deposit | 4.63 | 6.03 |
| Total income/working fund | 10.17 | 10.70 |
| Interest expenses/working fund | 3.80 | 3.50 |
| Non-interest expenses/working fund | 5.94 | 5.79 |
| Interest expense/interest income | 38.45 | 50.03 |
| Total expenses/working fund | 9.79 | 9.34 |
| Contingent liability/working fund | 30.85 | 46.30 |

**Source:** Compiled from the annual reports of Centurion Bank and Bank of Punjab.

The Table 6 shows that in pre-merger period interest expense to interest income is percentage 38.45 and interest expenses to working fund is percentage 3.8. But after the merger interest expense to interest income has increased to 50.03 percentage but interest expenses to working fund is lower as compared to pre-merger.

## Capital Adequacy Ratio

In India, banks are institutions where depositors place their hard-earned savings on the assumption that the risk shall be borne by the bank. In such a scenario, the banks must have enough capital to meet unforeseen contingencies. To fulfil this need, the RBI has laid down the norms of capital adequacy. The banks have to maintain the capital adequacy ratio specified by RBI from time to time. Capital adequacy indicates whether the bank has enough capital to absorb unexpected losses. It is required to maintain depositor's confidence and preventing the bank from going bankrupt.

As per the BASLE Committee norms, 8 per cent of a risk weighted asset should be the minimum capital for any banking institution. Capital adequacy ratio is nothing but expression of total capital of the bank as multiple of funded and non-funded assets and off the balance sheet item.

**Table 7**
**Capital Adequacy Ratio**

**(Percentage)**

| Item | Combined pre-merger (average) | Post-merger |
|---|---|---|
| Government securities/investment | 86.65 | 81.8 |
| Capital/deposits | 2.62 | 1.49 |
| Government securities/working fund | 26.8 | 21.04 |

**Source:** Compiled from the annual reports of Centurion Bank and Bank of Punjab.

The above Table shows that before the merger bank had enough government securities than the post-merger. Capital to deposit ratio is also low percentage 1.49 compared to pre-merger. Hence the Centurion Bank of Punjab has to maintain the capital adequacy in order to absorb unexpected losses.

## Resources Deployed Ratio

The resources obtained by banks through deposits and borrowings have to be developed properly to get the maximum return out of its in terms of profit and socio-economic objectives of the government. A substantial part of the resources is, however, prompted by the cash reserve and statutory liquidity ratio requirements of the remaining resources also a large chunk is subjective to RBI's regulation. The credit policy of the government and the rigidity which it is implemented to determine the amount of deployable resources available to a bank and also the areas where it can be profitably deployed.

**Table 8**
**Resources Deployed Ratio**

**(Percentage)**

| Item | Combined pre-merger (average) | Post-merger |
|---|---|---|
| Fixed assets/working fund | 3.41 | 2.70 |
| Advances/working fund | 49.17 | 57.40 |
| Advances/deposit | 59.10 | 69.50 |

**Source:** Compiled from the annual reports of Centurion Bank and Bank of Punjab.

The above Table represents that before the merger advances to deposit ratio is 59.1 percentage and fixed asset to working fund ratio is 3.41 percentage but after the merger fixed asset to working fund ratio is decreased due to increase in advances and deposit (i.e.) 69.5 percentage. Hence increase in deposits and borrowing have to be developed properly to get the maximum return in terms of profit.

**Table 9**
**Returns Ratio**

**(Percentage)**

| Item | Combined pre-merger (average) | Post-merger |
|---|---|---|
| PAT/working funds | 1.04 | 1.12 |
| PBDT/working funds | 1.63 | 2.02 |
| PAT/net worth | 10.24 | 12.54 |
| Operating income/working funds | 12.3 | 13 |

**Source:** Compiled from the annual reports of Centurion Bank and Bank of Punjab.

The above Table shows that before the merger the average operating income to total assets is 12.3 percentage and profit after tax to total assets ratio is 1.04 percentage but after the merger operating income to total asset is 12.3 percentage and profit after tax to total assets ratio is 1.04 but after the merger operating income to total asset ratio is high (i.e.) 13 per cent.

## Operating Performane Variables

Some more variables which are considered to be indicators of a banks operating performance have also been included to measure exactly the real impact of merger between Centurion Bank and Bank of Punjab.

The Table no.10 depicts that before the merger total income is 6.8% but after the merger total income has increased to 13%. Profit before tax also increased to 87.8 after the merger, so the banks operating performance is good

**Table 10**
**Performance Variables**

**(Percentage)**

| Item | Combined pre-merger (average) | Post-merger |
|---|---|---|
| Total income | 6.8 | 13 |
| EBT | 13.77 | 107.52 |
| PAT | 18.06 | 87.8 |

**Source:** Compiled from the annual reports of Centurion Bank and Bank of Punjab.

## Conclusion

Based on the analysis it can be concluded that there is an increase in financial performance of the Centurion Bank of Punjab after the merger compared to pre-merger period. Ratio analysis of the financial performance of the Centurion Bank of Punjab, were found to be very good. So we conclude that the merger between Centurion Bank and Bank of Punjab has turned to be successful.

## References

Books

*"Management accounting and financial analysis"* by Khan M.Y. and Jain P.K. published by Tata McGraw – Hill Publishing Company Ltd., New Delhi, 2003.

*"Finance management and policy"* by *Van Horne*, James.C Published by Hall of India Pvt. Ltd.

"*Banking theory, law and practice*" by *Sundram*, K.P.M. and Varshney, New Delhi, 2004.
"*Banking theory and practice*" by *Shekhar*, K.C. published by Vikas Publishing House Pvt. Ltd., 1997.

## Websites

1. http://www.centurionbop.co.in/site/aboutus.html
2. http://www.banknetindia.com/banking/bop.
3. html http://www.centurionbank.com/site/aboutus.html
4. http://finance.indiamart.com/investment_in_india/banks.
5. html http://www.centurionbank.com/site/AnnualRep0405.pdf
6. http://indiagateway.com/companies/banks.html

✦ ✦ ✦

Research Project 13

## 12.2 Direction of Exports of Commercial Agricultural Commodities

J.K. SACHDEVA[1]

### 1. Introduction

Agricultural commodities like tea, coffee, spices, oilseeds, cotton and cashew can be grouped under cash crops. They are traditional export items, which aggregate to 50% of total agricultural exports. These items are ready for consumption after some value addition. They are used as raw material in food and other industries. The commodities can be ranked high in hierarchy of demands after food items like wheat and rice. The economic status of the consumer plays a significant role in their demand. A review of the literature and expert views concerning the export of these commodities is undertaken in the subsequent section below. Objectives and research methodology have been discussed in Section3. Results are in Section4. Section5 concludes.

### 2. Literature Review

Indian tea has always been export oriented and has occupied an important place on the international tea map. The industry, however, has not been doing well on the export front in the recent years. In fact, in the decade of the 80s and in the earlier years of the 90s, it failed to repeat the performance it achieved in 1981. Barring occasional upswing, it has been a downhill journey thereafter. Intriguing developments, such as, cash crunch faced by the Iranian and Russian buyers, Lankan inroad into CIS markets, Poland turning to Kenya for cheaper teas or over supply of inferior teas leading to price crash at the tea auction centres were enough to play havoc with the fortunes of the Indian exporters (Kainth,1996a). India has the potential to exploit the enormous tea export opportunities by enhancing the production through increased yield rates. The quality aspect needs serious attention. China, Sri Lanka, Indonesia pose a competitive threat in this field and there is need for a number of policy initiatives so that India's advantages are reinforced and the disadvantages are neutralized. In this context a massive upgradation in the market information infrastructure in the country is a must. In addition, quality upgradation will have to be an ongoing process both in the field and in the factory (Talreja, 2003).

Next traditional item among cash crops is coffee. Veena et al. (1994) analyzed the direction of the changing situation of Indian coffee exports and found that India could not retain its previous market share to the U.S.A., the Netherlands, Yugoslavia and Italy during the decade prior to 1994. But the actual quantity exported to all these countries has increased. India has retained its previous market share to USSR, West Germany and others. West Germany and Italy prefer Indian coffee in the world market. The bulk of the coffee exported to the USSR was under bilateral agreement.

India has a long history of over 2,500 years in the spice trade. Its agro-climatic conditions have made the country the natural home of a variety of spices such as pepper, cardamom (small), cardamom (large), chilly, ginger, turmeric, garlic, coriander, cumin, fennel, fenugreek, celery, clove, nutmeg and saffron. Although Indian spices' exports have been increasing in quantity and value and cover a large number of countries, future prospects depend on exporters' ability to meet quality standards set by importing nations. The Indian spices industry has moved from only trade to consumer-oriented processing and production. Some of the companies have gone into joint ventures/marketing tie-ups with multinationals, (John, 2003). Kainth (1996) comments that

1 Dr. J K Sachdeva, Hon Editor, Journal of Global Economy. Author is obliged to Professor C. S. Murthy, Senior Fellow, CESS, Hyderabad, (Now in Ethiopia) and Dr. G.K. Mitra Fellow, CESS, Hyderabad, for their time to time guidance.

export performance of seed spices has a bearing on domestic prices. The production of seed spices has shown an increase during the last few years but the heavy domestic demand has rendered them uncompetitive at critical points of time. These are crops where farming practices play a key role in their production. Seed spices are comparatively minor exchange earners. Indian coriander finds a market in Singapore, the UAE, Sri Lanka and Oman while cumin is exported in sizable quantities to the US, Singapore, Japan, Saudi Arabia and the UK. Fennel is taken mostly by Saudi Arabia, Japan, the UAE, Sri Lanka, Kuwait and South Korea while bulk of the fenugreek export is to Canada, West Germany and Singapore. India exports spices in raw form and in bulk quantities. The importers process a large part of these into different end points and sell them at higher price. Important value added products are oils and oleoresins from various spices, curry powders and spices in consumer packs. Spice oils and oleoresins have registered the maximum growth in terms of volume and value. The major spice oils exported are pepper oil, ginger oil, celery seed oil, clove oil, cardamom oil. They are exported to the US, the UK, West Germany, France, the Netherlands, Yugoslavia and Australia (Kainth, 1996; John, 2003).

India exports oil seeds, but there are debatable issues whether India should export oil seeds and import edible oil or discourage exporters to export oilseeds. Chand (2002) writes that due to growing imbalance between demand and supply of edible oilseeds in post green revolution period, India had to import massive amounts of edible oil. Prior to 1994 oilseed sector was protected through QRs on imports and exports. Imports were canalized through State Trading Corporation and then sold through Public Distribution System at prices fixed by the government. Domestic prices of oilseeds were maintained at more than double the world prices (World Bank 1997 as quoted by Chand, 2002), Tariff rates on import were also quite high. From March 1, 1995 edible oils have been put under OGL and are regulated by import tariff, which is changed from time to time depending upon domestic and international price levels. Quota restrictions on export of rapeseed-mustard seed were lifted in May 1995, while export of oil remains restricted to 5 kg pack. Trade policy on edible oils has been caught between two opposing viewpoints. According to one view, India would be benefited by liberalising import of oil of rapeseed-mustard and other edible oils as their domestic prices have ruled higher than world reference prices for several years. Accordingly, resource use efficiency in edible oilseeds production was found to be low and oilseeds were found to be protected at the cost of cereals. Further, due to restrictions on imports, domestic prices were kept high. According to other view points the policy of import liberalization would have adverse impact on the oilseeds and Indian producers. Though India has been trying to be self-reliant in edible oilseed production, reliance on import has continued and increased in recent years. India's agro exports face certain constraints that arise from conflicting domestic policies relating to production, distribution, food security and pricing concerns. In the case of edible oils, the domestic price of two major edible oils – groundnut oil and mustard oil has been more than twice the international price of most globally traded oils. This is because India not only has little comparative price advantage in the production of oilseeds, but oil extraction is also based on obsolete traditional technology as edible oil production is still reserved for the small scale sector. Domestic supply of edible oils is unable to meet the domestic demand requirements and India imports about 4 million tonnes of edible oils annually. Low global prices had benefited India as it was able to import large volumes to meet the growing domestic demand for oils. However, the decline in international production of oilseeds and decline in stocks cause global availability of edible oils to decline thus pushing up international prices, (GOI, BUDGET, 2001-2002).

This study limits to the extent of export oilseeds to various countries and does not have the scope of edible oil import in details, but some factors cannot be ignored in controversies. Edible oils are 'essential' commodities and consumer interests are the major determinants of policies in this sector. High income elasticity of demand keeps demand buoyant and high price elasticity makes prices volatile. Though it has been argued that low world prices of edible oils are a consequence of high levels of protection and agricultural subsidies in developed countries, the Indian oilseed sector will remain under pressure even if these are properly adjusted. What make the oil sector uncompetitive are an inefficient processing sector and the policy of reservation for village and small industries. Both oils and oil meals suffer on this score, (Chand et al., 2004). The quest for raising self-sufficiency levels in edible oils remains a legitimate policy objective. Leaving aside the question of drain on foreign exchange reserves, import volumes have become too large and an upsurge in world prices of this politically sensitive commodity will have serious consequences. Bhupal (2003) observed that in Rajasthan and Haryana about 50 per cent processing units were closed down and the remaining were operating at 18 to 20 per cent below their capacity level. On the other hand farmers were shifting from oilseeds to wheat. Ramaswamy *et al.*, (2002) found that oilseeds markets and prices, in general show more fluctuations than other crops. The number of oilseeds and products, the jointness of meal and oil productions, the variability in substitution possibilities across crops and varying degrees of correlation between prices of different products are the many factors affecting technical relationships among oilseeds products. For instance, production and prices of palm oil in Malaysia and Indonesia influence the prices of oilseeds and edible oils in India. The excess production of edible oils in those countries and India's liberal import policy has depressing effects on prices in India. And farmers are not able to realise adequate returns. Farmers are, therefore, forced to stop cultivation of groundnut, mustard etc. India will become all the more totally dependent on imports if these conditions persist. The farmers are reluctant to diversify from wheat and rice to oil seeds

Cotton and garments are the important items exported by India. Cotton trade is highly complex. The number of grade specifications in which exports and imports are classified is very large. Besides, cotton is traded in various forms like raw cotton, yarn etc. India used to export small to moderate quantity of cotton but in the recent years dependence on import has increased substantially. The main reasons for this are (1) the stagnant production of cotton in the country, (2) international price fluctuations and (3) domestic demand. Due to very large number of specifications and quality variations it is difficult to undertake exact comparison of domestic and international prices. For instance, in most of the cases prices in US markets is found to be less than half of the prices quoted for Egyptian cotton, (Chand, 2002). Average price of cotton in US markets ruled higher than the Indian price in all the years. India has a very large milling capacity for textile and garments manufacturing and export of such items constitutes important share in the total export earnings. Therefore, export of raw cotton is not a good yardstick for export performance of the country. Excessive emphasis on cotton export can cause adverse impact on the agro-processing industry and also on export of value added products from the country. Thus, there is a need to study whether it is more advantageous to promote export of raw cotton or to promote export of the manufactured products. Domestic prices also play an important role in increasing the production. They should be remunerative to cotton growers. There is another dilemma. In the spinning sector, production of cotton yarn is influenced by many factors like export of cotton yarn, previous year's production and price of cotton. Exports significantly influence production of cotton yarn. But high spiral tendency in cotton price has adverse impact on cotton yarn production. Therefore, while maintaining remunerative cotton prices, the tendency in cotton prices to increase should be arrested through increasing the production of cotton. In the weaving sector, in both mill and decentralised units, export variable is important in determining the production of cotton fabrics, (Gopal, 1999).

The trend growth of the value of the Indian cotton exports declined in the post-liberalization period as compared to pre-liberalization period. In order to bring back the glory of Indian cotton in the global cotton trade map and to attain the competitive edge, it is necessary to adopt cost saving technologies and go for production of export-oriented long staple cotton varieties for improving the competitiveness of our cotton exports, (Mahesh, 2003). The price policy has failed to reduce price variability and contributes neither to farm income stability nor to protect the interest of the farmers. The support price fixed by the government does not reflect the market behaviour. The government should devise production-oriented price policies aimed at rational utilisation of scarce resources and in protecting the interests of the producers and consumers, (Rathi *et al.*, 2003).

Cashew is the most important component of agriculture export basket. India is the largest producer, processor and exporter of cashew in the world. Its share in world production ranged between 39 to 62 per cent during 1991-95. Liberalization policy since 1990s has positive effect on cashew export. The quantity of cashew kernels exported grew by 6.08 per cent during 1991-95. The positive growth rate in respect of cashew export was due to the increased domestic production and increased demand for cashew kernels in the international market. Variation in the exports of cashew depends upon domestic production, export price, domestic price, domestic consumption and world export. Further, the export price has slightly affected India's cashew exports, (Naik *et al.*,2003).

## 3.1 Objectives

1. Generally economists are of the view that only one commodity should be analysed at a time to do fair justice to research, but in the present study an attempt has been made to generalise whether export of commercial crops have increased after economic reforms and establishment of WTO by taking six sample commodities.
2. To analyse the exports of tea, coffee, spices, cotton, oilseeds and cashew.
3. To measure the export growth in the aftermath of economic reforms.
4. To study whether the past performance influences the future performance.
5. To study the volatility of export.
6. To explore the relationship between exports, imports and production.

## 3.2 Research Methodology

To achieve the above objectives four techniques have been used:

(i) Compounded growth rate (CGR)

(ii) Unit Root Technique

(iii) Instability Index (INS)

(iv) Regression on de-trended series

All the above techniques help to rank the countries with statistically significant growth, less volatility in export volumes and a good momentum of past performance.

Past performance can effect on future performance due to momentum. Statistically we say that time series have auto-correlation as succeeding years data is related to lag periods. Economist measure auto-correlation by Durbin Watson method with module $d = (\Sigma(e_t - e_{t-1})^2 / (\Sigma e^2)$ where 'e' is the error term "d" has a bound between 0 and 4. If there is no correlation d is expected to be 2, (Gujarthi, 1995).

Durbin Watson test has many limitations, as it does not have lagged dependent variable in calculations. As we are interested to know the lagged effect of both dependent and independent variable, Unit Root technique (Augmented Dickey fuller Test) has been used in preference to Durbin Watson test. This helps us to see not only the effect of lagged period but also sum total of all differences of lagged variables. There is not much literature on the subject except a few generalisations. Unit Root testing technique of time series is helpful to find whether business in past is temporary or permanent arrangement. If business momentum of past performance has impact on present performance. Customers are so loyal that they ignore slight variations in prices and other issue.

Remarks of Hoffmann *et al.*, (2002) are worth noting. They observe that when a time series contains unit roots, any shock – whether policy or random – would have a permanent impact on the series while a series without unit roots would be subject to a temporary effect. If any country's Y's exports to destination X contain unit roots, we can conclude that any shock to trade relationships between country Y and country X would have a permanent effect. Conversely, if the series does not show the presence of unit roots, any shock would be temporary in nature. Any exogenous shocks that may affect Y's exports to the markets with unit root may affect bi-lateral export relations permanently. While analysing the exports of Malaysia, Hoffmann cites that September 11th attacks in the heart of the US might have caused permanent damage to exports from Malaysia if American consumers tend to be more nationalistic in their purchase. In situations like this, it is imperative that the Malaysian government introduces policy initiatives to counter such damage. It must be emphasized here that such policy inducements would also tend to have a permanent effect on exports. Another instance is the introduction of the Euro and its effect on Malaysia's exports to the EU. If the euro proves to promote greater intra-EU trade at the expense of non-EU exports, it would pay for Malaysian officials to initiate trade missions to the EU to win contracts. In other words, for every negative shock a positive one has to be introduced to ensure a return to normality. Unit Root Technique is usually used to find how many times series should be differenced to de-trend it. We have used this technique to compare the series which have past performance momentum and to see a) countries where present strategies are working, b) where there is more momentum of past than present strategies. ADF module is

$$Y_t = \beta_1 + \beta_2 t + \delta Y_{t-1} + \alpha_i \ \Sigma\Delta Y_{t-1} + \varepsilon_t$$

Where $Y_T$ is amount of export at time t in time series, $Y_{t-1}$ is the lagged one year export, $\Sigma\Delta$ $\Sigma\Delta Y_{t-1}$ is the sum of all first differences and $_{\varepsilon t}$ is error term. Working on the above concept, the series were tested using tau ($\tau$) stat. This test may give an indication whether present strategies are working well or there is a past performance momentum.

All the above techniques help to rank the countries with statistically significant growth, less volatility in export volumes and a good momentum of past performance.

Basically the major present strategies are devaluation of rupee (due to economic reforms within India) and market access due to AoA of WTO. Period 1992 to 2003 cannot be sub-divided to see the effects separately as time period between the two is too short to see statistical significance due to less degree of freedom. Exports to and imports from only the major countries have been considered.

## 4. Results

### TEA

In year 2002, against the world trade of 2317.34 million US D, India, being third in rank of word exporters, exported tea valued at 326.63 million US D. In 2002, top tea exporters in the world were Sri Lanka, China, India, UK, Kenya and Indonesia. Top importers were UK, Russian Federation, Japan, USA, Egypt and Saudi Arabia. All developed countries are in re-export business, (**Table 1**).

**Table 1**
**World Tea Trade in Year 2002**

| Top Exporters | Value in US D Million | Top Importers | Value in US D Million |
|---|---|---|---|
| Sri Lanka | 650.4 | UK | 281.99 |
| China | 331.76 | Russian Fed | 288.67 |
| India | 326.64 | Japan | 179.55 |
| UK | 191.26 | USA | 173.70 |
| Kenya | 140.91 | Egypt | 141.81 |
| Indonesia | 103.43 | Saudi Arabia | 113.49 |
| World | 2317.34 | | |

**Table 2**
**World's and India's Tea Export in Value and Quantity and Production of Tea in India**

| Year | Total World Trade Value in US Dollars | World's weight '000 MTs | India total Value | India weight, '000 MT | Production of Tea in India |
|---|---|---|---|---|---|
| 1993 | 2314 | 1222.72 | 331.85 | 153.16 | 703.9 |
| 1994 | 2067 | 1061.40 | 308.40 | 150.87 | 753 |
| 1995 | 2278.3 | 1168.38 | 359.05 | 158.33 | 753.9 |
| 1996 | 2467.68 | 1213.66 | 282.58 | 138.36 | 761 |
| 1997 | 2982.16 | 1315.94 | 497.24 | 191.47 | 787 |
| 1998 | 3361.09 | 1422.44 | 518.26 | 201.80 | 836 |
| 1999 | 2787.88 | 1368.16 | 406.11 | 177.51 | 855 |
| 2000 | 2948.06 | 1489.21 | 431.60 | 200.87 | 835 |
| 2001 | 2833.56 | 1446.56 | 367.21 | 177.60 | 848 |
| 2002 | 2521.82 | 1354.51 | 326.63 | 181.62 | 847.25 |
| CGR | 2.92*** | 2.91* | 1.91 | 2.87*** | 2.09* |
| **INS** | 10.42 | 5.71 | 21.89 | 12.21 | 1.11 |
| ADF τ-STAT (Unit Root) # | −1.9363 | −1.8523 | −1.6789 | −1.3945 | −.8888 |

# Significance value for 5% level is -2.89 and for 10% level is -2.58

* Significance at 1% level, ** Significance at 5% level, *** Significance at 10% level.

During the period, 1993-2002, it is observed world trade of tea grew by 2.92% in dollar terms which is statistically significant at 10% level, while quantity of world exports grew by 2.91% which is statistically significant at 1% level. Difference in significance is due to slight price volatility during this period. Instability indices (INS) of value (10.42%) and quantity (5.71%) tell the same story, (**Table 2**). Nonetheless, comparatively this volatility appears to be negligible.

In comparison to World Trade, India exported comparatively more tea in quantity than value during the period under consideration. CGR of export quantity of tea is 2.87%, which is statistically significant 10% level while in dollar terms CGR is only 1.91% which is not statistically significant. This can be due to devaluation of rupee, (**Table 2**).

To see whether exports are related to production, de-trended export quantity series and de-trended production series were regressed on each other, among many results the following important result is worth noting.

$$U_{production} = .8448 \quad U_{export\ (t-1)}$$

$$(3.4288^*) \quad R^2 = .60 \quad n = 9$$

* Statistically significant at 1% level.

$U_{production}$ and $U_{export}$ are the residuals of productions and export time series such as where $Y_t = a + bt + U_t$ in which $Y_t$ is the export at time t. Figure in brackets is t-stat which is statistically significant at 1% level, which means proceeding year's exports effect succeeding years' production. Commercial crops usually have such relations, past exports may affect production or vice versa.

India's exports of tea to world and all major countries have Unit Roots at 5% significance level, which means past performance effects future outcomes. There is momentum and auto-correlation in all series, which means customer's loyalty plays a significant role than present strategies, even though rupee devaluation has played some part. Growth rate of tea exports to UAE, USA, Iraq, Netherlands, Kazakhstan, Australia and Turkey are statistically significant as shown in **Table 3.** Business to Netherlands, Germany, USA and UAE is stable as compared to other countries. Though CGR of exports to Iraq, Kazakhstan and Turkey is high and statistically significant but exports are highly volatile as shown by Instability Index (INS).

India is losing its business with Russian Fed, UK, Poland and Egypt. It may be noted that fall is due to lagged effect also. There is a Unit Root in all series. Exports to Poland, Iraq, Japan, Saudi Arabia, Kazakhstan and Australia are highly volatile.

**Table 3**
**Export of Tea to Major Countries (1993-2002)**

| Export Partner | CGR | INS | ADFτ-STAT(Unit Root) # |
|---|---|---|---|
| Russian Fed | –2.03 | 42.83 | –1.423 |
| UAE | 5.19** | 22.65 | –1.3442 |
| UK | –1.49 | 21.32 | –2.0307 |
| Poland | –8.96 | 41.66 | –1.8566 |
| USA | 8.57** | 19.63 | –1.1930 |
| Germany | 0.17 | 17.43 | –1.6713 |
| Iraq | 41.69** | 51.71 | –.7966 |
| Japan | 3.03 | 38.13 | –1.5909 |
| Saudil Arabia | 7.23 | 50.69 | –2.5039 |
| Netherlands | 5.04* | 14.31 | –.8452 |
| Kazakhstan | 48.01* | 37.28 | –1.0824 |
| Australia | 17.13* | 85.60 | .7337 |
| Iran | 0.77 | 72.06 | –1.7427 |
| Turkey | 35.08*** | 108.18 | –1.8353 |
| Egypt | –27.74 | 46.10 | –.9295 |
| Others | –1.96 | 16.49 | –3.2681@ |

# Significance value for 5% level is -2.89 and for 10% level is -2.58 @ no unit root

* **Significance at 1% level, ** Significance at 5% level, *** significance at 10% level.**

## Coffee

Coffee includes coffee, green and roasted, coffee extracts, essences, concentrates and preparations. In year 2002, world exported coffee worth 7.895 billion dollars. Worlds' top exporters were Brazil, Columbia, Germany, USA, Italy, Guatemala, Belgium, Indonesia, Mexico and India. India ranks tenth among Coffee exporters and exported coffee worth 204.56 million US D in year 2002, (**Table 4**).

Valuewise worlds' growth of coffee during the period 1993-2002 is negative but negligible (-.46%), however quantitywise coffee export in the world is growing at 3.07% which is statistically significant at 1% level. It means prices of coffee have fallen during this period. If we see India's export figures valuewise and quantitywise, India's CGR of coffee quantity export is 4.56% which is statistically significant at 1% level, but CGR in dollar terms is negative. CGR of -2.66% in value clearly shows that prices are falling but India's exports in quantity have risen due to devaluation effect (**Table 5**).

**Table 4**
**World Coffee Trade in Year 2002**

| Top Exporters | Value in US D Million | Top Importers | Value in US D Million |
|---|---|---|---|
| Brazil | 1384.79 | USA | 1796.3 |
| Columbia | 864.76 | Germany | 1111.4 |
| Germany | 835.75 | Japan | 666.67 |
| USA | 364.17 | France | 582.25 |
| Italy | 336.78 | Italy | 427.86 |
| Guatemala | 262.04 | Canada | 380.47 |
| Belgium | 245.74 | Belgium | 312.08 |
| Indonesia | 239.62 | UK | 308.63 |
| Mexico | 237.528 | Netherlands | 279.72 |
| India | 204.56 | Spain | 242.49 |
| World | 7895 | World # | 8741 |

# Difference due to CIF value and FOB value.

Do we produce for exports or does production affect exports? Coefficient of correlation between export and production is .73. De-trended time series export quantity and production quantity were regressed on each other. Out of many results, following result is worth noting.

$$U_{export\ (t)} = -.4412\ U_{production\ (t-1)} \quad \text{..........................} \quad (1)$$

$( -1.9839^{**})\ R^2 = .33 \quad n = 9$

**** Statistically significant 10% level**

$U_{production}$ and $U_{export}$ are the residuals of export time series such as where $Y_t = a + bt + U_t$ in which $Y_t$ is the export at time t. Figure in bracket is t-stat which is statistically significant at 10% level which means export is negatively related to production. Proceeding years' production affects succeeding years' exports. In commercial crops, such relation is but natural as one year lagged exports affect productions or vice versa.

India exports coffee to Russian Federation, Italy, Germany, USA, Spain, Belgium, Netherlands, Poland, Switzerland, Finland, Czech Republic and other countries as shown in **Table 6**. India's exports to Spain and Belgium are growing at CGR of 12.02% and 20.50%, which are statistically significant at 10% and 5% level. In dollar terms India's exports to Italy, Germany, USA, Japan, Poland, Switzerland, Finland and Czech Rep. are falling. Being momentum of past performance, there is a unit root in all time series of coffee exports, even the negative growth rates have lagged performance effect. As there is a vide fluctuation in prices, series show negative trend to most of the countries, (**Table 7**). As CGR of devaluation is 5.7%, if this devaluation CGR is added to dollar term growth of export, we shall arrive at approximate growth rate of exports in rupee term. In rupee term exports to Italy, Switzerland and Thailand are rising.

**Table 5**

**World and India's Export of Coffee in Value and Quantity, and Production in India Value in Million US D**

| Year | Total world trade (value) | world weight '000 MTs | India's production value | India export | India export weight'000 tonnes |
|---|---|---|---|---|---|
| 1993 | 5374.65 | 5184.63 | 162 | 174.04 | 121.76 |
| 1994 | 11527.69 | 5090.20 | 208 | 335.41 | 131.64 |
| 1995 | 14141.18 | 4712.36 | 180 | 448.48 | 158.48 |
| 1996 | 12307.41 | 5373.41 | 223 | 401.84 | 163.24 |
| 1997 | 15982.88 | 5528.88 | 205 | 454.97 | 153.83 |
| 1998 | 14830.68 | 5587.30 | 228 | 410.61 | 193.87 |
| 1999 | 12134.77 | 5918.08 | 265 | 331.05 | 190.56 |
| 2000 | 10717.13 | 6276.75 | 292 | 264.10 | 185.61 |
| 2001 | 7825.80 | 6237.30 | 301 | 232.24 | 177.19 |
| 2002 | 7895.56 | 6355.06 | 317 | 204.56 | 185.55 |
| CGR | –0.46 | 3.07* | 7.33* | –2.66 | 4.56* |
| INS | 20.62 | 3.12 | 6.02 | 19.59 | 5.95 |
| ADF τ-STAT(Unit Root) # | –.9781 | –.3285 | .7265 | –.9218 | –2.2294 |

# Significance value for 5% level is –2.89 and for 10% level is –2.58 @ no unit root

* Significance at 1% level, ** Significance at 5% level, *** Significance at 10% level.

**Table 6**

**India's Export of Coffee to Major Countries**

| Export Partner | CGR | INS | ADFτ-STAT(Unit Root) # |
|---|---|---|---|
| Rissian Fed | 2.42 | 30.87 | –2.5345 |
| Italy | –1.73 | 27.02 | –1.3624 |
| Germany | –7.26 | 31.07 | –.7185 |
| USA | –14.88 | 29.70 | –1.2766 |
| Spain | 12.02*** | 28.84 | –1.8562 |
| Belgium | 20.50** | 18.68 | –2.0346 |
| Netherlands | 2.91 | 38.39 | –2.3945 |
| Japan | –12.69 | 42.05 | –1.0456 |
| Poland | –17.65 | 62.99 | –1.5698 |
| Switzerland | –0.42 | 34.56 | –4.9215@ |

| Finland | -3.82 | 71.52 | -1.6776 |
|---|---|---|---|
| Czech Rep. | -50.98 | 94.24 | -.8781 |
| Others | 0.80 | 19.77 | -1.6454 |

# Significance value for 5% level is -2.89 and for 10% level is -2.58

@ no unit root

* Significance at 1% level, ** Significance at 5% level, *** Significance at 10% level.

## Spices

Since ages, India has been named as a gold mine. This gold mine has been created by exports of spices. Our analysis for the period 1993-2002 confirms the same. Among all the agricultural products, analyzed so far, spices show significant growth both quantitywise and valuewise. Spices exports are spread to all over the world.

India is number one exporter of spices. In year 2002, there was a world export of 2641.06 million US D. Top exporters were India, China, Indonesia, Singapore, USA, France, Brazil, Germany and Sri Lanka. Top importers were USA, Germany, Japan, France, Singapore, UK, Netherlands and India, (**Table** 7).

As against the world CGR of 6.22%, India' CGR is 6.56% which is statistically significant at 5% level, (**Table 8**). Exports are highly stable with instability index of 6.84% only. There is a significant growth of Indian spices to countries like Germany (6.56%), UK (9.32%), Japan (10.97%), France (6.80%), Malaysia (15.33%), Saudi Arabia (10.18%), Sri Lanka (12.85%), and Mexico (24.13%). CGRs are statistically significant as shown in (**Table 9**). India also exports spices to countries like USA, Singapore, Netherlands, Bangladesh and Italy, though growth rates are not statistically significant but seeing the UNIT root, t-stat and Instability index these growths are very important. There is no unit root to series for Singapore. Business to this country is volatile as in case of other commodities. In most commodities, business to Singapore and Japan is declining, but spices exports are rising.

**Table 7**

**World Spices Trade in Year 2002**

| Top Exporters | Value in US D Million | Top Importers | Value in USD Million |
|---|---|---|---|
| India | 337.52 | USA | 590.38 |
| China | 212.82 | Germany | 186.83 |
| Indonesia | 205.92 | Japan | 177.23 |
| Singapore | 174.11 | France | 160.70 |
| USA | 170.68 | Singapore | 137.18 |
| France | 126.84 | UK | 131.94 |
| Brazil | 112.41 | Netherlands | 113.42 |
| Germany | 106.99 | India | 110.14 |
| Sri LANKA | 96.39 | | |
| World | 2858.98 | WORLD# | 2641.06 |

# Difference due to CIF value and FOB value

**Table 8**
**World and India's Export of Spices in Value**
**Value in Million US D**

| Year | Total world trade (Value) | India's export |
|---|---|---|
| 1993 | 1473.19 | 195.25 |
| 1994 | 1809.39 | 202.94 |
| 1995 | 2214.72 | 253.73 |
| 1996 | 2155.94 | 340.96 |
| 1997 | 2589.16 | 389.54 |
| 1998 | 2687.50 | 387.90 |
| 1999 | 2821.40 | 414.12 |
| 2000 | 2760.74 | 365.82 |
| 2001 | 2679.87 | 318.59 |
| 2002 | 2641.06 | 337.52 |
| CGR | 6.22* | 6.56** |
| INS | 2.58 | 6.84 |
| ADF ô-STAT(Unit Root) # | −2.8966@ | −2.9423@ |

# Significance value for 5% level is −2.89 and for 10% level is −2.58

@ No unit root

* Significance at 1% level, ** Significance at 5% level, *** Significance at 10% level.

**Table 9**
**India's Export of Spices To Major Countries**

| Esport Partner | CGR | INS | ADFô-STAT(Unit Root) # |
|---|---|---|---|
| USA | 4.01 | 25.44 | −1.8148 |
| Germany | 6.56** | 22.28 | −1.5272 |
| UK | 9.32* | 4.40 | −3.2711@ |
| Japan | 10.97* | 11.29 | −1.4045 |
| France | 6.80* | 10.10 | −1.5805 |
| Singapore | 3.71 | 27.15 | −3.5891@ |
| Netherlands | 5.99 | 36.00 | −1.9430 |
| UAE | 3.67 | 24.79 | −2.8201@ |
| Bangladesh | 14.22 | 69.27 | −1.3268 |
| Malaysia | 15.33* | 26.67 | −2.2335 |
| Saudi Arabia | 10.18* | 30.12 | −1.1945 |
| Sri Lanka | 12.85** | 24.49 | −.8482 |
| Mexico | 24.13*** | 53.00 | −1.7885 |
| Italy | 2.66 | 22.42 | −1.4041 |
| Others | 6.00** | 8.86 | −2.2418 |

# Significance value for 5% level is −2.89 and for 10% level is −2.58

@ No unit root

* Significance at 1% level, ** Significance at 5% level, *** Significance at 10% level

India is in a leading position, China is the follower. Competition appears to be hard, we should prepare ourselves. India should play a driving seat role in price war and should try to maintain its position. Countries like Netherlands, Singapore, Bangladesh, Saudi Arabia and Mexico where exports are volatile should be concentrated. UK series has no Unit Root. Environment should be created so that present strategies have permanent effect on importers.

## Cotton

In year 2002 world (all countries) imported 5424.71 million US D worth cotton. Top importers were Indonesia, Turkey, Mexico, Italy, Rep of Korea, Japan, India, Russian Federation and China. Top exporters were USA, Australia, Egypt, Greece, Syria, Indonesia, France, Italy and Thailand. India exported cotton in year 1993, 1996 and 1977 to countries like Japan and Indonesia. Export series from 1993-2002 is highly volatile and had an insignificant negative growth, (**Table 10**).

As wheat has been exported and in succeeding imported, Cotton has been exported in good quantity in year 1993, 1996, and 1997, but has been imported in year 1994, 1995, 1999, 2001, 2001 and 2002 (**Table 11**). Relation of cotton production and import quantity has been calculated by regression on de-trended series as follows:

$$U_{export\ (t)} = .224\ U_{production\ (t-1)}$$

$$(-2.1802^*)\quad R^2 = .37 \quad n = 9$$

$$U_{import\ (t)} = -.2352\ U_{production\ (t-1)}$$

$$(-2.336^*)\quad R^2 = .40 \quad n = 9$$

$U_{production}$ and $U_{export}$ are the residuals of export time series such as where $Y_t = a + bt + U_t$ in which $Y_t$ is the export at time t. *t-stats in the above equations are statistically significant at 5% level. Above equations show that one proceeding year's production affects imports and exports.

India has imported more cotton than export during the period under consideration. Import series both valuewise and quantitywise show a significant high growth, but instability index is very high; high growth with high volatility can be termed as a good indication. High import demand by textile industry may be reason for high import. But volatile import and export has created problems at production level. In case of wheat, farmers are not affected as wheat import and export are related to stocks.

But in case of cotton, import and exports are linked with production; farmers are affected, when they are unable to sell their produce due to low exports and high imports. Present predicament is the outcome of a little protection to cotton, as **rate of Customs Duty on cotton is only 10%** (year 2003). It is worth noting that Customs duty on wheat is 100%, while on rice is 70%.

**Table 10**

**Export of Cotton Including Waste (Value in Million US D)**

| Year | Total world trade | India total | India's Weight exported in '000 tonnes | India's Production | Export to Japan | Export to Indonesia | Export to Others |
|---|---|---|---|---|---|---|---|
| 1993 | 3246.16 | 208.23 | 194.39 | 1825.97 | 29.87 | 28.23 | 150.14 |
| 1994 | 4879.20 | 44.35 | 34.76 | 2020.96 | 9.48 | 10.60 | 24.27 |
| 1995 | 7166.88 | 60.66 | 33.28 | 2186.37 | 12.71 | 2.27 | 45.69 |
| 1996 | 6936.28 | 443.33 | 269.51 | 2419.27 | 41.88 | 74.30 | 327.15 |

| | | | | | | | |
|---|---|---|---|---|---|---|---|
| 1997 | 6619.61 | 219.28 | 156.79 | 1844.67 | 17.95 | 38.31 | 163.02 |
| 1998 | 6016.13 | 49.16 | 41.95 | 2088.8 | 6.27 | 0.94 | 41.94 |
| 1999 | 4766.34 | 17.59 | 15.83 | 1960 | 6.42 | 0.00 | 11.18 |
| 2000 | 5265.67 | 19.76 | 18.55 | 1640.9 | 4.47 | 0.01 | 15.29 |
| 2001 | 5122.75 | 6.56 | 7.01 | 1987.3 | 2.89 | 0.00 | 3.67 |
| 2002 | 4838.54 | 10.21 | 11.76 | 1583 | 5.48 | 0.22 | 4.51 |
| CGR | 0.71 | −29.34 | −25.78 | −2.01 | −19.35 | −73.90 | −31.21 |
| INS | 14.13 | 159.80 | 146.55 | 15.04 | 108.97 | 198.75 | 161.72 |
| ADF τ-STAT(Unit Root) # | −2.3599 | −1.7762 | −1.8179 | −.9379 | 1.5181 | −1.8207 | −1.7955 |

**Table 11**

**Import of Cotton Including Waste (Value in Million US D)**

| Year | India's cotton '000 MTs | India total Import Value | Import weight '000 MT tonnes production |
|---|---|---|---|
| 1993 | 1825.97 | 5.86 | 3.82 |
| 1994 | 2020.96 | 161.56 | 80.87 |
| 1995 | 2186.37 | 155.47 | 69.62 |
| 1996 | 2419.27 | 8.88 | 2.92 |
| 1997 | 1844.67 | 21.67 | 9.97 |
| 1998 | 2088.8 | 90.67 | 57.40 |
| 1999 | 1960 | 288.59 | 236.75 |
| 2000 | 1640.9 | 263.38 | 212.13 |
| 2001 | 1987.3 | 434.75 | 386.87 |
| 2002 | 1583 | 254.28 | 233.82 |
| CGR | −2.00683 | 39.87*** | 51.45426** |
| INS | 15.04 | 58.56 | 58.41 |
| ADF τ-STAT (Unit Root) # | −.9379 | −.8492 | −.1995 |

# Significance value for 5% level is −2.89 and for 10% level is −2.58

@ No unit root

* Significance at 1% level, ** Significance at 5% level, *** Significance at 10% level

## Oil Seeds

This group comprises mustard, sunflower, rye and groundnuts. In year 2002, there was world trade of 16.31 billion US dollars. Top importers of oil seeds were China, Japan, Germany, Netherlands, Mexico, Spain, Belgium, UK and Rep. of Korea. Top exporters of world were USA, Brazil, Argentina, Canada, France, China, Australia, Netherlands and Paraguay, (**Table 12**). In year 2002, India exported oilseeds of value of 141.67 million US D. During the period 1993-2002, against the world growth of 4.32%, export of India's oil seeds grew at the rate of 7.55%, which is statistically significant at 10% level. World's instability index is 6.77% while India's instability index is 32.42% which means India's exports of oil seeds is highly volatile. As there is no Unit

Root in the series for the period under consideration, there is no momentum of past exports and only present strategies are working and these strategies are not of permanent nature according to statistical analysis. (**Table 13**).

**Table 12**
**World Oil Seeds Trade in Year 2002**

| Top Exporters | Value in US D Million | Top Importers | Value in US D Million |
|---|---|---|---|
| USA | 6076.00 | China | 2641.00 |
| Brazil | 3037.50 | Japan | 1987.90 |
| Argentina | 1280.62 | Germany | 1443.31 |
| Canada | 1050.34 | Netherlands | 1417.57 |
| France | 534.75 | Mexico | 1251.58 |
| China | 445.75 | Spain | 918.59 |
| Australia | 409.00 | Belgium | 634.70 |
| Netherlands | 369.35 | UK | 425.30 |
| Paraguay | 254.82 | Rep of Korea | 390.00 |
| | | World | 16310.00 |

**Table 13**
**World Trade in Oil Seeds (Value in Million US D)**

| Year | Total world trade | India total |
|---|---|---|
| 1993 | 8953.10 | 84.18 |
| 1994 | 11097.62 | 82.11 |
| 1995 | 11975.29 | 156.83 |
| 1996 | 15015.12 | 186.37 |
| 1997 | 16421.83 | 250.09 |
| 1998 | 14666.61 | 121.06 |
| 1999 | 12824.10 | 187.79 |
| 2000 | 13968.48 | 231.27 |
| 2001 | 14828.50 | 195.84 |
| 2002 | 15213.71 | 141.67 |
| CGR | 4.32** | 7.55*** |
| **INS** | 6.77 | 32.42 |
| UNIT ROOT | -2.2103 | -2.9066@ |

Growth rate of oil seeds to USA during 1993-2002 is 14.51%, which is statistically significant at 1% level. There is a good growth to other countries like Indonesia, Netherlands, Germany, Egypt, Turkey, Philippines, Malaysia and Russian Federation, but these growth rates are insignificant statistically, as exports volume is highly volatile from year to year. This is also shown by instability index. (**Table 14**).

**Table 14**
**India's Export of Oil Major Countries**

| Export Partner | CGR | INS | ADFτ-STAT(Unit Root) # |
|---|---|---|---|
| Indonesia | 4.57 | 53.02 | –3.6782@ |
| Netherlands | 2.09 | 36.21 | –3.0914@ |
| UK | –12.68 | 84.21 | –1.2680 |
| USA | 14.51* | 19.66 | –1.0233 |
| Germany | 2.47 | 24.02 | –2.9107@ |
| Egypt | 24.15 | 60.43 | –1.7826 |
| Turkey | 9.08 | 45.35 | –3.0535@ |
| Singapore | –3.49 | 51.47 | –1.7461 |
| Philippines | 6.03 | 94.47 | –1.6777 |
| Malasia | 15.50 | 57.00 | –3.8998@ |
| Russian Fed | 1.26 | 59.15 | –3.3150@ |
| Others | 14.09* | 29.11 | –1.8843 |

# Significance value for 5% level is less than -2.89 and for 10% level is –2.58

@ No unit root

* Significance at 1% level, ** Significance at 5% level, *** Significance 10% level

### Cashew

World imported cashew nuts (fresh and dried) valued at 1006.61 million US D in year 2002. India was the top exporter of cashew nuts with export of 422.215 million US D. India has almost 56% share (as world's export value is 755.36 million US D). Other exporters were Brazil, Cote d'Ivoire, Tanzania, Indonesia and Netherlands. Top importers were USA, India, Netherlands, UK, Germany, Canada, Australia and Japan, (**Table 15**). Among all the commodities analyzed so far cashew is the only commodity, in which India has good control as figures reveal that India is in the business of re-export. Against the world's import growth rate of 5.3%, India's export of cashew in dollar terms is growing at the rate of 2.7%. In tonnage terms it is growing at 5.9%, which means prices are falling. India is exporting more in quantity but receiving less in dollars. CGR in weight is significant at 1% level. Against the world's instability of 12.51%, India's instability in dollar term is 17.04%, but that of weight is 10.02%. It again means devaluation has played an important role.

India exports cashew to UK, USA, Netherlands, Japan, UAE, France, Saudi Arabia, Australia and other countries. CGR to USA, UAE, France and Saudi Arabia are statistically significant as shown in (**Table 17**). Volatile business to Russian Federation is clearly shown by high instability index. All series have Unit Root which means lagged effect have played major role than present strategies. Business to Japan, Russia and Australia is falling.

**Table 15**
**World Cashew Trade in Year 2002**

| Top Exporters | Value in USD Million | Top Importers | Value in USD Million |
|---|---|---|---|
| India | 422.22 | USA | 374.49 |
| Brazil | 105.65 | INDIA | 254.95 |
| Cote' d'Ivoire | 49.43 | NETHERLANDS | 58.04 |

| Tanzania | 47.23 | UK | 39.67 |
|---|---|---|---|
| Indonesia | 34.81 | GERMANY | 35.89 |
| Netherlands | 29.34 | CANADA | 31.09 |
| | | AUSTRALIA | 28.65 |
| | | JAPAN | 27.37 |
| | | | |
| World | 756.36 | WORLD# | 1000.61 |

# Difference due to CIF value and FOB value

**Table 16**

**World and India's Cashew Exports Value and Quantity (Value in Million US D)**

| Year | Total World Trade | Weight '000 MTs | India Value | India's Wt |
|---|---|---|---|---|
| 1993 | 656.69 | 288.33 | 334.50 | 69.83 |
| 1994 | 881.22 | 408.53 | 398.29 | 76.90 |
| 1995 | 815.43 | 336.72 | 383.07 | 70.07 |
| 1996 | 857.77 | 349.59 | 359.94 | 68.66 |
| 1997 | 937.52 | 416.52 | 377.99 | 76.54 |
| 1998 | 1013.91 | 398.89 | 390.59 | 76.94 |
| 1999 | 1339.16 | 595.75 | 596.64 | 96.66 |
| 2000 | 1198.17 | 508.28 | 456.41 | 89.15 |
| 2001 | 975.93 | 544.81 | 398.31 | 98.20 |
| 2002 | 1089.37 | 670.32 | 422.20 | 129.44 |
| CGR | 5.36* | 8.34* | 2.78 | 5.93* |
| INS | 12.51 | 17.04 | 18.66 | 10.02 |
| UNIT ROOT | −1.2331 | −.2398 | −1.7178 | −1.2595 |

**Table 17**

**India's Export of Cashew to major Countries**

| Export Partner | CGR | INS | ADFτ-STAT(Unit Root) # |
|---|---|---|---|
| UK | 5.44 | 30.44 | −1.4150 |
| USA | 7.57** | 26.25 | −1.0378 |
| Netherlands | −1.39 | 29.62 | −1.7482 |
| Japan | −3.78 | 17.39 | −2.9352@ |
| UAE | 9.16* | 19.33 | −1.1079 |
| France | 23.76* | 6.01 | −1.6868 |
| Saudi Arabia | 17.86* | 16.54 | −.9522 |
| Australia | −16.56 | 29.87 | −9879 |
| Russian Fed | −30.69 | 212.05 | −1.5555 |
| Others | 2.53 | 16.08 | −1.2389 |

# Significance value for 5% level is less than −2.89 and for 10% level is −2.58

@ No unit root * Significance at 1% level, ** Significance at 5% level, *** Significance 10% level

Table 18
Cashew Imports (Value in Million US D)

| Year | Total Value | Tanzania | Guinea Bissau | Cote d'Ivoire | Indonesia | Singapore | Others |
|---|---|---|---|---|---|---|---|
| 1993 | 153.88 | 46.74 | 14.31 | 15.14 | 16.30 | 5.35 | 56.04 |
| 1994 | 220.06 | 43.27 | 27.74 | 10.59 | 19.07 | 53.42 | 65.96 |
| 1995 | 226.72 | 80.03 | 34.19 | 23.46 | 18.21 | 0.27 | 70.55 |
| 1996 | 193.58 | 59.72 | 14.99 | 14.63 | 6.41 | 44.41 | 53.43 |
| 1997 | 206.15 | 56.70 | 43.14 | 22.42 | 29.45 | 6.12 | 48.33 |
| 1998 | 230.48 | 111.53 | 18.82 | 19.07 | 17.31 | 0.27 | 63.49 |
| 1999 | 276.40 | 98.52 | 36.07 | 37.50 | 22.23 | 0.34 | 81.73 |
| 2000 | 214.20 | 39.42 | 60.19 | 42.30 | 8.77 | 0.00 | 63.53 |
| 2001 | 91.40 | 33.48 | 9.76 | 19.75 | 5.94 | 0.02 | 22.45 |
| 2002 | 254.95 | 51.12 | 46.97 | 49.90 | 34.91 | 0.09 | 71.95 |
| | | | | | | | |
| CGR | –0.43 | –1.41 | 4.98 | 13.37* | –1.07 | –62.54 | –2.55 |
| INS | 26.60 | 45.34 | 39.64 | 56.18 | 50.68 | 201.16 | 31.64 |
| UNIT ROOT | –3.9615@ | –2.8225@ | –2.7805@ | –.9518 | –2.8718@ | 1.3337 | –8.087@ |

India imports cashew from West African coastal countries like Tanzania, Guinea Bissau, Cote d'Ivoire and Indonesia, (**Table 18**). Unit Roots tests, CGR and instability index clearly show that India does not depend on a permanent supplier. This is a very good strategy. Growth rates of imports from all countries are insignificant except Cote d'Ivoire, but it is highly instable. Cashew import-export business by India is best module, India should adopt for other commodities also like USA.

### Conclusions

Analysis of exports of cash crops like tea, coffee, cotton, spices, oilseeds and cashew reveal that devaluation has played a significant role in the exports of these commodities immediately after economic reforms. Tea and coffee are not performing well. Growth of tea is stagnant and coffee is negative in dollar term. However, if we see growth in rupee term it is slightly positive. In both the cases during last ten years (1993-2002), prices of these commodities have fallen and there is more export in quantity and value received is less. Production of tea and coffee is related to exports. In case of tea, exports of tea affect the production in the succeeding year. In case of coffee production affects the exports of succeeding year, competition is very hard. India exports tea and coffee to developed countries.

India is a top exporter of spices and cashew. Spices and cashew are exported to both developed and developing countries. Business of these commodities is very stable compared to other commodities.

Export of cotton and oil seeds raises many question marks. India's export of cotton and its imports in subsequent years has created a lot of problems to farmers as export and import are related with production. India's imports of edible oil and exports of oilseeds cannot be justified. India needs to protect cotton growers.

International prices of the commercial commodities fell after 1995 and it did not help developing countries to expand their business, however, India's export of commercial agricultural commodities to developed countries especially American and European countries has increased after establishment of WTO. Their export to Developed East Asian Countries fell after the onset of economic reforms and establishment of WTO.

## References


Bhupal D.S. (2003): "Impact of Liberal imports and Low Tariff on Edible Oil Sector in the Country: A Study of Rapeseed-Mustard, Soybeans and Palm Oil" in Indian Journal of Agricultural Economics, Vol 58 No.3, July-Sept, 2003.

Chand Ramesh (2002): "Trade liberalisation, WTO, and Indian Agriculture", Mittal Publication, New Delhi.

Chand Ramesh; Jha Dayanatha and Mittal Surabhi (2004): "WTO and Oilseeds Sector – Challenging of Trade Liberalisation" in EPW Vol XXXIX No. 6 Feb 7-13, 2004 (pp. 535-37).

John K. C. (2003): "Spices Export from India – Stock Taking" in EPW Vol XXXVIII No. 19 May 10-16, 2003 (pp. 1832-34).

Joshi, P.K; Gulati Ashok; Birthal Pratap S and Tewari Laxmi (2004): "Agriculture Diversification in South Asia –Patterns, Determinants and Policy Implications" in Economic and Political Weekly, Vol XXXIX No. 24, June 12-18, 2004.

Kainth Gursharan Singh (1996): "Export Potential of Indian Spices: Regaining Flavour" in Dr. Gursharan Singh Kainth (Ed), "Export Potential of Indian Agriculture", Regency Publication, New Delhi.

Kainth Gursharan Singh (1996a): "Exports of Tea Emerging Trends" in Dr. Gursharan Singh Kainth (Ed), "Export Potential of Indian Agriculture", Regency Publication, New Delhi.

Mahesh N. (2003): "Trade Liberalisation and its Impact on Indian Cotton Exports" in Indian Journal of Agricultural Economics, Vol 58 No.3, July-Sept, 2003.

Naik V.G. and Joshi, Milind G. (2003): "Impact of Liberalisation on Cashew Exports" in Indian Journal of Agricultural Economics, Vol 58 No.3, July-Sept, 2003.

Naik, Gopal and Jain, Sudhir Kumar (1999): Econometric Modelling of Indian Cotton Industry for Forecasting and Policy Implications" in Indian Journal of Agricultural Economics, Vol 54 No.2, April-June, 1999.

Ramamoorthy, K and Venugopal K.(1996): "Cotton Export potentiality under GATT" in Dr. Gursharan Singh Kainth (Ed.) "Export Potential of Indian Agriculture", Regency Publication, New Delhi.

Ramaswamy C. and Selvaraj K.N. (2002): "Pulses, Oilseeds and Coarse Cereals: Why are They Slow Growth Crops" in Indian Journal of Agricultural Economics, Vol 57 No.3, July-Sept, 2002.

Rao N. Chandrasekhra (2003): "Liberalisation and Suicides of Farmers in India" in Indian Journal of Agricultural Economics, Vol 58 No.3, July-Sept, 2003.

Rathi Deepak and Awasthi P.K. (2003): "Impact of Domestic Price Policy on Agricultural Production, Cropping Pattern and Productivity of Cotton in Madhya Pradesh" in Indian Journal of Agricultural Economics, Vol 58 No.3, July-Sept, 2003.

Talreja Usha (2003): "Growth and Export Competitiveness of Indian Tea in Liberalised Regime" in Indian Journal of Agricultural Economics, Vol 58 No.3, July-Sept, 2003.

Varadarajan S. and Elangovan S. (1996): "Exports Potential for Indian Coffee" in Dr. Gursharan Singh Kainth (Ed) "Export Potential of Indian Agriculture", Regency Publication, New Delhi.

Vashisht A.K. and Alka Singh (2003): "Impact of Liberalisation on India's Agricultural Exports: a Behavioural and Discriminant Approach" in Indian Journal of Agricultural Economics, Vol 58 No.3, July-Sept, 2003.

Veena, U.M., Suryaprakash S. and Lalith Achoth (1994): "Changing Direction of Indian Coffee Exports" in Indian Journal of Agricultural Economics, Vol 49 No.3, July-September, 1994.

✦ ✦ ✦

Research Project 14

# 12.3 Mini Milk Revolution: A Case of Youth Leadership for Village Economy

**R.M. Chennaveer**[1]

***Dr. Kurien, the father of white revolution in India, is not known in this village, but his mission is getting white here. Yelladgundi, a remote village in Karnataka, is getting white face-lift due to a transformative youth initiative. A handful of youths are striving for over the last two years to transform their village through self-help and milk dairy activities. Village is flooded with milky animals, youths are no more wasting time as earlier, women's purse is filled with bounty of rupees, shy educated youths are grazing cattle and working in fields, and lakhs of rupee revenue is drawn to the village. And so, the fields are filled with abode of happiness, as youth are working in the fields, once neglected considering it a low dignity work. Responsible youths are now affectionately pushing the elderly engaged in fields to homes for needed rest with a sigh of great relief.***

## Context

Yeladagundi is a tiny and quite interior village in Basava Kalyan Tehsil of Bidar district in Karnataka. Two streams and mountains surround the village. There are 300 families with 2000 population. Roads, school building and housing are getting better due to active role of Gram Panchayat. Agriculture is the mainstay of the villagers since time immemorial. The village has ample of water resources for drinking. It is nature's grace during the last four years the village received sufficient rains and witnessed bumper yield of tur dal, jawar, bajri, sunflower, green gram, black gram, ground nut and sugar cane; although drought persist in the nearby villages. The traditional occupations like carpentry, hair cutting, sheep grazing and farm labour form major means of livelihood for the backward communities. The village is composite of lingayat, dalit, backward communities and Muslims. Although upper caste lingayat possess high per capita land, dalits with sheer hard work are purchasing lands from the upper caste. The geo-ecological conditions are dry and the agriculture is dependent on rain. The youth and productive age group population, therefore, migrate seasonally to Mumbai, Pune and Hyderabad for their livelihood in tailoring and construction work. The hard earnings of labour, invest in the agriculture capital during rainy season. Lord Parameshwar, the village god is the symbol of unity and harmony for all castes and communities. Caste discrimination still persists, at times results in caste strife but gets settled amicably. However, the accommodative attitude is gaining among upper caste people, which is a gradual process. Villagers staying in different parts of the state and neighbouring states gather in the month of December every year to celebrate a fair for the village god. It is a mega event of culture and art as village youth perform dramas and people from around tens of villages gather and watch dramas all through the nights for two days and appease their recreational desire. Wrestling, the declining traditional sport, is a great amusement here.

Hotels have come up very recently followed by some small provision shops. For the past five years villagers have maintained frequent contacts with nearby talukas and cities for marketing agricultural produce and availing health services. Since, the village is on the boarder of Karnataka and Maharashtra, contacts with border cities have also increased these days for marketing and health services. Migration to Mumbai, Pune and Hyderabad cities is phenomenal since the village

1 Dr. R.M Channaveer, Lecturer, Dept. of Social Work, Walchand College, Solapur- 413006, Maharashtra. The article has been published in Vol 4 no. 2, April-June, 2007 issue, reprinted with permission from author and editors of Journal.

and whole India was struck by the 1972 famine, which forced people to move out. The push-pull conditions of 1972 drought increased the mobility of people to cities. Many families have settled there in tailoring and construction occupations and assist the mother families in the villages. Recently, the migration trend of youth has become seasonal (mainly summer) so as to support the agricultural activities and depending on the demand of the job in major cities. But the employment in organized sector is low. In the past five years girl child education is increasing and girls are going to nearby villages for high school education. Level of collegiate education is low, because youth taking interest in continuing collegiate education is countable, but slightly increasing these days. Early marriages are very rare, but dowry practice persists. Showing the characteristics of a healthy community, the village does not have any divorces or separations or marital conflicts or crimes for that matter. Caste Panchayat still prevails in the village to settle the family and property disputes.

### Swami Vivekanand Self-help Group

Anand, a village youth, attended a lecture of NABARD Bank at Gulbarga city, which is 60 km away from the village Yeladagundi. He was deeply inspired by the thoughts of the managers, who emphatically told the need of self-help groups for village development. Anand rushed to the village brooding over the self-help group concept. He shared the concept with his fellow friends. Mr. Khanderao was the first to respond positively to form a youth self-help group and other friends supported the idea, and all resolved to establish a youth self-help group. But hurdles started coming in the away one after another shattering their dream to form SHG. Taluka Panchayat office was never ready to register the SHG and Banks were also not ready for opening bank accounts. The reason cited was that there was no norm to open male youth SHG and only women SHGs can be registered and open their account. The youth were boiling and resolved not to leave the matter there itself, and fight till they get justice. They followed Gandhian means of Satyagraha. All the youths sat for dharana before the Taluka Panchyat. At the end, time came to their side. Taluka Panchayat agreed to their demand, and so the bank expressed readiness to allow opening of bank accounts. And thus the "Swami Vivekanand Self-help Group" became the first youth self-help group in Bidar district in the year 2004.

### Good Practices of the SHG

The Swami Vivekanand SHG has framed its own rules and objectives to maintain discipline, responsibility and accountability. Some of the important good practices are —

- Membership is fixed at 20
- Monthly contribution of ₹ 100/- for each member
- Money circulation among the members @ 2 per cent interest
- Penalty of ₹ 50/- for being absent to one SHG meeting
- Penalty of ₹ 10/- each day per member for delay in monthly contribution
- Meeting at every fortnight
- Participation in social activities of the village
- Contribution of money for village developmental activities

### Milk Dairy Initiative

The youth's zeal and vigour multiplied since the day of SHG's establishment. The youth started thinking seriously on only one question what should be done for the village? An idea struck them that milk dairy be the most feasible one. All the youth approached the Milk Dairy

Federation at Hudgi village in Humnabad Tehsil. Respecting the zeal and interest of the youths the dairy federation assured them to start a dairy unit. Special training was imparted to the members of the SHG in dairy unit. An initial need assessment for the potential milk providers was made through mobilizing 100 members required for running the dairy unit. People did not believe the initiative of the youth. They started doubting their ability and motive. Then the youth made it a campaign in mobilizing the youth of the village to become members of the dairy unit. And it worked favourably. The major problem was that there was not sufficient number of milk animals. Most of the families had sold them for not being able to maintain them properly. Yet again the youth took a courageous stand to purchase cows out of the money accumulated in the SHG. All the members purchased cows so as to collect minimum of 50 litres milk.

This zealous and adventurous story really touched the heart of a Bank Manager of Krishna Grameen Bank. The manager came forward to extend a financial assistance of ₹ 4 lakh to the members of the SHG. This step of the manager came like lightning in the village. Villagers turned to the side of the youth. Every family in the village purchased either cow or buffalo. Now youth have no difficulty in collecting 120 litres of milk everyday.

### Behavioural Change among Youths

1. The youth do not waste time as earlier they were without work
2. Disciplined life of the youth
3. Time management consciousness
4. Financial support to family
5. Organizational and associational feeling through affinity to SHG
6. Gained business knowledge
7. Youth have regained interest in agricultural activities
8. Youth have developed social contacts (interpersonal relations)
9. No need to migrate to city and the youth are enjoying family life, which they were deprived of
10. Self-employment for unemployed youth
11. Subsidiary employment to agriculture
12. Friendship is professionalized
13. Social strength gained
14. Saving habit is multiplied
15. 'No' to chemical fertilizer
16. Livelihood security achieved
17. Planning mini dairy unit for vertical and incremental growth
18. Timely help of money
19. Financial support for agricultural activities
20. Leadership initiative for developmental activities
21. Bank knowledge gained

22. Contacts with govt. agencies (ZP, Taluka Panchayat, Bank etc.). developed
23. No unnecessary expenditure (which was daily ₹ 100/- earlier)
24. Some youth stopped stone cutting jobs and are now engaged in cattle grazing
25. Economic security to 60 families in the village, who are sole milk producers now

### Milk Dairy Initiative: Impact

Two years passed, the SHG has made its distinct mark in the district. The zeal and vigour of youth has multiplied ever since the milk dairy unit has been established in the village. It also assured them of dignity and status. Villagers, especially the elderly, have developed positive frame of mind towards the village youth and appreciate them for the miraculous work that they have done in transforming the whole village life.

Following are the long lasting impact –

- Youth migration has nearly stopped
- Educated youth are holding work in fields with high dignity
- Grazing the cattle has become a habit of pride for the youth
- Youth are not wasting time as used to happen so earlier
- Solution to feminization of poverty, as women are earning out of selling the milk
- Monthly revenue to milk diary: ₹ 55000 to ₹ 1 lakh
- Loan assistance received:

  General Loan: ₹ 50,000/-

  Bank Loan to self-help group members: 4 lakh
- Assets of SHG: Insemination container, Training of insemination to a member and dairy equipments
- Livestock increased in the village
- Dung manure is the byproduct of the milk dairy initiative
- Purchase of chemical fertilizer has come down to 50 per cent as a result of accumulation of cow dung manure
- Some of the member of the SHG have stopped purchasing chemical fertilizer

**Qualitative and quantitative changes of youth**

| Sl.No. | Members of Self-help group | No. of Cows Added | No. of Buffaloes Added | Average Milk Sold (Litres) Min. Max. | Quantity of Cow Dung Manure (Tractor Qty.) | Yearly purchase of Chemical Fertilizer of 50 kg) | Current year purchase of Chemical Fertilizer (Bag of 50 kg) |
|---|---|---|---|---|---|---|---|
| 1 | Shanappa Hanumanth Oderaj | 1 | 2 | 5 | 4 | 2 | No purchase |
| 2 | Haji Ali | | 2 | 4 | 2 | 1 | No purchase |
| 3 | Mahadev Bhimrao Jangale | 1 | 1 | 4 to 20 | 3 | 6 | 3 |
| 4 | Shivanand Khanderao Jidde | 3 | – | 14 to 22 | 4 | 10 | 5 |
| 5 | Ramesh Parameshwar Inde | 6 | – | 8 to 24 | 10 | 10 | 6 |
| 6 | Deepak Reddy Pundlik Reddy | 1 | 1 | 8 to 24 | 10 | 10 | 6 |
| 7 | Revansiddappa Mahadevappa Niranjue | 2 | – | 4 | 2 | 3 | 2 |
| 8 | Baswaraj Gurlingappa Saje | 5 | – | 20 | 8 | 7 | No Purchase |
| 9 | Baswaraj Kalyanrao Bhange | 3 | 1 | 20 | 7 | 15 | 7 |
| 10 | Anand Gopalrao Patil | 2 | – | 12 | 4 | 10 | No purchase |
| 11 | Saibanna Bhimrao Jangale | 2 | – | 8 to 15 | 5 | 6 | 3 |
| 12 | Mallinath Chandrasha Kalashetty | 2 | – | 8 | 3 | 5 | 3 |
| 13 | Khanderao Madhurao Bhange | 1 | 1 | 7 | 3 | 6 | 3 |
| 14 | Apparao Gireppa Inde | – | 2 | 4 | 3 | 8 | 6 |
| 15 | Dattatrey Basawantrao Ghale | 2 | – | 8 | 2 | 15 | 12 |
| 16 | Gopinath Gurunath Inde | 2 | – | 9 to 14 | 4 | 6 | 3 |
| 17 | Shivappa Madhurao Tate | 2 | – | 10 | 5 | 20 | 15 |
| 18 | Omnath Gurunath Inde | 2 | – | 10 | 2 | 2 | No Purchase |
| 19 | Shivappa Gurlingappa Fulari | 1 | 1 | 4 to 14 | 3 | 2 | No Purchase |
| 20 | Ramesh Sidramappa Joti | 2 | – | 8 to 10 | 3 | No land | No Land |

### Conclusion

The youth are bubbling with new identity through constructivism in the village. Youth who were scolded for their laziness, carelessness and wasting of time unproductively are now respected, recognized and valued for performing an instrumental role in changing the scenario in the village. They wanted to establish milk dairy that was the change they thought to bring in the village. But byproduct changes are phenomenal that happened unexpectedly. It is an exemplary work of rural youth who led an initiative to support the agriculture through allied activities like dairy. The initiative is a matter for advocacy that the rural youth can transform their village economy. This can be simulated in any part of India. Such initiatives are replicated in many villages of India. The situation reminds us that the heritage of co-operative movement of our country could be transformed in a micro form at village level. Self-help, which is Indian concept, is a more evolved form of micro-finance concept of Prof. Mohd. Younus of Bangladesh. The MYRADA NGO of Karnataka is the pioneer in coining, promoting and practicing the self-help for women. On the other hand, the social capital of rural youth could be enhanced through enabling and empowering environment in the system both agency and community. Rural development through constructivism was the vision of Mahatma Gandhi. His lines for global change are revolutionary. He said, "Be the change that you seek in the world". The youth have proved it through their transformative dairy activity. Further the context of globalization gives ample opportunities to gain access to the global markets. This demands constructive action at the individual and group level.

✦ ✦ ✦

Research Project 15

## 12.4 Rising Prices and Financial Management Practices of Urban Families in India

By Suramaya Joshi[1]

### Introduction

Inflation, defined as a sustained rise in average prices of commodities and services, has been viewed as a major obstacle that most people face in achieving their financial goals and is found to be a major constraining factor in families' resource management. To illustrate, with a general rate of inflation of 4% and a saving account that has an interest rate of 6%, an investment of ₹ 1000 would grow to ₹ 1060 in a year's time. However, it will now require ₹ 1040.00 to purchase the same amount of goods and services that the original investment would have purchased. If one pays taxes on ₹ 60 or of interest at a tax rate of 28%, the tax contribution would be ₹ 16.8 (60*28%) and individual can keep ₹ 43.2 (60–16.80). Here, investment of ₹ 1000/– has only added ₹ 3.2 to the purchasing power. The situation will still be worse if the rate of inflation is 5%!

The consequences of rising prices and concomitant high cost of living are adverse and cause severe hardships to the families in the form of financial difficulties. The costs associated with financial difficulties are significant for the individuals involved. Personal stress, illness, marital discord, child abuse and loss of home often coincide with financial failure. More recently, some studies have addressed the issues of identification of vulnerable groups, coping strategies against macroeconomic shocks and patterns of overspending and financial management practices. Griffiths has noted a lack of incentives to save in view of inflation and high marginal tax rates and has mentioned the findings of an income and expenditure survey by the Australian Bureau of Statistics (ABS), which indicated that in all income groups the ability to fund consumption from current income deteriorated substantially. The close association between financial difficulties and stress related problems within families indicates the need to address and assess the issue of management practices adopted by the families, when confronting inflation.

This paper takes a more eclectic view by recognizing that families need to adapt and adjust to rising prices and financial difficulties by altering their priorities and reallocating their expenditure plans. Rising prices of consumer goods often compel families to drastically alter their consumption and the composition of their savings.

It should also be noted that the impact and incidence of inflation could differ across families with differing income levels. Families respond by employing different financial management practices through the management of their resources. A critical review of selected literature emerging from the African, Latin American, Caribbean and Asian countries that have adopted structural adjustment programmes throw light on the multidimensionality of effects at the household level and the cumulative gender implications. Major areas of concern involve around examining household survival strategies as ways of financial management practices with these impacts at the household level.

---

1 Dr. Suramaya Joshi, Department of Home Management, Faculty of Home Science, M.S.University of Baroda, Vadodara Gujarat

• The research paper has already been published in Vol 3 no. 1 of Journal of Global Economy. Repreinted with permissions from author and editors of Journal of Global Economy.

The term strategy more often connotes a continuum of adjustments made by households in response to internal and external factors to survive at the same level or attain upward mobility. Number of studies reported that households often respond by changing the way members generate income and organize expenditure and consumption. Many households cut costs and changed habits. More recent studies have identified the difficulties faced by urban poor and have argued that structural adjustment policies have created a favourable environment for intensification of multiple modes of livelihood strategies among salaried employees. Accordingly, survival strategies cannot be a substitute for equitable macroeconomic policies. The literature that repeatedly reinforced 'household survival strategies' and 'social capital' of the poor has over emphasized the resourcefulness of the poor and promoted a myth of 'survival'. The managerial sub-system incorporates financial management practices as well as coping strategies adopted by the families that ultimately facilitates meeting the demands called output in the form of quality of life Fig. 12.1.

### Objectives

The purpose of the study is to identify financial management practices adopted by different income groups in the wake of rising cost of living indices.

## Methodology

### Sample selection

It was recognized that the sample from all existing income groups should be drawn. A total 255 families were selected from five different income groups in Vadodara city of Gujarat state. For the multistage systematic random sampling technique, income slabs were provided by the municipal corporation and the residential areas were identified. Families were selected to reflect the composition of each identified residential area. The distribution of the sample according to the income groups is represented below.

**Table 1**

| Income groups | Income Range (₹/month) |
|---|---|
| Low Income (LIG) | Up to 2500 pm |
| Lower middle income (LMIG) | 2501 to 5500 |
| Middle income (MIG) | 5501 to 8500 |
| Higher middle income (HMIG) | 8501 to 10500 |
| Higher income (HIG) | 10501 and above |

## Data collection

The data were collected using a structured interview schedule during the months of March–May 2001. The questionnaire comprised seven sections incorporating questions pertaining to socio-economic and demographic profile of the families, their consumption expenditure during the base year (1995–1996) and the year (1999–2000) and the financial management practices adopted by the families.

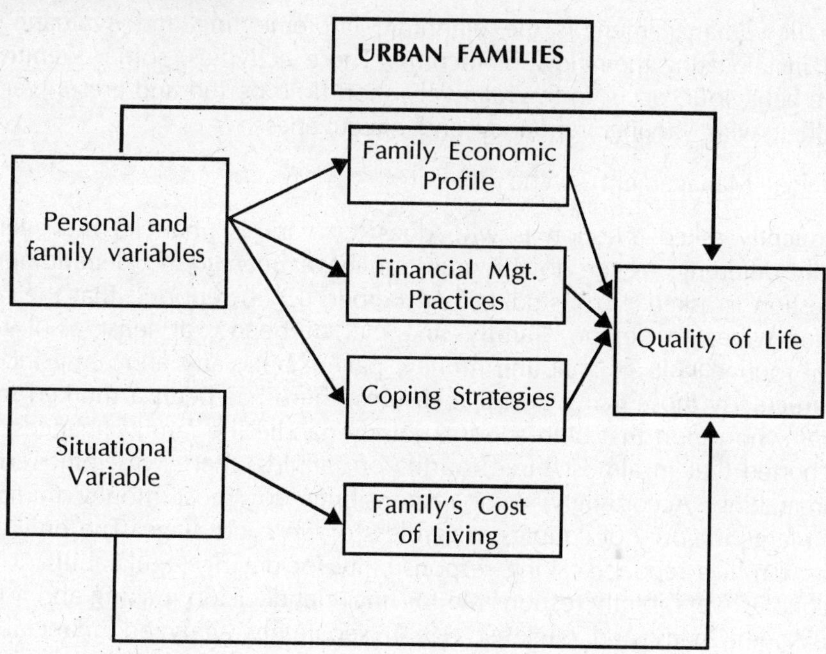


**Fig. 12.1 Conceptual Framework**

## Review of the Studies

Desai (1967) conducted cross sectional study with four income groups. According to Desai's findings, conscious money management practices were not followed by the families. Dhingra (1967) studied savings from the angle of practices and opinion of the families and had identified that most of the families opined about savings as essential and followed the practice of setting aside money for some purpose like higher education of children old age security and to meet emergency. Similar findings were obtained by Saikia (1979) in the study regarding time and money management practices of homemakers.

As far as expenditure patterns were concerned, Sumitra (1963), Desai (1967), Lasha Kumari (1974) and Saikia (1979) studied expenditure pattern of low and middle income groups on different household items. Desai (1967) and Lasha Kumari (1974) revealed that of all the items of expenditure the highest percentage of families income was spent on food and related expenditure. Other items of expenditure, in order of importance were, clothing, education, housing, miscellaneous, health and recreation. Lasha Kumari's (1974) findings were supporting the findings by Bhatnagar (1973) about income expenditure ratio. According to the findings, higher the income, greater were, the eating out practices and expenditure on readymade food. The share on vegetables, ghee and oil too was raising with the increase in income level. Sinha (1977) conducted a comparative study of money expenditure on selected ceremonies by two Hindu communities and found that the savings was in form of ornaments and savings accounts with banks. Similar were the findings by Gupta (1980) regarding major investment area as saving schemes with the banks.

Much of the literature on family financial management is descriptive in nature, including extensive discussion of what families should do in managing their financial resources. Despite the importance of effective financial management in families' lives, relatively little empirical research has focused on what families actually do. Even less research has focused on whether the prescribed financial management practices are effective in producing positive results for families. Here is one of the aspects of family financial management.

Family cash flow management is the planning, implementing and evaluating practices of families involved in allocating their flow of income. These activities, some cognitive and others overtly observable behaviour, occur in the relatively short time period and are universally engaged in by families (albeit with varying frequency and effectiveness).

Family Financial Management : Who does it?

Another frequently asked question is who does the various financial management tasks in families. Decidedly different answers to this question have been found depending on how and of whom this question is asked. Early studies (e.g. Ferber, 1973) reported that the most common arrangement is for wives to be the "family financial of head", at least as it relates to the implementation of routine tasks of handling money, paying bills, and allocating income. In more recent studies, particularly those using global measures, there has been a marked increase in the number of families who report that both spouses jointly handle the family finances. For example, Dollar, (1983) reported that in almost three fourths of couples, there was joint responsibility for financial decision-making. Accordingly, joint responsibility for most money management tasks was reported by a large majority of couples, regardless of life cycle stage. The only exception was that wives in most families reported taking responsibility for paying regular bills. It was observed that 59% of the couples were jointly responsible for financial decision making and implementation. However, when Abdel-Ghany and Nickols, (1984) separately analyzed financial management decision and implementation tasks, they found that husbands tended to handle the implementation tasks, such as paying bills, balancing cheque books, and reconciling financial accounts, whereas wives were more involved in decision tasks, such as policy decisions concerning the methods of savings, the number and ownership of checking accounts and the system of budgeting.

Another outcome of families' cash flow management is the subjective financial well-being of families or their level of satisfaction with their current financial situation. A few studies have examined the relationship between the financial management behaviour of families and their level of satisfaction with their finances. Some studies have found mixed results (e.g., Godwin & Carroll, 1985; Shepard, 1984, Mueller and Hira, 1984). For example, Godwin and Carroll (1985) found a positive relationship between the extensiveness of financial management behaviour and husbands' satisfaction, but not wives' satisfaction, whereas Shepard, (1985) found the opposite (i.e., more extensive financial management positively influenced women's satisfaction but was not significantly related to men's). Several research works studying married college students, found no relationship between their satisfaction with their finances and budgeting and record keeping of expenditures. The only practice which was related to their satisfaction was record keeping of checks. In their study of Japanese families' financial management practices and satisfaction, Mueller and Hira (1984) found two behaviours – having retirement plans and less frequent arguing about money—to be positively related to spouses' satisfaction with their financial situation.

Rosenfeld, (1982) analyzed the effect of family resources, demands, and perceptions on the financial satisfaction of both spouses, even when such factors as family income and net worth were included. Spouses' aspirations for the future were also strongly related to their satisfaction with their current financial status. Bryant, (1986) studying influences on spousal satisfaction with savings, found that, regardless of the objective situation of the family's income or net worth, couples' feelings about the importance of savings and their values regarding financial security were strongly predictive of their satisfaction. This research suggests that families' subjective financial well-being is more strongly related to their attitudes and perceptions rather than any observable management behaviour or their objectively measurable financial status.

## Data Analysis and Results

### Financial management practices followed by the families

Financial management practices were classified under planning, controlling and evaluation practices. Families had respondents in terms of never, sometimes and always. Scores were allotted to the responses as 1, 2, 3 respectively. The scores were then added to derive at the score at each respondent. Present section deals with the extent to which planning, controlling and evaluation practices were followed by the respondents.

### Planning

First step of any management process is planning. For managing the resource what is most essential is to plan out the allocation of that resource on desired goals. For financial management, money income need to be allotted for various expenditures. Families may or may not undergo conscious efforts for financial management and methods and the same may vary from family to family.

Nearly half of the respondents were following this practice of estimating monthly expenditure from each income class. Fifty four per cent of the total respondents were following this practice. Forty four per cent families from low income group were always following this practice, whereas out of lower middle income group, higher middle income group and higher income group, respectively 59.6%, 46% and 54% of the families where regularly estimating monthly expenditure. In case of middle income group 66% of the families were always following this practice.

Out of total respondents 37.6% were following checking of past months budget regularly. Fifty two per cent families of middle income group had reported that past month's records were checked while making monthly budget. This practice was otherwise followed by less than 40 per cent of the families from all other income groups, that is by 26% families from lower income group, 32.7% families from lower middle income group and 38% families from higher middle and higher income group. Sixty seven per cent of total families reported that expenditure was handled by a single person. Planning the expenditure was handled by a single individual in more than 70% families from low income and lower middle income groups. In case of 67.3% of the families from lower middle income group, expenditure planning was always handled by a single individual. This practice was followed to the greatest extent by the families from middle income group. i.e. 90.6%. From higher middle income group and higher income group, respectively 46% and 60% of the families always followed this practice. Forty three per cent of the total respondents always kept aside funds for savings in monthly budget. Half of the respondents from HMIG, HIG and LIG were following this practice, whereas this practice was rarely followed by LMIG families. Thirty nine per cent of the middle income families followed the practice of keeping aside funds for saving regularly.

Specific amount was kept aside only for food items at the time of planning money expenditure by 23% of the total families. This practice was followed by 38% of the families from LIG and 35% from MIG. It was reported to be never followed by majority of the families from other income groups. For other items fixed amount was never planned and kept aside by the families from LIG and LMIG. Expenditure on non-food items was planned regularly by 48% of the HMIG families. By the families from MIG and HIG respectively 43% and 40% were rarely following this practice.

Monthly income was allotted for each and every item on expected expenses by more than 60 to 65 per cent families belonging to higher middle income and higher income groups. Amount for personal entertainment was not planned by most of the families of all income groups. Other than higher income group, families from all other groups had reported the practice of planning fixed amount to be spent on vegetables and milk every month. As far as distributing income between husband and wife was concerned this practice was followed by 20% of the total families and 36% of the MIG families. Otherwise in case of all other income groups this practice was followed by very few families. Regular allotment of funds for tax and bills was nil in case of low income families, whereas in case of middle income and higher income families nearly 60 per cent were following this practice. Forty two per cent of total families used to plan expenditure for seasonal items. Nearly 50 to 55 per cent families belonging to low income, middle income and higher middle income groups were planning for expenditure on seasonal food items. Hence, planning the expenditure was observed most in case of low income and middle income groups.

To purchase the commodities, as and when need arises was the practice always followed by 49% of the total families. In case of low income and high income groups, more than 70 per cent families reported the purchase accessing to the need, rather than planned expenditure. Majority of the families from all income classes were taking care of priorities and requirements of the family members while planning the monthly budget. Fifty six per cent of total families always used to follow this practice and 58% to 64% families from LMIG, MIG, HMIG and HIG were following this practice.

### Controlling

Planning the use of resource makes sense only when it is implemented. For the present study, controlling was studied as part of financial management practices along with planning and evaluation.

Estimating the expenditure for each month was the practice followed by families in more than 60 per cent of cases. It was found that it was rather an opposite picture in the case of implementing the practice to stick to the estimated expenditure. Yet 60% of the middle income families had shown the strict implementation and in the case of higher middle income group it was found in 48 per cent cases. High income group families rarely implemented this practice and low income families rather never used to implement it (54 per cent). Higher middle and higher income families and middle-income families followed actual saving practice for education of children, respectively 76%, 60% and 58.5% of families.

Expenditure was being planned for food products more in case of low income families. Similarly the practice to stick to the estimate while spending on eatables too was found in case of the same income group. Overall 46.7% of the families used to do so. In case of middle income group, expenditure on food was incurred as per planning by 50.9% of the families and for other income groups that is, lower middle, higher middle and higher income groups it was respectively 38% and 44%. In case of fluctuation in price of vegetables the quantity was increased or decreased by almost 40 per cent families from all income groups except the higher income group. As far as making changes in the quantities of and quality of seasonal grains was concerned, lower middle and middle income families followed this practice, that is, 84.6 and 67.9% of the families were following this practice regularly. From other income groups, 56% of low income and higher middle income families and 40% of higher income families followed this practice regularly. According to current price level, the quantity and quality of the product was being decided to bring income and expenditure in alignment.

For clothing, out of the total respondents 60% were always trying to meet the estimate. From low income group, 72%, lower middle income group 63.5%, middle income group 47.2%, higher middle income group 68% and higher income group 52% did follow this practice. Making the expenditure as per planning on vehicle petrol was never followed by 43% families out of the total sample. Yet 58% of families from HMIG did follow this practice regularly.

Planning the amount to be spent on non-food items was followed in case of higher middle income families and the purchase of clothing and transportation expenditure too was found to be strictly followed by same income group families that is, 58%. Whereas 43% and 41% of lower middle and middle income families and 38% of higher income families used to try to meet the estimate on vehicle petrol while actually spending on it.

Expenditure on entertainment was checked by families from all income groups. It never used to exceed in case of 66.7% cases overall. From lower income group, in 90% cases and from lower middle, middle, higher middle, and higher income group respectively in 67%, 56% and 64% cases actual expenditure on entertainment never used to exceed the estimate.

Expenditure on social rituals was incurred according to the planned amount by 47% of total families, 46% families in case of lower and higher income groups, by 52% and 56% families of middle income and higher middle income group and 36.5% families of lower middle income group. Expenditure on religion was incurred by 48 per cent families regularly from higher middle and higher income groups only.

To meet the exceeding expenditure compared to planned expenditure, the practice of postponed payment was followed by 28.6% families from all income groups except higher income group. Charge account system was availed by nearly 40 per cent families from lower income and 42.3% families of lower middle income groups, otherwise it was not found to be commonly used. To allow the planned and actual expenditure to meet in case of transportation expenditure, nearly 55 per cent families from lower income and lower middle income reported that they preferred to walk under such conditions. Forty five per cent of middle income families and 40% of higher middle income families too followed this practice. Planning the income was followed by the practice of maintaining the records of expenditure which was handled by single individual. Fifty six per cent families reported the use of diary to maintain and check expenditure records. Nearly 72% per cent families from low income group and middle income group followed this record keeping practice. Sixty six per cent families from higher middle income group, 60% of the families from higher income group and 63.5% of the families from lower middle income group followed this practice. Maintaining the collection of cash and credit bills was the practice followed by 38% per cent cases from all income groups. This practice was most regularly followed by the families from middle income group, that is 60.4%. In case of 50% of middle income 46% of lower middle income and 44% of higher middle families the practice of collecting bills of one place was never followed. From higher income group, 38% families always followed this practice.

The practice to visit the market after making a list was always followed by total 58.4% families. This practice was followed by 70% families from higher income group, 66% and 63.5% of families from middle income and lower middle income groups and 56% of the families from higher middle income group, whereas from low income group this practice was rarely followed by 54% families.

To purchase the goods as and when the need arise was always done by 82% of the families from low income group, 71% of lower middle income group and 70% of higher income group. This practice was also found in case of middle income group, that is by 52.8% families, whereas in case of higher middle income families this practice was rarely found.

The practice to curtail pre-planned expenditure on essentials due to unforeseen entertainment expenditure was never found in total 47.8% of cases. From low income families, 84% families never followed this practice.

**Evaluation**

Along with planning and controlling evaluation was the part of management process applied to money resource by families.

The difference between actual expenditure and planned expenditure was checked and studied by 47 per cent of the families from middle income group only. More than 55 per cent families from higher income. Higher middle income and lower middle income group families were utilizing the feedback from evaluation of meeting the demands of family members and were then prioritizing the purchase plan for the left demands in next month's plan. As far as taking decisions regarding seasonal bulk purchase was concerned past records were certainly checked by 71 per cent and 62 per cent families respectively from lower middle income and middle groups. Whereas in case of rest of the income groups, by 42 to 48 per cent families this practice was followed.

While incurring expenditure on religious and social reasons, nearly 40 to 60 per cent families used to check past records to take decisions, from all the three middle income groups. It was never practised by 52 per cent families from higher income group and was rarely followed by majority of the families from low income group.

Out of total families 45.5% expressed that educational expenditure was never maintained as per the estimate. This fact was identified by following the evaluation practice. Eighty two per cent of lower income families, 40.4% of lower middle income families, 28.3% of middle income families and respectively 44% and 34% of higher middle and higher income families revealed that it was not possible to maintain the expenditure on education as per the estimated figure.

Regarding educational expenditure exceeding the planned figure, 74% of the families from low income group expressed that it rarely happened, whereas 46% of lower middle income families and 54% of higher middle income families expressed that educational expenditure always exceeded the planned figure. From middle income and higher income groups nearly 30% of the families did express the same.

Forty nine per cent of the total families responded that heavy expenditure was rarely made on the rituals and 38% revealed that it was always made. Thirty six per cent families from lower income group, 30.8% of lower middle income group, 28.3% from middle income group and 48% families from higher middle and higher income group were making heavy expenditure on rituals.

By following the evaluation practice, 60.8% of the total families identified that the fulfilment of monetary requirements of the family members as per planning was ensured. Though compared to other income groups in case of low income groups it was found only in 34% cases. Evaluation was always carried out to ensure the fulfilment of monetary requirements by 77% of the families from middle income group, 60% from high income group and nearly 65% of the families from lower middle and higher middle income groups.

Through evaluation, 39% of the total families found that total actual expenditure always exceeded the estimated expenditure. This was found by 46% of low income families, nearly 40% of lower middle income and middle income families, and 36% and 34% of high middle income and high income families.

Out of total number of families 41% reported that payments were postponed when expenditure was found exceeding the capacity of paying the bills. This was found mainly in case of lower income (30%) and lower middle income (34.6%) families compared to the other three income groups.

Planned budget was evaluated after expenditure was incurred on all the items during the month. This was done through the notebook method, where accounts were noted down. This practice was followed by 38.8% of total families. Higher middle income, middle income and lower middle income families used to regularly follow evaluation practice for expenditure using notebook method, respectively, 48%, 47% and 40.4% cases. Whereas from high income group 32% of the families always used to evaluate the expenditure using notebook method.

For evaluating the expenditure, cross checking was done through collected bills by 40.4 of the total families. In case of middle income and higher middle income groups this practice was followed by 56% of the families. This was less frequently followed by low income families. Out of high income families 42% did follow this practice.

Matching the difference between actual expenditure and estimated expenditure was always done by 30.6% of the total number of families. The same was never done by 34% of the total families and was rarely done by 35.3% of the total families. This practice was followed most by the families from middle income group (47.2%) compared to other income groups.

Through evaluation, items were identified to be given the priority for purchase. These were the items which were left un-purchased in the previous month. Fifty per cent of the total respondents had followed this practice. Fifty six per cent of the families from higher middle income and higher income group and 59.6% of those from middle income group followed this evaluation practice. Forty five per cent of the families from middle income group were following this practice, whereas 46% families from low income group rarely followed this evaluation practice. Feedbacks through the past records were utilized for the purchase of seasonal goods by 54% of the total families. This practice was followed by 71% of the lower middle income group families and 62% of the middle income group families. In case of lower income, higher middle income and higher income group it was followed by 46%, 48% and 42% of the families. Similarly the past records were examined while deciding expenditures on rituals and social expenditures by 37.6% of the total families. Forty six per cent families from higher middle group always used to follow this practice while 46% of the families from low income group rarely followed this practice. From higher income group only 22% of the families followed this practice of taking feedback from past records and from lower middle income and middle income groups respectively 42.3% and 41.5% of the families followed this evaluation practice.

**Table 2**

**Percentage Distribution: Financial Management Practices**

| Financial Management | Income Group | | | | | |
|---|---|---|---|---|---|---|
| Score – Range | LIG N=50 | LMIG N=52 | MIG N=53 | HMIG N=50 | HIG N=50 | Total |
| Planning | N % | N % | N % | N % | N % | N % |
| Low (15-25) | 15 30.0 | 13 25.0 | 6 11.3 | 17 34.0 | 5 10.0 | 56 22.0 |
| Medium (26-35) | 31 62.0 | 31 59.6 | 27 50.9 | 13 26.0 | 33 66.0 | 135 52.9 |
| High (36-45) | 4 8.0 | 8 15.4 | 20 37.7 | 20 40.0 | 12 24.0 | 64 25.1 |
| Total | 50 100 | 52 100 | 52 100 | 50 100 | 50 100 | 255 100 |
| Mean | 28.4 | 29.3 | 33.0 | 32.2 | 32.0 | 31.0 |
| S.D. | 4.2 | 4.9 | 4.8 | 6.5 | 4.9 | 5.4 |
| Controlling | N % | N % | N % | N % | N % | N % |
| Low (18-34) | 14 28.0 | 16 30.8 | 9 17.0 | 17 34.0 | 13 26.0 | 69 27.1 |
| Medium (35-44) | 28 56.0 | 34 65.4 | 31 58.5 | 13 26.0 | 31 62.0 | 137 53.7 |
| High (45-54) | 8 16.0 | 2 3.8 | 13 24.5 | 20 40.0 | 6 12.0 | 49 19.2 |
| Total | 50 100 | 52 100 | 52 100 | 50 100 | 50 100 | 255 100 |
| Mean | 36.9 | 37.8 | 40.5 | 41.0 | 38.6 | 39.0 |
| S.D. | 5.9 | 5.3 | 7.2 | 7.4 | 5.9 | 6.5 |
| Evaluation | N % | N % | N % | N % | N % | N % |
| Low (12-20) | 18 36.0 | 10 19.2 | 9 17.0 | 8 16.0 | 8 16.0 | 53 20.8 |
| Medium (21-28) | 28 56.0 | 18 34.6 | 14 26.4 | 18 36.0 | 28 56.0 | 106 41.6 |

| High (29-36) | 4 8.0 | 24 46.2 | 30 56.6 | 24 48.0 | 14 28.0 | 96 37.6 |
|---|---|---|---|---|---|---|
| Total | 50 100 | 52 100 | 52 100 | 50 100 | 50 100 | 255 100 |
| Mean | 21.8 | 24.4 | 26.2 | 25.3 | 24.5 | 24.5 |
| S.D. | 4.0 | 3.6 | 3.6 | 3.6 | 4.0 | 4.0 |

In order to obtain a view regarding the extent to which financial management practices were followed by families from different income group, the responses were given weighted scores. Scores obtained for various financial management practices were added to arrive at a total score of each respondent. The respondents were categorized into low, medium and high categories on equal interval basis.

As seen from the table 1, planning of expenditure as a part of financial management was followed less frequently by families from all income groups. Majority of the families had medium affinity towards planning. Higher middle income group had relatively higher scores for planning the expenditure. Similarly, controlling was also not exercised more frequently by other income group families but the middle income and higher middle income groups. On the other hand, expenditure pattern was evaluated by the families belonging to all the three middle income groups.

As far as planning of expenditure is concerned, an observation can be made that lower income families due to severe scarcity of money-resource do not have enough room to plan the expenditure wide variety of commodities. While for high income families, the abundance of the monetary resource makes it insignificant for them to plan the expenditure in advance. It is the middle income group which shows conscious managerial behaviour towards money.

## Conclusion

**Financial management practices followed by the families**

1. Planning practices were followed by nearly half of the total respondents.
2. Majority of the respondents planned the expenditure on food items.
3. Compared to higher income groups, families belonging to low income groups followed planning practices to a lesser extent due to lack of funds.
4. Majority of the respondents were estimating the expenditure on various items.
5. Respondents from HIG, HMIG and LIG had the practice of keeping aside the sum for savings. This practice was less frequently followed by the families from lower middle income group and middle income group.
6. For the consumption of consumer durables expenditure planning was not followed. Similarly no provision in expenditure planning was made for health care.
7. Regarding controlling practices, majority of the families followed regular record keeping practice. Family finance records were handled by a single person in 66 per cent cases out of the total sample.
8. Changes in expenditure were made for eatables with the change in price by nearly 40 to 47 per cent families from all income groups except higher income group.
9. Expenditure incurred was regularly evaluated by nearly 60 per cent of the families out of which, middle income families most frequently followed this practice.
10. Compared to other income groups, more number of low income families expressed that actual expenditure used to exceed planned expenditure every month.

11. Using the feed back from previous months expenditure was the practice followed by lower middle and middle income families compared to those from other income groups.

### Implications of the study

Findings of the study brought out a number of implications for action programmes for various social service institutions, educationalists, economists, policy makers and home scientists.

Certain implications have been enlisted below:

1. Families were reluctant to change their savings and investment pattern. This fact endorses the truth that families are more cautious about the safety of principle rather than income yield on their principle. The reason behind this reluctance may be the ignorance about the pros and cons of different savings and investment plans. Knowledge regarding the same should be imparted to the families in layman's language. This task can be taken up by economists, journalists and home scientists.
2. Controlling practices were more frequently adopted by the families for financial management compared to planning. This behaviour indicated lack of careful budget making on part of urban families. Home-scientists and educationists should combine their efforts to create skill amongst the families and impart adequate information about financial management to the family money managers.
3. High prices of essential commodities of daily requirements cause burden on low income, lower middle income and middle income group families. This fact was identified through the results of the present study. Families from these three groups were forced to cut down the expenditure on items of daily requirement. Further to maintain the level of living with increasing cost of living, families were forced to go for lower quality of edible items. This problem is the cardinal problem of our society. Policy makers need to take concrete steps against constant increase in the price of essential items. 'Inflation hits the poor the most' is the fact which needs to be dealt with.
4. Further, the study is significant because it reflects the picture of how families cope with their problems. Social organizations can take up the task of enlightening people regarding effective strategies to cope with the financial problems. Researchers and specialists from the field of home management can further contribute through imparting knowledge to the families regarding the ways to improve quality of life. By helping families to gain knowledge and skills to i) manage their financial resources ii) improve their economic profile and iii) adopting effective and successful coping strategies, home management specialist can impart remarkable contribution to the society.

## References

Abdel-Ghany, M. and Nickols, S.Y. (1984) "Consumer, consumption and family economics/ household management research, 1972-82 : Survey of the past and outlook for the future". Home Economics Research Journal, 12, 265-278.

Abramovitz, M. (1959) "The welfare interpretation of secular trends in national income and product", in M. Abramovitz (ed.), The allocation of Economics Resources : Essays in Honor of Bernard Francis Haley Stanford, CA : Stanford Uni. Press.

Ackerman, N. and Paolucci, B (1983) "Objective and Subjective income adequacy : their relationship to perceived life quality measures", Social Indicators Research, 12, 25-48.

Adams, B. (1975) The family : A sociological interpretation (2nd ed.), Chicago : Rand McNally.

Allen, R.G.D. (1975) Index numbers in Theory & Practice, The Macmillan Press Ltd.

Bartley, M., Blane, D and Montgomery, S. (1997) "Health and the life course : why safety nets matter", British Medical Journal, 314, 1194-1196.

Baye, Michael R., (1985) "Price Dispersion and Functional Price Indices", Econometrica, January, 53:1, 217-23.

Beutler I.F. and Mason, J.W. (1987) "Family cash flow budgeting", Home Economics Research Journal, 16, 3-12.

Bracht, N (1988) "Quantity and quality in social research", Unwin Hyman, Boston.

Bryant, W.K. (1986) "Assets and debts in a consumer portfolio", The Journal of Consumer Affairs, 20, 14-35.

Bubolz, M.M. and Sontag, M.S. (1993) "Human Ecology Theory", in Pauline G.B., William J.D. Ralph, L. Walter, R.S. and Suzanne, K.S. (ed) Source books of family theory and methods – a contextual approach (pp 419-450) New York : Plenum Press.

Burr, Wesley (1973) Theory construction and the sociology of the family, New York : Wiley.

Byrne, D. (1964) "Repression-Sensitization as a Dimension of Personality". in B.A. Maher (ed.), Progress in Experimental Personality Research, Vol. I. New York : Academic Press, 169-220.

Cynthia, L.Jennings (1981) – White house conference on families recommendations relating to the economic well being of families. *Family economics review*, **winter**, pp. 36-38.

Davis, E., and Helmik, S. (1983) "Composite measures of financial satisfaction : An analysis of two indices", M. M. Dunsing (Ed.) Proceedings of the Symposium on Perceived Economic well-being. Urbana : Agricultural Experiment Station, University of Illionois, 27-39.

Deacon R.E. and Firebaugh F.M. (1975) Home Management : context and concepts, Henghton Aviffin Company.

Deacon, R.E. and Firebaugh, F.M. (1981): Family Resource Management : Principles and Applications, New York : Allyn and Bacon.

Desai Chitra, (1967), A study of expenditure patterns and attitudes of selected urban families towards money management. An unpublished Ph.D. Dissertation, Department of Home Management, M.S.University of Baroda.

Devi N. Sumitra, (1969) "The income and expenditure patterns of a hundred and fifty selected families in Coimbatore City", Abstracts of home science series-2, Avinashlingam, Home Science College, Coimbatore.

Dhingra Sunita, (1967) Practices and opinions of families on saving pattern, Masters Thesis, Department of Home Management, M.S. University of Baroda.

Diewert, W.E., (1983) "The theory of the Cost-of-living Index and the Measurement of Welfare Change", in W.E. Diewert and C. Montmarquette, eds., Price Level Measurement, Statistics, Canada, 163-233.

Dollar P.G. (1983) The financial management practices and satisfaction with those practices of female-headed and dual-headed families, unpublished M.S. Thesis, IOWA State University, Ames, IA.

Dubey Aruna, (1984) A study of management of time and money by mothers of orthopaedically handicapped children, An unpublished Ph.D. Dissertation, Department of Home Management, M.S.University of Baroda.

Edwards, Kay P. (1977), "A theoretical approach to goal-oriented family behaviour", pp. 146-149 in Dynamics of Family Management (ed.), Baker G. and Hogan M.J.

Ferber, R. (1973) "Consumer Economics, A survey", Journal of Economic Literature, 11.

Gandotra Veena, (1983) Management problems and practices of homemakers with disabled member in the family, Doctoral thesis, Department of Home Management, M.S.University of Baroda.

Ghai Kiran, (1982) A study of money management practices of retired people and their attitude towards money management and retirement, (April), Department of Home Management, M.S.University of Baroda.

Godwin, D.D. and Carroll, D.D. (1986) "Financial management attitudes and behaviour of husbands and wives", Journal of Consumer Studies and Home Economics, 10, 77-96.

Gore, M.S. (1960) Urbanisation and Family Change, McGraw-Hill.

Gross I., Crandall E. & Knoll M. (1980) – Management for Modern Families, Prentice Hall Inc, Engleword Cliffs, London.

Gupta, S.P., (1998) Statistical Methods, Sultan Chand and Co.

Hafstrom, J.L. and Dunsing, M.M. (1973) "Level of living : Factors influencing the homemakers' satisfaction", Home Economics Research Journal, 2.

Hefferan, C., (1982) "Determinants and patterns of family savings", Home Economic Research Journal, 47-56.

Iyengar N. and Gopalkrishna M. (1985) "Appropriate criteria for measurement of levels of living", Indian Economic Review Vol. 20, issue 2, p. 191.

Jhaveri, J. (1974) "Erosion of Incomes of Income-Tax Payers through inflation", Economic and Political Weekly, issue 41, Vol. 9.

Jorgenson, Dale, W and Daniel, T. Slenick, (1983) "Individual and social cost of living indexes", in W.E. Diewert and C. Montmarguette eds., Price Level Measurement, Statistics Canada, 241-323.

Kerlinger Fred N. (1983) Foundations of behavioural research, Surjeet Publications.

Kothari, C.R. (1990) Research methodology – methods and techniques, Vishwa Prakashan, New Delhi.

Lasch, C. (1977) Haven in a Heartless World, New York : Basic Books.

Lincoln, Y.S. (1995) Emerging Criteria for quality in qualitative and interpretive research, Qualitative Inquiry, 1, 275-289.

Mammen, S., Helmick, S. and Metzen, E. (1983) "Factors affecting perceived adequacy of income", in M.M. Dunsing (ed.), Proceedings of the Symposium on Perceived Economic wellbeing, Urbana : Agricultural Experiment Station, University of Illinois.

Marlowe, J. (1981) "Financial variables associated with successful debt liquidation", Home Economics Research Journal, June, Vol. 9, No. 4.

Mattessich, P. and R. Hill (1987) "Life cycle and family development", in : M.B. Sussman and S.K. Steinmetz, eds., Handbook of Marriage and the Family, New York: Plenum Press, pp. 437-470.

Metzen, E.J., Williams, F.L., Shul, J. and Keefe, D.R. (1980) "Project description". in E.J. Metzen (ed.), Quality of life as affected by Area of residence (North Central Regional Research Publication No. 270), Columbia.

Milbrath, I., (1982) "A conceptualization and research strategy for the study of ecological aspects of the quality of life", Social Indicators Research, 14, 385-419.

Mikyeong Bae, Sherman Hanna and Suzanne Lindamood(1997), *Patterns of overspending in US households*, AFCPE.

Minhas B.S., Jain LR and Sulaja M.R., (1990) "State Specific Urban Consumer Price differentials relative to All India for middle Fractiles and Total Population : 1961-1983", Indian Economic Review Vol. 25, p. 75.

Moos, R. H. and B.S. Moos (1981) Family Environment Scale (Manual), Palo Alto, Calif: Consulting Psychologists Press.

Mueller, M.J. and Hira, T.K. (1984) "Impact of select money management practices on household solvency status", in K.P. Goebel (ed.), Proceedings of the 30th annual Conference of the American Council On Consumer Interests, Columbia, MO : American Council on Consumer Interests.

## 12.6 How to Do?

Jolly and Dolly discussed again.

Dolly: "I just wish to discuss research procedure again. We have read 15 research projects, I just wish to discuss, objectives, research methodology and findings in each project."

Jolly: "Let us see the research project No. 'A Case Study on Financial Performance of Centurion Bank and Bank of Punjab–In Pre and Post Merger Period' by Dr. P. Chellasamy and J. Udhaya Kumar."

Dolly: "The authors first describe merger and acquisition. The benefits of mergers are given in brief. Bank of Punjab has been introduced. Later it is described how Centurion and Bank of Punjab got merged on 1-10-2005. Later authors describe how both banks gained from merger. Should we take these, specially the paragraph 'gains from merger' as hypothesised statements?"

Jolly: "See, in methodlogy section, researchers state 'The whole evaluation is based on the principle that if one plus one gives a figure greater than two then the variable under study has resulted in synergy. In other words the study adopts a before and after approach for evaluating the merger's impact.' Reseachers have taken only two years data and compared to see the effects of mergers."

Dolly: "I have read somewhere that comparison of data is not called a good reseach"

Jolly: "Do not go just by words, try to understand the underlying concept. Here researchers want to see the impact of merger."

Dolly: "The first two tables show how increase/decrease in balance sheet items and income items. See after merger, the profit after merger has increased by 386%."

Jolly: "Then Spread Burden Model has been used to see bank's profitability."

Dolly: "There is confusion, are they comparing average or total."

Jolly: "Yes, researcher is taking pre-merger average while post-merger they are taking total."

Dolly: "We have already discussed, if research methodology is not written properly in report, reader can get confused, as the confusion increases with Table no. 4 and 5."

Jolly: "The position is clear with Table no. 8, 9 and 10. Authors conclude, 'Based on the analysis it can be concluded that there is an increase in financial performance of the Centurion Bank of Punjab after the merger compared to pre-merger period. Ratio analysis of the financial performance of the Centurion Bank of Punjab, were found to be very good. So we conclude that the merger between Centurion Bank and Bank of Punjab has turned to be successful'."

Dolly: "Don't you think there are lot of gaps in the study. We can take up this study again."

Jolly: "Research is a cyclic process."

Dolly: "Despite, some debatable issue in research, authors have done their best to collect and analyse the data."

Jolly: "Let us see the next project report, 'Direction of Exports of Commercial agricultural commodities' by J.K. Sachdeva."

Dolly: "After reviewing the available literature, author sets the objectives of study. There are six objectives, don't you think author wishes to study lot of things in one study."

Jolly: "Yes, usually a good researcher studies one item at a time in detail. Second important things is that external trade depends more on relationship within the countries, and it is more of political nature. So any study of export and import will have extraneous factors which are rarely taken into consideration."

Dolly: "So you think the findings cannot be generalized or in other words, they may lack external validity."

Jolly: "To some extent you are right. But authors appears to generalise the commercial commodity trade."

Dolly: "We have not read much about de-trended series."

Jolly: "All the course curriculum have some limitations due to syllabus, time and space constraints."

Dolly: "You want to say we should study more techniques as described in this book."

Jolly : "Sky is limit for a researcher."

Dolly: "It is descriptive, exploratory and empirical study."

Jolly: "Authors use all possible methods to achieve their objectives. In case of tea, author first describes the exports of tea, finds its growth rate and attempts to find out the determinant of exports. Tea production depends upon lagged year export."

Dolly: "Can we generalize it?"

Jolly: "R-Square is only 0.60, which means 60% of production depends on lagged export. So goodness of fit is only 60%. People will raise their doubts when you try to generalize."

Dolly: "So author has attempted to analyse the exports to various countries by three methods – compounded growth rate, instability index and Unit Root technique."

Jolly: "Similarly, coffee, spices, oilseeds, cotton and cashew have been analysed."

Dolly: "The conclusions are based on findings!"

Jolly: "Every research has gaps."

Dolly: "Can we say gaps are drawbacks?"

Jolly: "I feel no. Drawbacks mean type I or Type II error. They may be due to limitations of study."

Dolly: "In this case important finding is that devaluation gave a booster to exports of agricultural commodities."

Jolly: "Yes, author depends upon literature review as well as on empirical analysis."

Dolly: "Though hypotheses have not been clearly written, but they have tested to achieve the objectives."

Jolly: "Next project is a case study 'Mini Milk Revolution – A case of Youth leadership for village economy' by Dr. R.M. Channaveer."

Dolly: "The author describes the village setup, customs, social background and economy in brief."

Jolly: "Then hero, Mr. Anand, arrives at the scene and joins hands with one Mr. Khanderao for forming a Self Help Group. Formation of Swami Vivekananda SHG was not an easy task. Anyway all is well that ends well."

Dolly: "See, how rules were made for membership fees, absenteeism etc."

Jolly: "Starting milk dairy was not easy. People were not coming forward, however when it starts others always follow. Starting from scratch, milk dairy's monthly revenue reached to ₹ 55000 to one lakh."

Dolly: "It is an exemplary work of rural youth who led an initiative to support the agriculture through allied activities like dairy. The initiative is a matter for advocacy that the rural youth can transform their village economy. This can be simulated in any part of India. Such initiatives are replicated in many villages of India. The situation reminds us that the heritage of co-operative movement of our country could be transformed in a micro form at village level. Self-help, which is Indian concept, is a more evolved form of micro-finance concept of Prof. Mohd. Younus of Bangladesh. The MYRADA NGO of Karnataka is the pioneer in coining, promoting and practising the self-help for women. On the other hand, the social capital of rural youth could be enhanced through enabling and empowering environment in the system both agency and community."

Jolly: "It is a case study, many things can be generalized from the findings."

Dolly: "Comparative study of group members show how they have changed overtime."

Jolly: "We should work on such cases so that we may find new process and change agents. We can frame our hypothesis also to test them with the case."

Dolly: "Next project is 'Rising Prices and Financial Management Practices of Urban Families in India' by Dr. Suramaya Joshi, from Department of Home Managment, Faculty of Home Science, M.S. University of Baroda, Vadodara."

Jolly: "This report is a very good example of exploratory, descritptive and empirical technique synergy. The researcher, first, discusses the problem in general, then sets the objectives. Methodlogy is decided. Review literature is the part of methodology."

Dolly: "The sample has been taken with proper planning. A total 255 families were selected from five different income groups in Vadodara city of Gujarat state. For the multistage systematic random sampling technique, income slabs were provided by the municipal corporation and the residential areas were identified. Families were selected to reflect the composition of each identified residential area."

Jolly: "The data were collected using a structured interview schedule during the months of March–May 2001. The questionnaire comprised seven sections incorporating questions pertaining to socio-economic and demographic profile of the families, their consumption expenditure during the base year (1995–1996) and the year (1999–2000) and the financial management practices adopted by the families."

Dolly: "After reviewing the literature, author has described how finanacial management is classified, i.e. planning, controlling and evaluation practices. The author further describes how families manage their expenses and distribution of data."

Jolly: "Major findings are fifty per cent families manage especially on food items. Low income familes are unable to manage because of lack of funds. Families do not plan for health care. Expenditure of low income families usually exceed the planned expenditure."

Dolly: "The study is significant because it reflects the picture of how families cope with their problems. Social organizations can take up the task of enlightening people regarding effective strategies to cope with the financial problems. Researchers and specialists from the field of home management can further contribute through imparting knowledge to the families regarding the ways to improve quality of life. What if I wish to continue study with the data?

Jolly: "You can approach the researcher and ask for the data explaining purpose. This is a good way to carry out further research."

Dolly: "Dear, we have discussed a lot on research. We have learnt many techniques of research, qualitative research and quantitative research. Now is time to do it practically."

Jolly: "Start with an easy topic with secondary data. Do not go immediately for applied research."

Dolly: "I feel discussion is fruitful and I wish to continue with my friends. I shall take a good research journal, select one article, discuss its objectives, methodology and findings. I shall also try to see the validity of the findings."

Jolly: "Go ahead, I wish you best of luck."

CHAPTER

# APPENDICES

## Structure

## 13.1 Business Research Methodology Question Bank

1. What do you mean by research? Explain its significance in modern times.
2. Explain difference between research method and research methodology.
3. "A research scholar has to work as a judge and derive the truth and not as a pleader who is only eager to prove his case in favour of his plaintiff." Discuss the statement pointing out the objectives of research.
4. Briefly describe the different steps involved in a research process.
5. Explain the criteria of a good research.
6. "Research is much concerned with proper fact finding, analysis and evaluation." Do you agree with this statement? Give reason in support of your answers.
7. Explain the types of research in detail.
8. "Empirical research in India in particular creates so many problems for researchers."
9. State the problems that are usually faced by such researchers.
10. Why is it important to define research problem appropriately?
11. Explain in detail techniques involved in defining a research problem.
12. "The task of defining the research problem is often follows a sequential pattern." Explain.
13. Write short notes on following:
    (a) Ex post facto research
    (b) Motivation in research
    (c) Pilot survey
14. In the research process, why is the problem definition stage probably the most important stage? What are the key issues that need to be addressed at that stage?
15. Explain the meaning and significance of research design.
16. How does formulating a research design differ from developing an approach to a problem?
17. "Research design in exploratory studies must be flexible but in descriptive studies, it must minimize bias and maximize reliability." Discuss.
18. Differentiate between exploratory and descriptive research.
19. Write short notes on following:
    (a) Extraneous variable
    (b) Confounded relationship
    (c) Research hypothesis
    (d) Experimental and control group.
20. Write short note on "experience survey" explaining fully its utility in exploratory research studies.

21. Under what circumstances you recommend:
    (a) A probability sample
    (b) A non-probability sample
    (c) A cluster sample
22. What are the major purposes for which descriptive research is conducted?
23. List the steps involved in implementing the post-test only control group design. Describe the design symbolically.
24. What are the limitations of Latin square design?
25. "For any research to be successful it must be well designed." Justify this statement.
26. What do you mean by sample design? What points should be taken into consideration by a researcher in developing a sample design for this research project?
27. How would you differentiate between simple random sampling and complex random sampling?
28. Why probability sampling is generally preferred in comparison to non-probability sampling?
29. Explain the procedure of selecting a sample random sampling.
30. Distinguish between:
    (a) Restricted and unrestricted sampling
    (b) Convenience and purposive sampling
    (c) Systematic and stratified sampling
    (d) Cluster and area sampling
31. Under what circumstances stratified random sampling design is considered appropriate? How would you select such sample? Explain with the help of an example.
32. Under what circumstances you recommend:
    (a) A probability sample
    (b) A non-probability sample
    (c) A cluster sample
33. "A systematic bias results from error in sampling procedure." What do you mean by such a systematic bias? Describe the important causes responsible for such a bias.
34. What is the major difference between a sample and a census? Under what condition would a sample be preferable to a census? A census preferable to a sample?
35. What is a sampling unit? How is it different from the population element?
36. Describe the sampling design process.
37. How should the target population be defined?
38. Highlight various methods used in selecting a sample from the population. Point out their merits and demerits.

39. "Random sampling owes its importance to the fact that we can assess the results obtained from it in terms of probabilities otherwise the reliability of the estimates remains a matter of individual opinion." Elucidate this statement.

40. "A sample may be large yet worthless because it is not random; or it may be random but unreliable because it is small." Comment upon the above statement and explain the importance of sampling in daily life.

41. What is the least expensive and least time-consuming of all sampling techniques?

42. What are the major limitations of this technique?

43. Explain the difference between judgmental and convenience sampling.

44. What is the relationship between quota and judgmental sampling?

45. Explain the characteristics of a good sample design.

46. Write short note on following:

    (a) Need of sampling

    (b) Sampling frame

47. Define the appropriate target population and the sampling frame in each of following situation:

    (a) The manufacturer of a new cereal brand wants to conduct product usage test in India.

    (b) A local TV station wants to determine households' viewing habits and programming preference.

48. What do you mean by sampling frame and sampling design? What points should be taken into consideration while developing the sampling design for studying the problems of domestic airline passengers?

59. A Local newspaper wants to ascertain the extent to which the inclusion of a daily stock market page might increase its circulation. Which type of data collection would you like to propose for this? Explain the unit of analysis and the population size for the data collection. Prepare at least eight questions in a questionnaire to collect the pertinent information.

50. What are the different methods of data collection? Which one is most suitable for conducting enquiry regarding employee welfare programme in India?

51. How would you differentiate between primary and secondary data?

52. What do you understand by secondary data and why is it important to obtain secondary data before primary data?

53. Differentiate between internal and external secondary data.

54. What are the advantages and limitations of secondary data? And also list the sources of published secondary data.

55. "It is never safe to take published statistics at their face value without knowing their meaning and limitation". Elucidate this statement by enumerating and explaining the various points which you would consider before using any published data.

56. What do you understand by primary data and explain its advantages and limitations?

57. What do you mean by observation and also list its advantages and limitations?

58. What do you understand by the term "survey"? Name the major modes for obtaining information via survey.

59. Explain the difference between:

    (a) Survey and observation

    (b) Survey and case study

    (c) Survey and experiments

60. Describe some of the major projective techniques and evaluate their significance as a tool of scientific social research.

61. Describe the case study method. And analyse the merits and limitations of case study methods.

62. Explain why questionnaires are popular tools for data collection in research. Discuss qualities of a good questionnaire.

63. Explain the procedure of designing a good questionnaire.

64. Explain the difference between collection of data through questionnaire and schedules.

65. Explain the following terms:

    (a) Open ended question

    (b) Multiple choice question

    (c) Dichotomous question

66. Design a questionnaire to study customer's satisfaction towards services provided by State Bank of India. (Make necessary assumptions)

67. Describe the issues involved in pre-testing a questionnaire.

68. What are the reasons that respondents are unable to answer the question asked?

69. Explain about structured and unstructured questions with their advantages and limitations.

70. Design an open ended question to determine whether households are engaged in gardening. Also develop a multiple choice and a dichotomous question to obtain same information. Which one will be most desirable?

71. Discuss interview as a technique of data collection.

72. What are the main aspects of a questionnaire?

73. Railway commuters have been facing various problems during travel. You have been assigned the task of finding their problems. Design a suitable questionnaire to be used in this study. Use Likert scale for designing ten questions.

74. Mention six differences between survey and experiment.

75. What is the meaning of measurement in research? What are the different types of scales?

76. Point out the possible sources of error in measurement. Describe the test of sound measurement.

77. Discuss the relative merits and demerits of:
    (a) Rating vs. Ranking scale
    (b) Summated vs. cumulative scale
    (c) Scalogram analysis vs. factor analysis
78. Differentiate between nominal and ordinal scale.
79. What are the implications of having an arbitrary zero point in an interval scale?
80. What are the advantages of a ratio scale over an interval scale? Are these advantages significant?
81. Write short note on
    (a) Comparative rating scale
    (b) Paired comparison.
82. Describe the constant sum scale. How is it different from the other comparative rating scales?
83. Describe the Q-sort methodology.
84. What is a semantic differential scale? For what purpose is this scale is used?
85. What are the differences between staple scale and the semantic differential? Which scale is more popular?
86. What are the major decisions involved in constructing an itemized rating scale?
87. Develop a Likert and semantic differential scale for measuring store loyalty.
88. Develop a Likert scale for measuring the attitude of students towards the internet as a source of general information.
89. "Scaling describes the procedure by which numbers are assigned to various degrees of opinion, attitude and other concepts." Discuss.
90. What are the bases of scale classification?
91. Write short note on following:
    (a) Arbitrary scale
    (b) Multidimensional scaling
92. How would you select a particular scaling technique?
93. Explain in detail Thurstone type scale.
94. What do you mean by validity? How would you assess the validity of a multi item scale?
95. Explain the term reliability and also explain the relationship between reliability and validity.
96. Describe the term association technique. Give an example of a situation in which this technique is especially useful.
97. What do you understand by sentence completion test? Explain its advantages.

98. Write a short note on Thematic Apperception Test.

99. Suppose Baskin Robbins wants to know why some people don't eat ice-cream regularly. Develop a sentence completion test for this purpose.

100. If a semantic differential has seven scale items, should all the seven items have to be phrased as either positive or negative statements. Or can both positive and negative statements be used? Your answer should be supported by example.

101. Write short notes on:

    (a) Dependent and Independent Variables.

    (b) Concept of Measurement.

102. Observe the number of cars passing on a highway for one hour and count the number Maruti cars passing during the hour. Find simple percentage. Now search from internet and find out market share of Maruti. Does your result match with actual market share of Maruti. If not, why? If yes, why? Write a simple explanation and discuss with your colleagues, why there is a difference?

103. Research is not information gathering. Critically comment.

104. Discuss the critical elements of a research proposal or synopsis. Why should we write a research proposal in advance?

105. Critically discuss the importance of induction and deduction.

106. Discuss the importance of deduction in scientific enquiry.

107. Make two groups of 30 students in the class. Separate them in two classrooms. Tell one group in the class that you are going test their knowledge of political history (you can change the actual topic) during 1978 to 1991. Don't tell anything to the other group. Give one hour time to the first group for searching on internet and learn. Set a common question paper (this is your tool) with 25 objective type questions with four options. Compare the results. Find mean and standard deviation of each group. Which mean is better and why? What is the benefit of learning in advance. Find the difference in simple means? Do you think it right way to compare the results?

108. What are informal experimental research designs? Discuss critically.

109. List formal research designs. Explain the procedure of one way ANOVA.

110. Explain the terms Type I and Type II errors.

111. Why quantitative is better than qualitative? Comment critically.

112. (a) You have observed that there is lot of energy wastage in your institute. Lights are on even after the classes. Fans are not switched off. Whose responsibility is it to save energy? Frame 10 questions on Liker scale. Discuss among yourself how to analyse the responses.

    (b) Frame 10 questions on Likers scale and 5 questions on demography to ask opinion about job scenario in India. Survey 500 students, analyse data and write a report.

    (c) What are the sources of primary data? What are the benefits of primary data?

    (d) What are the sources of secondary data? What are the benefits of secondary data?

(e) Write short notes on

(i) Survey Methods

(ii) Question methods

(iii) In-depth interview

(iv) Focus group

113. Review 10 research papers on management education in education. You get such peer-reviewed articles from ebscohost database. Prepare abstracts. Now list 10 problems discussed in these papers. Frame 10 questions on these problems. Survey 200 students and write a report. Do you think sample size is good for such survey?

114. List probability and non-probability sampling procedures. Explain each briefly.

115. Write short notes on

(a) Sample frame

(b) Sample size

(c) Population

(d) Sampling error

(e) Parameter and statistics

## 13.2 Answers to Problems for Practice

### Chapter 7

1. (a) 0.0228 (b) 0.1587 (c) 0.9544
2. 0.001
3. 41
4. 0.063
5. (a) 0.011 (b) 0.011 (c) 0.99
6. .001, 0.2148, 0.499
7. 0.971, 0.029
8. 2.311, 0.05
9. 0.01
10. 0.0016
11. 96.925 mm to 53.079
12. 1.338 to 4.662
13. 267
14. 10%, S D = 0.94%, Range at 5% confidence level 11.84 and 8.16
15. 51.2465 and 48.7534

16. 0.962, 0.038
17. Z = 2.1, reject $H_0$ (Hint take p= ½)
18. Z = 4.5, reject $H_0$
19. Z = 1.79
20. Accept $H_0$

**Chapter 9.1.2**

1. No. of large industries = 50, no. of small industries = 100
2. 350 units
3. 7.42
4. 22.37%
5. 53.34
6. Average deviation = 90.39, Coefficient of average deviation = 0.374
7. 0.2034
8. Skewness = 0, (Distribution is symmetrical), Kurtosis = 2.89 which is less than 3. (Distribution is pltykurtik)
9. CV (X) = 40%, CV(Y) = 35.55%
10. 0.5

**Chapter 9.2.3.2**

11 Z of sample mean is –56 reject $H_0$. The sales of the product has decreased.
12. Z of sample mean is –1.75 accept $H_0$. The sales of the product has not improved.
13. Z of sample mean is –16.53 reject $H_0$.
14 Z of sample mean is 11.317 reject $H_0$.
15. Z of sample mean is 1.292 accept $H_0$
16. Z of sample mean is –4.8 reject $H_0$
17. t = 3.75, reject $H_0$
18. t = 2.485, reject $H_0$
19. Z = 2.933, reject $H_0$
20. Z = –2.29, reject $H_0$
21. Z = 0.827, accept $H_0$
22. Z = –0.831, accept $H_0$
23. $\chi^2$ = 3,735 – accept $H_0$

**Chapter 9.5.5.2**

1. F = .8175, accept $H_{0,}$ No difference in EPS
2. F = 0.23, No difference

3. Fertilizer F = .429 (No difference), Plots F = 1.676 (No difference)
4. Cars F=1.217 (accept $H_0$), Position F= 0.683, Tires F = 0.603
5. F = 1.86 For Batch, F = 3.74 for Subject, F = 1.65 for Faculty
6. F = 1.089 for profession, F = 0.228 for income, F = 1.291 for interaction
7. F = 3.76 for salesmen, F = 2.633 for region, F = 9.013 for interaction
8. Rows F = .3629, Columns F = 3.5105
9. Rows F = 0.75 Columns F = 1.53

**Chapter 9.6.3.1**

1. $\chi^2$ = 3.735 accept $H_0$
2. $\chi^2$ = 4.3 accept $H_0$
3. $\chi^2$ = 5.86 reject $H_0$
4. $\chi^2$ = 13.30 reject $H_0$
5. $\chi^2$ = 40 reject $H_0$
6. $\chi^2$ = 0.29 accept $H_0$ (No difference)
7. $\chi^2$ = 3.33 accept $H_0$ (No difference)

**Chapter 9.9.7.1**

1. a = 11.6949, b= 1.525, $R^2$ = 0.92, F = 35.166
2. C= 48.8+0.42Y, $R^2$ = 0.96, F = 82.6875, Consumption = 111800
3. Y=-1.968+0.8136X,
4. Sales = 7.87+1.0209 adv,
9. Sales = −1.35714 + 10.107t
10. Y = $9.67+0.077X_1 + 0.065X_z$

**Refer to www.himpub.com for solution and answers (teacher's manual)**

## 13.3 Statistical Tables

Area between 0 and z

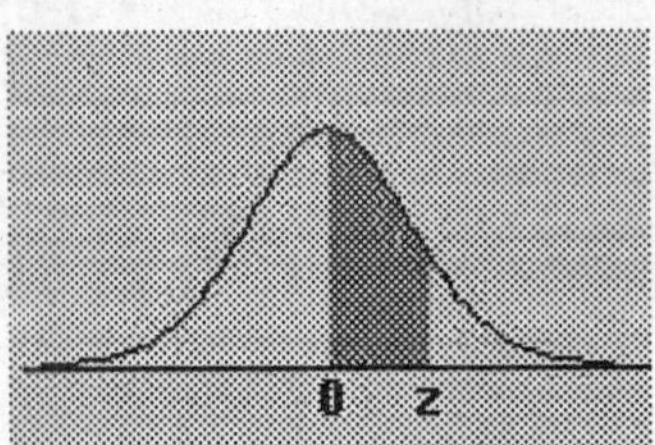


| | 0.00 | 0.01 | 0.02 | 0.03 | 0.04 | 0.05 | 0.06 | 0.07 | 0.08 | 0.09 |
|---|---|---|---|---|---|---|---|---|---|---|
| **0.0** | 0.0000 | 0.0040 | 0.0080 | 0.0120 | 0.0160 | 0.0199 | 0.0239 | 0.0279 | 0.0319 | 0.0359 |
| **0.1** | 0.0398 | 0.0438 | 0.0478 | 0.0517 | 0.0557 | 0.0596 | 0.0636 | 0.0675 | 0.0714 | 0.0753 |
| **0.2** | 0.0793 | 0.0832 | 0.0871 | 0.0910 | 0.0948 | 0.0987 | 0.1026 | 0.1064 | 0.1103 | 0.1141 |
| **0.3** | 0.1179 | 0.1217 | 0.1255 | 0.1293 | 0.1331 | 0.1368 | 0.1406 | 0.1443 | 0.1480 | 0.1517 |
| **0.4** | 0.1554 | 0.1591 | 0.1628 | 0.1664 | 0.1700 | 0.1736 | 0.1772 | 0.1808 | 0.1844 | 0.1879 |
| **0.5** | 0.1915 | 0.1950 | 0.1985 | 0.2019 | 0.2054 | 0.2088 | 0.2123 | 0.2157 | 0.2190 | 0.2224 |
| **0.6** | 0.2257 | 0.2291 | 0.2324 | 0.2357 | 0.2389 | 0.2422 | 0.2454 | 0.2486 | 0.2517 | 0.2549 |
| **0.7** | 0.2580 | 0.2611 | 0.2642 | 0.2673 | 0.2704 | 0.2734 | 0.2764 | 0.2794 | 0.2823 | 0.2852 |
| **0.8** | 0.2881 | 0.2910 | 0.2939 | 0.2967 | 0.2995 | 0.3023 | 0.3051 | 0.3078 | 0.3106 | 0.3133 |
| **0.9** | 0.3159 | 0.3186 | 0.3212 | 0.3238 | 0.3264 | 0.3289 | 0.3315 | 0.3340 | 0.3365 | 0.3389 |
| **1.0** | 0.3413 | 0.3438 | 0.3461 | 0.3485 | 0.3508 | 0.3531 | 0.3554 | 0.3577 | 0.3599 | 0.3621 |
| **1.1** | 0.3643 | 0.3665 | 0.3686 | 0.3708 | 0.3729 | 0.3749 | 0.3770 | 0.3790 | 0.3810 | 0.3830 |
| **1.2** | 0.3849 | 0.3869 | 0.3888 | 0.3907 | 0.3925 | 0.3944 | 0.3962 | 0.3980 | 0.3997 | 0.4015 |
| **1.3** | 0.4032 | 0.4049 | 0.4066 | 0.4082 | 0.4099 | 0.4115 | 0.4131 | 0.4147 | 0.4162 | 0.4177 |
| **1.4** | 0.4192 | 0.4207 | 0.4222 | 0.4236 | 0.4251 | 0.4265 | 0.4279 | 0.4292 | 0.4306 | 0.4319 |
| **1.5** | 0.4332 | 0.4345 | 0.4357 | 0.4370 | 0.4382 | 0.4394 | 0.4406 | 0.4418 | 0.4429 | 0.4441 |
| **1.6** | 0.4452 | 0.4463 | 0.4474 | 0.4484 | 0.4495 | 0.4505 | 0.4515 | 0.4525 | 0.4535 | 0.4545 |
| **1.7** | 0.4554 | 0.4564 | 0.4573 | 0.4582 | 0.4591 | 0.4599 | 0.4608 | 0.4616 | 0.4625 | 0.4633 |
| **1.8** | 0.4641 | 0.4649 | 0.4656 | 0.4664 | 0.4671 | 0.4678 | 0.4686 | 0.4693 | 0.4699 | 0.4706 |
| **1.9** | 0.4713 | 0.4719 | 0.4726 | 0.4732 | 0.4738 | 0.4744 | 0.4750 | 0.4756 | 0.4761 | 0.4767 |
| **2.0** | 0.4772 | 0.4778 | 0.4783 | 0.4788 | 0.4793 | 0.4798 | 0.4803 | 0.4808 | 0.4812 | 0.4817 |
| **2.1** | 0.4821 | 0.4826 | 0.4830 | 0.4834 | 0.4838 | 0.4842 | 0.4846 | 0.4850 | 0.4854 | 0.4857 |
| **2.2** | 0.4861 | 0.4864 | 0.4868 | 0.4871 | 0.4875 | 0.4878 | 0.4881 | 0.4884 | 0.4887 | 0.4890 |
| **2.3** | 0.4893 | 0.4896 | 0.4898 | 0.4901 | 0.4904 | 0.4906 | 0.4909 | 0.4911 | 0.4913 | 0.4916 |
| **2.4** | 0.4918 | 0.4920 | 0.4922 | 0.4925 | 0.4927 | 0.4929 | 0.4931 | 0.4932 | 0.4934 | 0.4936 |
| **2.5** | 0.4938 | 0.4940 | 0.4941 | 0.4943 | 0.4945 | 0.4946 | 0.4948 | 0.4949 | 0.4951 | 0.4952 |
| **2.6** | 0.4953 | 0.4955 | 0.4956 | 0.4957 | 0.4959 | 0.4960 | 0.4961 | 0.4962 | 0.4963 | 0.4964 |
| **2.7** | 0.4965 | 0.4966 | 0.4967 | 0.4968 | 0.4969 | 0.4970 | 0.4971 | 0.4972 | 0.4973 | 0.4974 |
| **2.8** | 0.4974 | 0.4975 | 0.4976 | 0.4977 | 0.4977 | 0.4978 | 0.4979 | 0.4979 | 0.4980 | 0.4981 |
| **2.9** | 0.4981 | 0.4982 | 0.4982 | 0.4983 | 0.4984 | 0.4984 | 0.4985 | 0.4985 | 0.4986 | 0.4986 |
| **3.0** | 0.4987 | 0.4987 | 0.4987 | 0.4988 | 0.4988 | 0.4989 | 0.4989 | 0.4989 | 0.4990 | 0.4990 |

t table with right tail probabilities

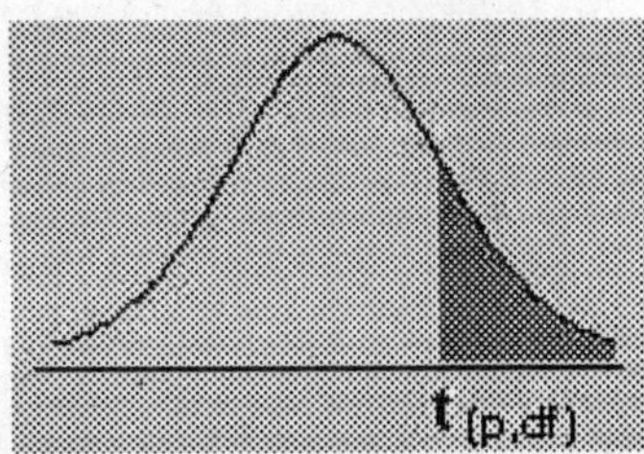


| df\p | 0.40 | 0.25 | 0.10 | 0.05 | 0.025 | 0.01 | 0.005 | 0.0005 |
|---|---|---|---|---|---|---|---|---|
| 1 | 0.324920 | 1.000000 | 3.077684 | 6.313752 | 12.70620 | 31.82052 | 63.65674 | 636.6192 |
| 2 | 0.288675 | 0.816497 | 1.885618 | 2.919986 | 4.30265 | 6.96456 | 9.92484 | 31.5991 |
| 3 | 0.276671 | 0.764892 | 1.637744 | 2.353363 | 3.18245 | 4.54070 | 5.84091 | 12.9240 |
| 4 | 0.270722 | 0.740697 | 1.533206 | 2.131847 | 2.77645 | 3.74695 | 4.60409 | 8.6103 |
| 5 | 0.267181 | 0.726687 | 1.475884 | 2.015048 | 2.57058 | 3.36493 | 4.03214 | 6.8688 |
| 6 | 0.264835 | 0.717558 | 1.439756 | 1.943180 | 2.44691 | 3.14267 | 3.70743 | 5.9588 |
| 7 | 0.263167 | 0.711142 | 1.414924 | 1.894579 | 2.36462 | 2.99795 | 3.49948 | 5.4079 |
| 8 | 0.261921 | 0.706387 | 1.396815 | 1.859548 | 2.30600 | 2.89646 | 3.35539 | 5.0413 |
| 9 | 0.260955 | 0.702722 | 1.383029 | 1.833113 | 2.26216 | 2.82144 | 3.24984 | 4.7809 |
| 10 | 0.260185 | 0.699812 | 1.372184 | 1.812461 | 2.22814 | 2.76377 | 3.16927 | 4.5869 |
| 11 | 0.259556 | 0.697445 | 1.363430 | 1.795885 | 2.20099 | 2.71808 | 3.10581 | 4.4370 |
| 12 | 0.259033 | 0.695483 | 1.356217 | 1.782288 | 2.17881 | 2.68100 | 3.05454 | 4.3178 |
| 13 | 0.258591 | 0.693829 | 1.350171 | 1.770933 | 2.16037 | 2.65031 | 3.01228 | 4.2208 |
| 14 | 0.258213 | 0.692417 | 1.345030 | 1.761310 | 2.14479 | 2.62449 | 2.97684 | 4.1405 |
| 15 | 0.257885 | 0.691197 | 1.340606 | 1.753050 | 2.13145 | 2.60248 | 2.94671 | 4.0728 |
| 16 | 0.257599 | 0.690132 | 1.336757 | 1.745884 | 2.11991 | 2.58349 | 2.92078 | 4.0150 |
| 17 | 0.257347 | 0.689195 | 1.333379 | 1.739607 | 2.10982 | 2.56693 | 2.89823 | 3.9651 |
| 18 | 0.257123 | 0.688364 | 1.330391 | 1.734064 | 2.10092 | 2.55238 | 2.87844 | 3.9216 |
| 19 | 0.256923 | 0.687621 | 1.327728 | 1.729133 | 2.09302 | 2.53948 | 2.86093 | 3.8834 |
| 20 | 0.256743 | 0.686954 | 1.325341 | 1.724718 | 2.08596 | 2.52798 | 2.84534 | 3.8495 |
| 21 | 0.256580 | 0.686352 | 1.323188 | 1.720743 | 2.07961 | 2.51765 | 2.83136 | 3.8193 |
| 22 | 0.256432 | 0.685805 | 1.321237 | 1.717144 | 2.07387 | 2.50832 | 2.81876 | 3.7921 |
| 23 | 0.256297 | 0.685306 | 1.319460 | 1.713872 | 2.06866 | 2.49987 | 2.80734 | 3.7676 |
| 24 | 0.256173 | 0.684850 | 1.317836 | 1.710882 | 2.06390 | 2.49216 | 2.79694 | 3.7454 |
| 25 | 0.256060 | 0.684430 | 1.316345 | 1.708141 | 2.05954 | 2.48511 | 2.78744 | 3.7251 |
| 26 | 0.255955 | 0.684043 | 1.314972 | 1.705618 | 2.05553 | 2.47863 | 2.77871 | 3.7066 |
| 27 | 0.255858 | 0.683685 | 1.313703 | 1.703288 | 2.05183 | 2.47266 | 2.77068 | 3.6896 |
| 28 | 0.255768 | 0.683353 | 1.312527 | 1.701131 | 2.04841 | 2.46714 | 2.76326 | 3.6739 |
| 29 | 0.255684 | 0.683044 | 1.311434 | 1.699127 | 2.04523 | 2.46202 | 2.75639 | 3.6594 |
| 30 | 0.255605 | 0.682756 | 1.310415 | 1.697261 | 2.04227 | 2.45726 | 2.75000 | 3.6460 |
| inf | 0.253347 | 0.674490 | 1.281552 | 1.644854 | 1.95996 | 2.32635 | 2.57583 | 3.2905 |

**Right tail areas for the *Chi-square* Distribution**

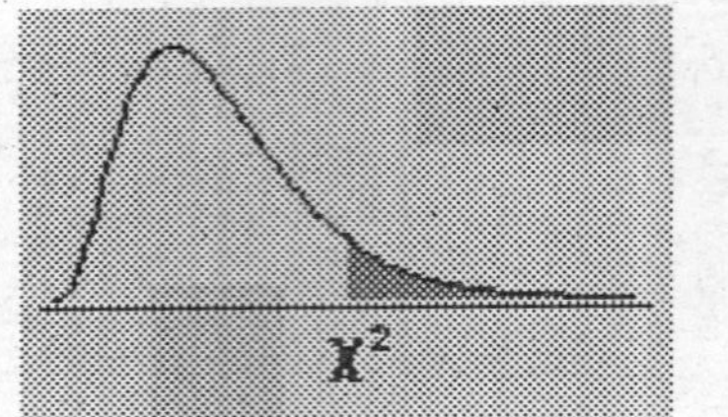


| df\area | .995 | .990 | .975 | .950 | .900 | .750 | .500 | .250 | .100 | .050 | .025 | .010 | .005 |
|---|---|---|---|---|---|---|---|---|---|---|---|---|---|
| 1 | 0.00004 | 0.00016 | 0.00098 | 0.00393 | 0.01579 | 0.10153 | 0.45494 | 1.32330 | 2.70554 | 3.84146 | 5.02389 | 6.63490 | 7.87944 |
| 2 | 0.01003 | 0.02010 | 0.05064 | 0.10259 | 0.21072 | 0.57536 | 1.38629 | 2.77259 | 4.60517 | 5.99146 | 7.37776 | 9.21034 | 10.59663 |
| 3 | 0.07172 | 0.11483 | 0.21580 | 0.35185 | 0.58437 | 1.21253 | 2.36597 | 4.10834 | 6.25139 | 7.81473 | 9.34840 | 11.34487 | 12.83816 |
| 4 | 0.20699 | 0.29711 | 0.48442 | 0.71072 | 1.06362 | 1.92256 | 3.35669 | 5.38527 | 7.77944 | 9.48773 | 11.14329 | 13.27670 | 14.86026 |
| 5 | 0.41174 | 0.55430 | 0.83121 | 1.14548 | 1.61031 | 2.67460 | 4.35146 | 6.62568 | 9.23636 | 11.07050 | 12.83250 | 15.08627 | 16.74960 |
| | | | | | | | | | | | | | |
| 6 | 0.67573 | 0.87209 | 1.23734 | 1.63538 | 2.20413 | 3.45460 | 5.34812 | 7.84080 | 10.64464 | 12.59159 | 14.44938 | 16.81189 | 18.54758 |
| 7 | 0.98926 | 1.23904 | 1.68987 | 2.16735 | 2.83311 | 4.25485 | 6.34581 | 9.03715 | 12.01704 | 14.06714 | 16.01276 | 18.47531 | 20.27774 |
| 8 | 1.34441 | 1.64650 | 2.17973 | 2.73264 | 3.48954 | 5.07064 | 7.34412 | 10.21885 | 13.36157 | 15.50731 | 17.53455 | 20.09024 | 21.95495 |
| 9 | 1.73493 | 2.08790 | 2.70039 | 3.32511 | 4.16816 | 5.89883 | 8.34283 | 11.38875 | 14.68366 | 16.91898 | 19.02277 | 21.66599 | 23.58935 |
| 10 | 2.15586 | 2.55821 | 3.24697 | 3.94030 | 4.86518 | 6.73720 | 9.34182 | 12.54886 | 15.98718 | 18.30704 | 20.48318 | 23.20925 | 25.18818 |
| | | | | | | | | | | | | | |
| 11 | 2.60322 | 3.05348 | 3.81575 | 4.57481 | 5.57778 | 7.58414 | 10.34100 | 13.70069 | 17.27501 | 19.67514 | 21.92005 | 24.72497 | 26.75685 |
| 12 | 3.07382 | 3.57057 | 4.40379 | 5.22603 | 6.30380 | 8.43842 | 11.34032 | 14.84540 | 18.54935 | 21.02607 | 23.33666 | 26.21697 | 28.29952 |
| 13 | 3.56503 | 4.10692 | 5.00875 | 5.89186 | 7.04150 | 9.29907 | 12.33976 | 15.98391 | 19.81193 | 22.36203 | 24.73560 | 27.68825 | 29.81947 |
| 14 | 4.07467 | 4.66043 | 5.62873 | 6.57063 | 7.78953 | 10.16531 | 13.33927 | 17.11693 | 21.06414 | 23.68479 | 26.11895 | 29.14124 | 31.31935 |
| 15 | 4.60092 | 5.22935 | 6.26214 | 7.26094 | 8.54676 | 11.03654 | 14.33886 | 18.24509 | 22.30713 | 24.99579 | 27.48839 | 30.57791 | 32.80132 |
| | | | | | | | | | | | | | |
| 16 | 5.14221 | 5.81221 | 6.90766 | 7.96165 | 9.31224 | 11.91222 | 15.33850 | 19.36886 | 23.54183 | 26.29623 | 28.84535 | 31.99993 | 34.26719 |

| | | | | | | | | | | | | | |
|---|---|---|---|---|---|---|---|---|---|---|---|---|---|
| **17** | 5.69722 | 6.40776 | 7.56419 | 8.67176 | 10.08519 | 12.79193 | 16.33818 | 20.48868 | 24.76904 | 27.58711 | 30.19101 | 33.40866 | 35.71847 |
| **18** | 6.26480 | 7.01491 | 8.23075 | 9.39046 | 10.86494 | 13.67529 | 17.33790 | 21.60489 | 25.98942 | 28.86930 | 31.52638 | 34.80531 | 37.15645 |
| **19** | 6.84397 | 7.63273 | 8.90652 | 10.11701 | 11.65091 | 14.56200 | 18.33765 | 22.71781 | 27.20357 | 30.14353 | 32.85233 | 36.19087 | 38.58226 |
| **20** | 7.43384 | 8.26040 | 9.59078 | 10.85081 | 12.44261 | 15.45177 | 19.33743 | 23.82769 | 28.41198 | 31.41043 | 34.16961 | 37.56623 | 39.99685 |
| | | | | | | | | | | | | | |
| **21** | 8.03365 | 8.89720 | 10.28290 | 11.59131 | 13.23960 | 16.34438 | 20.33723 | 24.93478 | 29.61509 | 32.67057 | 35.47888 | 38.93217 | 41.40106 |
| **22** | 8.64272 | 9.54249 | 10.98232 | 12.33801 | 14.04149 | 17.23962 | 21.33704 | 26.03927 | 30.81328 | 33.92444 | 36.78071 | 40.28936 | 42.79565 |
| **23** | 9.26042 | 10.19572 | 11.68855 | 13.09051 | 14.84796 | 18.13730 | 22.33688 | 27.14134 | 32.00690 | 35.17246 | 38.07563 | 41.63840 | 44.18128 |
| **24** | 9.88623 | 10.85636 | 12.40115 | 13.84843 | 15.65868 | 19.03725 | 23.33673 | 28.24115 | 33.19624 | 36.41503 | 39.36408 | 42.97982 | 45.55851 |
| **25** | 10.51965 | 11.52398 | 13.11972 | 14.61141 | 16.47341 | 19.93934 | 24.33659 | 29.33885 | 34.38159 | 37.65248 | 40.64647 | 44.31410 | 46.92789 |
| | | | | | | | | | | | | | |
| **26** | 11.16024 | 12.19815 | 13.84390 | 15.37916 | 17.29188 | 20.84343 | 25.33646 | 30.43457 | 35.56317 | 38.88514 | 41.92317 | 45.64168 | 48.28988 |
| **27** | 11.80759 | 12.87850 | 14.57338 | 16.15140 | 18.11390 | 21.74940 | 26.33634 | 31.52841 | 36.74122 | 40.11327 | 43.19451 | 46.96294 | 49.64492 |
| **28** | 12.46134 | 13.56471 | 15.30786 | 16.92788 | 18.93924 | 22.65716 | 27.33623 | 32.62049 | 37.91592 | 41.33714 | 44.46079 | 48.27824 | 50.99338 |
| **29** | 13.12115 | 14.25645 | 16.04707 | 17.70837 | 19.76774 | 23.56659 | 28.33613 | 33.71091 | 39.08747 | 42.55697 | 45.72229 | 49.58788 | 52.33562 |
| **30** | 13.78672 | 14.95346 | 16.79077 | 18.49266 | 20.59923 | 24.47761 | 29.33603 | 34.79974 | 40.25602 | 43.77297 | 46.97924 | 50.89218 | 53.67196 |

# F Table for alpha=.10

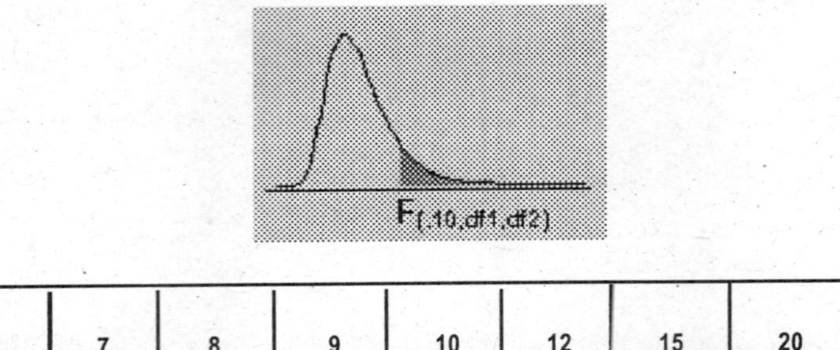


| df2/ df1 | 1 | 2 | 3 | 4 | 5 | 6 | 7 | 8 | 9 | 10 | 12 | 15 | 20 | 24 | 30 | 40 | 60 | 120 | INF |
|---|---|---|---|---|---|---|---|---|---|---|---|---|---|---|---|---|---|---|---|
| 1 | 39.86346 | 49.50000 | 53.59324 | 55.83296 | 57.24008 | 58.20442 | 58.90595 | 59.43898 | 59.85759 | 60.19498 | 60.70521 | 61.22034 | 61.74029 | 62.00205 | 62.26497 | 62.52905 | 62.79428 | 63.06064 | 63.32812 |
| 2 | 8.52632 | 9.00000 | 9.16179 | 9.24342 | 9.29263 | 9.32553 | 9.34908 | 9.36677 | 9.38054 | 9.39157 | 9.40813 | 9.42471 | 9.44131 | 9.44962 | 9.45793 | 9.46624 | 9.47456 | 9.48289 | 9.49122 |
| 3 | 5.53832 | 5.46238 | 5.39077 | 5.34264 | 5.30916 | 5.28473 | 5.26619 | 5.25167 | 5.24000 | 5.23041 | 5.21562 | 5.20031 | 5.18448 | 5.17636 | 5.16811 | 5.15972 | 5.15119 | 5.14251 | 5.13370 |
| 4 | 4.54477 | 4.32456 | 4.19086 | 4.10725 | 4.05058 | 4.00975 | 3.97897 | 3.95494 | 3.93567 | 3.91988 | 3.89553 | 3.87036 | 3.84434 | 3.83099 | 3.81742 | 3.80361 | 3.78957 | 3.77527 | 3.76073 |
| 5 | 4.06042 | 3.77972 | 3.61948 | 3.52020 | 3.45298 | 3.40451 | 3.36790 | 3.33928 | 3.31628 | 3.29740 | 3.26824 | 3.23801 | 3.20665 | 3.19052 | 3.17408 | 3.15732 | 3.14023 | 3.12279 | 3.10500 |
| 6 | 3.77595 | 3.46330 | 3.28876 | 3.18076 | 3.10751 | 3.05455 | 3.01446 | 2.98304 | 2.95774 | 2.93693 | 2.90472 | 2.87122 | 2.83634 | 2.81834 | 2.79996 | 2.78117 | 2.76195 | 2.74229 | 2.72216 |
| 7 | 3.58943 | 3.25744 | 3.07407 | 2.96053 | 2.88334 | 2.82739 | 2.78493 | 2.75158 | 2.72468 | 2.70251 | 2.66811 | 2.63223 | 2.59473 | 2.57533 | 2.55546 | 2.53510 | 2.51422 | 2.49279 | 2.47079 |
| 8 | 3.45792 | 3.11312 | 2.92380 | 2.80643 | 2.72645 | 2.66833 | 2.62413 | 2.58935 | 2.56124 | 2.53804 | 2.50196 | 2.46422 | 2.42464 | 2.40410 | 2.38302 | 2.36136 | 2.33910 | 2.31618 | 2.29257 |
| 9 | 3.36030 | 3.00645 | 2.81286 | 2.69268 | 2.61061 | 2.55086 | 2.50531 | 2.46941 | 2.44034 | 2.41632 | 2.37888 | 2.33962 | 2.29832 | 2.27683 | 2.25472 | 2.23196 | 2.20849 | 2.18427 | 2.15923 |
| 10 | 3.28502 | 2.92447 | 2.72767 | 2.60534 | 2.52164 | 2.46058 | 2.41397 | 2.37715 | 2.34731 | 2.32260 | 2.28405 | 2.24351 | 2.20074 | 2.17843 | 2.15543 | 2.13169 | 2.10716 | 2.08176 | 2.05542 |
| 11 | 3.22520 | 2.85951 | 2.66023 | 2.53619 | 2.45118 | 2.38907 | 2.34157 | 2.30400 | 2.27350 | 2.24823 | 2.20873 | 2.16709 | 2.12305 | 2.10001 | 2.07621 | 2.05161 | 2.02612 | 1.99965 | 1.97211 |
| 12 | 3.17655 | 2.80680 | 2.60552 | 2.48010 | 2.39402 | 2.33102 | 2.28278 | 2.24457 | 2.21352 | 2.18776 | 2.14744 | 2.10485 | 2.05968 | 2.03599 | 2.01149 | 1.98610 | 1.95973 | 1.93228 | 1.90361 |
| 13 | 3.13621 | 2.76317 | 2.56027 | 2.43371 | 2.34672 | 2.28298 | 2.23410 | 2.19535 | 2.16382 | 2.13763 | 2.09659 | 2.05316 | 2.00698 | 1.98272 | 1.95757 | 1.93147 | 1.90429 | 1.87591 | 1.84620 |
| 14 | 3.10221 | 2.72647 | 2.52222 | 2.39469 | 2.30694 | 2.24256 | 2.19313 | 2.15390 | 2.12195 | 2.09540 | 2.05371 | 2.00953 | 1.96245 | 1.93766 | 1.91193 | 1.88516 | 1.85723 | 1.82800 | 1.79728 |
| 15 | 3.07319 | 2.69517 | 2.48979 | 2.36143 | 2.27302 | 2.20808 | 2.15818 | 2.11853 | 2.08621 | 2.05932 | 2.01707 | 1.97222 | 1.92431 | 1.89904 | 1.87277 | 1.84539 | 1.81676 | 1.78672 | 1.75505 |
| 16 | 3.04811 | 2.66817 | 2.46181 | 2.33274 | 2.24376 | 2.17833 | 2.12800 | 2.08798 | 2.05533 | 2.02815 | 1.98539 | 1.93992 | 1.89127 | 1.86556 | 1.83879 | 1.81084 | 1.78156 | 1.75075 | 1.71817 |
| 17 | 3.02623 | 2.64464 | 2.43743 | 2.30775 | 2.21825 | 2.15239 | 2.10169 | 2.06134 | 2.02839 | 2.00094 | 1.95772 | 1.91169 | 1.86236 | 1.83624 | 1.80901 | 1.78053 | 1.75063 | 1.71909 | 1.68564 |
| 18 | 3.00698 | 2.62395 | 2.41601 | 2.28577 | 2.19583 | 2.12958 | 2.07854 | 2.03789 | 2.00467 | 1.97698 | 1.93334 | 1.88681 | 1.83685 | 1.81035 | 1.78269 | 1.75371 | 1.72322 | 1.69099 | 1.65671 |
| 19 | 2.98990 | 2.60561 | 2.39702 | 2.26630 | 2.17596 | 2.10936 | 2.05802 | 2.01710 | 1.98364 | 1.95573 | 1.91170 | 1.86471 | 1.81416 | 1.78731 | 1.75924 | 1.72979 | 1.69876 | 1.66587 | 1.63077 |
| 20 | 2.97465 | 2.58925 | 2.38009 | 2.24893 | 2.15823 | 2.09132 | 2.03970 | 1.99853 | 1.96485 | 1.93674 | 1.89236 | 1.84494 | 1.79384 | 1.76667 | 1.73822 | 1.70833 | 1.67678 | 1.64326 | 1.60738 |
| 21 | 2.96096 | 2.57457 | 2.36489 | 2.23334 | 2.14231 | 2.07512 | 2.02325 | 1.98186 | 1.94797 | 1.91967 | 1.87497 | 1.82715 | 1.77555 | 1.74807 | 1.71927 | 1.68896 | 1.65691 | 1.62278 | 1.58615 |
| 22 | 2.94858 | 2.56131 | 2.35117 | 2.21927 | 2.12794 | 2.06050 | 2.00840 | 1.96680 | 1.93273 | 1.90425 | 1.85925 | 1.81106 | 1.75899 | 1.73122 | 1.70208 | 1.67138 | 1.63885 | 1.60415 | 1.56678 |
| 23 | 2.93736 | 2.54929 | 2.33873 | 2.20651 | 2.11491 | 2.04723 | 1.99492 | 1.95312 | 1.91888 | 1.89025 | 1.84497 | 1.79643 | 1.74392 | 1.71588 | 1.68643 | 1.65535 | 1.62237 | 1.58711 | 1.54903 |
| 24 | 2.92712 | 2.53833 | 2.32739 | 2.19488 | 2.10303 | 2.03513 | 1.98263 | 1.94066 | 1.90625 | 1.87748 | 1.83194 | 1.78308 | 1.73015 | 1.70185 | 1.67210 | 1.64067 | 1.60726 | 1.57146 | 1.53270 |
| 25 | 2.91774 | 2.52831 | 2.31702 | 2.18424 | 2.09216 | 2.02406 | 1.97138 | 1.92925 | 1.89469 | 1.86578 | 1.82000 | 1.77083 | 1.71752 | 1.68898 | 1.65895 | 1.62718 | 1.59335 | 1.55703 | 1.51760 |
| 26 | 2.90913 | 2.51910 | 2.30749 | 2.17447 | 2.08218 | 2.01389 | 1.96104 | 1.91876 | 1.88407 | 1.85503 | 1.80902 | 1.75957 | 1.70589 | 1.67712 | 1.64682 | 1.61472 | 1.58050 | 1.54368 | 1.50360 |
| 27 | 2.90119 | 2.51061 | 2.29871 | 2.16546 | 2.07298 | 2.00452 | 1.95151 | 1.90909 | 1.87427 | 1.84511 | 1.79889 | 1.74917 | 1.69514 | 1.66616 | 1.63560 | 1.60320 | 1.56859 | 1.53129 | 1.49057 |
| 28 | 2.89385 | 2.50276 | 2.29060 | 2.15714 | 2.06447 | 1.99585 | 1.94270 | 1.90014 | 1.86520 | 1.83593 | 1.78951 | 1.73954 | 1.68519 | 1.65600 | 1.62519 | 1.59250 | 1.55753 | 1.51976 | 1.47841 |
| 29 | 2.88703 | 2.49548 | 2.28307 | 2.14941 | 2.05658 | 1.98781 | 1.93452 | 1.89184 | 1.85679 | 1.82741 | 1.78081 | 1.73060 | 1.67593 | 1.64655 | 1.61551 | 1.58253 | 1.54721 | 1.50899 | 1.46704 |
| 30 | 2.88069 | 2.48872 | 2.27607 | 2.14223 | 2.04925 | 1.98033 | 1.92692 | 1.88412 | 1.84896 | 1.81949 | 1.77270 | 1.72227 | 1.66731 | 1.63774 | 1.60648 | 1.57323 | 1.53757 | 1.49891 | 1.45636 |
| 40 | 2.83535 | 2.44037 | 2.22609 | 2.09095 | 1.99682 | 1.92688 | 1.87252 | 1.82886 | 1.79290 | 1.76269 | 1.71456 | 1.66241 | 1.60515 | 1.57411 | 1.54108 | 1.50562 | 1.46716 | 1.42476 | 1.37691 |
| 60 | 2.79107 | 2.39325 | 2.17741 | 2.04099 | 1.94571 | 1.87472 | 1.81939 | 1.77483 | 1.73802 | 1.70701 | 1.65743 | 1.60337 | 1.54349 | 1.51072 | 1.47554 | 1.43734 | 1.39520 | 1.34757 | 1.29146 |
| 120 | 2.74781 | 2.34734 | 2.12999 | 1.99230 | 1.89587 | 1.82381 | 1.76748 | 1.72196 | 1.68425 | 1.65238 | 1.60120 | 1.54500 | 1.48207 | 1.44723 | 1.40938 | 1.36760 | 1.32034 | 1.26457 | 1.19256 |
| inf | 2.70554 | 2.30259 | 2.08380 | 1.94486 | 1.84727 | 1.77411 | 1.71672 | 1.67020 | 1.63152 | 1.59872 | 1.54578 | 1.48714 | 1.42060 | 1.38318 | 1.34187 | 1.29513 | 1.23995 | 1.16860 | 1.00000 |

# F Table for alpha=.05

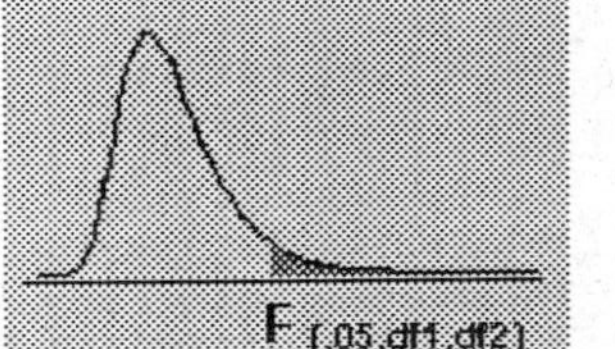


| df2/df1 | 1 | 2 | 3 | 4 | 5 | 6 | 7 | 8 | 9 | 10 | 12 | 15 | 20 | 24 | 30 | 40 | 60 | 120 | INF |
|---|---|---|---|---|---|---|---|---|---|---|---|---|---|---|---|---|---|---|---|
| 1 | 161.4476 | 199.5000 | 215.7073 | 224.5832 | 230.1619 | 233.9860 | 236.7684 | 238.8827 | 240.5433 | 241.8817 | 243.9060 | 245.9499 | 248.0131 | 249.0518 | 250.0951 | 251.1432 | 252.1957 | 253.2529 | 254.3144 |
| 2 | 18.5128 | 19.0000 | 19.1643 | 19.2468 | 19.2964 | 19.3295 | 19.3532 | 19.3710 | 19.3848 | 19.3959 | 19.4125 | 19.4291 | 19.4458 | 19.4541 | 19.4624 | 19.4707 | 19.4791 | 19.4874 | 19.4957 |
| 3 | 10.1280 | 9.5521 | 9.2766 | 9.1172 | 9.0135 | 8.9406 | 8.8867 | 8.8452 | 8.8123 | 8.7855 | 8.7446 | 8.7029 | 8.6602 | 8.6385 | 8.6166 | 8.5944 | 8.5720 | 8.5494 | 8.5264 |
| 4 | 7.7086 | 6.9443 | 6.5914 | 6.3882 | 6.2561 | 6.1631 | 6.0942 | 6.0410 | 5.9988 | 5.9644 | 5.9117 | 5.8578 | 5.8025 | 5.7744 | 5.7459 | 5.7170 | 5.6877 | 5.6581 | 5.6281 |
| 5 | 6.6079 | 5.7861 | 5.4095 | 5.1922 | 5.0503 | 4.9503 | 4.8759 | 4.8183 | 4.7725 | 4.7351 | 4.6777 | 4.6188 | 4.5581 | 4.5272 | 4.4957 | 4.4638 | 4.4314 | 4.3985 | 4.3650 |
| 6 | 5.9874 | 5.1433 | 4.7571 | 4.5337 | 4.3874 | 4.2839 | 4.2067 | 4.1468 | 4.0990 | 4.0600 | 3.9999 | 3.9381 | 3.8742 | 3.8415 | 3.8082 | 3.7743 | 3.7398 | 3.7047 | 3.6689 |
| 7 | 5.5914 | 4.7374 | 4.3468 | 4.1203 | 3.9715 | 3.8660 | 3.7870 | 3.7257 | 3.6767 | 3.6365 | 3.5747 | 3.5107 | 3.4445 | 3.4105 | 3.3758 | 3.3404 | 3.3043 | 3.2674 | 3.2298 |
| 8 | 5.3177 | 4.4590 | 4.0662 | 3.8379 | 3.6875 | 3.5806 | 3.5005 | 3.4381 | 3.3881 | 3.3472 | 3.2839 | 3.2184 | 3.1503 | 3.1152 | 3.0794 | 3.0428 | 3.0053 | 2.9669 | 2.9276 |
| 9 | 5.1174 | 4.2565 | 3.8625 | 3.6331 | 3.4817 | 3.3738 | 3.2927 | 3.2296 | 3.1789 | 3.1373 | 3.0729 | 3.0061 | 2.9365 | 2.9005 | 2.8637 | 2.8259 | 2.7872 | 2.7475 | 2.7067 |
| 10 | 4.9646 | 4.1028 | 3.7083 | 3.4780 | 3.3258 | 3.2172 | 3.1355 | 3.0717 | 3.0204 | 2.9782 | 2.9130 | 2.8450 | 2.7740 | 2.7372 | 2.6996 | 2.6609 | 2.6211 | 2.5801 | 2.5379 |
| 11 | 4.8443 | 3.9823 | 3.5874 | 3.3567 | 3.2039 | 3.0946 | 3.0123 | 2.9480 | 2.8962 | 2.8536 | 2.7876 | 2.7186 | 2.6464 | 2.6090 | 2.5705 | 2.5309 | 2.4901 | 2.4480 | 2.4045 |
| 12 | 4.7472 | 3.8853 | 3.4903 | 3.2592 | 3.1059 | 2.9961 | 2.9134 | 2.8486 | 2.7964 | 2.7534 | 2.6866 | 2.6169 | 2.5436 | 2.5055 | 2.4663 | 2.4259 | 2.3842 | 2.3410 | 2.2962 |
| 13 | 4.6672 | 3.8056 | 3.4105 | 3.1791 | 3.0254 | 2.9153 | 2.8321 | 2.7669 | 2.7144 | 2.6710 | 2.6037 | 2.5331 | 2.4589 | 2.4202 | 2.3803 | 2.3392 | 2.2966 | 2.2524 | 2.2064 |
| 14 | 4.6001 | 3.7389 | 3.3439 | 3.1122 | 2.9582 | 2.8477 | 2.7642 | 2.6987 | 2.6458 | 2.6022 | 2.5342 | 2.4630 | 2.3879 | 2.3487 | 2.3082 | 2.2664 | 2.2229 | 2.1778 | 2.1307 |
| 15 | 4.5431 | 3.6823 | 3.2874 | 3.0556 | 2.9013 | 2.7905 | 2.7066 | 2.6408 | 2.5876 | 2.5437 | 2.4753 | 2.4034 | 2.3275 | 2.2878 | 2.2468 | 2.2043 | 2.1601 | 2.1141 | 2.0658 |
| 16 | 4.4940 | 3.6337 | 3.2389 | 3.0069 | 2.8524 | 2.7413 | 2.6572 | 2.5911 | 2.5377 | 2.4935 | 2.4247 | 2.3522 | 2.2756 | 2.2354 | 2.1938 | 2.1507 | 2.1058 | 2.0589 | 2.0096 |
| 17 | 4.4513 | 3.5915 | 3.1968 | 2.9647 | 2.8100 | 2.6987 | 2.6143 | 2.5480 | 2.4943 | 2.4499 | 2.3807 | 2.3077 | 2.2304 | 2.1898 | 2.1477 | 2.1040 | 2.0584 | 2.0107 | 1.9604 |
| 18 | 4.4139 | 3.5546 | 3.1599 | 2.9277 | 2.7729 | 2.6613 | 2.5767 | 2.5102 | 2.4563 | 2.4117 | 2.3421 | 2.2686 | 2.1906 | 2.1497 | 2.1071 | 2.0629 | 2.0166 | 1.9681 | 1.9168 |
| 19 | 4.3807 | 3.5219 | 3.1274 | 2.8951 | 2.7401 | 2.6283 | 2.5435 | 2.4768 | 2.4227 | 2.3779 | 2.3080 | 2.2341 | 2.1555 | 2.1141 | 2.0712 | 2.0264 | 1.9795 | 1.9302 | 1.8780 |
| 20 | 4.3512 | 3.4928 | 3.0984 | 2.8661 | 2.7109 | 2.5990 | 2.5140 | 2.4471 | 2.3928 | 2.3479 | 2.2776 | 2.2033 | 2.1242 | 2.0825 | 2.0391 | 1.9938 | 1.9464 | 1.8963 | 1.8432 |
| 21 | 4.3248 | 3.4668 | 3.0725 | 2.8401 | 2.6848 | 2.5727 | 2.4876 | 2.4205 | 2.3660 | 2.3210 | 2.2504 | 2.1757 | 2.0960 | 2.0540 | 2.0102 | 1.9645 | 1.9165 | 1.8657 | 1.8117 |
| 22 | 4.3009 | 3.4434 | 3.0491 | 2.8167 | 2.6613 | 2.5491 | 2.4638 | 2.3965 | 2.3419 | 2.2967 | 2.2258 | 2.1508 | 2.0707 | 2.0283 | 1.9842 | 1.9380 | 1.8894 | 1.8380 | 1.7831 |
| 23 | 4.2793 | 3.4221 | 3.0280 | 2.7955 | 2.6400 | 2.5277 | 2.4422 | 2.3748 | 2.3201 | 2.2747 | 2.2036 | 2.1282 | 2.0476 | 2.0050 | 1.9605 | 1.9139 | 1.8648 | 1.8128 | 1.7570 |
| 24 | 4.2597 | 3.4028 | 3.0088 | 2.7763 | 2.6207 | 2.5082 | 2.4226 | 2.3551 | 2.3002 | 2.2547 | 2.1834 | 2.1077 | 2.0267 | 1.9838 | 1.9390 | 1.8920 | 1.8424 | 1.7896 | 1.7330 |
| 25 | 4.2417 | 3.3852 | 2.9912 | 2.7587 | 2.6030 | 2.4904 | 2.4047 | 2.3371 | 2.2821 | 2.2365 | 2.1649 | 2.0889 | 2.0075 | 1.9643 | 1.9192 | 1.8718 | 1.8217 | 1.7684 | 1.7110 |
| 26 | 4.2252 | 3.3690 | 2.9752 | 2.7426 | 2.5868 | 2.4741 | 2.3883 | 2.3205 | 2.2655 | 2.2197 | 2.1479 | 2.0716 | 1.9898 | 1.9464 | 1.9010 | 1.8533 | 1.8027 | 1.7488 | 1.6906 |
| 27 | 4.2100 | 3.3541 | 2.9604 | 2.7278 | 2.5719 | 2.4591 | 2.3732 | 2.3053 | 2.2501 | 2.2043 | 2.1323 | 2.0558 | 1.9736 | 1.9299 | 1.8842 | 1.8361 | 1.7851 | 1.7306 | 1.6717 |
| 28 | 4.1960 | 3.3404 | 2.9467 | 2.7141 | 2.5581 | 2.4453 | 2.3593 | 2.2913 | 2.2360 | 2.1900 | 2.1179 | 2.0411 | 1.9586 | 1.9147 | 1.8687 | 1.8203 | 1.7689 | 1.7138 | 1.6541 |
| 29 | 4.1830 | 3.3277 | 2.9340 | 2.7014 | 2.5454 | 2.4324 | 2.3463 | 2.2783 | 2.2229 | 2.1768 | 2.1045 | 2.0275 | 1.9446 | 1.9005 | 1.8543 | 1.8055 | 1.7537 | 1.6981 | 1.6376 |
| 30 | 4.1709 | 3.3158 | 2.9223 | 2.6896 | 2.5336 | 2.4205 | 2.3343 | 2.2662 | 2.2107 | 2.1646 | 2.0921 | 2.0148 | 1.9317 | 1.8874 | 1.8409 | 1.7918 | 1.7396 | 1.6835 | 1.6223 |
| 40 | 4.0847 | 3.2317 | 2.8387 | 2.6060 | 2.4495 | 2.3359 | 2.2490 | 2.1802 | 2.1240 | 2.0772 | 2.0035 | 1.9245 | 1.8389 | 1.7929 | 1.7444 | 1.6928 | 1.6373 | 1.5766 | 1.5089 |
| 60 | 4.0012 | 3.1504 | 2.7581 | 2.5252 | 2.3683 | 2.2541 | 2.1665 | 2.0970 | 2.0401 | 1.9926 | 1.9174 | 1.8364 | 1.7480 | 1.7001 | 1.6491 | 1.5943 | 1.5343 | 1.4673 | 1.3893 |
| 120 | 3.9201 | 3.0718 | 2.6802 | 2.4472 | 2.2899 | 2.1750 | 2.0868 | 2.0164 | 1.9588 | 1.9105 | 1.8337 | 1.7505 | 1.6587 | 1.6084 | 1.5543 | 1.4952 | 1.4290 | 1.3519 | 1.2539 |
| inf | 3.8415 | 2.9957 | 2.6049 | 2.3719 | 2.2141 | 2.0986 | 2.0096 | 1.9384 | 1.8799 | 1.8307 | 1.7522 | 1.6664 | 1.5705 | 1.5173 | 1.4591 | 1.3940 | 1.3180 | 1.2214 | 1.0000 |

To index

# F Table for alpha=.025

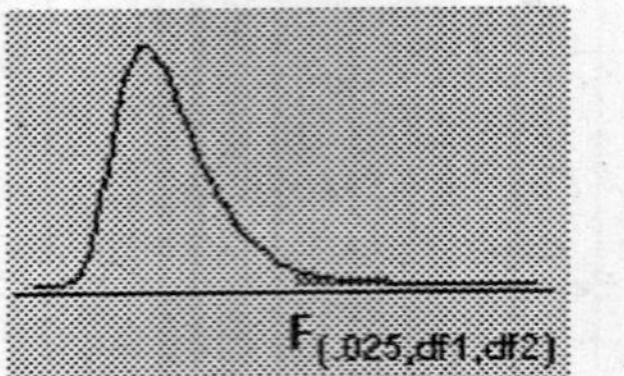


| df2/df1 | 1 | 2 | 3 | 4 | 5 | 6 | 7 | 8 | 9 | 10 | 12 | 15 | 20 | 24 | 30 | 40 | 60 | 120 | INF |
|---|---|---|---|---|---|---|---|---|---|---|---|---|---|---|---|---|---|---|---|
| 1 | 647.7890 | 799.5000 | 864.1630 | 899.5833 | 921.8479 | 937.1111 | 948.2169 | 956.6562 | 963.2846 | 968.6274 | 976.7079 | 984.8668 | 993.1028 | 997.2492 | 1001.414 | 1005.598 | 1009.800 | 1014.020 | 1018.258 |
| 2 | 38.5063 | 39.0000 | 39.1655 | 39.2484 | 39.2982 | 39.3315 | 39.3552 | 39.3730 | 39.3869 | 39.3980 | 39.4146 | 39.4313 | 39.4479 | 39.4562 | 39.465 | 39.473 | 39.481 | 39.490 | 39.498 |
| 3 | 17.4434 | 16.0441 | 15.4392 | 15.1010 | 14.8848 | 14.7347 | 14.6244 | 14.5399 | 14.4731 | 14.4189 | 14.3366 | 14.2527 | 14.1674 | 14.1241 | 14.081 | 14.037 | 13.992 | 13.947 | 13.902 |
| 4 | 12.2179 | 10.6491 | 9.9792 | 9.6045 | 9.3645 | 9.1973 | 9.0741 | 8.9796 | 8.9047 | 8.8439 | 8.7512 | 8.6565 | 8.5599 | 8.5109 | 8.461 | 8.411 | 8.360 | 8.309 | 8.257 |
| 5 | 10.0070 | 8.4336 | 7.7636 | 7.3879 | 7.1464 | 6.9777 | 6.8531 | 6.7572 | 6.6811 | 6.6192 | 6.5245 | 6.4277 | 6.3286 | 6.2780 | 6.227 | 6.175 | 6.123 | 6.069 | 6.015 |
| 6 | 8.8131 | 7.2599 | 6.5988 | 6.2272 | 5.9876 | 5.8198 | 5.6955 | 5.5996 | 5.5234 | 5.4613 | 5.3662 | 5.2687 | 5.1684 | 5.1172 | 5.065 | 5.012 | 4.959 | 4.904 | 4.849 |
| 7 | 8.0727 | 6.5415 | 5.8898 | 5.5226 | 5.2852 | 5.1186 | 4.9949 | 4.8993 | 4.8232 | 4.7611 | 4.6658 | 4.5678 | 4.4667 | 4.4150 | 4.362 | 4.309 | 4.254 | 4.199 | 4.142 |
| 8 | 7.5709 | 6.0595 | 5.4160 | 5.0526 | 4.8173 | 4.6517 | 4.5286 | 4.4333 | 4.3572 | 4.2951 | 4.1997 | 4.1012 | 3.9995 | 3.9472 | 3.894 | 3.840 | 3.784 | 3.728 | 3.670 |
| 9 | 7.2093 | 5.7147 | 5.0781 | 4.7181 | 4.4844 | 4.3197 | 4.1970 | 4.1020 | 4.0260 | 3.9639 | 3.8682 | 3.7694 | 3.6669 | 3.6142 | 3.560 | 3.505 | 3.449 | 3.392 | 3.333 |
| 10 | 6.9367 | 5.4564 | 4.8256 | 4.4683 | 4.2361 | 4.0721 | 3.9498 | 3.8549 | 3.7790 | 3.7168 | 3.6209 | 3.5217 | 3.4185 | 3.3654 | 3.311 | 3.255 | 3.198 | 3.140 | 3.080 |
| 11 | 6.7241 | 5.2559 | 4.6300 | 4.2751 | 4.0440 | 3.8807 | 3.7586 | 3.6638 | 3.5879 | 3.5257 | 3.4296 | 3.3299 | 3.2261 | 3.1725 | 3.118 | 3.061 | 3.004 | 2.944 | 2.883 |
| 12 | 6.5538 | 5.0959 | 4.4742 | 4.1212 | 3.8911 | 3.7283 | 3.6065 | 3.5118 | 3.4358 | 3.3736 | 3.2773 | 3.1772 | 3.0728 | 3.0187 | 2.963 | 2.906 | 2.848 | 2.787 | 2.725 |
| 13 | 6.4143 | 4.9653 | 4.3472 | 3.9959 | 3.7667 | 3.6043 | 3.4827 | 3.3880 | 3.3120 | 3.2497 | 3.1532 | 3.0527 | 2.9477 | 2.8932 | 2.837 | 2.780 | 2.720 | 2.659 | 2.595 |
| 14 | 6.2979 | 4.8567 | 4.2417 | 3.8919 | 3.6634 | 3.5014 | 3.3799 | 3.2853 | 3.2093 | 3.1469 | 3.0502 | 2.9493 | 2.8437 | 2.7888 | 2.732 | 2.674 | 2.614 | 2.552 | 2.487 |
| 15 | 6.1995 | 4.7650 | 4.1528 | 3.8043 | 3.5764 | 3.4147 | 3.2934 | 3.1987 | 3.1227 | 3.0602 | 2.9633 | 2.8621 | 2.7559 | 2.7006 | 2.644 | 2.585 | 2.524 | 2.461 | 2.395 |
| 16 | 6.1151 | 4.6867 | 4.0768 | 3.7294 | 3.5021 | 3.3406 | 3.2194 | 3.1248 | 3.0488 | 2.9862 | 2.8890 | 2.7875 | 2.6808 | 2.6252 | 2.568 | 2.509 | 2.447 | 2.383 | 2.316 |
| 17 | 6.0420 | 4.6189 | 4.0112 | 3.6648 | 3.4379 | 3.2767 | 3.1556 | 3.0610 | 2.9849 | 2.9222 | 2.8249 | 2.7230 | 2.6158 | 2.5598 | 2.502 | 2.442 | 2.380 | 2.315 | 2.247 |
| 18 | 5.9781 | 4.5597 | 3.9539 | 3.6083 | 3.3820 | 3.2209 | 3.0999 | 3.0053 | 2.9291 | 2.8664 | 2.7689 | 2.6667 | 2.5590 | 2.5027 | 2.445 | 2.384 | 2.321 | 2.256 | 2.187 |
| 19 | 5.9216 | 4.5075 | 3.9034 | 3.5587 | 3.3327 | 3.1718 | 3.0509 | 2.9563 | 2.8801 | 2.8172 | 2.7196 | 2.6171 | 2.5089 | 2.4523 | 2.394 | 2.333 | 2.270 | 2.203 | 2.133 |
| 20 | 5.8715 | 4.4613 | 3.8587 | 3.5147 | 3.2891 | 3.1283 | 3.0074 | 2.9128 | 2.8365 | 2.7737 | 2.6758 | 2.5731 | 2.4645 | 2.4076 | 2.349 | 2.287 | 2.223 | 2.156 | 2.085 |
| 21 | 5.8266 | 4.4199 | 3.8188 | 3.4754 | 3.2501 | 3.0895 | 2.9686 | 2.8740 | 2.7977 | 2.7348 | 2.6368 | 2.5338 | 2.4247 | 2.3675 | 2.308 | 2.246 | 2.182 | 2.114 | 2.042 |
| 22 | 5.7863 | 4.3828 | 3.7829 | 3.4401 | 3.2151 | 3.0546 | 2.9338 | 2.8392 | 2.7628 | 2.6998 | 2.6017 | 2.4984 | 2.3890 | 2.3315 | 2.272 | 2.210 | 2.145 | 2.076 | 2.003 |
| 23 | 5.7498 | 4.3492 | 3.7505 | 3.4083 | 3.1835 | 3.0232 | 2.9023 | 2.8077 | 2.7313 | 2.6682 | 2.5699 | 2.4665 | 2.3567 | 2.2989 | 2.239 | 2.176 | 2.111 | 2.041 | 1.968 |
| 24 | 5.7166 | 4.3187 | 3.7211 | 3.3794 | 3.1548 | 2.9946 | 2.8738 | 2.7791 | 2.7027 | 2.6396 | 2.5411 | 2.4374 | 2.3273 | 2.2693 | 2.209 | 2.146 | 2.080 | 2.010 | 1.935 |
| 25 | 5.6864 | 4.2909 | 3.6943 | 3.3530 | 3.1287 | 2.9685 | 2.8478 | 2.7531 | 2.6766 | 2.6135 | 2.5149 | 2.4110 | 2.3005 | 2.2422 | 2.182 | 2.118 | 2.052 | 1.981 | 1.906 |
| 26 | 5.6586 | 4.2655 | 3.6697 | 3.3289 | 3.1048 | 2.9447 | 2.8240 | 2.7293 | 2.6528 | 2.5896 | 2.4908 | 2.3867 | 2.2759 | 2.2174 | 2.157 | 2.093 | 2.026 | 1.954 | 1.878 |
| 27 | 5.6331 | 4.2421 | 3.6472 | 3.3067 | 3.0828 | 2.9228 | 2.8021 | 2.7074 | 2.6309 | 2.5676 | 2.4688 | 2.3644 | 2.2533 | 2.1946 | 2.133 | 2.069 | 2.002 | 1.930 | 1.853 |
| 28 | 5.6096 | 4.2205 | 3.6264 | 3.2863 | 3.0626 | 2.9027 | 2.7820 | 2.6872 | 2.6106 | 2.5473 | 2.4484 | 2.3438 | 2.2324 | 2.1735 | 2.112 | 2.048 | 1.980 | 1.907 | 1.829 |
| 29 | 5.5878 | 4.2006 | 3.6072 | 3.2674 | 3.0438 | 2.8840 | 2.7633 | 2.6686 | 2.5919 | 2.5286 | 2.4295 | 2.3248 | 2.2131 | 2.1540 | 2.092 | 2.028 | 1.959 | 1.886 | 1.807 |
| 30 | 5.5675 | 4.1821 | 3.5894 | 3.2499 | 3.0265 | 2.8667 | 2.7460 | 2.6513 | 2.5746 | 2.5112 | 2.4120 | 2.3072 | 2.1952 | 2.1359 | 2.074 | 2.009 | 1.940 | 1.866 | 1.787 |
| 40 | 5.4239 | 4.0510 | 3.4633 | 3.1261 | 2.9037 | 2.7444 | 2.6238 | 2.5289 | 2.4519 | 2.3882 | 2.2882 | 2.1819 | 2.0677 | 2.0069 | 1.943 | 1.875 | 1.803 | 1.724 | 1.637 |
| 60 | 5.2856 | 3.9253 | 3.3425 | 3.0077 | 2.7863 | 2.6274 | 2.5068 | 2.4117 | 2.3344 | 2.2702 | 2.1692 | 2.0613 | 1.9445 | 1.8817 | 1.815 | 1.744 | 1.667 | 1.581 | 1.482 |
| 120 | 5.1523 | 3.8046 | 3.2269 | 2.8943 | 2.6740 | 2.5154 | 2.3948 | 2.2994 | 2.2217 | 2.1570 | 2.0548 | 1.9450 | 1.8249 | 1.7597 | 1.690 | 1.614 | 1.530 | 1.433 | 1.310 |
| inf | 5.0239 | 3.6889 | 3.1161 | 2.7858 | 2.5665 | 2.4082 | 2.2875 | 2.1918 | 2.1136 | 2.0483 | 1.9447 | 1.8326 | 1.7085 | 1.6402 | 1.566 | 1.484 | 1.388 | 1.268 | 1.000 |

To index

## F Table for alpha=.01

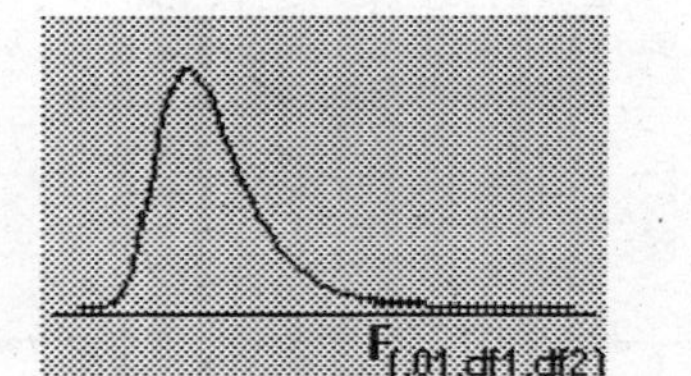


| f2/ df1 | 1 | 2 | 3 | 4 | 5 | 6 | 7 | 8 | 9 | 10 | 12 | 15 | 20 | 24 | 30 | 40 | 60 | 120 | INF |
|---|---|---|---|---|---|---|---|---|---|---|---|---|---|---|---|---|---|---|---|
| 1 | 4052.181 | 4999.500 | 5403.352 | 5624.583 | 5763.650 | 5858.986 | 5928.356 | 5981.070 | 6022.473 | 6055.847 | 6106.321 | 6157.285 | 6208.730 | 6234.631 | 6260.649 | 6286.782 | 6313.030 | 6339.391 | 6365.864 |
| 2 | 98.503 | 99.000 | 99.166 | 99.249 | 99.299 | 99.333 | 99.356 | 99.374 | 99.388 | 99.399 | 99.416 | 99.433 | 99.449 | 99.458 | 99.466 | 99.474 | 99.482 | 99.491 | 99.499 |
| 3 | 34.116 | 30.817 | 29.457 | 28.710 | 28.237 | 27.911 | 27.672 | 27.489 | 27.345 | 27.229 | 27.052 | 26.872 | 26.690 | 26.598 | 26.505 | 26.411 | 26.316 | 26.221 | 26.125 |
| 4 | 21.198 | 18.000 | 16.694 | 15.977 | 15.522 | 15.207 | 14.976 | 14.799 | 14.659 | 14.546 | 14.374 | 14.198 | 14.020 | 13.929 | 13.838 | 13.745 | 13.652 | 13.558 | 13.463 |
| 5 | 16.258 | 13.274 | 12.060 | 11.392 | 10.967 | 10.672 | 10.456 | 10.289 | 10.158 | 10.051 | 9.888 | 9.722 | 9.553 | 9.466 | 9.379 | 9.291 | 9.202 | 9.112 | 9.020 |
| 6 | 13.745 | 10.925 | 9.780 | 9.148 | 8.746 | 8.466 | 8.260 | 8.102 | 7.976 | 7.874 | 7.718 | 7.559 | 7.396 | 7.313 | 7.229 | 7.143 | 7.057 | 6.969 | 6.880 |
| 7 | 12.246 | 9.547 | 8.451 | 7.847 | 7.460 | 7.191 | 6.993 | 6.840 | 6.719 | 6.620 | 6.469 | 6.314 | 6.155 | 6.074 | 5.992 | 5.908 | 5.824 | 5.737 | 5.650 |
| 8 | 11.259 | 8.649 | 7.591 | 7.006 | 6.632 | 6.371 | 6.178 | 6.029 | 5.911 | 5.814 | 5.667 | 5.515 | 5.359 | 5.279 | 5.198 | 5.116 | 5.032 | 4.946 | 4.859 |
| 9 | 10.561 | 8.022 | 6.992 | 6.422 | 6.057 | 5.802 | 5.613 | 5.467 | 5.351 | 5.257 | 5.111 | 4.962 | 4.808 | 4.729 | 4.649 | 4.567 | 4.483 | 4.398 | 4.311 |
| 10 | 10.044 | 7.559 | 6.552 | 5.994 | 5.636 | 5.386 | 5.200 | 5.057 | 4.942 | 4.849 | 4.706 | 4.558 | 4.405 | 4.327 | 4.247 | 4.165 | 4.082 | 3.996 | 3.909 |
| 11 | 9.646 | 7.206 | 6.217 | 5.668 | 5.316 | 5.069 | 4.886 | 4.744 | 4.632 | 4.539 | 4.397 | 4.251 | 4.099 | 4.021 | 3.941 | 3.860 | 3.776 | 3.690 | 3.602 |
| 12 | 9.330 | 6.927 | 5.953 | 5.412 | 5.064 | 4.821 | 4.640 | 4.499 | 4.388 | 4.296 | 4.155 | 4.010 | 3.858 | 3.780 | 3.701 | 3.619 | 3.535 | 3.449 | 3.361 |
| 13 | 9.074 | 6.701 | 5.739 | 5.205 | 4.862 | 4.620 | 4.441 | 4.302 | 4.191 | 4.100 | 3.960 | 3.815 | 3.665 | 3.587 | 3.507 | 3.425 | 3.341 | 3.255 | 3.165 |
| 14 | 8.862 | 6.515 | 5.564 | 5.035 | 4.695 | 4.456 | 4.278 | 4.140 | 4.030 | 3.939 | 3.800 | 3.656 | 3.505 | 3.427 | 3.348 | 3.266 | 3.181 | 3.094 | 3.004 |
| 15 | 8.683 | 6.359 | 5.417 | 4.893 | 4.556 | 4.318 | 4.142 | 4.004 | 3.895 | 3.805 | 3.666 | 3.522 | 3.372 | 3.294 | 3.214 | 3.132 | 3.047 | 2.959 | 2.868 |
| 16 | 8.531 | 6.226 | 5.292 | 4.773 | 4.437 | 4.202 | 4.026 | 3.890 | 3.780 | 3.691 | 3.553 | 3.409 | 3.259 | 3.181 | 3.101 | 3.018 | 2.933 | 2.845 | 2.753 |
| 17 | 8.400 | 6.112 | 5.185 | 4.669 | 4.336 | 4.102 | 3.927 | 3.791 | 3.682 | 3.593 | 3.455 | 3.312 | 3.162 | 3.084 | 3.003 | 2.920 | 2.835 | 2.746 | 2.653 |
| 18 | 8.285 | 6.013 | 5.092 | 4.579 | 4.248 | 4.015 | 3.841 | 3.705 | 3.597 | 3.508 | 3.371 | 3.227 | 3.077 | 2.999 | 2.919 | 2.835 | 2.749 | 2.660 | 2.566 |
| 19 | 8.185 | 5.926 | 5.010 | 4.500 | 4.171 | 3.939 | 3.765 | 3.631 | 3.523 | 3.434 | 3.297 | 3.153 | 3.003 | 2.925 | 2.844 | 2.761 | 2.674 | 2.584 | 2.489 |
| 20 | 8.096 | 5.849 | 4.938 | 4.431 | 4.103 | 3.871 | 3.699 | 3.564 | 3.457 | 3.368 | 3.231 | 3.088 | 2.938 | 2.859 | 2.778 | 2.695 | 2.608 | 2.517 | 2.421 |
| 21 | 8.017 | 5.780 | 4.874 | 4.369 | 4.042 | 3.812 | 3.640 | 3.506 | 3.398 | 3.310 | 3.173 | 3.030 | 2.880 | 2.801 | 2.720 | 2.636 | 2.548 | 2.457 | 2.360 |
| 22 | 7.945 | 5.719 | 4.817 | 4.313 | 3.988 | 3.758 | 3.587 | 3.453 | 3.346 | 3.258 | 3.121 | 2.978 | 2.827 | 2.749 | 2.667 | 2.583 | 2.495 | 2.403 | 2.305 |
| 23 | 7.881 | 5.664 | 4.765 | 4.264 | 3.939 | 3.710 | 3.539 | 3.406 | 3.299 | 3.211 | 3.074 | 2.931 | 2.781 | 2.702 | 2.620 | 2.535 | 2.447 | 2.354 | 2.256 |
| 24 | 7.823 | 5.614 | 4.718 | 4.218 | 3.895 | 3.667 | 3.496 | 3.363 | 3.256 | 3.168 | 3.032 | 2.889 | 2.738 | 2.659 | 2.577 | 2.492 | 2.403 | 2.310 | 2.211 |
| 25 | 7.770 | 5.568 | 4.675 | 4.177 | 3.855 | 3.627 | 3.457 | 3.324 | 3.217 | 3.129 | 2.993 | 2.850 | 2.699 | 2.620 | 2.538 | 2.453 | 2.364 | 2.270 | 2.169 |
| 26 | 7.721 | 5.526 | 4.637 | 4.140 | 3.818 | 3.591 | 3.421 | 3.288 | 3.182 | 3.094 | 2.958 | 2.815 | 2.664 | 2.585 | 2.503 | 2.417 | 2.327 | 2.233 | 2.131 |
| 27 | 7.677 | 5.488 | 4.601 | 4.106 | 3.785 | 3.558 | 3.388 | 3.256 | 3.149 | 3.062 | 2.926 | 2.783 | 2.632 | 2.552 | 2.470 | 2.384 | 2.294 | 2.198 | 2.097 |
| 28 | 7.636 | 5.453 | 4.568 | 4.074 | 3.754 | 3.528 | 3.358 | 3.226 | 3.120 | 3.032 | 2.896 | 2.753 | 2.602 | 2.522 | 2.440 | 2.354 | 2.263 | 2.167 | 2.064 |
| 29 | 7.598 | 5.420 | 4.538 | 4.045 | 3.725 | 3.499 | 3.330 | 3.198 | 3.092 | 3.005 | 2.868 | 2.726 | 2.574 | 2.495 | 2.412 | 2.325 | 2.234 | 2.138 | 2.034 |
| 30 | 7.562 | 5.390 | 4.510 | 4.018 | 3.699 | 3.473 | 3.304 | 3.173 | 3.067 | 2.979 | 2.843 | 2.700 | 2.549 | 2.469 | 2.386 | 2.299 | 2.208 | 2.111 | 2.006 |
| 40 | 7.314 | 5.179 | 4.313 | 3.828 | 3.514 | 3.291 | 3.124 | 2.993 | 2.888 | 2.801 | 2.665 | 2.522 | 2.369 | 2.288 | 2.203 | 2.114 | 2.019 | 1.917 | 1.805 |
| 60 | 7.077 | 4.977 | 4.126 | 3.649 | 3.339 | 3.119 | 2.953 | 2.823 | 2.718 | 2.632 | 2.496 | 2.352 | 2.198 | 2.115 | 2.028 | 1.936 | 1.836 | 1.726 | 1.601 |
| 120 | 6.851 | 4.787 | 3.949 | 3.480 | 3.174 | 2.956 | 2.792 | 2.663 | 2.559 | 2.472 | 2.336 | 2.192 | 2.035 | 1.950 | 1.860 | 1.763 | 1.656 | 1.533 | 1.381 |
| inf | 6.635 | 4.605 | 3.782 | 3.319 | 3.017 | 2.802 | 2.639 | 2.511 | 2.407 | 2.321 | 2.185 | 2.039 | 1.878 | 1.791 | 1.696 | 1.592 | 1.473 | 1.325 | 1.000 |

## Critical Values for the Two-sample Kolmogorov-Smirnov Test (2-sided)

**Table gives critical D-values for ± = 0.05 (upper value) and ± = 0.01 (lower value) for various sample sizes. * means you cannot reject $H_0$ regardless of observed D.**

| $n_2 \backslash n_1$ | 3 | 4 | 5 | 6 | 7 | 8 | 9 | 10 | 11 | 12 |
|---|---|---|---|---|---|---|---|---|---|---|
| 1 | *<br>* | *<br>* | *<br>* | *<br>* | *<br>* | *<br>* | *<br>* | *<br>* | *<br>* | *<br>* |
| 2 | *<br>* | *<br>* | *<br>* | *<br>* | *<br>* | 16/16<br>* | 18/18<br>* | 20/20<br>* | 22/22<br>* | 24/24<br>* |
| 3 | *<br>* | *<br>* | 15/15<br>* | 18/18<br>* | 21/21<br>* | 21/24<br>24/24 | 24/27<br>27/27 | 27/30<br>30/30 | 30/33<br>33/33 | 30/36<br>36/36 |
| 4 | | 16/16<br>* | 20/20<br>* | 20/24<br>24/24 | 24/28<br>28/28 | 28/32<br>32/32 | 28/36<br>32/36 | 30/40<br>36/40 | 33/44<br>40/44 | 36/48<br>44/48 |
| 5 | | | *<br>* | 24/30<br>30/30 | 30/35<br>35/35 | 30/40<br>35/40 | 35/45<br>40/45 | 40/50<br>45/50 | 39/55<br>45/55 | 43/60<br>50/60 |
| 6 | | | | 30/36<br>36/36 | 30/42<br>36/42 | 34/48<br>40/48 | 39/54<br>45/54 | 40/60<br>48/60 | 43/66<br>54/66 | 48/72<br>60/72 |
| 7 | | | | | 42/49<br>42/49 | 40/56<br>48/56 | 42/63<br>49/63 | 46/70<br>53/70 | 48/77<br>59/77 | 53/84<br>60/84 |
| 8 | | | | | | 48/64<br>56/64 | 46/72<br>55/72 | 48/80<br>60/80 | 53/88<br>64/88 | 60/96<br>68/96 |
| 9 | | | | | | | 54/81<br>63/81 | 53/90<br>70/90 | 59/99<br>70/99 | 63/108<br>75/108 |
| 10 | | | | | | | | 70/100<br>80/100 | 60/110<br>77/110 | 66/120<br>80/120 |
| 11 | | | | | | | | | 77/121<br>88/121 | 72/132<br>86/132 |
| 12 | | | | | | | | | | 96/144<br>84/144 |

For larger sample sizes, the approximate critical value Dα is given by the equation

$$D\alpha = c(\alpha) * \sqrt{\frac{n_1 + n_2}{n_1 n_2}}$$

where the coefficient is given by the table below.

| α | 0.10 | 0.05 | 0.025 | 0.01 | 0.005 | 0.001 |
|---|---|---|---|---|---|---|
| c(α) | 1.22 | 1.36 | 1.48 | 1.63 | 1.73 | 1.95 |

## Critical Values for the One-sample Kolmogorov-Smirnov Test (2-sided)

| Sample size | 0.10 | 0.05 |
|---|---|---|
| 1 | .95 | .975 |
| 2 | .776 | .842 |
| 3 | .642 | .708 |
| 4 | .564 | .624 |
| 5 | .510 | .565 |
| 6 | .470 | .521 |
| 7 | .438 | .486 |
| 8 | .411 | .457 |
| 9 | .388 | .432 |
| 10 | .368 | .410 |
| 11 | .352 | .391 |
| 12 | .338 | .375 |
| 13 | .325 | .361 |
| 14 | .314 | .349 |
| 15 | .304 | .338 |
| 20 | .264 | .294 |
| 25 | .24 | .27 |
| 30 | .22 | .24 |
| 35 | .21 | .23 |
| Over 35 | $1.22/\sqrt{n}$ | $1.36/\sqrt{n}$ |

## Wilcoxon Rank-Sum Test

**Significance level: 0.05 one-tailed, 0.1 two-tailed**

| | | | | | | | | n2 | | | | | | | | |
|---|---|---|---|---|---|---|---|---|---|---|---|---|---|---|---|---|
| | | 6 | 7 | 8 | 9 | 10 | 11 | 12 | 13 | 14 | 15 | 16 | 17 | 18 | 19 | 20 |
| | 6 | 28 | 30 | 32 | 34 | 35 | 37 | 39 | 41 | 43 | 44 | 46 | 48 | 50 | 52 | 53 |
| | 7 | | 39 | 41 | 43 | 46 | 48 | 50 | 52 | 54 | 57 | 59 | 61 | 63 | 66 | 68 |
| | 8 | | | 52 | 54 | 57 | 60 | 62 | 65 | 67 | 70 | 73 | 75 | 78 | 81 | 83 |
| | 9 | | | | 66 | 69 | 72 | 75 | 78 | 81 | 84 | 87 | 90 | 94 | 97 | 100 |
| | 10 | | | | | 83 | 86 | 90 | 93 | 96 | 100 | 103 | 107 | 110 | 114 | 117 |
| | 11 | | | | | | 101 | 105 | 109 | 112 | 116 | 120 | 124 | 128 | 132 | 136 |
| n1 | 12 | | | | | | | 121 | 125 | 130 | 134 | 138 | 142 | 147 | 151 | 155 |
| | 13 | | | | | | | | 143 | 148 | 152 | 157 | 162 | 166 | 171 | 176 |
| | 14 | | | | | | | | | 167 | 172 | 177 | 182 | 187 | 192 | 197 |
| | 15 | | | | | | | | | | 192 | 198 | 203 | 209 | 215 | 220 |
| | 16 | | | | | | | | | | | 220 | 226 | 232 | 238 | 244 |
| | 17 | | | | | | | | | | | | 249 | 256 | 262 | 269 |
| | 18 | | | | | | | | | | | | | 281 | 287 | 294 |
| | 19 | | | | | | | | | | | | | | 314 | 321 |
| | 20 | | | | | | | | | | | | | | | 349 |

**Wilcoxon Matched-Pairs Test**

| N | Significance | |
|---|---|---|
| | 0.05 one-tailed (0.10 two-tailed) | 0.025 one-tailed (0.05 two-tailed) |
| 6 | 2 | 1 |
| 7 | 4 | 2 |
| 8 | 6 | 4 |
| 9 | 8 | 5 |
| 10 | 11 | 8 |
| 11 | 14 | 10 |
| 12 | 18 | 14 |
| 13 | 21 | 17 |
| 14 | 26 | 21 |
| 15 | 31 | 25 |
| 16 | 36 | 30 |
| 17 | 41 | 35 |
| 18 | 47 | 40 |
| 19 | 54 | 46 |
| 20 | 60 | 52 |

## 13.4 Bibliography and References


Aaker David A, Kumar V and Day Geroge S (2002): "Market Research", John Wiley and Sons, New York.

Achen, C.H. (1982). "Interpreting and using regression", Sage Publication.

Ackoff, Russell L. (1961): "The Design of Social Research," University of Chicago Press.

Afifi, A.A. and V. Clark (1984): "Computer-aided Multivariate Analysi", Lifetime Learning Publications, California, 1984.

Alien, T. Harrell (1978): "New Methods in Social Science Research", Praeger Publishers, New York.

Anderson, Sweeny and Williams (2006): "Quantitative Methods in Business", Thomson, South Western.

Baker T.L. (1994): "Doing Social Research", 2nd Edition, McGraw-Hill, New York.

Belson, W.A. (1986): "Validity in Social Research", Gower.

Best, John W., and Kahn, James V. (1986): "Research in Education," 5th Ed., Prentice-Hall of India Pvt. Ltd., New Delhi.

Bhat Sridhar K. (2007): "Essentials of Operation Research & Quantitative Techniques", Himalaya Publishing House, Mumbai.

Bhattacharya, Srinibas, (1972.): "Psychometrics & Behavioural Research", Sterling Publishers Pvt. Ltd., New Delhi.

Black, J. A., & Champion, D. J. (1976): "Methods and Issues in Social Research", New York: Wiley.

Blalock, H.M. (1984): "Basic Dilemmas in the Social Sciences", Sage.

Boot, John C.G., and Cox, Edwin B. (1979): "Statistical Analysis for Managerial Decisions", McGraw-Hill Publishing Co. Ltd., (International Student Edition), New Delhi.

Bordens, K.S. & Abbott, B.B. (1988): "Research Design and Methods: A Process Approach", Mayfield.

Brinberg, D., & McGrath, J.E. (1988): "Validity and the Research Process", Sage.

Cook, T.D., & Campbell, D.T. (1979): "Quasi-experimentation", Houghton, Mifflin.

Cooley, William W., and Lohnes, Paul R (1971), "Multivariate Data Analysis", New York: John Wiley & Sons.

Cooper Donald R, and Schindler Pamela S (2006): "Business Research Methods", Tata McGraw-Hill.

Croxton, F.E., Cowden, D.J., and Klein, S (1975): " Applied General Statistic", Prentice-Hall of India Pvt. Ltd., New Delhi.

Danielson, W.A. & Mullen, J.J. (1965). A Basic Space Unit for Newspaper Content Analysis, Journalism Quarterly, pp. 108-110.

Devi Prasad, B. & Sampath Kumar, R.D. (1991), Opinion Moulding by the Press: An Analysis of the Election Related Content of Editorials and Letters to the Editors, Media Asia, 18(1): 24-29.

Dhillon Sharanjit S and Manjinder Kaur (2007): "Foreign Institutional Investors and Stock Market Volatility in India – an Empirical Analysis" in Journal of Global Economy, Vol 3 no. 5, December, 2007.

Duggan James E (1979): "On Measuring the Instability of Time Series Data" in Oxford Bulletin of Eco and Statistics, Vol 41 No. 5, Aug, 1979.

Fowler, F.J. (1993): "Survey Research Methods" (2nd ed.), Sage.

Ghosh, B.N. (1982): "Scientific Methods and Social Research", Sterling Publishers Pvt. Ltd., New Delhi.

Glyn Winter (2000): "A Comparative Discussion of the Notion of 'Validity' in Qualitative and Quantitative Research". The Qualitative Report, Volume 4, Numbers 3 & 4, March, 2000 (http://www.nova.edu/ssss/QR/QR4-3/winter.html).

Goodman, S.E. and S.T. Hedetniemi (1977), "Introduction to the Design and Analysis or Algorithms", McGraw-Hill, Singapore.

Guilford, J.P.(1954) : "Psychometric Methods", McGraw-Hill, Inc., New York.

Gujarati, Damodar N (1995): "Basic Econometric", McGraw-Hill International Edition.

Hammersley, M. (1987): "Some notes on the terms 'validity' and 'reliability", British Educational Research Journal, 13(1), pp. 73-81.

Janet M. Ruane (2004): "Essentials of Research Methods – A Guide to Social Science Research", Blackwell Publishing.

Jhunjhunwala Bharat (2008): "Business Statistics", S Chand & Co., New Delhi.

Johanston, (1997): "Econometric Methods", the McGraw-Hill Companies Inc., New Delhi.

Johnson, R.A. and G.K. Bhattacharyya(1996): "Statistics: Principles and Methods", John Wiley & Sons, New York.

Judd, C.M., Smith, E.R., & Kidder, L.H. (1991): "Research Methods in Social Relations", HBJ.

Kalton, G. (1983): "Introduction to Survey Sampling", Sage Publication.

Kanji Gopal K (1993): "100 Statistical Tests", Sage Publication, New Delhi.

Karson, Marvin J.(1982) : "Multivariate Statistical Methods", The Lowa State University Press.

Kerlinger, F.N., (1973): "Foundation of Behavioral Research," Holt, Rinehard & Winston, New York.

Kish, L. (1965): "Survey Sampling", John Wiley and Sons.

Kothari C.R. (2004): "Research Methodology", New Age International, New Delhi.

Kothari, C.R. (1984): "Quantitative Techniques", Delhi.

Kotler, Philip (1996): "Marketing Management — Analysis, Planning, Implementation, and Control", Prentice-Hall of India, New Delhi.

Krathwohl, D.R. (1985): "Social and Behavioural Science research", Jossey-Bass.

Krishnaswami O.R. and Ranganatham M.(2007), "Methodology of Research in Social Sciences", Himalaya Publishing House, Mumbai.

Leedy, P.D. (1997) "Practical Research: Planning and Design" (6th Ed.), Upper Saddle River, NJ: Prentice-Hall, Inc., pp. 232-233.

Levin, Richard I and Rubin David S (1994), "Statistics for Management", 5th Edition: New Delhi, Prentice-Hall of India Pvt. Ltd.

Lewin, M. (1979): "Understanding Psychological Research", Wiley.

Marjit, S. and Raychaudhari, A., (1997): "An Analytical Study: India's Exports", Oxford University Press, New Delhi.

Marshall, C., Rossman, G.B (1989): "Designing Qualitative Research", Sage Publications Ltd., Beverly Hills, California.

Marshall, Catherine; Rossman, Gretchen B.( 1989): "Designing Qualitative Research", Sage Publications, Beverly Hills, California.

Maxwell, J. A. (1992): "Understanding and Validity in Qualitative Research", Harvard Educational Review, 62(3), pp. 279-300.

Nachmias, D. & Nachmias, C. (1976). Content analysis. In Research methods in the social sciences (pp.132-139), UK: Edward Arnold.

Neena Malhotra (2006): "Growth, Structure and Determinant of India's Import 1980-81 to 2000-01", in Journal of Global Economy, Mumbai, Jan-March, 2006.

Norusis, M.J. (1990) "SPSS Advanced Statistics: Student Guide".

Osgood, C.E., G.J. Suci, and O.H. Tannenbaum (1957): "The Measurement of Meaning", University of Illinois Press, Urbana.

Pandey Alok Kumar (2006): "Export and Economic Growth in India, Causal Interpretation", in Journal of Global Economy, Vol 2, No.4, Dec, 2006.

Paneerselvam R (2007): "Research Methodology", Prentice Hall of India, New Delhi.

Prasad A R (2005): "Engel's Law and Expenditure Elasticities of Specific Food Items in India: 1950-51 to 1999-2000", in Journal of Global Economy, Mumbai, 2005.

Reich, J.W. (1982): "Experimenting in Society, Scott, Foresman.

Sachdeva J K (2006): "Export of Agricultural Commodities in the Context of WTO and Economic Reforms", in Journal of Global Economy, April-July, 2006.

Sachdeva J K (2006): "Quantitative Modelling (Series -1), Unit Root Technique -(Augmented Dickey Fuller Test) for Analysis of Series – Economists' dilemma", Journal of Global Economy, Vol. 2 No. 3, Oct, 2006.

Sachdeva J K (2007): "Diversification and Export of Agricultural Commodities – Prospects to revamp Drought Prone Areas", Paper presented at UGC sponsored National Seminar on Geo- Eco Interventions to Revamp DPA, Walchand College, Solapur, 2007.

Sadhu, A.N., and Singh, Amarjit, (1980): "Research Methodology in Social Sciences", Himalaya Publishing House, Mumbai.

Sekhar C S C (2003): "Volatility of Agricultural Prices – An Analysis of Major International and Domestic Markets", Indian Council for Research on International Economic Relations, Core-6A, 4th Floor, India Habitat Centre, Lodi Road, New Delhi-110 003, June 2003.

Sharma S.D. (2005): "Operations Research", Kedar Nath Ram Nath & Co., Meerut.

Srivastava U K, Shenoy G V and Sharma S C (2005): "Quantitative Techniques for Managerial Decision", New Age International Publishing, New Delhi.

Stewart, D.W. (1984): "Secondary Research: Information Sources and Methods", Sage Publication.

Tandon, B.C.(1979): "Research Methodology in Social Sciences", Chaitanya Publishing House, Allahabad.

Thurstone, L.L.(1959): "The Measurement of Values", University of Chicago Press, Chicago.

Thurstone, L.L., The Measurement of Values, Chicago: University of Chicago Press, 1959.

Trochin William M.K.( 2006): "Research Methods", Biztantra, New Delhi.

Verma Renu and Deepak Khanna (2006): "Agriculture, where does the problem lie", Journal of Global Economy, Vol 2 no. 2, April-June, 2006.

Vohra N.D. (2007): "Quantitative Techniques in Management", Tata McGraw-Hill, New Delhi.

Wilkinson, T.S. and Bhandarkar, PL.(1979): "Methodology and Techniques of Social Research", Himalaya Publishing House, Mumbai.

...✎...✎...✎

# INDEX